Double Dividend

Double Dividend: Environmental Taxes and Fiscal Reform in the United States

Dale W. Jorgenson
Richard J. Goettle
Mun S. Ho
Peter J. Wilcoxen

The MIT Press
Cambridge, Massachusetts
London, England

MIT Press books may be purchased at special quantity discounts for business or sales promotional use. For information, please email special_sales@mitpress.mit.edu.

This book was set in Palatino by Toppan Best-set Premedia Limited. Printed and bound in the United States of America.

Library of Congress Cataloging-in-Publication Data

Jorgenson, Dale W. (Dale Weldeau), 1933–
Double dividend : environmental taxes and fiscal reform in the United States / Dale W. Jorgenson, Richard Goettle, Mun S. Ho, and Peter Wilcoxen.
pages cm
Includes bibliographical references and index.
ISBN 978-0-262-02709-0 (hardcover : alk. paper)
1. Environmental impact charges—United States. 2. Taxation—United States. 3. Fiscal policy—United States. I. Title.
HJ5316.J67 2013
336.2'7833370973—dc23
2013035500

10 9 8 7 6 5 4 3 2 1

Contents

List of Figures

List of Tables

Preface

The first task for environmental policy is to assure that users of fossil fuels bear the incremental costs of health and other environmental damages. The second task for environmental policy is to improve economic performance by joining market-based policies to fiscal reform. The third task of environmental policy is to evaluate alternative energy and environmental policies by linking market outcomes to consumer welfare. In this book we present a new approach for designing energy and environmental policies for the United States that accomplishes all three tasks.

The simplest and most transparent approach for assuring that users of fossil fuels bear the incremental costs of health and other environmental damages is to levy taxes on emissions that are equal to these costs. Market participants would then internalize the costs and incorporate them into decisions. Environmental taxes would be cost-effective because users of energy would face the same tax rates and there would be no opportunities for reducing the costs of pollution control by shifting among alternative energy sources.

Although we emphasize energy taxes in designing new energy and environmental policies, we have also analyzed policies that would impose a cap on emissions. By enforcing the cap and allowing market participants to trade emissions permits, the price of permits would be the same for all participants and environmental policy would be cost-effective. We refer to energy taxes and tradable permits as market-based policies. Market-based environmental policies could generate substantial government revenues and these could be substituted for revenues raised by other taxes, such as income taxes or sales taxes.

Environmental taxes must be integrated with fiscal reform in order to improve economic performance. The substitution of environmental taxes for other taxes would affect energy markets directly and would have far-reaching ramifications for other markets. To trace out these ramifications, we consider the effects of these taxes on all markets at every point in time. We show that the substitution of environmental taxes for other taxes could offset the costs of pollution control and produce a *double dividend* by improving the environment and the economy simultaneously.

We emphasize throughout this book that the double dividend of our title is not simply a matter of logic. We present numerous examples of policies that combine environmental taxes and fiscal reform that fail to achieve simultaneous improvements in environmental quality and economic performance. The existence of a double dividend requires careful policy design and must be verified empirically in every case. This requires the precise evaluations of alternative energy and environmental policies, which we provide.

Our final objective is to link market outcomes to consumer welfare in order to evaluate alternative energy and environmental policies. For this purpose we compare these policies in terms of their impacts on individual consumers. Individual welfare depends on the prices faced by consumers and consumer budgets. Social welfare depends on information about consumer preferences but also incorporates value judgments about horizontal and vertical equity. We emphasize the role of equity by comparing policy evaluations for different measures of social welfare.

To summarize: In this book we consider market-based approaches to energy and environmental policy that would internalize the incremental health costs and environmental damages from using energy. We integrate environmental taxes and tradable permits into the government budget in order to capture the economic benefits of fiscal reforms. Finally, we evaluate alternative policies in terms of the impacts of market outcomes on the welfare of individual consumers.

Our approach to the design of energy and environmental policies is based on a new model of the U.S. economy presented in chapter 1. Changes in energy and environmental policies result in changes in current prices and expectations of future prices. Current prices are especially important because they are reflected in the economic data. Expectations of future prices are determined along with current prices and incorporate the same information. Since our model includes markets for all commodities at every point of time, we refer to this as the Intertemporal General Equilibrium Model of the U.S. economy; for brevity we use the acronym IGEM.

In chapter 2 we describe the features of our general equilibrium model in greater detail. The core of the supply side is a new model of producer behavior introduced by Jin and Jorgenson (2010). This model incorporates extensive time series data for the industries that make up the U.S. economy. Our model of producer behavior represents substitution among inputs in response to changes in energy taxes. The model distinguishes input substitution from changes in technology in response to price changes.

The core of the demand side of IGEM is a new model of consumer behavior introduced by Jorgenson and Slesnick (2008). This model incorporates prices of energy and other commodities as well as total expenditures as determinants of consumer demand. To deal with the heterogeneity of consumers, the model includes the demographic characteristics of households as demand determinants. For this purpose we introduce extensive survey data on individual households, covering almost three decades.

Total demand for each commodity in IGEM includes consumer demands for private consumption and demands by producers for inputs into production. Total demand also includes public consumption in the government sector and demands for exports to the rest of the world. Total supply for each commodity comprises domestic production by all industries as well as imports. The intertemporal price system modeled by IGEM equilibrates demands and supplies for all markets at every point of time.

In chapter 3 we describe our model of consumer behavior. Full consumption includes demand for leisure as well as goods and services. Each household allocates a time endowment between work and leisure. Full wealth is the value of assets owned by the household as well as the value of the household's time endowment. Our model allocates full wealth among levels of full consumption in different time periods. Combining demand for leisure with the time endowment, we obtain a model of labor supply for each household.

Our model for an individual household includes the household's labor supply as well as the household's demands for goods and services. We incorporate household demands for goods and services and supplies of labor into IGEM by summing over demands and supplies for all households. The resulting model of aggregate consumer behavior depends on wages and prices, as well as the distribution of full consumption and demographic characteristics throughout the U.S. population.

To link market outcomes to consumer welfare, we recover demand and supply functions for individual households from the aggregate demand and supply functions in IGEM. We use the household demands and supplies to generate measures of individual welfare. We combine measures of individual welfare into a measure of social welfare that reflects principles of horizontal and vertical equity. We employ individual and social welfare functions to provide rankings of alternative energy and environmental policies.

In chapter 4 we present models of producer behavior for the 35 sectors that comprise the supply side of the U.S. economy. These include five energy-producing sectors—Coal Mining, Crude Petroleum and Natural Gas Mining, Petroleum Refining, Electric Utilities, and Gas Utilities. The remaining 30 sectors include Agriculture, Manufacturing, Services, and Trade. The model for each of the 35 industries allocates the value of output among capital, labor, energy, and materials inputs.

Our models of producer behavior incorporate input prices as determinants of input demands. We represent substitution among inputs by parameters estimated from extensive time series data. Input demands are also determined by price-induced changes in technology, represented by latent variables. By projecting these latent variables into the future, we incorporate trends in productivity and changes in the structure of production into our projections of U.S. economic growth.

Our models of producer behavior determine the supply prices for the 35 commodity groups included in IGEM. Using these prices, we allocate energy demands among the alternative sources of energy. We also allocate materials demands among the producing sectors of the economy. By summing energy and materials demands across industries, we obtain the inputs into domestic production in IGEM. We combine domestic supplies of energy and materials with imports from the rest of the world to provide the supply side of the model.

Chapter 5 completes the demand side of IGEM by describing our models of government and the rest of the world. The government sector plays a crucial role in our analysis of the impact of energy and environmental policies. Revenues from energy and environmental taxes enter the government budget and can be substituted for revenues from other taxes. This creates the link to reform of the government budget that we discuss in more detail in subsequent chapters.

In IGEM we distinguish among investment, capital stock, and capital services for each commodity that enters investment demand. The demands for investment goods depend on relative prices. As an illustration, rapidly declining prices of information technology equipment and software have generated a steady rise in the proportion of information technology in the overall value of investment. The allocation of investment also depends on changes in technology that we model by means of latent variables.

Finally, we treat imports as substitutes for domestically produced commodities and exports as substitutes for commodities consumed domestically. The trade balance is the value of exports less the value of imports. Our projections of U.S. economic growth treat the trade balance as exogenous. In chapter 5 we show how the exchange rate of the dollar against other currencies is determined endogenously.

Demography and technology are the driving forces in U.S. economic growth. We describe demography in terms of the growth of the U.S. population, the time endowment, and the quality of labor services determined by education and experience. Our population projections are based on official projections by the U.S. Bureau of the Census. We describe technology in terms of the growth of productivity and changes in composition in the 35 industrial sectors of IGEM.

The evolution of the government and rest-of-the-world sectors are important determinants of U.S. economic growth and the composition of economic activity. In chapter 5 we describe how to derive projections of the federal government from official projections by the Congressional Budget Office and other agencies. We derive projections for the rest-of-the-world sector from the projections of the International Monetary Fund.

In chapter 6 we describe the solution of our model to obtain base case projections of the growth of the U.S. economy from our studies of recent legislative proposals for the U.S. Environmental Protection Agency (EPA). We have calibrated our base case projections to the *Annual Energy Outlook*, published by the Energy Information Administration. In chapter 6 we show how the projections can be harmonized to make the results consistent.

The first step in analyzing energy and environmental policies with IGEM is to prepare a base case projection of the U.S. economy with no change in policy. The second step is to determine the environmental and economic impacts of policy changes. For this purpose we prepare an alternative projection of the future growth of the U.S. economy with the change in policy that we refer to as a policy case. Each policy case requires a new solution of IGEM.

In chapter 7 we describe emissions of pollutants as externalities, since these emissions are external to the markets represented in IGEM. We describe the accounting framework for energy and environmental outcomes of policy changes by presenting emissions coefficients for the activities that generate pollution. These include product emissions linked to production and process emissions linked to consumption. As described in more detail in chapter 7, we have calibrated our projections of these externalities to inventories of pollutants published by EPA.

In analyzing alternative energy and environmental policies we report emissions of the main greenhouse gases—carbon dioxide, methane, nitrous oxides, and high global warming potential gases. For convenience we express emissions in terms of the global warming potential of an equivalent amount of carbon dioxide, the most important greenhouse gas. We also present emissions of EPA's criterion air pollutants, including sulfur dioxide and particulates.

In chapter 7 we show how IGEM can be extended to technologies that are not in commercial use. An example is carbon capture and storage, a technology that could become a significant source of pollution abatement for carbon dioxide. We summarize the technology in terms of a marginal abatement cost schedule derived from engineering studies. Marginal abatement cost schedules are also useful in describing proposed environmental and energy policies, such as complex trading rules and subsidies for particular sectors, that greatly broaden the scope of policy responses analyzed by means of IGEM. In chapter 7 we illustrate this by means of policies from recent legislative proposals.

In chapter 8 we evaluate alternative energy and environmental policies for the United States. We present the IGEM base case for U.S. economic growth and a wide variety of policy cases. A carbon tax would target emissions of greenhouse gases as the U.S. contribution to an international effort to moderate changes in the climate. The tax would be imposed on greenhouse gas emissions in proportion to their global warming potential, denominated in terms of equivalent emissions of carbon dioxide. We consider a tax on carbon to illustrate the design of new energy and environmental policies.

We consider different carbon tax trajectories and different methods for utilizing the tax revenues. We first analyze the impact of carbon taxes on pollution abatement. Emissions of greenhouse gases decline with increases in carbon tax rates, but at a diminishing rate. Substitution of carbon tax revenues for reductions in capital income tax rates reduces the cost of capital and stimulates capital formation. The increased supply of capital offsets the adverse impacts of carbon taxes.

We evaluate alternative policies for recycling carbon tax revenues in terms of their impacts on individual and social welfare. Reductions in capital taxes generate the largest gain in social welfare benefits over the costs of pollution control and emerge as the preferred policy for revenue recycling. This provides a striking illustration of the potential role of intertemporal general equilibrium modeling in designing new energy and environmental policies for the United States.

A frequent objection to energy and environmental taxes is that they would reduce equity in the distribution of individual welfare. In chapter 8 we decompose changes in social welfare into changes in efficiency and equity. We emphasize the role of value judgments by measuring the losses in equity for different social welfare functions. We find that gains in efficiency from recycling carbon tax revenues would greatly outweigh the modest declines in equity, however these are evaluated.

In chapter 9 we quantify the uncertainties in the IGEM base case projections of the U.S. economy by means of confidence intervals. We present econometric techniques introduced by Tuladhar and Wilcoxen (1998) for determining confidence intervals for base case consumption, production, and prices. These intervals are accompanied by probabilities that provide precise quantitative measures of the uncertainties. We derive these probabilities from the measures of uncertainty for our parameter estimates.

The distinguishing feature of IGEM is that we estimate the parameters of our models of producer and consumer behavior econometrically. We use extensive time series data in our models of production. We introduce detailed survey data for individual households to capture the heterogeneity of consumer preferences. We employ econometric methods to quantify the uncertainties in our estimates by means of confidence intervals for the unknown parameters.

Our evaluations of energy and environmental policies involve comparisons between the IGEM base case projections and projections under alternative policies. We present new techniques for determining confidence intervals for the consequences of changes in policy. The probabilities associated with these intervals measure the uncertainties in our policy evaluations. In chapter 9 we provide a detailed analysis of the uncertainties in evaluating the substitution of carbon tax revenues for reductions in capital income tax rates.

In chapter 10 we summarize the key innovations in our design of new energy and environmental policies in an epilogue to the book. The most important innovation is to link the markets for all commodities in every time period by means of our Intertemporal General Equilibrium Model of the United States. The prices determined by markets for capital services and investment goods summarize the expectations of future prices needed by market participants in making current decisions.

We illustrate the practical consequences of the intertemporal price system captured by IGEM by linking environmental taxes to fiscal reform. The substitution of carbon tax revenues for reductions in the tax rates for capital income reduces the cost of capital, a price determined in the market for capital services. This stimulates capital formation by means of the price determined in the market for investment goods. The increase in the supply of capital in future time periods offsets the costs of controlling environmental pollution and produces the double dividend of simultaneous improvements in environmental quality and economic performance.

Our evaluation of alternative energy and environmental policies depends on the impacts of these policies on individual and social welfare. The traditional approach for comparing policies in terms of the distributions of individual welfare fails to provide a clear-cut ranking of these policies. Our innovation is to introduce measures of social welfare that combine equity and efficiency and lead to a complete ordering of alternative policies. We show how value judgments enter into social welfare valuations by comparing results for different social welfare functions.

The principal innovation in our aggregate model of consumer behavior is to incorporate the heterogeneity of individual consumers through data on the demographic characteristics of households. For this purpose we use a large body of individual household survey data. We combine data on individual households with price data that vary over cross sections of households as well as over time. A second major innovation in our modeling of consumer behavior is the recovery of measures of individual welfare from aggregate demands and supplies.

Substitution among goods and services in response to price changes is the key to understanding the economic impacts of energy and environmental policies. We have employed these price changes in modeling producer behavior at the industry level, as well as consumer behavior at the individual level. Our most important innovation in modeling producer behavior is to distinguish changes in technology induced by price changes from substitution in response to prices for a given technology. For this purpose we represent technology by means of latent variables and use these variables in projecting changes in technology into the future.

The innovation in IGEM that sets it apart from other models of energy and environmental policy is that we estimate the parameters of our models of producer and consumer behavior econometrically. We extend these econometric methods to include demands for public consumption by the government sector and demands for imports and supplies of exports by the rest of the world. Our econometric estimates are based on extensive survey data for individual households and a large body of time series data for individual industries, as well as the government and rest-of-the-world sectors.

Our final innovation is to quantify the uncertainties that arise in projecting the growth of the U.S. economy into the future. We also quantify the uncertainties that arise in evaluating the outcomes of changes in energy and environmental policies. Our methodology exploits the econometric estimates of the unknown parameters of our models of producer and consumer behavior. We transform the uncertainties from these estimates into measures of uncertainty in model outcomes based on precise probabilities.

To sum up: Our overall conclusion is that the design of new energy and environmental policies for the United States requires a market-based approach. The price mechanisms that determine capital formation are critical in designing energy and environmental policies that work through the intertemporal price system. We have illustrated these mechanisms by analyzing the substitution of revenues from environmental taxes for reductions in tax rates on capital incomes. This substitution reduces the cost of capital and stimulates capital formation.

Since market-based approaches like environmental taxes and tradable permits would generate substantial government revenues, environmental policies must be integrated with the government budget. This opens the possibility of enhancing environmental quality and improving economic performance through fiscal reform, the double dividend of our title. Finally, energy and environmental policies must be evaluated in terms of their impacts on individual and social welfare.

For this purpose we use measures of individual and social welfare that incorporate information about consumer preferences from the econometric model of consumer behavior in IGEM.

Acknowledgments

The original version of our Intertemporal General Equilibrium Model was presented by Jorgenson and Wilcoxen (1990). A wide range of applications of this model are discussed in Jorgenson (1998b). We present version 16 of the model in chapter 8 of the *Handbook of Computable General Equilibrium Modeling*, edited by Peter Dixon and Dale Jorgenson (2012). This book presents version 18 of the model, which we have developed for the U.S. Environmental Protection Agency. We are very grateful for support of our research, but nothing in the book should be interpreted as an official position of the agency.

We are greatly indebted to Eric Smith, our project manager at EPA, and to Allen Fawcett, Acting Director of the Climate Change Division of the Office of Air and Radiation, and his predecessors at EPA for their support and advice on the project. We are also indebted to Al McGartland, Director of the National Center for Environmental Economics (NCEE), and David Evans, our project manager at NCEE, as well as Richard Garbaccio of the NCEE staff, for their support and advice. Mun Ho is grateful to Resources for the Future, where he was a Visiting Fellow during much of his work on this book.

In designing the latest version of our model, we have greatly benefited from the recommendations of the *Peer Review Panel for IGEM and ADAGE* (2010), Charles Kolstad, Chair, Gilbert Metcalf, Ian Sue Wing, and Roberton Williams. The panel's full report is available on EPA's Climate Economics website. The peer review included our studies of legislative initiatives on climate policy. These are fully documented on EPA's Legislative Analyses website and summarized in chapter 8 of the *Handbook of Computable General Equilibrium Modeling*.

We are greatly indebted to Daniel Slesnick for his contributions to the model of consumer behavior and the measures of individual and social welfare presented in chapter 3. He is the co-author of the article by Jorgenson and Slesnick (2008) that presents this model, and of chapter 17 of the *Handbook of Computable General Equilibrium Modeling* (Dixon and Jorgenson 2012), summarizing the econometric methodology. His collaboration in modeling consumer behavior and measuring welfare has been essential throughout the project.

We are grateful to Hui Jin for her collaboration on the model of producer behavior presented in chapter 4. She is the co-author of the article by Jin and Jorgenson (2010) that presents this model and the summary of the methodology in chapter 17 of the *Handbook of Computable General Equilibrium Modeling*. We are indebted to Kun-Young Yun for his collaboration on the representation of the U.S. tax structure used in IGEM. His contributions are summarized in Jorgenson and Yun (2001) and in chapter 10 of the *Handbook*.

Finally, we are very grateful to Jon Samuels for his collaboration on the time series data set for the industry-level production account used in our econometric modeling of producer behavior in chapter 4. This data set is reported in greater detail in Jorgenson, Ho, and Samuels (2012). We are indebted to Yu Shi for her contributions to the covariance formulas for the production model used in chapter 9 and to Ankur Patel for simulations of the model in constructing confidence intervals for the outcome variables in chapter 9.

Trina Ott of the Department of Economics at Harvard University, with the assistance of Robert "Sully" Winn, assembled the manuscript for the book in machine-readable form, edited the individual chapters, and prepared them for typesetting. We are grateful to Nancy Benjamin at Books By Design for managing the project, including copyediting, proofreading, and indexing. We would like to thank Toppan Best-set Premedia Ltd. for the typesetting and The MIT Press for the artwork. The editorial staff of The MIT Press, especially Jane Macdonald and Emily Taber, was helpful at every stage of the project. As always, the authors retain sole responsibility for any remaining deficiencies in the volume.

1 Designing Energy and Environmental Policies

1.1 Introduction

In this book we present a new approach for designing energy and environmental policies in the United States. Developing and implementing a coherent energy and environmental policy has always been problematic. This arises from the fact that the production and use of energy are characterized by large and well-documented "hidden costs." These costs are described in a congressionally mandated study by the National Research Council (NRC).[1] The most important hidden costs of energy result from the environmental effects of burning fossil fuels. In the absence of environmental policy, these costs are ignored by economic decision makers and are not reflected in energy prices.

Since economic statistics depend largely on market transactions, the hidden costs of producing and consuming energy are invisible in our national accounts and other economic reports. The U.S. government produces very detailed official statistics on energy prices and quantities, the production and consumption of energy, and its distribution among households and industries.[2] These outcomes reflect the market effects of using energy. The costs are taken into account by economic decision makers and are reflected in energy markets and energy statistics. However, the U.S. government does not provide official statistics on the hidden costs associated with energy use. This poses a major challenge for the formulation and implementation of energy and environmental policies.

Despite the lack of official statistics, it is important not to exaggerate the difficulties of documenting and using information on the hidden costs of energy. The U.S. Environmental Protection Agency (EPA) generates a great deal of information on the effects of energy use as well as the use of many other products that create environmental hazards.

A recent example is the study, *Benefits and Costs of the Clean Air Act: Second Retrospective Study—1990 to 2020*, issued in March 2011.[3] This study is devoted to evaluation of the Clean Air Act of 1970 and the Clean Air Act Amendments of 1990.

The effects of energy use are an active area for investigation by economists. New results have recently been reported by Muller, Mendelsohn, and Nordhaus in their important paper, "Environmental Accounting for Pollution in the United States Economy."[4] The methodology employed in this study is also used by the NRC in *Hidden Costs of Energy* and the EPA in the *Second Retrospective Study*. This information can be used for designing energy policies, including energy taxes, that would enable markets to incorporate the effects of the hidden costs of energy production and use.

In the absence of the hidden costs of energy, the role of government policy would be to maintain competitive and smoothly functioning energy markets. However, energy production is carried out around the globe and involves a substantial portion of U.S. international trade.[5] This results in important national security costs for maintaining access to foreign energy supplies. In addition, the production of energy is itself subject to hidden costs. An important illustration is the ongoing controversy over the environmental effects of hydraulic fracturing, or "fracking," in the production of petroleum and natural gas.

The most important hidden costs of energy are those associated with environmental pollution. A textbook example is a power plant that emits smoke and sulfur dioxide as by-products of electricity production. These emissions are dispersed to the surrounding population, and smoke and sulfate particles find their way into people's lungs, resulting in disease and premature death. Failure to restrict emissions produces an inefficient outcome. As an example, Muller, Mendelsohn, and Nordhaus (2011) estimate that environmental damages for coal-fired power plants in the United States are more than double the value added by these plants.[6]

An environmental policy for dealing with the hidden costs of energy requires that users of fossil fuels, firms and households, bear the incremental costs of the health and environmental damages. The objective of environmental policy is to enable economic decision makers to "internalize" these incremental costs. This could be achieved by levying taxes on emissions that are equal to the incremental damages.[7] These taxes would be cost-effective, since every user of energy would face the same taxes for damages associated with different forms of energy. This would reduce costs of pollution control to a minimum, since there would be no opportunities for reducing cost by shifting costs among alternative energy sources.

For example, environmental taxes could be levied on emissions of EPA's six criterion air pollutants from fossil fuel combustion. These are coarse particulate matter or smoke; fine particulate matter, also from smoke; sulfur dioxide; nitrogen oxides; volatile organic compounds; and ammonia. Using the data on the hidden costs of energy from their work with Nordhaus, Muller and Mendelsohn (2009) have designed a system of taxes based on these emissions.[8] One result of empirical studies of the hidden costs of energy is that pollution is greatest in relationship to heat production for coal, next greatest for petroleum products, and least for natural gas.[9]

Climate change is an important environmental cost of using energy. This arises from the release of by-products of fossil fuel combustion, such as carbon dioxide, into the atmosphere. These gases absorb heat radiated by the earth's surface and radiate some of this heat back to the earth's surface, resulting in global warming. Climate scientists refer to this as the "greenhouse effect." Gases that absorb heat and radiate it back to the earth are labeled "greenhouse gases." Since carbon dioxide is the most important of these gases, emissions of greenhouse gases are often converted to equivalent amounts of carbon dioxide in terms of global warming potential.

Nordhaus (2008) has designed a carbon tax, that is, a tax on the greenhouse gas content of fossil fuels, that would internalize the hidden costs of energy due to global warming.[10] The greenhouse gas content of fossil fuels is highly correlated with emissions of the criterion pollutants. Coal has the highest carbon dioxide content per unit of heat production, oil has the next highest content, and natural gas the least. A system of environmental taxes on fossil fuel combustion would generate both health and environmental benefits and also reduce the contribution of this combustion to global climate change.

A carbon tax is sometimes advocated in the absence of environmental taxes for the EPA's criterion air pollutants. The benefits that accrue from reduction in conventional pollutants are then treated as "ancillary" to the control of emissions of greenhouse gases. Muller and Mendelsohn (2009) have designed a system of energy taxes that includes both of these hidden costs of using energy. This approach is also used by the National Research Council in quantifying the *Hidden Costs of Energy* and by the EPA in the *Second Retrospective Study*.

One alternative to environmental taxes is a cap-and-trade system, like the one used for sulfur dioxide in the United States since the Clean Air Act Amendments of 1990.[11] Under this system emissions permits are issued up to a "cap" and market participants are then allowed to trade permits until the cost of emissions is equalized for all participants. A cap-and-trade system for greenhouse gas emissions is employed in the European Union Emission Trading Scheme. A cap-and-trade system for greenhouse gases was proposed by U.S. members of Congress Henry Waxman and Edward Markey in the American Clean Energy and Security Act of 2009.[12]

A second alternative to energy taxes is a set of energy conservation standards, such as the Corporate Average Fuel Economy (CAFE) standards imposed on automobiles. The incremental cost of reducing pollution varies widely among the different programs and different producers within each program. This results in an effective but expensive approach to pollution reduction.[13] A "market-based" approach, based on environmental taxes or tradable permits, would reduce costs of pollution control to a minimum. The same arguments apply to tax incentives for substituting renewable sources of energy for fossil fuels in electricity production.[14] The costs vary substantially among different renewable energy sources. Cost-ineffective regulations and tax incentives impose an unnecessary burden on the U.S. economy.

Parry and Williams (2012) and Parry and Krupnick (2011) have pointed out that a major proportion of the reduction in carbon dioxide reductions resulting from climate policy in the United States would result from fuel switching in the generation of electricity, in particular, the substitution of natural gas for coal. This is already taking place on a broad scale, due to the decline in the price of natural gas. Many of the benefits of a market-based approach could be achieved by a well-designed carbon dioxide intensity standard for electricity generation. Burtraw (2012) has observed that the federal system of government in the United States is a major obstacle to implementation of market-based approaches.

Targeted and technology-neutral subsidies for energy production are intended to deal with a different market failure, namely, hidden costs of energy production. These costs are also reflected in the environmental regulation of extractive industries that require remediation of production sites and mitigation of other environmental damages. While energy production policies deal with important market failures, they are not a cost-effective method for internalizing the hidden costs of energy use. These policies fail to reflect the substantial differences in these hidden costs associated with the different fossil fuels—coal, oil, and natural gas.

1.2 Energy and Environmental Policies

In this book we focus on energy taxes in designing energy and environmental policies for the United States. Energy taxes would put renewable energy sources not subject to these taxes onto a level playing field with the nonrenewable sources that will continue to provide a major part of our energy supply. Moreover, energy taxes would reflect the highly important differences in the hidden costs of energy associated with the combustion of different fossil fuels—coal, oil, and natural gas. Finally, we are able to exploit four decades of experience with the energy conservation that results from higher energy prices in modeling the reactions of producers and consumers to energy taxes.

Energy taxes would internalize the hidden costs of energy through energy markets. Our approach to designing energy and environmental policies is based on modeling the impact of these taxes on energy prices. For this purpose we employ a general equilibrium model for the United States that includes supplies and demands for energy and other commodities.[15] This enables us to capture all the ramifications of energy taxes in the formation of prices for energy and other commodities.

Our modeling framework for the U.S. economy is provided by the Intertemporal General Equilibrium Model (IGEM) introduced by Jorgenson and Wilcoxen (1990).[16] Version 16 of IGEM was developed for the U.S. Environmental Protection Agency.[17] The novel feature of IGEM is that the equilibrium concept is based on an intertemporal price system, linking prices in the current time period to future prices through markets for investment goods and capital assets. An intertemporal price system incorporates the impact of energy taxes on current prices of energy and other commodities and also on expectations about these prices in the future. This is crucial for capturing the impact of changes in energy and environmental policies on the expectations of market participants about future prices.

Since economic growth is an important determinant of U.S. demand for energy, an essential first step in evaluating alternative energy and environmental policies is to analyze the determinants of U.S. economic growth. This theory has been developed in the form appropriate for modeling the interrelationships among energy, the environment, and U.S. economic growth by Cass (1965) and Koopmans (1967).[18] The time path of output in a neoclassical model depends on energy and environmental policies through the impact of these policies on current and future prices. This is captured by the intertemporal price system modeled in IGEM.

In disaggregating the economic impacts of U.S. energy and environmental policies, we preserve the key features of more highly aggregated intertemporal general equilibrium models. Maler (1974, 1975) and Uzawa (1975, 1988) have presented neoclassical theories of economic growth with pollution abatement.[19] Solow (1974a, 1974b) has developed a theory of economic growth that includes an exhaustible resource.[20] In this book we focus on pollution abatement, since the U.S. economy is relatively open to trade in natural resources, including coal, oil, and natural gas.

The long-run determinants of economic growth are independent of energy and environmental policies. However, the neoclassical theory of economic growth also provides a framework for analyzing intermediate-run growth trends. These trends depend on energy and environmental policies through their effects of capital accumulation and rates of productivity growth. In this context the "intermediate-run" refers to the time needed for the capital-to-output ratio to converge to a steady state. This often requires decades, so that modeling the impact of energy and environmental policies on intermediate-run trends is critical for policy evaluation.

The slowdown of the U.S. economy during the 1970s and 1980s and the acceleration of growth during the 1990s are striking examples of changes in intermediate-run trends. Two events associated with the slowdown—more restrictive environmental policies and an increase in world petroleum prices—have led to a substantial literature on the interactions of energy supplies and prices, environmental quality and its cost, and the sources of economic growth.[21] Similarly, Jorgenson (2009a) has demonstrated that the rapid development of information technology is the key to more rapid growth in the 1990s and 2000s. Despite the U.S. financial crisis of 2007–2009, Jorgenson and Vu (2011) have shown that the outlook for the growth of the U.S. economy remains relatively favorable in the intermediate run.

The neoclassical theory of economic growth provides the framework for the important studies of climate policy by Nordhaus (2008, 2010).[22] Nordhaus (2008) presents the latest version of the Dynamic, Integrated

Climate-Economy (DICE) model. This is a one-sector neoclassical growth model that integrates a production function for the world economy with a model of intertemporal choice for a representative consumer. Nordhaus combines these familiar elements with a model of the impact of climate change on productivity. This model links climate change to world output through a series of dynamic relationships based on the well-known greenhouse effect.

The organizing mechanism for the DICE model, like that for IGEM, is an intertemporal price system. Changes in the global climate are generated by economic activity, especially the combustion of fossil fuels. The parameters of the model are calibrated to extensive data on the growth of the world economy. The physical model of climate change incorporates the principal features of simulation models developed by climate scientists. Climate change feeds back to economic activity by reducing productivity levels. These mechanisms provide the basis for the design of climate policy by application of a tax on greenhouse gas emissions.

Clarke, Böhringer, and Rutherford (2009) have provided a recent survey of models employed for the evaluation of alternative climate policies. This is based on a report on EMF 22, a comparative study of simulations from 18 models, including IGEM and other economic models, technology-based models, and integrated assessment models combining economic and physical models, like Nordhaus's DICE model. The study was conducted by the Energy Modeling Forum (EMF) at Stanford University and is one of an extended series of studies comparing alternative models for analyzing energy and environmental policies.[23]

The DICE model provides a very valuable perspective on world climate policy through the integration of economic and physical models. However, the design and implementation of energy and environmental policies requires a much more detailed modeling approach for the U.S. economy. To capture the heterogeneity of energy producers and consumers, we distinguish among industries and demographic groups within the United States. An econometric approach to modeling the impact of energy and environmental policies is essential in describing the behavior of different industries and different demographic groups.[24]

An important dimension for disaggregation of the U.S. economy is to distinguish among industries and commodities, especially different forms of energy, in order to measure policy impacts for narrower segments of the U.S. economy. We model the policy impact on different fuels, as well as differences among industries in responses to the imposition of energy taxes. A second avenue for disaggregation is to distinguish among households by level of wealth and demographic characteristics. We model differences in responses to price changes and environmental taxes for different households. We also use the effects of energy and environmental policies on different households to capture the distributional effects of energy and environmental policies, as in Jorgenson, Slesnick, and Wilcoxen (1992), Jorgenson, Goettle, Ho, Slesnick, and Wilcoxen (2010), and chapter 8 of this book.[25]

1.3 General Equilibrium Model

We next summarize the features of the latest version (version 18) of our Intertemporal General Equilibrium Model, which was prepared for the U.S. Environmental Protection Agency and which is discussed in more detail in chapter 2. The household sector, modeled by Jorgenson and Slesnick (2008), is the core of the demand side of IGEM presented in chapter 3. This is supplemented by the models of investment and government demand and models of exports to the rest of the world discussed in chapter 5. The core of the supply side of the model is the domestic production sector, modeled by Jin and Jorgenson (2010) and described in chapter 4. This is augmented by the models of imports from the rest-of-the-world sector discussed in chapter 5.

Our household model has three stages. In the first stage *lifetime full income* is allocated between consumption and savings. Full income includes leisure as well as income from the supply of capital and labor services. Consumption consists of commodities and leisure; we refer to this as *full consumption*. In the second stage full consumption is allocated to leisure and three commodity groups—nondurables, capital services, and services. In the third stage the three commodity groups are allocated to the 36 commodities, including the five types of energy. We describe the household model in more detail in chapter 3.

By constructing a model of consumer demand through aggregation over individual demands, we are able to incorporate the restrictions implied by the theory of individual consumer behavior. In addition, we incorporate demographic information about individual households from the Consumer Expenditure Survey (CEX), published by the Bureau of Labor Statistics (BLS). For the period beyond the sample, we project the distribution of the population by age, sex, and race of the head of the household along with the size of the population. Our population projections are discussed in more detail in chapter 6.

In modeling the domestic production sector in chapter 4 we distinguish among 35 industries and commodities, including five energy-producing sectors—Coal Mining, Petroleum and Natural Gas Mining, Petroleum Refining, Electric Utilities, and Gas Utilities. The combustion of fossil fuels is captured by the use of coal, natural gas, and petroleum. Noncomparable imports are a thirty-sixth commodity that is not produced domestically but enters as an input into the domestic production sectors.

Our model of producer behavior captures substitution among inputs in response to price changes and changes in technology. Modeling price substitution is especially important for analyzing the economic impacts of energy and environmental policies that induce substantial price changes. However, production patterns also depend on changes in output per unit of input, or *total factor productivity*, and *biases of technical change*, or changes in the composition of inputs unrelated to price changes. For example, energy use may decline in intensity due to energy-saving changes in technology, as well as substitution away from higher-priced energy.

We employ a production function for each of the 35 industries in IGEM. These industries include the five energy producers. The output of each industry is produced by using capital, labor, and intermediate inputs of energy, materials, and services. The value of capital services consists of all property-type income—profits and other operating surplus, depreciation, and taxes on property. The price of capital services is the price of the corresponding asset, multiplied by an annualization factor that we denote the *cost of capital*. The cost of capital consists of the rate of return, the rate of depreciation, less capital gains or plus capital losses, all adjusted for taxes.[26]

The construction of the price of capital services and the cost of capital is described in Jorgenson, Ho, and Stiroh (2005), chapter 5, and summarized in appendix B. This is based on the detailed development in Jorgenson and Yun (2001, 2012). The quantity of capital services for each industry is an aggregate of the service flows from all asset types. Our database identifies 62 asset categories, including equipment and software, structures, land, and inventories. We emphasize that the price of capital services is distinct from the price of capital stock. The price of capital services is an annualized rental, while the capital stock price is the price for acquiring an asset.

Data on capital input in IGEM are derived from investments in structures, producers' durable equipment, land, inventories, and consumers' durables. This differs from the definition of investment in the National Income and Product Accounts (NIPAs), which excludes consumers' durables.[27] There are two sides to the private capital account. The capital stock is rented to the producers, as described in chapter 5, and the annual rental payment is the capital income of the household sector. The flow of investment is purchased annually to replace and augment the capital stock. We consider both aspects of the capital market.

We assume that the supply of capital is determined by past investments. We also assume that there are no installation or adjustment costs in converting new investment goods into capital stocks or transferring assets among industries. Under these simplifying assumptions the savings decision by the household is identical to the investment decision. We analyze the savings-investment decision in detail to clarify the role of the cost of capital, a key equation of IGEM. Since capital formation is the outcome of intertemporal optimization, decisions today are based on expectations of future prices and rates of return. Policies announced today that affect future prices will affect investment decisions today. This is an important feature of the intertemporal price system modeled in IGEM.

Similarly, the quantity of labor input for each industry is an aggregate over the hours for workers with different demographic categories, where the weights are the rates of hourly compensation, including wages and salaries and benefits. Our database identifies seven age groups, six education groups, and the two genders. The construction of the labor input indices is described in Jorgenson, Ho, and Stiroh (2005), chapter 6, and summarized in appendix B.

The construction of capital and labor inputs is a critical feature of our historical data set. Simple sums of hours worked or asset quantities would not fully capture the substitution possibilities within each aggregate. For example, a simple sum of hours worked would not adequately characterize the impact on labor input of the substitution toward more highly educated workers as the educational attainment of the labor force increases. Similarly, a simple sum of computers and industrial buildings would fail to reflect the impact on capital input of substitution toward information technology equipment and software as prices of these inputs decline relative to buildings.

Intermediate inputs are divided among 35 commodity groups consisting of domestically produced energy, materials, and services and competitive imports of these commodities There is a thirty-sixth input consisting of noncomparable imports, defined to include goods not produced in the United States, such as coffee, natural rubber, and foreign port services. The generation of our data on industry-level outputs and intermediate inputs is described by Jorgenson, Ho, and Stiroh (2005), chapter 4, and summarized in appendix B.

The output of the production sector is divided among 35 commodities, each the primary product of one of the 35 industries. Many industries produce secondary products as well, for example, the petroleum-refining industry produces refined petroleum products and secondary products that are the primary outputs of the chemicals industry. The relation between industries and commodity output is given by the *make* matrix (or supply matrix) in the official input-output accounts. We model joint production of primary and secondary products as well as substitution among inputs and technical change for each industry.

The model of producer behavior introduced by Jin and Jorgenson (2010) captures the changes in patterns of production revealed in the data. Latent variables representing biases of technical change are required to track the changes in inputs that are not explained by price changes. Finally, a latent variable representing the level of technology is needed to capture differences in productivity growth rates across industries and over time. Simplified formulations, like those described in the next section, would lead to inaccurate estimates of the cost of policy changes, generating costs that are far too high.

1.4 Consumer Behavior

A model of a representative consumer is a common approach for modeling consumer behavior in general equilibrium models. Aggregate demand functions are treated as if they could be generated by a single utility-maximizing individual.[28] This has the advantage of incorporating restrictions implied by the theory of consumer behavior. The disadvantage of this approach is that aggregate demand functions can also be expressed as sums of demand functions for individual households and must reflect the heterogeneity of consumer behavior observable in census and survey data.

Gorman (1953) has provided a set of restrictions on individual demand functions implied by the model of a representative consumer. These restrictions are satisfied by the linear expenditure system proposed by Klein and Rubin (1947) and estimated by Stone (1954). This is the most common model of consumer behavior used in the construction of computable general equilibrium models. Muellbauer (1975) provides a less restrictive set of conditions for the model of a representative consumer. These conditions are satisfied, for example, by the demand system proposed by Deaton and Muellbauer (1980).

Browning, Hansen, and Heckman (1999) have emphasized the importance of heterogeneity of consumers in studies based on household-level data on consumer behavior. This is a particularly crucial issue in the calibration of macroeconomic models from microeconomic data, following the program of research proposed by Lucas (1980).[29] Browning, Hansen, and Heckman provide a detailed survey of the very extensive literature on microeconomic models of the type considered by Lucas. They conclude that the "gulf" between macroeconomic and microeconomic models is so great that the "large shelf" of micro estimates available for application to macro modeling is "virtually empty."

The gap between Lucas's calibration approach and the microeconometric modeling summarized by Browning, Hansen, and Heckman (1999) can be successfully bridged by the model of consumer behavior we summarize in chapter 3. This model is based on extensive microeconomic data for individual households and reflects the heterogeneity of these households. We drop the representative consumer model for aggregate demand functions employed in many computable general equilibrium models but retain the theory of consumer behavior at the individual household level.

Jorgenson, Lau, and Stoker (1982) developed a model of consumer behavior that dispenses with the notion of a representative consumer.[30] The demand functions are generated by direct aggregation over individual demand functions, but the individual demand functions can be recovered from the aggregate demand functions. Like the model of a representative consumer, this model of consumer behavior incorporates all the implications of the theory of individual consumer behavior.

The model introduced by Jorgenson, Lau, and Stoker includes the demographic characteristics of individual households, as well as prices and household expenditures, as determinants of consumer behavior.

These characteristics capture the enormous heterogeneity of the U.S. population. Jorgenson and Slesnick (1987) have implemented the model from time series data on personal consumption expenditures and the prices of consumer goods, including energy, as well as cross-section data on total expenditure and its composition for different types of households. This model is the core of the demand side of the intertemporal equilibrium model of Jorgenson and Wilcoxen (1990).

Jorgenson and Slesnick (2008) have extended their model of consumer behavior to include labor supply and the intertemporal allocation of full wealth. Full wealth includes the value of the household's human wealth, as well as the tangible and financial wealth of the household. Jorgenson and Slesnick (2008) implement this model of aggregate demand for goods and leisure for the United States using 150,000 individual household observations from the Consumer Expenditure Survey and price data from the Consumer Price Index for 1980–2006. The results are summarized in chapter 3 and presented in detail in appendix C.

Following Slesnick (2002) and Kokoski, Cardiff, and Moulton (1994), Jorgenson and Slesnick generate price data for U.S. regions at different points of time. They also construct quality-adjusted wages from the Consumer Expenditure Survey that vary across regions and over time and incorporate the human capital of individual workers.[31] We present the Jorgenson-Slesnick model of consumer behavior in chapter 3. We employ this model in evaluating alternative energy and environmental policies in chapter 8.

1.5 Producer Behavior

We next outline our econometric methodology for modeling producer behavior. We recognize at the outset that the predominant tradition in general equilibrium modeling does not employ econometric methods. This originated with the static input-output model of Leontief (1951). Leontief (1953) gave a further impetus to the development of general equilibrium modeling by introducing a dynamic input-output model. This is an important progenitor of the IGEM described in chapter 2.

By linearizing technology and preferences Leontief solved at one stroke the two fundamental problems in practical implementation of general equilibrium models. First, the resulting model can be solved as a system of linear equations with constant coefficients. Second, the unknown parameters describing technology and preferences, the "input-output coefficients," can be determined from a single inter-industry transactions table. The data required are available for countries that have implemented the United Nations' (2009) *System of National Accounts* (2008 SNA).[32]

The obvious objection to the fixed-coefficients approach in modeling energy and environmental policies is that the purpose of these policies is to change the input-output coefficients. For example, the purpose of imposing taxes on fossil fuels is to induce producers and consumers to substitute less polluting forms of energy for more polluting ones. A more specific example is the substitution of low-sulfur coal for high-sulfur coal by electric utilities in response to price incentives to reduce sulfur-dioxide emissions.

Johansen (1974) constructed the first successful applied general equilibrium model without Leontief's fixed-coefficients assumption. Johansen retained Leontief's fixed coefficients assumption in determining demands for intermediate goods, including energy, but employed linear-logarithmic, or Cobb-Douglas, production functions in modeling substitution between capital and labor services. Johansen also replaced Leontief's fixed-coefficients assumption for household behavior by a system of demand functions originated by Frisch (1959). He developed a method for representing the growth rates in his general equilibrium model as unknowns in a system of linear equations. Johansen's multi-sectoral growth (MSG) model of Norway is another important progenitor for the IGEM described in chapter 2.[33]

For linear logarithmic production functions, the relative shares of capital and labor inputs are fixed and can be estimated from a single data point. The capital and labor input coefficients are not fixed but change in inverse proportion to changes in relative prices. In describing producer behavior, Johansen employed econometric modeling in estimating constant rates of productivity growth. Similarly, the unknown parameters of the demand system proposed by Frisch can be determined from a single point, except for a single parameter estimated econometrically.

The essential features of Johansen's approach have been preserved in the general equilibrium models surveyed by Dixon and Parmenter (1996) and Dixon and Rimmer (2013).[34] The unknown parameters describing technology and preferences in these models are determined by calibration, supplemented by a small number of parameters estimated econometrically. The Johansen approach, like input-output analysis, can absorb the enormous amounts of detail now available for a single data point. For example, Dixon and Parmenter (1996) describe a model of Australia with 120 industries, 56 regions, 280 occupations, and several hundred family types.

The obvious disadvantage of the calibration approach is the highly restrictive assumptions on technology and preferences required to make calibration feasible. Many general equilibrium models retain the fixed-coefficients assumption of Leontief and Johansen for modeling the demand for intermediate goods, including energy. However, this assumption is directly contradicted by massive empirical evidence of price-induced energy conservation in response to higher world energy prices beginning in 1973 and again in the aftermath of the oil price spike of June 2008. Models that include substitution among energy, capital, and labor inputs frequently retain the fixed-coefficients assumption for materials. This is inconsistent with the empirical evidence that we summarize in chapter 4.

British Petroleum's (2012) *Energy Outlook 2030* shows that world energy use per unit of gross domestic product (GDP) peaked in the early 1970s and fell by more than 50% through 2011. The reductions in energy utilization induced by successive energy crises in the 1970s and the higher level of energy prices prevailing in the 1980s has been documented in great detail by Schipper and Meyers (1992). This extensive survey covers nine countries in the Organization for Economic Co-operation and Development (OECD), including the United States, for the period 1970 through 1989 and describes energy conservation in residential, manufacturing, other industry, services, passenger transport, and freight transport sectors. Reductions in energy-output ratios for these activities average 15 to 20%.

A representation of technology and preferences that overcomes the limitations of the Johansen approach requires econometric methods. A common extension of Johansen's methodology employs constant elasticities of substitution between capital and labor inputs. This model of substitution between capital and labor inputs was proposed by Arrow, Chenery, Minhas, and Solow (1961). Armington (1969) has employed this approach to model the substitution between domestic and imported varieties of a particular commodity.[35] Unfortunately, constant elasticities of substitution among more than two inputs imply, essentially, that elasticities of substitution among all inputs must be the same, as Uzawa (1962) and McFadden (1963) have shown.

A less restrictive approach to econometric modeling of producer behavior is to generate complete systems of equations for the inputs of capital, labor, energy, materials, and services (KLEMS). Each system gives quantities of inputs as functions of prices of the inputs and the level of output. The new version of IGEM discussed in this book employs the model of technical change introduced by Jin and Jorgenson (2010). The system of equations representing demand for inputs is augmented by latent variables representing the rate and biases of technical change.

The approach to modeling producer behavior employed in IGEM was originated by Christensen, Jorgenson, and Lau (1973).[36] An important application by Berndt and Jorgenson (1973) was used in modeling the impact of U.S. energy policies by Hudson and Jorgenson (1974).[37] This approach to modeling producer behavior was extended to include technical change by Jorgenson and Fraumeni (2000).[38] Their model forms the core of the supply side of the original version of IGEM developed by Jorgenson and Wilcoxen (1990) and the models surveyed by Jorgenson (1998b).

Despite the limitations of calibration of models of producer behavior to a single data point, this approach has its defenders. For example, Dawkins, Srinivasan, and Whalley (2001) have advocated calibration to a single point. Their argument is buttressed by the lack of data for implementation of econometric methods like those of Jin and Jorgenson (2010). These methods require an extensive time series of data on outputs, inputs, and productivity growth.

Data suitable for econometric modeling of producer behavior were generated for the United States by Jorgenson, Gollop, and Fraumeni (1987). These data provided the empirical basis for the econometric models employed by Jorgenson and Wilcoxen (1990). The U.S. data used in the new version of IGEM cover the time period 1960 to 2005 and are based on those of Jorgenson, Ho, and Stiroh (2005). These data augment the framework of Jorgenson, Gollop, and Fraumeni by distinguishing between capital inputs that employ information technology equipment and software and other capital inputs.

The completion of the European Union (EU) KLEMS project represents a major breakthrough for econometric modeling of producer behavior. This project has involved a massive collaboration among 18 European research institutes, using a common methodology for generating the data described by Schreyer's (2001, 2009) OECD manuals for the measurement of productivity and capital. These manuals are consistent with the new United Nations' (2009) *2008 System of National Accounts* and the "new architecture" for the U.S. national accounts proposed by Jorgenson and Landefeld (2006) and Jorgenson (2009b).[39]

The EU KLEMS project has generated time series data on prices and quantities of capital, labor, energy, materials, and services inputs for 25 of the 27 EU members. For the major European economies the data cover the time period 1970 to 2005.[40] The project also includes similar data for Australia, Canada, Japan, Korea, and the United States, using the methodology of Jorgenson, Ho, and Stiroh (2005). The results of the EU KLEMS project are summarized by Timmer, Inklaar, O'Mahony, and van Ark (2010) and Mas and Stehrer (2012).

The World KLEMS Initiative formed at Harvard University on August 19–20, 2010, will extend the EU KLEMS database to include major emerging and transition economies—Argentina, Brazil, Chile, China, India, Indonesia, Mexico, Russia, Taiwan, and Turkey.[41] Jorgenson and Schreyer (2013) have developed a methodology for linking aggregate and industry-level production accounts. They present data for outputs, inputs, and productivity appropriate for modeling producer behavior within the framework of the United Nations' *2008 System of National Accounts* used by national accountants around the world.

Industry-level KLEMS data have been incorporated into the official national accounts for Australia, Canada, Denmark, Finland, Italy, The Netherlands, Sweden, and the United States.[42] Data are available for many countries for implementing the econometric methods required to overcome the limitations of Johansen-type models. These data will be updated annually and will provide the basis for implementation of econometric models of producer behavior like those of Jin and Jorgenson (2010), summarized in chapter 4 and presented in detail in appendix C.

1.6 Government and the Rest of the World

The U.S. government sector plays an important role in IGEM. Government spending affects household welfare directly through transfer payments and direct spending on goods and services for consumers. Taxes to raise government revenue affect household welfare by inserting tax wedges between supply prices for commodities and the prices paid by consumers. Our model for the government sector is presented in chapter 5. We set tax rates exogenously and take the shares of public expenditure by commodity to be exogenous, so that government revenues are endogenous. We set the government deficit exogenously, allowing the level of real government purchases to be endogenous.

The government collects revenues for the social insurance trust funds and transfers these funds to households. In the new architecture for the U.S. national accounts proposed by Jorgenson and Landefeld (2006) and Jorgenson (2009b), the trust funds are treated as part of household assets. For example, Social Security contributions and benefits are regarded as transfers within the household sector and not accounted as government revenue and expenditures. The tax rate on labor income in IGEM thus includes federal and state and local income taxes but not social insurance contributions.

We simplify tax codes of the federal, state, and local governments in order to highlight the key distortions. We represent sales taxes, import tariffs, capital income taxes, labor income taxes, property taxes, and wealth or estate taxes explicitly in IGEM. While the U.S. Internal Revenue Code includes standard deductions, progressive rate schedules, alternative minimum taxes, and federal-state interactions, we summarize these features by distinguishing between average and marginal tax rates for labor income. These two labor tax rates capture the key feature that marginal rates are higher than average rates.

In IGEM we allow for a consumption tax, that is, a tax on personal consumption expenditures but not on intermediate purchases. We also modify taxes on capital, for example, by changing the deductibility of household mortgage interest from income for tax purposes. These features allow for the simulation of tax reforms combined with environmental taxes. In policy simulations we often impose a new tax or subsidy but maintain revenue neutrality. Where the new subsidy is offset by a lump sum tax, we represent this tax by a variable that is subtracted from household income and added to government revenues.

The total revenue of the government sector is the sum of sales taxes, tariffs, property taxes, capital income taxes, labor income taxes, wealth taxes, nontax revenues, unit output taxes, energy and environmental taxes, imputed capital consumption, income from government enterprises, and lump sum taxes. Total government expenditures are the sum of purchases, transfers, and interest payments both to domestic households and to the rest of the world. The public deficit is total outlays less total revenues, a concept equal to the official net borrowing requirement. Since we set tax rates exogenously and set the deficit exogenously, IGEM generates economic activity and government revenues endogenously. Government transfers and interest are also set exogenously. The remaining item, general government final purchases, is determined residually.

The government deficit adds to the public debt, which is separated between debt held by U.S. residents and debt held by foreigners. The "Integrated Macroeconomic Accounts," constructed by the Bureau of Economic Analysis and the Board of Governors of the Federal Reserve System, provide this information.[43] Similarly, the stock of debt to the rest of the world is the accumulation of the foreign borrowing. The deficit and stocks of debt in IGEM correspond to actual values for the sample period and official projections beyond that, as described in more detail in chapter 6.

Since IGEM is a U.S. model, the supply of goods by the rest of the world and the demand for U.S. exports are exogenous. We treat imports and domestic outputs as imperfect substitutes, which is reasonable at our level of aggregation. For example, while imports of a particular type of steel may be a perfect substitute for the domestically produced variety, the output of the primary metals industry is a composite of many types of steel and other commodities, so that this output is not a perfect substitute for imports of primary metals. We also assume that U.S. demand is not sufficient to affect world relative prices.

Imports into the United States have risen rapidly not only in absolute terms but as a share of domestic output. This cannot be explained by prices alone so we employ latent variables like those introduced by Jin and Jorgenson (2010) in modeling changes in the pattern of imports not induced by price changes. We have now closed the loop in the flow of commodities. We began with each production sector purchasing intermediate inputs and selling output. The price of intermediates is the total supply price given as a function of domestic and imported commodities.

For each commodity group, we model the allocation of total supply between domestic consumption and exports. We use Jin and Jorgenson's (2010) approach to technical change to track the historical changes in exports that cannot be explained by price movements. The current account balance in dollars is the value of exports less imports, plus net interest receipts, and less private and government transfers. The current account surplus, less the portion due to government foreign investment, adds to the stock of net private U.S. foreign assets.

Different closures of the external sector are employed in general equilibrium models of international trade.[44] The current account could be set exogenously, allowing world prices to adjust. Alternatively, world prices could be taken to be exogenous and the current account balance to be endogenous. In a dynamic model the second option would require a portfolio choice model to determine the demand for foreign assets and hence the path of current account balances.[45] This is beyond the scope of IGEM, and we set the current account exogenously, making the world price endogenous, as described in chapter 5. We discuss projections of this price and other exogenous variables in the rest-of-the-world sector in chapter 6.

The model closure conditions in IGEM require that government and current account deficits are not affected by changes in energy and environmental policies. With energy tax revenues as a new source of government revenue, this treatment of the government budget is a key assumption in analyzing the economic impact of policy changes in chapter 8.

To simplify welfare comparisons we treat real aggregate government expenditures under energy tax policies as exogenous. We hold real expenditures on goods equal to the base case and preserve only deficit neutrality. Although we do not model price inflation in IGEM, there are large changes in relative prices due to changes in the policy. Variations in U.S. saving fully account for the variations in U.S. investment and capital formation, so that there can be no crowding out or crowding in of private investment.

1.7 Model Solution

The organizing mechanism of IGEM is an intertemporal price system balancing demands and supplies for all products and factors of production. This price system links the prices of assets in every time period to the discounted values of future capital services. In IGEM forward-looking behavior of producers and consumers in response to expectations of future price changes is combined with backward linkages among investment, capital stock, and capital services in modeling the dynamics of economic growth.

The IGEM determines a unique growth path for the U.S. economy. This leads naturally to the development of the algorithm for solving the model. Like the Cass-Koopmans neoclassical model of economic growth, IGEM has a saddle-point property: In IGEM the capital stock generated by investment is the state variable. Full consumption determined by intertemporal optimization by households is the costate variable. Given the initial value of capital stock, there is a unique value of full consumption for which the model converges to a steady state.

There are many state variables in IGEM, such as the government debt, claims on foreigners, and the latent variables estimated by Jin and Jorgenson (2010) and described in chapter 4. These state variables are not determined by optimizing behavior and have no associated costate variables. We take these state variables to be exogenous and project them into the future on the basis of historical trends. For example, in a disaggregated model like IGEM a well-defined steady state requires that all industries have the same rate of productivity growth. In IGEM we focus on an intermediate term of 75 years and impose a zero rate of productivity growth in the long run. This assumption allows us to specify a productivity growth rate for each industry in the intermediate term that replicates the observed variety of economic behavior.

We first describe the equilibrium within each period, given the inherited capital stock and an initial guess of full consumption for that period. We then describe the intertemporal equilibrium linking full consumption across time periods. In the commodity markets the demand side of the economy consists of intermediate demands by producers, household consumption, investment demand, government demand, and exports. The supply of each commodity comes from domestic producers and imports. Under the assumptions of constant returns to scale and factor mobility, the equilibrium prices clear all markets for each period.

In capital market equilibrium the demand from all industries and households is equal to the supply from the inherited stock of capital. Capital income is equal to the aggregate price multiplied by the flow of capital services given by the capital stock. Since we assume that capital is mobile across sectors, only a single rate of return is needed to clear this market. However, we observe different rates of return in the historical data. To reconcile this with our simplifying assumption of capital mobility, we treat the industry rental prices as proportional to the economy-wide rental price. Turning to the labor market, supply comes from the household demand for leisure and the demand is the sum over the demands from the 35 industries and government. We treat the industry wage rates as proportional to the economy-wide wage rate.

Three additional equations must hold in equilibrium. The government deficit is exogenous, so that government spending on goods and services is determined endogenously. The current account surplus is also exogenous, so that the world relative price is endogenous. To determine the equilibrium of saving and investment, household saving is first allocated to lending to the government to finance the public deficit and lending to the rest of the world, both adjusted for government borrowing from abroad. The remainder is allocated to investment in domestic private capital. Investment and savings decisions are identical in IGEM.

The steady state of IGEM is reached when the state and costate variables are stationary. The two dynamic equations—capital accumulation and household optimization—determine the steady state. Along the transition path from the initial state variables to the steady state, the capital accumulation equation and the equation for household optimization must hold. In addition, the cost of capital links the marginal product of capital with the rate of return.

We approximate the steady state of IGEM at 120 periods after the initial conditions. We structure the algorithm to solve our model in a sequence of steps summarized in chapter 2 and described in more detail in appendix D. Briefly, this algorithm consists of (i) solving for the steady state, (ii) guessing a path of full consumption and capital stock, (iii) calculating equilibrium in each period conditional on these guesses; and (iv) deriving an implied new stock of capital from the investment in each period. We reiterate this sequence of steps until the capital stock satisfies the initial condition and the equation for household optimization holds for all time periods.

As described so far, IGEM has some 4000 endogenous variables for each period. In solving the model we triangulate the system into a series of nested loops. Each loop involves only a small number of equations and unknowns. This algorithm solves the resulting system quickly and is relatively easy to debug. After the base case described in chapter 6 is determined, alternative policy cases require usually only seconds to compute.[46]

1.8 Externalities

Externalities arising from energy use are represented by IGEM by variables that capture the emissions of pollutants. These variables include emissions of EPA's six criterion air pollutants and emissions of carbon dioxide and other greenhouse gases from combustion of fossil fuels. For the analysis of climate policy in chapter 8, we define a single variable that represents total greenhouse gas emissions from all sources, expressed in terms equivalent to carbon dioxide in global warming potential.

We derive our measures of emissions from detailed historical data in EPA (2010b), *Inventory of U.S. Greenhouse Gas Emissions and Sinks*.[47] The emissions data are sorted and aggregated to create the totals. These totals are then allocated to the output and inputs of each industry and each final demand category, as described in chapter 7. For projections beyond the sample period, the emission coefficients are set to follow historical trends that taper to a steady state, as described in chapter 6. Trends in the industry-level aggregates reflect changes in composition as well as trends in emissions of individual greenhouse gases.

Emissions abatement occurs through three mechanisms—output reductions, input substitutions, and price-induced technical change. The model of producer behavior presented in chapter 4 captures these effects. To illustrate the effects in their simplest form, we consider simulations of the model that exclude non-CO_2 abatement, such as bioelectricity generation, carbon capture and storage technologies, domestic sequestration and other offsets, and international permit trading. In chapter 7 we illustrate the methodology appropriate for modeling these abatement options. The energy taxes and economic costs are higher than in simulations that include these policy options.[48]

In chapter 8 we compare alternative energy tax policies with a base case generated by the model in order to isolate economic impacts implied by the supply and demand components of IGEM. A typical approach in policy assessments is to calibrate the base case to patterns of energy consumption and economic growth. For example, the EPA instructions to policy analysts often include calibration to base case projections of economic growth and energy consumption from the Energy Information Administration of the U.S. Department of Energy, as described in chapter 6. This facilitates comparisons among the simulation results from different models.

1.9 Policy Evaluation

The most important objective of our Intertemporal General Equilibrium Model is to evaluate alternative energy and environmental policies. For this purpose we first project the time path of the U.S. economy with no change in policy. We refer to this as the *base case*. We then project the time path with a policy change and refer to this as the *policy case*. For example, the base case described in chapter 6 assumes no change in energy and environmental policy, while the policy cases considered in chapter 8 impose energy and environmental taxes intended to reduce greenhouse gas emissions.

The base case and the policy case correspond to complete projections of the future growth of the U.S. economy. Each time path is characterized by an intertemporal price system that equates demands and supplies for all commodities and factors of production in every time period. In addition, the intertemporal price system must satisfy forward-looking relationships between current asset prices and the future prices of capital services for each category of assets. Finally, the model must satisfy backward-looking restrictions relating current capital stock to past investments.

The intertemporal price system is the key to avoiding the Lucas (1976) critique of policy evaluations in economic models, including econometric models and computable general equilibrium models.[49] Expectations of future prices are determined as part of the model solution for both base case and policy cases of the model. Each solution incorporates all the information used to specify each policy, as well as the other information used to generate time paths of U.S. economic growth. The key point of the Lucas critique is that expectations change when policies change. This is a crucial feature of the determination of the intertemporal price system in our model.

To evaluate alternative energy and environmental policies we quantify the impact of policy changes on individual welfare. For this purpose we employ the model of consumer behavior presented in detail in chapter 3. This model is based on aggregate demand functions obtained by direct aggregation over demand functions for individual households. By recovering individual demand functions from the aggregate demand functions we are able to compare energy and environmental policies in terms of their impact on individual welfare.

In chapter 8 we present measures of individual welfare for alternative energy and environmental policies. Under the Pareto principle a policy change can be recommended only if all households are at least as well off under the policy change and at least one household is better off. The advantage of this approach is that comparisons of levels of individual welfare among households are not required. Furthermore, only ordinal measures of individual welfare, based on the household's ordering of alternative policy outcomes, are needed. The disadvantage of policy evaluations based on the Pareto principle is that the ordering of alternative policies is incomplete. The typical result of the policy evaluations presented in chapter 8 is that some households are made better off and others worse off, so that no recommendations for changes in policy can be made under the Pareto principle.

In chapter 3 we present the approach to general equilibrium evaluation of alternative economic policies originated by Jorgenson and Slesnick (1985) and summarized by Jorgenson (1997b). This begins with measures of individual welfare for all households recovered from our model of aggregate consumer behavior. These measures of individual welfare are cardinal, rather than ordinal, and permit interpersonal comparisons of welfare levels among all households. Jorgenson and Slesnick (1985) have combined these measures by means of a social welfare function.[50] This requires the introduction of normative principles, such as horizontal and vertical equity. Unlike the Pareto principle, the social welfare function generates a complete ordering of economic policies.

Jorgenson, Slesnick, and Wilcoxen (1992) have employed a social welfare function to combine measures of individual welfare based on lifetime consumption. In chapter 3 we extend this to include lifetime full consumption, involving nonwork time as well as the consumption of goods and services. For this purpose we use Jorgenson and Slesnick's (2008) model of consumer behavior. We evaluate energy and environmental policies in terms of their impact on social welfare in chapter 8. Measures of social welfare can be decomposed into measures of efficiency and equity, so that we are able to bring distributional impacts to bear in evaluating alternative energy and environmental policies.

In chapter 8 we consider the substitution of energy taxes for other taxes, such as income taxes and sales taxes. We find that the use of revenues from energy taxes to reduce the rate of taxation on capital income produces a double dividend consisting of substantial reductions in pollution and an improvement in economic performance. The mechanism is that reductions in capital income taxes reduce the cost of capital and increase the rate of capital formation. The increased supply of capital offsets the costs of pollution abatement and enhances economic performance.

We evaluate energy and environmental policies in terms of their impacts on individual and social welfare. A common objection to energy taxes is that they reduce equity. We find that the modest reductions in equity from substitution of energy taxes for capital income taxes would be more than offset by gains in efficiency, so that this tax substitution would enhance social welfare, however equity is measured. This is a dramatic illustration of the potential of intertemporal general equilibrium modeling in designing new energy and environmental policies for the United States.

We conclude that market-based environmental policies are required to internalize the hidden costs of energy in a cost-effective way. These policies must be integrated with reform of the government budget and the tax system in order to offset the costs of pollution control with improvements in economic performance. Finally, energy and environmental policies must be evaluated in terms of their impacts on individual and social welfare.

1.10 Confidence Intervals

Confidence intervals for outcomes of the analysis of energy and environmental policies are an important feature of the new version of IGEM presented in this book. Previous applications of the econometric approach to general equilibrium modeling have provided confidence intervals for the parameters of the models of producer and consumer behavior.[51] Using the new methodology presented in chapter 9, we derive confidence intervals for measures of the impact of policies on outcomes of policy changes. This requires a transformation of random variables from the parameter estimates to the variables that describe the outcomes of policy changes.[52]

The confidence intervals for outputs of IGEM must be carefully distinguished from the "sensitivity" studies often presented for computable general equilibrium models. These studies provide estimates for the endogenous outcomes of a model, corresponding to different values of the input data. While sensitivity studies provide valuable information about the response of model outcomes to changes in model inputs, these studies omit the critical feature of a confidence interval, namely, the associated probability statement. This limitation is easily overlooked, given the nearly universal absence of probability statements for the outcomes of general equilibrium models.

1.11 Summary and Conclusion

The approach to designing energy and environmental policies presented in this book incorporates a number of significant innovations discussed in detail in chapter 10. We have presented new models of consumer and producer behavior that capture features of behavior that are very important for policy evaluations. The model of consumer behavior presented in chapter 3 incorporates labor-leisure choice, the choice between saving and consumption, and the selection of goods and services. This model of consumer behavior also provides the measures of individual welfare for all households that we employ in evaluating alternative policies.

Combining measures of individual welfare based on our econometric model of consumer behavior with normative principles such as horizontal and vertical equity, we obtain a powerful new criterion for the evaluation of energy and environmental policies. Our social welfare function generates a complete ordering of policies, rather than the incomplete ordering provided by the Pareto principle. In addition, we are able to incorporate equity as well as efficiency into the evaluation of alternative policies. We describe the social welfare function in chapter 3 and present the results of our evaluations of alternative policies in chapter 8.

The model of producer behavior presented in chapter 4 includes substitutions between energy and other inputs in response to price changes. We also model the impact of changes in technology, including the rate of technical change and biases of technical change for energy and other inputs. Using this approach to modeling producer behavior, we are able to separate changes in technology that are not affected by changes in input prices from changes in technology in response to price changes.

In constructing IGEM we combine models of consumer and producer behavior presented in chapters 3 and 4 with models of the government and rest of the world in chapter 5. We solve the resulting model for an intertemporal price system that introduces forward-looking prices as well as the backward-looking dynamics of capital accumulation. Since the resulting time path of prices for the U.S. economy incorporates all the information used in constructing the model, we have avoided the Lucas (1976) critique of economic models that fail to model expectations of future prices.

Jorgenson (1998b) provides a survey of the extensive applications of the econometric approach to general equilibrium modeling. This approach was incorporated into the official guidelines for preparing economic analyses of environmental policies by the U.S. Environmental Protection Agency (2000, 2010a). The new version of the IGEM model presented in this book is employed for the evaluation of proposed legislation on climate policy by EPA (2012b). A detailed list of legislative initiatives analyzed by means of IGEM is given on EPA's *Climate Economics* website.[53]

EPA (2010a) emphasizes that development of a computable general equilibrium model like that described in this book is a costly undertaking. The implementation of the econometric approach to general equilibrium modeling requires the new architecture for the national accounts proposed by Jorgenson and Landefeld (2006) and Jorgenson (2009). These macroeconomic data must be combined with microeconomic data to generate econometric estimates for models of producer and consumer behavior like those presented in chapters 3 and 4.

In chapter 8 we compare alternative energy and environmental policies that involve substitutions between energy taxes and other taxes, such as taxes on capital and labor incomes. We find that the use of government revenues from energy taxes to reduce rates of capital income taxes is the most promising approach for designing new energy and environmental policies for the United States. This works through the intertemporal price system modeled in IGEM by reducing the cost of capital and stimulating capital formation. Higher prices of energy reduce pollution and lower costs of capital offset the cost of pollution control with enhanced economic performance. We find that the modest reduction in equity is more than offset by an increase in efficiency, producing substantial gains in social welfare.

The econometric approach to general equilibrium modeling incorporates long-established principles for producer and consumer behavior while dealing with the heterogeneity of industries and households revealed by microeconomic data. The econometric approach also fulfills the promise of general equilibrium modeling by generating verifiable statements about the outcomes of changes in economic policies, accompanied by the associated probabilities. These probability statements require the transformation of random variables to provide confidence intervals for policy outcomes, as described in chapter 9.

Notes

1. See National Research Council (2010), *Hidden Costs of Energy: Unpriced Consequences of Energy Production and Use,* Washington, DC, National Academies Press. This report was mandated by the Energy Policy Act of 2005. See www.nap.edu/catalog.php?record_id=12794.

2. Much of this is produced by the Energy Information Administration, a highly respected statistical agency within the U.S. Department of Energy.
3. U.S. Environmental Protection Agency (2011), *Benefits and Costs of the Clean Air Act of 1970: Second Retrospective Study —1990 to 2020*, March.
4. Nicholas Z. Muller, Robert Mendelsohn, and William Nordhaus (2011), "Environmental Accounting for Pollution in the United States Economy," *American Economic Review* 100, no. 3 (August): 1649–1675.
5. In 2006, prior to the Great Recession of 2007–2009, petroleum products comprised 13.5% of U.S. imports.
6. See Muller, Mendelsohn, and Nordhaus (2011), table 2, p. 1665. "Value added" is the value of all capital and labor inputs used in power production.
7. The use of environmental taxes to control emissions was originally proposed by Arthur C. Pigou (1920), *The Economics of Welfare* (London: Macmillan).
8. Nicholas Muller and Robert Mendelsohn (2009), "Efficient Pollution Regulation: Getting the Prices Right," *American Economic Review* 99, no. 5 (December): 1714–1739.
9. National Research Council (2010), *Hidden Costs of Energy: Unpriced Consequences of Energy Production and Use* (Washington, DC: National Academies Press), table 7.3, p. 361. See www.nap.edu/catalog.php?record_id=12794.
10. William Nordhaus (2008), *A Question of Balance: Weighing the Options on Global Warming Policies* (New Haven, CT: Yale University Press).
11. For a history of the Clean Air Act Amendments and an analysis of their economic impact, see Gabriel Chan, Robert Stavins, Robert Stowe, and Richard Sweeney (2012), "The SO_2 Allowance Trading System and the Clean Air Act Amendments of 1990: Reflections on Twenty Years of Policy Innovation," Harvard Environmental Economics Program, Cambridge, MA: Harvard Kennedy School, January. See www.hks.harvard.edu/fs/rstavins/Monographs_&_Reports/SO2-Brief.pdf.
12. This Waxman-Markey legislation was passed by the House of Representatives but died in the Senate. Our analysis of this legislation is available on the Environmental Protection Agency Climate Economics website: www.epa.gov/climatechange/EPAactivities/economics/legislativeanalyses.html#americanClan.
13. See Joint Committee on Taxation (2012), *Present Law and Analysis of Energy-Related Tax Expenditures* (JCX-28-12), March 23, table 1, p. 27. See www.jct.gov.
14. Ibid.
15. A handbook of general equilibrium modeling is presented in two volumes edited by Peter B. Dixon and Dale Jorgenson (2012), *Handbook of Computable General Equilibrium Modeling* (Amsterdam, North-Holland).
16. Applications of the first version of IGEM are summarized by Jorgenson and Wilcoxen (1993a) and Jorgenson (1998b). Additional applications of IGEM are presented by Ho (2000) and Wilcoxen (2000).
17. Version 16 of IGEM and its applications are summarized by Jorgenson, Goettle, Ho, and Wilcoxen (2012) in chapter 8 of Dixon and Jorgenson (2012), pp. 477–552. A concise summary of the model and details on its many applications are given on EPA's Climate Economics website. See www.epa.gov/climatechange/EPAactivities/economics/modeling.html#intertemporal.
18. Barro and Sala-i-Martin (2004) provide a standard textbook treatment.
19. Brock and Taylor (2005) survey the extensive literature on this topic.
20. The classic textbook treatment of this topic remains that of Dasgupta and Heal (1979), who also give a detailed survey of the literature.
21. This literature is surveyed by Tietenberg and Lewis (2012).
22. More details are given by Nordhaus (2012) in chapter 16 of Dixon and Jorgenson (2012), pp. 1069–1132.

23. See http://emf.stanford.edu/research/emf22/. Bergman (2005) provides a detailed survey of computable general equilibrium models of energy and the environment.
24. Econometric methods for general equilibrium modeling are summarized by Jorgenson, Jin, Slesnick, and Wilcoxen (2012) in chapter 17 of Jorgenson and Dixon (2012), pp. 1133–1212. An important application of the econometric approach to general equilibrium modeling is the G-cubed model of the world economy constructed by McKibbin and Wilcoxen (1999). A survey of applications of the G-cubed model is presented by McKibbin and Wilcoxen (2012), chapter 15 of Dixon and Jorgenson (2012), pp. 995–1068.
25. Fullerton (2010) provides a survey of recent literature on distributional aspects of energy and environmental policies.
26. The cost of capital was introduced by Jorgenson (1963). A survey of applications of the cost of capital is presented by Lau (2000). This concept was used in modeling investment behavior by Jorgenson (1963, 1996a) and in measuring productivity by Jorgenson (1966, 1995a). Surveys of models of investment behavior, emphasizing the cost of capital, are given by Jorgenson (1971) and Hayashi (2000). Surveys of productivity measurement are provided by Jorgenson (2002, 2009b).
27. Land is not part of investment in the U.S. GDP. The rental from land is included in gross domestic income.
28. The first version of our model of consumer behavior was developed by Christensen, Jorgenson, and Lau (1975). This is based on the theory of a representative consumer and incorporates the cost of capital into the price of capital services from housing and consumers' durables. Applications of this model are summarized by Jorgenson (1997a). The model was incorporated into an intertemporal general equilibrium model by Jorgenson and Yun (1990, 2001, 2012) and has been used in analyzing the impact of U.S. tax policies on economic growth, beginning with the Tax Reform Act of 1986. Applications of this model are summarized by Jorgenson (1996b) and Yun (2000).
29. Dawkins, Srinivasan, and Whalley (2001) include the Lucas program in their list of calibration methods for computable general equilibrium models.
30. Surveys of aggregation in modeling consumer behavior are given by Stoker (1993, 2000), Jorgenson (1997a), and Blundell and Stoker (2005).
31. A further extension would incorporate investment in human capital along the lines discussed by Browning, Hansen, and Heckman (1999), tables 2.3 and 2.4, pp. 585–586. This would be appropriate for modeling changes in long-run trends in demographic behavior induced by changes in economic policies, such as social insurance. Our focus throughout this book is on intermediate-run trends.
32. The World Input-Output Database (WIOD) develops internationally comparable input-output tables for 40 countries, covering more than 90% of world GDP. See www.wiod.org/.
33. Holmøy (2013) describes the current version of the Multisectoral Growth Model of Norway. Holmøy and Strom (2012), chapter 3 of Dixon and Jorgenson (2012), pp. 105–158, present applications of this model to financial sustainability of the Norwegian government.
34. See chapter 2 of Dixon and Jorgenson (2012), pp. 23–104.
35. Hillberry and Hummels (2012), chapter 18 of Dixon and Jorgenson (2012), pp. 1213–1270, provide a survey of econometric methods for estimating trade elasticities.
36. This model of producer behavior was incorporated into an intertemporal general equilibrium model by Jorgenson and Yun (1990, 2001, 2012).
37. Surveys of econometric general equilibrium modeling are given by Jorgenson (1998a) and Jorgenson, Jin, Slesnick, and Wilcoxen (2012).
38. Jorgenson (1986, 2000) provides surveys of econometric modeling of producer behavior. Jaffe, Newell, and Stavins (2003) survey the literature on induced technical change in energy and environmental economics.

39. A system of accounts for the private sector was presented by Christensen and Jorgenson (1973). Applications of this system are summarized by Jorgenson (1995a) and Fraumeni (2000).
40. Updated data are available at the EU KLEMS website: www.euklems.net/.
41. See the World KLEMS website: www.worldklems.net/.
42. See Fleck, Rosenthal, Russell, Strassner, and Usher (2012), "A Prototype BEA/BLS Industry-Level Production Account for the United States," *Survey of Current Business* 92, no. 11: 44–50. Annual data covering the period 1998 to 2010 are available at http://bea.gov/industry/index.htm#integrated.
43. See Teplin et al. (2006). For current data see www.bea.gov/national/nipaweb/Ni_FedBeaSna/Index.asp.
44. See Dixon, Koopman, and Rimmer (2012) and Hertel (2012), chapters 2 and 12 in Jorgenson and Dixon (2012), pp. 23–104 and 815–877, for surveys of the literature on modeling trade in single country and global models, respectively.
45. See, for example, McKibbin and Wilcoxen (2012), chapter 15 in Jorgenson and Dixon (2012), pp. 995–1069.
46. A survey of software platforms employed in general equilibrium modeling is provided by Horridge, Meeraus, Pearson, and Rutherford (2012) in chapter 20 of Dixon and Jorgenson (2012), pp. 1331–1382.
47. See www.epa.gov/climatechange/ghgemissions/usinventoryreport.html.
48. To see the impact of these external abatement opportunities in reducing allowance prices and the economic costs of mitigation policy, see EPA (2012a) www.epa.gov/climatechange/economics/economicanalyses.html.
49. More details on the Lucas critique are provided by Schmidt and Wieland (2012) in chapter 22 of Dixon and Jorgenson (2012), pp. 1439–1512.
50. Surveys of social welfare measurement are provided by Jorgenson (1990, 1997b, 1998b), Jorgenson and Slesnick (2012), and Slesnick (1998, 2000, 2001).
51. Econometric general equilibrium modeling was introduced by Hudson and Jorgenson (1974). Applications of this approach are surveyed by Jorgenson (1998a).
52. We employ the "delta" method introduced by Tuladhar and Wilcoxen (1998) and discussed in detail by Tuladhar (2003). Recent applications of this method are presented by Jorgenson, Jin, Slesnick, and Wilcoxen (2012), chapter 17 in Jorgenson and Dixon (2012), *Handbook of Computable General Equilibrium Modeling* (Amsterdam: Elsevier), vol. 1B, pp. 1133–1212.
53. See www.epa.gov/climatechange/economics/modeling.html.

2 Structure of the Intertemporal General Equilibrium Model

2.1 Introduction

The Intertemporal General Equilibrium Model (IGEM) presented in chapter 1 is a comprehensive model of the U.S. economy. The defining characteristic of a general equilibrium model is that prices are determined together with quantities through the interactions between supply and demand. In this chapter we describe the production sector that is central to the supply side of the model and the household sector that forms the core of the demand side.

In the factor markets the household sector supplies capital and labor services, while the production sector demands these services as inputs. The model is completed by market-clearing conditions that determine supplies and demands for all commodities and all factors along with the corresponding prices. In chapter 5 we describe the role of investment demand, government demand, and demand for exports in the demand side of the model. We also consider the role of imports from the rest of the world in the supply side of the model.

The intertemporal equilibrium defined by IGEM requires that market-clearing conditions be satisfied for each commodity and each factor at every point of time. In addition, the markets are linked by investments in capital goods and asset prices. Asset pricing imparts forward-looking dynamics to IGEM because the price of an asset is equal to the discounted value of the prices of capital services over the asset's future lifetime. Capital services are generated by stocks of assets accumulated through past investments, so that capital accumulation provides backward-looking dynamics for the model.

A distinguishing feature of IGEM is that unknown parameters of the behavioral equations are estimated econometrically rather than calibrated. This is essential in capturing the heterogeneity of the industries and households that make up the U.S. economy, as well as providing confidence intervals for model outcomes, as in chapter 9. We defer a description of the econometrics of the demand side of the model to chapter 3. Similarly, we defer the estimation of the producer model and import demands to chapters 4 and 5, respectively.

The model determines the flows of goods and factor services among the four main sectors of the economy—production, household, government, and rest of the world. The flows of payments among these sectors determine the expenditure patterns for the economy as a whole, including expenditures on consumption, investment, government, exports, and imports. In this chapter we show how the demands and supplies interact in markets to arrive at the intertemporal equilibrium prices. We also describe the solution algorithm for determining the equilibrium prices.

A complete list of the equations in IGEM is given in appendix A with all the distinguishing subscripts. Section A.8 of that appendix provides a glossary of the symbols we have used. In describing the model in this chapter we have simplified the notation in order to avoid a proliferation of symbols. For example, where this can be done without creating confusion, we suppress the variables that index industries, commodities, and households.

2.2 Producer Behavior and Technical Change

Market-based policies, such as energy and environmental taxes and tradable permits, insert tax wedges between supply and demand prices and generate government revenue. The supply and demand for tradable permits can be modeled along with demands and supplies for commodities. The costs associated with market-based policies are determined through the price responses to changes in policy.

The key to analyzing the economic impacts of energy and environmental policy is the substitutability among productive inputs, especially energy inputs, in response to price changes induced by policy. While production patterns reflect substitutability among inputs in response to price changes, these patterns also depend on changes in technology. Our model of producer behavior incorporates both substitution among inputs and technical change.

In the long run the material well-being of the population depends on the rate of technical change. Part of technical change is induced by changes in relative prices of inputs, while another part is autonomous with respect to these price changes. In addition, the relative demands for inputs may be altered by biased technical change. For example, energy use may decline in intensity due to energy-saving changes in technology, as well as substitution away from higher-priced energy.

Estimates for the parameters that describe substitutability and technical change for the industrial sectors that comprise the U.S. economy are not available in the literature. Since the changes in the patterns of production are complex, specification and estimation of models of production suitable for the analysis of energy and environmental policy require econometric methods. In chapter 4 we discuss the issues that arise in specifying and estimating the parameters that characterize substitution and technical change.

We subdivide the business sector into the 35 industries listed in table 2.1.The government and household sectors also purchase energy inputs but are excluded from the business sector. Five of the industries are energy producers—Coal Mining (industry 3), Oil and Gas Mining (4), Petroleum Refining (16), Electric Utilities (30), and Gas Utilities (31). We have chosen the classification of "non-energy" industries to distinguish sectors that differ in the intensity of utilization of different inputs, especially energy, and exhibit different patterns of technical change.

The output of the production sector is divided among 35 commodities, each the primary product of one of the 35 industries. For example, steel is a primary product of the Primary Metals industry, while brokerage services are included in the Finance, Insurance, and Real Estate industry. Many industries produce secondary products as well. For example, Petroleum Refining produces commodities that are the primary outputs of the Chemicals industry. The model permits joint production for all sectors and all commodities. We model joint production together with substitution and technical change for each industry.

The parameters of our production model are estimated econometrically from a historical database covering the period 1960–2005. This database is described in appendix B, and includes a time series of input-output tables in current and constant prices, as well as data on the prices and quantities of capital and labor services. These data comprise the industry-level production account of the "new architecture" for the U.S. national accounts developed by Jorgenson (2009b) and Jorgenson and Landefeld (2006). The methodology for constructing the data is presented in Jorgenson, Ho, and Stiroh (2005).

Table 2.1
Industry output and energy inputs, year 2005

		Coal Input ($ml)	Electricity ($ml)	Total Energy ($ml)	Energy Share of Output (%)
1	Agriculture	0.0	4120.6	18719.3	4.41
2	Metal Mining	15.5	1134.0	2450.5	9.79
3	Coal Mining	1500.6	402.2	3197.2	12.53
4	Petroleum and Gas	0.0	1605.3	19740.8	7.60
5	Nonmetallic Mining	47.2	780.1	2882.9	12.26
6	Construction	0.0	3260.9	36482.9	2.69
7	Food Products	165.4	4507.1	10464.3	1.76
8	Tobacco Products	14.9	72.6	205.8	0.66
9	Textile Mill Products	26.1	1112.8	1943.0	3.23
10	Apparel and Textiles	2.8	280.9	520.9	1.45
11	Lumber and Wood	2.6	1500.7	3727.0	2.88
12	Furniture and Fixtures	14.8	702.5	1958.1	1.93
13	Paper Products	252.1	3514.9	7446.7	4.43
14	Printing and Publishing	0.0	1289.6	2633.3	1.15
15	Chemical Products	263.1	8350.6	25577.8	4.91
16	Petroleum Refining	10.7	4707.1	214660.4	51.25
17	Rubber and Plastic	14.0	3047.6	4649.8	2.47
18	Leather Products	0.9	74.8	170.7	2.69
19	Stone, Clay, and Glass	436.9	2949.2	7660.6	5.92
20	Primary Metals	1160.8	7510.1	12752.2	5.08
21	Fabricated Metals	8.2	3715.0	6448.9	2.18
22	Industrial Machinery and Equipment	11.7	2927.9	5368.2	1.27
23	Electronic and Electric Equipment	2.9	2718.9	4490.5	1.36
24	Motor Vehicles	34.0	2122.5	3824.5	0.87
25	Other Transportation Equipment	20.0	1524.3	2860.8	1.26
26	Instruments	40.5	1212.9	2056.1	0.99
27	Miscellaneous Manufacturing	1.6	389.5	1114.3	1.84
28	Transport and Warehouse	7.7	7269.7	87450.0	13.09
29	Communications	0.0	2364.8	3997.5	0.76
30	Electric Utilities	14887.2	4611.8	52863.6	14.17
31	Gas Utilities	21.0	204.1	42556.6	54.99
32	Trade	21.5	41705.0	79064.1	3.18
33	FIRE	6.9	24836.7	33751.5	1.23
34	Services	21.0	35390.1	74215.3	1.70
35	Government Enterprises	0.0	8717.8	25489.8	7.78

Note: "Energy input" includes feedstocks.

The input-output tables consist of *use* and *make* matrices for each year. The use matrix gives the inputs used by each industry—intermediate inputs supplied by other industries, noncomparable imports, capital services, and labor services. This matrix also gives commodity use by each category of final demand—consumption, investment, government, exports, and imports.

The use matrix is illustrated in figure 2.1. The rows of this table correspond to commodities, while the columns correspond to industries. Each entry in the table is the amount of a given commodity used by a particular industry. The sum of all entries in a row is equal to the total demand for the commodity, while the sum of all entries in a column is the value of all the inputs used in a given industry.

The make, or supply, matrix is illustrated in figure 2.2. This matrix describes an essential part of the technology of the U.S. economy. The rows of the make matrix correspond to industries, while the columns correspond to commodities. Each entry in the table is the amount of a commodity supplied or "made" by a given industry. The domestic supply of the commodity is the sum of all the entries in the corresponding column, while the sum of all the entries in a row represents the value of the commodities produced by a given industry.

In short, the interindustry accounts of the system of U.S. national accounts are critical components of the historical database for IGEM. The interindustry accounts in current and constant prices are discussed in detail in appendix B.1. The use matrix includes the values of capital and labor inputs for each industry. These values are divided into prices and quantities, like the values of the interindustry flows.

The value of capital services consists of all property-type income—profits and other operating surplus, depreciation, and taxes on property and property-type income. The price of capital services consists of the price of the corresponding asset, multiplied by an annualization factor that we denote as the *cost of capital*. The cost of capital consists of the rate of return plus the rate of depreciation, less capital gains or plus capital losses, all adjusted for taxes. The price of capital services and the cost of capital are discussed in appendix B.3, which is based on the detailed development in Jorgenson and Yun (2001, 2012).

The quantity of capital services is the annual flow from a given asset. The assets included in our historical database are plant, equipment, inventories, and land. Plant and equipment are subdivided into detailed subcategories. For example, equipment includes items ranging from motor vehicles and construction equipment to computers and software.

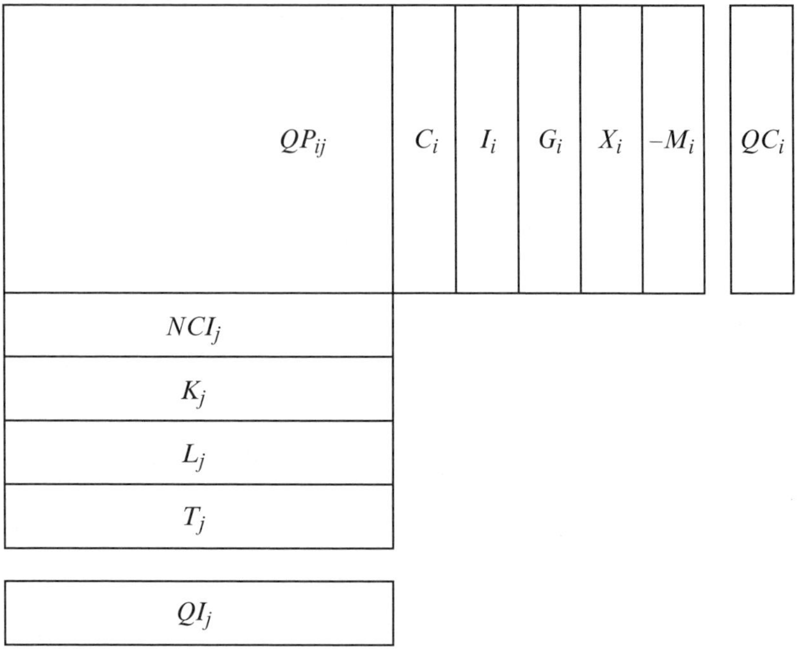

QP_{ij}	C_i	I_i	G_i	X_i	$-M_i$	QC_i
NCI_j						
K_j						
L_j						
T_j						
QI_j						

Notes:

QI_j : industry j output
QC_i : quantity of domestic commodity i
K_j : capital input
L_j : labor input
T_j : sales tax
NCI_j : noncomparable imports
QP_{ij} : quantity of intermediate input i into j
C_i, I_i, G_i, X_i, M_i, : final demands for commodity i
M_{ji} : quantity of commodity i made by industry j

Figure 2.1
Input-output USE table.

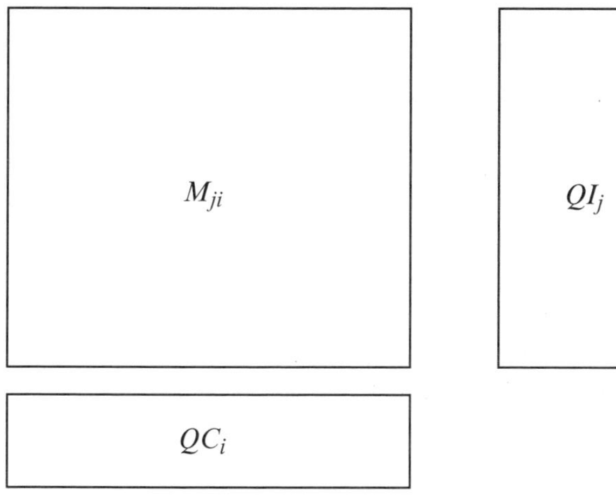

Notes:

QI_j : industry j output

QC_i : quantity of domestic commodity i

M_{ji} : quantity of commodity i made by industry j

Figure 2.2
Input-output MAKE table.

We aggregate over the prices and quantities of capital services from these asset types to obtain a price and a quantity index of capital services.

To obtain a quantity index each type of capital stock is weighted by the rental price of capital services. Similarly, we aggregate over asset types to obtain a price and quantity index of capital stock. Each type of capital stock is weighted by the asset price to obtain a quantity index of capital stock. The price and quantity of capital services and capital stocks are described in more detail in appendix B.2.

Similarly, the value of labor services includes all labor-type income—wages and salaries, labor income from self-employment, supplements such as contributions to social insurance, and taxes such as payroll taxes. The quantity of labor input for each demographic category is hours worked. We construct a price and a quantity index of labor services by weighting the hours worked for each demographic group by labor compensation per hour. These groups range from young workers with only secondary education to mature workers with advanced degrees. The price and quantity of labor services are described in more detail in appendix B.2.

Our methods for aggregating over detailed categories of capital and labor services are an essential feature of the historical data set. Arithmetic aggregates consisting of sums of hours worked or capital stocks would not accurately represent the substitution possibilities within each aggregate. For example, a simple sum of computers and software with industrial buildings would not reflect the impact of a shift in composition toward information technology equipment and software on capital input. Similarly, a simple sum of hours worked over college-educated and non-college-educated workers would not reveal the impact on labor input of increases in educational attainment of the U.S. work force.

2.2.1 *Notation*

To describe our submodel for producer behavior we begin with notation. The general system is to use P for prices, Q for quantities, and Greek letters for parameters.

QI_j—quantity of output of industry j.

PO_j—price of output to producers in industry j.

PI_j—price of output to purchasers from industry j.

QP_{ij}^j—quantity of commodity input i into industry j.

PS_i—price of commodity i to buyers.

KD_j—quantity of capital input into j.

LD_j—quantity of labor input into j.

E_j—index of energy intermediate input into j.

M_j—index of total non-energy intermediate input into j.

$P_{E,j}$—price of energy intermediate input into j.

$P_{M,j}$—price of total non-energy intermediate input into j.

PKD_j—price of total capital input to industry j.

PLD_j—price of total labor input to industry j.

v—value shares.

QC_i—quantity of domestically produced commodity i.

PC_i—price of domestically produced commodity i.

$M_{j,i}$—MAKE matrix; value of commodity i made by industry j.

2.2.2 *Top-Tier Production Functions with Technical Change*

The production function represents output as a function of capital services, labor services, and intermediate inputs. Output also depends on the level of technology t, so that the output of industry takes the form:

$$QI_j = f(KD_j, LD_j, QP_1^j, QP_2^j, \ldots, QP_m^j, QP_{NCI}^j, t), \quad (j = 1, 2, \ldots, 35). \tag{2.1}$$

The dimensionality of this form of the production function is too great to be tractable.

To reduce the dimensionality of the production function we assume that this function is separable in energy and materials inputs. Output depends on inputs of energy and non-energy materials, as well as inputs of capital and labor services:

$$QI_j = f(KD_j, LD_j, E_j, M_j, t); \quad E_j = E(QP_3^j, \ldots); \quad M_j = M(QP_1^j, \ldots). \tag{2.2}$$

In the second stage of the production model the energy and non-energy inputs depend on the components of each of these aggregates. For example, energy input depends on inputs of coal, crude oil, refined petroleum products, natural gas, and electricity. These are primary outputs of Coal Mining, Oil and Gas Mining, Petroleum Refining, Electric Utilities, and Gas Utilities industries. Similarly, non-energy input depends on inputs of all the non-energy commodities listed in table 2.1, plus inputs of noncomparable imports. The tier structure of the production model is given in table 2.2.

We assume constant returns to scale and competitive markets, so that the production function (2.2) is homogeneous of degree one and the value of output is equal to the sum of the values of all inputs:

$$\begin{aligned} PO_{jt}QI_{jt} &= PKD_{jt}KD_{jt} + PLD_{jt}LD_{jt} + P_{Ejt}E_{jt} + P_{Mjt}M_{jt}. \\ P_{Ejt}E_{jt} &= PS_{3t}QP_{3t}^j + PS_{4t}QP_{4t}^j + \ldots + PS_{31t}QP_{31t}^j. \\ P_{Mjt}M_{jt} &= PS_{1t}QP_{1t}^j + PS_{2t}QP_{2t}^j + \ldots + PS_{NCI,t}QP_{NCI,t}^j. \end{aligned} \tag{2.3}$$

Under constant returns to scale the price function expresses the price of output as a function of the input prices and technology, so that for industry j:

$$PO_j = p(PKD_j, PLD_j, P_{Ej}, P_{Mj}, t). \tag{2.4}$$

Since we assume that all producers within a sector face the same prices, the aggregate price function can be represented as a function of

Table 2.2
Tier structure of industry production function

	Symbol	Name	Components
1	Q	Gross output	Capital, labor, energy, materials Q = f(K, L, E, M).
2	E	Energy	Coal mining, petroleum & gas mining, petroleum refining, electric utilities, gas utilities E = f(X3, X4, X16, X30, X31).
3	M	Materials (non-energy)	Construction, agriculture mat, metallic materials, nonmetallic materials, services materials M = f(X6, MA, MM, MN, MS).
4	MA	Agriculture materials	Agriculture, food manufacturing, tobacco, textile-apparel, wood-paper MA = f(X1, X7, X8, TA, WP).
5	MM	Metallic materials	Fabricated-other metals, machinery materials, equipment MM = f(FM, MC, EQ).
6	MN	Nonmetallic materials	Nonmetal mining, chemicals, rubber, stone, miscellaneous manufacturing MN = f(X5, X15, X17, X19, X27).
7	MS	Services materials	Transportation, trade, FIRE, services, OS MS = f(X28, X32, X33, X34, OS).
8	TA	Textile-apparel	Textiles, apparel, leather TA = f(X9, X10, X18).
9	WP	Wood-paper	Lumber-wood, furniture, paper, printing WP = f(X11, X12, X13, X14).
10	OS	Other services	Communications, govt. enterprises, NC imports OS = f(X29, X35, X_N).
11	FM	Fabricated-other metals	Metal mining, primary metals, fabricated metals FM = f(X2, X20, X21).
12	MC	Machinery materials	Industrial machinery, electric machinery MC = f(X22, X23).
13	EQ	Equipment	Motor vehicles, other transportation equipment, instruments EQ = f(X24, X25, X26).

these prices. To characterize substitution and technical change we find it convenient to work with the price function rather than the production function (2.1).[1]

In order to represent substitutability among inputs and technical change in a flexible manner we have chosen the translog form of the price function, following Jin and Jorgenson (2010):

$$\ln PO_t = \alpha_0 + \sum_i \alpha_i \ln p_{it} + \frac{1}{2}\sum_{i,k} \beta_{ik} \ln p_{it} \ln p_{kt} + \sum_i \ln p_{it} f_{it}^p + f_t^p. \tag{2.5}$$

$$p_i, p_k = \{PKD, PLD, P_E, P_M\}.$$

For simplicity we have dropped the industry j subscript. The parameters—α_i, β_{ik}, and α_0—are estimated separately for each industry.

The vector of latent variables

$$\xi_t = (1, f_{Kt}^p, f_{Lt}^p, f_{Et}^p, f_{Mt}^p, \Delta f_t^p)'$$

is generated by a first-order vector autoregressive scheme:

$$\xi_t = F\xi_{t-1} + v_t. \tag{2.6}$$

The p superscript denotes that these are latent variables for the production sector. We introduce additional latent variables for the consumption, investment, and import functions. We estimate these latent variables by means of the Kalman filter, following Jin and Jorgenson (2010).

The production submodel (2.5) and (2.6) achieves considerable flexibility in the representation of substitution and technical change. An important advantage of this model is that it generates equations for the input shares that are linear in the logarithms of the prices and the latent variables. Differentiating equation (2.5) with respect to the logarithms of the prices, we obtain equations for the shares of inputs. For example, if we differentiate with respect to the price of capital services, we obtain the share of capital input:

$$v_K = \frac{PKD_t KD_t}{PO_t QI_t} = \alpha_K + \sum_k \beta_{Kk} \ln P_k + f_{Kt}^p. \tag{2.7}$$

The parameters $\{\beta_{ik}\}$ are share elasticities, giving the change in the share of the ith input in the value of output with respect to a proportional change in the price of the kth input. These parameters represent the degree of substitutability among the capital (K), labor (L), energy

(E), and non-energy (M) inputs. If the share elasticity is positive, the value share increases with a change in the price of the input; if the share elasticity is negative, the share decreases with a change in the price. A zero share elasticity implies that the value share is constant, as in the linear-logarithmic, or Cobb-Douglas, specification of technology used by Johansen.

The price function is homogeneous of degree one, so that a doubling of input prices results in a doubling of the output price. This implies that the row and column sums of the matrix of share elasticities must be equal to zero:

$$\sum_i \beta_{ik} = 0 \quad \text{for each } k; \quad \sum_k \beta_{ik} = 0 \quad \text{for each } i. \tag{2.8}$$

Symmetry of the price effects implies that the matrix of share elasticities is symmetric. Monotonicity and concavity restrictions on the price function are discussed in chapter 4.

The level of technology f_t^p and the biases of technical change $\{f_{it}^p\}$ evolve according to equation (2.6). The latent variables $\{f_{it}^p\}$ describe the biases of technical change. For example, if the energy share declines, holding prices of all inputs constant, the bias with respect to energy is negative and we say that technical change is energy-saving. Similarly, a positive bias implies that technical change is energy-using. Note that while the parameters describing substitution are constant, reflecting responses to varying price changes, the biases of technical change may vary from time to time, since historical patterns involve both energy-using and energy-saving technical change.

The latent variable f_t^p represents the level of technology. The first difference of the level of technology takes the form:

$$\Delta f_t^p = F_{p1} + F_{pK} f_{K,t-1}^p + F_{pL} f_{L,t-1}^p + F_{pE} f_{E,t-1}^p + F_{pM} f_{M,t-1}^p + F_{pp} \Delta f_{t-1}^p + v_{pt}. \tag{2.9}$$

A more detailed description of the production submodel, including the price function, is presented in chapter 4.

2.2.3 *Lower Tier Production Functions for Intermediate Inputs*

In modeling producer behavior in section 2.1.2 we have introduced multistage allocation in order to avoid an intractable specification of the production function (2.1). In the lower tiers of the model, energy and non-energy materials inputs are allocated to individual commodities, as summarized in table 2.2. The energy and materials submodels are represented as:

$$E_j = E(QP_3^j, QP_4^j, QP_{16}^j, QP_{30}^j, QP_{31}^j); \quad M_j = M(QP_1^j, \ldots, QP_{NCI}^j). \tag{2.10}$$

As in the top tier, we work with the price function instead of the production function. To illustrate the elements of the tier structure we consider the translog price function for energy input:

$$\ln P_{Et} = \alpha_0 + \sum_{i \in energy} \alpha_i \ln P_{it}^{P,E} + \frac{1}{2}\sum_{i,k} \beta_{ik} \ln P_{it}^{P,E} \ln P_{kt}^{P,E} + \sum_{i \in energy} f_{it}^{node=E} \ln P_{it}^{P,E}$$
$$P_i^{P,E} \in \{PS_3, PS_4, PS_{16}, PS_{30}, PS_{31}\}. \tag{2.11}$$

The share equations are obtained by differentiating with respect to the logarithms of the prices. For coal, the first input, the share in the value of energy inputs, is:

$$v_3 = \frac{PS_3 QP_3}{P_E E} = \alpha_3 + \sum_{k \in energy} \beta_{3k} \ln P_k^{P,E} + f_{3t}^{node=E}. \tag{2.12}$$

The other four energy input demands correspond to crude petroleum, refined petroleum products, electricity, and natural gas. As before, the parameters $\{\beta_{ik}\}$ are share elasticities and represent the degree of substitutability among the five types of energy commodities. The latent variables $\{f_{it}^p\}$ represent biases of technical change.

The components of the non-energy materials (M) input include 30 commodities in table 2.1 and noncomparable imports (NCI), commodities not produced domestically and denoted X_{NCI} in figure 2.1. We model the demand for individual commodities within the non-energy materials aggregate for each industry j by means of a hierarchical tier structure of translog price functions. The set of nodes for the production sector is denoted I_{PNODE} and the full set of price functions is given in appendix A.

The price functions for the subtiers (2.11) differ from the price function for the top tier (2.5), since the subtiers do not include a latent variable representing the level of technology. This reflects the fact that the price of energy for the subtier is constructed from the prices of the individual components, while the price of output in the top tier is measured separately from the prices of capital, labor, energy, and non-energy materials inputs. The price of output would fall, relative to the input prices, as productivity rises.

The latent variables of the subtier $\{f_{it}^{node}\}$ represent the biases of technical change. For example, an increase in the latent variable $f_{30t}^{node=E}$ implies that the electricity share of total energy input is increasing, so that technical change is electricity-using, while a decrease in this latent variable implies that technical change is electricity-saving. The latent variables are generated by a vector autoregression, as in (2.6).

The non-energy materials input consists of five subaggregates—construction, agriculture materials, metal materials, nonmetal materials, and services. Each of these subaggregates in turn is a function of subtiers until all the 31 non-energy commodities are included. Each node to the tier structure employs a translog price function like equation (2.11) and includes latent variables that represent the biases of technical change.

2.2.4 *Commodities, Industries, and Output Taxes*

Production or sales taxes may be proportional to the value of output or expressed as a tax per quantity unit. We refer to taxes proportional to the value of output as ad valorem taxes. In the base case we represent all taxes on production as ad valorem taxes. In the policy simulations we introduce additional ad valorem taxes in order to represent energy and environmental taxes and tradable permits. These taxes are included for all 35 sectors of the production model and introduce wedges between the prices faced by sellers and buyers.

Denoting the purchaser's price of the output of industry j byPI_j, we have

$$PI_j = (1 + tt_j^{full})PO_j, \tag{2.13}$$

where PO_j is the seller's price given in (2.4). The full superscript on the output tax tt_j^{full} indicates that this is the sum of various output taxes that are described below. The value of industry j's output is denoted

$$VT_j^{QI} = PI_j QI_j. \tag{2.14}$$

We have noted above that each industry makes a primary product and many industries make secondary products that are the primary outputs of other industries. We denote the price, quantity, and value of commodity i by PC_i, QC_i, and V_i^{QC}, respectively, all from the purchasers' point of view. For column i in the make matrix, let the shares contributed by the various industries to that commodity in the base year T be denoted

$$m_{ji} = \frac{M_{ji,t=T}}{V_{i,t=T}^{QC}}; \quad \sum_j m_{ji} = 1. \tag{2.15}$$

For row j we denote the shares of the output of industry j be allocated to the various commodities as follows:

$$m_{ji}^{row} = \frac{M_{ji,t=T}}{VT_{j,t=T}^{QI}}; \quad \sum_i m_{ji}^{row} = 1. \tag{2.16}$$

The shares (2.15) and (2.16) are fixed for all periods after the base year. We assume that the production function for each commodity is a linear logarithmic, or Cobb-Douglas, aggregate of the outputs from the various industries. The weights are the base-year shares, that is, we write the price of commodity i as a linear logarithmic function of the component industry inputs:

$$PC_i = PI_1^{m_{1i}}, \ldots, PI_m^{m_{mi}} \quad \text{for } i = 1, 2, \ldots, 35. \tag{2.17}$$

The values and quantities of commodity i are given by

$$V_{it}^{QC} = \sum_j m_{ji}^{row} PI_{jt} QI_{jt} \quad \text{for } i = 1, 2, \ldots, 35. \tag{2.18}$$

$$QC_i = \frac{V_i^{QC}}{PC_i}. \tag{2.19}$$

2.3 Consumer Behavior and Demography

Policies that affect energy prices have different impacts on different households, so that econometric methods are essential for capturing the heterogeneity observed in microeconomic data. On average, households in warmer regions have larger electricity bills for cooling, elderly persons drive less, and households with children drive more. To capture these differences we subdivide the household sector into demographic groups. We treat each household as a consuming unit, that is, a unit with preferences over commodities and leisure.

Our household model has three stages. In the first stage lifetime full income is allocated between consumption and savings. Full income includes leisure as well as income from the supply of capital and labor services. Consumption consists of commodities and leisure and we refer to this as full consumption. In the second stage full consumption is allocated to leisure and three commodity groups—nondurables, capital services, and services. In the third stage the three commodity groups are allocated to the 36 commodities, including the five types of energy.

2.3.1 *Notation*

We next describe the three stages of the household model, beginning with the notation:

A_k—vector of demographic characteristics of household *k*.

C_i^X—quantity of consumption of commodity *i*.

C_{ik}—quantity of consumption of commodity *i* by household *k*.

F_t—quantity of full consumption.

R_t—quantity of aggregate leisure.

R_k^m—quantity of leisure.

LS_t—quantity of aggregate labor supply.

m_k—value of full expenditures of household *k*.

KS_t—quantity of aggregate capital stock at end of period *t*.

n_t—growth rate of population.

PF_t—price of F_t.

P_t^L—price of labor to employer, economy average.

P_t^K—rental price of capital, economy average.

r_t—rate of return between *t–1* and *t*.

Y_t—household disposable income.

S_t—household savings.

2.3.2 *First Stage: Intertemporal Optimization*

Let V_{kt} denote the utility of household *k* derived from consuming goods and leisure during period *t*. In the first stage household *k* maximizes an additively separable intertemporal utility function:

$$\max_{F_{kt}} U_k = E_t\left\{\sum_{t=1}^{T}(1+\rho)^{-(t-1)}\left[\frac{V_{kt}^{(1-\sigma)}}{(1-\sigma)}\right]\right\} \tag{2.20}$$

subject to the lifetime budget constraint

$$\sum_{t=1}^{T}(1+r_t)^{-(t-1)}PF_{kt}F_{kt}\le W_k, \tag{2.21}$$

where F_{kt} is the full consumption in period t, PF_{kt} is its price, r_t is the nominal interest rate, and W_k is the "full wealth" at time 0. The parameter σ represents intertemporal curvature and ρ is the subjective rate of time preference. The within-period utility function is logarithmic if σ is equal to one:

$$\max_{F_{kt}} U_k = E_t\left\{\sum_{t=1}^{T}(1+\rho)^{-(t-1)}\ln V_{kt}\right\}. \tag{2.22}$$

The term *full wealth* refers to the present value of future earnings from the supply of tangible assets and labor, plus transfers from the government, and imputations for the value of leisure. Tangible assets include domestic capital, government bonds and net foreign assets. Equations (2.20) and (2.21) are standard in economic growth models.

The first-order condition for optimality is expressed in the Euler equation:

$$\begin{aligned}\Delta\ln PF_{k,t+1}F_{k,t+1} = {} & (1-\sigma)\Delta\ln V_{k,t+1}+\Delta\ln(-D(p_{k,t+1}))+\ln(1+r_{t+1}) \\ & -\ln(1+\rho)+\eta_{kt},\end{aligned} \tag{2.23}$$

where $D(p_{kt})$ is a function of the prices of goods and leisure and η_{kt} is an expectational error. In chapter 3 we describe in more detail how the Euler equation is estimated from data for synthetic cohorts obtained by adding over all households in each cohort. From these household Euler equations we derive an aggregate Euler equation. This Euler equation is forward-looking, so that the current level of full consumption incorporates expectations about all future prices and discount rates.

In the simulations reported in chapter 8 we use a simplified version of the aggregate Euler equation with the curvature parameter σ equal to one. The aggregate version of the intertemporal optimization problem is written

$$U = E_t\sum_{t=1}^{\infty}N_0\prod_{s=1}^{t}\left(\frac{N_t^{eq}}{1+\rho}\right)\ln F_t. \tag{2.24}$$

The aggregate Euler equation derived from this is simply

$$\frac{F_t}{F_{t-1}} = \frac{(1+n_t)(1+r_t)}{1+\rho}\frac{PF_{t-1}}{PF_t} + \eta_t, \tag{2.25}$$

where n_t is the rate of growth of population. This is discussed in more detail in chapter 3, section 3.3.1.

2.3.3 *Second Stage: Goods and Leisure*

In the second stage of the household model, full consumption is divided between the value of leisure time and personal consumption expenditures on commodities. Given the time endowment of the household sector, the choice of leisure time also determines the supply of labor. The allocation of full consumption employs a very detailed household demand model that incorporates demographic characteristics of the population. The database for this model includes the Consumer Expenditure Survey (CEX) and Personal Consumption Expenditures (PCE) from the U.S. National Income and Product Accounts (NIPAs).

Conceptually, we determine the consumption C_{ik}^X of commodity i for household k by maximizing a utility function $U(C_{1k}^X, \ldots, C_{ik}^X \ldots, C_{Rk}^X; A_k)$, where C_{Rk}^X is leisure and A_k denotes the demographic characteristics of household k, such as the number of children and the number of adults. Summation over all households gives the total demand for commodity i:

$$PC_{it}^X C_{it}^X = \sum_k P_{ikt}^{CX} C_{ikt}^X \quad i = 1, 2, \ldots, R. \tag{2.26}$$

The price P_{ik}^{CX} is the price of good i faced by household k. The superscript X denotes that this is a CEX measure that must be distinguished from measures based on the NIPAs and interindustry transactions accounts discussed below. Similarly, total leisure demand is the sum over all households' leisure demands $(\sum_k P_{Rkt}^{CX} C_{Rkt}^X)$; and the sum of goods and leisure gives the full consumption determined in stage 1:

$$PF_t F_t = \sum_i PC_{it}^X C_{it}^X + PC_R C_R^X. \tag{2.27}$$

The list of commodities included in the household model is presented in table 2.3 along with the values in 2005. These are defined in terms of categories of PCEs and the last column of the table gives the precise definitions in the NIPAs. One major difference between our classification system and the PCE is the treatment of consumers'

Table 2.3
Personal consumption expenditures and leisure, IGEM categories, 2005

	IGEM Categories	Consumption ($bil)	NIPA PCE Category
1	Food	719.7	3
2	Meals	449.2	4
3	Meals-employees	12.3	5, 6
4	Shoes	54.9	12
5	Clothing	286.7	14, 15, 16
6	Gasoline	283.6	75
7	Coal	0.3	40
8	Fuel oil	20.7	40
9	Tobacco	88.3	7
10	Cleaning supplies	137.8	21, 34
11	Furnishings	43.3	33
12	Drugs	265.3	45
13	Toys	66.2	89
14	Stationery	19.5	35
15	Imports (travel)	7.3	111
16	Reading	61.4	88, 95
17	Rental	333.7	25, 27
18	Electricity	133.4	37
19	Gas	64.9	38
20	Water	64.0	39
21	Communications	133.0	41
22	Domestic service	19.9	42
23	Other household	64.4	43
24	Own transportation	262.9	74, 76, 77
25	Transportation	61.5	79, 80, 82, 83, 84, 85
26	Medical services	1350.0	47, 48, 49, 51, 55
27	Health insurance	141.3	56
28	Personal services	115.6	17, 19, 22
29	Financial services	498.6	61, 62, 63, 64
30	Other services	147.4	65, 66, 67
31	Recreation	357.8	94, 97, 98, 99, 100, 101, 102, 103
32	Education and welfare	450.9	105, 106, 107, 108
33	Foreign travel	99.9	110
34	Owner maintenance	202.2	our imputation
35	Durables flow	1972.4	our imputation
	Leisure	14432.3	our imputation

Note: NIPA PCE category refers to the line number in table 2.5.5 of Survey of Current Business (SCB), August 2006.

durables. Purchases of new housing are included in investment in the NIPAs, while only the annual rental value of housing is included in the PCE.

Purchases of consumer durables such as automobiles are treated as consumption expenditures in the PCE. In the new architecture for the U.S. national accounts discussed by Jorgenson (2009), these purchases are included in investment, while rental values are treated as consumption. This has the advantage of achieving symmetry in the treatment of housing and consumers' durables. The annual flow of capital services from these household assets is given as item 35 in table 2.3.

The dimensionality of a utility function written as $U(C_{1k}^X, \ldots, C_{Rk}^X; A_k)$ is intractable. Accordingly, we impose a tier structure much like the production model of section 2.1. At the top tier, utility function depends on nondurables, capital services, services, and leisure:

$$\begin{aligned} U &= U(C_{ND,k}, C_{K,k}, C_{SV,k}, C_{R,k}; A_k). \\ C_{ND} &= C(C_1, C_2, \ldots, C_{16}); \quad C_{SV} = C(C_{17}, \ldots, C_{NCI}). \end{aligned} \tag{2.28}$$

Consumer nondurables (C_{ND}) and services (C_{SV}) are further allocated to the 36 commodities in the third stage of the household model. For the remainder of this subsection we focus on the top tier. We first describe how the parameters are estimated from CEX data. We then indicate how the model for individual households is aggregated to obtain the model of the household sector in IGEM. The full details of the household model are given in chapter 3.

In order to characterize substitutability among leisure and the commodity groups, we find it convenient to derive household k's demands from a translog indirect utility function $V(p_k, m_k; A_k)$, following Jorgenson and Slesnick (2008):

$$-\ln V_k = \alpha_0 + \alpha^H \ln \frac{p_k}{m_k} + \frac{1}{2} \ln \frac{p_k}{m_k}' B^H \ln \frac{p_k}{m_k} + \ln \frac{p_k}{m_k}' B_A A_k, \tag{2.29}$$

where p_k is a vector of prices faced by household k; m_k is full expenditure of household k, α^H is a vector of parameters; B^H and B_A are matrices of parameters that describe price, total expenditure, and demographic effects; and A_k is a vector of variables that describe the demographic characteristics of household k.[2]

The value of full expenditure on leisure and the three commodity groups is

$$m_k = P_{ND}^C C_{NDk} + P_K^C C_{Kk} + P_{SV}^C C_{SVk} + P_R^C C_{Rk}. \tag{2.30}$$

In (2.29) the demands are allowed to be nonhomothetic, so that full expenditure elasticities are not constrained to unity. The commodity groups in (2.30) represent consumption of these commodities by household k.

The leisure time consumed by household k takes into account the opportunity costs of time of the individual members of the household. These opportunity costs are reflected in the after-tax wage p_R^m for each worker. We assume that the effective quantity of leisure of person m (R_k^m) is nonwork hours multiplied by the after-tax wage, relative to the base wage $q_k^m = p_R^m / p_R^0$.

We assume a time endowment of 14 hours per day for each adult. The annual leisure of person is the time endowment less hours worked:

$$R_k^m = q_k^m(\bar{H}_k^m - LS_k^m) = q_k^m(14 * 365 - \text{hours worked}_k^m). \tag{2.31}$$

The quantity of leisure for household k is the sum over all adult members:

$$C_{Rk} = \sum_m R_k^m, \tag{2.32}$$

and the value of household leisure is

$$P_R^C C_{Rk} = p_R^0 \sum_m R_k^m = \sum_m p_R^m(\bar{H}_k^m - LS_k^m). \tag{2.33}$$

The demand functions for commodities and leisure are derived from the indirect utility function (2.29) by applying Roy's identity:

$$\mathbf{w}_k = \frac{1}{D(p_k)}(\alpha^H + B^H \ln p_k - \iota' B^H \ln m_k + B_A A_k), \tag{2.34}$$

where $\mathbf{w}_k$ is the vector of shares of full consumption, ι is a vector of ones, and $D(p_k) = -1 + \iota' B^H \ln p_k$. For example, the demand for consumer nondurables is

$$w_{ND,k} = \frac{1}{D(p_k)}(\alpha_{ND}^H + B_{ND\bullet}^H \ln p_k - \iota B^H \ln m_k + B_{A,ND\bullet} A_k), \tag{2.35}$$

where $B_{ND\bullet}^H$ denotes the top row of the B^H matrix of share elasticities.

We require that the indirect utility function obey the restrictions

$$B^H = B^{H\prime}; \quad \iota' B^H \iota = 0, \quad \iota' B_A = 0, \quad \iota' \alpha^H = -1, \tag{2.36}$$

where B^H is the matrix of share elasticities representing the price effects and must be symmetric, while $\iota' B^H$ represents the full expenditure effect and must sum to zero. The matrix B_A determines how the expenditure shares differ among demographic groups and must sum to zero.

The restrictions in (2.36) are implied by the theory of individual consumer behavior and the requirement that individual demand functions can be aggregated exactly to obtain the aggregate demand functions used in the model. The restrictions are discussed in greater detail in chapter 3. The estimation of the parameters describing consumer demand from household survey data is described in chapter 3 as well.

The demographic characteristics employed in the model include the number of children; the four national census regions; and race, sex and three age groups for the head of household. Since it is infeasible to include demand functions for individual households in IGEM, we derive an aggregate version of the household demand functions (2.34). Let n_k be the number of households of type k. Then the vector of demand shares for the U.S. economy, $w = \left(\frac{P_{ND}^{CX} C_{ND}^X}{MF^X}, \frac{P_K^{CX} C_K^X}{MF^X}, \frac{P_{SV}^{CX} C_{SV}^X}{MF^X}, \frac{P_R^{CX} C_R^X}{MF^X} \right)'$, is obtained by aggregating over all types of households:

$$
\begin{aligned}
w &= \frac{\sum_k n_k m_k \mathbf{w}_k}{\sum_k n_k m_k} \\
&= \frac{1}{D(p)} \left[\alpha^H + B^H \ln p - \iota B^H \xi^d + B_A \xi^L \right],
\end{aligned}
\tag{2.37}
$$

where the distribution terms are

$$
\xi^d = \sum_k n_k m_k \ln m_k / M; \quad M = \sum_k n_k m_k.
\tag{2.38}
$$

$$
\xi^L = \sum_k n_k m_k A_k / M.
\tag{2.39}
$$

For example, the nondurables component of the aggregate share vector is

$$
w_{ND} = \frac{P_{ND}^{CX} C_{ND}^X}{MF^X},
\tag{2.40}
$$

where MF^X denote the national value of full consumption expenditures in CEX units:

$$
MF^X = \sum_k n_k m_k = P_{ND}^{CX} C_{ND}^X + P_K^{CX} C_K^X + P_{SV}^{CX} C_{SV}^X + P_R^{CX} C_R^X.
\tag{2.41}
$$

By constructing the model of consumer demand through exact aggregation over individual demands, we incorporate the restrictions implied by the theory of individual consumer behavior. In addition, we incorporate demographic information through the distribution terms (2.38) and (2.39). For the sample period we observe the actual values of these terms. For the period beyond the sample we project the distribution terms, using projections of the population by sex and race.

2.3.4 *Linking Survey Data to the National Accounts*

The top tier of the household model is estimated from data in the CEX. This is the only source of microeconomic data that includes the information necessary to characterize household demands for commodities and leisure in a consistent way. The CEX also includes the information on demographic characteristics of individual households that is required to capture the enormous heterogeneity of U.S. households.

Personal Consumption Expenditures in the NIPAs includes many items omitted from the CEX. Since we base IGEM on the NIPAs, we must reconcile the CEX-based estimates and the NIPAs-based estimates. We denote the quantity of consumption of item i in the NIPAs by N_i, and the price by PN_i, $i = 1, 2, \ldots, 35, R$, as listed in table 2.3. Corresponding to the CEX-based commodity groups for nondurables, C_{ND}, and services, C_{SV}, we have the quantities from the NIPAs, N^{ND} and N^{SV}, and their prices, PN^{ND} and PN^{SV}. The price of leisure PN^R is derived by aggregation over the population.

The share equations (2.37) allocate full consumption among the shares of commodities and leisure (w_{ND}, w_K, w_{SV}, and w_R). We denote the consumption shares based on the CEX as $SC_i^X = w_i$. We need to reconcile these to the shares based on NIPAs:

$$SC^N \equiv \left(\frac{PN^{ND}N^{ND}}{MF^N}, \frac{PN^K N^K}{MF^N}, \frac{PN^{CS}N^{CS}}{MF^N}, \frac{PN^R N^R}{MF^N} \right)', \tag{2.42}$$

where MF^N is full consumption.

Our reconciliation of the CEX and NIPAs data on consumption is accomplished by expressing the differences between the two sets of shares as an autoregressive process:

$$\Delta SC_{it} = SC_{it}^N - SC_{it}^X \quad i = \{ND, K, CS, R\}. \tag{2.43}$$

$$\Delta SC_{it} = \alpha + \beta \Delta SC_{it-1} + \varepsilon_{it} \quad \varepsilon_{it} = \rho \varepsilon_{it-1} + u_{it}. \tag{2.44}$$

We estimate (2.44) from sample period data and then project the differences forward. This provides an exogenous projection of the difference between the two sets of shares.

The value of full consumption in CEX units can be rewritten as the sum of the value of leisure and total expenditures on commodities:

$$\begin{aligned} MF^X &= P_{ND}^{CX} C_{ND}^X + P_K^{CX} C_K^X + P_{SV}^{CX} C_{SV}^X + P_R^{CX} C_R^X \\ &= P^{CC,X} CC^X + P_R^{CX} C_R^X. \end{aligned} \tag{2.45}$$

After rescaling to NIPA units the value of full consumption is

$$\begin{aligned} PF_t F_t &= P_t^{CC} CC_t + PN^R N^R \\ &= \sum_i PN_{it} N_{it} + PN^R N^R \end{aligned} \tag{2.46}$$

where $P_t^{CC} CC_t$ denotes the value of aggregate tangible consumption. This is the value that is matched to the Euler equation (2.23).

2.3.5 *Third Stage: Demands for Commodities*

In the third and final stage of the household model we allocate the quantities of nondurables, capital services, and other services (N^{ND}, N^K, and N^{CS}) to the 35 commodities, noncomparable imports, and capital services. We do not employ demographic information for this allocation but use a hierarchical model like the one employed for production in section 2.2. We impose homotheticity on each of the submodels.

There is a total of 34 commodity groups, one type of capital services, and one type of leisure, as listed in table 2.3. These are arranged in 17 nodes, as shown in table 2.4. This set of nodes is denoted I_{CNODE}. At each node m we represent the demand by a translog indirect utility function, $V^m(P^{Hm}, m_m; t)$:

$$\begin{aligned} -\ln V^m &= \alpha_0 + \alpha^{Hm} \ln \frac{P^{Hm}}{m_m} + \frac{1}{2} \ln \frac{P^{Hm}}{m_m}' B^{Hm} \ln \frac{P^{Hm}}{m_m} + f^{Hm} \ln \frac{P^{Hm}}{m_m} \quad m \in I_{CNODE}. \\ \ln P^{Hm} &\equiv (\ln PN_{m1}, \ldots, \ln PN_{mi}, \ldots, \ln PN_{m,im})' \quad i \in I_{CNODEm} \end{aligned} \tag{2.47}$$

The value of expenditures at node m is

$$m_m = PN_{m1} N_{m1} + \ldots + PN_{m,im} N_{m,im}. \tag{2.48}$$

The shares of full consumption derived from (2.47) exclude demographic variables and include latent variables representing changes in preferences f_t^{Hm}. When we impose homotheticity, by requiring that

Table 2.4
Tier structure of consumption function

	Symbol	Name	Components
1	F	Full consumption	Nondurables, capital, consumer services, leisure $F = F(N^{ND}, N_K, N^{CS}, N_R)$.
2	ND	Nondurables	Energy, food, consumer goods $N^{ND} = N^{ND}(N^{EN}, N^F, N^{CG})$.
3	EN	Energy	Gasoline, fuel-coal, electricity, gas $N^{EN} = N^{EN}(N_6, N^{FC}, N_{18}, N_{19})$.
4	F	Food	Food, meals, meals-employees, tobacco $N^F = N^F(N_1, N_2, N_3, N_9)$.
5	CG	Consumer goods	Clothing-shoe, household articles, drugs, miscellaneous goods $N^{CG} = N^{CG}(N^{CL}, N^{HA}, N_{12}, N^{MS})$.
6	CS	Consumer services	Housing, household operation, transportation, medical, miscellaneous services $N^{CS} = N^{CS}(N^H, N^{HO}, N^{TR}, N^{MD}, N^{MI})$.
7	FC	Fuel-coal	Coal, fuel oil $N^{FC} = N^{FC}(N_7, N_8)$.
8	CL	Clothing-shoes	Shoes, clothing $N^{CL} = N^{CL}(N_4, N_5)$.
9	HA	Household articles	Cleaning supplies, furnishings $N^{HA} = N^{HA}(N_{10}, N_{11})$.
10	MS	Misc. goods	Toys, stationery, imports, reading $N^{MS} = N^{MS}(N_{13}, N_{14}, N_{15}, N_{16})$.
11	H	Housing services	Housing rental, owner occupied maintenance $N^H = N^H(N_{17}, N_{34})$.
12	HO	Household operations	Water, communications, domestic service, other household $N^{HO} = N^{HO}(N_{20}, N_{21}, N_{22}, N_{23})$.
13	TR	Transportation	Own transportation, transportation $N^{TR} = N^{TR}(N_{24}, N_{25})$.
14	MD	Medical	Medical services, health insurance $N^{MD} = N^{MD}(N_{26}, N_{27})$.
15	MI	Misc. services	Personal services, business services, recreation, education $N^{MI} = N^{MI}(N_{28}, N^{BU}, N^{RC}, N_{32})$.
16	BU	Business services	Financial services, other services $N^{BU} = N^{BU}(N_{29}, N_{30})$.
17	RC	Recreation	Recreation, foreign travel $N^{RC} = N^{RC}(N_{31}, N_{33})$.

$\iota' B^{Hm} = 0$, the share demands simplify to an expression that is independent of the level of expenditures (m_m):

$$SN^m = \begin{bmatrix} PN_{m1}N_{m1} / PN^m N^m \\ \cdots \\ PN_{m,im}N_{m,im} / PN^m N^m \end{bmatrix} = \alpha^{Hm} + B^{Hm} \ln PN^{Hm} + f^{Hm}. \qquad (2.49)$$

Note that with homotheticity, the indirect utility function reduces to

$$-\ln V^m = \alpha^{Hm} \ln P^{Hm} + \frac{1}{2} \ln P^{Hm\prime} B^{Hm} \ln P^{Hm} + f^{Hm} \ln P^{Hm} - \ln m_m. \qquad (2.50)$$

The first three terms in (2.50) are analogous to the price function in the production model. We can define the price of the mth commodity group as

$$\ln PN^m = \alpha^{Hm} \ln P^{Hm} + \frac{1}{2} \ln P^{Hm\prime} B^{Hm} \ln P^{Hm} + f^{Hm} \ln P^{Hm}. \qquad (2.51)$$

Next, we express the value of expenditures as the price (2.51), multiplied by the corresponding quantity:

$$m_m = PN^m N^m. \qquad (2.52)$$

Substituting (2.51) and (2.52) into (2.50), we see that the utility index is the quantity of the mth commodity group, $V^m = N^m$.

As an example, in the $m = 3$ node the energy aggregate is a function of N_6 (gasoline), N^{FC} (fuel-coal aggregate), N_{18} (electricity), and N_{19} (gas), so that $N^{EN} = N^{EN}(N_6, N^{FC}, N_{18}, N_{19})$. The demand shares are functions of the prices of these four components and the state variables representing the biases:

$$SN^{m=3} = \begin{bmatrix} PN_6 N_6 / PN^{m=3} N^{m=3} \\ \cdots \\ PN_{19} N_{19} / PN^{m=3} N^{m=3} \end{bmatrix} = \alpha^{H3} + B^{H3} \ln PN^{H3} + f^{H3}. \qquad (2.53)$$

The value of energy purchases that appears in the next higher node for nondurables ($m = 2$) is

$$PN^{EN} N^{EN} = PN_6 N_6 + PN^{FC} N^{FC} + PN_{18} N_{18} + PN_{19} N_{19}. \qquad (2.54)$$

2.3.6 *Linking the National Accounts to the Interindustry Transactions Accounts*

The categories of PCE from the NIPAs are given in table 2.3. The expenditures are in purchasers' prices, which include the trade and transportation margins. These prices must be linked to the supply side of the model, where expenditures are in producers' prices. In the official input-output tables this link is provided by a bridge table,[3] for example, the PCE expenditures of \$32.9 billion in 1992 for "shoes" comprises the following commodity groups from the input-output tables: \$3.7 billion from rubber and plastic, \$11.2 billion from leather, \$0.12 billion from transportation, and \$17.8 billion from trade.

We denote the bridge matrix by H, where H_{ij} is the share of input-output commodity i in PCE item j. The value of total demand by households for commodity i is

$$VC_i = \sum_j H_{ij} PN_j N_j. \tag{2.55}$$

The prices from the NIPAs are also linked to input-output prices through this bridge matrix.

In section 2.1 we denoted the supply price of input i to the producing industries by PS_i, where we assumed that all industries pay the same price. We allow the sectors represented in the final demands to pay a different price PS_i^C; in particular, households may be charged a consumption tax. The price of PCE item j is thus expressed in terms of the commodity prices, and the transpose of the bridge matrix:

$$PN_j = \sum_i H_{ij}^T PS_i^C. \tag{2.56}$$

The quantity of commodity i consumed by the household sector is

$$C_i = VC_i / PS_i^C \quad i \in I_{COM}. \tag{2.57}$$

The value of total personal consumption expenditures is the sum over all commodities in either definition:

$$PCC_t CC_t = \sum_i VC_i = \sum_i PN_i N_i. \tag{2.58}$$

We emphasize again that the consumption expenditures in IGEM exclude the purchases of new consumer durables but include the service flow from the stock of durables. Purchases of new durables are treated as investment in order to preserve symmetry between housing and consumers' durables.

2.3.7 *Accounting for Leisure, the Time Endowment, and Full Income*

The demand for leisure in CEX units (C_R^X) is given by the fourth element of the share vector in (2.35). The aggregate demand for leisure in NIPA units (N^R) is obtained from C_R^X by applying the exogenous CEX-NIPA difference from (2.43). Individual leisure is related to hours supplied to the labor market.

We define the aggregate time endowment LH_t as an index number of the population, where individuals are distinguished by gender, age, and educational attainment. Let POP_{kt} denote the number of people in group k at time t, and the price of time is the after-tax hourly wage of person k, $(1-tl_t^m)P_{kt}^L$. The value of the aggregate time endowment with 14 hours per day to each person is

$$P_t^h LH_t = VLH_t = \sum_k (1-tl_t^m)P_{kt}^L \cdot 14 \cdot 365 \cdot POP_{kt}. \tag{2.59}$$

We express the value of time endowment as the product of the quantity LH and the price P^h. The Tornqvist index for the quantity of the time endowment is

$$\begin{aligned} d\ln LH_t &= \sum_k \frac{1}{2}(v_{kt}^L + v_{kt-1}^L) d\ln(14 \cdot 365 \cdot POP_{kt}), \\ v_{kt}^L &= \frac{(1-tl_t^m)P_{kt}^L \cdot 14 \cdot 365 \cdot POP_{kt}}{VLH_t} \quad k = \{\text{gender, age, education}\}. \end{aligned} \tag{2.60}$$

The price of aggregate time endowment is the value divided by this quantity index:

$$P_t^h = \frac{VLH_t}{LH_t}; \quad P_{baseyear}^h \equiv 1. \tag{2.61}$$

In a similar manner, we define the quantity of aggregate leisure by aggregating overall population groups, where the annual hours of leisure for a person in group k is denoted by H_{kt}^R:

$$\begin{aligned} d\ln N_t^R &= \sum_k \frac{1}{2}(v_{kt}^R + v_{kt-1}^R) d\ln(H_{kt}^R \cdot POP_{kt}), \\ v_{kt}^R &= \frac{(1-tl_t^m)P_{kt}^L \cdot H_{kt}^R \cdot POP_{kt}}{VR_t} \quad k = \{\text{gender, age, education}\}, \\ VR_t &= \sum_k (1-tl_t^m)P_{kt}^L H_{kt}^R POP_{kt}. \end{aligned} \tag{2.62}$$

The leisure hours of group k are derived from the accounts for hours worked used in estimating the quantity of industry labor input in section 2.1. The details of these labor accounts are given in appendix B.2. Individual leisure is equal to the annual time endowment, less the average hours worked for individuals in group k:[4]

$$H_{kt}^{R} = 14 \cdot 365 - h_{kt}. \tag{2.63}$$

The value of aggregate leisure is

$$VR_t = \sum_k (1 - tl_t^m) P_{kt}^L \cdot H_{kt}^R \cdot POP_{kt}. \tag{2.64}$$

The price of aggregate leisure is this value divided by the quantity index:

$$PN_t^R = \frac{VR_t}{N_t^R}; \quad PN_{baseyear}^R \equiv 1. \tag{2.65}$$

The price of aggregate time endowment (P_t^h) is not the same as the price of aggregate leisure even though they are the same at the level of the individual in group *k*. This is due to the differences in weights. We relate the two with a price aggregation coefficient:

$$PN_t^R = \psi_{Ct}^R P_t^h. \tag{2.66}$$

Taking the aggregation coefficient (2.66) into account, we define aggregate labor supply as time endowment, less adjusted leisure:

$$LS = LH - \psi_C^R N^R. \tag{2.67}$$

This implies that the price of labor supply is identical to the price of time endowment and the values are related as

$$P^h LH = P^h LS + PN^R N^R. \tag{2.68}$$

The value of labor supply is the gross payments by employers less the marginal tax on labor income:

$$P^h LS = (1 - tl^m) \sum_j PLD_j LD_j. \tag{2.69}$$

Labor income is the main source of household income. We can now describe the household financial accounts. In the lifetime budget constraint, W_0^F represents the present value of the stream of household full income, that is, tangible income plus the imputed value of leisure. Household tangible income, Y_t, is the sum of after-tax capital income (YK^{net}), labor income (YL), and transfers from the government (G^{TRAN}):

$$Y_t = YK_t^{net} + YL_t + G_t^{TRAN} - TLUMP_t - twW_{t-1}. \tag{2.70}$$

The term twW_{t-1} represents taxes on wealth, and $TLUMP_t$ represents lump-sum taxes that are zero in the base case but may be used in the policy cases.[5]

Labor income after taxes is

$$YL = P^h LS \frac{1-tl^a}{1-tl^m} = (1-tl^a)\sum_j PLD_j LD_j. \tag{2.71}$$

We distinguish between marginal tax rates and average tax rates. The price of the time endowment and leisure refers to the marginal price—the wage rate reduced by the marginal tax rate—while income is defined in terms of the wage rate less average taxes.

Capital income is the sum of dividend income from the private stock of physical assets and financial assets in the form of claims on the government and rest of the world:

$$YK_t^{net} = DIV - YK^{gov} + (1-tk)\left(GINT_t + Y_t^{row}\right). \tag{2.72}$$

The components of capital income are explained in more detail in section 2.4 on capital accounts, section 2.5 on government accounts, and section 2.6 on foreign accounts.

Full income includes the value of the time endowment and is equal to household tangible income Y_t plus the value of leisure:

$$YF_t = YK_t^{net} + YL_t + PN_t^N N_t^R + G_t^{TRAN} - TLUMP_t - twW_{t-1}. \tag{2.73}$$

Private household savings is income less consumption, nontax payments to the government (R_t^N), and transfers to rest of the world (H^{row}):

$$\begin{aligned} S_t &= YF_t - PF_t F_t - H_t^{row} - R_t^N + tcVCC^{exempt} \\ &= Y_t - P_t^{CC} CC_t - H_t^{row} - R_t^N + tcVCC^{exempt}. \end{aligned} \tag{2.74}$$

2.4 Investment and Cost of Capital

The primary factors of production are capital and labor services. Capital in IGEM includes structures, producer's durable equipment, land, inventories, and consumers' durables. Capital stocks are rented to producers and the annual rental value of capital services is included in the capital income of households. We focus on capital owned by the private sector in this section; government-owned capital is not part of the capital market and will be discussed in chapter 5.

We assume that the supply of capital is determined by past investments. We also assume that there are no installation or adjustment costs in converting new investment goods into capital stocks. With these simplifying assumptions the savings decision by households is identical to the investment decision. We analyze the savings-investment decision in more detail in order to clarify the role of the cost of capital, a key equation of IGEM that links investment, capital stock, and capital services.

The owner of the stock of capital chooses the time path of investment by maximizing the present value of the stream of after-tax capital income, subject to a capital accumulation constraint:

$$\text{Max}\sum_{t=u}^{\infty}\frac{(1-tk)(PKD_t\psi^K K_{t-1}-tpPK_{t-1})-(1-t^{ITC})PII_t I_t^a}{\prod_{s=u}^{t}1+r_s}, \tag{2.75}$$

such that

$$K_t=(1-\delta)K_{t-1}+\psi^I I_t^a. \tag{2.76}$$

After-tax capital income $(1 - tk)(PKD_t\psi^K K_{t-1} - tpPK_{t-1})$ is related to the capital income of households YK^{net} in (2.72). The discount rate r_s is the same as in the Euler equation for the household sector and the rental price of capital services is PKD_t. The stock of capital available at the end of the period is K_t. The remaining terms are the property tax rate tp, the capital income tax rate tk, and the price of the capital assets PK. We introduce the aggregation coefficient ψ^K to convert the capital stock measure to the flow of capital services.[6] Finally, I_t^a is the quantity of aggregate investment and $(1 - t^{ITC})PII_t$ is the price of investment, net of the investment tax credit. To simplify this model we have ignored details such as depreciation allowances and the distinction between debt and equity.

Aggregate investment includes commodities ranging from computers to structures. Capital stock is also an aggregate of these commodities but with different weights. At the level of the individual commodity, the capital accumulation equation is

$$K_{kjt}=(1-\delta_k)K_{kj,t-1}+I_{kjt}.$$

Aggregation over all the commodities results in the aggregate capital accumulation equation (2.76). The ψ_t^I aggregation coefficient converts the investment to capital stock and the aggregate depreciation rate is denoted δ. The issues involved in aggregation of capital services, capital stocks, and investment flows are discussed in more detail in appendix B.

The maximization of the present value of capital income after taxes results in the Euler equation:[7]

$$(1+r_t)\frac{(1-t^{ITC})PII_{t-1}}{\psi_{t-1}^I}=(1-tk)(PKD_t\psi_t^K-tpPK_{t-1})+(1-\delta)\frac{(1-t^{ITC})PII_t}{\psi_t^I}. \tag{2.77}$$

This equation describes the consequences of arbitrage between the market for investment goods and the market for capital services. If we were to put $(1 - t^{ITC})PII_{t-1}$ dollars in a bank in period t-1 we would earn a gross return of $(1 + r_t)(1 - t^{ITC})PII_{t-1}$ at time t. On the other hand, if we used those dollars to buy one unit of investment goods ($=\psi^I$ units of capital) we would collect a rental for one period, pay taxes, and the depreciated capital would be worth $(1 - \delta)(1 - t^{ITC})PII_t$ in period t prices. The Euler equation requires that these two returns be the same.

Our simplifying assumption of no installation costs implies that new investment goods are perfectly substitutable for existing capital in the capital accumulation equation. This implies that the price of capital stock is linked to the price of aggregate investment:

$$PK_t=\psi_t^{PK}PII_t(1-t^{ITC}). \tag{2.78}$$

The aggregation coefficient ψ_t^{PK} is used to transform asset prices to investment goods prices and plays a symmetrical role to ψ_t^I in the accumulation equation. The aggregation coefficients are taken to be exogenous in our policy simulations.

In equilibrium the price of one unit of capital stock (*PK*) is the present value of the discounted stream of rental payments (*PKD*). Capital rental prices, asset prices, prices of capital stock, rates of return, and interest rates for each period are related by the Euler equation (2.77). This incorporates the forward-looking dynamics of asset pricing into our model of intertemporal equilibrium. The asset accumulation equation (2.76) imparts backward-looking dynamics.

Combining the link between the prices of capital assets and investment goods (2.78) and the Euler equation (2.77), we obtain the well-known cost of capital equation:[8]

$$PKD_t=\frac{1}{(1-tk)}[(r_t-\pi_t)+\delta(1+\pi_t)+tp]PK_{t-1}, \tag{2.79}$$

where $\pi_t = (PK_t - PK_{t-1})/PK_{t-1}$ is the inflation rate for the asset price. The rental price of capital *PKD* equates the demands for capital by the 35 industries and households with the aggregate supply given by capital stock at the beginning of the period K_{t-1}.

The rental payment by industry j for capital services is $PKD_j\ KD_j$; the sum over all industries is the gross capital income in the objective function (2.75):

$$PKD_t \psi_t^K K_{t-1} = \sum_j PKD_{jt} KD_{jt}. \tag{2.80}$$

We denote the after-tax payments to capital by DIV. This notation evokes the notion of dividends, but the payments also include retained earnings. The payment to households is gross capital income less the capital income tax, the property tax, and taxes on owner-occupied housing RK^{hh}:

$$DIV = (1-tk)\left[\sum_j PKD_j KD_j - RK^{hh} - tpPK_t K_t\right]. \tag{2.81}$$

These after-tax payments are a major component of household capital income YK^{net} in (2.72).

2.5 Intertemporal Equilibrium

2.5.1 *Market Clearing Conditions*

We have now described the principal sources of supply and demand in the model. The other source of supply of commodities is imports and that is described in chapter 5. Government, investment, and export demand at the commodity level is also given in chapter 5. For the factors, the supply of labor is given in the household model above while the supply of capital is given in (2.80). We next characterize intertemporal equilibrium where demand and supply are balanced by an intertemporal price system. This is essential for an understanding of the algorithm for solving the model presented in the following section.

The Cass-Koopmans neoclassical model of economic growth has a saddle-path property: Given the initial value of the state variable, there is a unique value of the costate variable for which the model will converge to a steady state that satisfies a transversality condition. In this model there is only one state variable, the capital stock. The path of this stock is governed by the Euler equation derived by maximizing the household's objective function. We treat full consumption as the costate variable. Given the initial stock of capital, there is only one initial value of full consumption on the saddle path.

Additional state variables in the system include the government debt, claims on foreigners, and the latent variables in the behavioral equations. However, these state variables are not governed by optimizing behavior. They are set exogenously and do not have associated costate variables.[9] We first describe the equilibrium within each period, given the inherited capital stock and a guess of full consumption for that period. We then describe the intertemporal equilibrium where the Euler equation links full consumption across time periods.

With constant returns to scale and factor mobility, the equilibrium prices clear all markets for each period. In the commodity markets, the demand side of the economy consists of intermediate demands by producers, household consumption, investor demand, government demand, and exports. The supply comes from domestic producers and imports, as explained in chapter 5, equation 5.31. In the equilibrium for each period, the industry output prices PO_j equate supply and demand, so that for each commodity i

$$PQ_iQS_i = \sum_j PS_iQP_{ij} + PS_i(C_i + I_i + G_i) + PC_iX_i. \tag{2.82}$$

In capital market equilibrium, the demand for capital input from all industries and households is equal to the supply from the stock of inherited capital. In section 2.4 we have been careful to stress the distinction between the stock and flow of capital. The stock measures are related to the flow of services for each of the asset types and these stock and flow measures are independently aggregated. Capital income is equal to the capital service price multiplied by the service flow, which in turn is given by the capital stock multiplied by the aggregation coefficient ψ_t^K. The equilibrium condition in value terms is

$$PKD_t\psi_t^K K_{t-1} = \sum_j PKD_{jt}KD_{jt}. \tag{2.83}$$

Since we assume that capital is mobile across sectors, only one capital rental price is needed to clear this market. However, we observe different rates of return in our historical database for the period 1960–2005 presented in appendix B. To reconcile the actual movement in historical prices with our simplifying assumption of capital mobility, we treat the industry rental price as a constant times the economy-wide rental price:

$$PKD_{jt} = \psi_{jt}^K PKD_t. \tag{2.84}$$

In the sample period we calculate the aggregation coefficients ψ_{jt}^{K} from the actual data on industry costs of capital and the aggregate cost of capital. For the projection period we set these coefficients equal to the last sample observation, so that the ratios of marginal products of capital across industries are constant in the projection period. With these industry-specific adjustments, the economy-wide price PKD_t equates supply and demand for capital services:

$$\sum_{j=1}^{C} \psi_{jt}^{K} KD_{jt} = KD_t = \psi_t^{K} K_{t-1}. \tag{2.85}$$

An exception to the above treatment is the Petroleum and Gas Mining industry, industry number 4. The capital stock measure K_t includes land. Given the nonreproducible nature of this resource-based industry, we have allowed for two possible closures of the market for KD_{4t}: one is to treat it symmetrically with all other industries; and two is to assume that the stock of capital in this sector is fixed (no investment and no depreciation). In the second option, we have an endogenous rental price of this fixed stock of capital PKD_t^{oil} such that the demand for capital input is equal to the fixed supply:

$$KD_{j=4,t} = \overline{KD}^{oil}. \tag{2.86}$$

Turning to the labor market, the supply comes from the household demand for leisure and the time endowment. The demand is the sum over the demands from the 35 industries and government. The equilibrium condition in value terms is

$$P_t^h LS_t = P_t^h \left(LH_t - \psi_{Ct}^{R} N_t^{R} \right) = (1 - tl_t^m) \sum_j PLD_{jt} LD_{jt}. \tag{2.87}$$

The aggregation coefficient ψ_C^R links the time endowment to aggregate leisure.

Similarly, time trends in the industry labor prices are also different among industries. To reconcile the historical movements of these prices with the simplifying assumption of labor mobility, we first set the economy-wide wage rate equal to the price of the time endowment, adjusted for the marginal labor tax. We then use fixed constants to scale the industry wage rates to the economy-wide wage rate:

$$PLD_j = \psi_j^L \frac{P^h}{\left(1 - tl^m\right)}. \tag{2.88}$$

The price of aggregate time endowment P^h clears the market for labor:

$$LS_t = LH_t - \psi^R_{Ct} N^R_t = \sum_j \psi^L_{jt} LD_{jt}. \tag{2.89}$$

Our model of producer behavior is estimated over the sample period 1960–2005. In simulating the model beyond the sample period, projecting the hours available for work raises an issue about the treatment of business cycles. In particular, the actual data for 2008 and 2009 shows a sharp recession and fall in hours worked. The near-term projections are for a slow recovery with a period of above-average unemployment rates.

A simulation that begins in 2010 that ignores unemployment would overstate work, output, and energy use by a substantial margin. In order to project a baseline level of energy consumption that is consistent with the widely held views of below-trend output we introduce a simple adjustment for the time endowment:

$$LH^{adj}_t = (1 - u^{adj}_t) LH_t. \tag{2.90}$$

The construction of the unemployment adjustment ratio for above-trend unemployment is described in chapter 6, section 6.2.1.

Three additional equations must hold in equilibrium. The first is the exogenous government deficit, which is satisfied by the endogenous spending on goods. This is described in section 5.2.2, equation 5.9. The second is the exogenous current account surplus (5.34), which is satisfied by the world relative price e_t. The third item is the savings and investment balance:

$$S_t = P^I_t I^a_t + \Delta G_t + CA_t. \tag{2.91}$$

Household saving is first allocated to the two exogenous items—lending to the government to finance the public deficit (ΔG) and lending to the rest of the world (CA). The remainder is allocated to investment in domestic private capital. As we have explained in section 2.4, there are no separate savings and investment decisions in IGEM and (2.91) holds as a result of household intertemporal optimization.

2.5.2 *Steady State and Transition Path*

Our projections of the exogenous variables converge to long-run values. These include stocks of debt, the population, the latent variables in the price functions, and the aggregation coefficients. The steady state equilibrium is reached when all the conditions characterizing the market balance hold and, in addition, two further conditions are met:

$$K_t = K_{t-1}. \tag{2.92}$$

$$F_t = F_{t-1}. \tag{2.93}$$

The capital accumulation equation implies that investment exactly covers depreciation in the steady state:

$$\delta K_{ss} = \psi^I_{ss} I^a_{ss}. \tag{2.94}$$

The Euler equation implies that the steady state interest rate equals the rate of time preference:

$$r_{ss} = \rho. \tag{2.95}$$

The saddle-path feature of the Cass-Koopmans model is well known, as illustrated in figure 2.3. The locus of $\dot{K}_t = 0$ and $\dot{F}_t = 0$ intersect at the steady state values, (K_{ss}, F_{ss}). The saddle path is given by the dashed line going through (K_{ss}, F_{ss}). Given an initial capital stock K_0, the unique costate variable value that lies on the saddle path is F_0; this is the value of full consumption in the first period that is on an intertemporal equilibrium path that obeys the transversality condition.

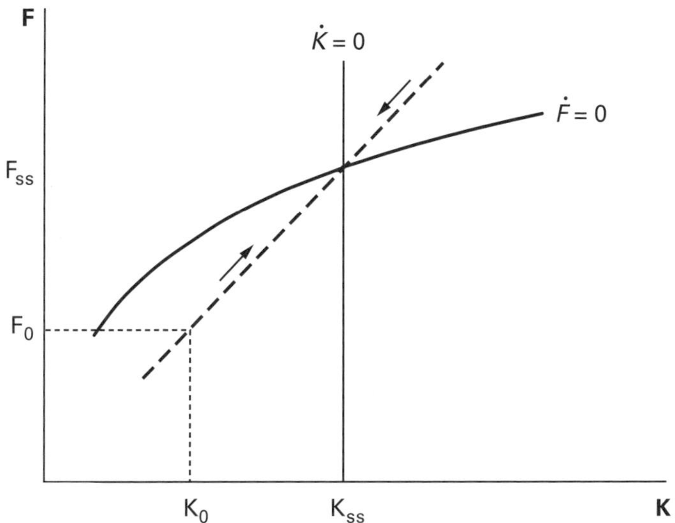

Figure 2.3
Phase diagram for state and costate variables.

Along the transition path from the first period to the steady state, the following equations must hold: (1) the capital accumulation equation, (2) the Euler equation linking full consumption between adjacent periods, and (3) the cost of capital equation linking the marginal product of capital with the rate of return and capital gains.

2.5.3 *Numeraire and Walras Law*

The model is homogenous in prices, so that doubling all prices will leave the equilibrium unchanged. We are free to choose a normalization for the price system and we use the price of time endowment P_t^h as the numeraire. For each period t, P_t^h is set to an exogenous value; for the sample period we set to the actual data and for the projection period we set to the value in the last year of the sample. Excess demands must sum to zero, that is, one of the market clearing equations is implied by the other equations and Walras law. In our solution algorithm we drop the labor market clearing equation.

2.6 Solution Algorithm

There are more than 4000 endogenous variables in IGEM in each time period, as summarized above and in chapter 5. We approximate the steady state at $T = 120$ periods after the initial shock. Roughly half a million values of the unknown variables must be determined. It would be difficult, if not impossible, to solve this system of equations for all the unknown variables simultaneously. The structure of our solution algorithm makes it possible to do this in a sequence of computational steps. The algorithm is implemented by us in Fortran and C programming languages. This is in contrast to most models that use a modeling package such as GAMS or GEMPACK.

Conceptually, the model consists of three main components: (1) an intratemporal module, (2) a steady state module, and (3) an intertemporal module. The intratemporal module computes a complete equilibrium for any given year t conditional on that year's exogenous variables and the values of two intertemporal variables: the capital stock available at the beginning of the period (K_{t-1}), and the value of aggregate full consumption ($PFF_t = PF_tF_t$).This intratemporal equilibrium is discussed in section 2.5.1.

The steady state, as described in section 2.5.2, contains all the equations of the intratemporal equilibrium, plus two conditions. Thus, in the steady state module we iterate over values of the state variable K_{ss} and the costate variable PFF_{ss}, and call the intratemporal module repeatedly until the accumulation and Euler equations (2.94 and 2.95) are satisfied.

Finally, the intertemporal module iterates over complete intertemporal trajectories of $\{K_t\}$ and $\{PFF_t\}$, $t = 1, 2, \ldots, T$, invoking the intratemporal module for every period until it finds a set that satisfies the model's accumulation and Euler conditions (2.76, 2.79, 2.25). In addition, the intertemporal module ensures that the trajectories satisfy two boundary conditions: (1) the initial capital stock matches the value of the capital stock in the model's data set and (2) the value of full consumption in the final period of the simulation matches its steady state value.

The solution algorithm is structured to solve the three modules efficiently. The process is illustrated in table 2.5. In the first step we solve the steady state module by using an enhanced version of Newton's method described in appendix D. A subroutine iterates over the $\{K_{ss}, PFF_{ss}\}$ pair until equations (2.94) and (2.95) are satisfied. For each guess of $\{K_{ss}, PFF_{ss}\}$, this subroutine invokes the intratemporal module in each time period $t = T$ to solve for all the other endogenous variables. The exogenous variables are set to their steady state values.

After the steady state has been determined the second step of the intertemporal algorithm is to determine the trajectories of $\{K_t\}_{t=1}^T$ and $\{PFF_t\}_{t=1}^T$, using the hybrid intertemporal algorithm described in appendix D.3. The algorithm is implemented in a subroutine and a second subroutine is called to evaluate each trajectory at each iteration. The procedure is illustrated in figure 2.4. We begin with an initial guess of the state and costate paths, say, $\{K_t^g\}_{t=1}^T$ and $\{PFF_t^g\}_{t=1}^T$. In figure 2.4 we only illustrate the path of the guess of full consumption, $\{PFF_t^g\}_{t=1}^T$.

For each period, given K_{t-1}^g and PFF_t^g, a subroutine calls the intratemporal module to solve for all the other endogenous variables. The intratemporal equilibria for the periods t and $t + 1$ determines the implied capital stock for the beginning of $t + 1$:

$$K_t = (1-\delta)K_{t-1}^g + \psi^I I_t^a, \tag{2.96}$$

and the interest rate r_{t+1} using the cost of capital equation:

$$PKD_{t+1} = \frac{1}{(1-tk)}[(r_{t+1} - \pi_{t+1}) + \delta(1+\pi_{t+1}) + tp]PK_t, \tag{2.97}$$

and, finally, the implied full consumption using the Euler equation:

Table 2.5
Algorithm to solve IGEM by triangulating the system

Solving the steady state module
Outer Loop
A subroutine *Newton_SS* iterates over $\{K_{ss}, PFF_{ss}\}$ to solve the two steady state conditions (2.86) and (2.87).
Inner Loop
For each trail pair of $\{Kss, PFFss\}$, call the intratemporal module to solve all other endogenous variables.
Solving the intratemporal module in period t, given a value for K_{t-1} and PFF_t
Outer Loop
A subroutine *Newton_FP* iterates over factor prices and other variables, $\{PKD, PKD\_oil, e, VII, VGG\}$, to solve 5 equations {2.76, 2.79, 5.42, 2.84, 5.10}.
The 5 "miss" distances are calculated in *Intra_miss*.
Inner Loop
For each iteration of *Newton_FP*, i.e., for each guess of the factor prices, call a subroutine *Newton_PO* that iterates over 35 industry prices to solve 35 industry cost equations {2.5}. The 35 "miss" distances are computed in subroutine *PO_miss*.
With these 35 commodity prices, and the guess of the outer loop variables, we can derive all demands and supplies with all intratemporal equations holding, except for the 5 listed.
Solving the intertemporal module
Outer Loop
A subroutine *FAIR_TAYLOR* iterates over the whole time path of $\{K_{t-1}, PFF_t\}$, $t = 1, 2, \ldots, T$ until the intertemporal equations (2.25, 5.22) are satisfied.
Inner Loop
For each guess of the path, a subroutine PATH is called to compute the implied values for $t + 1$. $\left\{K_t^g, PFF_t^g\right\}_{t=1}^{T}$ See figure 2.4. PATH calls the intratemporal module to compute the equilibrium for each t.
The miss distance between the guess and the values implied by the intertemporal equations is used to revise the guess. (See figure 2.4.)

$$PFF_{t+1} = \frac{(1+n_{t+1})(1+r_{t+1})}{1+\rho} PFF_t^g; \quad t = 1, 2, \ldots, T-1. \tag{2.98}$$

The implied values of the full consumption costate variable are marked by the arrows in figure 2.4. The difference between the guesses and the implied values are labeled "miss" in the figure:

$$miss_t^{PFF} = PFF_t - PFF_t^g; \quad miss_t^K = K_t - K_t^g. \tag{2.99}$$

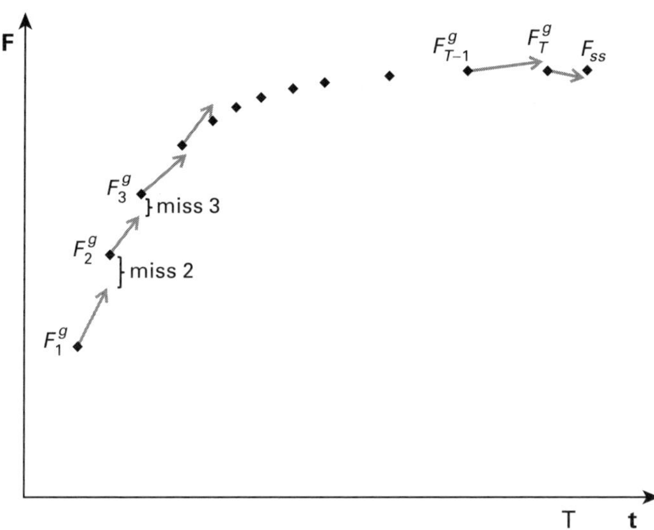

Figure 2.4
Solving for the intertemporal equilibrium path.

These *miss* values are used to update the guesses using a hybrid intertemporal algorithm that generalizes Fair and Taylor (1983) and employs certain features of the "multiple shooting" procedure[10] as described in appendix D. A straightforward implementation of Fair-Taylor will simply use a weighted average as the new guess:

$$PFF_t^{g+1} = \omega PFF_t + (1-\omega)PFF_t^g. \tag{2.100}$$

The hybrid algorithm introduced in Wilcoxen (1988) uses the *miss* values to compute a Jacobian that generates revised guesses that converge much faster.

The guess for the costate variable in the final period for each iteration is the steady state value: $PFF_T^g = PFF_{ss}$. The terminal period T is chosen such that the implied value of PFF_T after convergence differs from the steady state values by less than a chosen tolerance level for $T = 120$.

During both the steady state calculation and intertemporal calculation, the intratemporal module is invoked repeatedly. For computational efficiency, that module consists of a two-tiered suite of enhanced Newton's method algorithms as summarized in table 2.5. The outer loop is implemented in subroutine *Newton_FP* and iterates over a vector of factor prices and other variables. The corresponding miss distances are computed by subroutine *Intra_miss*. For each iteration of *Newton_FP*, an inner algorithm is called to determine industry output prices conditional on the guessed vector of factor prices. The inner algorithm is implemented in *Newton_PO* and the miss distances are calculated by *PO_miss*.

The design of the nested loops requires careful organization of the solution algorithm, rather a brute force approach for solving all of the equations at the same time. The result is an algorithm that solves the model quickly and is relatively easy to debug. After the base case transition path is obtained, the solutions for alternative policy cases usually require only seconds to solve.

2.7 Summary and Conclusion

In this chapter we have presented the Intertemporal General Equilibrium Model of the United States. The core of the demand side of the model presented in section 2.3 is a model of consumer behavior that consists of three stages. In the first stage full wealth is allocated to full consumption in each time period by means of an Euler equation. In the second stage full consumption is allocated among goods and services and leisure time. In the third and final stage the consumption of goods and services is allocated to the specific commodity groups that appear in IGEM.

Consumer demands, including leisure, depend on prices and full consumption as well as the demographic characteristics of individual households. These characteristics enable us to capture the heterogeneity of the households that make up the U.S. population. Combining the time endowment for each household with the demand for leisure, we obtain the supply of labor. We sum over the demands and supplies of individual households to obtain the model of aggregate consumer behavior that appears in IGEM. We discuss the household model in more detail in chapter 3.

The core of the supply side of IGEM is the models of producer behavior for the 35 industrial sectors presented in section 2.2. Each model determines the supply price for the industry, as well as the allocation of the value of output to the inputs of capital and labor services and intermediate inputs of energy and materials. The model also allocates energy among 5 energy sources and materials among 30 types of non-energy goods and services. We obtain total intermediate demands for each type of energy and materials as well and capital and labor services by summing over the 35 industrial sectors.

For each investment good included in the model we include investment, capital stock, and capital services, and the corresponding prices. The price of investment goods is linked to the demand for capital services through the cost of capital. The prices determined in markets for investment goods and capital services in each time period summarize the information about expectations of future prices that is relevant for current decisions. We discuss the model of producer behavior in more detail in chapter 4.

Each solution of IGEM determines an intertemporal equilibrium, consisting of the balance between demands and supplies for all commodities in every time period. This balance is achieved by the intertemporal price system, consisting of current prices as well as expectations of future prices. The effects of energy taxes work through markets for both energy and non-energy commodities and through current and expected future prices determined in these markets. We consider the solution of the model in greater detail in appendix D.

Notes

1. The price function contains the same information about technology as the production function. For further details, see Jorgenson (1986).
2. The aggregation properties of this indirect utility function are discussed in Jorgenson and Slesnick (2008).
3. For the 1992 benchmark in the *Survey of Current Business*, November 1997, this is given in table D, Input-Output Commodity Composition of NIPA Personal Consumption Expenditure Categories.
4. The average hours worked for people of type k are derived from the data that correspond to the h_{scaej} variable in appendix B, equation (B.29).
5. Taxes on wealth are estate taxes and are described more fully in section 2.4.1.
6. These concepts are explained in appendix B.3.1.5 describing the construction of historical data for aggregate investment and capital.
7. The Hamiltonian for the maximization problem is given in appendix A, equation A.3.3.
8. See Jorgenson (1963).
9. A model with portfolio choice allocating savings between capital and government debt is presented by McKibbin and Wilcoxen (1998, 2012). This requires an additional costate variable for the price of the debt.
10. See Lipton et al. (1982).

3 Modeling Consumer Behavior

3.1 Introduction

The objective of this chapter is to present a new econometric model of aggregate consumer behavior for the United States. The model allocates full wealth among time periods for households distinguished by demographic characteristics and determines the within-period demands for leisure, consumer goods, and consumer services. An important feature of the model is a closed form representation of aggregate demand and labor supply that accounts for the heterogeneity in household behavior observed in microlevel data. These aggregate demand and labor supply functions are the key component of the demand side of the Intertemporal General Equilibrium Model (IGEM) for the United States presented in chapter 2.

We combine expenditure data for over 150,000 households from the Consumer Expenditure Surveys (CEX) with price information from the Consumer Price Index (CPI) between 1980 and 2006. Following Slesnick (2002) and Kokoski, Cardiff, and Moulton (1994), we exploit the fact that the prices faced by households vary across regions of the United States as well as over time periods. We use the CEX to construct quality-adjusted wages for individuals with different characteristics that also vary across regions and over time. In order to measure the value of leisure for individuals who are not employed, we impute the opportunity wages they face from the wages earned by employees.

Cross-sectional variation of prices and wages is considerable and provides an important source of information about the determinants of patterns of consumption and labor supply. The demographic characteristics of households are also significant determinants of consumer expenditures and the supply of labor. The final determinant of consumer behavior is the value of the time endowment for households.

Part of this endowment is allocated to the labor market. This reduces the time available for consumption in the form of leisure.

In modeling household demands for goods and leisure we employ a generalization of the translog indirect utility function introduced by Jorgenson, Lau, and Stoker (1997). This indirect utility function generates demand functions with rank two in the sense of Gorman (1981). The rank-extended translog indirect utility function proposed by Lewbel (2001) has Gorman rank three. We present empirical results for the original translog demand system as well as the rank-extended system. Although the differences are not large, we conclude that the rank-three system more adequately represents the variations in consumer behavior over our extensive cross section of households.

Our model of consumption and labor supply is based on two-stage budgeting, similar to the framework described and implemented by Blundell, Browning, and Meghir (1994). However, their study is limited to consumption goods and does not include labor supply. Our first stage allocates full wealth, including assets and the value of the time endowment, among time periods, using the Euler equation approach introduced by Hall (1978). Since the CEX does not provide annual panel data at the household level, we employ synthetic cohorts, introduced by Browning, Deaton, and Irish (1985) and utilized by Attanasio and Weber (1995), Blundell, Browning, and Meghir (1994), and many others.

The second stage of our model of consumer behavior allocates full consumption among four subaggregates—nondurables, capital services, consumer services, and leisure. The third stage allocates these subaggregates to the 35 commodity groups identified in IGEM. Table 2.3 in chapter 2 gives the value of consumption by these 35 commodities and leisure time in 2005. We next describe historical trends in consumption.

Full consumption is first allocated to nondurables (ND), capital services (K), consumer services (SV), and leisure (R), as in equations (2.39) and (2.40):

$$\begin{aligned} PF_tF_t &= P_t^{CC}CC_t + PN_t^RN_t^R \\ &= PN_t^{ND}N_t^{ND} + PN_t^KN_t^K + PN_t^{CS}N_t^{CS} + PN_t^RN_t^R. \end{aligned} \tag{3.1}$$

Quantities of consumption are denoted N and variables denoted PN are the corresponding prices. Capital services are the annual rental flow of services from owner-occupied housing and consumer durables. Electricity and other forms of energy are included in nondurables.

Table 3.1
Aggregate consumption in the United States, top tier

	1960	1970	1980	1990	2000	2005
Value (billions of dollars)						
Nondurables	161.4	287.7	754.1	1351.9	2091.9	2714.8
Capital Services	81.9	154.7	416.1	892.6	1613.6	1972.4
Consumer Services	99.2	222.8	649.9	1711.8	3280.1	4303.1
Leisure	641.3	1386.6	3316.2	7053.4	10452.2	14432.3
Full Consumption	983.8	2051.9	5136.3	11009.7	17437.7	23422.6
Share of Full Consumption (%)						
Nondurables	16.4	14.0	14.7	12.3	12.0	11.6
Capital Services	8.3	7.5	8.1	8.1	9.3	8.4
Consumer Services	10.1	10.9	12.7	15.5	18.8	18.4
Leisure	65.2	67.6	64.6	64.1	59.9	61.6

Table 3.1 gives the values of the four subaggregates in current prices and the shares of these subaggregates in full consumption at various points of time from 1960 to 2005. Figure 3.1 plots the shares of these subaggregates in full consumption. The share of leisure fell from a high of 67.8% in 1971 to 59.9% in 2000 as the female labor force participation rate increased. In figure 3.2 we show how the labor supply and leisure grew relative to the total population. Our measure of the quantity of leisure is a Tornqvist index with rates of labor compensation as weights, as shown in equation (2.62).

The U.S. population grew at 1.08% per year between 1960 and 1990, but labor input grew at 1.71% per year. This reflects an increase in the quality of labor input due to the increased education and experience of workers. The quantity of leisure grew more slowly at 1.57% per year. Population growth accelerated to 1.21% per year during 1990–2000, while leisure growth decelerated to 1.46%. Only a small part of the rise in labor input during this boom period can be attributed to an increase in female labor force participation. The participation rate and annual hours of work rose during the boom for the population as a whole. Since 2000 the United States has undergone "jobless growth" and the growth rate of labor input has fallen substantially.

The share of nondurables fell almost continuously from 16.4% in 1960 to 12.0% in 2000, while the share of consumer services rose from 10.1% to 18.8%. The share of capital services was volatile but showed no distinct trend. Over the entire 1960–2005 period the leisure share

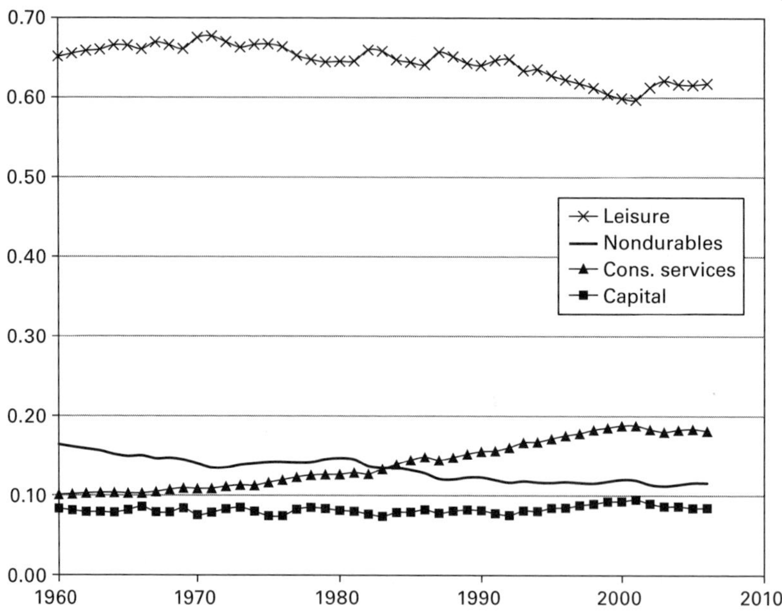

Figure 3.1
Consumption shares at top tier.

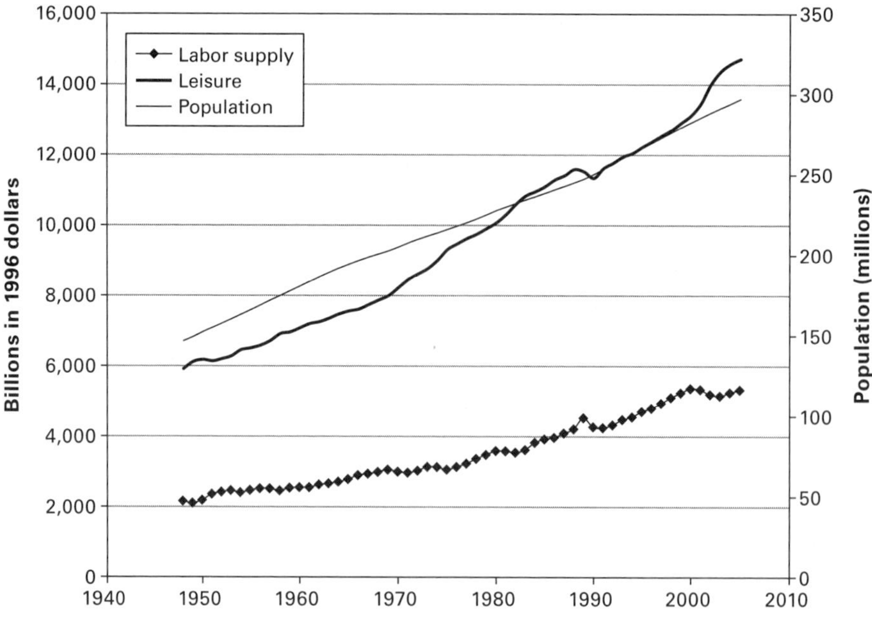

Figure 3.2
Labor supply and leisure (billions in 1996 dollars, left scale); Population (millions, right scale).

first rose, then fell, and then rose again during the 2000s; the rise in the services share mirrors the decline in the nondurables share.

The allocation of the consumption subaggregates—nondurables, capital services, and consumer services—to the 35 commodities identified in IGEM is given in table 2.4. This tier structure has 17 nodes and table 3.2 gives the value in current prices for each node for year 2005. Full consumption is dominated by leisure (14.4 trillion out of a total of 23.4 trillion), with consumer services contributing 4.30 trillion. Consumer Services has five components, the largest of which is Miscellaneous Services (1.7 trillion) and Medical Services (1.5 trillion). Miscellaneous Services include Business Services (646 billion) and Education & Welfare (451 billion).

The Nondurables group contributes 2.7 trillion and consists of Energy, Food, and Consumer Goods. The Energy node comes to 503 billion and consists of Gasoline and oil (284 billion), Coal and Fuel oil (21 billion), Electricity (133 billion) and Gas (65 billion). Transportation services are energy-intensive, and households purchased 62 billion in 2005. We note the carbon emissions from these services are counted as emissions from Transportation, while emissions from household gasoline use are allocated to Households. "Own transportation" comes to 263 billion and refers to expenditures on repair, car rental, insurance, and other services.

In figure 3.3 we plot the energy share of the Nondurables group and the energy share of Personal Consumption Expenditures (PCE). The share of energy increased dramatically with the oil shocks in the 1970s, rising from 14.8% of nondurables in 1972 to 21.7% in 1981. The share of energy then declined sharply in the mid-1980s and continued to fall, reaching 14.5% in 1999 when oil prices were low. With higher oil prices the energy share rose to 18.5% by 2005. The energy share in PCE rose from 6.1% in 1972 to 8.9% in 1981, then gradually declined to 4.3% in 1998 and rose to 5.6% in 2005.

Within the energy group gas consumption is relatively stable at about 12–13% of total energy expenditures. The electricity share rose from 21.1% in 1960 to 35.6% in 1995 before falling back to 26.5% in 2005. The gasoline share fell from the 54.8% peak in 1981 to 46.4% in 1998 and rose to more than 56% in 2005.

The increase in computers and communications is one of the signal economic events of the recent decades.[1] The share of "computers, peripherals, and software" in PCE rose from 0.23% in 1990 to 0.65% in 2007, despite the dramatic decline in prices. The share of PCE allocated

Table 3.2
Tier structure of consumption function, 2005 (billions of dollars) (NIPA-PCE categories)

Nondurables 2715	Energy 503	Gasoline and oil	284		
		Fuel—coal	21	Coal	0.3
				Fuel—oil	21
		Electricity	133		
		Gas	65		
	Food 1270	Food	720		
		Meals	449		
		Meals—employee	12		
		Tobacco	88		
	Consumer goods 942	Clothing—shoe	342	Shoes	55
				Clothing	287
		Household articles	181	Toilet articles; cleaning	138
				Furnishings	43
		Drugs	265		
		Miscellaneous goods	154	Toys	66
				Stationery	20
				Imports	7
				Reading materials	61

Table 3.2 (continued)

Full consumption 23423	Capital services 1972					
	Consumer services 4303	Housing 536	Rental housing	334		
			Owner maintenace	202		
		Household operation 281	Water	64		
			Communications	133		
			Domestic service	20		
			Other household	64		
		Transportation 324	Own transportation	263		
			Transportation services	62		
		Medical 1491	Medical services	1350		
			Health insurance	141		
		Miscellaneous services 1670	Personal services	116		
			Business services	646	Financial services	499
					Other business services	147
			Recreation	458	Recreation	358
					Foreign travel	100
			Education and welfare	451		
	Leisure 14432					

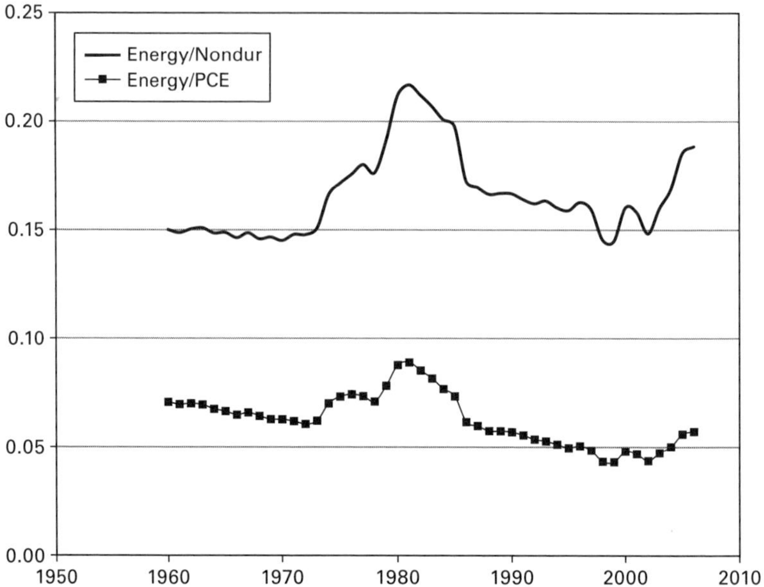

Figure 3.3
Energy consumption shares of Personal Consumption Expenditures (PCEs).

to "Communications" rose from 1.36% in 1960 to 1.88% in 1990 before falling back to 1.46% in 2007. Communications is represented in our consumption function under Consumer services–Household operations.

We turn next to our econometric model of demand for goods and services and labor supply. We introduce our model of consumer behavior in section 3.2. We first consider the second stage of the model, which allocates full consumption among leisure, goods, and services. We then present the first stage of the consumer model, describing the allocation of full wealth across time periods. In section 3.3 we discuss data issues, including the measurement of price and wage levels that show substantial variation across regions and over time.

In section 3.4 we present the estimation results for the rank-two and rank-three specifications of our second-stage model. We provide estimates of price and income elasticities for goods and services as well as leisure. We find that the wage elasticity of household labor supply is essentially zero, but that the compensated elasticity is large and positive. Leisure and consumer services are income elastic, while capital services and nondurable goods are income inelastic. We find that the aggregate demands and labor supplies predicted by our model accurately replicate the patterns in the data despite our relatively straightforward representation of household labor supply.

In section 3.5 we present a model of the intertemporal allocation of full consumption. We partition the sample of households into 17 cohorts based on the birth year of the head of the household. There are 27 time series observations for each cohort from 1980 through 2006. We use these data to estimate the unknown parameters of the Euler equation. Our methods exploit the longitudinal features of the data. Section 3.6 describes our model to allocate the three subaggregates—nondurables, capital services, and consumer services—to the 35 commodity groups employed in the Intertemporal General Equilibrium Model presented in chapter 2.

We present our methodology for measuring the welfare effects of policy changes in section 3.7. We employ our econometric model of consumer behavior to derive an intertemporal expenditure function for each household, giving the full wealth required to attain a given level of intertemporal utility. Our money metric of the welfare effects of a change in policy is the equivalent variation in full wealth. This is the wealth required to attain the welfare associated with the new policy at prices in the base case, less the wealth required to attain base case welfare at these prices. If this equivalent variation is positive, the policy produces a gain in welfare.

Section 3.8 presents our approach to measuring social welfare. We combine our econometric model of consumer behavior with a social welfare function to derive a social expenditure function. We define a money metric of the welfare effects of a change in policy as the equivalent variation in aggregate full wealth. This is the wealth required to attain the social welfare associated with a new policy at prices of the base case, less the wealth required to attain base case social welfare at these prices. Section 3.9 concludes the chapter.

3.2 Econometric Modeling

We next consider the econometric model of consumer behavior. We assume that household consumption and labor supply are allocated in accord with two-stage budgeting. In the first stage, full expenditure is allocated over time so as to maximize a lifetime utility function subject to a full wealth constraint. Conditional on the chosen level of full expenditure in each period, households allocate expenditures across consumption goods and leisure so as to maximize a within-period utility function.

To describe the second stage model in more detail, we assume that households consume n consumption goods in addition to leisure. The within-period demand model for household k can be described using the following notation:

$x_k = (x_{1k}, x_{2k}, \ldots, x_{nk}, R_k)$ are the quantities of goods and leisure.

$\rho_k = (p_k, p_{Lk})$ are prices and wages faced by household k. These prices vary across geographic regions and over time.

$w_{ik} = p_{ik}x_{ik}/M_k$ is the expenditure share of good i for household k.

$w_k = (w_{1k}, w_{2k}, \ldots, w_{nk}, w_{Rk})$ is the vector of expenditure shares for household k.

A_k is a vector of demographic characteristics of household k.

M_k is the full expenditure of household k, where p_{Lk} is the wage rate and R_k is the quantity of leisure consumed:

$$M_k = \sum_i p_{ik}x_{ik} + p_{Lk}R_k. \tag{3.2}$$

To obtain a closed form representation of aggregate demand and labor supply, we use a model that is consistent with exact aggregation, as originally defined by Lau (1977). Specifically, we focus on models for which the aggregate demands are the sums of microlevel demand functions rather than assume that they are generated by a representative consumer. Exact aggregation is possible if the demand function for good i by household k is of the form

$$x_{ik} = \sum_{j=1}^{J} b_{ij}(\rho)\psi_j(M_k). \tag{3.3}$$

Gorman (1981) showed that if demands are consistent with consumer rationality, the matrix $\{b_{ij}(\rho)\}$ has rank that is no larger than three.[2]

We assume that household preferences can be represented by a translog indirect utility function that generates demand functions of rank three. Lewbel (2001) has proposed an indirect utility function $V_k(p_k, M_k)$ that can be exactly aggregated:

$$(\ln V_k)^{-1} = \left[\alpha_0 + \ln\left(\frac{\rho_k}{M_k}\right)' \alpha_p + \frac{1}{2}\ln\left(\frac{p_k}{M_k}\right)' B_{pp} \ln\left(\frac{p_k}{M_k}\right) + \ln\left(\frac{p_k}{M_k}\right)' B_{pA} A_k\right]^{-1}$$
$$- \ln\left(\frac{p_k}{M_k}\right)' \gamma_p, \qquad (3.4)$$

where we assume $B_{pp} = B'_{pp}$, $\iota' B_{pA} = 0$, $\iota' B_{pp}\iota = 0$, $\iota'\alpha_p = -1$, and $\iota'\gamma_p = 0$.

To simplify notation, define $\ln G_k$ as

$$\ln G_k = \alpha_0 + \ln\left(\frac{p_k}{M_k}\right)' \alpha_p + \frac{1}{2}\ln\left(\frac{p_k}{M_k}\right)' B_{pp} \ln\left(\frac{p_k}{M_k}\right) + \ln\left(\frac{p_k}{M_k}\right)' B_{pA} A_k. \qquad (3.5)$$

Application of Roy's identity to equation (3.4) yields budget shares of the form

$$w_k = \frac{1}{D(p_k)}\left(\alpha_p + B_{pp} \ln\frac{p_k}{M_k} + B_{pA} A_k + \gamma_p [\ln G_k]^2\right), \qquad (3.6)$$

where $D(p_k) = -1 + \iota' B_{pp} \ln p_k$

With household demand functions of the form (3.4), the aggregate budget shares, denoted by the vector w, can be represented explicitly as functions of prices and summary statistics of the joint distribution of full expenditure and household attributes:

$$w = \frac{\sum_k M_k w_k}{\sum_k M_k}$$
$$= \frac{1}{D(\rho)}\left[\alpha_p + B_{pp} \ln\rho - i' B_{pp} \frac{\sum M_k \ln M_k}{\sum M_k}\right. \qquad (3.7)$$
$$\left. + B_{pA} \frac{\sum M_k A_k}{M_k} + \gamma_p \frac{\sum M_k (\ln G_k)^2}{\sum M_k}\right].$$

In the implementation of IGEM we use the simpler form where $\gamma_p = 0$, which generates demand functions with rank two in the sense of Gorman (1981):

$$w_k = \frac{1}{D(p_k)}\left(\alpha_p + B_{pp} \ln\frac{p_k}{M_k} + B_{pA} A_k\right). \qquad (3.8)$$

This provides own-price and cross-price elasticities for the four commodity groups, as well as unrestricted full expenditure elasticities. The aggregate budget shares in (3.7) then simplify to

$$w = \frac{1}{D(p)}\left[\alpha_p + B_{pp}\ln p - \iota' B_{pp}\frac{\sum M_k \ln M_k}{\sum M_k} + B_{pA}\frac{\sum M_k A_k}{M_k}\right]. \tag{3.9}$$

3.3 Data Issues

3.3.1 *Consumer Expenditure Survey*

In the United States the only comprehensive sources of information on consumer expenditures and labor supply are the Consumer Expenditure Surveys (CEX) published by the Bureau of Labor Statistics (BLS). These surveys are representative national samples conducted for the purpose of establishing weights for the Consumer Price Index (CPI). The surveys were administered approximately every 10 years until 1980. Since then the surveys have been conducted quarterly for every year.

Detailed information on labor supply is provided by the CEX only after 1980, so that we use a sample that covers the period 1980 through 2006. Expenditures are recorded on a quarterly basis and our sample sizes range from 4000 to 8000 households per quarter. To avoid issues related to seasonality, we use only the set of households that were interviewed in the second quarter of each year.[3]

In order to obtain a comprehensive measure of consumption, we modify the total expenditure variable reported in the surveys. We delete gifts and cash contributions as well as pensions, retirement contributions, and Social Security payments. Outlays on owner-occupied housing, such as mortgage interest payments, insurance, and the like, are replaced with households' estimates of the rental equivalents of their homes. Durable purchases are replaced with estimates of the services received from the stocks of goods held by households.[4] After these adjustments, our estimate of total expenditure is the sum of spending on nondurables and services (a frequently used measure of consumption) and the service flows from consumer durables and owner-occupied housing.

3.3.2 *Measuring Price Levels*

The CEX records expenditures on hundreds of items but provides no information on prices. This makes it necessary to link the surveys with price data from the CPI. While BLS provides time series of price indexes from the CPI for different cities and regions, the agency does not publish information on price levels. Kokoski, Cardiff, and Moulton (1994) (KCM) use the 1988 and 1989 CPI database to estimate the prices of a variety of goods and services in 44 urban areas.

We use the KCM estimates of prices for rental housing, owner-occupied housing, food at home, food away from home, alcohol and tobacco, household fuels (electricity and piped natural gas), gasoline and motor oil, household furnishings, apparel, new vehicles, professional medical services, and entertainment.[5] We extrapolate the price levels for 1988 and 1989 backward and forward to obtain prices before and after the benchmark period, using price indexes for the 44 urban areas published by the BLS. Most of these indexes cover the period from December 1977 to the present at either monthly or bimonthly frequencies, depending on the year and the commodity group.[6]

We link prices from the CPI to expenditure data from the CEX. The publicly available CEX data do not report households' cities of residence in an effort to preserve the confidentiality of survey participants. This necessitates aggregation across urban areas to obtain prices for the four major census regions: the Northeast, Midwest, South, and West. Since BLS does not collect nonurban price information, rural households are assumed to face the prices of Class D–sized urban areas.[7]

3.3.3 *Measuring Wages in Efficiency Units*

The primitive observation unit in the CEX is a "consumer unit" and expenditures are aggregated over all members. We model labor supply at the same level of aggregation by assuming that male and female leisure are perfect substitutes when measured in quality-adjusted units. The price of leisure (per efficiency unit) is estimated from a wage equation defined over full-time workers, those who work more than 40 weeks per year and at least 30 hours per week. The wage equation for worker i is given by

$$\ln P_{Li} = \sum_j \beta_j^z z_{ji} + \sum_j \beta_j^s (S_i^* z_{ji}) + \sum_j \beta_j^{nw} (NW_i^* z_{ji}) + \sum_l \beta_l^g g_{li} + \varepsilon_{it}, \qquad (3.10)$$

where

P_{Li} is the wage of worker i;

z_i is a vector of demographic characteristics that includes the age, age squared, years of education, and years of education squared of worker i;

S_i is a dummy variable indicating whether the worker is female;

NW_i is a dummy variable indicating whether the worker is nonwhite; and

g_i is a vector of region-year dummy variables.

We estimate the wage equation (3.10) using the CEX from 1980 through 2006 with the usual sample selection correction. The quality-adjusted wage for a worker in region-year s is given by $p_L^s = \exp(\hat{\beta}_s^g)$. The parameter estimates (excluding the region-year effects) are presented in table 3.3.

In figure 3.4 we present our estimates of quality-adjusted hourly wages in the urban Northeast, Midwest, South, and West, as well as rural areas from 1980 through 2006. The reference worker, whose quality is normalized to one, is a white male, age 40, with 13 years of education. The levels and trends of the wages generally accord with expectations; the highest wages are in the Northeast and the West and the lowest are in rural areas. Perhaps more surprising is the finding that real wages, shown in figure 3.5, have decreased over the sample period and exhibit substantially less variation across

Table 3.3
Parameter estimates of wage equation

Variable	Estimate	SE
CONST	0.04507	0.0783
AGE	0.06014	0.0024
AGESQ	–0.00056	0.00003
EDUC	0.03609	0.0058
EDUCSQ	0.00118	0.0002
FEM*AGE	–0.02322	0.0028
FEM*AGESQ	0.00022	0.00003
FEM*EDUC	–0.00808	0.0082
FEM*EDUCSQ	0.00075	0.0003
NW*AGE	–0.01340	0.0035
NW*AGESQ	0.00014	0.00004
NW*EDUC	–0.02971	0.0088
NW*EDUCSQ	0.00127	0.0003
MAR	0.09257	0.0044
NW	0.38577	0.0882
FEM	0.30830	0.0772
INVMILLS	–0.21600	0.0204

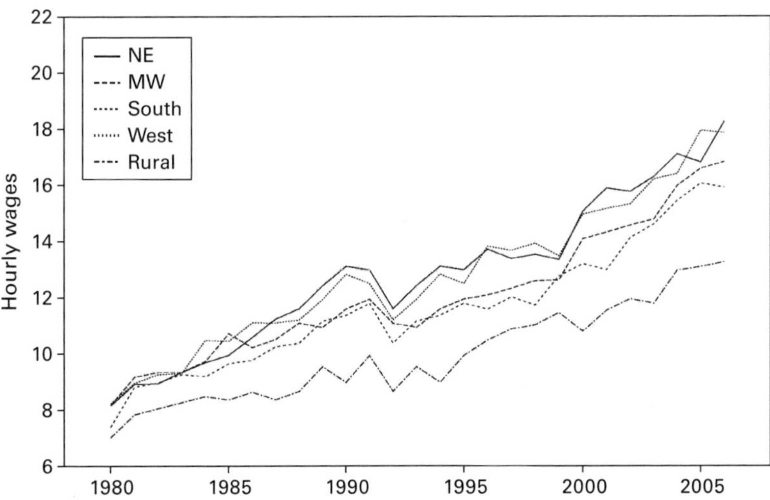

Figure 3.4
Regional wages (current dollars).

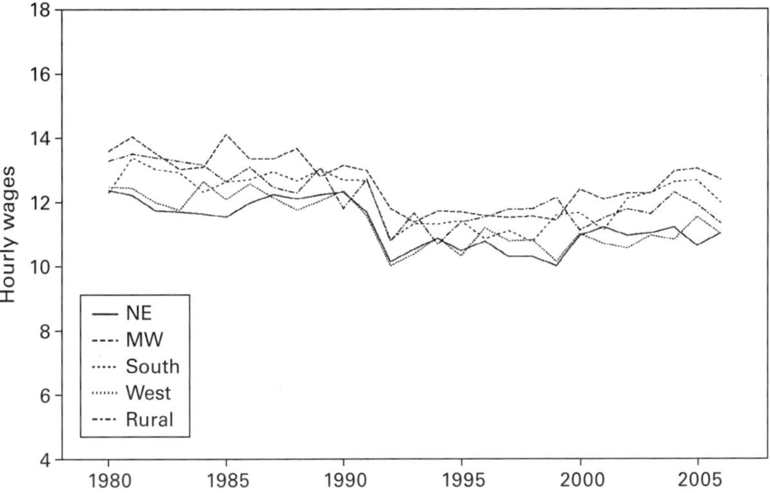

Figure 3.5
Regional real wages (Northeast region, 1989 dollars)

regions. Adjustments for differences in the cost of living across geographical regions reduce the between-region wage dispersion.

3.3.4 *Measuring Household Leisure*

Estimates of the quantity of leisure consumed are easily obtained for workers. The earnings of individual m in household k at time t are

$$E_{kt}^{m} = p_{Lt} q_{kt}^{m} H_{kt}^{m}, \tag{3.11}$$

where p_{Lt} is the wage at time t per efficiency unit, q_{kt}^{m} is the quality index of the worker, and H_{kt}^{m} is the observed hours of work. With observations on wages and the hours worked, the quality index for worker m is

$$q_{kt}^{m} = \frac{E_{kt}^{m}}{p_{Lt} H_{kt}^{m}}. \tag{3.12}$$

If the daily time endowment is 14 hours, the household's time endowment measured in efficiency units is $T_{kt}^{m} = q_{kt}^{m} \cdot (14)$ and leisure consumption is $R_{kt}^{m} = q_{kt}^{m}(14 - H_{kt}^{m})$.

For nonworkers we impute a nominal wage for individual m in household k, $\hat{p}_{Lkt}^{m}$, using the fitted values of a wage equation similar to equation (3.6). The estimated quality adjustment for nonworkers is

$$\hat{q}_{kt}^{m} = \frac{\hat{p}_{Lkt}^{m}}{p_{Lt}}, \tag{3.13}$$

and the individual's leisure consumption is calculated as $R_{kt}^{m} = \hat{q}_{kt}^{m} \cdot (14)$. Given estimates of leisure for each adult in the household, full expenditure for household k is computed as

$$M_{kt} = p_{Lt} R_{kt} + \sum_{i} p_{ik} x_{ik}, \tag{3.14}$$

where

$$R_{kt} = \sum_{m} R_{kt}^{m} \tag{3.15}$$

is total household leisure computed as the sum over all adult members.

In figure 3.6 we present tabulations of per capita full consumption (goods and leisure) as well as per capita consumption (goods only). For both series, expenditures are deflated by price and wage indexes that vary over time and across regions. Per capita consumption grew at an average annual rate of 1.1% per year in the period from 1980 through 2006, compared to 1.0% per year for per capita full consumption.

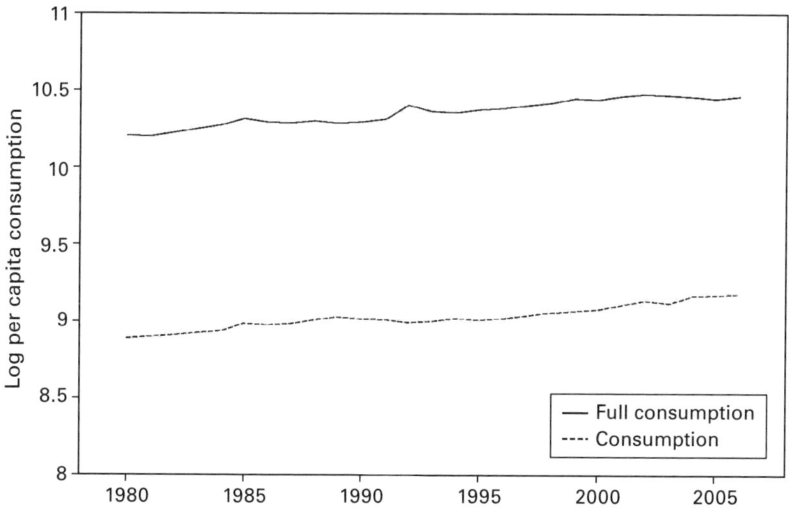

Figure 3.6
Log consumption per capita (constant dollars).

Figure 3.7 shows the average level of quality-adjusted leisure consumed per adult. The average annual hours increased by approximately 18% over the 26 years from 2656 in 1980 to 3177 in 2006. Figure 3.8 shows that the inclusion of household leisure lowers the dispersion in consumption, the variance of log per capita full consumption is about 25% lower than the variance of log per capita consumption. The trends of the two series, however, are similar.

3.3.5 *Reconciling Survey Data with the National Accounts*

Personal Consumption Expenditures (PCE) from the National Income and Product Accounts (NIPAs) define the scope of consumption in the Intertemporal General Equilibrium Model (IGEM) presented in chapter 2. The Consumer Expenditure Survey (CEX) used to estimate aggregate demand and supply functions is less comprehensive.[8] For example, the CEX includes only the out-of-pocket component of health care spending, while PCE includes all components of household health expenditures, imputations for financial services, activities of nonprofit institutions, and so on.

Section 2.1 in chapter 2 describes the bridge equation (2.44) that reconciles the differences in coverage. In section 3.4 below we describe how the aggregate demand equations are estimated using the CEX

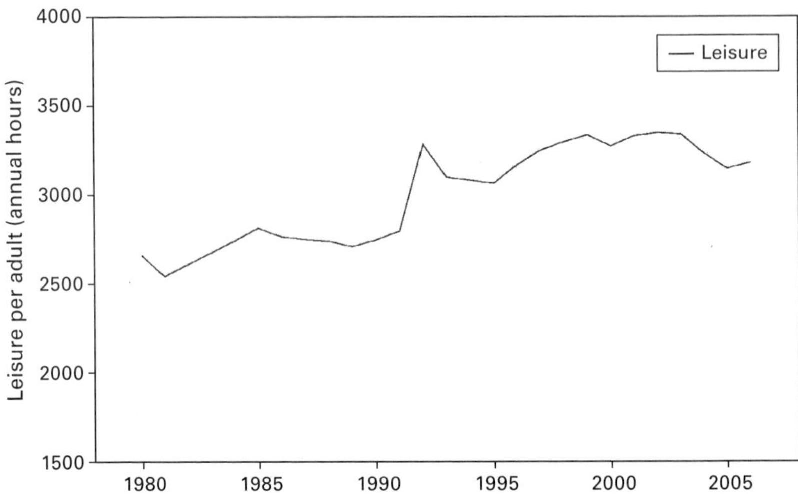

Figure 3.7
Quality-adjusted leisure per adult.

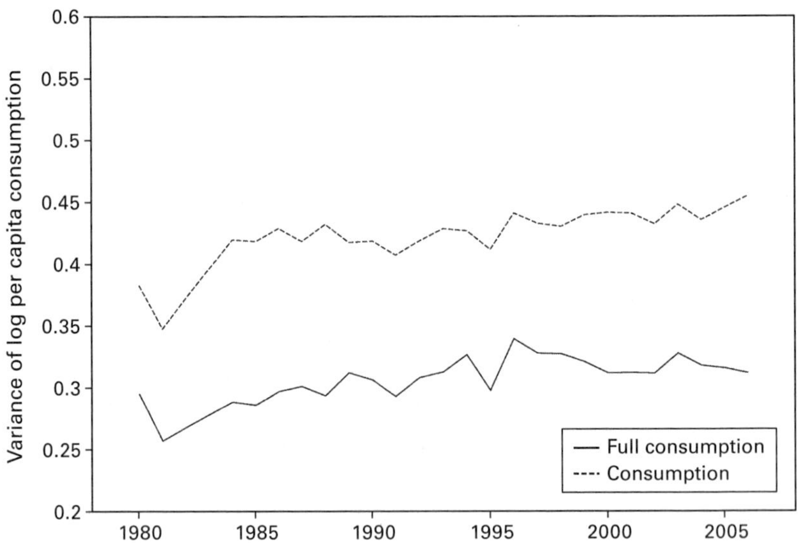

Figure 3.8
Variance of log per capita consumption.

Table 3.4
Expenditure shares from CEX versus PCE (NIPA)

	Consumer Expenditure Survey		Personal Consumption Expenditures (NIPA)	
	1980	2006	1980	2006
Nondurables	0.118	0.106	0.147	0.116
Capital Services	0.103	0.125	0.081	0.085
Consumer Services	0.062	0.061	0.127	0.182
Leisure	0.718	0.708	0.646	0.618

data. The aggregate shares that are based on the CEX data have an X superscript, and the shares based on the NIPAs[9] are distinguished by an N superscript:

$$SC^N \equiv \left(\frac{PN^{ND}N^{ND}}{MF^N}, \frac{PN^K N^K}{MF^N}, \frac{PN^{CS}N^{CS}}{MF^N}, \frac{PN^R N^R}{MF^N}\right)'.$$

These two sets of shares are given in table 3.4 for 1980 and 2006. At the start of the sample period the NIPA share of nondurables in full consumption was 14.7% while the CEX share was 11.8%, and the shares for consumer services were 12.7% versus 6.2%. This reflects the smaller coverage of consumer services in the CEX. Correspondingly, the NIPA shares for capital and leisure are smaller than the CEX shares.

While the CEX share for nondurables had only fallen by 0.8 percentage points by 2006, the NIPA share had fallen 3.1 percentage points. The share for consumer services in the CEX stayed at 6% but rose by almost a half in the NIPAs. The two definitions of the consumer services share are plotted in figure 3.9 to show how the gap is steadily growing over this 1980–2006 period. The trends in the NIPA-based shares for the other commodity groups are presented in figure 3.1.

We have modeled the differences between the NIPA and CEX shares as an AR(1) process. This is described in chapter 2, equations (2.43) and (2.44), reproduced here:

$$\Delta SC_{it} = SC_{it}^N - SC_{it}^X \quad i = \{ND, K, CS, R\}. \tag{2.43}$$

$$\Delta SC_{it} = \alpha + \beta \Delta SC_{it-1} + \varepsilon_{it} \quad \varepsilon_{it} = \rho \varepsilon_{it-1} + u_{it}. \tag{2.44}$$

The data partly presented in table 3.4 and figure 3.9 are used to estimate the autoregression (2.44). The estimated equations are used to project the difference in the CEX and NIPA shares beyond the sample. The results are plotted in figure 3.10. These show that the projected

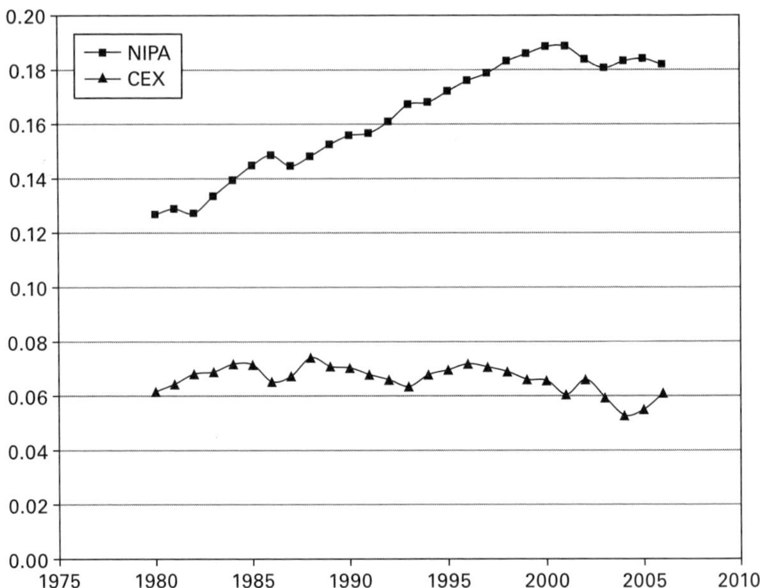

Figure 3.9
Trends in share of consumer services in full consumption; CEX versus NIPA.

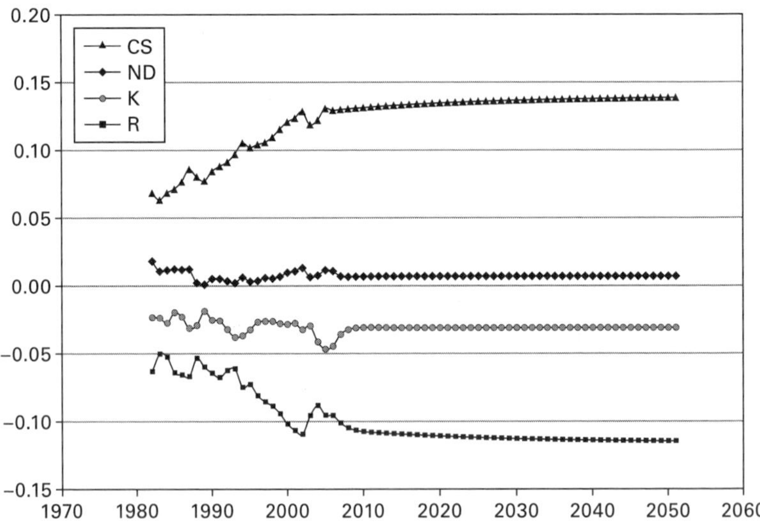

Figure 3.10
Projections of the difference between CEX- and NIPA-based consumption shares based on an AR(1) model.

difference between the CEX and NIPA will change only modestly. We emphasize that the absolute value of the gap is substantial in all years of the projection.

3.4 Demands for Goods and Leisure

The four commodity groups identified in the second stage model are given in table 3.2. To reiterate, these four subaggregates are

Nondurables—Energy, food, clothing, and other consumer goods.

Consumer Services—Medical care, transportation, entertainment, and the like.

Capital Services—Owner-occupied housing and consumer durables.

Household Leisure—The sum of leisure over all adult members of the household.

The demographic characteristics used to control for heterogeneity in household behavior are given in table 3.5. There is a potential total of $4 \times 3 \times 4 \times 2 \times 2 \times 2 = 384$ household types. However, only 244 types are nonzero in the sample, with few observations of rural households.

In table 3.6 we present summary statistics of the variables used in the estimation of the demand system. On average, household leisure comprises almost 70% of full expenditure, although the dispersion is greater than for the other commodity groups. As expected, the price of capital services (which includes housing) shows substantial variation in the sample, as does the price of consumer services. The average number of adults is 1.9 and the average number of children is 0.7. Female-headed households account for over 28% of the sample and almost 16% of all households have nonwhite heads.

Table 3.5
Demographic groups identified in household consumption model

Number of children	0, 1, 2, 3, or more
Number of adults	1, 2, 3, or more
Region	Northeast, Midwest, South, West
Location	Urban, rural
Gender of head	Male, female
Race of head	White, nonwhite

Table 3.6
Sample summary statistics (Sample size: 154,180)

Variable	Mean	Standard Error	Minimum	Maximum
Share NON	0.101	0.052	0.0009	0.695
Share CAP	0.133	0.076	0.0001	0.895
Share CS	0.072	0.054	0.00004	0.787
Share LEIS	0.694	0.123	0.0001	0.991
Log PNON	0.116	0.212	–0.510	0.877
Log PCAP	–0.090	0.280	–1.101	0.526
Log PCS	0.144	0.333	–0.828	0.702
Log wage	–0.304	0.234	–0.933	0.137
Log full exp.	11.547	0.605	8.241	15.281
No. children	0.717	1.121	0.000	12.000
No. adults	1.887	0.841	1.000	13.000
White dummy	0.844	0.363	0.000	1.000
Nonwhite dummy	0.156	0.363	0.000	1.000
Male dummy	0.715	0.451	0.000	1.000
Female dummy	0.285	0.451	0.000	1.000
Urban dummy	0.905	0.293	0.000	1.000
Rural dummy	0.095	0.293	0.000	1.000
Northeast dummy	0.198	0.398	0.000	1.000
Midwest dummy	0.249	0.433	0.000	1.000
South dummy	0.311	0.463	0.000	1.000
West dummy	0.242	0.428	0.000	1.000

We model the within-period allocation of expenditures across the four commodity groups using the rank-extended translog model defined in equation (3.4). We assume that the disturbances of the demand equations are additive so that the system of estimating equations is

$$\mathbf{w}_k = \frac{1}{D(\rho_k)}\left(a_{\mathbf{p}} + B_{pp}\ln\frac{p_k}{F_k} + B_{pA}\mathbf{A}_k + \gamma_{\mathbf{p}}[\ln G_k]^2\right) + \varepsilon_k, \tag{3.16}$$

where the vector ε_k is assumed to be mean zero with variance-covariance matrix Σ. We compare these results to those obtained using the rank-two translog demand system (3.8), originally developed by Jorgenson, Lau, and Stoker (1997):

$$\mathbf{w}_k = \frac{1}{D(\rho_k)}\left(a_{\mathbf{p}} + B_{pp}\ln\frac{p_k}{F_k} + B_{pA}\mathbf{A}_k\right) + \mu_k. \tag{3.17}$$

We note, as before, that the two specifications coincide if the elements of the vector γ_p are equal to zero.

Both the rank-two and rank-three demand systems are estimated using nonlinear, full information maximum likelihood with leisure as the omitted equation of the singular system. The parameter estimates of both models are presented in tables 3.7 and 3.8. The level of precision of the two sets of estimates is high, as would be expected given the large number of observations. Less expected is the fact that the rank-two and rank-three estimates are similar for all variables other than full expenditure. Note, however, that the parameters γ_p are statistically significant and that any formal test would strongly reject the rank-two model in favor of the rank-three specification (the likelihood ratio test statistic is over 978).

In table 3.9 we compute price and income elasticities for the three consumption goods and leisure. In all cases the elasticities are calculated for a household with two adults and two children, living in the urban Northeast, with a male, white head of the household with $100,000 of full expenditure in 1989. Both nondurables and consumer services are price inelastic while capital services have price elasticities exceeding unity. The compensated own-price elasticities are negative for all goods and differences between the rank-two and rank-three models are small. The uncompensated wage elasticity of household labor supply is negative but close to zero while the expenditure elasticity is quite high. The compensated wage elasticity is around 0.70 and, as with the consumption, the differences between the two types of demand systems are small.[10]

If the rank-two and rank-three models differ, they are likely to show different effects of full expenditure on demand patterns. To assess this possibility we present the fitted shares from both systems for the reference household at different levels of full expenditure in table 3.10. The predicted shares from the two models are similar for levels of full expenditure in the range $25,000 to $150,000. They diverge quite sharply, however, in both the upper and lower tails of the expenditure distribution. For example, when full expenditure is $7,500, the share of nondurables in the rank-two model is 0.227 compared with 0.268 for the rank-three model. At high levels of full expenditure ($350,000), the fitted share of household leisure is 0.734 in the rank-two model and 0.711 in the rank-three model.

Both the rank-two and rank-three demand systems are consistent with exact aggregation. Closed form representations of aggregate demands for the four goods are given by

Table 3.7
Parameter estimates, rank-two model

Variable	Estimate	SE	Estimate	SE
	Nondurables		Capital Services	
CONST	–0.53660	0.0027	–0.29696	0.0041
PNON	–0.01576	0.0014	–0.02430	0.0013
PCAP	–0.02430	0.0013	0.05172	0.0022
PSERV	0.05024	0.0009	–0.04291	0.0012
WAGE	–0.04689	0.0019	0.00632	0.0026
FULLC	0.03670	0.0002	0.00916	0.0004
CHILD	–0.01482	0.0002	–0.00256	0.0004
CHILSQ	0.00152	0.0001	0.00066	0.0001
ADULT	0.00360	0.0006	0.04338	0.0007
ADULTSQ	–0.00048	0.0001	–0.00407	0.0001
REGMW	–0.00390	0.0004	0.00865	0.0007
REGS	–0.00824	0.0004	0.01163	0.0007
REGW	0.00057	0.0004	–0.00753	0.0005
NONWHITE	0.01115	0.0003	0.01341	0.0005
FEMALE	0.00823	0.0003	0.00285	0.0004
RURAL	–0.01264	0.0004	0.03158	0.0008
	Consumer Services		Leisure	
CONST	–0.03032	0.0030	–0.13615	0.0063
PNON	0.05024	0.0009	–0.04689	0.0019
PCAP	–0.04291	0.0012	0.00632	0.0026
PSERV	–0.02309	0.0013	0.02110	0.0018
WAGE	0.02110	0.0018	0.05999	0.0045
FULLC	–0.00535	0.0003	–0.04052	0.0006
CHILD	–0.00077	0.0003	0.01815	0.0006
CHILSQ	0.00053	0.0001	–0.00271	0.0002
ADULT	0.01814	0.0007	–0.06511	0.0011
ADULTSQ	–0.00139	0.0001	0.00594	0.0002
REGMW	–0.01280	0.0005	0.00805	0.0010
REGS	–0.01857	0.0005	0.01519	0.0010
REGW	–0.00216	0.0004	0.00913	0.0009
NONWHITE	0.01139	0.0004	–0.03594	0.0008
FEMALE	–0.00776	0.0003	0.00333	0.0007
RURAL	–0.01141	0.0005	–0.00752	0.0011

Table 3.8
Parameter estimates, rank-three model

	Estimate	SE	Estimate	SE
Variable	Nondurables		Capital Services	
CONST	−0.42468	0.2143	−0.20158	0.1835
PNON	−0.01508	0.0039	−0.02232	0.0043
PCAP	−0.02232	0.0043	0.0533	0.0039
PSERV	0.05108	0.0018	−0.04132	0.0034
WAGE	−0.04136	0.0086	0.00886	0.0053
FULLC	0.02768	0.0177	0.00148	0.0151
FULLCSQ	−0.00678	0.0002	−0.0059	0.0003
CHILD	−0.01474	0.0004	−0.00257	0.0004
CHILDSQ	0.0015	0.0001	0.00065	0.0001
ADULT	0.00112	0.0007	0.0409	0.0011
ADULTSQ	0.00003	0.0001	−0.0036	0.0001
REGMW	−0.004	0.0004	0.00851	0.0007
REGS	−0.00816	0.0005	0.01151	0.0007
REGW	−0.00054	0.0004	−0.00747	0.0006
NONWHITE	0.01079	0.0005	0.01306	0.0006
FEMALE	0.00848	0.0003	0.00312	0.0004
RURAL	−0.01274	0.0005	0.03112	0.0008
	Consumer Services		Leisure	
CONST	0.03746	0.1305	0.4112	0.5281
PNON	0.05108	0.0018	−0.04136	0.0086
PCAP	−0.04132	0.0034	0.00886	0.0053
PSERV	−0.02203	0.0022	0.0231	0.0046
WAGE	0.0231	0.0046	0.02773	0.0608
FULLC	−0.01082	0.0107	−0.01833	0.0435
FULLCSQ	−0.00428	0.0002	0.01696	0.0005
CHILD	−0.0008	0.0003	0.01811	0.0008
CHILDSQ	0.00052	0.0001	−0.00267	0.0002
ADULT	0.01649	0.0008	−0.05851	0.002
ADULTSQ	−0.00106	0.0001	0.00462	0.0002
REGMW	−0.01275	0.0005	0.00824	0.0011
REGS	−0.01847	0.0006	0.01512	0.0012
REGW	−0.00215	0.0004	0.00907	0.0009
NONWHITE	0.01113	0.0005	−0.03497	0.0013
FEMALE	−0.00748	0.0003	−0.00412	0.0007
RURAL	−0.0115	0.0005	−0.00687	0.0011

Table 3.9
Price and income elasticities

Good	Uncompensated Price Elasticity		Compensated Price Elasticity		Full Expenditure Elasticity	
	Rank 2	Rank 3	Rank 2	Rank 3	Rank 2	Rank 3
Nondurables	–0.918	–0.903	–0.822	–0.809	0.722	0.724
Capital Services	–1.428	–1.432	–1.314	–1.319	0.926	0.93
Consumer Services	–0.613	–0.614	–0.548	–0.548	1.088	1.096
Leisure	0.012	0.014	–0.323	–0.314	1.059	1.056
Labor Supply	–0.026	–0.030	0.698	0.698	–2.289	–2.342

Reference household: 2 adults, 2 children, NE urban, male, white, full expenditure = $100,000.

Table 3.10
Full expenditure and household budget shares at different expenditure levels

Expenditure level ($)	Rank 2	Rank 3	Rank 2	Rank 3
	Nondurables		Capital Services	
7500	0.227	0.268	0.147	0.183
25000	0.183	0.192	0.136	0.145
75000	0.143	0.140	0.126	0.125
150000	0.117	0.116	0.120	0.119
275000	0.095	0.100	0.114	0.119
350000	0.086	0.095	0.112	0.120
	Consumer Services		Leisure	
7500	0.047	0.073	0.579	0.476
25000	0.053	0.060	0.627	0.603
75000	0.059	0.058	0.672	0.677
150000	0.063	0.062	0.700	0.702
275000	0.066	0.070	0.725	0.711
350000	0.067	0.073	0.734	0.711

Reference household: 2 adults, 2 children, NE urban, male, white.

$$w = \frac{\sum_k M_k w_k}{\sum_k M_k} = P_t + Y_t + D_t, \tag{3.18}$$

where P_t, Y_t, and D_t are summary statistics similar to those described by Jorgenson, Lau, and Stoker (1997). Specifically, the price factor is the full expenditure weighted average of the price terms in the share equations in each time period:

$$P_t = \frac{\sum_k M_{kt} D(\rho_{kt})^{-1}(\alpha_p + B_{pp} \ln \rho_{kt})}{\sum_k M_{kt}}, \tag{3.19}$$

and Y_t, and D_t are defined similarly for the full expenditure and demographic components of the aggregate demand system:

$$Y_t = \frac{\sum_k M_{kt} D(\rho_{kt})^{-1}(\gamma_p (\ln G_{kt})^2 - i' B_{pp} \ln M_{kt})}{\sum_k M_{kt}}.$$

$$D_t = \frac{\sum_k M_{kt} D(\rho_{kt})^{-1}(B_{pA} A_{kt})}{\sum_k M_{kt}}. \tag{3.20}$$

How well do the fitted demands reflect aggregate expenditure patterns and their movements over time? In table 3.11 we compare the fitted aggregate shares for the rank-three system with sample averages tabulated for each of the four commodity groups. The rank-three demand system provides an accurate representation of both the levels and movements of the aggregate budget shares over time. With few exceptions, the fitted shares track the sample averages closely in terms of both the absolute and relative differences. Table 3.11 also reports the R-squared statistic to assess the normalized within-sample performance of the predicted household-level budget shares. At this level of disaggregation, the nondurables and leisure demand equations fit better than the other two commodity groups in most years.

The aggregation factors show that essentially all of the movement in the aggregate shares was the result of changes in prices and full

Table 3.11
Aggregate budget shares

Year	Sample Shares	Fitted Shares	R-squared	Aggregation Factors		
				Price	Expenditure	Demographics
Nondurables						
1980–1981	0.1145	0.1074	0.1273	0.3985	–0.3009	0.0098
1985–1986	0.0993	0.1003	0.1609	0.4009	–0.3090	0.0084
1990–1991	0.0967	0.0990	0.1793	0.4051	–0.3141	0.0080
1995–1996	0.0898	0.0892	0.2198	0.3996	–0.3181	0.0077
2000–2001	0.0846	0.0852	0.1910	0.4011	–0.3235	0.0076
2005–2006	0.0864	0.0845	0.1806	0.4055	–0.3279	0.0068
Capital Services						
1980–1981	0.0956	0.1162	0.0296	0.2100	–0.0141	–0.0797
1985–1986	0.1134	0.1178	0.1003	0.2103	–0.0143	–0.0782
1990–1991	0.1186	0.1213	0.1292	0.2132	–0.0145	–0.0774
1995–1996	0.1222	0.1240	0.1161	0.2161	–0.0150	–0.0771
2000–2001	0.1306	0.1272	0.1226	0.2193	–0.0154	–0.0766
2005–2006	0.1403	0.1344	0.1134	0.2255	–0.0155	–0.0756
Consumer Services						
1980–1981	0.0566	0.0561	0.0018	–0.0439	0.1202	–0.0202
1985–1986	0.0626	0.0668	0.0111	–0.0370	0.1236	–0.0199
1990–1991	0.0706	0.0678	0.0317	–0.0379	0.1258	–0.0201
1995–1996	0.0734	0.0750	0.0318	–0.0326	0.1270	–0.0193
2000–2001	0.0724	0.0747	0.0420	–0.0350	0.1289	–0.0192
2005–2006	0.0748	0.0678	0.0245	–0.0434	0.1308	–0.0195
Leisure						
1980–1981	0.7333	0.7203	0.1506	0.4354	0.1948	0.0902
1985–1986	0.7247	0.7151	0.1532	0.4257	0.1997	0.0897
1990–1991	0.7141	0.7119	0.1804	0.4197	0.2028	0.0895
1995–1996	0.7146	0.7117	0.1791	0.4170	0.2060	0.0887
2000–2001	0.7124	0.7129	0.1758	0.4147	0.2100	0.0882
2005–2006	0.6985	0.7133	0.1458	0.4124	0.2126	0.0883

expenditure. The demographic factors are important in explaining cross-sectional variation but showed very little movement over time for any of the four commodity groups. This is especially true of leisure, where the effects of prices and full expenditure on the aggregate shares changed significantly in opposite directions while the influence of demographic variables showed little temporal variation.

As a final assessment of our within-period demand model, we examine the statistical fit of the leisure demand equations for subgroups of the population for which our model might perform poorly. In order to develop a model of aggregate labor supply, we have made the simplifying assumption that quality-adjusted male and female leisure are perfect substitutes within the household. If this assumption turns out to be overly strong, we might expect the demand system to predict less well for groups for which the assumption is likely to be contrary to fact.

In table 3.12 we compare the aggregate leisure demands of male-headed households with at least two adults. It seems reasonable to expect that the presence of children complicates the labor supply decisions of adults. Since we do not explicitly model this interaction, it is possible that our model might not fit the data as well for this subgroup as for others. Instead, we find that for both types of household, the fitted aggregate demands for leisure are quite close to the sample averages for the subgroups. Moreover, the R-squared computed for households with children is actually higher than that computed for those without.

Table 3.12
Group budget shares of leisure (Male household head with 2 or more adults)

	At Least 1 Child			No Children		
Year	Sample Share	Fitted Share	R-squared	Sample Share	Fitted Share	R-squared
1980–1981	0.7347	0.7236	0.1144	0.7522	0.7412	0.0277
1985–1986	0.7221	0.7167	0.0774	0.7467	0.7391	0.0171
1990–1991	0.7171	0.7136	0.0730	0.7342	0.7366	0.0811
1995–1996	0.7161	0.7138	0.0799	0.7364	0.7343	0.0612
2000–2001	0.7115	0.7158	0.0633	0.7405	0.7358	0.0528
2005–2006	0.7029	0.7161	0.0421	0.7200	0.7360	0.0349

3.5 Intertemporal Allocation

In the first stage full expenditure M_{kt} is allocated across time periods so as to maximize lifetime utility U_k for household k:

$$\max_{F_{kt}} U_k = E_t\left\{\sum_{t=1}^{T}\frac{1}{(1+\rho)^{t-1}}\left[\frac{V_{kt}^{(1-\sigma)}}{(1-\sigma)}\right]\right\} \tag{3.21}$$

subject to the lifetime budget constraint:

$$\sum_{t=1}^{T}(1+r_t)^{-(t-1)}M_{kt} \leq W_k, \tag{3.22}$$

where r_t is the nominal interest rate, σ is an intertemporal curvature parameter, and ρ is the subjective rate of time preference. We expect ρ to be between zero and one, and the within-period utility function is logarithmic if σ is equal to one:

$$\max_{F_{kt}} U_k = E_t\left\{\sum_{t=1}^{T}(1+\rho)^{-(t-1)}\ln V_{kt}\right\}. \tag{3.23}$$

The first-order conditions for this optimization yield Euler equations of the form

$$(V_{kt})^{-\sigma}\left[\frac{\partial V_{kt}}{\partial M_{kt}}\right] = E_t\left[(V_{k,t+1})^{-\sigma}\left(\frac{\partial V_{k,t+1}}{\partial M_{k,t+1}}\right)\frac{(1+r_{t+1})}{1+\rho}\right]. \tag{3.24}$$

If the random variable η_{kt} embodies expectational errors for household k at time t, equation (3.24) becomes

$$(V_{kt})^{-\sigma}\left(\frac{\partial V_{kt}}{\partial M_{kt}}\right) = \left[(V_{k,t+1})^{-\sigma}\left(\frac{\partial V_{k,t+1}}{\partial M_{k,t+1}}\right)\frac{(1+r_{t+1})}{1+\rho}\right]\eta_{k,t+1}. \tag{3.25}$$

We can simplify this equation by noting that, for the indirect utility function given in equation (3.4), we obtain

$$\frac{\partial V_{kt}}{\partial M_{kt}} = \frac{V_{kt}}{M_{kt}}[-D(p_{kt})][1-(\gamma_p' \ln p_{kt})\cdot G_{kt}]^{-2}. \tag{3.26}$$

The last term in the square bracket is equal to one in the rank-two case (and approximately equal to one in the data for the rank-three case), so that taking logs of both sides of equation (3.26) yields

$$\Delta\ln M_{k,t+1} = (1-\sigma)\Delta\ln V_{k,t+1} + \Delta\ln[-D(p_{k,t+1})] + \ln(1+r_{t+1}) - \ln(1+\rho) + \eta_{kt}. \tag{3.27}$$

Equation (3.27) serves as the estimating equation for σ and the subjective rate of time preference ρ. Since we do not have longitudinal data on full consumption, we create synthetic panels from the CEX similar to those described by Blundell, Browning, and Meghir (1994) and Attanasio and Weber (1995) for consumption alone. The estimating equation for this stage of the consumer model is

$$\Delta \ln M_{c,t+1} = (1-\sigma)\Delta \ln V_{c,t+1} + \Delta \ln[-D(p_{c,t+1})] + \ln(1+r_{t+1}) - \ln(1+\rho) + v_{ct} \tag{3.28}$$

where:

$$\Delta \ln F_{c,t+1} = \sum_{k\varepsilon c} \ln F_{k,t+1} - \sum_{k\varepsilon c} \ln F_{k,t}, \tag{3.29}$$

$$\Delta \ln V_{c,t+1} = \sum_{k\varepsilon c} \ln V_{k,t+1} - \sum_{k\varepsilon c} \ln V_{k,t}, \tag{3.30}$$

$$\Delta \ln[-D(\rho_{c,t+1})] = \sum_{k\varepsilon c} [-D(\rho_{k,t+1})] - \sum_{k\varepsilon c} [-D(\rho_{k,t})]. \tag{3.31}$$

The summations above are over all households in cohort c at time t.

To implement the Euler equation we first partition the sample of households in the CEX into 17 cohorts based on the birth year of the head of the household. There are 27 time series observations from 1980 through 2006 for all but the oldest and youngest cohorts and we use these data to estimate σ and ρ using methods that exploit the longitudinal features of the data.

The birth cohorts are defined over five-year age bands on the basis of the age of the head of the household. In 1982 and 1983 the BLS did not include rural households in the survey and, to maintain continuity in our sample, we use data from 1984 through 2006. The characteristics of the resulting panel are described in table 3.13. The oldest cohort was born between 1900 and 1904 and the youngest cohort was born between 1980 and 1984. The cell sizes for most of the cohorts were typically several hundred households, although the range is substantial.

The age profiles of consumption per capita and of household leisure per capita are presented in figures 3.11 and 3.12 for the cohorts in the sample. The consumption per capita is relatively flat for the younger households but rises quite steeply for those aged between 40 and 60. Per capita leisure remains relatively constant until age 35, increases until age 60, and then decreases. Given the large weight of leisure, the profile of per capita full consumption is similar to the age profile of

Table 3.13
Synthetic cohorts

Cohort	Cohort Birth Year	Average No. Observations	Range of No. Observations	Years Covered
1	1900–1904	108	52–169	1980–1989
2	1905–1909	158	78–229	1980–1994
3	1910–1914	195	92–305	1980–2000
4	1915–1919	261	176–347	1980–2000
5	1920–1924	284	53–415	1980–2005
6	1925–1929	337	234–417	1980–2006
7	1930–1934	337	272–469	1980–2006
8	1935–1939	354	289–446	1980–2006
9	1940–1944	437	341–554	1980–2006
10	1945–1949	546	432–705	1980–2006
11	1950–1954	622	457–817	1980–2006
12	1955–1959	650	382–910	1980–2006
13	1960–1964	580	120–870	1980–2006
14	1965–1969	484	103–768	1985–2006
15	1970–1974	464	83–742	1990–2006
16	1975–1979	397	71–594	1995–2006
17	1980–1984	331	45–473	2000–2006

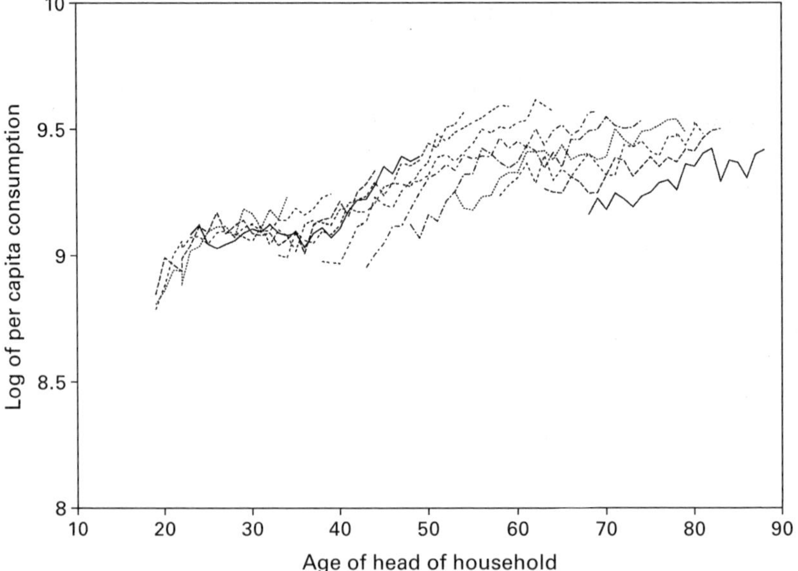

Figure 3.11
Age profile of per capita consumption.

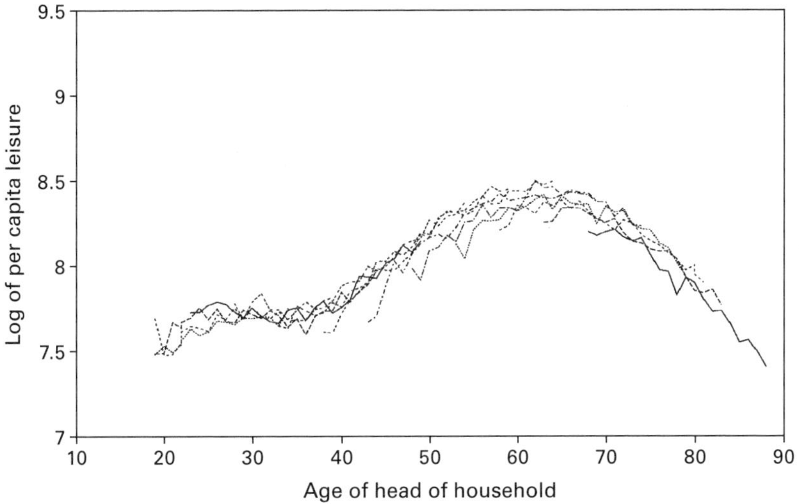

Figure 3.12
Age profile of per capita leisure.

household leisure. Figure 3.13 shows the age profile of the average within-period utility levels ($\ln V_k$), which plays a critical role in the estimation of equation (3.28).

The statistical properties of the disturbances v_{ct} in equation (3.28) that are constructed from synthetic panels in the CEX are described in detail by Attanasio and Weber (1995). They note that the error term is the sum of expectational error as well as measurement error associated with the use of averages tabulated for each cohort. We present estimates of δ and σ using ordinary least squares, least squares weighted by the cell sizes of each cohort in each year, and a random effects estimator that exploits the panel features of our synthetic cohort data. The first panel in table 3.14 shows that estimates of ρ are consistently around 0.015 while the estimates of σ are approximately 0.1.

We re-estimate (3.28) using a variety of instruments to account for expectational and measurement error associated with synthetic cohorts. The results shown in the second panel of table 3.14 are based on different sets of instruments. The first estimator (IV1) uses a constant, the average age of the cohort, a time trend, and the two-period lagged average marginal tax rate on earnings as instruments. The second estimator IV2 uses, in addition, the two period lags of wages, interest rates, and prices of capital services and consumer services. The third estimator IV3 also includes the third period lags. Regardless of the instrument

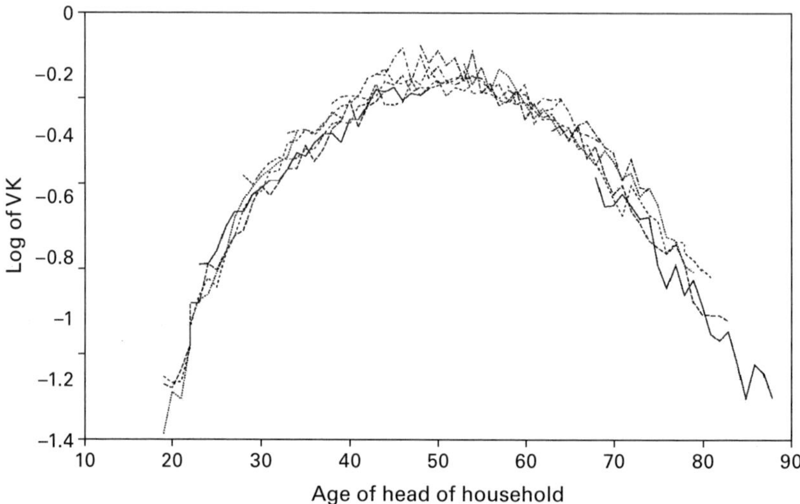

Figure 3.13
Age profile of ln VK.

Table 3.14
Parameter estimates, intertemporal model

	Least Squares Estimates					
	OLS		Weighted OLS		Random Effects	
Variable	Estimate	SE	Estimate	SE	Estimate	SE
ρ	0.01471	0.0011	0.01185	0.0011	0.01460	0.0016
**σ	0.08226	0.0194	0.11280	0.0218	0.10183	0.0202
	Instrumental Variables Estimators					
	IV1		IV2		IV3	
Variable	Estimate	SE	Estimate	SE	Estimate	SE
ρ	0.01253	0.0012	0.01251	0.0012	0.01249	0.0011
σ	0.03414	0.0357	0.05521	0.0350	0.08150	0.0337

set, the point estimates of the subjective rate of time preference remains around 0.0125 while the estimates of σ are in the range between 0.0341 and 0.0815.

In the earlier versions of IGEM the intertemporal parameters are not those estimated from (3.28) using the synthetic cohorts but were estimated using only national aggregate full consumption. The simpler aggregate approach is kept as an option in IGEM and for completeness we also report how this aggregate Euler equation is implemented. This is described in chapter 2, where equation (2.24) is the aggregate household intertemporal utility function as a discounted sum of log full consumption:

$$U = \sum_{t=1}^{\infty} N_0 \prod_{s=1}^{t} \left(\frac{N_t^{eq}}{1+\rho} \right) \ln F_t. \tag{3.32}$$

This gives the following Euler equation to be estimated:

$$\frac{F_t / N_t}{F_{t-1} / N_{t-1}} = \frac{(1+r_t)}{1+\rho} \frac{P_{t-1}^F}{P_t^F}. \tag{3.33}$$

We assume that the errors in this first stage of the household model can be expressed in the following stochastic form:

$$\ln \frac{F_t / N_t}{F_{t-1} / N_{t-1}} = \ln \frac{(1+r_t)}{1+\rho} + \ln \frac{P_{t-1}^F}{P_t^F} + \varepsilon_t^F. \tag{3.34}$$

The disturbance terms are serially uncorrelated by construction.

Equation (3.34) is estimated using nonlinear, three-stage least squares using instruments described in section 4.3.2. The value of ρ is estimated to be 0.0263 with a standard error of 0.004. This estimated rate of time preference is higher than the estimate for our model of synthetic cohorts.

3.6 Allocating Full Consumption

In chapter 2, section 2.2, we have described the allocation of the three subaggregates—nondurables, capital services, and consumer services—to the 35 commodity groups in table 2.3. These groups are based on Personal Consumption Expenditures (PCE) in the National Income and Product Accounts (NIPAs). Expenditure on each of the commodity groups is expressed in purchasers' prices and includes trade and transportation margins. The tier structure of the allocation to these 35 groups is given in table 2.4, and we have presented expenditures in purchasers' prices for 2005 in table 3.2.

The prices and quantities of aggregate consumption of commodity group i are denoted PN_i and N_i, where the letter N is used to indicate that the classifications are based on the NIPAs. The value of expenditures at node m is

$$M^m = PN^m N^m = PN_{m1}N_{m1} + \ldots + PN_{m,im}N_{m,im}. \tag{3.35}$$

The allocation of consumer nondurables, capital services, and consumer services to individual commodity groups is derived from the price function implied by a homothetic indirect utility function $V^m = V(P^{Hm}, M^m)$.

Trends in the consumption shares cannot be completely explained by movements in relative prices. We include latent variables (f^{Hm}) in the share equations for our model of consumer behavior. These play a similar role to the latent variables in the input share equations for the model of producer behavior described in more detail in chapter 4. The price function for mode m takes the form

$$\ln PN^m = \alpha^{Hm\prime} \ln P^m + \frac{1}{2} \ln P^{m\prime} B^{Hm} \ln P^m + \ln P^{m\prime} f^{Hm}. \tag{3.36}$$

The share equations are derived by applying Roy's identity to the price function (3.36). We add a stochastic term and a first-order autoregressive model for the latent variables:

$$SN^m = \begin{bmatrix} PN_{m1}N_{m1} / PN^m N^m \\ \cdots \\ PN_{m,im}N_{m,im} / PN^m N^m \end{bmatrix} = \alpha^{Hm} + B^{Hm} \ln PN^{Hm} + f^{Hm} + \varepsilon_t^{Hm}. \tag{3.37}$$

$$f_t^{Hm} = F^{Hm} f_{t-1}^{Hm} + v_t. \tag{3.38}$$

We estimate the unknown parameters of this model and the latest variables by means of the Kalman filter.

The results from estimating the latent variables model are given in table 3.15. This model is used for the 35 items in nodes 2 through 17 given in table 2.4. The coefficients are generally well estimated for the nodes with two or three inputs. The price elasticities for the nodes with four or five inputs are less satisfactory. For nodes 7 (fuel-coal) and 14 (medical services) the share elasticities were set equal to zero, $B^{Hm} = 0$. The estimated share elasticities range from –0.9 to 0.16, but most are between –0.1 and 0.1. Of the 43 own-price share elasticities, 22 are negative, so that the own-price elasticity is greater than one.

There are strong nonprice trends for many of the commodity groups, so that the latent variables play an important role in explaining the sample variations in the shares. We have projected the latent variables, using equation (3.38). Figure 3.14 shows the latent terms for energy during the sample period, as well as the projections for gasoline, fuel-coal, electricity, and gas.

The latent term for electricity rises between the 1960s and 1990 and has flattened since then. The projected value of these latent terms will increase the electricity share only modestly. The latent share for gasoline was flat for most of the sample period and the projection is also very flat. The latent term for natural gas is declining during most of the sample period and is projected to decline a bit more.

The latent term for the energy share in total Nondurables (node 2) is given in figure 3.15. This shows the rise in the share with the oil shocks in the 1970s, followed by a period of decline until 2001, when oil and gas prices rose again.

3.7 Measuring Household Welfare

Our methodology for measuring the welfare effects of policy changes was introduced by Jorgenson, Slesnick, and Wilcoxen (1992). As presented in section 3.3 above, the household sector comprises infinitely lived households that we refer to as dynasties. Each household takes commodity prices, wage rates, and rates of return as given. All dynasties are assumed to face the same vector of prices time t, p_t^C, and the same nominal rate of return r_t. The quantity of a commodity, including leisure, consumed by dynasty d in period t is x_{ndt} and full expenditure of dynasty d on consumption in period t is $M_{dt} = \sum_{n=1}^{N} p_{nt}^C x_{ndt}$, where N is the number of commodities (see equation 3.2).

When the equilibrium solution path is solved we obtain aggregate consumption and income for all periods. The aggregate value of full expenditures (2.21) is allocated to the different household types according to their mean share in the base year:

$$\bar{M}_{dt} = \frac{\bar{M}_{d,2006}}{\sum_d N_{d,2006} \bar{M}_{d,2006}} PF_t F_t. \tag{3.39}$$

Table 3.15
Estimated parameters of consumption functions, lower tiers

Node	Inputs	Alpha	(SE)	Beta1	(SE)	Beta2
2	Nondurables	Energy	0.196	(0.025)	0.083	(0.01)
		Food	1.095	(0.003)	–0.064	(0.01)
		Consumer goods	–0.291	(0.025)	–0.019	(0.01)
3	Energy	Gasoline	0.080	(0.007)	0.160	(0.04)
		Fuel—coal	–0.329	(0.008)	0.015	(0.04)
		Electricity	–0.210	(0.086)	–0.119	(0.02)
		Gas	1.459	(0.087)	–0.056	(0.05)
4	Food	Food	0.199	(0.072)	0.011	(0.05)
		Meals	0.043	(0.093)	0.021	(0.07)
		Meal—employee	0.010	*	0.000	*
		Tobacco	0.748	(0.118)	–0.031	(0.09)
5	Consumer goods	Clothing—shoes	0.337	(0.055)	0.093	(0.03)
		Household articles	0.224	(0.007)	–0.035	(0.07)
		Drugs	0.099	(0.018)	–0.023	(0.05)
		Misc. goods	0.341	(0.059)	–0.035	(0.09)
6	Consumer services	Housing	–0.014	(0.048)	–0.079	(0.47)
		HH operation	0.060	(0.089)	0.054	(0.63)
		Transportation	0.078	(0.122)	–0.045	(0.26)
		Medical	–0.052	(1.240)	–0.092	(0.19)
		Misc. services	0.927	(1.250)	0.163	(0.86)
7	Fuel—coal	Fuel—oil	0.014	*	0.000	*
		Coal	0.986	*	0.000	*
8	Clothing—shoes	Shoes	0.009	(0.034)	–0.0003	(0.01)
		Clothing	0.991	(0.034)	0.0003	(0.01)
9	Household articles	Cleaning supplies	0.737	(0.021)	0.001	(0.00)
		Furnishings	0.263	(0.021)	–0.001	(0.00)
10	Misc. goods	Toys	0.049	(0.012)	–0.050	(0.04)
		Stationery	0.034	(0.011)	0.002	(0.03)
		Imports	–0.028	(0.006)	0.013	(0.00)
		Reading material	0.945	(0.017)	0.035	(0.05)
11	Housing services	Housing rental	1.238	(0.073)	–0.210	(0.07)
		Owner maintenance	–0.238	(0.073)	0.210	(0.07)

(SE)	Beta3	(SE)	Beta4	(SE)	Beta5	(SE)		Number of Beta Est	Number Negative on Diagonal Beta
–0.064	(0.01)	–0.019	(0.01)					3	2
–0.019	(0.01)	0.082	(0.01)						
0.082	(0.01)	–0.063	(0.02)						
0.015	(0.04)	–0.119	(0.02)	–0.056	(0.05)			4	1
–0.001	(0.06)	–0.002	(0.00)	–0.011	(0.07)				
–0.002	(0.00)	0.138	(0.05)	–0.017	(0.05)				
–0.011	(0.07)	–0.017	(0.05)	0.085	(0.10)				
0.021	(0.07)	0.000	*	–0.031	(0.09)			3	1
–0.025	(0.09)	0.000	*	0.004	(0.12)				
0.000	*	0.000	*	0.000	*				
0.004	(0.12)	0.000	*	0.027	(0.15)				
–0.035	(0.07)	–0.023	(0.05)	–0.035	(0.09)			4	0
0.077	(0.04)	–0.003	(0.08)	–0.038	(0.11)				
–0.003	(0.08)	0.018	(0.03)	0.008	(0.10)				
–0.038	(0.11)	0.008	(0.10)	0.065	(0.17)				
0.054	(0.63)	–0.045	(0.26)	–0.092	(0.19)	0.163	(0.86)	5	5
–0.107	(1.17)	–0.016	(0.53)	–0.103	(0.77)	0.172	(1.63)		
–0.016	(0.53)	–0.062	(0.97)	–0.101	(0.15)	0.224	(1.14)		
–0.103	(0.77)	–0.101	(0.15)	–0.056	(6.22)	0.353	(6.27)		
0.172	(1.63)	0.224	(1.14)	0.353	(6.27)	–0.911	(6.64)		
0.000	*							0	0
0.000	*								
0.0003	(0.01)							2	0
–0.0003	(0.01)								
–0.001	(0.00)							2	0
0.001	(0.00)								
0.002	(0.03)	0.013	(0.00)	0.035	(0.05)			4	4
–0.095	(0.04)	0.006	(0.01)	0.087	(0.04)				
0.006	(0.01)	–0.086	(0.03)	0.067	(0.03)				
0.087	(0.04)	0.067	(0.03)	–0.189	(0.07)				
0.210	(0.07)							2	0
–0.210	(0.07)								

(continued)

Table 3.15 (continued)

Node	Inputs	Alpha	(SE)	Beta1	(SE)	Beta2
12	Household operation	Water	0.179	(0.165)	0.041	(0.09)
		Communications	0.226	(0.031)	0.005	(0.04)
		Domestic services	−0.015	(0.189)	0.021	(0.08)
		Other hh services	0.610	(0.253)	−0.067	(0.13)
13	Transportation	Own transportation	1.045	(0.203)	0.118	(0.02)
		Transportation	−0.045	(0.203)	−0.118	(0.02)
14	Medical	Medical services	0.931	*	0.000	*
		Health insurance	0.069	*	0.000	*
15	Misc. services	Personal services	0.022	(0.542)	−0.001	(0.01)
		Business services	−0.006	(0.272)	0.005	(0.03)
		Recreation	0.078	(0.037)	0.018	(0.05)
		Education	0.905	(0.608)	−0.021	(0.06)
16	Business services	Financial services	0.552	(4.649)	−0.224	(0.03)
		Other business services	0.448	(4.649)	0.224	(0.03)
17	Recreation	Recreation	1.357	(0.029)	−0.231	(0.31)
		Foreign travel	−0.357	(0.029)	0.231	(0.31)

Note: * denotes parameters that are not estimated.

Equation (3.39) will be used in chapter 8, equation (8.1), to compute the welfare effects of a policy.

We assume that each dynasty maximizes an additive intertemporal utility function of the form, as in equation (3.23),

$$V_d = \sum_{t=0}^{\infty} \delta^t \ln V_{dt}, \tag{3.40}$$

where $\delta = 1/(1+\rho)$ and ρ is the subjective rate of time preference. The intratemporal indirect utility function V_{dt} in (3.40) is expressed in terms of "household equivalent members," N_{dt}:

(SE)	Beta3	(SE)	Beta4	(SE)	Beta5	(SE)	Number of Beta Est	Number Negative on Diagonal Beta
0.005	(0.04)	0.021	(0.08)	−0.067	(0.13)		4	2
−0.074	(0.03)	0.079	(0.08)	−0.010	(0.09)			
0.079	(0.08)	−0.086	(0.14)	−0.013	(0.18)			
−0.010	(0.09)	−0.013	(0.18)	0.091	(0.24)			
−0.118	(0.02)						2	0
0.118	(0.02)							
0.000	*						0	0
0.000	*							
0.005	(0.03)	0.018	(0.05)	−0.021	(0.06)		4	3
0.079	(0.14)	−0.053	(0.01)	−0.031	(0.14)			
−0.053	(0.01)	−0.126	(0.14)	0.161	(0.15)			
−0.031	(0.14)	0.161	(0.15)	−0.109	(0.21)			
0.224	(0.03)						2	2
−0.224	(0.03)							
0.231	(0.31)						2	2
−0.231	(0.31)							
							43	22

$$\ln V_{dt} = \alpha_p' \ln p_t + \frac{1}{2} \ln p_t' B_{pp} \ln p_t - D(p) \ln \frac{M_{dt}}{N_{dt}}. \tag{3.41}$$

where $\ln N_{dt} = \frac{1}{D(p_t)} \ln p_t' B_A A_d$ and A_d is a vector of attributes of the dynasty allowing for differences in preferences among households.[11] $D(p)$ has the form (see 3.6)

$$D(p_t) = -1 + \iota' B_{pp} \ln p_t. \tag{3.41b}$$

The utility function V_d is maximized subject to the lifetime budget constraint

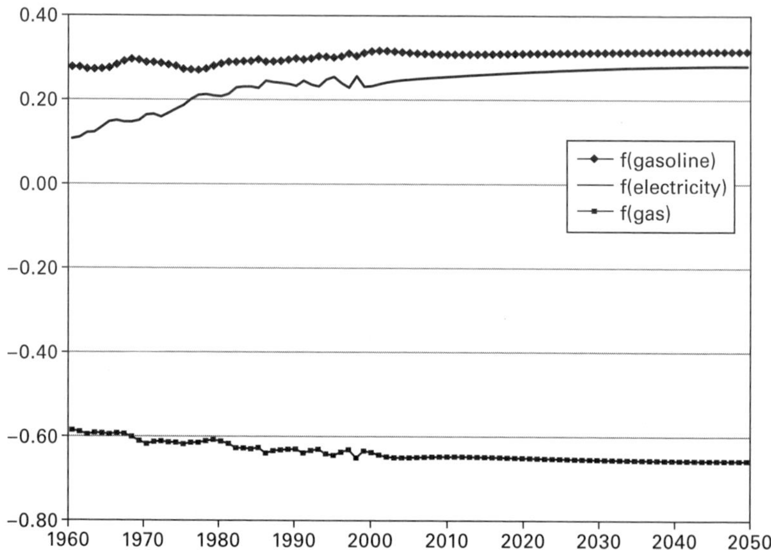

Figure 3.14
Projection of latent term (*ft*) in node 3: Energy = *f*(gasoline,fuel,electricity,gas).

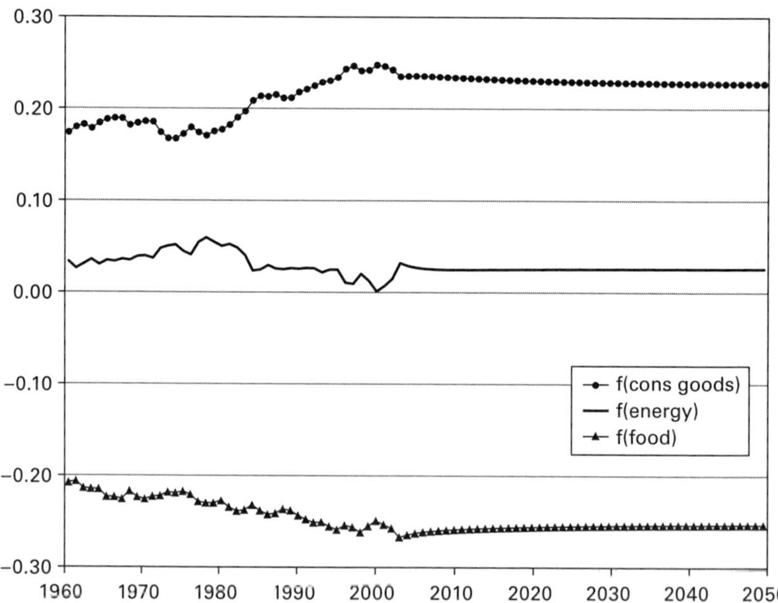

Figure 3.15
Projection of latent term (*ft*) in node 2: Nondurables = *f*(energy,food,consumer goods).

$$\sum_{t=0}^{\infty} \gamma_t M_{dt}(p_t, V_{dt}, A_d) = \Omega_d \tag{3.42}$$

where $\gamma_t = \prod_{s=0}^{t} \frac{1}{1+r_s}$,

and Ω_d is the full wealth of the dynasty. In this representation $M_{dt}(p_t, V_{dt}, A_d)$ is the intratemporal full expenditure function[12] and takes the form

$$\ln M_{dt}(p_t, V_{dt}, A_d) = \frac{1}{D(p_t)}\left[\alpha_p' \ln p_t + \frac{1}{2}\ln p_t' B_{pp} \ln p_t - \ln V_{dt}\right] + \ln N_{dt}. \tag{3.43}$$

The necessary conditions for a maximum of the intertemporal utility function, subject to the wealth constraint, are given by the discrete time Euler equation:

$$\ln V_{dt} = \frac{D_t}{D_{t-1}} \ln V_{dt-1} + D_t \ln\left(\frac{D_{t-1}\gamma_t N_{dt} P_t}{\delta D_t \gamma_{t-1} N_{dt-1} P_{t-1}}\right). \tag{3.44}$$

where we have used D_t to denote $D(p_t)$ and the aggregate price term, P_t, denotes

$$P_t = \exp\left(\frac{\alpha_p' \ln p_t + \frac{1}{2}\ln p_t' B_{pp} \ln p_t}{D_t}\right). \tag{3.45}$$

The Euler equation implies that the current level of utility of the dynasty can be represented as a function of the initial level of utility and the initial and future prices and discount factors:

$$\ln V_{dt} = \frac{D_t}{D_0} \ln V_{d0} + D_t \ln\left(\frac{D_0 \gamma_t N_{dt} P_t}{\delta^t D_t N_{d0} P_0}\right). \tag{3.46}$$

Equation (3.46) enables us to represent dynastic utility as a function of full wealth and initial and future prices and interest rates. We begin by rewriting the intertemporal budget constraint (3.42) as

$$\sum_{t=0}^{\infty} \gamma_t N_{dt} P_t V_{dt}^{-1/D_t} = \Omega_d. \tag{3.47}$$

Substituting (3.46) into (3.47), and simplifying, yields the following for initial utility:

$$\ln V_{d0} = -D_0 \ln\left(\frac{\Omega_d}{N_{d0}R}\right). \tag{3.48}$$

where $R = \frac{P_0}{D_0}\sum_{t=0}^{\infty}\delta^t D_t$. This allows us to evaluate dynastic utility (3.39) in terms of full wealth by first substituting in (3.46) and then substituting in (3.48):

$$\begin{aligned} V_d &= \sum_{t=0}^{\infty}\delta^t \ln V_{dt} \\ &= \sum_{t=0}^{\infty}\delta^t\left[\frac{D_t}{D_0}\ln V_{d0} + D_t \ln\left(\frac{D_0\gamma_t N_{dt}P_t}{\delta^t D_t N_{d0}P_0}\right)\right] \\ &= \sum_{t=0}^{\infty}\delta^t\left[-D_t \ln\frac{\Omega_d}{R} + D_t \ln\left(\frac{D_0\gamma_t N_{dt}P_t}{\delta^t D_t P_0}\right)\right]. \end{aligned} \tag{3.49}$$

Simplifying with $S = \sum_{t=0}^{\infty}\delta^t D_t$, we get

$$\begin{aligned} V_d &= S\ln R - S\ln\Omega_d + \sum_{t=0}^{\infty}\delta^t D_t \ln\left(\frac{D_0\gamma_t N_{dt}P_t}{\delta^t D_t P_0}\right) \\ &= S\ln\frac{P_0 S}{D_0} - S\ln\Omega_d + \sum_{t=0}^{\infty}\delta^t D_t \ln\left(\frac{D_0\gamma_t N_{dt}P_t}{\delta^t D_t P_0}\right). \end{aligned}$$

Solving this for full wealth as a function of prices and utility yields the intertemporal expenditure function of the dynasty:

$$\ln\Omega_d(\{p_t\},\{\gamma_t\},V_d) = \frac{1}{S}\left[S\ln\frac{P_0 S}{D_0} + \sum_{t=0}^{\infty}\delta^t D_t \ln\left(\frac{D_0\gamma_t N_{dt}P_t}{\delta^t D_t P_0}\right) - V_d\right], \tag{3.50}$$

where $\{p_t\}$ is the time profile of prices and $\{\gamma_t\}$ is the profile of discount factors.

We employ the expenditure function (3.50) in measuring the monetary equivalent of the effect on welfare of a change in policy. We let $\{p_t^0\}$ and $\{\gamma_t^0\}$ represent the time profiles of prices and discount factors for the base case and V_d^0 the resulting level of welfare. Denoting the welfare of the dynasty after the imposition of the new policy by V_d^1, the equivalent variation in full wealth is

$$\Delta W_d = \Omega_d(\{p_t^0\},\{\gamma_t^0\},V_d^1) - \Omega_d(\{p_t^0\},\{\gamma_t^0\},V_d^0). \tag{3.51}$$

The equivalent variation in full wealth (3.51) is the wealth required to attain the welfare associated with the new policy at prices in the base case, less the wealth required to attain base case welfare at these prices. If this equivalent variation is positive, the policy produces a gain in welfare; otherwise, the policy change results in a welfare loss. Equivalent variations in full wealth enable us to rank the base case policy and any number of alternative policies in terms of a money metric of dynastic welfare.

In reporting the welfare effects it is often more meaningful to have the equivalent variation given as a percentage of full wealth rather than in absolute dollars; that is, we graph

$$\%EV_d = \frac{\Delta W_d}{\Omega_d(\{p_t^0\},\{\gamma_t^0\},V_d^0)} \tag{3.52}$$

instead of ΔW_d.

Table 3.5 gives a total of 384 household types. However, the number of types with a positive number of households is only 244. In the results given in chapter 8 we report the equivalent variations of full wealth resulting from changes in energy and environmental policies for all 244 types. We calculate the equivalent variations at mean wealth, half the mean wealth, and twice the mean wealth to illustrate the magnitude of the income effects.

3.8 Measuring Social Welfare

While the distribution of equivalent variations across dynasties is useful for policy analysis, it is also important to assess the change in social welfare that results from the imposition of a carbon tax. Jorgenson and Slesnick (1997) discuss the forms of social welfare functions that can provide a basis for social cost-of-living measurement. Given the results there, we define an intertemporal social welfare function over the distribution of dynastic welfare functions given in (3.49). Let x be the matrix of dynasty consumption, x_{ndt}, and $u = \{V_d\}$ be the vector of dynastic welfare functions. The intertemporal social welfare function is defined as a weighted sum of the dynastic welfare ($\bar{V}$) and a measure of deviations from this weighted average:

$$W(u,x) = \bar{V} - \eta\left[\sum_{d=1}^{D} a_d \left|V_d - \bar{V}\right|^{-\mu}\right]^{-1/\mu}, \tag{3.53}$$

where D is the number of dynasties, and

$$\bar{V} = \sum_{d=1}^{D} a_d V_d; \quad -\infty < \mu < -1.$$

In this representation of the social welfare function, the parameter η is chosen so as to assure that social welfare is increasing in the levels of individual welfare; this is the familiar Pareto principle. The parameter μ is a measure of social aversion to inequality and can take values ranging from minus one to minus infinity. The maximum value of minus one gives the greatest weight to equity relative to efficiency. Allowing this parameter to go to minus infinity generates a utilitarian social welfare function and gives the least relative weight to equity considerations.

If we require that all transfers of wealth from rich dynasties to poor dynasties must increase social welfare, then Jorgenson and Slesnick (1997) show that the weights on the individual welfare levels must be given by

$$a_d = \frac{\exp\left\{\sum_t \delta^t D_t \ln N_{dt} / S\right\}}{\sum_{l=1}^{D} \exp\left\{\sum_t \delta^t D_t \ln N_{lt} / S\right\}}. \tag{3.54}$$

The maximum level of social welfare for fixed prices and fixed total wealth is attained by reallocating wealth among dynasties to equalize dynastic welfare. This occurs when the wealth of dynasty d is

$$\Omega_d^* = a_d \Omega, \tag{3.55}$$

where Ω is total wealth.

The maximum level of social welfare can be represented as

$$W_{\max} = S \ln R - S \ln \Omega + S \ln N + \sum_{t=0}^{\infty} \delta^t D_t \ln\left(\frac{D_0 \gamma_t P_t}{\delta^t D_t P_0}\right), \tag{3.56}$$

where N is the sum over all dynasties of a function of the number of household equivalent members in dynasty l:

$$N = \sum_{l=1}^{D} \exp\left\{\sum_t \delta^t D_t \ln N_{lt} / S\right\}.$$

This is a representative agent version of equation (3.49) above and can be interpreted as the welfare level of a dynasty with size equal to the number of household equivalent members in the whole population.

To derive a money measure of social welfare, we define the social expenditure function as the minimum level of total wealth required to attain a specified level of social welfare at given prices and interest rates:

$$\Omega(\{p_t\},\{\gamma_t\},W)=\min\left[\Omega:W(u,x)\geq W;\Omega=\sum_{d=1}^{D}\Omega_d\right]. \quad (3.57)$$

Our representation of the social expenditure function is obtained by solving the welfare function for the representative agent shown in (3.56) for aggregate wealth as a function of social welfare, the initial and future prices, and interest rates:

$$\ln\Omega(\{p_t\},\{\gamma_t\},W)=\frac{1}{S}\left[S\ln R+S\ln N+\sum_{t=0}^{\infty}\delta^t D_t\ln\left(\frac{D_0\gamma_t P_t}{\delta^t D_t P_0}\right)-W\right]. \quad (3.58)$$

This is the expenditure function of a representative agent with welfare level given by (3.56).

The social expenditure function enables us to evaluate the monetary equivalent of the change in social welfare that results from the imposition of a new policy. Let W^0 be the level of social welfare under the base case and let W^1 be the corresponding level of social welfare after the policy change. The monetary measure of the change in social welfare, the equivalent variation of the policy, is given by

$$\Delta W=\Omega(\{p_t^0\},\{\gamma_t^0\},W^1)-\Omega(\{p_t^0\},\{\gamma_t^0\},W^0). \quad (3.59)$$

If this equivalent variation is positive, then social welfare has increased as a result of the policy. Otherwise, the policy decreases social welfare or leaves it unaffected.

Policies for control of carbon dioxide emissions are often evaluated solely in terms of their impact on economic efficiency. Accordingly, we can define the change in efficiency to be the change in social welfare at a perfectly egalitarian distribution of wealth. For this distribution, social welfare is a maximum for a given level of wealth and corresponds to the potential level of welfare associated with a particular policy. This measure of efficiency is independent of the distribution of welfare among dynasties. If $W_{\max}^0$ is the maximum level of social welfare in the base case and $W_{\max}^1$ is the corresponding level after the imposition of the policy, our monetary measure of the change in efficiency is

$$\Delta E=\Omega(\{p_t^0\},\{\gamma_t^0\},W_{\max}^1)-\Omega(\{p_t^0\},\{\gamma_t^0\},W_{\max}^0). \quad (3.60)$$

This definition of the change in efficiency (3.60) suggests a decomposition of the change in social welfare (3.59) into efficiency and equity components:

$$\Delta W = \Delta E + \Delta EQ, \tag{3.61}$$

where ΔEQ is a monetary measure of the change in equity. The difference between the level of potential welfare and the level of actual welfare is the loss due to an inequitable distribution of dynastic welfare. Our measure of equity is the monetary value of the change in this welfare loss due to the policy:

$$\begin{aligned}\Delta EQ = &[\Omega(\{p_t^0\},\{\gamma_t^0\},W^1) - \Omega(\{p_t^0\},\{\gamma_t^0\},W_{\max}^1)] \\ &- [\Omega(\{p_t^0\},\{\gamma_t^0\},W^0) - \Omega(\{p_t^0\},\{\gamma_t^0\},W_{\max}^0)].\end{aligned} \tag{3.62}$$

A positive value of ΔEQ indicates that equity has increased due to the imposition of the policy.

We have developed a framework for evaluating the impact of a policy on the level of social welfare. A separate but closely related issue is the progressivity of the policy. Following Slesnick (1986) we can classify a policy as progressive if it induces greater equality in the distribution of welfare. However, equality can be measured in absolute or relative terms. In the context of the model presented above, an absolute index of equality is given by

$$AEQ(\{p_t^0\},\{\gamma_t^0\},W,W_{\max}) = [\Omega(\{p_t^0\},\{\gamma_t^0\},W)] - [\Omega(\{p_t^0\},\{\gamma_t^0\},W_{\max})]. \tag{3.63}$$

This measure of equality is the monetary value of the loss in social welfare due to an inequitable distribution of welfare. It is nonpositive and invariant to equal absolute additions to the money measures of potential and social welfare.

A relative measure of equality can be defined as the ratio of money metric social welfare to the monetary measure of potential welfare:

$$REQ(\{p_t^0\},\{\gamma_t^0\},W,W_{\max}) = \frac{\Omega(\{p_t^0\},\{\gamma_t^0\},W)}{\Omega(\{p_t^0\},\{\gamma_t^0\},W_{\max})}. \tag{3.64}$$

This measure of equality lies between zero and one and attains the value of unity when the actual distribution of welfare is the perfectly egalitarian distribution. The measure of relative equality is invariant to equal proportional changes in money metric potential and social welfare. This will occur with equal proportional changes in the wealth of all dynasties.

An absolute measure of progression of a policy is the change in the absolute measure of equality:

$$AP = AEQ(\{p_t^0\},\{\gamma_t^0\},W^1,W_{\max}^1) - AEQ(\{p_t^0\},\{\gamma_t^0\},W^0,W_{\max}^0). \tag{3.65}$$

The measure of absolute progressivity is identical to the measure of the change in equity (3.62). A positive value indicates that the carbon tax is absolutely progressive. A negative value indicates absolute regressivity. The corresponding relative measure of progressivity is defined similarly:

$$RP = REQ(\{p_t^0\},\{\gamma_t^0\},W^1,W_{\max}^1) - REQ(\{p_t^0\},\{\gamma_t^0\},W^0,W_{\max}^0). \tag{3.66}$$

It is easily demonstrated that a policy that is absolutely progressive need not be relatively progressive and vice versa.

3.9 Summary and Conclusion

Jorgenson and Slesnick (2008) have successfully exploited variation across households to characterize the allocation of full wealth, including the assets and time endowment of each household, over time. We have also characterized the allocation of full consumption within each time period among goods and services and leisure, incorporating variations in prices and wages across households. We find that leisure and consumer services are income elastic, while nondurable goods and capital services are income inelastic. Leisure and capital services are price elastic, while nondurable goods and consumer services are price inelastic.

Compared to earlier vintages of IGEM, we have greatly extended our translog model of aggregate consumer expenditures by incorporating leisure and utilizing a less restrictive approach for representing income effects. While the less restrictive rank-three system fits better for the households with very low or very high expenditures, the elasticities are similar, so that we implement the simpler rank-two model in IGEM.

The allocation of full consumption among goods and services and leisure also depends on the composition of individual households. The share of leisure greatly predominates, accounting for around 70% of full consumption. This increases considerably with the number of adults in the household and declines slightly with the number of children for a given number of adults. The shares of goods and services decline with the number of adults, while the share of nondurable goods rises and the shares of capital and other consumer services fall with the number of children.

An important challenge for general equilibrium modeling has been to capture the heterogeneity of behavior of individual households in a tractable way, as emphasized by Browning, Hansen, and Heckman (1999). In IGEM we employ exact aggregation over households in order to incorporate this heterogeneity. Our exact aggregate model also encompasses the responses of the household sector to variations in wages and prices, as well as variations in full expenditures and its distribution over households. Finally, this model incorporates all of the restrictions implied by the traditional model of consumer behavior into the responses of individual households.

Notes

1. This is discussed in more detail in Jorgenson, Ho, and Stiroh (2005).
2. See Blundell and Stoker (2005) for further discussion.
3. Surveys are designed to be representative only at a quarterly frequency. We use the second quarter to avoid seasonality of spending associated with the summer months and holiday spending at the end of the calendar year.
4. The methods used to compute the rental equivalent of owner-occupied housing and the service flows from consumer durables are described in Slesnick (2001).
5. In 1988 and 1989 these items constituted approximately 75% of all expenditures.
6. A detailed description of this procedure can be found in Slesnick (2002).
7. These areas correspond to nonmetropolitan urban areas and are cities with fewer than 50,000 persons. Examples of cities of this size include Yuma, Arizona, in the West; Fort Dodge, Iowa, in the Midwest; Augusta, Maine, in the Northeast; and Cleveland, Tennessee, in the South.
8. A detailed discussion of the differences between the CEX and PCE is given in Slesnick (1992) and Fixler and Jaditz (2002).
9. As described above, we use our own imputations of capital services and our value of leisure is derived from the data on hours worked and value of compensation. There is no official estimate of the value of leisure.
10. In the calculation of the wage elasticities, unearned income is assumed to be zero and the value of the time endowment is equal to full expenditure.
11. Further details on equivalence scales are given in Jorgenson and Slesnick (1987). Strictly speaking, there is a constant term in the expression for $\ln N_{dt}$, but that may be ignored.
12. The expenditure function $e(p,u)$ is the inverse of the indirect utility function and is the minimum cost of achieving utility u given price p.

4 Modeling Producer Behavior

4.1 Introduction

The objective of this chapter is to present a new approach to econometric modeling of producer behavior. The index number approach to productivity measurement has been the work horse of empirical research for half a century.[1] This salient concept has generated a vast literature on productivity measurement, recently surveyed by Jorgenson variable in a neo-classical production function. Under appropriate assumptions the rate of technical change is the residual between the growth rate of output and the growth rate of inputs. Using index numbers for these growth rates, we can recover the level of technology without estimating the unknown parameters of the production function.

Recently attention has shifted to the biases of technical change.[2] This shift is motivated by the fact that the rate of technical change accounts for only a modest proportion of economic growth.[3] In addition, biases of technical change have found a wide range of applications, such as changes in the distribution of income, emphasized in the survey by Acemoglu (2002b), and determinants of energy conservation, highlighted in the survey by Jaffe, Newell, and Stavins (2003). However, biases of technical change are not directly observable. In this chapter we present a new econometric approach to measuring both the rate and the biases of technical change. Our key contribution is to represent the rate and biases by unobservable or latent variables.

The standard econometric approach to modeling the rate and biases of technical change was introduced by Binswanger (1974a, 1974b) and described in the surveys by Binswanger and Ruttan (1978), Jorgenson (1986), and Ruttan (2001). Binswanger's approach is to represent price effects by the translog function of the input prices introduced by

Christensen, Jorgenson, and Lau (1973). He represents the rate and biases of technical change by constant time trends and fits the unknown parameters by econometric methods. This approach to modeling technical change is widely employed, for example, by Jorgenson and Fraumeni (1983), Jorgenson, Gollop, and Fraumeni (1987, chapter 7), and, more recently, by Feng and Serletis (2008).

Binswanger's approach exploits the fact that price effects depend on observable variables, such as the prices of output and inputs and the shares of inputs in the value of output. The key to modeling these effects is to choose a flexible functional form that admits a variety of substitution patterns.[4] Our model of substitution, like Binswanger's, is based on the translog price function, giving the price of output as a function of the prices of inputs. The measures of substitution are unknown parameters that can be estimated from observable data on prices and value shares.

Our novel contribution is to replace the constant time trends that describe the rate and biases of technical change in Binswanger's model by latent or unobservable variables. An important advantage of the translog price function in this setting is that the resulting model is linear in the latent variables. We recover these variables by applying the Kalman (1960, 1963) filter, a standard statistical technique in macroeconomics and finance, as well as many areas of engineering.

An important feature of the Kalman filter is that latent variables representing the rate and biases of technical change can be recovered for the sample period. A second and decisive advantage of the Kalman filter is that the latent variables can be projected into the future, so that the rate and biases of technical change can be incorporated into econometric projections.[5] The rate of technical change captures trends in productivity, while biases of technical change describe changes in the structure of production.

We implement our new approach for modeling substitution and technical change for the post-war U.S. economy, 1960–2005. This period includes substantial changes in the prices of fossil fuels and the wage rate. Energy crisis periods with dramatic increases in energy prices alternating with periods of energy price collapse are particularly valuable for our purposes. By modeling substitution and technical change econometrically, we are able to decompose changes in the price of output and the input value shares between price effects and the effects of technical change. Empirically, these two sets of effects are comparable in magnitude.

We also decompose the rate of technical change between an autonomous part, unaffected by price changes, and an induced part, responsive to price changes. The rate of induced technical change links the rate and biases of technical change through the correlation between the input prices and the latent variables representing biases. Efforts to economize on an input that has become more expensive or to increase the utilization of an input that has become cheaper will affect the rate of technical change. Although modest in size, rates of induced technical change are generally opposite in sign to rates of autonomous technical change.

The list of industries included in the Intertemporal General Equilibrium Model (IGEM) described in chapter 2 is presented in table 2.1. Industries 7–27 comprise manufacturing, and industries 28–35 make up services. The remaining industries are agriculture, the four mining sectors, and construction. We refer to these 35 industries as the "business sector." Two additional sectors, households and general government, also employ capital and labor services.

There are five energy-related industries in IGEM—Coal Mining, Petroleum and Gas Mining, Petroleum Refining, Electric Utilities, and Gas Utilities. The Electric Utilities sector in IGEM includes both private and government-owned producers. Only private firms are included in the National Income and Product Accounts (NIPAs). Table 4.1 gives output, intermediate input, capital input, and the number of workers employed for all 37 sectors in the year 2005. Households and general government have no intermediate inputs, so that output is equal to value added.

The largest industries in terms of gross output are Services; Finance, Insurance, and Real Estate (FIRE); and Trade. The largest manufacturing industries are Food, Chemicals, Motor Vehicles, and Industrial Equipment. In terms of value added, the largest manufacturing industries are Food, Motor Vehicles, Chemicals, and Petroleum Refining. Outside manufacturing, the largest industry is Services with a value added that is 20.6% of gross domestic product (GDP), followed by Trade and FIRE. The energy group is a small share of the U.S. economy and the value added by the energy industries was only 4.4% of GDP in 2005.

The business sector with the largest capital input is FIRE ($1183 billion). This is considerably smaller than capital input in the household sector, which is the annualized value of owner-occupied housing and consumer durables. Among the energy industries, the largest user

Table 4.1
Industry characteristics, 2005

	Industry	Output ($mil)	Intermediate Input ($mil)	Value Added ($mil)	Capital Input ($mil)	Workers (mil)
1	Agriculture	424010	240366	183644	103928	3427
2	Metal Mining	25023	15702	9321	6748	32
3	Coal Mining	25507	11180	14327	9764	80
4	Petroleum and Gas	259579	76429	183150	150555	369
5	Nonmetallic Mining	23515	10379	13135	8849	108
6	Construction	1355663	772639	583024	146613	9107
7	Food Products	595414	400716	194698	85394	1635
8	Tobacco Products	30995	22508	8487	4612	31
9	Textile Mill Products	60180	38438	21741	8152	348
10	Apparel and Textiles	35993	20950	15043	1918	364
11	Lumber and Wood	129542	81356	48186	16352	840
12	Furniture and Fixtures	101267	55835	45432	9155	479
13	Paper Products	168010	95537	72473	26854	526
14	Printing and Publishing	229739	87465	142274	51835	1342
15	Chemical Products	521438	288887	232551	141413	940
16	Petroleum Refining	418828	281766	137062	109542	115
17	Rubber and Plastic	187904	103277	84627	24591	858
18	Leather Products	6347	4026	2322	564	42
19	Stone, Clay, and Glass	129354	66340	63015	23549	543
20	Primary Metals	251132	174115	77017	43371	527
21	Fabricated Metals	296458	167543	128915	48235	1353
22	Industrial Machinery and Equipment	424034	239807	184227	45841	1561
23	Electronic and Electric Equipment	330537	176514	154024	54123	1227
24	Motor Vehicles	442156	355975	86181	26820	856
25	Other Transportation Equipment	227460	115185	112275	19787	759
26	Instruments	207399	87887	119511	22883	776
27	Miscellaneous Manufacturing	60531	34852	25679	11470	402
28	Transport and Warehouse	667845	355519	312326	116000	4870
29	Communications	527862	235594	292268	180655	1412
30	Electric Utilities	372987	130236	242751	174264	823
31	Gas Utilities	77393	54422	22971	15597	111
32	Trade	2487860	975584	1512276	468047	32634
33	FIRE	2752265	961589	1790676	1183313	8873
34	Services	4353650	1556446	2797203	551327	49644
	Government Enterprises	327507	111594	215913	98254	1789
	Private Households	1911067	0	1911067	1911067	0
	General Government	1572675	0	1572675	364631	22262

of capital in 2005 is Petroleum and Gas Mining. The largest employers of workers are Services, Trade, and Government. Only a tiny 1% of U.S. workers is employed in the energy industries.

Table 4.2 presents growth rates of output, intermediate input, and value added for all 37 sectors for the period 1960–2005. Output growth is most rapid for the information technology (IT) industries—Industrial Machinery, Electrical Machinery, and Communications. During this period GDP grew at 3.3% per annum, while the IT industries grew in excess of 5.6%. Growth of intermediate input is also high for many of these industries, however, the IT manufacturing industries also enjoy rapid productivity growth and do not have the highest growth rates for intermediate inputs.

The exceptional performance of the IT-producing industries—Industrial Machinery and Electrical Machinery—is discussed in detail by Jorgenson, Ho, and Stiroh (2005, henceforward JHS). They show that the IT-producing industries not only grew the most rapidly but also had the highest acceleration in growth rates during the IT investment boom of 1995–2000. In appendix table B.9 we compare 1960–1973, 1973–1995, and 1995–2005 subperiods in order to show how industries recovered from the low-growth period following the energy crisis period of the 1970s and how growth accelerated after 1995.

We next describe the sources of economic growth at the industry level. Table 4.3 presents the sources of growth for each industry, where the growth of output is the sum of the contributions of capital, labor, intermediate inputs, and productivity growth. Our methodology follows JHS. The considerable impact of intermediate inputs on the growth of industry output is strikingly apparent in table 4.3. Intermediate input is the key contributor to industry growth in most of the manufacturing industries, including Petroleum Refining. However, this input makes a negative contribution in Petroleum and Gas Mining and Textiles.

Investments in tangible assets and human capital are very important contributors to the growth of output. The contributions of capital input are positive for every industry, even those which had declines in output. The business sectors with particularly significant growth in capital input are Petroleum and Gas Mining, Electric Utilities, Gas Utilities, Communications, and FIRE. We note that JHS divides capital between IT capital and non-IT capital. All industries had rapid growth of IT capital input, including those with low or negative output growth. This is described in greater detail in appendix table B.24.

Table 4.2
Industry output, intermediate input, and value-added growth, 1960–2005

	Industry	Output	Intermediate Input	Value Added
1	Agriculture	2.00	1.30	3.16
2	Metal Mining	0.67	2.17	–1.32
3	Coal Mining	2.21	2.65	2.37
4	Petroleum and Gas	0.40	0.08	0.94
5	Nonmetallic Mining	1.56	1.69	1.48
6	Construction	1.60	2.82	0.08
7	Food Products	2.01	1.56	3.25
8	Tobacco Products	–0.83	0.68	–2.53
9	Textile Mill Products	1.17	–0.12	3.75
10	Apparel and Textiles	–0.28	–0.98	0.79
11	Lumber and Wood	2.03	2.22	1.82
12	Furniture and Fixtures	3.27	3.11	3.47
13	Paper Products	2.04	1.72	2.48
14	Printing and Publishing	1.83	1.77	1.83
15	Chemical Products	2.81	2.55	3.16
16	Petroleum Refining	1.63	1.65	4.56
17	Rubber and Plastic	4.21	3.42	5.24
18	Leather Products	–2.36	–2.29	–2.48
19	Stone, Clay, and Glass	1.90	1.76	2.05
20	Primary Metals	0.84	0.94	0.66
21	Fabricated Metals	1.94	1.97	1.89
22	Industrial Machinery	5.92	4.32	7.97
23	Electronic and Electric Equipment	6.50	3.61	9.79
24	Motor Vehicles	3.22	3.36	2.83
25	Other Transportation Equipment	1.91	2.27	1.54
26	Instruments	4.32	4.10	4.52
27	Miscellaneous Manufacturing	2.18	1.83	2.61
28	Transport and Warehouse	3.01	2.79	3.23
29	Communications	5.65	5.36	5.93
30	Electric Utilities	2.94	2.58	3.12
31	Gas Utilities	–0.45	0.13	–4.38
32	Trade	3.72	3.36	3.98
33	FIRE	4.19	4.41	4.08
34	Services	3.93	4.42	3.61
	Government Enterprises	2.43	2.83	2.25
	Private Households	4.09	0.00	4.09
	General Government	1.98	0.00	1.98
	Average	2.33	2.06	2.54

Note: All figures are average annual growth rates.

Table 4.3
Sources of growth of industry output, 1960–2005

			Input Contributions			
		Output	Capital	Labor	Inter-mediate	Total Factor Productivity
1	Agriculture	2.00	0.18	–0.34	0.76	1.40
2	Metal Mining	0.67	0.48	–0.60	1.40	–0.60
3	Coal Mining	2.21	0.64	–0.35	0.75	1.17
4	Petroleum and Gas	0.40	1.05	0.04	–0.11	–0.58
5	Nonmetallic Mining	1.56	0.82	–0.20	0.67	0.27
6	Construction	1.60	0.19	0.46	1.55	–0.61
7	Food Products	2.01	0.19	0.14	1.17	0.52
8	Tobacco Products	–0.83	0.55	–0.08	0.22	–1.52
9	Textile Mill Products	1.17	0.09	–0.43	–0.04	1.56
10	Apparel and Textiles	–0.28	0.17	–0.84	–0.59	0.97
11	Lumber and Wood	2.03	0.26	0.24	1.38	0.15
12	Furniture and Fixtures	3.27	0.26	0.63	1.69	0.69
13	Paper Products	2.04	0.37	0.14	1.06	0.47
14	Printing and Publishing	1.83	0.63	0.53	0.83	–0.15
15	Chemical Products	2.81	0.68	0.11	1.46	0.55
16	Petroleum Refining	1.63	0.15	0.09	1.31	0.08
17	Rubber and Plastic	4.21	0.45	0.93	1.97	0.87
18	Leather Products	–2.36	0.00	–1.24	–1.44	0.33
19	Stone, Clay, and Glass	1.90	0.32	0.15	0.89	0.54
20	Primary Metals	0.84	0.07	–0.15	0.60	0.32
21	Fabricated Metals	1.94	0.30	0.06	1.08	0.51
22	Industrial Machinery	5.92	0.61	0.33	2.34	2.65
23	Electronic and Electric Equipment	6.50	0.76	0.01	1.92	3.81
24	Motor Vehicles	3.22	0.24	0.13	2.57	0.27
25	Other Transportation Equipment	1.91	0.19	0.25	1.18	0.28
26	Instruments	4.32	0.53	0.90	1.79	1.10
27	Miscellaneous Manufacturing	2.18	0.33	–0.04	1.00	0.88
28	Transport and Warehouse	3.01	0.36	0.41	1.26	0.99
29	Communications	5.65	1.88	0.38	2.23	1.16
30	Electric Utilities	2.94	1.24	0.30	1.10	0.30
31	Gas Utilities	–0.45	0.43	0.01	–0.03	–0.86
32	Trade	3.72	0.89	0.73	1.27	0.84
33	FIRE	4.19	1.42	0.50	1.51	0.77
34	Services	3.93	0.77	1.69	1.74	–0.27
	Government Enterprises	2.43	1.02	0.32	0.90	0.19
	Private Households	4.09	4.09	0.00	0.00	0.00
	General Government	1.98	0.76	1.23	0.00	0.00

Notes: Output and total factor productivity are average annual growth rates. Capital, labor, and intermediate inputs are average annual contributions (share-weighted growth rates).

Labor input makes large positive contributions to the growth of Services, Construction, and Trade but is not an important contributor to growth of the energy industries. Many industries had negative contributions of labor input, including Agriculture, Metal Mining, Coal Mining, Leather, and Textiles and Apparel. Since labor input is an important source of aggregate economic growth, these negative contributions are outweighed by positive contributions in other industries.

We note that JHS divides labor between college-educated workers and those with less than a college education. Rapid growth of college-educated workers characterizes almost all industries. However, growth of college-educated labor input for the economy as a whole is concentrated in trade, finance, and service industries—which have high levels of employment.

The final source of economic growth identified in table 4.3 is the growth of productivity. Electrical Machinery has the most dramatic contribution of productivity growth with 3.8 out of the 6.5 annual percentage growth rate of output. This industry is followed by the other IT-manufacturing industry, Industrial Machinery, with 2.6 out of the 5.9 percentage growth rate of output. Productivity growth is also relatively important in Agriculture, Coal Mining, Textiles, Apparel, Instruments, and Communications.

In the energy group, productivity contributed 0.30 percentage points of the 2.94 percentage growth rate of output for Electric Utilities. For Coal Mining, productivity accounted for 1.17 percentage points out of the growth rate of 2.21%. For Petroleum Refining, productivity growth was only 0.08 points of the growth rate of output of 1.63%. Petroleum and Gas Mining and Gas Utilities had negative productivity growth. A total of seven industries had negative productivity growth for the period 1960–2005, including Construction and Services. Negative productivity growth is not at all paradoxical and reflects resource depletion, deterioration in the level of competition in the labor market in a few of the labor-intensive industries, and increases in the stringency of environmental regulation.

Measures of average performance over the period 1960–2005 may conceal changes in trends over time. Table 4.4 provides growth rates of productivity for the 35 industries for the entire period and for the subperiods 1960–1973, 1973–1995, and 1995–2005. Productivity growth was highest during 1960–1973, decelerated dramatically during 1973–1995, and revived substantially during 1995–2005. However, the two IT-producing manufacturing industries had accelerating productivity

Table 4.4
Growth of industry total factor productivity by subperiod

		1960–2005	1960–1973	1973–1995	1995–2005
1	Agriculture	1.40	0.03	2.04	1.79
2	Metal Mining	–0.60	–1.40	0.74	–2.51
3	Coal Mining	1.17	0.41	0.99	2.58
4	Petroleum and Gas	–0.58	0.97	–1.49	–0.62
5	Nonmetallic Mining	0.27	1.26	–0.63	0.96
6	Construction	–0.61	–0.36	–0.62	–0.90
7	Food Products	0.52	0.53	0.59	0.37
8	Tobacco Products	–1.52	0.61	–1.94	–3.36
9	Textile Mill Products	1.56	1.09	1.55	2.18
10	Apparel and Textiles	0.97	1.03	0.66	1.58
11	Lumber and Wood	0.15	0.01	0.09	0.46
12	Furniture and Fixtures	0.69	0.99	0.17	1.44
13	Paper Products	0.47	1.12	–0.36	1.45
14	Printing and Publishing	–0.15	0.54	–1.08	0.97
15	Chemical Products	0.55	1.93	–0.28	0.55
16	Petroleum Refining	0.08	0.36	0.79	–1.87
17	Rubber and Plastic	0.87	1.47	0.39	1.14
18	Leather Products	0.33	0.17	0.34	0.50
19	Stone, Clay, and Glass	0.54	1.09	0.16	0.68
20	Primary Metals	0.32	0.46	–0.21	1.31
21	Fabricated Metals	0.51	1.06	0.23	0.41
22	Industrial Machinery and Equipment	2.65	1.29	2.39	4.98
23	Electronic and Electric Equipment	3.81	2.62	3.62	5.77
24	Motor Vehicles	0.27	0.62	–0.15	0.76
25	Other Transportation Equipment	0.28	0.95	–0.12	0.31
26	Instruments	1.10	1.70	0.56	1.51
27	Miscellaneous Manufacturing	0.88	1.35	0.34	1.47
28	Transport and Warehouse	0.99	1.57	0.56	1.17
29	Communications	1.16	1.27	1.11	1.12
30	Electric Utilities	0.30	1.54	–0.48	0.40
31	Gas Utilities	–0.86	0.67	–1.77	–0.85
32	Trade	0.84	0.84	0.60	1.36
33	FIRE	0.77	0.48	0.88	0.90
34	Services	–0.27	0.23	–0.72	0.05
35	Government Enterprises	0.19	–0.42	0.84	–0.43
	Private Households	0.00	0.00	0.00	0.00
	General Government	0.00	0.00	0.00	0.00

Note: All figures are average annual growth rates.

growth. Industrial Machinery, including computers, accelerated from 1.29% during 1960–1973 to an unprecedented 5.0% during 1995–2005 while Electrical Machinery, including semiconductors, accelerated from 2.62 to 5.8% per year.

The energy industries exhibit a wide variety of behavior. Coal Mining had accelerating productivity growth, reaching 2.58% per year during 1995–2005. Electric Utilities followed the national average with a sharp deceleration to –0.48% per year during 1973–1995, followed by a revival to 0.40% during 1995–2005. Productivity growth in Petroleum Refining accelerated from 0.36% in 1960–1973 to 0.79% in 1973–1995 and then fell sharply to –1.87%. Petroleum and Gas Mining, and Gas Utilities were the poor performers; both had negative productivity growth after 1973, with a less negative growth after 1995.

We conclude from this brief discussion that a model of producer behavior must incorporate changes in technology as well as substitution among inputs in response to price changes. Since productivity growth rates vary substantially over time, it is important to have a flexible representation of technical change that reflects this fact. Time trends with constant rates of productivity growth do not adequately capture the empirical reality we have described. Finally, patterns of output growth, input utilization, and the growth of productivity differ widely among the industry groups we have identified. This is especially true for the energy sectors that are critical for an understanding of the impacts of changes in energy and environmental policy. We have now set the stage for the new approach to modeling producer behavior presented in this chapter.

In section 4.2 we present our econometric model of producer behavior. We augment the translog price function by introducing latent variables that represent the rate and biases of technical change. In section 4.3 we apply an extension of the Kalman filter to estimate the unknown parameters of the model and generate the latent variables. In section 4.4 we extend the standard framework for the Kalman filter to include endogenous prices by introducing instrumental variables. We propose a two-step procedure based on two-step Maximum Likelihood Estimation and derive two diagnostic tests for the validity of the instruments.

In section 4.5 we present our empirical results on producer behavior. We find that substitution and technical change are both important in representing changes in patterns of production. In particular, biases of technical change are quantitatively significant for all inputs. The rates of technical change decompose neatly between a negative rate of induced technical change and a positive rate of autonomous technical change, which generally predominates. This implies that biased technical change, a change in technology directed to a particular input, reduces the rate of technical change. In section 4.6 we turn to the estimation of input demands in the subtiers for the aggregate energy and non-energy intermediate input. Section 4.7 concludes the chapter.

4.2 Econometric Modeling

In our data set, production is disaggregated into 35 separate commodities produced by one or more of the 35 industries making up the U.S. economy and listed in table 2.1. The industries generally match two-digit sectors in the North American Industry Classification System (NAICS). Industries produce a primary product and may produce one or more secondary products. Each industry is modeled by a system of equations that represents possible substitutions among the inputs of capital, labor, energy and materials and the rate and biases of technical change.

Our data set for the U.S. economy is based on a new data set constructed by Jorgenson, Ho, Samuels, and Stiroh (2007). On June 30, 2008, the European Union released similar data sets for the 25 member states (prior to the enlargement to include Bulgaria and Romania).[6] The Research Institute for Economy, Trade and Industry in Japan has developed data sets of this type for China, Japan, Korea, and Taiwan.[7] Our new methods for modeling producer behavior can be applied to these economies and others with similar data sets.

The production function expresses output as a function of capital, labor, m intermediate inputs, noncomparable imports (QP^j_{NCI}) and technology (t); for industry j:

$$QI_j = f(KD_j, LD_j, QP^j_1, QP^j_2, \ldots, QP^j_m, QP^j_{NCI}, t), \quad (j = 1, 2, \ldots, 35). \tag{4.1}$$

At the first stage the value of each industry's output is allocated to four input groups—capital, labor, energy, and non-energy materials:

$$QI_j = f(KD_j, LD_j, E_j, M_j, t). \tag{4.2}$$

The second stage allocates the energy and non-energy materials groups to the individual intermediate commodities. This stage is discussed further in Section 4.6 below.

Assuming constant returns to scale and calculating the cost of capital as the residual that exhausts the value of output, the value of output is equal to the value of the four inputs:

$$PO_{jt}QI_{jt} = PKD_{jt}K_{jt} + PLD_{jt}L_{jt} + P_{Ejt}E_{jt} + P_{Mjt}M_{jt}. \quad (4.3)$$

In representing substitution and technical change it is more convenient to work with the dual price function instead of the production function in (4.2).[8] The price function expresses the unit output price as a function of all the input prices and technology, $PO_j = p(PKD_j, PLD_j, P_{Ej}, P_{Mj}, t)$.

We assume that the price function has the *translog* form:

$$\ln PO_{jt} = \alpha_0^j + \sum_i \alpha_i^{Pj} \ln p_{it} + \frac{1}{2}\sum_{i,k} \beta_{ik}^{Pj} \ln p_{it} \ln p_{kt} + \sum_i \ln p_{it} f_{it}^{Pj} + f_t^j \quad i,k = \{\mathrm{K,L,E,M}\}. \quad (4.4)$$

We refer to the translog price function (4.4) as the *state-space model of producer behavior*. The superscript P denotes parameters of the producer function, as distinguished from parameters of the investment and import functions in the rest of IGEM. We drop the j superscript for the jth industry in the rest of this discussion for simplicity. The parameters α_0, α_i^P, and β_{ik}^P are estimated separately for each industry. The latent variables f_{it}^P and f_t are also estimated separately for each industry, using the Kalman filter described in section 4.3 below. Changes in the latent variables f_{it} represent biases of technical change and the latent variable f_{pt} represents the level of technology.

An important advantage of the translog price function in this application is that it generates input share equations that are linear in the latent variables representing the biases of technical change. Differentiation of the price function (4.4) with respect to the log of input prices yields the input share equations. For example, the demand for capital is derived from the capital share equation:

$$v_{Kt} = \frac{PKD_tKD_t}{PO_tQI_t} = \alpha_K^P + \sum_k \beta_{Kk}^P \ln p_{kt} + f_{Kt}^P. \quad (4.5)$$

The share of capital is a linear function of the logarithms of the input prices and a latent variable corresponding to the bias of technical change.

The biases of technical change are the changes in the shares of inputs, holding the input prices constant, for example,

$$\Delta v_{Kt} = f_{Kt} - f_{K,t-1}. \quad (4.6)$$

The biases capture patterns of increasing or decreasing input use over time after accounting for price changes. If the latent variable f_{Kt} in (4.5) is increasing with time, the bias of technical change is "capital-using." For a given set of input prices the share of capital is higher as a consequence of the change in technology. Alternatively, if f_{Kt} is decreasing, the bias of technical change is "capital-saving." It is important to emphasize that technical change may be capital-using at one point of time and capital-saving at another. This would be ruled out by the constant time trends used in Binswanger's approach. There is a separate bias for each of the productive inputs—capital, labor, energy, and materials.

The rate of technical change between t and $t-1$ is the negative of the rate of change in the price of output, holding the input prices constant:

$$\Delta T_t = -\sum_{i=1}^{n} \ln P_{it}(f_{it}^P - f_{i,t-1}^P) - (f_t - f_{t-1}). \tag{4.7}$$

As technology progresses for a given set of input prices, the price of output falls. The first term in the rate of technical change (4.7) depends on the prices and the biases of technical change. We refer to this as the rate of *induced* technical change. If, for example, the price of capital input falls and the bias of technical change (4.6), corresponding to a change in the latent variable f_{Kt}, is capital-using, the rate of technical change in (4.7) will increase. However, if the bias of technical change is capital-saving, a decrease in the price for capital will retard the rate of productivity growth. The second term in (4.7) depends only on changes in the level of technology f_t, so that we refer to this as the rate of *autonomous* technical change.

The rate of technical change (4.7) is the sum of induced and autonomous rates of technical change. Ordinarily, the autonomous rate of technical change would be positive, while the induced rate of technical change could be positive or negative. The rate of induced technical change is simply the negative of the covariance between the logarithms of the input prices and the biases of technical change. If lower input prices are correlated with higher biases of technical change, then the rate of induced technical behavior change is positive.

The parameters β_{ik} capture the price responsiveness of demands for inputs for a given state of technology. These parameters are called *share elasticities* and represent the degree of substitutability among the inputs. For example, a lower price of capital leads to greater demand for capital input. This may lead to a higher or lower share of capital input, depending on the substitutability of other inputs for capital; this substitutability is captured by the share elasticity for capital input. Share elasticities may be positive or negative, so that the share of capital may increase or decrease with the price of capital input. When all share elasticities β_{ik} are zero, the cost function reduces to the Cobb-Douglas or linear logarithmic form and the shares are independent of input prices.

In estimating the unknown share elasticities, restrictions derived from production theory must be imposed on the translog price function (4.4). In more compact vector notation the price function can be written as

$$\ln PO_t = \alpha_0 + \alpha^{P\prime} \ln p_t + \frac{1}{2} \ln p_t' B^P \ln p_t + \ln p_t' f_t^P + f_t + \varepsilon_t^p \qquad (4.4)'$$

and input share equations take the form:

$$v_t = \alpha^P + B^P \ln p_t + f_t^P + \varepsilon_t^v \qquad (4.5)'$$

where $p = (PKD, PLD, P_E, P_M)'$, $v = (v_K, v_L, v_E, v_M)'$, $f_t^p = (f_{Kt}^p, f_{Lt}^p, f_{Et}^p, f_{Mt}^p)'$ and $B^P = [\beta_{ik}]$. We have added disturbance terms ε_t^p and ε_t^v, random variables with mean zero, to represent shocks to producer behavior for a given state of technology.

Homogeneity restrictions on the price function imply that doubling of all input prices doubles the output price, so that

$$\alpha_K + \alpha_L + \alpha_E + \alpha_M = 1. \qquad (4.8)$$

$$\sum_i \beta_{ik} = 0 \quad \text{for each k.}$$

In addition, the matrix of share elasticities must be symmetric, so that

$$\beta_{ik} = \beta_{ki}. \qquad (4.9)$$

Finally, the price function must be "locally concave" when evaluated at the prices observed in the sample period; note that this does not imply that the cost function is "globally concave" at all possible prices. The concavity condition implies that

$$B + v_t v_t' - V_t \qquad (4.10)$$

must be nonpositive definite at each t in the sample period,[9] where B^P is the matrix of parameters in (4.4) and V_t is a diagonal matrix with the shares along the diagonal. These restrictions on the parameter estimates are easily implemented by means of standard optimization code.[10]

Since the shares for all four inputs sum to unity, the latent variables representing biases of technical change f_{it} must sum to zero, $\Sigma_i f_{it} = 0$. Similarly, the shocks to producer behavior for a given state of technology ε_t^v sum to zero. We solve out these constraints on the shocks, as well as the homogeneity constraints (4.8), by expressing the model (4.4′) and (4.5′) in terms of relative prices and dropping one of the equations (4.5′) for the shares and one of the latent variables representing biases of technical change.

We assume that the latent variables corresponding to biases of technical change f_{it} are stationary, since the value shares v_t are nonnegative and sum to unity. We assume, further, that the level of technology is nonstationary but the first difference, $\Delta f_t = f_t - f_{t-1}$, is stationary, so that technology evolves in accord with a stochastic trend or unit root. To implement a model of production based on the price function equation (4.4′), we express the technology state variables as a vector autoregression (VAR).

Let $\tilde{\xi}_t = (1, f_{Kt}^p, f_{Lt}^p, f_{Et}^p, \Delta f_t)'$ denote the vector of stationary state variables. The *transition equation* is

$$\tilde{\xi}_t = \tilde{F}\tilde{\xi}_{t-1} + \varepsilon_t, \tag{4.11}$$

where $\tilde{\xi}_t$ is a random vector with mean zero representing technology shocks and $\tilde{F}$ is a matrix of unknown parameters of a first-order VAR. The transition equation (4.11) determines a vector of latent variables, including the biases as well as the determinants of the rate of technical change. This equation is employed in projecting the vector of latent technology variables, given the values of these variables during the sample period and estimates of the unknown parameters of the coefficient matrix $\tilde{F}$.

4.3 Latent Variables

The econometric technique for identifying the rate and biases of technical change is a straightforward application of the Kalman filter, introduced by Kalman (1960, 1963) and presented in detail by Hamilton (1994, chapter 13) and others. In the empirical research described in the following section, the Kalman filter is used to model production in each of the 35 sectors of our data set. The latent variables in the state-space specification of the price function (4.4) determine current and future patterns of production along with relative prices, which are the covariates of the Kalman filter.

The model underlying the Kalman filter is as follows:

$$\underset{(r\times1)}{\xi_t} = \underset{(r\times r)}{F}\,\underset{(r\times1)}{\xi_{t-1}} + \underset{(r\times1)}{\varepsilon_t}, \tag{4.12}$$

$$\underset{(n\times1)}{y_t} = \underset{(n\times k)}{A'}\,\underset{(k\times1)}{x_t} + \underset{(n\times r)}{H'}\,\underset{(r\times1)}{\xi_t} + \underset{(n\times1)}{w_t}, \tag{4.13}$$

where ξ_t, $t = 0, 1, 2, \ldots, T$ is the vector of unobserved latent variables and y_t, t = 1, 2, … , T is the vector of observations on the dependent variables. The vector y_t is determined by ξ_t and x_t, the vector of observations on the explanatory variables. The subscript t denotes time and indexes the observations.

In the model underlying the Kalman filter the *state equation* is (4.12) and the *observation equation* is (4.13), where x_t is exogenous, that is, uncorrelated with the disturbance w_t. The shocks v_t and w_t are assumed uncorrelated at all lags and

$$E(\varepsilon_t\varepsilon_\tau') = \begin{cases} \underset{(r\times r)}{Q} & t=\tau \\ 0 & otherwise \end{cases}$$
$$E(w_t w_\tau') = \begin{cases} \underset{(n\times n)}{R} & t=\tau \\ 0 & otherwise \end{cases} \tag{4.14}$$

where Q and R are the covariance matrices for the disturbances. The matrices A, H, F, R, and Q include unknown parameters, but some of their elements may be known. For simplicity, we denote the unknown components of these matrices by the parameter vector θ.

Computation of the standard Kalman filter involves two procedures, *filtering* and *smoothing*. In filtering we use the Maximum Likelihood Estimator (MLE) to estimate the unknown parameter vector θ. The log-likelihood function, based on the normal distribution, is computed by the forward recursion described by Hamilton (1994):

$$\max_\theta l(\theta \mid Y_T) = \max_\theta \sum_{t=1}^{T} \log N(y_t \mid \hat{y}_{t|t-1}, V_{t|t-1}), \tag{4.15}$$

where the matrix,

$$Y_t = (y_t', y_{t-1}', \ldots, y_1', x_t', x_{t-1}', \ldots, x_1')',$$

consists of the observations up to time t and the mean and variance are

$$\hat{y}_{t|t-1} = E(y_t \mid Y_{t-1}); \quad V_{t|t-1} = E[(y_t - \hat{y}_{t|t-1})(y_t - \hat{y}_{t|t-1})']. \tag{4.16}$$

Both are functions of θ and the data, calculated in the forward recursion. We use numerical methods to calculate the covariance matrix of the maximum likelihood estimator $\hat{\theta}$. In smoothing, we estimate the latent vector ξ_t, given the maximum likelihood estimator, using the backward recursion described by Hamilton (1994).

The econometric model we have presented in section 4.2 can be expressed in the form required by the Kalman filter with the following definitions:

$$y_t = \begin{bmatrix} v_{Kt} \\ v_{Lt} \\ v_{Et} \\ \ln \dfrac{PO_t}{P_{Mt}} \end{bmatrix}; \quad x_t = \begin{bmatrix} 1 \\ \ln \dfrac{P_{Kt}}{P_{Mt}} \\ \ln \dfrac{P_{Lt}}{P_{Mt}} \\ \ln \dfrac{P_{Et}}{P_{Mt}} \\ \dfrac{1}{2}\left(\ln \dfrac{P_{Kt}}{P_{Mt}}\right)^2 \\ \dfrac{1}{2}\left(\ln \dfrac{P_{Lt}}{P_{Mt}}\right)^2 \\ \dfrac{1}{2}\left(\ln \dfrac{P_{Et}}{P_{Mt}}\right)^2 \\ \ln \dfrac{P_{Kt}}{P_{Mt}} \ln \dfrac{P_{Lt}}{P_{Mt}} \\ \ln \dfrac{P_{Kt}}{P_{Mt}} \ln \dfrac{P_{Et}}{P_{Mt}} \\ \ln \dfrac{P_{Lt}}{P_{Mt}} \ln \dfrac{P_{Et}}{P_{Mt}} \end{bmatrix};$$

$$\xi_t = \begin{bmatrix} 1 \\ f_{Kt} \\ f_{Lt} \\ f_{Et} \\ f_{pt} \\ f_{pt-1} \end{bmatrix}; \quad w_t = \begin{bmatrix} \varepsilon_{Kt}^{v} \\ \varepsilon_{Lt}^{v} \\ \varepsilon_{Et}^{v} \\ \varepsilon_t^{p} \end{bmatrix}; \quad \varepsilon_t = \begin{bmatrix} 0 \\ \varepsilon_{Kt} \\ \varepsilon_{Lt} \\ \varepsilon_{Et} \\ \varepsilon_{dpt} \\ 0 \end{bmatrix}. \tag{4.17}$$

$$A' = \begin{bmatrix} \alpha_K & \beta_{KK} & \beta_{KL} & \beta_{KE} & 0 & 0 & 0 & 0 & 0 & 0 \\ \alpha_L & \beta_{KL} & \beta_{LL} & \beta_{LE} & 0 & 0 & 0 & 0 & 0 & 0 \\ \alpha_E & \beta_{KE} & \beta_{LE} & \beta_{EE} & 0 & 0 & 0 & 0 & 0 & 0 \\ \alpha_0 & \alpha_K & \alpha_L & \alpha_E & \beta_{KK} & \beta_{LL} & \beta_{EE} & \beta_{KL} & \beta_{KE} & \beta_{LE} \end{bmatrix};$$

$$H' = \begin{bmatrix} 0 & 1 & 0 & 0 & 0 & 0 \\ 0 & 0 & 1 & 0 & 0 & 0 \\ 0 & 0 & 0 & 1 & 0 & 0 \\ 0 & \ln\dfrac{P_{Kt}}{P_{Mt}} & \ln\dfrac{P_{Lt}}{P_{Mt}} & \ln\dfrac{P_{Et}}{P_{Mt}} & 1 & 0 \end{bmatrix};$$

$$F' = \begin{bmatrix} 1 & 0 & 0 & 0 & 0 & 0 \\ \chi_K & \delta_{KK} & \delta_{KL} & \delta_{KE} & \delta_{Kp} & -\delta_{Kp} \\ \chi_L & \delta_{LK} & \delta_{LL} & \delta_{LE} & \delta_{Lp} & -\delta_{Lp} \\ \chi_E & \delta_{EK} & \delta_{EL} & \delta_{EE} & \delta_{Ep} & -\delta_{Ep} \\ \chi_p & \delta_{pK} & \delta_{pL} & \delta_{pE} & \delta_{pp}+1 & -\delta_{pp} \\ 0 & 0 & 0 & 0 & 1 & 0 \end{bmatrix}.$$

4.4 Instrumental Variables

We require two modifications of the standard Kalman filter. First, we impose the concavity constraints (4.10) at each data point in the sample period by simply adding these constraints to the computation of the MLE, converting this from an unconstrained to a constrained optimization. Second, the explanatory variables are prices determined by the balance of demand and supply, so that they may be endogenous. We introduce exogenous instrumental variables, say z_t, to deal with the potential endogeneity of the prices.[11] We assume that the vector z_t includes the observations on these variables at time t and satisfies the equation

$$\underset{(k\times 1)}{x_t} = \underset{(k\times m)}{\Pi}\ \underset{(m\times 1)}{z_t} + \underset{(k\times 1)}{\eta_t}, \tag{4.18}$$

where z_t is uncorrelated with η_t and w_t, and η_t is correlated with w_t but uncorrelated with ε_t.

Combining equation (4.18) with the observation equation (4.13), we construct a new observation equation:

$$\begin{bmatrix} y_t \\ x_t \end{bmatrix} = \begin{bmatrix} A'\Pi \\ \Pi \end{bmatrix} z_t + \begin{bmatrix} H' \\ O \end{bmatrix} \xi_t + \begin{bmatrix} A'\eta_t + w_t \\ \eta_t \end{bmatrix}, \tag{4.19}$$

or

$$\underset{[(n+k)\times 1]}{\tilde{y}_t} = \underset{[(n+k)\times m]}{\tilde{A}'}\underset{(m\times 1)}{\tilde{x}_t} + \underset{[(n+k)\times r]}{\tilde{H}'}\underset{(r\times 1)}{\xi_t} + \underset{[(n+k)\times 1]}{\tilde{w}_t}. \tag{4.20}$$

The state equation (4.12) is unchanged. The new model satisfies the exogeneity requirement of the Kalman filter. This would be a promising approach if the size of Π were small; however, in our application, this matrix involves 120 unknown parameters.

A more tractable approach is the two-step Kalman filter, obtained by a direct application of the two-step MLE (Wooldridge, 2010, chapter 13). If the parameter Π were known, we could replace x_t with $\Pi z_t + \eta_t$ and formulate a new observation equation, $y_t = A'\Pi z_t + H'\xi_t + (A'\eta_t + w_t)$, where z_t is the exogenous explanatory variable. Motivated by this idea, we proceed in two steps:

Step 1: Estimate $\hat{\Pi} = XZ'(ZZ')^{-1}$ using OLS to obtain a consistent estimator of Π, where X and Z represent the matrices of observations on x_t and z_t, t = 1, 2, … , T.

Step 2: Replace X in the standard Kalman filter with $\hat{X} = \hat{\Pi}Z$, that is, replace x_t with the fitted value $\hat{x}_t$ at time t, and use the standard filtering procedure to obtain the two-step MLE of the unknown parameters in the matrices A, H, F, R, Q.[12]

Wooldridge (2010, chapter 13) shows that $\hat{\theta}$ is a consistent estimator of the parameter θ. In addition, it is asymptotically normal with

$$\begin{aligned}
\sqrt{N}\left(\hat{\theta}-\theta_0\right) &= \frac{A_0^{-1}}{\sqrt{N}}\sum_{t=1}^{N}[-g_t(\theta_0;\Pi_0)] + o_p(1) \\
&= -A_0^{-1}\left[\frac{1}{\sqrt{N}}\sum_{t=1}^{N}\frac{\partial \log f(y_t \mid x_t, y_{t-1};\theta_0,\Pi_0)}{\partial\theta}\right. \\
&\quad \left. + \sqrt{N}E\left(\frac{\partial^2 \log f(y_t \mid x_t, y_{t-1};\theta_0)}{\partial\theta\partial\Pi}\right)\times(\hat{\Pi}-\Pi_0)\right] + o_p(1) \\
&= -A_0^{-1}\left[\frac{1}{\sqrt{N}}\sum_{t=1}^{N}s_t + \sqrt{N}F_0(\hat{\Pi}-\Pi_0)\right] + o_p(1) \\
&= -A_0^{-1}\left\{\frac{1}{\sqrt{N}}\sum_{t=1}^{N}s_t + \sqrt{N}F_0\left[\left(\sum_{t=1}^{N}Z_t'Z_t\right)^{-1}\left(\sum_{t=1}^{N}Z_t'\eta_t\right)\right]\right\} + o_p(1) \\
&= -A_0^{-1}\left\{\frac{1}{\sqrt{N}}\sum_{t=1}^{N}s_t + \frac{1}{\sqrt{N}}F_0\left[\left(\frac{1}{N}\sum_{t=1}^{N}Z_t'Z_t\right)^{-1}\left(\sum_{t=1}^{N}Z_t'\eta_t\right)\right]\right\} + o_p(1) \\
&= -\frac{A_0^{-1}}{\sqrt{N}}\sum_{t=1}^{N}\left[s_t + F_0\left(\frac{1}{N}\sum_{t=1}^{N}Z_t'Z_t\right)^{-1}Z_t'\eta_t\right] + o_p(1) \\
&= -\frac{A_0^{-1}}{\sqrt{N}}\sum_{t=1}^{N}[s_t + F_0 r_t] + o_p(1)
\end{aligned} \tag{4.21}$$

where we employ the following definitions:

$$A_0 = E\frac{\partial^2 \log f(y_t \mid x_t, y_{t-1}; \theta_0)}{\partial\theta\partial\theta'}.$$

$$F_0 = E\frac{\partial^2 \log f(y_t \mid x_t, y_{t-1}; \theta_0, \Pi_0)}{\partial\theta\partial\Pi}.$$

$$r_t = \left(\frac{1}{N}\sum_{t=1}^{N} Z_t' Z_t\right)^{-1} Z_t'\eta_t.$$

$$s_t = \frac{\partial \log f(y_t \mid x_t, y_{t-1}; \theta_0, \Pi_0)}{\partial\theta}.$$

So, $\sqrt{N}\left(\hat{\theta} - \theta_0\right)$ can be expressed as

$$\sqrt{N}\left(\hat{\theta} - \theta_0\right) = -\frac{A_0^{-1}}{\sqrt{N}}\sum_{t=1}^{N}[s_t + F_0 r_t] + o_p(1).$$

The asymptotic variance of the unknown parameter $\hat{\theta}$ is

$$\begin{aligned} AVar\sqrt{N}\left(\hat{\theta} - \theta_0\right) &= \frac{1}{N}A_0^{-1}E\{[-g_t(\theta_0; \Pi_0)][-g_t(\theta_0; \Pi_0)]'\}A_0^{-1} \\ &= \frac{1}{N}A_0^{-1}D_0A_0^{-1} \end{aligned} \tag{4.22}$$

given

$$D_0 = E\{[-g_t(\theta_0; \Pi_0)][-g_t(\theta_0; \Pi_0)]'\}.$$

Therefore, the variance of the unknown parameter $\hat{\theta}$ should be

$$Var\left(\hat{\theta} - \theta_0\right) = \frac{1}{N^2}A_0^{-1}D_0A_0^{-1}.$$

To estimate the asymptotic covariance matrix consistently, we apply the law of large numbers to the following sample statistics:

$$\hat{A}_0 = \frac{1}{N}\sum_{t=1}^{N}\frac{\partial^2 \log f(y_t \mid x_t, y_{t-1}; \hat{\theta}, \hat{\Pi})}{\partial\theta\partial\theta'}$$

$$\hat{F}_0 = \frac{1}{N}\sum_{t=1}^{N}\frac{\partial^2 \log f(y_t \mid x_t, y_{t-1}; \hat{\theta}, \hat{\Pi})}{\partial\theta\partial\Pi}$$

$$\hat{r}_t = \left(\frac{1}{N}\sum_{t=1}^{N} Z_t' Z_t\right)^{-1} Z_t'\eta_t$$

$$\hat{s}_t = \frac{\partial \log f(y_t \mid x_t, y_{t-1}; \hat{\theta}, \hat{\Pi})}{\partial \theta}$$

$$\hat{D}_0 = \frac{1}{N}\sum_{t=1}^{N}\{[-\hat{g}_t(\theta_0;\Pi_0)][-\hat{g}_t(\theta_0;\Pi_0)]'\}$$
$$= \frac{1}{N}\sum_{t=1}^{N}\left[(\hat{s}_t + \hat{F}_0\hat{r}_t)(\hat{s}_t + \hat{F}_0\hat{r}_t)'\right],$$

so that a consistent estimator of the covariance matrix is

$$Var\left(\hat{\theta} - \theta_0\right) = \frac{1}{N^2}\hat{A}_0^{-1}\hat{D}_0\hat{A}_0^{-1}.$$

Table 4.5 provides a list of the instrumental variables and figure 4.1 displays the instruments graphically. These are treated as exogenous variables in IGEM. We employ two tests to check the validity of our instrumental variables. Fortunately, we have more instrumental variables than endogenous explanatory variables; in fact, there are 11 nonconstant instruments in z_t and 9 endogenous explanatory variables

Table 4.5
Instrumental variables

1	Constant
2	Average marginal tax rate on personal labor income
3	Effective corporate income tax rate
4	Average marginal tax rate on dividends
5	Rate of taxation on consumption goods
6	Time endowment in 2000 dollars/lagged private wealth including claims on government and the ROW
7	Lagged price of personal consumptions expenditure/lagged price index of private domestic labor input
8	Lagged price of leisure and unemployment/lagged price index of private domestic labor input
9	Lagged price of capital services for household/ lagged price index of private domestic labor input
10	Lagged real full consumption/lagged private wealth including claims on government and the ROW
11	U.S. population/lagged private wealth including claims on government and the ROW
12	Government demand/lagged private wealth including claims on government and the ROW

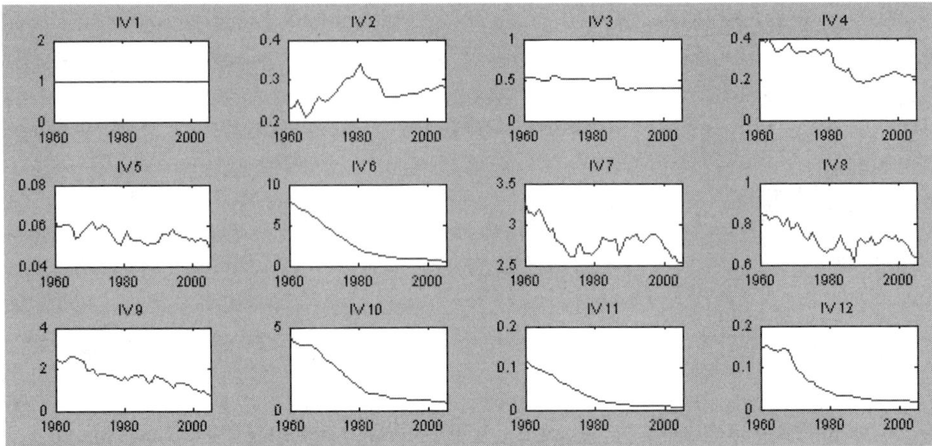

Figure 4.1
Instrumental variables.

in x_t. This enables us to conduct a test of overidentifying restrictions to confirm the exogeneity of the instruments.

We carry out the test of overidentifying restrictions as follows: First, we select any two nonconstant instrumental variables out of the eleven $z_t^{(m-k)}$, where $m - k = 12 - 10 = 2$. Second, in the second-stage Kalman filter, we include $z_t^{(m-k)}$ as an exogenous variable in the observation equation and keep the state equation the same as before:

$$\begin{aligned} \underset{(n\times1)}{y_t} &= \underset{(n\times k)}{A'}\,\underset{(k\times1)}{\hat{x}_t} + \underset{[n\times(m-k)]}{C'}\,\underset{[(m-k)\times1]}{z_t^{(m-k)}} + \underset{(n\times r)}{H'}\,\underset{(r\times1)}{\xi_t} + \underset{(n\times1)}{w_t^{(m-k)}} \\ \underset{(r\times1)}{\xi_t} &= \underset{(r\times r)}{F}\,\underset{(r\times1)}{\xi_{t-1}} + \underset{(r\times1)}{v_t}\,. \end{aligned} \tag{4.23}$$

Note that $\hat{X}$, the observation matrix of $\hat{x}_t$, t = 1, 2, …, T, satisfies $\hat{X} = \hat{\Pi}Z = XZ'(ZZ')^{-1}Z$ with rank $k = 10$; therefore, selection of any two nonconstant instrumental variables yields the same test statistic. Moreover, if our null hypothesis that z_t is uncorrelated with w_t is true, the addition of $z_t^{(m-k)}$ to the observation equation will not affect the original Kalman filter. We perform a Likelihood Ratio Test of the hypothesis that C is zero by comparing l and l_g, the log-likelihood values before and after the introduction of $z_t^{(m-k)}$. Under the null hypothesis of exogeneity the difference is asymptotically chi squared:

$$2(l_g - l) \overset{a}{\sim} \chi^2_{n\times(m-k)}.$$

The results presented in table 4.6 show that the instrumental variables are exogenous.

Table 4.6
Tests for overidentification

Industry	l_g	l	$2(l_g - l)$	p-value	p-value*35
1	563.48	562.65	1.67	0.990	34.63
2	454.21	447.07	14.28	0.075	2.62
3	481.81	478.00	7.61	0.473	16.55
4	509.39	508.64	1.50	0.993	34.74
5	550.44	547.61	5.66	0.685	23.97
6	714.71	712.61	4.19	0.839	29.38
7	730.60	727.74	5.72	0.679	23.75
8	604.98	604.94	0.07	1.000	35.00
9	704.31	702.58	3.47	0.902	31.56
10	709.93	708.88	2.11	0.978	34.21
11	638.50	637.66	1.68	0.989	34.62
12	691.26	688.36	5.82	0.668	23.37
13	630.64	627.61	6.07	0.640	22.40
14	722.78	719.49	6.59	0.581	20.33
15	620.06	618.78	2.55	0.959	33.57
16	531.17	526.66	9.01	0.342	11.96
17	702.20	699.77	4.86	0.772	27.03
18	597.88	596.47	2.82	0.945	33.08
19	660.17	658.94	2.47	0.963	33.71
20	647.79	641.26	13.07	0.109	3.83
21	702.88	700.86	4.03	0.854	29.90
22	701.61	697.96	7.30	0.505	17.67
23	648.23	648.00	0.47	1.000	35.00
24	674.59	670.90	7.38	0.496	17.36
25	648.00	642.70	10.61	0.225	7.87
26	700.77	695.14	11.26	0.187	6.56
27	673.38	669.86	7.06	0.530	18.56
28	607.55	602.54	10.01	0.264	9.26
29	781.95	776.59	10.72	0.218	7.64
30	595.61	594.48	2.25	0.972	34.03
31	560.82	552.14	17.35	0.027	0.93
32	703.84	699.63	8.43	0.392	13.73
33	765.86	760.74	10.24	0.248	8.69
34	726.58	721.86	9.43	0.307	10.76
35	572.33	564.66	15.34	0.053	1.85

Notes:
(1) The number of degrees of freedom for the LR test for each sector is 8.
(2) The null hypothesis is that the instrumental variables are exogenous.
(3) High p-values indicate that we cannot reject the null hypothesis of exogeneity.
(4) The last column presents p-values adjusted for simultaneous inference.

Table 4.7
Tests of validity of the instrumental variables

Industry	LR	p-value
1	677.89	<0.001
2	580.45	<0.001
3	679.11	<0.001
4	762.29	<0.001
5	717.90	<0.001
6	646.73	<0.001
7	672.32	<0.001
8	646.00	<0.001
9	782.78	<0.001
10	643.17	<0.001
11	541.68	<0.001
12	600.82	<0.001
13	668.19	<0.001
14	743.66	<0.001
15	732.65	<0.001
16	692.95	<0.001
17	734.26	<0.001
18	625.93	<0.001
19	829.69	<0.001
20	626.03	<0.001
21	726.69	<0.001
22	696.75	<0.001
23	791.19	<0.001
24	601.69	<0.001
25	596.51	<0.001
26	777.20	<0.001
27	588.84	<0.001
28	568.53	<0.001
29	762.82	<0.001
30	657.10	<0.001
31	748.91	<0.001
32	856.78	<0.001
33	755.03	<0.001
34	715.89	<0.001
35	764.75	<0.001

Second, we apply a Likelihood Ratio Test to the hypothesis of zero correlation between endogenous explanatory variables and instrumental variables. Let $\hat{\Sigma}$ represent the empirical covariance matrix of $\dot{x}_t$, the nine nonconstant elements of x_t, and $\tilde{\Sigma}$ represent the corresponding empirical covariance matrix of $\dot{x}_t - \dot{\Pi} z_t$, the residuals from the fitted values of the $\dot{x}_t$'s in the linear regression, where $\dot{\Pi}$ represents the corresponding submatrix of Π. The log-likelihood for the latter is

$$\begin{aligned}\ln \tilde{L} &= -\frac{(k-1)T}{2}\ln|2\pi| - \frac{T}{2}\ln|\tilde{\Sigma}| - \frac{1}{2}\sum_{t=1}^{T}(\dot{x}_t - \dot{\Pi}z_t)'\tilde{\Sigma}^{-1}(\dot{x}_t - \dot{\Pi}z_t) \\ &= -\frac{(k-1)T}{2}\ln|2\pi| - \frac{T}{2}\ln|\tilde{\Sigma}| + \frac{(k-1)T}{2}. \end{aligned} \tag{4.24}$$

The quadratic term is replaced by a constant due to the ML process of the linear regression. For $\hat{\Sigma}$, we can derive a similar log-likelihood:

$$\ln \hat{L} = -\frac{(k-1)T}{2}\ln|2\pi| - \frac{T}{2}\ln|\hat{\Sigma}| + \frac{(k-1)T}{2}. \tag{4.25}$$

This is a linear regression, where the parameters before the constant term in z_t are unconstrained and all other parameters in $\dot{\Pi}$ are fixed at zero.

The Likelihood Ratio Test statistic is

$$LR = -2\left(\ln \hat{L} - \ln \tilde{L}\right) = T\left(\ln|\tilde{\Sigma}| - \ln|\hat{\Sigma}|\right). \tag{4.26}$$

This statistic is asymptotically chi-squared, where the number of degrees of freedom is equal to the number of parameters that are constrained, $(m-1)\cdot(k-1) = 11 \cdot 9 = 99$ in our model. The results presented in table 4.7 show that the instrumental variables are highly correlated with the endogenous variables. We conclude that both diagnostic tests confirm the validity of our instruments.

4.5 Empirical Results

In this section we present the rate and biases of technical change for the state-space model of producer behavior equation (4.4) for each of the 35 sectors of the U.S. economy listed in table 4.1. In figures 4.2–4.5 we give the changes in input shares of the four inputs—capital, labor, energy, and materials—over the period 1960–2005. These are the dependent variables for the value share of capital input in equation (4.5) and the remaining value shares. The industries are ordered by the

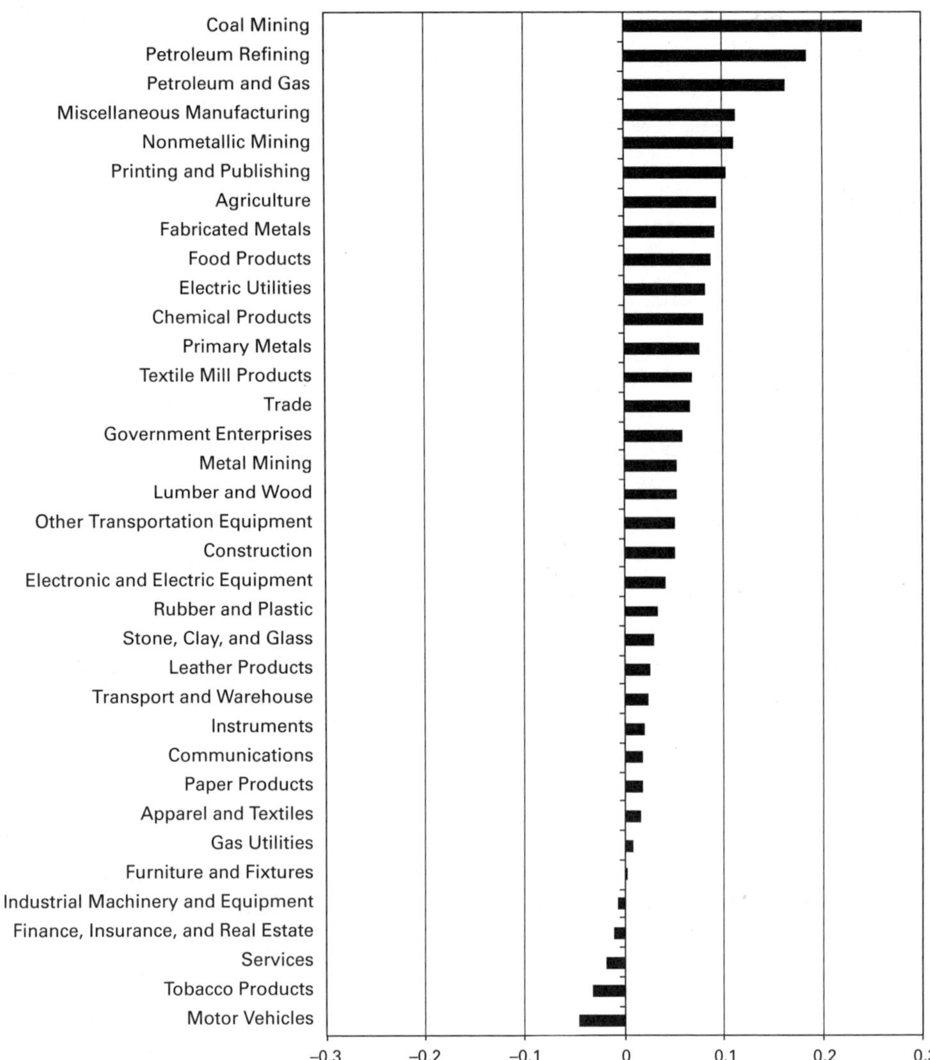

Figure 4.2
Change of capital input share, 1960–2005. $v_{K,2005} - v_{K,1960}$

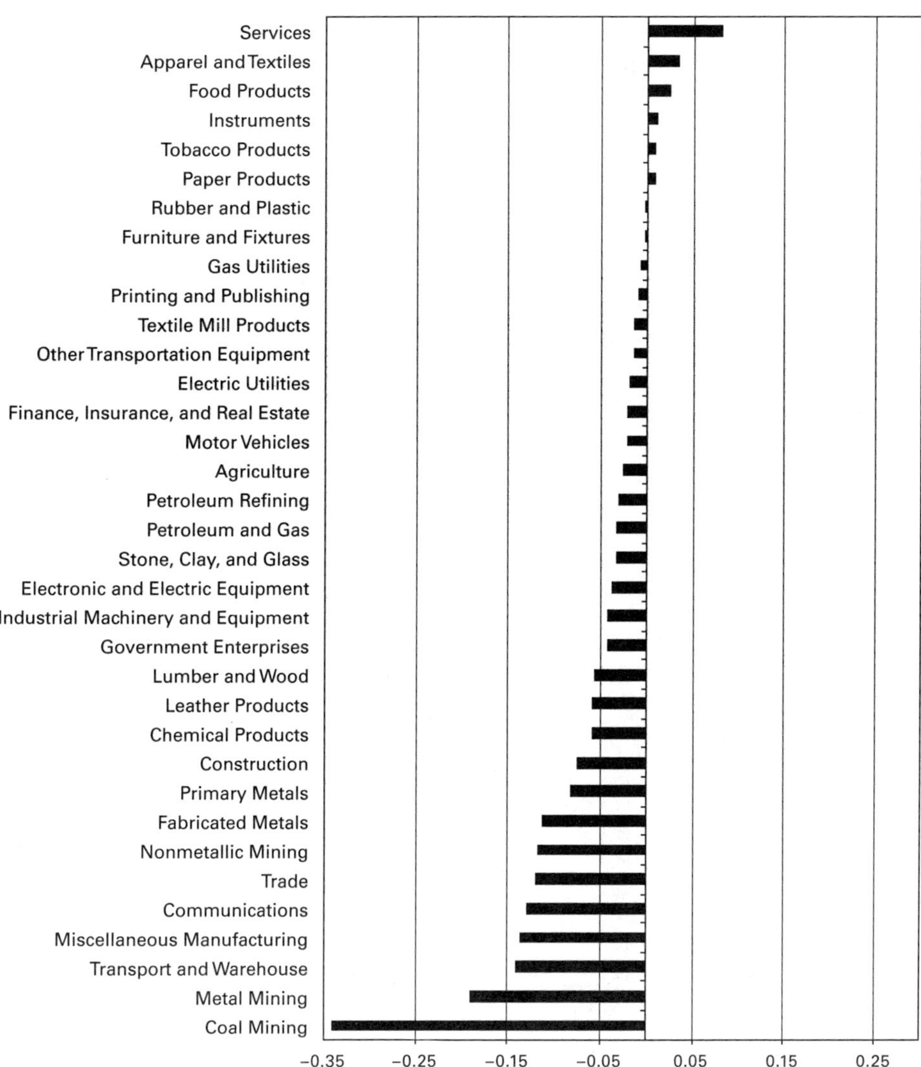

Figure 4.3
Change of labor input share, 1960–2005. $v_{L,2005} - v_{L,1960}$

Figure 4.4
Change of energy input share, 1960–2005. $v_{E,2005} - v_{E,1960}$

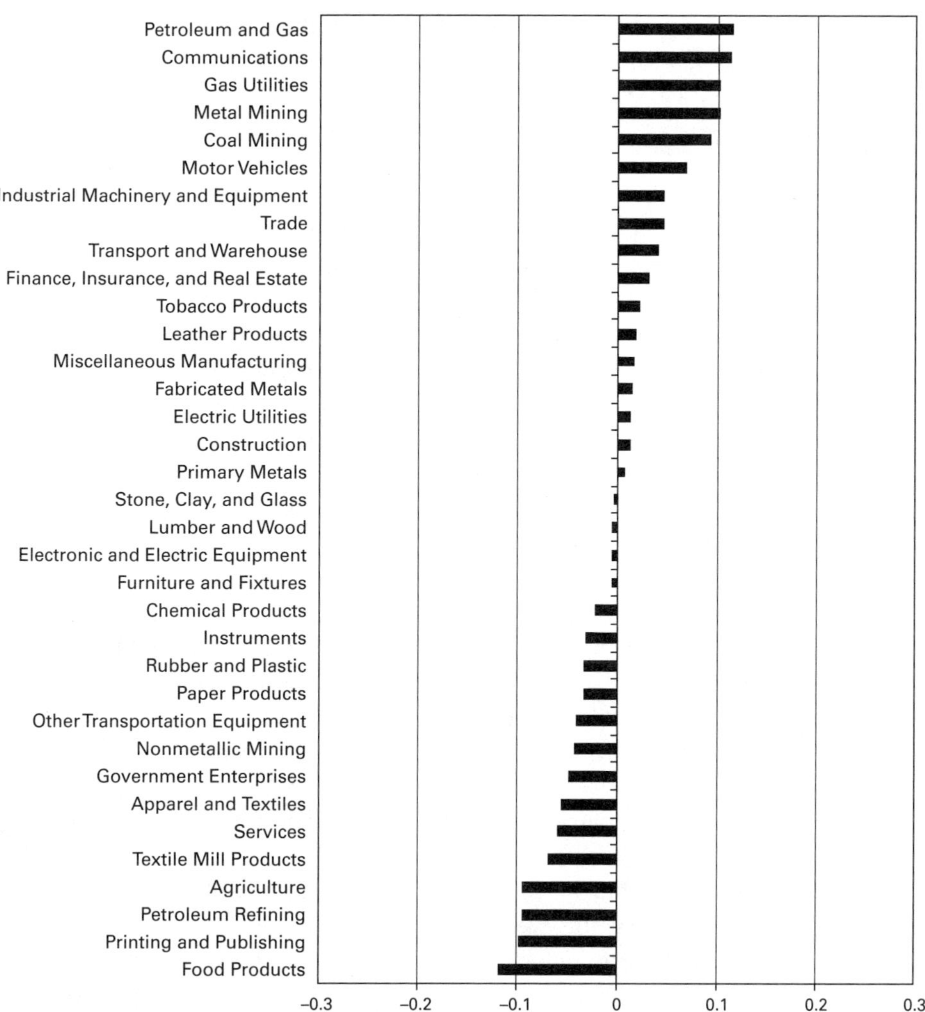

Figure 4.5
Change of material input share, 1960–2005. $v_{M,2005} - v_{M,1960}$

magnitude of the changes. In general, the capital input shares have increased, some of them very substantially. With some notable exceptions the labor shares have decreased and the energy shares have increased slightly. The materials shares are almost evenly divided between increases and decreases.

We next allocate changes in the input shares between a price effect, corresponding to the second term in (4.5), and the bias of technical change (4.6), corresponding to the third term in (4.5). The price effects presented in figures 4.6–4.9 represent the responses of production patterns to price changes through substitution among inputs. These responses are substantial but appear to be evenly balanced between negative and positive effects for capital and energy. The labor price effects are predominantly negative, reflecting increases in wages relative to prices, while the materials price effects are predominantly positive. These price effects rule out a Cobb-Douglas or linear logarithmic specification for the price function (4.4).

We present the biases of technical change (4.6) in figures 4.10–4.13. The biases of technical change for capital input are predominantly capital-using and substantial in magnitude, especially for Coal Mining and Government Enterprises. The biases are capital-saving but relatively small for Paper Products and Services. The biases of technical change for labor input are divided between labor-saving technical change for industries like Leather Products and Coal Mining and labor-using change for industries such as Food Products and Textile Mill Products.

The biases of technical change for energy are relatively small in magnitude, reflecting the small size of the energy shares for most industries. The bias for energy is energy-using for Agriculture and Transportation and energy-saving for Petroleum and Gas Mining, Electric and Gas Utilities, and Coal Mining. Finally, the biases of technical change for materials are predominantly materials-saving and substantial in size, especially for Chemical Products and Government Enterprises. However, the biases are materials-using for Petroleum and Gas Mining and Instruments.

We conclude that the biases of technical change are comparable in magnitude to the price effects. Substitution among inputs and biased technical change are both important determinants of changes in the input shares. However, the biases also play a significant role in our state-space model of producer behavior as determinants of the rate of induced technical change. We turn next to changes in the price of

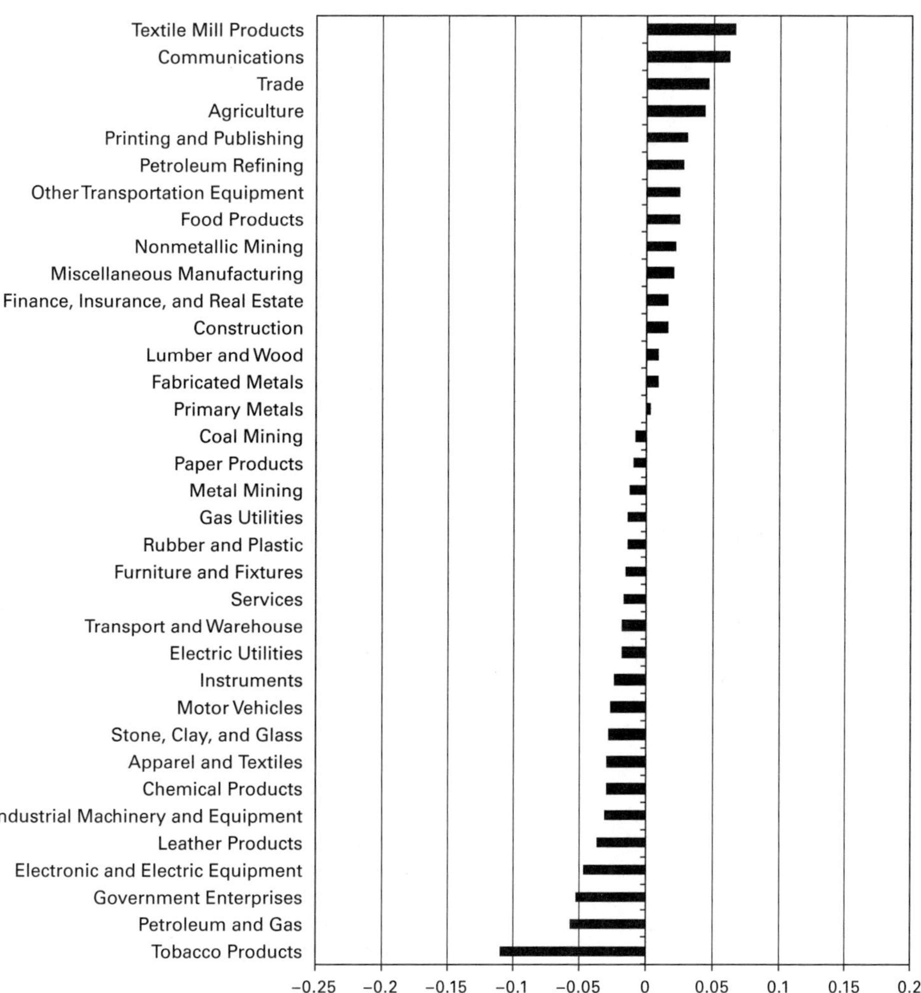

Figure 4.6
Price effect of capital input share change, 1960–2005.

$$\sum_k \beta_{Kk} \Delta \ln P_{kt} = \left(\beta_{KK} \ln \frac{P_{K2005}}{P_{K1960}} + \beta_{KL} \ln \frac{P_{L2005}}{P_{L1960}} + \beta_{KE} \ln \frac{P_{E2005}}{P_{E1960}} + \beta_{KM} \ln \frac{P_{M2005}}{P_{M1960}} \right)$$

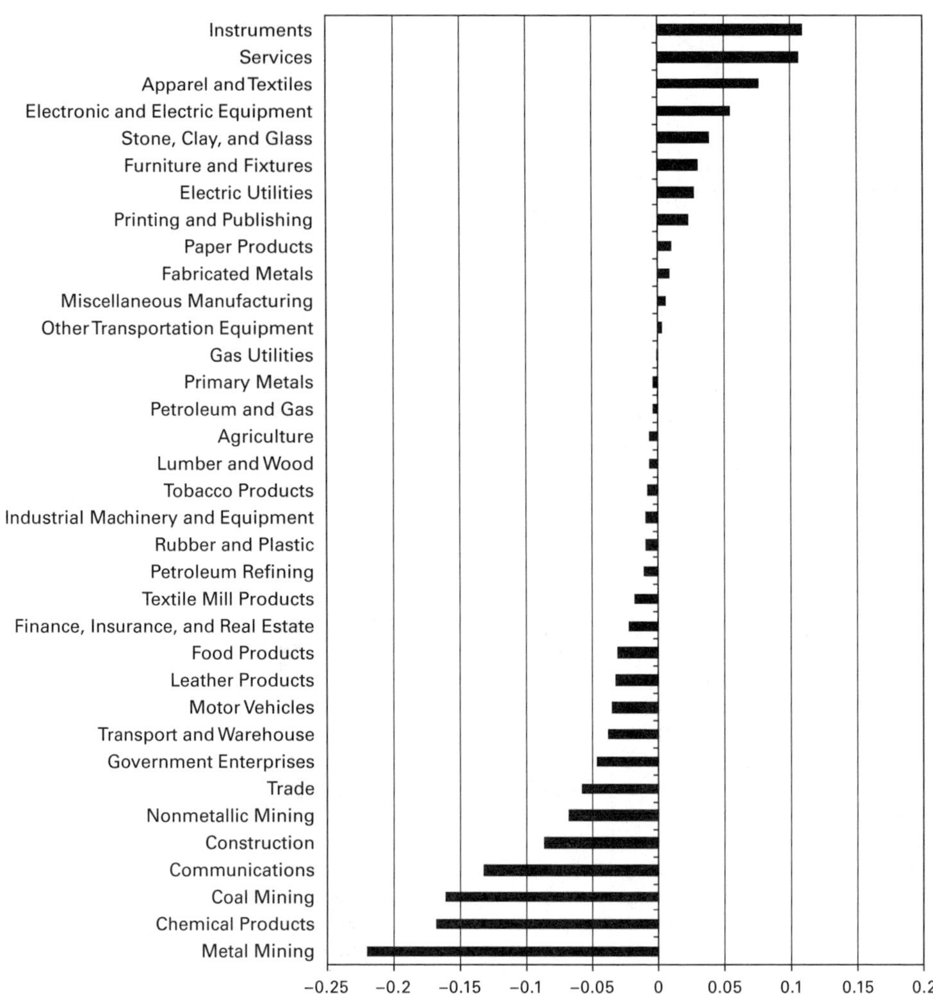

Figure 4.7
Price effect of labor input share change, 1960–2005.

$$\sum_k \beta_{Lk} \Delta \ln P_{kt} = \left(\beta_{LK} \ln \frac{P_{K2005}}{P_{K1960}} + \beta_{LL} \ln \frac{P_{L2005}}{P_{L1960}} + \beta_{LE} \ln \frac{P_{E2005}}{P_{E1960}} + \beta_{LM} \ln \frac{P_{M2005}}{P_{M1960}} \right)$$

Figure 4.8
Price effect of energy input share change, 1960–2005.

$$\sum_k \beta_{Ek} \Delta \ln P_{kt} = \left(\beta_{EK} \ln \frac{P_{K2005}}{P_{K1960}} + \beta_{EL} \ln \frac{P_{L2005}}{P_{L1960}} + \beta_{EE} \ln \frac{P_{E2005}}{P_{E1960}} + \beta_{EM} \ln \frac{P_{M2005}}{P_{M1960}} \right)$$

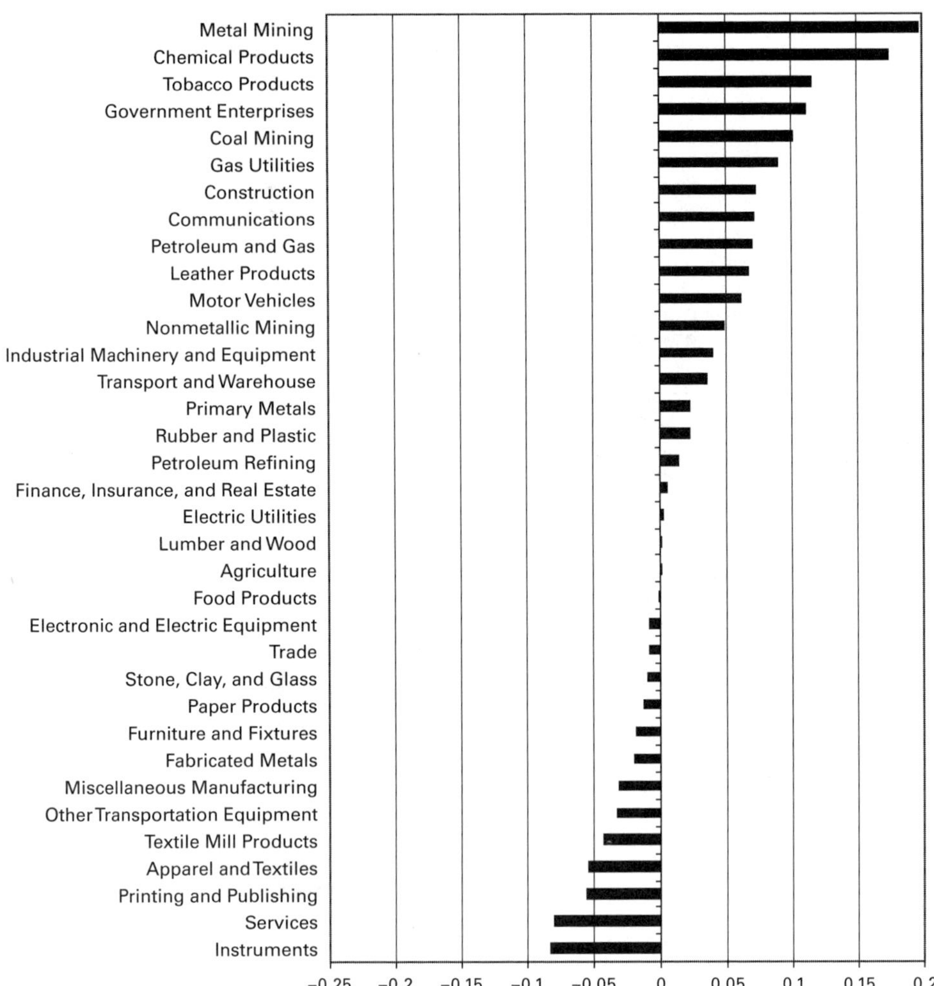

Figure 4.9
Price effect of material input share change, 1960–2005.

$$\sum_k \beta_{Mk}\Delta \ln P_{kt} = \left(\beta_{MK}\ln\frac{P_{K2005}}{P_{K1960}} + \beta_{ML}\ln\frac{P_{L2005}}{P_{L1960}} + \beta_{ME}\ln\frac{P_{E2005}}{P_{E1960}} + \beta_{MM}\ln\frac{P_{M2005}}{P_{M1960}}\right)$$

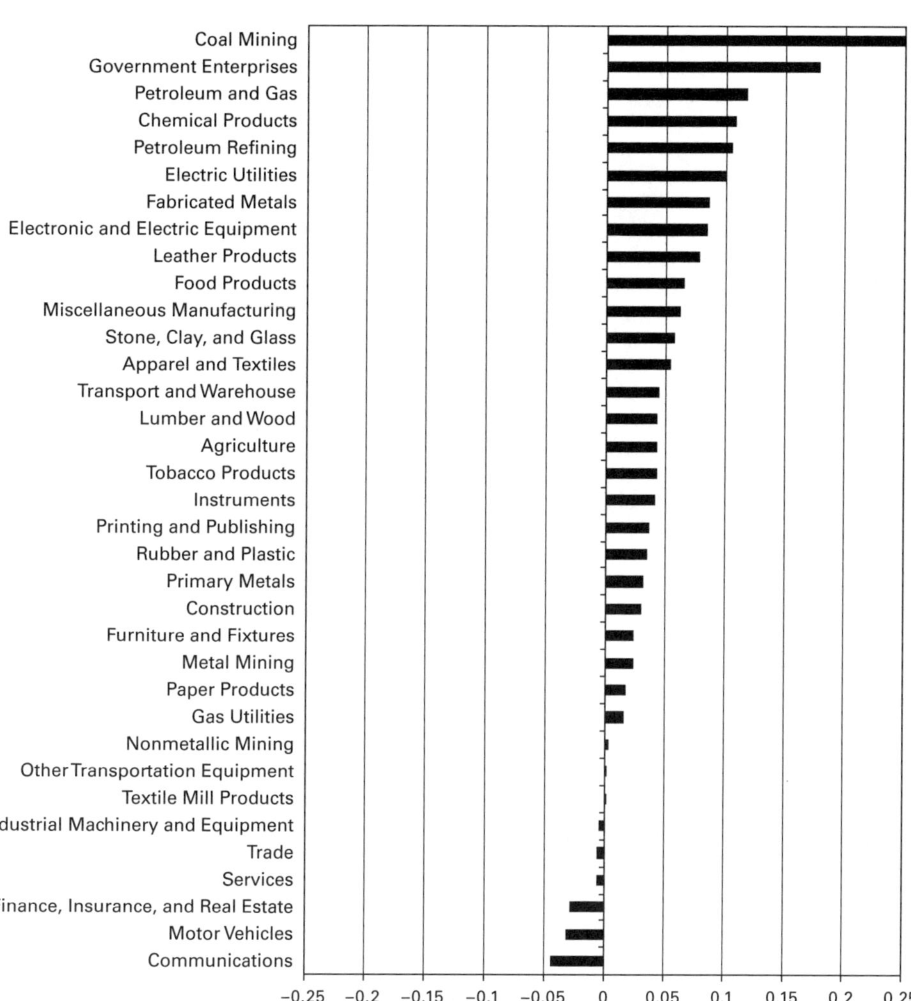

Figure 4.10
Bias of technical change for capital input, 1960–2005. $f^{P}_{K,2005} - f^{P}_{K,1960}$

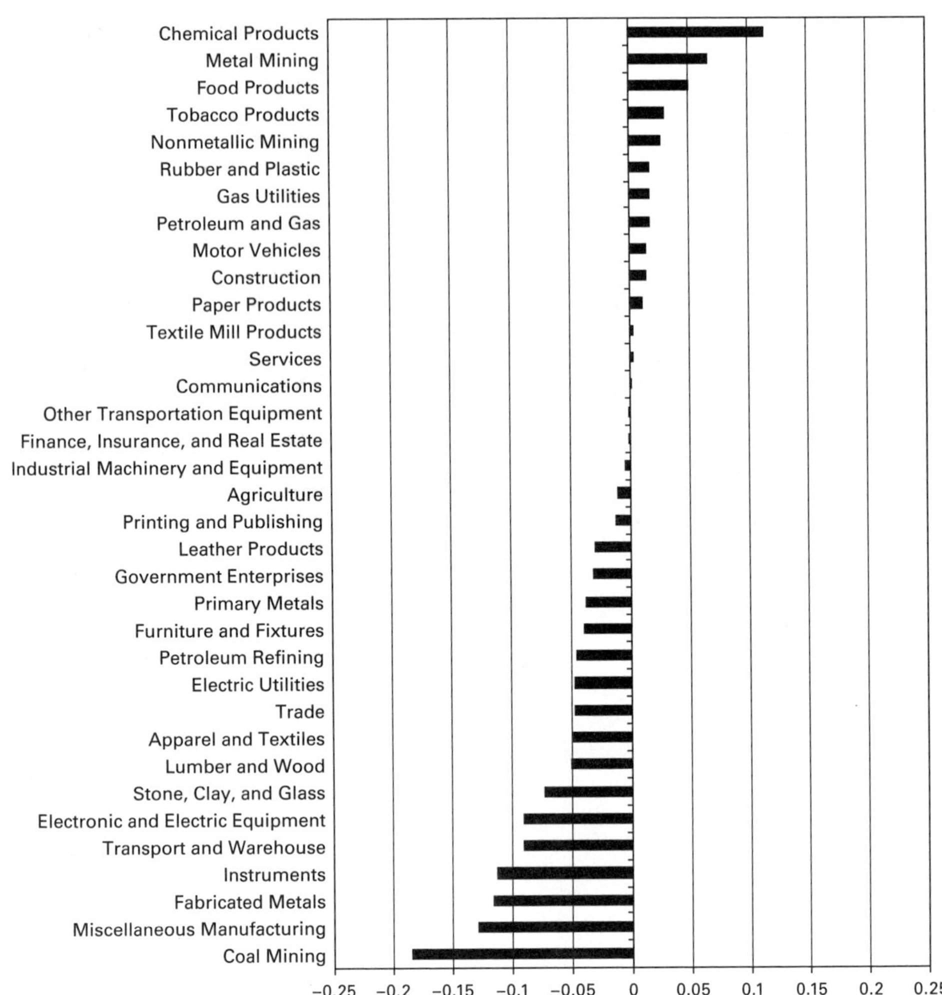

Figure 4.11
Bias of technical change for labor input, 1960–2005. $f^P_{L,2005} - f^P_{L,1960}$

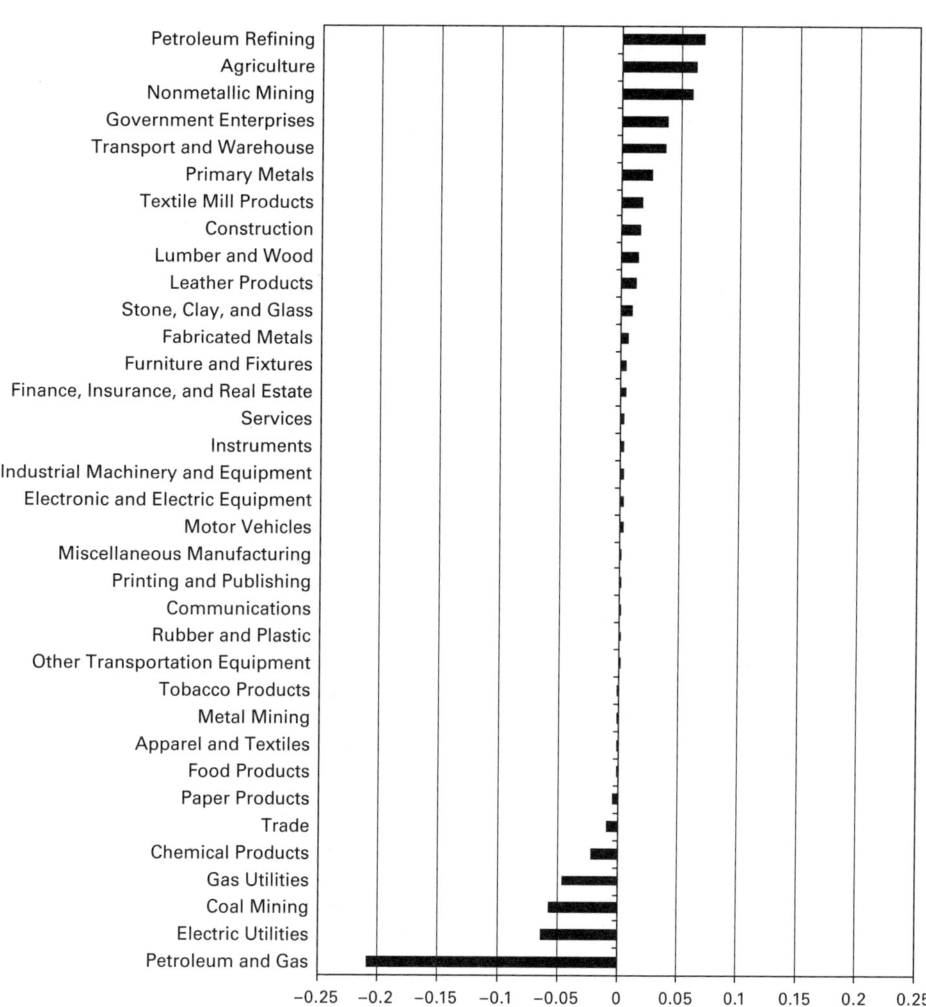

Figure 4.12
Bias of technical change for energy input, 1960–2005. $f^{P}_{E,2005} - f^{P}_{E,1960}$

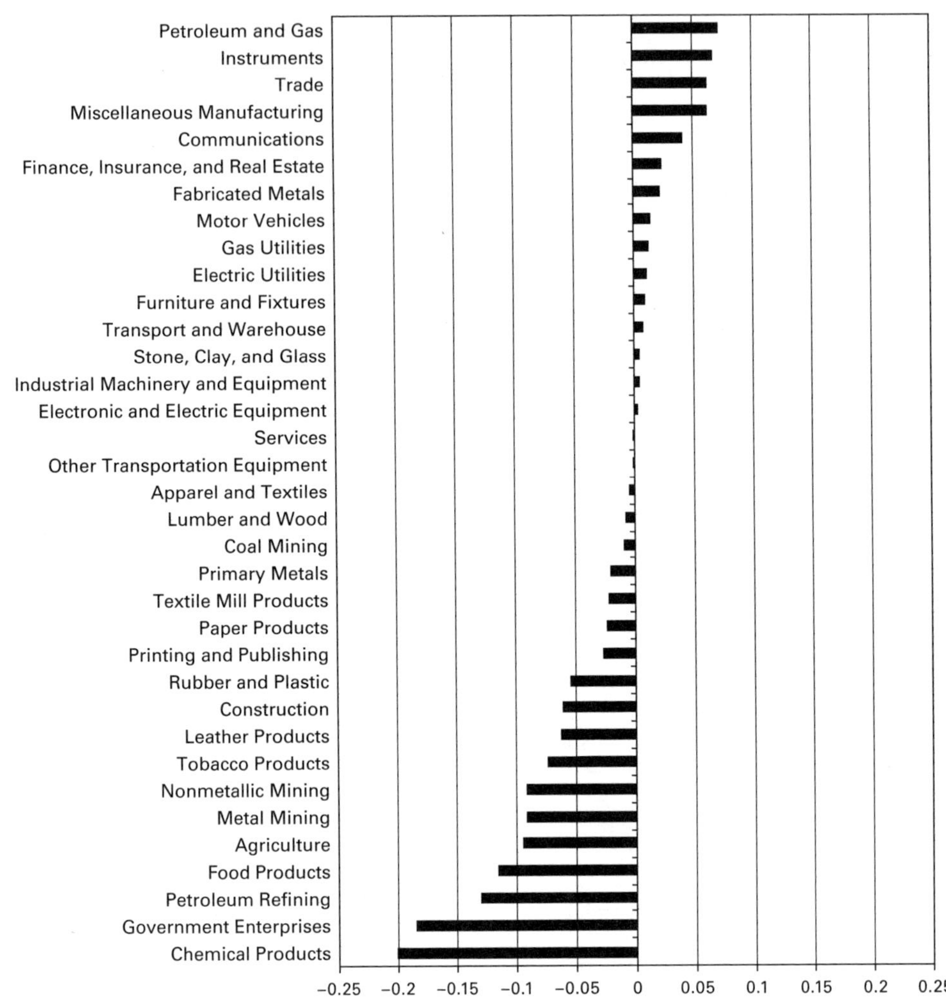

Figure 4.13
Bias of technical change for material input, 1960–2005. $f^P_{M,2005} - f^P_{M,1960}$

output and its decomposition into a price effect, corresponding to the second and third terms in (4.4), and the rates of induced and autonomous technical change in (4.6).

Figure 4.14 presents reductions in the logarithms of prices of the outputs of the 35 industries, relative to the prices of materials inputs in each sector. For example, large positive values represent substantial reductions in prices. Not surprisingly, these price changes are almost evenly divided between positive and negative values with the large reductions for Electronic and Electrical Equipment and Industrial Machinery and Equipment as the outstanding exceptions. The Electronic and Electrical Equipment industry produces semiconductor components for computers and other electronic equipment, while Industrial Machinery and Equipment includes computers. Technical change has resulted in a very dramatic fall in the prices of outputs for these industries, relative to the materials they consume.

We decompose the output price reductions represented in figure 4.14 into three parts—the price effects, the induced technical change, and the autonomous technical change:

$$\begin{aligned}
-(\ln PO_{jt} - \ln PO_{j,t-1}) = -\Bigg\{ & \sum_i \alpha_i^{Pj} (\ln p_{it} - \ln p_{i,t-1}) \\
& + \frac{1}{2} \sum_{i,k} \beta_{ik}^{Pj} (\ln p_{it} \ln p_{kt} - \ln p_{it-1} \ln p_{kt-1}) \\
& + \sum_i (\ln p_{it} - \ln p_{i,t-1}) f_{it}^{Pj} \Bigg\} \\
& - \sum_i \ln p_{i,t-1} (f_{it}^{Pj} - f_{i,t-1}^{Pj}) - (f_t^j - f_{t-1}^j). \qquad (4.27)
\end{aligned}$$

The price effects presented in figure 4.15 are differences between the price reductions in figure 4.14 and the rates of technical change in (4.7); that is, the first curly bracketed term on the right of (4.27). These price effects result from substitution among inputs and are dominated by increases in wage rates, relative to prices of materials inputs. The contribution of induced technical change, corresponding to the first term in (4.7), is given by second term on the right of (4.27). The contribution of the rate of autonomous technical change, corresponding to the second term in (4.7), is represented by the last term in (4.27).

The rates of autonomous technical change given in figure 4.17 are predominantly positive and substantial in magnitude. Electronic and Electric Equipment leads all other industries with a rate of autonomous technical change that exceeds even the very dramatic rate of decline

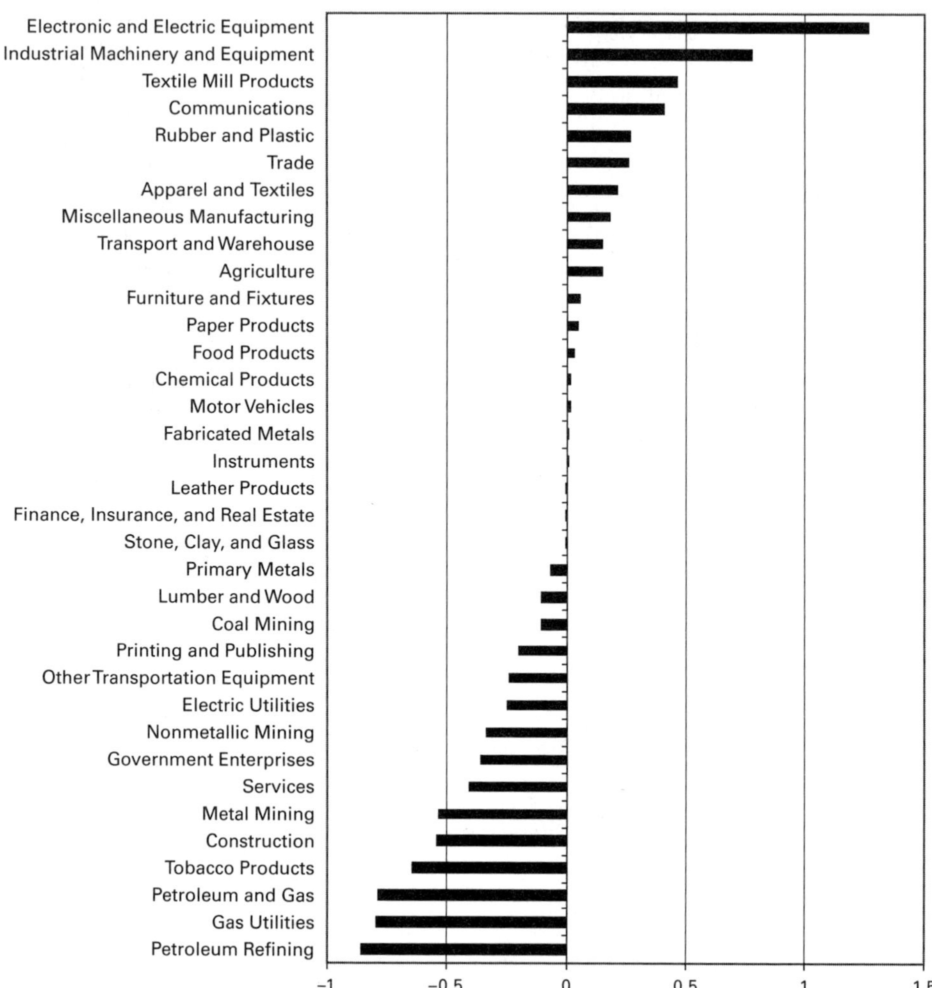

Figure 4.14
Reduction of log relative output price, 1960–2005. $-\ln\left(\frac{PO_{j2005}}{P_{Mj2005}} - \ln\frac{PO_{j1960}}{P_{Mj1960}}\right)$

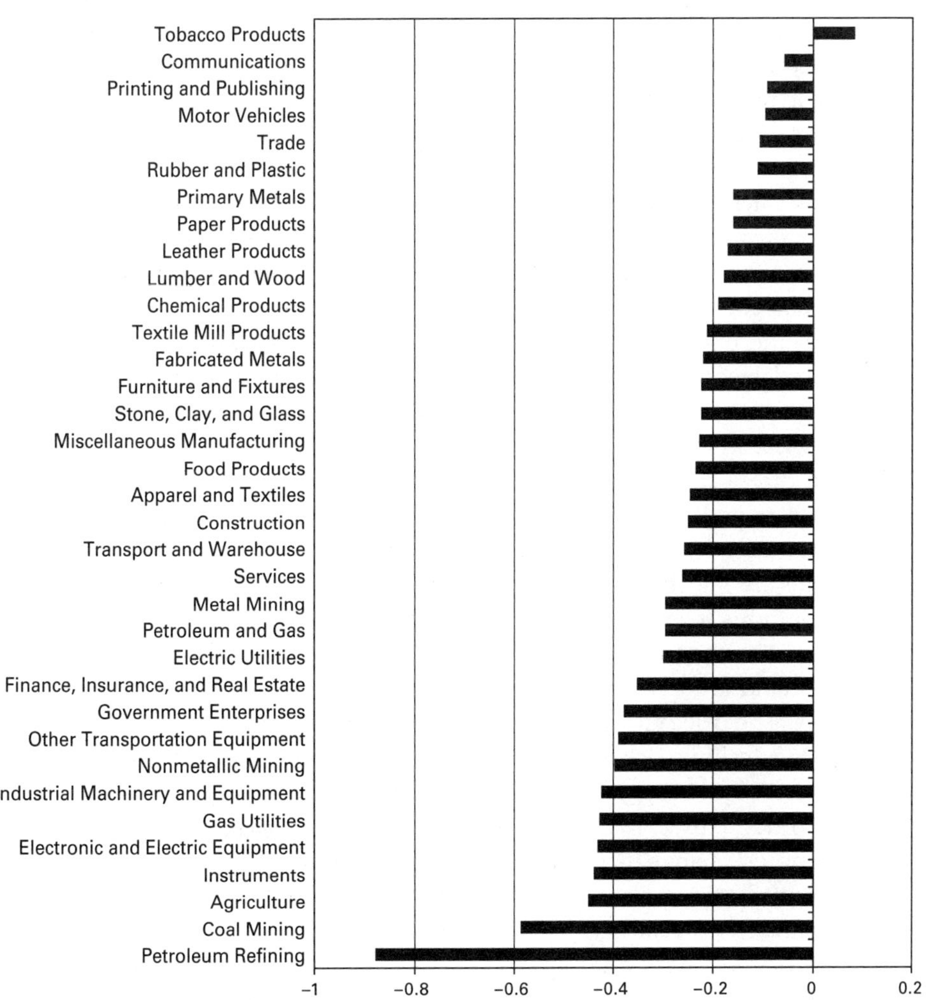

Figure 4.15
Price effects for log relative output price change, 1960–2005.

$$-\left\{ \sum_{i=KLEM} \alpha_i^{Pj}(\ln p_{i2005} - \ln p_{i1960}) + \frac{1}{2}\sum_{i,k} \beta_{ik}^{Pj}(\ln p_{i2005} \ln p_{k2005} - \ln p_{i1960} \ln p_{k1960}) + \sum_{t=1961}^{2005} \sum_{i=KLEM} (\ln p_{it} - \ln p_{i,t-1}) f_{it}^{Pj} \right\}$$

of the relative price of the industry's output. Industrial Machinery and Equipment, the industry that includes computers, has the second largest rate of autonomous technical change. The Tobacco Products industry and Gas Utilities have sizable negative rates of autonomous technical change.

The rates of induced technical change in figure 4.16, corresponding to the second term on the right of (4.27), depend on the correlations between prices of inputs and biases of technical change. If this correlation is negative, input-using technical change corresponds to low input prices and input-saving change to high input prices, so that the rate of induced technical change is positive. The rates of induced technical change presented in figure 4.16 show more negative changes than positive ones, so that input-using technical change is correlated with high input prices and input-saving technical change with low input prices.

Our overall conclusion from the empirical results presented in figures 4.14–4.17 is that rates of autonomous and induced technical change are substantial in magnitude and opposite in sign. However, autonomous technical change predominates, so that rates of technical change are positive for most industries. Rates of technical change are large relative to the price effects associated with substitution among inputs. The price effects exert upward pressure on output prices while induced technical change exerts pressure in the same direction, but both are offset by positive rates of autonomous technical change.

In order to explore changes in the direction and magnitude of biases in technical change in greater detail, we subdivide the biases for energy input into two subperiods—1960–1980 in figure 4.18 and 1980–2005 in figure 4.19. Recall that the biases of technical change are first differences of the latent variables, as in (4.6). In figures 4.18 and 4.19 the biases are both energy-saving and energy-using for the seven most intensive energy-using sectors during the sample period—Petroleum Refining; Electric and Gas Utilities; Transportation and Warehousing; Coal Mining; Chemical Products; and Stone, Clay, and Glass. These changes in the bias of technical change would have been concealed by constant time trends.

There is a common pattern of energy-using change from 1960 to 1980 and energy-saving change from 1980 to 2005, except for a few industries such as Metal Mining, Petroleum Refining, and Agriculture. The turning point was the Second Oil Crisis, when energy prices reached their postwar peaks in real terms. We conclude that high energy prices after 1980 are correlated with energy-saving change, while low energy

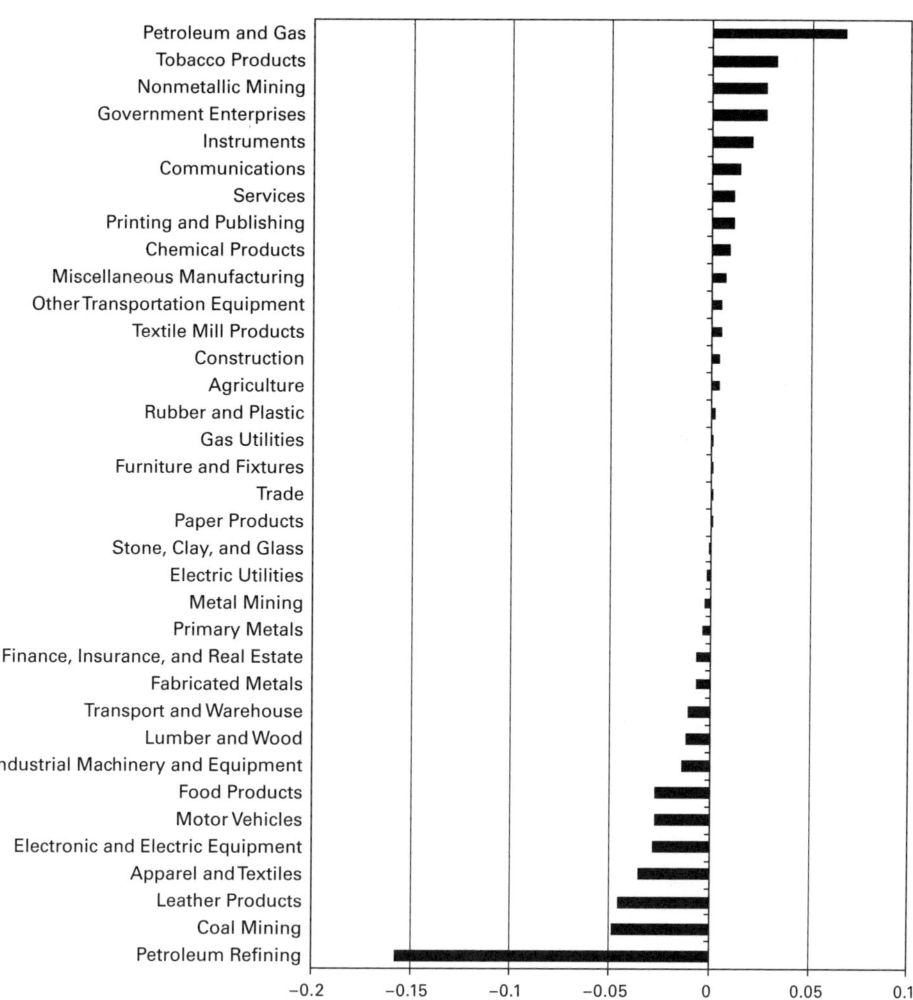

Figure 4.16
Rate of induced technical change, 1960–2005. $-\sum_{t=1961}^{2005}\sum_{i=KLEM}\ln p_{i,t-1}(f_{it}^{Pj}-f_{i,t-1}^{Pj})$

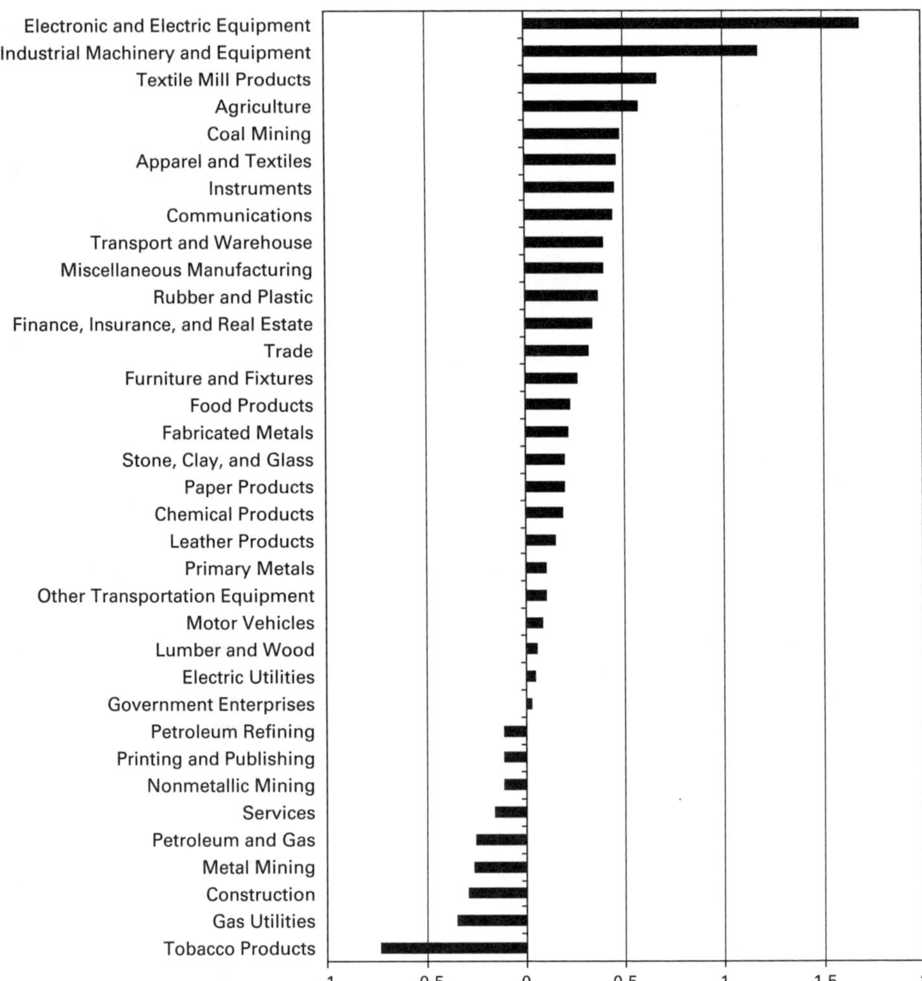

Figure 4.17
Rate of autonomous technical change, 1960–2005. $-(f_{2005} - f_{1960})$

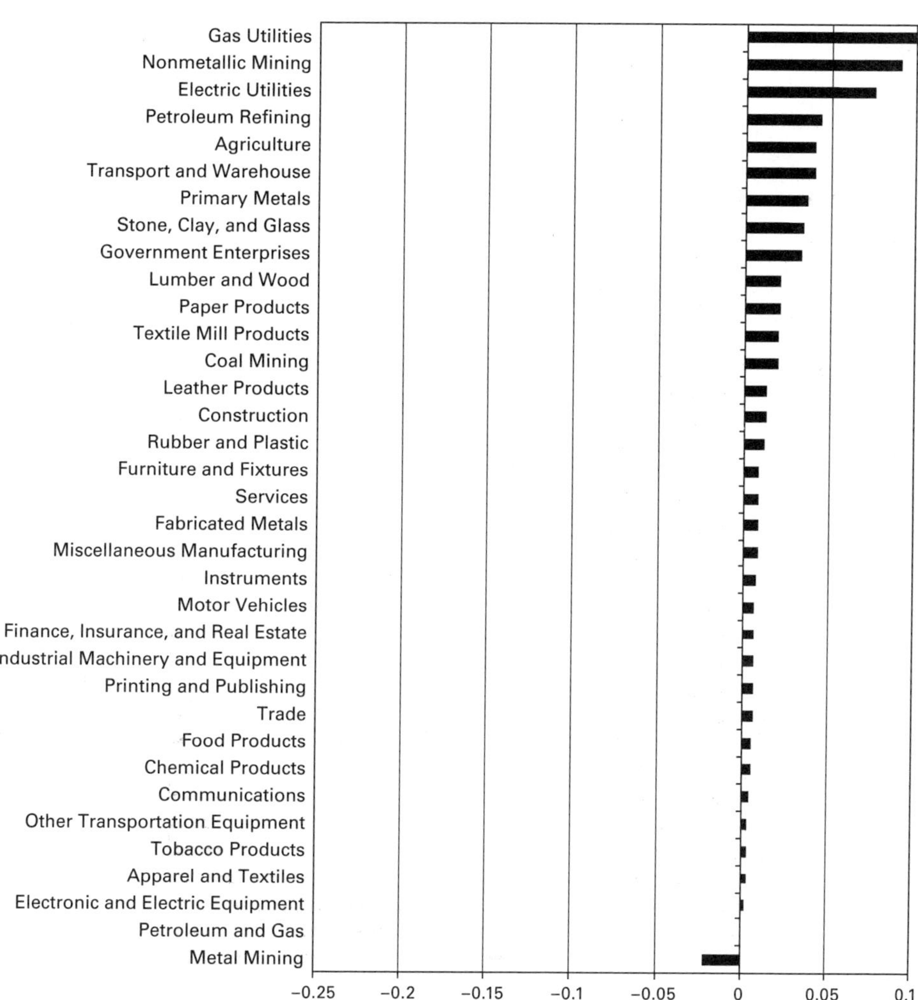

Figure 4.18
Bias of technical change for energy input, 1960–1980. $f^P_{E,1980} - f^P_{E,1960}$

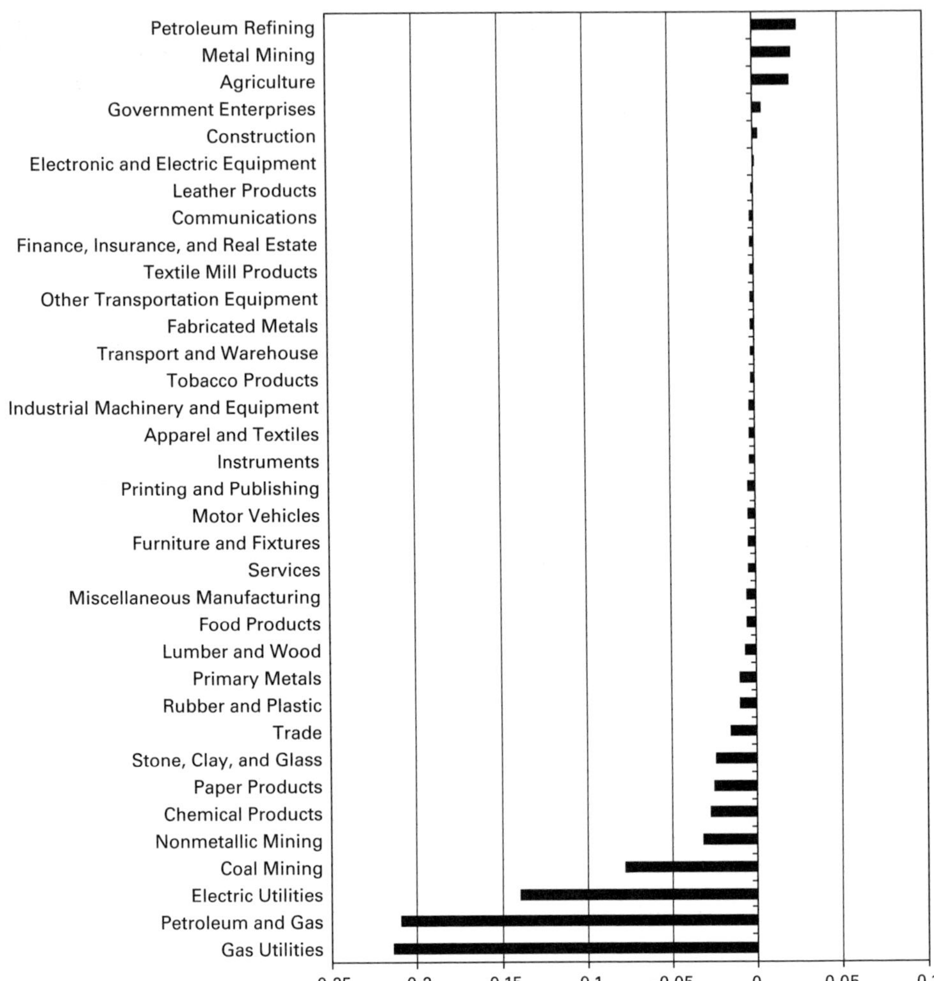

Figure 4.19
Bias of technical change for energy input, 1980–2005. $f^P_{E,2005} - f^P_{E,1980}$

prices before 1980 are correlated with energy-using change. This pattern would also have been concealed by constant time trends.

The latent variables f_{it} converge to constants, so that biases of technical change corresponding to changes in these variables converge to zero. In figure 4.20 we present projections of the biases of technical change for energy for the period 2006–2030. Note that the projected biases for the seven most energy-intensive industries are not simple extrapolations of the trends toward energy conservation we have identified after 1980. Projected biases are energy-saving for Electric Utilities, Petroleum Mining, Coal Mining, and Transportation and Warehousing. However, projected biases are energy-using for Gas Utilities, Agriculture, and Paper Products. As before, these projections are inconsistent with the constant time trends in Binswanger's approach.

In figures 4.21–4.23 we give projections of biases of technical change for capital, labor, and materials for the period 2006–2030. These projections are not simple extrapolations of biases during the sample period and many alternate between input-using and input-saving bias, as we noted for the particularly pronounced differences in the case of energy input. For example, in Transportation and Warehousing, we observed a labor-saving bias during the sample period 1960–2005 but project a labor-using bias for the 2006–2030 period. We conclude that the latent variables representing biases of technical change must be sufficiently flexible to capture variations between input-using and input-saving technical change.

The levels of technology f_t converge to linear trends, corresponding to constant rates of autonomous technical change. Recalling that we employ the dual representation of technology (4.4), falling trends correspond to positive rates of technical change, while rising trends represent negative rates. In figures 4.24 and 4.25 we give projections of the rates of induced and autonomous technical change. Rates of induced technical change are relatively small in magnitude and are evenly divided between positive and negative values. Rates of autonomous technical change are predominantly positive in sign and substantial in magnitude. The projections for Electronic and Electric Equipment, including semiconductors, have very rapid rates of technical change. Projected rates of technical change for Industrial Machinery and Equipment, including computers, are the next most rapid, also extrapolating trends during the sample period. Negative rates of autonomous technical change are substantial in magnitude for Petroleum and Gas Mining and Tobacco Products.

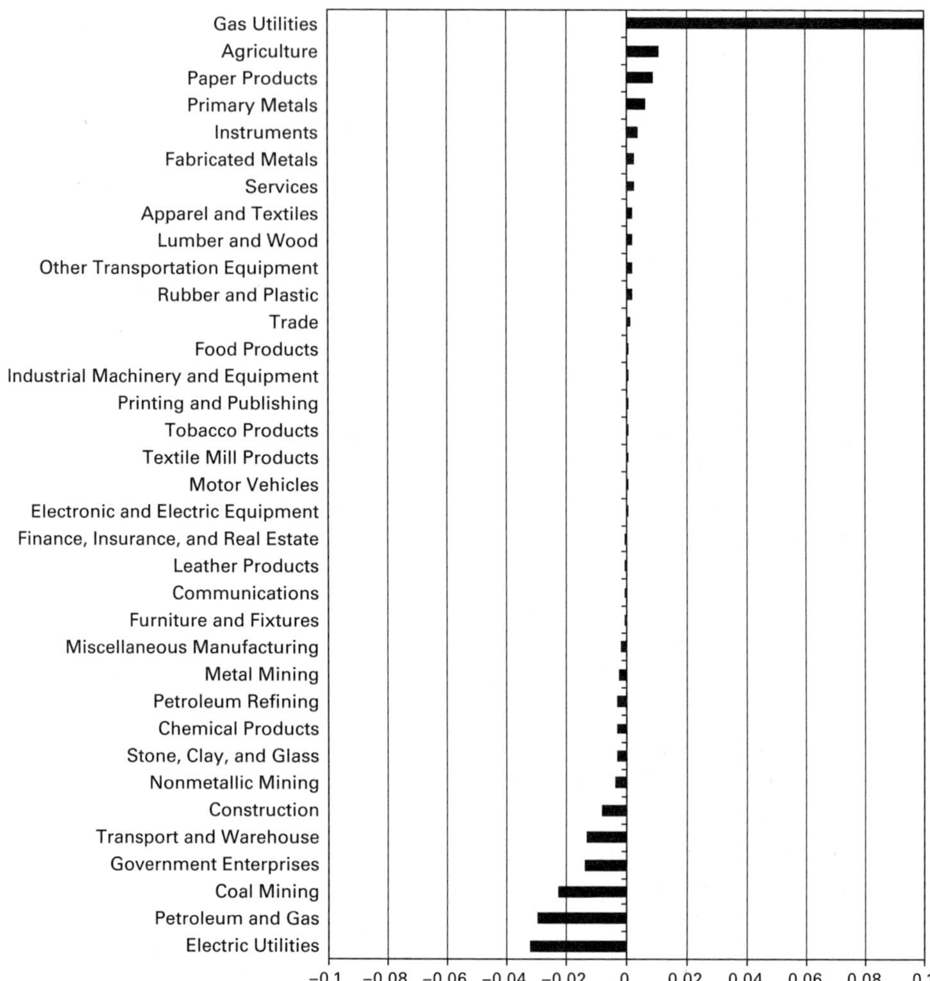

Figure 4.20
Projection of the bias of technical change for energy input, 2005–2030. $f^P_{E,2030} - f^P_{E,2005}$

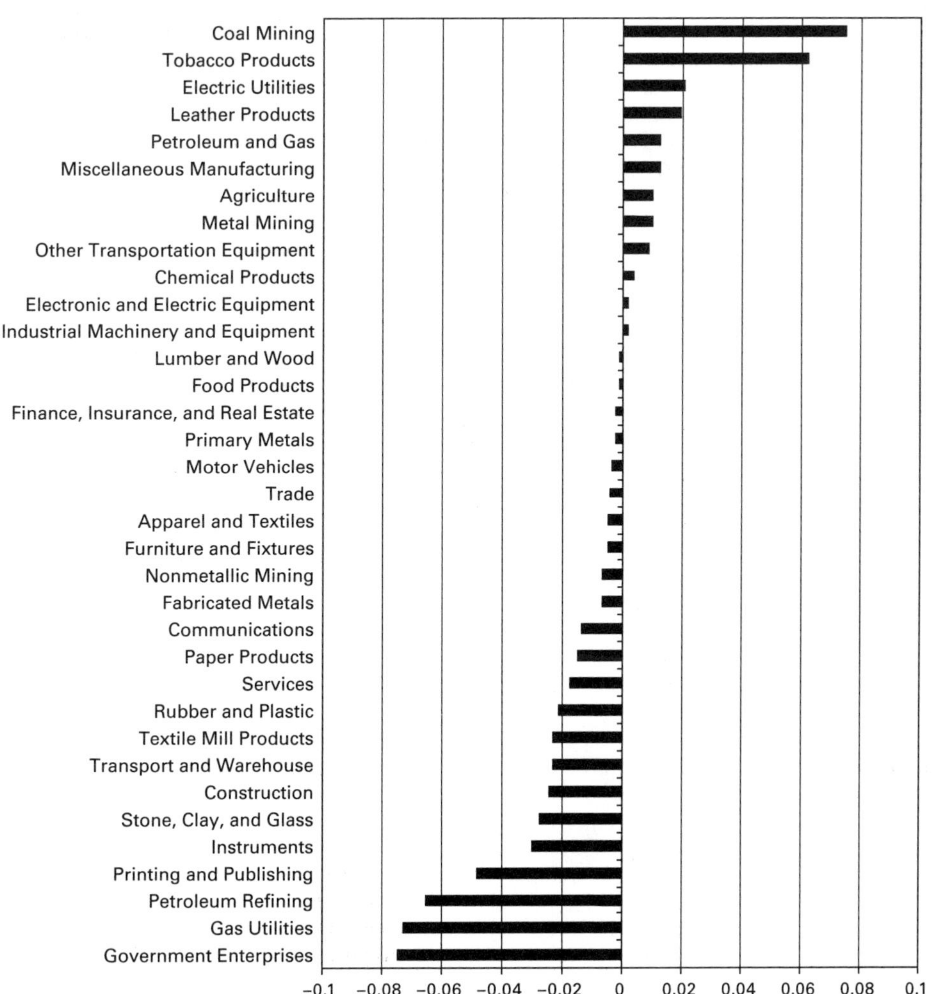

Figure 4.21
Projection of the bias of technical change for capital input, 2005–2030. $f^P_{K,2030} - f^P_{K,2005}$

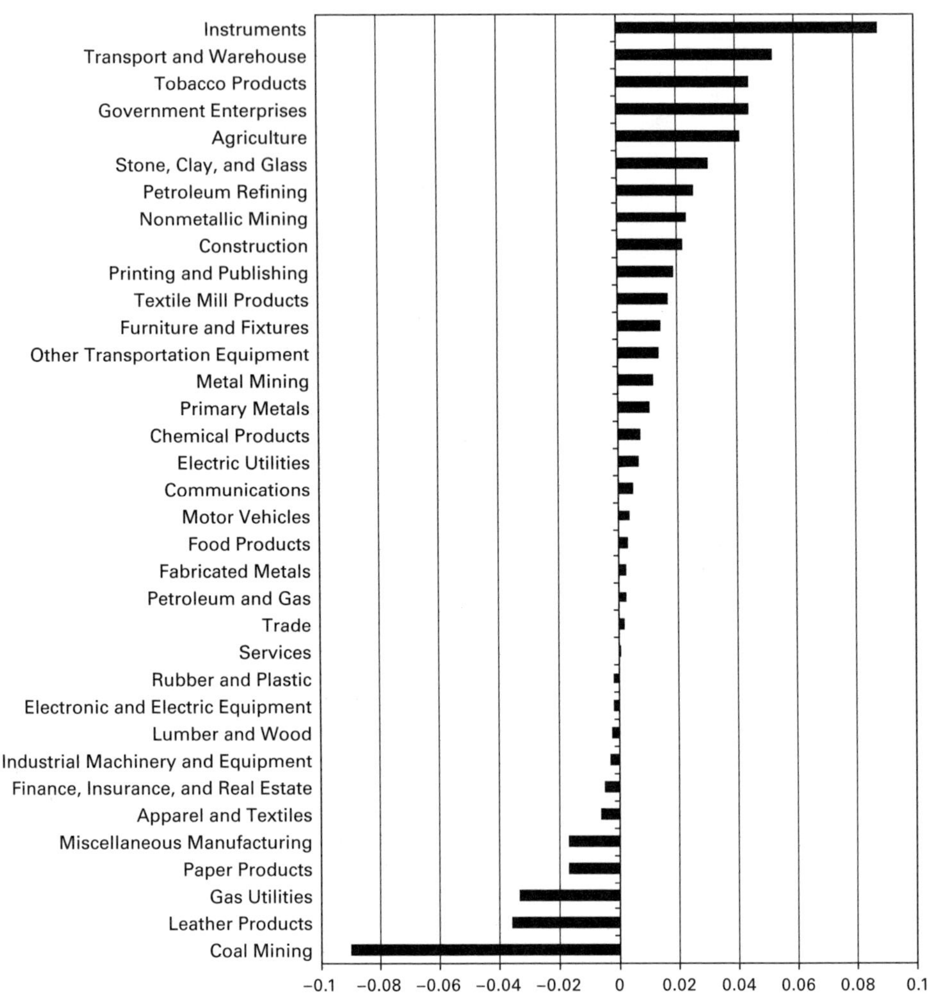

Figure 4.22
Projection of the bias of technical change for labor input, 2005–2030. $f^P_{L,2030} - f^P_{L,2005}$

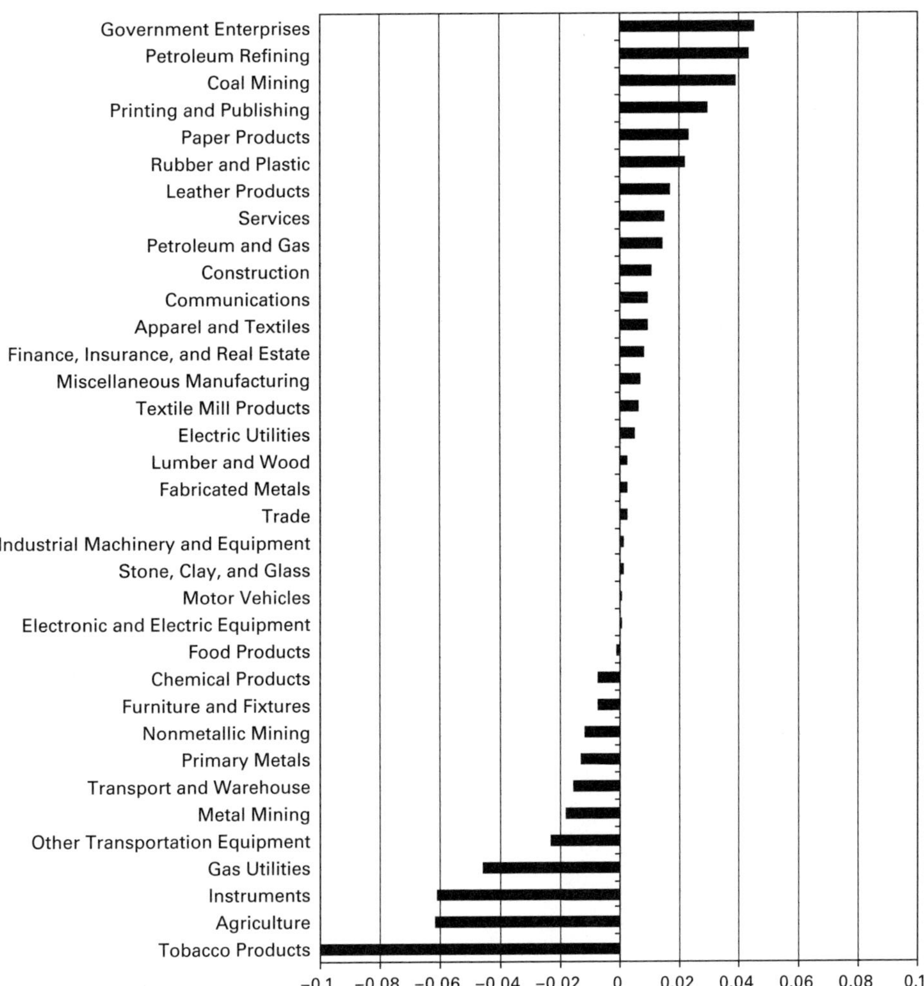

Figure 4.23
Projection of the bias of technical change for material input, 2005–2030. $f^P_{M,2030} - f^P_{M,2005}$

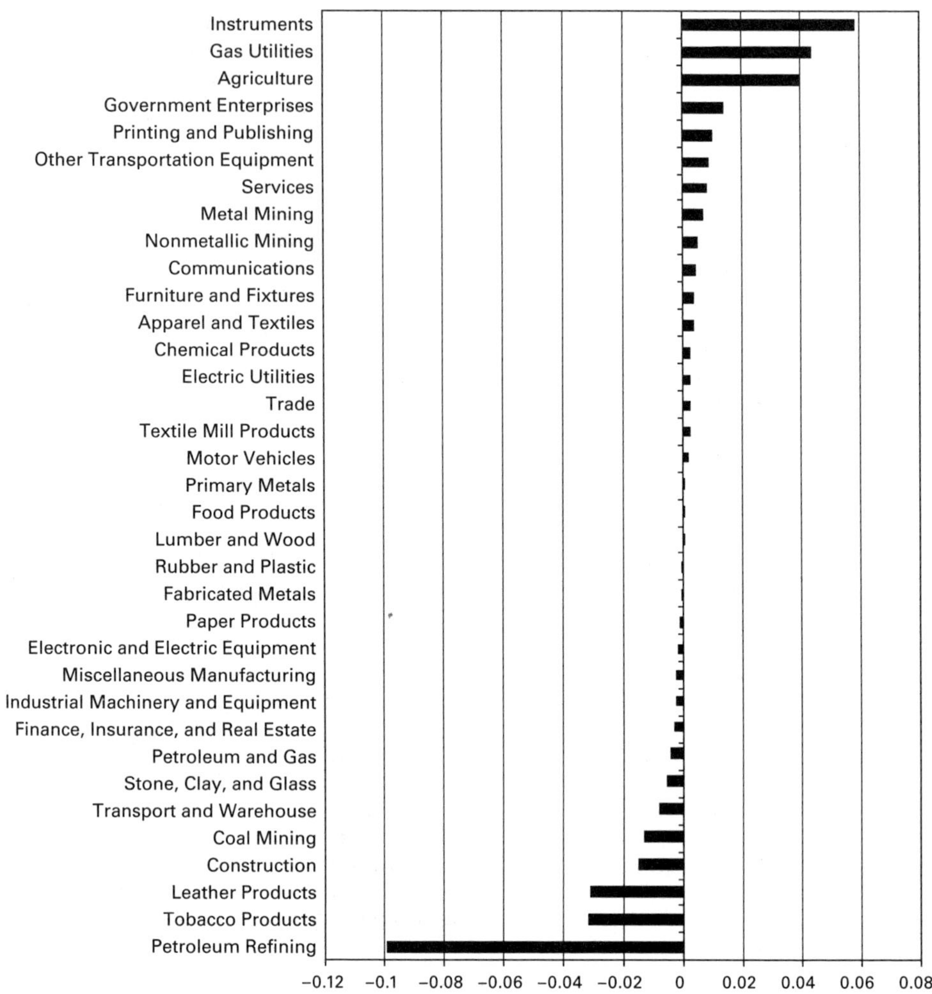

Figure 4.24
Projected rate of induced technical change, 2005–2030.

$$-\left[\ln\frac{P_{KT}}{P_{MT}}(f_{K2030}-f_{K2005})+\ln\frac{P_{LT}}{P_{MT}}(f_{L2030}-f_{L2005})+\ln\frac{P_{ET}}{P_{MT}}(f_{E2030}-f_{E2005})\right]$$

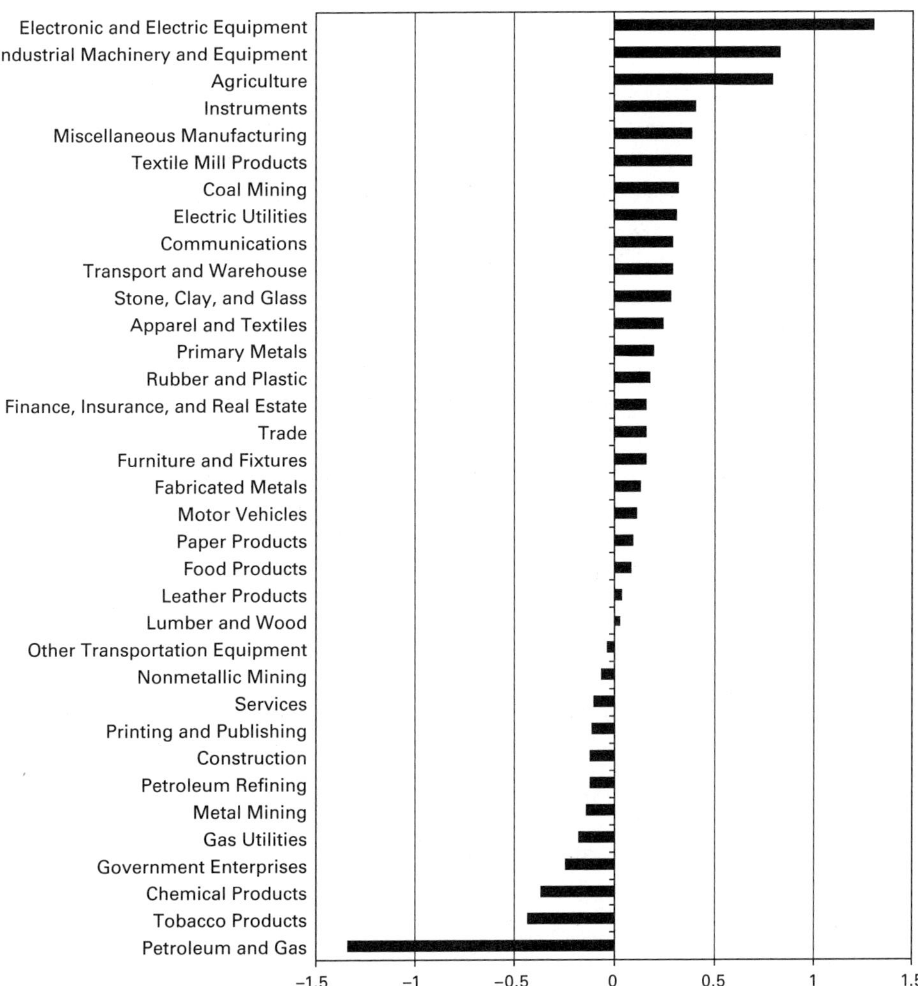

Figure 4.25
Projected rate of autonomous technical change, 2005–2030. $-(f_{2030} - f_{2005})$

4.6 Allocating Energy and Materials

The industry production model we have discussed determines demands for capital, labor, energy, and materials (KLEM) inputs. Our next task is to model the allocation of energy and materials aggregates among the 35 individual commodities. These commodities are the primary products of the 35 sectors and noncomparable imports. The demands for these commodities are derived from a hierarchical tier structure of price functions.

The tier structure for our production model is given in table 2.2 of chapter 2. There is a total of 13 nodes, including the top tier we have already described. The energy node is part of the second tier and determines the allocation of energy input to crude oil and natural gas, coal, refined petroleum products, electricity, and deliveries from gas utilities. The remaining 11 nodes allocate non-energy materials to the 30 commodity groups and noncomparable imports. This involves a hierarchical tier structure with 11 nodes.

As an example, the value of energy input is the sum of the values of five components—coal, crude petroleum and natural gas, refined petroleum products, electricity, and deliveries from gas utilities. Denoting the energy industries by $I_E = \{3, 4, 16, 30, 31\}$, the value of energy input is the product of price and quantity for each industry j:

$$P_{Ejt}E_{jt} = PS_{3t}QP^j_{3t} + PS_{4t}QP^j_{4t} + PS_{16t}QP^j_{16t} + PS_{30t}QP^j_{30t} + PS_{31t}QP^j_{31t} \tag{4.28}$$

and the price function takes the form

$$\ln P_{Et} = \alpha_0 + \sum_{i \in I_E} \alpha_i^E \ln P_{it}^{P,E} + \frac{1}{2}\sum_{i,k} \beta_{ik}^E \ln P_{it}^{P,E} \ln P_{kt}^{P,E} + \sum_{i \in I_E} f_{it}^E \ln P_{it}^{P,E} \tag{4.29}$$

where the input prices are denoted $P_i^{P,E} = \{PS_3, PS_4, PS_{16}, PS_{30}, PS_{31}\}$, the latent variables generating biases of technical change are denoted $\{f_{it}^E\}$ and the industry superscripts have been dropped for simplicity. Note that there is no latent variable for the level of technology, since the price of energy input is a function of the five energy input prices.

The input share equations are derived by differentiating the price function (2.11) with respect to the logarithms of prices. In matrix notation the vector of input shares for the energy node example is written

$$v_t^E = \begin{bmatrix} PS_3QP_3 / P_EE \\ \cdots \\ PS_{31}QP_{31} / P_EE \end{bmatrix} = \alpha^E + B^E \ln P^{P,E} + f_t^E. \tag{4.30}$$

We construct a similar system of equations for each node of the hierarchical tier structure of price functions for each industry.

The latent variables describing biases of technical change are a novel feature of IGEM. In the historical data we observe changes in the composition of inputs that cannot be explained by price changes. The latent variables representing biases of technical change are assumed to follow a first-order VAR for each *node* and each industry *j*:

$$\begin{aligned} \xi_t^{node,j} &= F^{node,j}\xi_{t-1}^{node,j} + \varepsilon_t^{node,j} \quad node = 2,\ldots,13;\ j = 1,\ldots,35 \\ \xi_t^{node} &\equiv (f_{1t}^{node},\ldots,f_{nt}^{node})'. \end{aligned} \tag{4.31}$$

Our econometric methodology for estimating the parameters of the system of equations (4.30) and (4.31) is analogous to that discussed for the top tier. Homogeneity, symmetry, and concavity restrictions are imposed in a similar way:

$$\begin{aligned} &\sum_i \alpha_i^E = 1 \quad \sum_i \beta_{ik}^E = 0 \quad \text{for each } k; \\ &\beta_{ik}^E = \beta_{ki}^E; \\ &L_t D_t L_t' = B + v_t v_t' - V_t; \quad D_{ii,t} < 0. \end{aligned} \tag{4.32}$$

As a consequence of these restrictions, we estimate only four of the five equations for the input shares in the energy node, and use four relative prices.

In order to estimate the unknown parameters and the latent variables, we apply the two-step Kalman filter given above. For the energy node where we estimate four share equations and the VAR generating the latent variables, we implement this by making the following definitions:

$$y_t = \begin{bmatrix} v_{3t}^E \\ \vdots \\ v_{30t}^E \end{bmatrix}; \quad x_t = \begin{bmatrix} 1 \\ \ln\dfrac{PS_{3t}}{PS_{31t}} \\ \vdots \\ \ln\dfrac{PS_{30t}}{PS_{31t}} \end{bmatrix}; \quad \xi_t = \begin{bmatrix} 1 \\ f_{3t}^E \\ \vdots \\ f_{30t}^E \end{bmatrix}; \quad w_t = \begin{bmatrix} \varepsilon_{3t}^{Ev} \\ \vdots \\ \varepsilon_{30t}^{Ev} \end{bmatrix}; \quad \varepsilon_t = \begin{bmatrix} 0 \\ \varepsilon_{3t}^E \\ \varepsilon_{7t}^E \end{bmatrix}. \tag{4.33}$$

The instrumental variables used to deal with the endogeneity of the prices are the same as those used in the top tier.

For many of our nodes some inputs are zero for many industries. For example, the output of Metal Mining is used by only a few industries. For the remaining industries the parameters for Metal Mining are set equal to zero. Where the inputs are very small, estimation becomes difficult and we set the relevant parameters equal to zero. Ignoring the parameters of the state equation, there are 13 nodes in the hierarchical tier structure shown in table 2.2, yielding a total of 164 parameters. Of these, 106 are independent after imposing the homogeneity and symmetry constraints. Ignoring the parameters set equal to zero, there is a total 3710 parameters (106 × 35 industries) to be estimated for the production model as a whole.

It is difficult to summarize the large number of parameters and latent variables representing biases of technical change succinctly, so that we consider only a few of the most important features. To give a sense of the estimates and the issues involved, we focus on the Electric Utilities industry. In table 4.8 we report the estimated coefficients for all 13 subtiers of this industry. The structure of this table and abbreviations follow that in table 2.2. We first note the wide range of estimates for the share elasticities among the intermediate inputs. This implies that the Leontief framework, imposing fixed input-output coefficients, is far too inflexible and imposes an artificially high welfare cost for policy changes.

To visualize the role played by the latent variables f_{it}^{node} in tracking changes in demands not due to price effects, the last column in table 4.8 gives the change in these terms between 1960 and 2005. The value shares in (4.30) are additive in the latent variables f_{it}^{node}. The contribution of the bias of technical change is sizable in most cases. In the particular example of the Electric Utilities industry, intermediate input demand has shifted towards financial and other services at the expense of transportation, communications, and government enterprises. The latent variable f_{it}^{OS} for communications fell by 0.07 during 1960–2005, a 7 percentage point fall in the value share, which stood at 60% in 1996.

The latent variables are projected for the simulation period. To illustrate the projection, figure 4.26 plots the latent variables f_{it}^{MS} for Transportation and Services in the Services Materials node (MS) for the Electric Utilities industry. The plots cover the estimated values during the sample period 1960–2005 and the projected values for 2006–2035. The 27 percentage point fall in the bias term for Transportation is a steady decline through the late 1990s, followed by stable share. The trend for Services is almost the exact opposite, rising substantially in the 1960–1998 period. The other inputs in this node—Trade, FIRE, and Other Services—have small changes and are not plotted in figure 4.5.

Table 4.8
Estimates of production functions in subtier structure of Electric Utilities

Node		Name	α_i	β_{ik}					Δf_{it} 1960–2005
1	Q	Gross output							
2	E	Energy							
		Coal	0.364	–0.065	0.065	–0.040	–0.008	0.048	–0.106
		Oil Mining	0.198	0.065	0.051	–0.012	–0.029	–0.075	–0.052
		Refining	0.092	–0.040	–0.012	–0.003	0.023	0.031	0.180
		Electric Utilities	0.097	–0.008	–0.029	0.023	0.006	0.008	–0.024
		Gas Utilities	0.249	0.048	–0.075	0.031	0.008	–0.012	0.002
3	M	Materials							
		Construction	–0.035	–0.041	0.000	0.065	0.000	–0.024	–0.095
		Agriculture Materials	0.000	0.000	0.000	0.000	0.000	0.000	0.000
		Metallic Materials	0.014	0.065	0.000	–0.017	0.000	–0.048	0.015
		Nonmetallic Materials	0.000	0.000	0.000	0.000	0.000	0.000	0.000
		Services Materials	1.021	–0.024	0.000	–0.048	0.000	0.072	0.079
4	MA	Agriculture Materials							
		Agriculture	0.000	0.000	0.000	0.000	0.000	0.000	0.000
		Food	0.000	0.000	0.000	0.000	0.000	0.000	0.000
		Tobacco	0.000	0.000	0.000	0.000	0.000	0.000	0.000
		Textile—Apparel	0.000	0.000	0.000	0.000	0.000	0.000	0.000
		Wood—Paper	1.000	0.000	0.000	0.000	0.000	0.000	0.000

(continued)

Table 4.8 (continued)

Node		Name	α_i	β_{ik}					Δf_{it} 1960–2005
5	MM	Metallic Materials							
		FM	0.005	–0.043	0.015	0.028			–0.032
		MC	–0.289	0.015	0.082	–0.097			–0.003
		EQ	1.285	0.028	–0.097	0.069			0.035
6	MN	Nonmetallic Materials							
		Nonmetal Mining	0.000	0.000	0.000	0.000	0.000	0.000	0.000
		Chemicals	–0.148	0.000	0.069	–0.011	–0.058	0.000	–0.029
		Rubber—Plastics	0.252	0.000	–0.011	–0.116	0.127	0.000	0.045
		Stone—Clay—Glass	0.896	0.000	–0.058	0.127	–0.069	0.000	–0.016
		Misc. Mfg.	0.000	0.000	0.000	0.000	0.000	0.000	0.000
7	MS	Services Materials							
		Transportation	0.044	0.106	–0.047	–0.022	–0.028	–0.010	–0.274
		Trade	0.017	–0.047	0.077	–0.024	0.003	–0.009	–0.009
		FIRE	0.137	–0.022	–0.024	0.008	0.090	–0.052	0.052
		Services	0.866	–0.028	0.003	0.090	–0.111	0.046	0.244
		OS	–0.064	–0.010	–0.009	–0.052	0.046	0.024	–0.013
8	TA	Textile—Apparel							
		Textiles	1.081	–0.397	0.397	0.000			0.137
		Apparel	–0.081	0.397	–0.397	0.000			–0.137
		Leather	0.000	0.000	0.000	0.000			0.000

Table 4.8 (continued)

Node		Name	α_i	β_{ik}				Δf_{it} 1960–2005
9	WP	Wood—Paper						
		Lumber Wood	0.160	0.099	0.000	−0.055	−0.043	0.240
		Furniture	0.000	0.000	0.000	0.000	0.000	0.000
		Paper	−0.120	−0.055	0.000	0.061	−0.005	−0.065
		Printing	0.961	−0.043	0.000	−0.005	0.049	−0.175
10	OS	Other Services						
		Communications	0.851	−0.239	0.239	0.000		−0.074
		Govt. Enterp	0.149	0.239	−0.239	0.000		0.074
		Non-Comp. Imports	0.000	0.000	0.000	0.000		0.000
11	FM	Fab—Other Metals						
		Metal Mining	0.000	0.000	0.000	0.000		0.000
		Primary Metals	−0.068	0.000	0.183	−0.183		−0.048
		Fabricated Metals	1.068	0.000	−0.183	0.183		0.048
12	MC	Machinery Materials						
		Industrial Machinery	0.770	0.225	−0.225			−0.004
		Electrical Mach.	0.230	−0.225	0.225			0.004
13	EQ	Equipment						
		Motor Vehicles	−0.082	0.102	0.000	−0.102		0.194
		Other Transp Equip	0.000	0.000	0.000	0.000		0.000
		Instruments	1.082	−0.102	0.000	0.102		−0.194

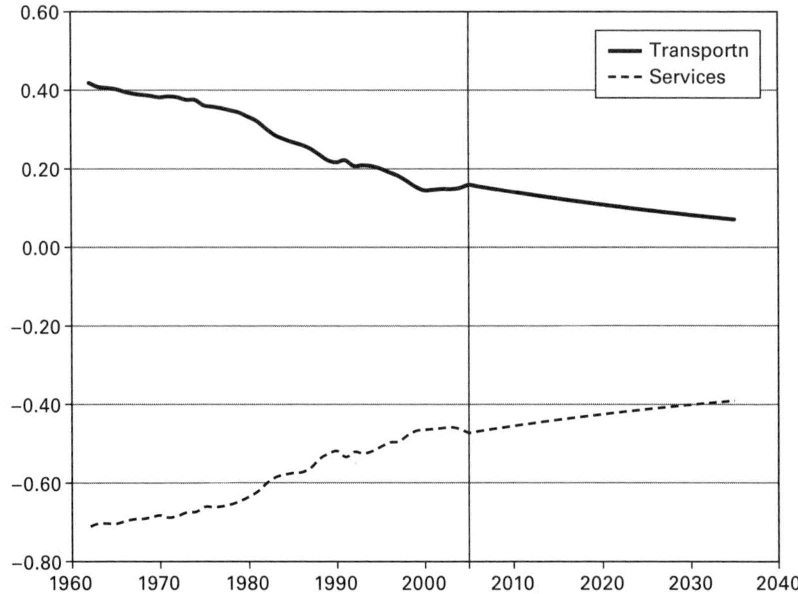

Figure 4.26
Latent bias terms for the Services Materials subtier of Electric Utilities; Transportation and Services inputs $f^{MS}_{Transp,t}$, $f^{MS}_{Services,t}$.

The complete set of projections of the latent terms in the subtiers is given in appendix C, table C3. Recall that the latent variables for the bias terms converge to a constant.

4.7 Summary and Conclusion

We have presented a new approach to econometric modeling of producer behavior. This combines a flexible representation of the responses of inputs to changes in prices with a state-space model of the rate and biases of technical change. The state-space model generates the rate and biases of technical change as latent variables. The latent variables supersede the fixed time trends employed in previous research. The empirical results reveal that biases of technical change may be input-saving or input-using for the same industry, which is inconsistent with fixed time trends.

Changes in the use of inputs are responsive to price changes as well as biases of technical change. Quantitatively, our results show that price changes and biases of technical change are equally important in accounting for changes in input use. The empirical evidence shows that the fixed coefficients approach of the Leontief framework is highly oversimplified and would result in gross overestimation of the cost of changes in energy and environmental policies. The Johansen approach, using constant value shares for capital and labor services, is an improvement. However, this is also strongly contradicted by historical evidence for the period 1960–2005.

Productivity growth accounts for only a modest portion of the sources of U.S. economic growth. However, this is vital to the long-run growth of the American economy. The state-space model also includes a latent variable representing the level of technology. This is essential for capturing differences in productivity growth rates across industries and over time. Fixed productivity growth rates like those employed in the Johansen framework are inconsistent with the extensive empirical evidence. Rates of productivity growth vary dramatically over time and differ substantially among industries. This variation is captured by the state-space model of producer behavior.

Partly as a consequence of the relatively modest contribution of productivity growth to the sources of U.S. economic growth, emphasis in the recent literature has focused on biases of technical change. These imply that the rate of technical change can be decomposed into technical change induced by changes in relative prices and technical change that is autonomous. For most industries autonomous technical change is positive and induced technical change is negative. However, both are essential for representing wide variations in rates of technical change among industries and over time.

Finally, in implementing our econometric model of producer behavior, we employ a very detailed breakdown of energy supply and demand. This is critical in evaluating the impact of alternative energy and environmental policies. Energy intensity, the price responsiveness of energy demand, and the bias of technical change for energy all differ substantially among industries.

Notes

1. For further details see Diewert and Morrison (1986).
2. Acemoglu (2002a) presents models of biased technical change and reviews applications to macroeconomics, development economics, labor economics, and international trade. Acemoglu (2007) surveys more recent developments in the literature and presents detailed results on relative and absolute biases of technical change. Acemoglu, Aghion, Bursztyn, and Hemous (2012) present applications to environmental economics.
3. See Jorgenson (2009).

4. Additional details are given by Jorgenson (2000). Barnett and Serletis (2008) provide a detailed survey of flexible functional forms used in modeling consumer demand, including parametric, semiparametric, and nonparametric approaches.
5. The IGEM model presented in chapter 2 incorporates the dynamics of capital accumulation and asset pricing, so that we do not include these features in the specification of our models of producer behavior.
6. See Timmer, Inklaar, O'Mahony, and van Ark (2010).
7. See Jorgenson, Kuroda, and Motohashi (2007).
8. The dual price function is equivalent to the primal production function in that all the information expressed in one is recoverable from the other. Further details are given by Jorgenson (2000).
9. More detail on the implications of imposing concavity at all data points in the sample is provided by Gallant and Golub (1984).
10. For additional details see Gallant and Golub (1984).
11. The endogeneity of the input and output prices for each of the 35 sectors is clear in the general equilibrium framework of IGEM.
12. Estimates of the unknown parameters of our model are presented in appendix C. A similar approach for estimation of models with time-varying parameters has been introduced by Kim (2006) and Kim and Nelson (2006).

5 Government and the Rest of the World

5.1 Introduction

In chapter 2 we presented the Intertemporal General Equilibrium Model (IGEM). We outlined the equations of the production sector, which is the core of the supply side of the model. Our model of producer behavior is presented in more detail in chapter 4. We also discussed the equations of the household sector, which forms the center of the demand side of the model. Our model of consumer behavior is presented in more detail in chapter 3. Finally, in chapter 2 we presented the solution algorithm for determining the system of intertemporal equilibrium prices that equilibrates supply and demand.

In this chapter we complete the description of the demand side of the model by presenting demands for commodities and factors of production by the government sector, as well as demands for investment and exports. We complete the description of the supply side by describing demands for imports. Like our models of consumer and producer behavior, the parameters of our models of investment, imports, and exports are estimated econometrically, using time series database and econometric methods like those employed in chapters 3 and 4.

The treatment of the government sector in IGEM is described in section 5.2. We show how revenues are related to tax rates and how revenues and government expenditures are linked to the public sector deficit. We then describe how government expenditures are allocated among the commodity groups employed in IGEM and tax rates are constructed from the data. We also describe the projections of the exogenous components of the government sector beyond the sample period.

The government sector in IGEM corresponds to "general government" in the National Income and Product Accounts (NIPAs), a category that excludes the government enterprises. The output and purchases of government enterprises are included in industry 35 in the business sector. The surpluses of these enterprises are recorded as revenues of the general government. The general government sector covers federal and state and local government accounts.

In IGEM the social insurance trust funds, including Social Security and Medicare, are treated as part of the household assets. The payroll tax for social insurance is regarded as a contribution to the trust funds that generates benefits to be paid from in the future. The benefits from the trust funds are assumed to equal the contributions in present value terms. We do not include the payroll tax rate in the gap between employer payments and worker receipts. Similarly, we do not include transfers from the trust funds in household income.

The determination of the optimal path of investment is discussed in section 5.3. This is the result of maximizing the present value of rental income from the stock of capital. We have derived the cost of capital, linking the rental price of capital with the rate of return, the depreciation rate, and the price of capital goods. This is the key to the incorporation of forward-looking price dynamics into IGEM, since asset prices reflect future rental prices.

In section 5.3.2 we describe how aggregate investment is built up from data on investment by detailed asset classes within the broad groups of structures, producer durable equipment, and consumer durables. Expenditures on each asset type are linked to the input-output commodity classification via a bridge table. For example, the $43.6 billion investment in computers and peripheral equipment in 1992 is made up of the following input-output commodities at producers' prices: $32.7 billion from machinery, $3.4 billion from services, $0.4 billion from transportation, and $7.1 billion from trade.

In section 5.4 we define the supply of a commodity as the sum of the domestic and imported varieties. The total supply and the corresponding demands for domestic and imported goods are functions of the commodity prices and modeled like the lower tiers in the production function. Data on domestic and imported prices are used to construct the supply price and quantity for each sector.

Latent variables like those used in our models of producer and consumer behavior are essential for tracking the historical evolution of U.S. imports and exports. The econometric approach outlined in chapter 4 permits the incorporation of future trends in the latent variables into the projections of IGEM. For example, U.S. exports have risen as a share of GDP during the postwar decades, although not as rapidly as imports, resulting in a large trade deficit. In this chapter we show how to project these trends into the future.

5.2 Accounting for Government

5.2.1 *Government Receipts and Expenditures*

The government sector plays an important role in IGEM. Government spending affects household welfare directly through transfer payments and health spending and indirectly through public capital that improves private sector productivity. Taxes introduce wedges between prices faced by buyers and sellers and distort the allocation of resources. We do not specify a model for public goods and taxation but set tax rates exogenously and take the shares of public expenditure by commodity as exogenous. We also set the government deficit exogenously.

In the new architecture for the U.S. national accounts discussed by Jorgenson (2009), the social insurance trust funds are treated as part of household assets. For example, Social Security contributions and benefits are regarded as transfers within the household sector and are not included in government revenues and expenditures. The tax on labor income in IGEM includes federal and state and local income taxes but not social insurance contributions.

The tax codes of the federal, state, and local governments are very complex with progressive rates and numerous credits and deductions. We simplify these codes by introducing average and marginal tax rates on labor incomes in order to obtain a tractable representation that captures the key distortions. In IGEM the taxes that are explicitly recognized are sales taxes, import tariffs, capital income taxes, labor income taxes, property taxes, and wealth or estate taxes.

Taxes on production tt_j^{full} create a wedge between the prices faced by buyers and sellers. These taxes include sales taxes, as well as energy and environmental taxes. The average sales tax rate is chosen to match the revenues collected less subsidies. Labor taxes give the effective price of leisure as the price paid by employers less the marginal tax rate tl^m. Similarly, labor income received is the price after deducting the average tax rate tl^a. The two labor tax rates in IGEM capture the key feature that marginal rates are higher than average rates.

The effective capital income tax tk creates a wedge between payments by producers and receipts by households. The average tax rate represents the combined effect of the corporate tax and the personal income tax. The property tax *tp* also appears in the cost of capital; this is mostly state and local property taxes. The wealth tax *tw* is a deduction from household income. Tariffs *tr* are described below. Nontax receipts, denoted R_t^N, include various fees charged by governments and appear as a household expenditure. The effective rates are chosen to replicate the actual revenues; these are close, but not identical, to the statutory rates. The construction of effective tax rates is described in more detail in appendix B.5.

In addition to taxes that are currently collected we introduce new taxes required by energy and environmental policies. Environmental taxes may be imposed on unit values or quantities (per dollar or per gallon, for example). The environmental tax on the sales value of industry *j*'s output is denoted tx_j^v, while the unit tax is tx_j^u.[1] Other, nonenvironmental, unit taxes are denoted tu_j. The result is that the total tax on a dollar of industry *j*'s output is

$$tt_j^{full} = tt_j + tx_j^v + \frac{tu_j + tx_j^u}{PO_j}.$$

This is the tax on the industry output price PO_j introduced in equation (2.13).

The model also allows a new consumption tax, that is, a tax on personal consumption expenditures but not on intermediate purchases. We normally assume that the same consumption tax rate applies to all goods, that is, $tc_i = tc$, and this drives a wedge between the supply price and the consumer price PS_i^C:

$$PS_i^C = (1 + tc_i)PS_i \quad i \in I_{COM}. \tag{5.1}$$

Given the complexity of the various consumption tax reforms that have been proposed, we also allow for the possibility of a threshold for the consumption tax, an exemption below a certain level, so that the revenue is

$$R\_CON^{net} = \sum_{I_{COM}} tc_i PS_i C_i - tcVCC^{exempt}. \tag{5.2}$$

Finally, we allow an adjustment in taxes that applies only to capital used by the households KD_{36}. An example is a change in the tax deductibility of interest from mortgages on owner-occupied residential property. This is represented by a revenue item for the government which may be positive or negative:

$$RK^{hh} = \frac{tk^{hh}}{1 - tk^{hh}} PKD_{36} KD_{36}. \tag{5.3}$$

On the other side of the ledger, this is represented as a reduction of after-tax capital income.

In policy simulations we often impose a new tax or subsidy but maintain revenue neutrality by an offsetting lump sum tax. To implement this scenario we introduce a lump sum transfer variable *TLUMP*, which is subtracted from household income and added to government revenues. New taxes are offset by a negative *TLUMP*. A lump sum transfer could be implemented by increasing the standard deduction under the individual income tax.

Government expenditures fall into four major categories—goods and services purchased from the private sector, transfers to the household and foreigners, interest payments on debt to household and foreigners, and subsidies. The first three are denoted VGG, $G^{TRAN} + G^{tran,row}$, and $GINT + GINT^{row}$. Subsidies are regarded as negative sales taxes and included in the calculation of the output tax tt_j in (5.1). Transfers and interest payments are set exogenously under our standard closure for IGEM; they are scaled to projections from the Congressional Budget Office.[2]

Total government spending on commodities, including labor and capital services, is denoted VGG. Government consumption VG_i of commodity i is set to actual purchases in the sample period. For projections we assume fixed shares of each commodity in total spending, using shares α_i^G from the final year:

$$\begin{aligned} &VG_{it} = PS_{it} G_{it} = \alpha_i^G VGG_t \quad i \in I_{COM}. \\ &PLD_{Gt} LD_{Gt} = \alpha_L^G VGG_t \quad VG_{GK,t} = \alpha_K^G VGG_t. \end{aligned} \tag{5.4}$$

The quantity of public consumption G_i is the value divided by the supply price. The government owns the stock of public capital. In the NIPAs the "consumption of government fixed capital" is an imputed flow of services. This imputation is added to the expenditure side and the income side of the government accounts. We represent this flow of capital consumption by VKG_t and add this to government revenue. This should not be confused with government purchases of investment goods, which are included in VGG.

In simulating energy and environmental policies we frequently treat real government purchases as exogenous, so that welfare comparisons are limited to changes in private consumption. We define the price index of aggregate government purchases as

$$PGG_t = \prod_i PS_{it}^{\alpha_i^G} \tag{5.4b}$$

and the index of real aggregate government purchases as the value divided by this price:

$$GG = VGG / PGG. \tag{5.4c}$$

5.2.2 Government Deficits and Debt

The total revenue of the government sector is the sum of all the taxes we have mentioned. These include sales taxes, tariffs, property taxes, capital income taxes, labor income taxes, wealth taxes, nontax revenues, unit output taxes, externality taxes, imputed capital consumption, income from government enterprises (industry 35), consumption taxes, and lump sum taxes:

$$\begin{aligned} R\_TOTAL = {} & R\_SALES + R\_TARIFF + R\_P + R\_K + RK^{hh} \\ & + R\_L + R\_W + R^N + R\_UNIT + R\_EXT + R\_ITC \\ & + VG_{GK} + YK^{gov} + R\_CON^{net} + TLUMP \end{aligned} \tag{5.5}$$

where

(a) $R\_SALES = \sum_j tt_j PO_j QI_j$

(b) $R\_TARIFF = \sum_i tr_i PM_i M_i$

(c) $R\_P = tpPK_{t-1}K_{t-1}$

(d) $R\_K = tk(YK - R\_P) + tkGINT + tkY^{ROW}$

(e) $R\_L = tl^a P^h LS / (1 - tl^m) = tl^a \sum_j PLD_j LD_j$

(f) $R\_W = tw(PK.K + BG + BF)$

(g) $R\_UNIT = \sum_j tu_j QI_j$

(h) $R\_EXT = \sum_j tx_j^v PI_j QI_j + \sum_i tx_i^{rv} PM_i M_i + \sum_j tx_j^u QI_j + \sum_i tx_i^{ru} M_i$

(i) $YK^{gov} = (1 - tk)PKD_{35}KD_{35}$
R_CON^{net} is eq. (5.3); RK^{hh} is equation (5.4)

(j) R_ITC: adjustment to revenues for investment tax credit

(k) R^N and VG_{GK}: non-tax receipts and government capital consumption[3]

The estimation of government revenues is described below. The largest component is labor income taxes, followed by capital income taxes. Government expenditures are the sum of purchases, transfers and interest payments both to domestic households and to foreigners:

$$EXPEND = VGG + G^{tran} + G^{tran,row} + GINT + GINT^{row}. \quad (5.6)$$

Given our treatment of the social insurance funds as household assets, the government interest payments to domestic bond holders is the sum of the official payments plus payments to social insurance trust ($GINT^{ss}$), minus payments from the funds to the government for operating expenses (R_SS):

$$GINT = GINT^{hh} + GINT^{ss} - R\_SS. \quad (5.7)$$

In IGEM interest payments $\left(\overline{GINT}^{hh} + \overline{GINT}^{ss}\right)$ may be set exogenously as a function of the projected deficits and accumulated government debt. An alternative formulation links the interest rate on the debt to the endogenous rate of return r_t:

$$GINT_t^{endog} = \frac{r_t}{1-tk} BG_{t-1}. \quad (5.8)$$

Government expenditures by these categories are given for 2005 in the bottom half of table 5.1.

The National Income and Product Accounts (NIPAs) distinguish between current expenditures and investment spending and between current receipts and capital transfers (wealth taxes). This results in a current deficit that is distinct from the net borrowing requirement. We do not make this distinction in IGEM and define the public deficit of the entire government as total outlays less total revenues, a concept equal to the official net borrowing requirement.

Denoting the government deficit by ΔG, this is equal to the difference between expenditures and revenues:

$$\Delta G_t = EXPEND_t - R\_TOTAL_t. \quad (5.9)$$

Deficits add to the public debt. This is separated between debt held by U.S. residents and debt held by foreigners, $BG + BG^*$. The construction of the debt series and the other government sector

Table 5.1
Tax rates, main revenues, and expenditures in 2005

Model Code Name	Appendix A Symbol	2005
Tax rates		
Marginal tax rate on labor income	tl^m	0.2452
Average tax rate on labor income	tl^a	0.1183
Property tax rate	tp	0.0099
Wealth tax rate	tw	0.0006
Tax rate on capital income	tk	0.1344
Investment tax credit	t^{ITC}	0.0000
Tax rate on consumption	tc	0.0000
Revenues and expenditures		(2005 bil $)
Sales tax revenue (net subsidies)	R_SALES	470.0
Property tax revenue	R_P	454.2
Capital income tax revenue	R_K	702.7
Labor income tax revenue	R_L	893.6
Nontax receipts	R^N	71.4
Import tariff revenue	R_TARIFF	25.3
Wealth tax revenue	R_W	30.3
Consumption tax revenue	R_CON	0
Transfers to domestic residents (not social insurance)	G^{tran}	560.7
Transfers to rest of the world	GR	35.3
Net interest to domestic residents	$GINT$	148.5
Net interest to rest of the world	$GINTR$	101.5
Interest to social insurance funds	$GINT^{SS}$	120.2
Expenditures on goods and services	VGG	2369.9
Capital consumption (excl Enterprises)	VKG	208.7
Government surplus (net lending)	$-\Delta G$	–453.2
Government foreign investment	GFI	–273.9
Stocks of debt		
Debt to domestic residents	BG	5091.2
Debt to rest of the world	BG^*	2169.9

variables is described in appendix B.5. In both cases we count only the net debt. The increase in the domestic debt is the total deficit less the portion financed by foreigners, $BG_t = BG_{t-1} + \Delta G_t + GFI$.

Government debt is not estimated in the NIPAs but rather in the Flow of Funds Account by the Federal Reserve Board. As a consequence the stock of debt is not reconciled with the net borrowing requirement in the NIPAs. For the sample period we introduce a variable BG^{disc} for the statistical discrepancy between the two accounts. The stocks of debt are estimated at market values, so that we adjust for the inflation effect using a variable ΔP_t^{BG}:

$$BG_t = BG_{t-1} + \Delta G_t + GFI_t + \Delta P_t^{BG} + BG_t^{disc}. \tag{5.10}$$

Similarly, the stock of debt to foreigners is the accumulation of government net foreign investment, GFI, plus the inflation adjustment:

$$BG_t^* = BG_{t-1}^* - GFI - \Delta P_t^{BG^*}. \tag{5.11}$$

The deficit, stock of debt, and other elements in the equations (5.10) and (5.11) are set to actual values for the sample period. For the projection period the discrepancies are set to zero, the capital gains terms are set to zero, and the deficits are set to official projections.

5.2.3 *Data Sources*

The sources of government revenues we have explicitly identified are those from sales taxes, tariffs, property taxes (R_P), capital income tax (R_K), labor income tax (R_L), wealth (estate) tax (R_W), nontax receipts (R^N), externality taxes (R_EXT), and some minor items. The main expenditure items are final purchases (VGG), transfers (G^{tran}) and interest payments ($GINT$). The government deficits ΔG_t cumulate into government debt. The portion of the deficit funded by foreigners is denoted $-GFI_t$, the negative of government foreign investment.

The data for our government accounts are taken directly from the National Income and Product Accounts.[4] These include revenues from income taxes, other personal taxes, property taxes, taxes on production, customs duties, corporate income taxes, capital transfers (estate taxes), and surpluses of government enterprises. On the expenditure side, the NIPAs include details on government consumption expenditures, government investment, benefits from social insurance (SI) funds, other government transfers, interest payments, subsidies, and capital transfers. These expenditures for domestic residents and foreigners are separately identified. The consumption of fixed capital (*VKG*) is an imputed item that appears on both sides of the ledger; it is a part of consumption expenditures and a part of revenues. This accounting recognizes the fact that this imputation does not change government borrowing requirements.

In the top section of table 5.1 we give the values of the main tax rates used in IGEM for 2005. The variable symbols used in the above equations and in appendix A are given in the table, together with model simulation codes. For brevity tax rates that differ by industry, such as sales taxes and tariffs, are not included. Note that the marginal tax rate on labor income is much higher than the average tax rate. Investment tax credits and taxes on consumption are zero in 2005 and in the projections of the base case; they may, of course, be introduced for policy simulations.

In the second section of table 5.1 we give the main components of general government revenue and expenditures for 2005 (5.6 and 5.7). The largest category is the tax on labor income with $894 billion, followed by taxes on capital income with $703 billion. These two items are derived from personal income taxes and the corporate income tax. The other major sources of revenue are property taxes ($454 billion) and nontax receipts such as fees ($71 billion).

The expenditures derived from the NIPAs include transfers other than social insurance to domestic residents ($561 billion), transfers to foreigners ($35 billion), interest paid to domestic residents ($148 billion), interest paid to foreigners ($101 billion), and interest paid to the social insurance trust funds ($120 billion). Spending on goods and services was $2,370 billion, including both consumption and investment; consumption includes the imputations for government capital consumption. By comparison social insurance benefits were $922 billion and contributions to the trust funds were $877 billion in 2005.

The average tax rates are calculated by dividing revenue estimates from the NIPAs by the tax base. The definitions of the taxes are given in Jorgenson and Yun (2001).The tax bases are scaled to value added in the NIPAs and industry outputs. Personal income taxes are allocated between labor and capital income taxes using data from the U.S. Internal Revenue Service (IRS). The IRS data on taxes paid by income categories are used to estimate the marginal labor tax rate.[5]

Since there are no similar data for state and local taxes on personal income, we scale the marginal and average rates for federal taxes to include total revenues for state and local income taxes. The government deficit in 2005 is $453 billion, of which $274 billion is financed by the rest of the world. Finally, the stock of government debt to domestic residents is estimated at $5.1 trillion and the net public debt to foreigners is $2.2 trillion.

Government purchases of the output of the business sector and the primary factors of labor and capital are denoted *VGG* in equation (5.5). We note that the conventions of the NIPAs make this a net measure. Government sales to the household sector such as fees collected for colleges and hospitals are netted out. Not all the salaries for public employees are included in *VGG*. For example, the portion paid as tuition fees to public colleges and universities is included in personal consumption expenditures. In IGEM we follow this convention. Although the NIPAs distinguish between government consumption and government investment, *VGG* refers to the sum of these items. The government purchases of each commodity are expressed as shares of total spending. The shares α_i^G for 2005 are given in table 5.2.

The largest government expenditure is on wages and salaries, more than 46% in 2005. This is followed by purchases from Construction and the imputed value of government capital consumption. It should be emphasized that capital services are those from the government-owned stock of capital. The largest item purchased from the manufacturing group is Other Transportation Equipment for aircraft and ships. Energy purchases are substantial and 1.5% of government purchases each go to Petroleum Refining and Electric Utilities. Purchases from Petroleum Refining were between 1% and 1.5% for most of the sample period, except during the second oil shock when it rose above 2%. The share going to electricity has been steadily rising since 1970, from 1.0% to 1.6% in 2000.

In figure 5.1 we plot the share of GDP going to government purchases (*VGG*), the share going to total expenditures *EXPEND*, and the revenue share of GDP. These are based on the IGEM definitions given above, not consolidated government expenditures and revenues, including social insurance funds. The share going to final purchases has fluctuated between 17% and 23% with a sharp rise during the Great Recession. The share going to total expenditures reached over 30% in the early 1990s and in the 2008–2009 recession. Revenues, excluding payroll taxes, were close to 25% for much of the period before 1995 but fell with the tax cuts of 2001 and fell dramatically in the Great Recession. In the next section we describe how we project the exogenous elements of the government accounts going forward.

Table 5.2
Government expenditures by commodity, 2005 (% of total purchases)

1	Agriculture	0.11
2	Metal Mining	–0.01
3	Coal Mining	0.00
4	Petroleum and Gas	–0.01
5	Nonmetallic Mining	0.00
6	Construction	16.73
7	Food Products	1.00
8	Tobacco Products	0.00
9	Textile Mill Products	0.03
10	Apparel and Textiles	0.14
11	Lumber and Wood	0.02
12	Furniture and Fixtures	0.33
13	Paper Products	0.30
14	Printing and Publishing	0.56
15	Chemical Products	0.85
16	Petroleum Refining	1.52
17	Rubber and Plastic	0.21
18	Leather Products	0.03
19	Stone, Clay, and Glass	0.05
20	Primary Metals	0.03
21	Fabricated Metals	0.49
22	Industrial Machinery	1.16
23	Electronic and Electric Equipment	1.09
24	Motor Vehicles	1.00
25	Other Transportation Equipment	3.76
26	Instruments	2.27
27	Miscellaneous Manufacturing	0.24
28	Transport and Warehouse	1.66
29	Communications	0.85
30	Electric Utilities	1.51
31	Gas Utilities	0.27
32	Trade	1.36
33	FIRE	2.18
34	Services	4.53
35	Government Enterprises	0.28
36	Noncomparable Imports	0.59
	Capital Services	8.04
	Labor Services	46.82

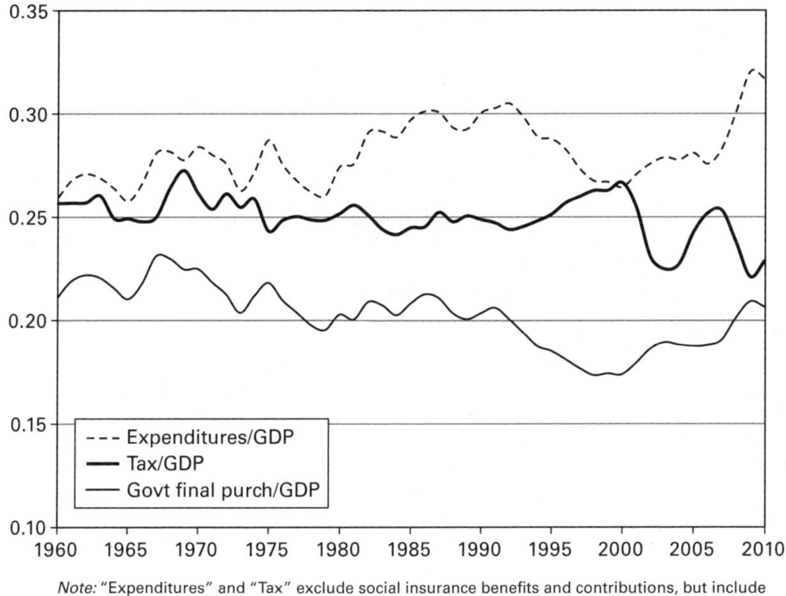

Note: "Expenditures" and "Tax" exclude social insurance benefits and contributions, but include estate taxes.

Figure 5.1
Government expenditures and revenues (model definition) as share of GDP.

5.2.4 Projecting the Exogenous Components of Government

The Congressional Budget Office (CBO) is the main source of our intermediate-term projections of variables related to the government accounts. CBO (2010a) provides 11-year projections to 2020 for the federal deficit, balances of the social insurance trust funds, interest payments, transfers and other major items.[6] These are based on their detailed projections of GDP and unemployment over this horizon. A more aggregated methodology is used to project over a longer horizon in CBO (2010b) with some variables projected to 2084.

Unfortunately there are no authoritative projections for the state and local government budgets and we construct our own estimates of revenues and expenditures. We treat the state and local social insurance trust funds consistently with the federal social insurance trust funds. In IGEM these are part of private assets, so that we ignore the contributions and benefits.

The state and local governments typically run small current surpluses and we retain that feature in our projections. The net borrowing requirement is the current surplus combined with investment

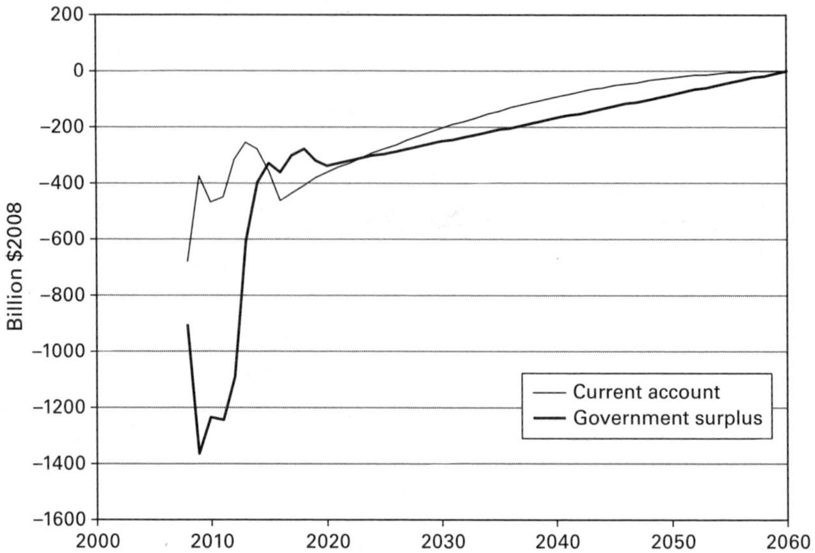

Figure 5.2
Projections of government and current account deficits.

spending, capital transfers, and other minor items. We assume that these items grow at the same rate as the GDP projected by CBO and thus generate a projection of the net borrowing by state and local governments. This is combined with the CBO projection of the federal budget to project the consolidated government surplus to 2020. This consolidated projection is given in figure 5.2; the deficit was $1.41 trillion in 2009[7] and projected to be $1.35 trillion in 2010 and $1.03 trillion in 2011 (current dollars). Following the CBO projections, our deficit falls to $613 billion in 2014 before rising to $843 billion in 2020.

Beyond the 10-year projection window we assume that the government deficit falls steadily to zero by 2060. The projection of the total debt, together with the sample period data, is plotted in figure 5.3. The graphs give the debt (domestic plus foreign) and surplus deflated by our labor price index. The total debt (right-hand axis) was $5.42 trillion at the end of 2005 and rises to $12.5 trillion in 2020 under the projections derived from CBO (2010a) and continue to rise to $19.6 trillion by 2060 under our assumption of falling deficits.

The government deficits cumulate into the stock of debt to U.S. residents and foreigners as given in equations (5.11) and (5.12). For the sample period we have estimates of government foreign investment (*GFI*) derived from data on foreign asset holdings.[8] As shown in figure

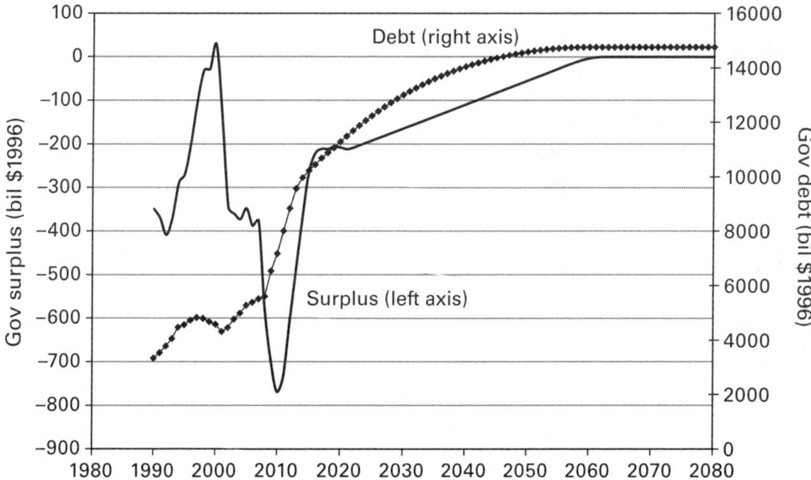

Figure 5.3
Projections of consolidated government surplus and total debt.

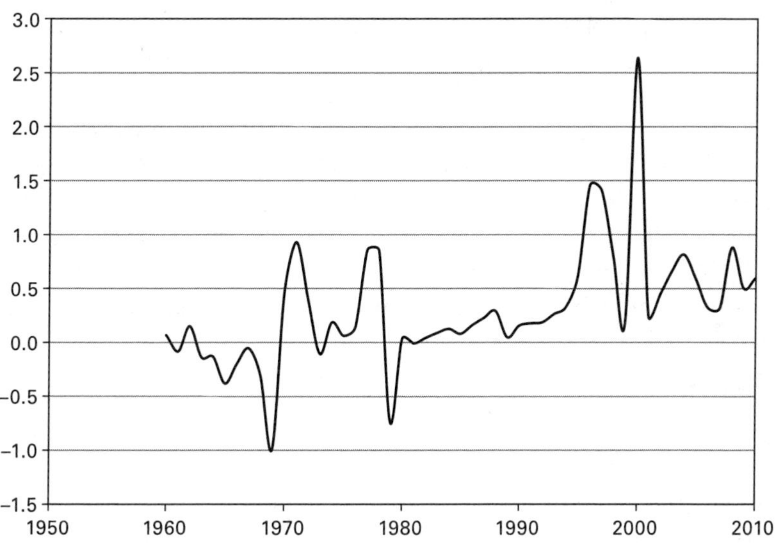

Figure 5.4
Share of government borrowing financed by foreigners.

5.4, the share of deficit financed by foreigners is highly unstable; in the 1980s it was about 10–20%, fluctuated wildly in the 1990s, reaching more than 100% in 1996, and averaged 50% during 2001–2006. During the Great Recession the ratio fell as U.S. savings rose. We extrapolate the 2009 value, assuming that this share will fall gradually to zero by 2040. This is in line with our assumptions of falling current account deficits described in chapter 6.

The expenditure items in equation (5.7), other than final purchases, *VGG*, are exogenous in our standard projections for IGEM. For the 10-year CBO projection window we follow the projections for transfers in CBO (2010a), which include the high transfers associated with the Great Recession. We scale the CBO projections for the federal budget to include the state and local government transfers.

Beyond the end of the 10-year budget window, ending in 2020, when the domestic transfer share of GDP (α^{GTRAN}) is projected at 3.7%, we assume that it will fall gradually to 3.1% in 75 years. Transfers to foreigners are about 0.2–0.3% of GDP at the end of the sample period and we assume that this eventually falls to 0.2%. For these exogenous transfers, we multiply the projected shares by the GDP projections in the CBO Long-Term Projection in CBO (2010b) to generate G_t^{tran} and $G_t^{tran,row}$. The projections are plotted in figure 5.5.

Transfers to households (not including social insurance) were $416 billion in 2005, measured in 1996 dollars. After a sharp rise for the recession, these are projected to fall back to $483 billion in 2020 by the CBO and rise to $960 billion by 2060 by our assumptions. Transfers to foreigners were $20 billion in 2005 and projected to be $29 billion in 2060. An alternative approach would be to make the transfers endogenous and set them equal to exogenous shares multiplied by the endogenous GDP.

$$G_t^{tran} = \alpha_t^{GTRAN} GDP_t. \tag{5.12}$$

$$G_t^{tran,row} = \alpha_t^{GTR\_R} GDP_t. \tag{5.13}$$

Interest payments to residents and foreigners are set exogenously according to the projected debt graphed in figure 5.3. For the 2010–2020 period, CBO (2010a, tables 1–3) gives the net interest payable by the federal government. Given our estimate of the stock of federal debt embodied in figure 5.3, we can derive an implied average interest rate from these CBO projections. To this estimate of federal government payments we add the interest paid by the state and local governments. We project this by multiplying the implied interest rate by the stock of state and local debt.

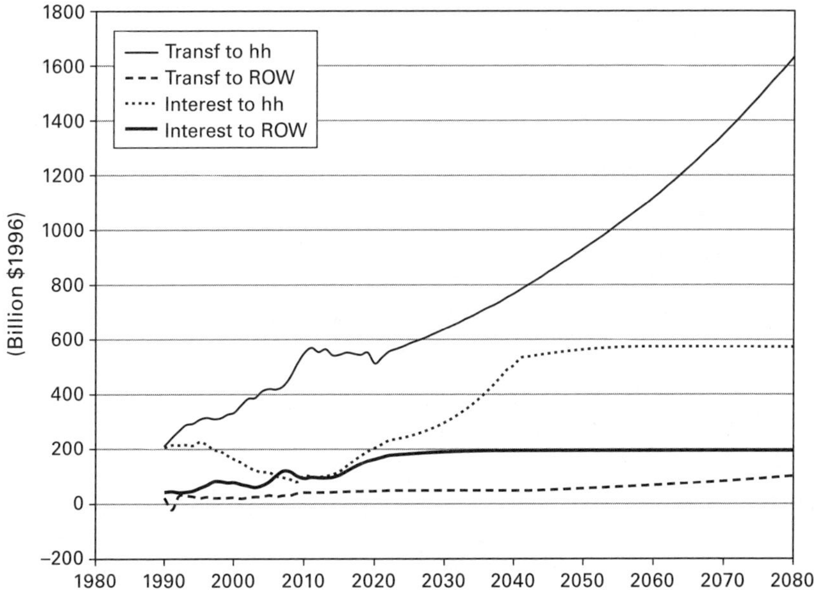

Figure 5.5
Projections of exogenous components of government expenditures.

For the period beyond 2020 we assume that the domestic interest rate stays at the 2020 level of 5.47% and project the interest paid by multiplying this rate by the stock of domestic debt. The foreign interest rate is assumed to follow the same trend. These projections of interest payments are also plotted in figure 5.5, again deflated using our labor price to 1996 dollars. Interest paid to domestic residents is projected to rise from $106 billion (1996 dollars) in 2006 to $306 billion in 2020 and to $927 billion by 2060. Interest paid to foreigners by the government was $93 billion (1996 dollars) in 2006 and will rise rapidly to $92 billion in 2020 before stabilizing at $252 billion in 2040 by our assumptions.

On the revenue side, all elements except one are given by an exogenous tax rate multiplied by an endogenous tax base. The exception is the nontax revenue given in figure 5.6. This is projected to rise proportionately with GDP from $59 billion in 2008 to $154 billion in 2060.

5.3 Investment by Commodity

The determination of the optimal path of aggregate investment is discussed in chapter 2, section 2.4. This is the result of maximizing the

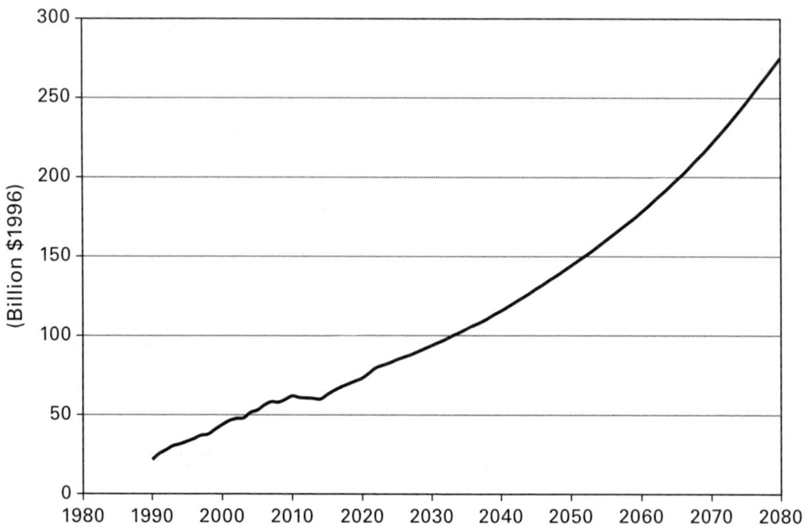

Figure 5.6
Projections of nontax revenue (exogenous).

present value of rental payments for the stock of capital. As part of this calculation we derived the cost of capital, linking the rental cost with the rate of return, the depreciation rate, and the price of capital goods.

Our methodology consistently aggregates over types of investment, asset types, and capital services. The capital accumulation equation (2.76) is written

$$K_t = (1-\delta)K_{t-1} + \psi^I I_t^a. \tag{5.14}$$

The function ψ_t^I is an aggregation coefficient that reconciles the different compositions of aggregate investment (I_t^a) and aggregate capital stock (K_t). The stock is dominated by long-lived assets such as structures and land, while investment is heavily weighted toward short-lived assets such as computers.

Between 1960 and 2005 the aggregation coefficient ψ_t^I has been falling at 0.05% per year as the composition of investment has shifted towards short-lived assets, as shown in figure 5.7. The structure of investment is discussed in detail in appendix B.3. The share of IT investment, a short-lived asset, is given in figure B.12. We project this change in ψ_t^I to continue at a slower rate in the future.

The flow of aggregate capital services is given in (2.80) as the capital stock multiplied by an aggregation coefficient ψ_t^K which reconciles the

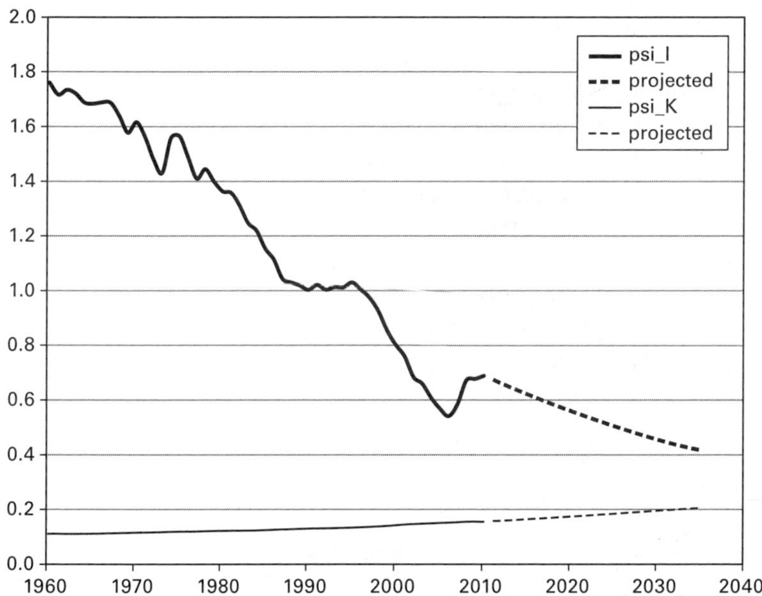

Figure 5.7
Aggregation coefficients for capital investment (ψ^I) and capital quality (ψ^K).

difference in composition between the stock and the flow. Capital stock K_t is aggregated over asset types, using prices of capital goods as weights, while the flow of capital services KD_t is weighted by the rental cost of capital services. This coefficient is called the *quality of capital* in Jorgenson, Ho, and Stiroh (2005), since a shift in composition from assets with long service lives and low rental rates to assets with short lives and high rental rates is an increase in the quality of the aggregate stock.

Capital stock, capital services, and capital quality are given in table B.22. Over the period 1960–2005, the quality of capital rose at 1.1% per year, and we project this to continue rising before tapering to a steady state in 2050. This growth in the quality of capital is a major source of growth and contributed 0.78 percentage points out of the 3.1% U.S. GDP growth over 1977–2000.[9] This contribution is omitted in models that do not introduce capital services or simplify equations (5.15) and (2.80) by assuming constant aggregation coefficients.

The quantity of investment demanded by the investor in period t is I_t^a when the price is PII_t. In the NIPAs this total is an aggregate of investment by detailed asset classes structures, producer durable equipment, consumer durables, and inventories. The value of investment by these asset types in 2005 is given in table 5.3.[10] In the benchmark input-output tables, expenditures in purchaser's prices are linked to producer prices via bridge tables in an identical manner to personal consumption expenditures, as described in section 2.2.5.[11] Using these bridge tables, we have constructed a time series of investment demands by the 35 commodity groups employed in IGEM.

We allocate investment demand I_t^a to the 35 individual commodities by means of a hierarchical tier structure of production models, similar to the demand for intermediate inputs in our model of producer behavior. At the top tier we express this as a function of fixed and inventory investment:

$$\begin{aligned} I^a &= I(I^{fixed}, I^{inventory}) \\ I^{fixed} &= I^f(IF_1, IF_2, \ldots, IF_{35}). \end{aligned} \tag{5.15}$$

We denote the value of private investment by VII:

$$VII_t = PII_t I_t^a = VII^{\text{fixed}} + VII^{\text{inventory}}. \tag{5.16}$$

In order to have a tractable model of demand for intermediate inputs by the producers we have used a hierarchical tier structure of translog price functions. Similarly, we derive fixed investment commodity demands from a nested structure of investment price functions. This tier structure is given in table 5.4; there are a total of 15 nodes dominated by construction, vehicles, and machinery. The set of nodes is denoted I_{INV}.

Table 5.3
Private investment by asset class, 2005 (bil. $)

Total Private Investment	3101.1
Nonresidential structures	334.6
Residential structures	759.2
Equipment and software	946.5
Household furniture	1.9
Other furniture	36.5
Other fabricated metal products	14.2
Steam engines	4.3
Internal combustion engines	1.2
Farm tractors	10.8
Construction tractors	3.9

Table 5.3 (continued)

Total Private Investment	3101.1
Agricultural machinery, ex tractors	10.5
Construction machinery, ex tractors	25.3
Mining and oilfield machinery	7.5
Metalworking machinery	26.0
Special industry machinery, n.e.c.	30.6
General industrial equipment	58.7
Computers and peripheral equipment	89.0
Service industry machinery	19.0
Communication equipment	86.2
Electrical trans., distrib., and industrial app.	21.4
Household appliances	0.2
Other electrical equipment, n.e.c.	6.8
Trucks, buses, and truck trailers	96.7
Autos	31.9
Aircraft	15.0
Ships and boats	4.8
Railroad equipment	4.6
Instruments (scientific and engineering)	79.9
Photocopy and related equipment	3.6
Other nonresidential equipment	56.0
Other office equipment	6.2
Software	193.8
Consumers durables	1023.9
Autos	227.1
Trucks	190.8
Other (RVs)	27.0
Furniture	79.9
Kitchen appliance	36.8
China, glassware	36.6
Other durable	85.8
Computers and software	56.5
Video, audio	82.7
Jewelry	24.3
Ophthalmic	76.2
Books and maps	58.4
Wheel goods	41.8
Land	—
Inventories	36.9

Table 5.4
Tier structure of investment function

	Symbol	Name	Components
	A	Aggregate Investment	Fixed investment, inventory investment $I^a = I(I^{FX}, I^{IY})$.
	IY	Inventory	All 35 commodities in flat Cobb-Douglas function VII^{IY}.
1	FX	Fixed	Long-lived assets, short-lived assets $I^{FX} = I(IF^{LG}, IF^{SH})$.
2	LG	Long-lived Assets	Construction, Finance-Insurance-Real Estate $IF^{LG} = I(IF_6, IF_{33})$.
3	SH	Short-lived Assets	Vehicles, Machinery, Services $IF^{SH} = I(IF^{VE}, IF^{MC}, IF^{SV})$.
4	VE	Vehicles	Motor vehicles, Other Transportation Equip. $IF^{VE} = I(IF_{24}, IF_{25})$.
5	MC	Machinery	Industrial Mach., Electrical Mach., Other Machinery $IF^{MC} = I\ (IF_{22}, IF_{23}, IF^{MO})$.
6	SV	Services	Services, Other Services $IF^{SV} = I\ (IF_{32}, IF^{SO})$.
7	MO	Other Machinery	Gadgets, Wood Products, Nonmetallic Products, Other Misc. $IF^{MO} = I(IF^{GD}, IF^{WD}, IF^{MN}, IF^{OO})$.
8	SO	Other Services	Services, Transport-Communication $IF^{SO} = I(IF_{34}, IF^{TC})$.
9	GD	Gadgets	Primary Metals, Fabricated Metals, Instruments $IF^{GD} = I(IF_{20}, IF_{21}, IF_{26})$.
10	WD	Wood Products	Lumber & Wood, Furniture & Fixtures $IF^{WD} = I(IF_{11}, IF_{12})$.
11	MN	Nonmetallic Products	Chemicals, Rubber, Stone-Clay-Glass, Misc. Mfg. $IF^{MN} = I(IF_{15}, IF_{17}, IF_{19}, IF_{27})$.
12	OO	Other Misc.	Mining Aggregate, Textile Aggregate, Paper $IF^{OO} = I(IF^{TX}, IF_{13}, IF^{MG})$.
13	TC	Transport Communications	Transportation, Communications $IF^{TC} = I(IF_{28}, IF_{29})$.
14	TX	Textile Aggregate	Textile, Apparel, Leather, Noncompetitive Imports $IF^{TX} = I(IF_9, IF_{10}, IF_{18}, IF_{NCI})$.
15	MG	Mining Aggregate	Metal Mining, Petroleum Mining $IF^{MG} = I(IF_2, IF_4)$.

We have constructed a time series of investment expenditures, classified by the 35 IGEM commodities based on the input-output classification, as described in appendix B.3. The values for fixed investment by these commodities in 2000 and 2005 are given in producer's prices in table 5.5. Of the total \$2538 billion of investment at the peak of the investment boom in 2000, the largest is Construction (\$634 billion) followed by Motor Vehicles (\$331 billion). Trade margins are significant for investment goods and are valued at \$446 billion. At the end of the investment slump of the 2000s in 2005, the share of investment going to Industrial Machinery and Equipment, including computers, fell substantially, offset by a rise for Finance, Insurance, and Real Estate and Petroleum and Gas Mining.

Investment (I_t^a) is the sum of fixed investment and changes in business inventory. Aggregate fixed investment is a function of the 35 commodity groups in IGEM, $I^{fixed} = I(IF_1, IF_2, \dots IF_{35})$, and this is implemented as a nested set of demand functions. The tier structure was given in table 5.4 where node 1 allocates fixed investment to "long-lived" commodities and "short-lived" commodities and node 15 allocates "mining" to "metal mining" and "petroleum mining" commodities.

Of the 35 commodities, only 25 have positive contributions to fixed investment. We have noted that the main contributors are Construction (\$634 billion) and Trade (\$446 billion). The recent importance of information technology equipment is shown by the \$279 billion in Industrial Machinery of the total fixed investment of \$3084 billion in 2005.

The translog price function for node m is a function of the component prices $\{PII_{m1}, \dots, PII_{m,im}\}$ and the latent variables f_t^{Im}. For each node m, there are im inputs and the set of inputs at that node is denoted I_{INVm}. The price function is written in vector form as

$$\begin{aligned} \ln PII^m &= \alpha^{Im\prime} \ln P^{Im} + \frac{1}{2} \ln P^{Im\prime} B^{Im} \ln P^{Im} \\ &\quad + \ln P^{Im\prime} f_t^{Im} + \log \lambda^I \quad m \in I_{INV}. \\ \ln P^{Im} &\equiv (\ln PII_{m1}, \dots, \ln PII_{mi}, \dots, \ln PII_{m,im})' \quad i \in I_{INVm}. \end{aligned} \tag{5.17}$$

Since there are trends in the investment demands that cannot be explained by the price variation we also include a latent term f_t^{Im} that follows an autoregressive form, as in our model of producer behavior:

$$f_t^{Im} = F^{Im} f_{t-1}^{Im} + v_t. \tag{5.18}$$

Table 5.5
Tier structure of investment function in IO categories (bil. $)

	Commodity	2000	2005
1	Agriculture	0.0	0.0
2	Metal Mining	0.6	1.4
3	Coal Mining	0.0	0.0
4	Petroleum and Gas	34.0	83.8
5	Nonmetallic Mining	0.0	0.0
6	Construction	634.2	823.8
7	Food Products	0.0	0.0
8	Tobacco Products	0.0	0.0
9	Textile Mill Products	13.2	17.7
10	Apparel and Textiles	2.3	2.9
11	Lumber and Wood	11.7	13.1
12	Furniture and Fixtures	62.4	81.5
13	Paper Products	0.0	0.0
14	Printing and Publishing	18.8	24.2
15	Chemical Products	3.0	2.6
16	Petroleum Refining	0.0	0.0
17	Rubber and Plastic	15.6	21.9
18	Leather Products	0.9	1.6
19	Stone, Clay, and Glass	4.9	5.5
20	Primary Metals	0.5	0.7
21	Fabricated Metals	17.9	22.4
22	Industrial Machinery and Equipment	255.1	278.6
23	Electronic and Electric Equipment	147.6	160.7
24	Motor Vehicles	331.2	376.8
25	Other Transportation Equipment	55.8	59.9
26	Instruments	88.6	103.9
27	Miscellaneous Manufacturing	44.2	59.9
28	Transport and Warehouse	24.4	28.1
29	Communications	11.6	9.5
30	Electric Utilities	0.0	0.0
31	Gas Utilities	0.0	0.0
32	Trade	446.2	532.2
33	FIRE	64.7	111.1
34	Services	248.1	260.3
35	Government enterprises	0.0	0.0
	Total	2537.8	3083.8

The shares of commodity groups at node m corresponding to the price function are:

$$SI^m = \begin{bmatrix} PII_{m1}IF_{m1} / PII^m IF^m \\ \cdots \\ PII_{m,im}IF_{m,im} / PII^m IF^m \end{bmatrix} = \alpha^{Im} + B^{Im} \ln PII^{Im} + f_t^{Im} \quad \begin{matrix} m \in I_{INV} \\ m,i \in I_{INVm} \end{matrix}. \tag{5.19}$$

We add a stochastic term to it and estimate the following system subject to homogeneity, symmetry, and concavity restrictions, as in the production model

$$SI^{\mathrm{m}} = \alpha^{Im} + B^{Im} \ln PII^{Im} + f_t^{Im} + \varepsilon_t^{Im}. \tag{5.20}$$

As an example, the Transportation Equipment subaggregate (node 4) is made of Motor Vehicles (I24) and Other Transportation Equipment (I25), and the share of Motor Vehicles is given by

$$\begin{aligned} \frac{PII_{24}I_{24}}{PII^{m=4}IF^{m=4}} &= \alpha_1^{I,m=4} + B_{11}^{I,m=4} \ln \frac{PII_{24}}{PII_{25}} + f_1^{I,m=4} + \varepsilon_t \\ f_{1,t}^{Im=4} &= F_{1,1}^{Im=4} f_{1,t-1}^{Im=4} + v_{1,t}. \end{aligned} \tag{5.21}$$

The results are given in table 5.6. Fifteen of the 39 own-share elasticities (the B_{ii}'s) are negative, so that substitution is more elastic than with a Cobb-Douglas function. The remaining B_{ii}'s are positive with an elasticity of substitution less than one. Examples of the estimated latent variable and the projections are given in figure 5.8 for the first input in node 1 and node 5. Node 1 gives total fixed investment as a function of long-lived assets and short-lived assets. The plot marked by squares shows how the latent variable for long-lived assets ($f_{longlived,t}^{Im=1}$) is falling in the sample period and is projected to continue falling.

Node 5 gives Machinery as a function of Industrial Machinery, Electrical Machinery, and Other Machinery. Industrial Machinery's share shows no long-term trend that is not explained by prices and this is projected as constant. The projections of the latent variables in the other nodes of the investment tier structure are plotted in appendix C, figure C5. Most nodes show a pattern more similar to the plot for Industrial Machinery, that is, with no distinct sustained trend in the sample period.

As another example, in node 4 for Transportation Equipment the share of Motor Vehicles fell from the early 1960s to hit bottom after the oil shocks and later recovered. One other node shows a clear trend: In node 8 comprising Services and Moving Services (Transportation and

Table 5.6
Estimated parameters of investment functions; lower tiers

	Node	Input	Alpha	Beta1	Beta2	Beta3	Beta4
1	Fixed Investment	Long-lived	–0.002	0.106	–0.106		
		Short-lived	1.002	–0.106	0.106		
2	Long-lived	Construction	0.428	–0.108	0.108		
		Fin., Insur., Real Estate	0.572	0.108	–0.108		
3	Short-lived	Transport. Equip.	–0.171	–0.244	0.062	0.183	
		Machinery	0.002	0.062	0.014	–0.076	
		Services	1.169	0.183	–0.076	–0.107	
4	Transportation Equipment	Motor Vehicles	0.515	0.065	–0.065		
		Other Transp. Equip.	0.485	–0.065	0.065		
5	Machinery	Industrial Machinery	0.075	0.062	–0.077	0.015	
		Electrical Machinery	0.058	–0.077	0.114	–0.037	
		Other Machinery	0.868	0.015	–0.037	0.022	
6	Services	Trade	0.366	0.076	–0.076		
		Other services	0.634	–0.076	0.076		
7	Other Machinery	Gadgets	0.251	0.068	–0.111	0.080	–0.038
		Wood	0.388	–0.111	0.081	0.093	–0.063
		Nonmetal Inventory	0.280	0.080	0.093	–0.155	–0.018
		Other Machinery	0.082	–0.038	–0.063	–0.018	0.119
8	Other Services	Services	1.634	0.104	–0.104		
		Moving Services	–0.634	–0.104	0.104		
9	Gadgets	Primary Metals	0.000	0.000	0.000	0.000	
		Fabricated Metals	0.005	0.000	0.017	–0.017	
		Instruments	0.995	0.000	–0.017	0.017	
10	Wood	Lumber and Wood	–0.088	–0.029	0.029		
		Furniture and Fixtures	1.088	0.029	–0.029		
11	Nonmetal Investment	Chemicals	0.026	–0.069	0.008	–0.081	0.142
		Rubber and Plastics	–0.094	0.008	–0.229	0.164	0.056
		Nonmetal Minerals	–0.098	–0.081	0.164	–0.088	0.005
		Other Manufacturing	1.166	0.142	0.056	0.005	–0.203

Table 5.6 (continued)

	Node	Input	Alpha	Beta1	Beta2	Beta3	Beta4
12	Other	Printing and Publishing	–0.024	0.049	0.033	–0.082	
	Other Machinery	Textile—Apparel	0.213	0.033	0.041	–0.073	
		Mining	0.811	–0.082	–0.073	0.155	
13	Moving Services	Transportation	0.561	–0.095	0.095		
		Communications	0.439	0.095	–0.095		
14	Textile—Apparel	Textile	–0.155	–0.226	0.240	–0.014	0.000
		Apparel	–0.102	0.240	–0.225	–0.015	0.000
		Leather	1.257	–0.014	–0.015	0.029	0.000
		Noncompeting Imports	0.000	0.000	0.000	0.000	0.000
15	Mining	Metal Mining	–0.440	0.016	–0.016		
		Petroleum Mining	1.440	–0.016	0.016		

Note: Coefficients without standard errors are those that are not estimated (alpha set to sample average, beta = 0).

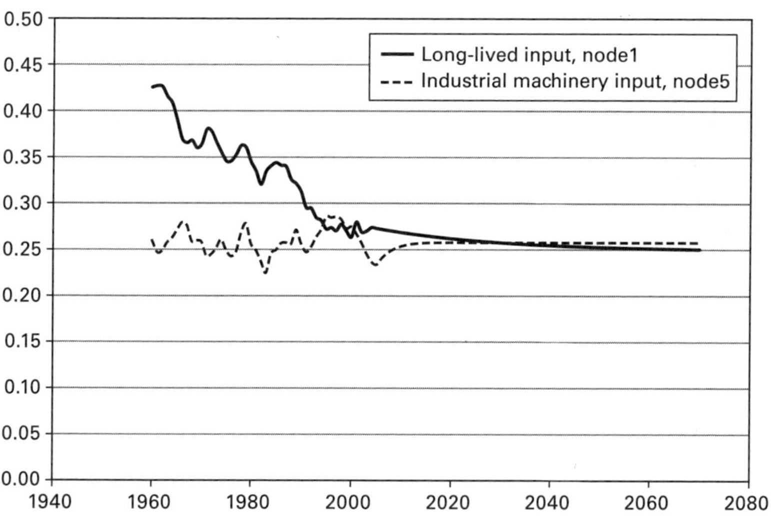

Figure 5.8

Projection of latent term in investment. Node 1: total = *f*(long, short-lived). Node 5: machinery = *f*(industrial machinery, electric machinery, other machinery).

Communications), the latent term for Services (commodity 34), is rising during most of the sample period before tapering off in the 2000s. The projection of $f^{Im=8}_{Services,t}$ is thus essentially flat.

Change in business inventories (CBI) fluctuates with the business cycle that we do not model, so that we specify inventory investment as an exogenous share of aggregate investment:

$$VII^{inventory} = \alpha^{IY} VII, \tag{5.22}$$

where the share α^{IY} is taken from sample data. Total inventory demand is specified as a Cobb-Douglas function of the commodities, using actual shares in the sample period and the share for the final year of the sample for projections. The value of inventory investment in commodity i is

$$VII_i^{\text{invy}} = \alpha_i^{IY} VII^{\text{invy}} \qquad i \in I_{\text{COM}}. \tag{5.23}$$

The total investment demand for commodity i is the sum of the fixed investment and inventory components:

$$\begin{aligned} VI_i &= VI_i^{fixed} + VI_i^{inventory} \\ PS_i I_i &= PII_i IF_i + VI_i^{inventory}. \end{aligned} \tag{5.24}$$

This set of equations is specified in greater detail in appendix A (A.3.24).

5.4 Imports, Exports, and Total Supply

Since IGEM is a one-country model, the supply of goods by the rest of the world (ROW) is not modeled explicitly for each commodity. We follow the standard treatment in one-country models of treating imports and domestic output as imperfect substitutes. This is often called the Armington assumption and is reasonable at our level of aggregation.[12] We also assume that U.S. demand is not sufficient to change world relative prices.

The total supply of commodity i at period t is an aggregate of the domestic and imported varieties:

$$QS_{it} = QS(QC_i, M_i, t). \tag{5.25}$$

Domestic commodity supply QC_i is given in equation (2.19), while M_i denotes the quantity of competitive imports.[13] The price of imports is the world price multiplied by an effective exchange rate e_t, plus tariffs tr and, possibly, new externality taxes tx:

$$PM_{it} = (1 + tr_{it} + tx_i^{rv})e_t PM_{it}^* + tx_i^{ru}. \tag{5.26}$$

The role of the exchange rate will be made clear after the discussion of the current account balance below. We use the term "landed price" to refer to the border price in dollars, before tariffs:

$$PM_{it}^{land} = e_t PM_{it}^*. \tag{5.27}$$

We treat the total supply function in a manner similar to that for the production model—writing the supply price as a function of the domestic price and imported price. We derive the demand for domestic and imported varieties from a translog price function for the total supply price:

$$\begin{aligned}\ln PS_{it} = {} & \alpha_{ct} \ln PC_{it} + \alpha_{mt} \ln PM_{it} + \frac{1}{2}\beta_{cc} \ln^2 PC_{it} + \frac{1}{2}\beta_{mm} \ln^2 PM_{it} \\ & + \beta_{cm} \ln PC_{it} \ln PM_{it} + f_{ct}^M \ln PC_{it} + f_{mt}^M \ln PM_{it}.\end{aligned} \tag{5.28}$$

The demands in share form derived from this cost function are

$$\frac{PM_{it}M_{it}}{PS_{it}QS_{it}} = \alpha_{mt} + \beta_{mm} \ln \frac{PM_{it}}{PC_{it}} + f_t^{Mi}. \tag{5.29}$$

When the share elasticity is zero, $\beta_{mm} = 0$, the demand for imports has unit price elasticity, while a positive value implies an inelastic demand for imports and a negative value implies an elastic demand. The value of the supply of commodity i to the domestic market and exports is

$$PS_{it}QS_{it} = PC_{it}QC_{it} + PM_{it}M_{it}. \tag{5.30}$$

The import price is the U.S. border price in dollars, inclusive of tariffs, just as the domestic price is the producers' price, including sales taxes but excluding transport and trade margins. Combining this value with the supply price from (5.29) we obtain the quantity of total supply QS_i of the commodity.

At this point we should note that we have now closed the loop in describing the flow of commodities. In chapter 2 we began with producing sectors purchasing intermediate inputs at price PS_i and selling output at price PO_j in equations (2.5) and (2.11). The price of intermediates is the price of total supply given in (5.29). We assume that all buyers buy the same bundle of domestic and imported varieties for each type of commodity i.

Imports into the United States have been rising rapidly during our sample period, not only in absolute terms but as a share of domestic output. This change cannot be explained by price movements alone. We employ the econometric approach used for the production and consumption subtiers to capture changes in technology. The right-hand side of (5.30) contains a latent state variable f_{it}^{M} modeled as a vector autoregression. The estimation of this function is described in section 5.4.1 below.

The inputs into the industry production functions include noncomparable imports. The demands for these goods are derived through a hierarchical tier structure. In the production function the value of such imports by industry j is $PNCI_j QP_{NCI}^{j}$. The price of these imports is specified in the same way as competitive imports in (5.27) above:

$$PNCI_{it} = (1 + tr_{it})e_t PNCI_{it}^{*}. \tag{5.31}$$

Beyond the sample period world prices PM_{it}^{*} are projected to change at the same rate as the productivity growth in U.S. industry prices. The productivity of industry j, as represented by the latent term in the price function discussed in chapter 4, is assumed to apply to productivity in commodity i in the rest of the world. The rate of change of PM_{it}^{*} is thus set equal to the change in the latent variable f_{it}^{p}.

The demand for U.S. exports depends on world income and prices. We use a translog price function and the corresponding share equations with latent state variables to allocate supply between domestic supply and exports. The actual export prices received in the sample period behave differently from prices of imports into the United States. The commodities traded are different, due to differences in subclassification, location, or timing, even if they are both classified under the same commodity group.

To simplify IGEM we use a single world price for each commodity. We write the allocation function in terms of the import price PM_{it}:

$$SX_t^{i} = \frac{PC_{it}X_{it}}{PC_{it}QC_{it}} = \alpha_{xt} + \beta_{xx}\ln\frac{PM_{it}}{PC_{it}} + f_{it}^{X}. \tag{5.32}$$

As before, we introduce a latent variable to track historical changes that cannot be explained by price movements alone.

When the allocation function (5.33) is estimated, as described below, we use the import prices instead of the actual export prices. Note that this function is derived from profit maximization of the supplier and is not symmetrical with the cost minimization that underlies the input demands. In particular, the implied price function is convex, not concave like the price function that describes producer behavior.

During the projection period we assume that the world price of commodity i falls at the same rate as the change in productivity in the U.S. industry i, so there is no bias towards exports over time.

The trade balance in dollars is exports less both types of imports:

$$TB_t = \sum_i PC_i X_i - \sum_i e_t PM_i^* M_i - \sum_j ePNCI_j^* NCI_j. \tag{5.33}$$

The current account balance is the trade balance, plus net interest receipts, and less private and government transfers:

$$CA_t = TB_t + Y_t^{row} - GINT^{row} - CR_t - GTRAN_t^{row}. \tag{5.34}$$

The current account surplus, less the portion due to government foreign investment, adds to the stock of net private U.S. foreign assets:

$$BF_t = BF_{t-1} + CA_t - GFI. \tag{5.35}$$

Another way to express this is that the current account equals the change in total claims on the rest of the world:

$$BF_t - BG_t^* = BF_{t-1} - BG_{t-1}^* + CA_t. \tag{5.36}$$

Since 2007 the system of Integrated Macroeconomic Accounts produced jointly by BEA and the Federal Reserve Board reconciles the stocks and flows in (5.36).[14] These accounts include an item for statistical discrepancy. Our estimates of the stock of net private assets include this discrepancy (BF^{disc}) and allow for capital gains (ΔP^{BF}), and we re-write (5.36) as

$$BF_t = BF_{t-1} + CA_t - GFI + BF^{disc} + \Delta P^{BF}. \tag{5.37}$$

The closure of the external sector is treated in various ways in different trade models. We could set the current account exogenously and let the world relative price, e_t, adjust. Alternatively, we could set e_t exogenously and let the current account balance be endogenous. The second option is difficult to implement in a dynamic model where we need to have a clearly defined steady state. We therefore chose the first method, that is, the price of imports and exports move with the endogenous e_t so that (5.35) is satisfied.

5.4.1 *Estimating Import and Export Functions*

Equation (5.29) expresses the aggregate supply price as a translog function of the price of domestic variety PC_i and the price of imports PM_i.

We note that there is no independent observation on the total supply price PS_i, since only the domestic and imported prices are observed and these are used to construct the aggregate supply price and quantity. As in the lower tiers of the price functions for producer behavior, there is no latent variable corresponding to growth in productivity.

In the *state-space* model (5.29) the latent variables for the biases of trade changes that do not result from price substitution are specified as a vector autoregressive scheme (VAR):

$$f_{mt}^{Mi} = F^{Mi} f_{m,t-1}^{Mi} + \varepsilon_t^i. \tag{5.38}$$

The state variable f_{mt}^{Mi} in the share equation for import demand (5.30) allows us to track historical changes in imports that cannot be explained by changes in prices. This is important because of the rapid rise in the import shares for almost all commodities during the period 1960–2005. The rising proportion of trade to GDP reflects the extension of global supply chains to many countries. Models that specify import demands as functions of prices and income often yield implausible elasticities, since they fail to capture the effects of globalization.

The share equation (5.30) and VAR (5.39) are estimated for all commodities; however, there are seven commodities with zero imports, so that we estimate only 28 equations. The import shares in total supply for 2000 are given in the first column of table 5.7. The commodity with the largest import share is 72% for Leather Products, where imports exceed domestic output. Next are Apparel with a 57% import share and Miscellaneous Manufacturing with 52%, also exceeding domestic output. The energy commodities have very high shares as well. Petroleum and Gas Mining had a 39% import share and Petroleum Refining had 29%. The nontraded industries are Construction, Communications, Gas Utilities, Trade, and Government Enterprises.

The estimated parameters α_m^M and β_{mm}^M are given in table 5.7. The estimated share elasticities β_{mm}^M's are quite elastic; many are negative, so that the substitution elasticity between imported and domestic goods is greater than unity. The share elasticities for Petroleum Refining and Petroleum and Gas Mining are somewhat inelastic. Petroleum is not a homogenous commodity, crude oil of a particular grade, but an aggregate of many commodities that have their own price behavior. This leads to estimated elasticities that are relatively small.

To demonstrate the importance of the latent variable representing the bias of trade change, we also report in the last column the change in f_{mt}^M between the first and last year of the sample. The rise in the latent

Table 5.7
Estimates of import demand functions

		Import Share	Estimated Coefficients		Estimated
		2000 (%)	α	β	ft(2005)–ft(1960)
1	Agriculture	7.0	0.0040	0.0059	0.0761
2	Metal Mining	0.0	0.0993	0.0195	0.1264
3	Coal Mining	3.8	0.0115	0.0012	0.0379
4	Petroleum and Gas	39.2	0.0066	0.0150	0.4294
5	Nonmetallic Mining	12.9	0.0000		0.0000
6	Construction	0.0	0.0000		0.0000
7	Food Products	6.7	0.0000	–0.0208	0.0560
8	Tobacco Products	6.1	0.0292	0.0047	0.0610
9	Textile Mill Products	14.8	0.0314	–0.0983	0.1562
10	Apparel and Textiles	57.0	0.0005	0.0206	0.4567
11	Lumber and Wood	14.2	0.1313	0.0196	0.0700
12	Furniture and Fixtures	21.8	0.0547	0.0150	0.1914
13	Paper Products	11.5	0.0170	–0.0056	0.1299
14	Printing and Publishing	3.2	0.0020	–0.0068	0.0267
15	Chemical Products	17.1	0.0000	0.0169	0.1339
16	Petroleum Refining	29.0	0.0000	0.0185	0.1327
17	Rubber and Plastic	14.4	0.0234	–0.0305	0.1325
18	Leather Products	72.5	0.2999	0.0546	0.6280
19	Stone, Clay, and Glass	14.4	0.1440	0.0131	0.1498
20	Primary Metals	20.2	0.0068	–0.2053	0.2814
21	Fabricated Metals	9.6	0.1219	–0.1240	0.1094
22	Industrial Machinery	22.1	0.0180	–0.1226	0.1356
23	Electronic and Electric Equip.	24.2	0.0000	0.0949	0.0627
24	Motor Vehicles	30.7	0.0000	0.0518	0.2367
25	Other Transportation Equip.	16.8	0.1099	0.0091	0.1263
26	Instruments	21.6	0.1667	0.0070	0.1809
27	Miscellaneous Mfg.	51.9	0.0000	0.0506	0.4401
28	Transport and Warehouse	2.3	0.0018	–0.0009	0.0217
29	Communications	0.0	0.0000		0.0000
30	Electric Utilities	0.9	0.0020	–0.0244	0.0104
31	Gas Utilities	0.0	0.0000		0.0000
32	Trade	0.0	0.0000		0.0000
33	FIRE	0.2	0.0000	0.0003	0.0014
34	Services	0.3	0.0000	–0.0074	0.0030
35	Government Enterprises	0.0	0.0000	0.0000	0.0000

variable indicates a rise in the share of imports that is not explained by price substitution. In the manufacturing industries we see very large increases in import penetration. The largest changes are in Leather Products (0.63), Apparel (0.46), and Miscellaneous Manufacturing (0.44). The energy-intensive industries also see large increases in import shares—Primary Metals (0.28), Stone-Clay-Glass (0.15), and Chemicals (0.13). In the energy group, the large increase in oil imports generated a 0.43 unit change in the latent variable for Petroleum and Gas Mining, and a 0.13 change for Petroleum Refining.

To illustrate the role of the latent variable f_{mt}^{M} in the time series behavior, figure 5.9 plots this variable for Motor Vehicles for the sample period 1960–2004 and for the projection period 2005–2050. We see a steady rise in the latent variable from the mid-1970s to the mid-1980s, tracking the rise in value shares, followed by a stable period during the 1990s and an increase in the 2000s. The projection of f_{mt}^{M} using (5.39) shows a small rise in the import share going forward. As we noted for the production subtiers in section 4.4, these terms converge to a constant. The projections of the other imports are plotted in appendix C, figure C5. The steady rise in the import share due to nonprice factors can be seen in almost all commodities except for the mining and services sectors. The imports of transportation services, of course, rose with the imports of tangible goods.

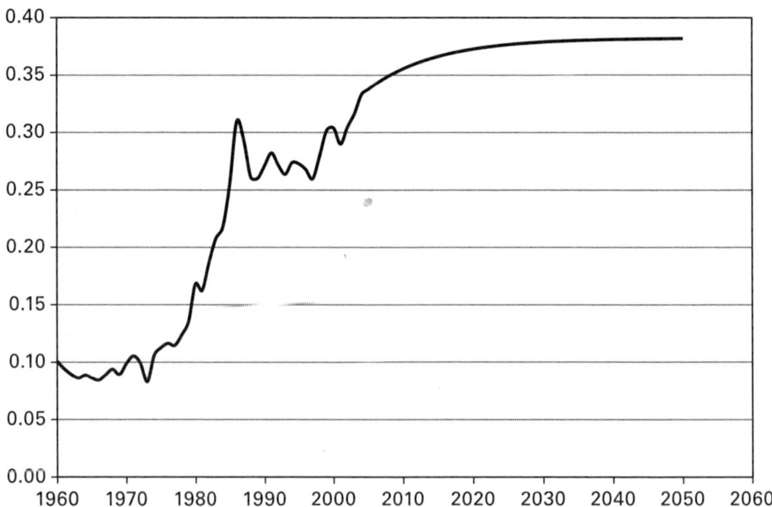

Figure 5.9
Projection of latent term in imports; Motor Vehicles.

Turning next to the export function, the first column of table 5.8 gives the share of domestic output going to exports in 2005. The major exported manufactures are Other Transportation Equipment (which includes aircraft), Instruments, Chemicals, Motor Vehicles, and Electrical Equipment. The other major commodities are Metal Mining and Transportation Services. The large export share for Leather Products in 2005 comes after a long period of declining domestic production; as we noted above, this sector has the largest share of imports in total supply.

We add a stochastic term to export share equation (5.33) and estimate the following function:

$$\frac{PC_{it}X_{it}}{PC_{it}QC_{it}} = \alpha_{xt} + \beta_{xx}\ln\frac{PM_{it}}{PC_{it}} + f_{it}^{X} + \varepsilon_{it}^{X}. \qquad (5.39)$$

The price function underlying equation (5.33) allocates total supply between exports and domestic consumption. This function is convex, unlike the price function for the allocation of domestic output, which is concave. The results are reported in table 5.8. The fitted share for year 1996, when the prices are normalized to 1, would be given by the sum of the α_{xt} and f_{it}^{X} terms. The estimated share elasticity, β_{xx}, ranges from 0.02 to 0.40, ignoring the tiny share in Construction, with the largest share elasticities in Coal Mining, Other Transportation Equipment, Industrial Machinery, and Electrical Equipment.

The latent term captures the trend of rising export shares between 1960 and 1980 for most commodities. The U.S. economic boom in the second half of the 1990s led to a decline in export shares as more output was allocated to the domestic market. These are illustrated in figure 5.10 for three commodities—Chemicals, Other Transportation Equipment, and Transportation Services.

The strong upward trend for Chemicals was interrupted with the oil shock of the 1970s and another pause in the 2000s; the estimated autoregressive parameter then projects a quick stabilization of the share. Transportation Services also grew strongly since 1980 and is projected to continue, but at a rate much slower than the sample period. Other Transportation Equipment (mainly aerospace) was quite volatile with a declining share in the 2000s; the estimated parameters projected a quick stabilization of this share at a level close to the sample average for 1980–2005.

The latent terms projected for the other commodities are given in appendix C, figure C7. Exports of energy were not very important,

Table 5.8
Estimates of export allocation functions

		Export Share	Estimated Coefficients		Estimated
		2005 (%)	α	β	ft(2005)– ft(1960)
1	Agriculture	7.2	0.8591	0.1117	0.0217
2	Metal Mining	16.5	0.5767	0.1397	0.1907
3	Coal Mining	6.0	0.0999	0.4004	0.2049
4	Petroleum and Gas	1.9	0.0645	0.0404	0.0154
5	Nonmetallic Mining	4.6	0.2073	0.0885	–0.0469
6	Construction	0.1	0.2364	0.0017	0.0028
7	Food Products	6.5	0.0044	0.0746	0.0579
8	Tobacco Products	11.2	0.0511	0.1773	0.0648
9	Textile Mill Products	14.4	0.0833	0.2277	–0.0402
10	Apparel and Textiles	10.6	0.0168	0.0726	–0.0110
11	Lumber and Wood	4.2	0.3222	0.0607	0.0034
12	Furniture and Fixtures	5.1	0.0937	0.1456	–0.0739
13	Paper Products	9.0	0.0871	0.0806	0.0273
14	Printing and Publishing	4.6	0.1800	0.0454	0.0243
15	Chemical Products	20.2	0.0942	0.1344	0.0983
16	Petroleum Refining	22.5	0.0955	0.0857	0.0101
17	Rubber and Plastic	9.3	0.1859	0.1274	–0.0102
18	Leather Products	40.4	0.0467	0.0895	0.0082
19	Stone, Clay, and Glass	5.6	0.0014	0.0984	0.0066
20	Primary Metals	10.2	0.0000	0.1071	0.0369
21	Fabricated Metals	7.7	0.1498	0.1353	0.0319
22	Industrial Machinery	13.1	0.0876	0.2900	–0.0264
23	Electronic and Electric Equipment	13.4	0.3296	0.2415	–0.2672
24	Motor Vehicles	13.9	0.2202	0.1770	–0.1115
25	Other Transportation Equipment	30.5	0.1000	0.3082	0.0089
26	Instruments	21.5	0.1002	0.2012	0.0463
27	Miscellaneous Mfg.	20.4	0.1290	0.0860	–0.0281
28	Transport and Warehouse	13.4	0.1047	0.1525	0.1123
29	Communications	2.2	0.1514	0.0303	0.0137
30	Electric Utilities	1.7	0.0441	0.0676	0.0157
31	Gas Utilities	1.5	0.1648	0.0278	0.0229
32	Trade	4.2	0.0408	0.0493	0.0477
33	FIRE	5.3	0.0185	0.0578	0.0199
34	Services	1.7	0.0141	0.0229	0.0145
35	Government Enterprises	0.3	0.1831	0.1678	0.3694

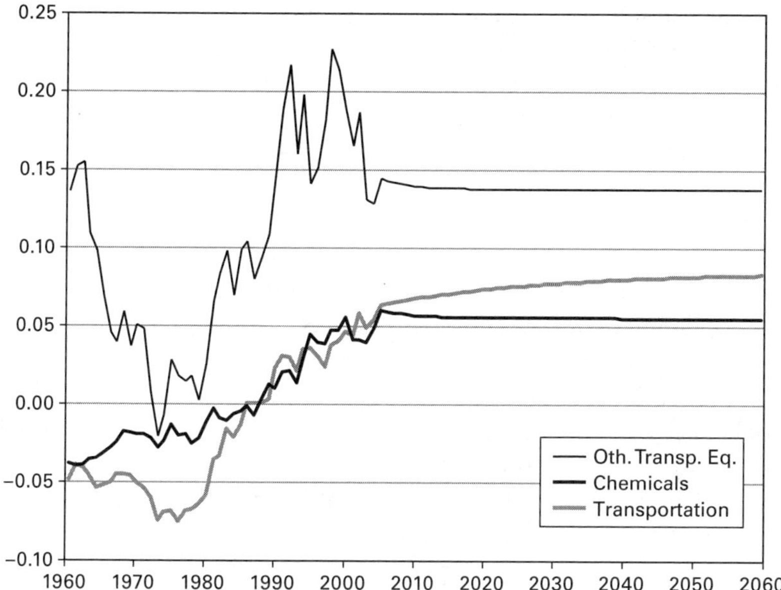

Figure 5.10
Latent term for exports; selected commodities.

except for Petroleum Refining. There is no particular trend in the latent term for Petroleum Refining exports and we project a latent variable close to the value at the end of the sample period. The value share of coal going to exports has been falling until the early 2000s when it started to rise again to 6.0% in 2005. Coal exports have risen substantially in the more recent years; this is, however, beyond the sample period used to estimate our model and we project only a modest growth in the latent term for coal exports. We should emphasize that a projected boom in world prices of coal represented in the exogenous variable $PM^{*}_{coal,t}$ will raise the export shares in our model to the extent allowed by the elasticity $\beta_{xx}^{i=coal}$.

The sectors with the greatest rate of productivity growth are Industrial Machinery, which includes computers, and Electrical Machinery, which includes semiconductors. These sectors show the largest fall in relative prices. The latent terms in the export equation for these sectors are volatile. During the period 1995–2000, when investment in IT hardware and software boomed, the share of their output going to exports fell. Our projected trends for the latent variables for both Industrial Machinery and Electrical Machinery are essentially flat at the last sample point, a low point since the peak in the early 1990s. The latent variables are essential to capture the trends observed in the data. A simpler model reflecting only price substitution between exports and domestically consumed products would fail to capture these trends.

5.5 Summary and Conclusion

In this chapter we have completed the demand side of IGEM by incorporating demands for all commodities and services by governments, for domestic investment, and for exports. We have added imports to domestic production to complete the supply side of the model. Our models of the government and rest of the world include both capital and current accounts for both sectors. The revenue side of the government budget is particularly critical in analyzing the impacts of energy and environmental taxes and the substitution of these taxes for other revenue sources or revenue recycling in chapter 8.

We model investment by commodity in the same way as the subtiers of our models of consumer and producer behavior in chapters 3 and 4. We distinguish empirically between substitution in response to price changes, for example, the decline in the relative prices of information technology and equipment, and price-induced changes in technology. We project these changes into the future, using autoregressive schemes that generate the latent variables that describe changes in technology. Unlike our models of producer behavior, there is no change in the overall level of technology.

We model imports as imperfect substitutes for domestically produced commodities and exports as imperfect substitutes for domestic consumption. The novel feature of our model of the rest of the world is that we distinguish between substitution in response to price changes and price-induced changes in technology. Both imports and exports have been affected by substantial price-induced technical change resulting from the development of global supply chains. This is a key phenomenon in globalization and has been greatly facilitated by the decline in tariff and nontariff barriers to international trade.

This chapter has closed the loop for the commodity flows modeled in IGEM. We have now accounted for both demands and supplies of all commodities, including capital and labor services. We are now prepared to project the future growth of the U.S. economy in chapter 6. Demography and technology are the driving forces in our projections.

Investment is the primary enabling factor, but this is determined endogenously in IGEM, using our models of investment, capital stock, and capital services and the corresponding prices. In chapter 7 we extend the scope of the model to incorporate emissions of greenhouse gases and conventional pollutants. In chapter 8 we apply our projections in designing new energy and environmental policies for the United States.

Notes

1. Chapter 7 gives a complete description of the environmental accounts.
2. IGEM allows for a standard closure where transfers are set exogenously in constant dollars or the alternative closure with exogenous shares of GDP, described in more detail in appendix A, equation A.4.30.
3. Note that government capital consumption, VG_{GK}, is not a market transaction but an imputed value in the national accounts; it is added to current consumption expenditures (5.5) and makes the net borrowing requirement smaller than the "current deficit."
4. See *Survey of Current Business*, August 2007, pp. 89–107.
5. The calculation of tax rates is discussed in Section 7.4 of Jorgenson and Yun (2001).
6. The *Budget and Economic Outlook*, released in January 2009, was followed by *The Treatment of Federal Receipts and Expenditures in the National Income and Product Accounts*, released in June 2009. The *Budget and Economic Outlook* released in January 2010 was not accompanied by this additional NIPA-based information and we made some simple conversions to the NIPA system. The GDP and unemployment projections are given in table E-1 of CBO (2010a) and in a file Year-by-YearForecast.xls available on their website (www.cbo.gov/ftpdocs/108xx/doc10871/BudgetOutlook2010_Jan.cfm). Projections of the federal government and trust fund surpluses are in table 1.3, government debts in table 1.7 and D2, expenditures are in table 3.3 (these tables also in the web file budget-projections.xls).
7. This is according to our definitions of the government accounts, in the official NIPA in the *Survey of Current Business*, August 2010, the net borrowing was $1593 billion in 2009.
8. Since 2007 the Bureau of Economic Analysis (BEA) has published a set of Integrated Macroeconomic Accounts that include a reconciliation of the Current Account with the Changes in the Balance Sheet accounts. See Bond et al. (2007), table 7. More recent updates are given in the BEA website: www.bea.gov/national/nipaweb/Ni_FedBeaSna/Index.asp.
9. See Jorgenson, Ho, and Stiroh, *Information Technology and the U.S. Growth Resurgence* (Cambridge, MA: The MIT Press, 2005), table 8.1.
10. The sources of data are described in appendix B.3.2.
11. In the 1992 Input-Output Benchmark this bridge table is table E in the *Survey of Current Business*, November 1997. For example, the $43.6 billion investment in the asset "computers and peripheral equipment" is made up of the following commodities at producer prices: 32.7 from machinery, 3.4 from services, 0.4 from transportation, and 7.1 from trade.
12. That is, while we may regard the imports of steel of a particular type as perfectly substitutable, the output of the entire primary metals industry is a basket of many commodities and would have an estimated substitution elasticity that is quite small. The literature on econometric modeling of import demands is surveyed by Russell Hillberry

and David Hummels, "Trade Elasticity Parameters for a Computable General Equilibrium Model." Chap. 18 in Dixon and Jorgenson, *Handbook of Computable General Equilibrium Modeling*, vol. 1B (Amsterdam: Elsevier, 2012).

13. We have used the notation M_j to denote the inputs of non-energy materials into the industry production function. The distinction from M_i as commodity imports should be clear from the context.

14. See "Integrated Macroeconomic Accounts for the United States," *Survey of Current Business*, February 2007, p. 14.

6 Model Solution

6.1 Introduction

In this chapter we describe IGEM's projection of the U.S. economy. We show how the various elements of the model determine overall GDP growth and the composition of economic activity, including energy use. Among the main drivers of growth are exogenous variables such as the population, the time endowment, labor quality and capital quality growth, current account deficits, government deficits, and tax policies. In addition, the exogenous state variables of the production, consumption, and trade models derive growth and the composition of activity. We describe how these exogenous values are chosen from official projections and from our own extrapolations.

Our discussion of the base case is intended to illustrate how the exogenous variables affect the future time path of the U.S. economy. The main point of using models such as IGEM is to study how changes in energy and environmental policies affect the time path of the economy. For example, how are changes in endogenous variables, such as the GDP or the level of coal use, determined by exogenous policy changes? The size of endogenous changes is mainly determined by the substitution parameters. The exogenous state variables have a smaller effect in most situations.[1] In summary, the main application of IGEM is in analyzing the impact of policy changes or external shocks or analyzing sensitivity to exogenous assumptions. We illustrate these applications in considerable detail in chapter 8.

We first describe the projections of exogenous variables in section 6.2 and then describe the base case path as generated by these exogenous values in section 6.3. In many policy studies, however, the model is calibrated to exogenous projections before simulating the impact of a policy shock. An example is the U.S. Environmental Protection

Agency (EPA) requirement that analysis of climate legislation must be consistent with the medium-term projections of GDP and energy use made by the Energy Information Administration (EIA) of the U.S. Department of Energy. This is described in *EPA Analysis of the American Clean Energy and Security Act of 2009* (EPA 2009), using the IGEM and ADAGE models. In section 6.4 we describe how we calibrate IGEM to such external requirements.

6.2 Projecting the Exogenous Variables

Exogenous variables are those whose values are specified before model simulations of the endogenous variables. In most cases the distinction is obvious: Prices other than the numeraire are endogenous and the state variables of the production and consumption models are exogenous. The classification of variables depends on the desired closure of the model. For example, the rate of taxation of carbon emissions may be exogenous and the emissions themselves endogenous. Alternatively, we may choose an exogenous cap on carbon emissions, using an endogenous tax rate on emissions as a policy instrument. Another example is the government deficit and expenditures on final purchases. Either variable may be set exogenously with the other treated as a policy instrument and determined endogenously.

The values for the entire time path must be specified for each exogenous variable. We specify that IGEM must converge to a stationary steady state in order to satisfy transversality conditions. For convergence of the model the time path for each exogenous variable must be chosen to stabilize eventually. For the policies that we examine, the time frame of interest is usually in the medium range of 25 to 50 years. However, emissions targets in the Waxman-Markey House Resolution 2454 are set for 2080. To accommodate these policies, we specify the exogenous variables according to official projections, where available, through 75 years. Beyond this period of interest, we set the exogenous variables to converge to a stationary value.

We have described the projections of government sector variables, such as budget deficits and tax rates, in chapter 5, section 5.1.2. The projections of the latent variables representing technical change in the top tier of the cost functions are described in section 4.3., following the discussion of the estimation results. The projections of the lower-tier cost functions are given in section 4.4. The projections of the latent variables representing nonprice changes in aggregate consumption patterns for commodities in the lower tiers is described in section 3.6. The projection of the growth in capital quality is given in figure 5.7. In this section we describe the projection of additional exogenous variables related to population in section 6.2.1 and those related to the rest-of-the-world sector in section 6.2.2.

6.2.1 Population and Time Endowment

Population growth and the composition of the population are key exogenous variables in determining the size of the economy. For example, changes in the size and composition of the population determine the time available for labor supply. We refer to this as the time endowment. We begin with population projections from the Bureau of the Census by sex and individual year of age.[2]

During the sample period we allocate the population to six educational attainment categories, using data from the Current Population Survey. The calculations parallel those used in measuring labor input and described in appendix B.2, table B.12.[3] We divide the population into seven age groups. The time endowment for each adult is 14 hours a day, allocated between work and leisure. The number of hours for each sex-age-education category is then weighted by the labor compensation rates from our labor database and aggregated to form the time endowment, as described in chapter 2, section 2.3.7.

For convenience we reproduce equation (2.60) for the Tornqvist index of time endowment, LH:

$$\begin{aligned} d\ln LH_t &= \sum_k \frac{1}{2}(v_{kt}^L + v_{kt-1}^L)d\ln(14\cdot 365\cdot POP_{kt}). \\ v_{kt}^L &= \frac{(1-tl_t^m)P_{kt}^L\cdot 14\cdot 365\cdot POP_{kt}}{VLH_t} \quad \text{k = \{gender, age, education\}}, \end{aligned} \tag{6.1}$$

where POP_{kt} is the population in group k projected for year t and P_{kt}^L is the hourly compensation rate for group k. The value of the aggregate time endowment VLH_t is derived as the sum over the values of all groups.

In making projections beyond the sample period we use the Census Bureau projections by sex and age. We assume that educational attainment of those aged 35 or younger will be the same as the last year of the sample period; that is, a person who becomes 22 years old in 2020 will have the same chance of having a bachelor's degree as a person in 2006, our base year for the population data. Those aged 55 and older

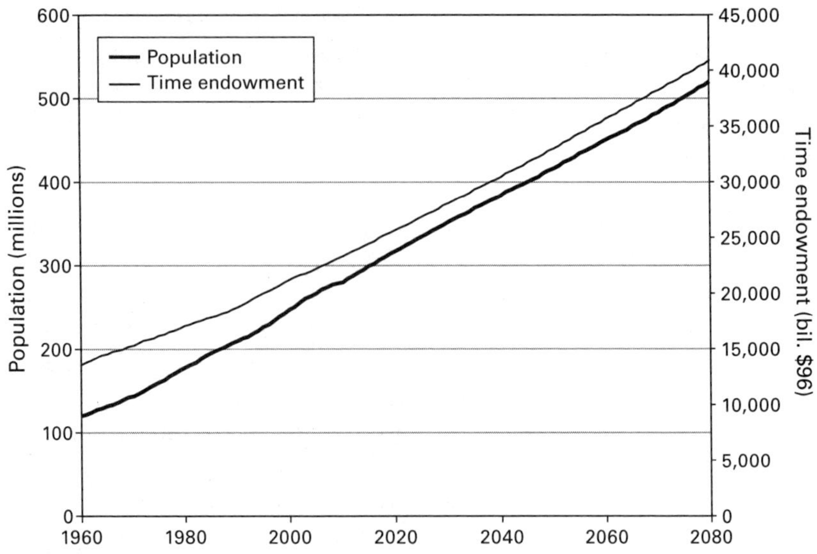

Figure 6.1
Population and household time endowment.

carry their education attainment with them as they age. For example, the educational distribution of 70-year-olds in 2010 is the same as that of 60-year-olds in 2000, assuming that death rates are independent of educational attainment. We combine these two assumptions for individuals between ages 35 and 55. This results in a smooth improvement in educational attainment that is consistent with the observed profile in 2006.

Our projections of the time endowment are illustrated in figure 6.1 along with projections for the total population. In these projections the population is expected to grow at 0.94% per year for the next 25 years (2010–2035) and eventually reach 545 million persons by 2080. The gradual improvement in educational attainment implies that the time endowment grows at a modestly faster rate of 1.18% over the same 25 years. Over the longer horizon, 2010–2080, the growth in educational attainment is slower; the difference between growth rates of the time endowment and the population is only 0.08 percentage points. Our projected rate of U.S. population growth exceeds the projected world population growth of 0.75% per year during the period 2010–2050.[4]

We project a second set of exogenous variables that provide the distribution terms in the aggregate consumption share equations. The vector of shares for nondurables, capital services, services, and leisure was given in (2.37), and the distribution terms for the demographic effects are in (2.38) and (2.39). These equations are repeated here:

$$w_t = \frac{1}{D(p_t)}\left[\alpha^H + B^H \ln p_t - \iota B^H \xi_t^d + B_A \xi_t^L\right]. \tag{6.2}$$

$$\xi_t^d = \sum_k n_{kt} m_k \ln m_k \,/\, M. \tag{6.3}$$

$$\xi_t^L = \sum_k n_{kt} m_k A_k \,/\, M. \tag{6.4}$$

m_k is the expenditure of households of type k, and n_k is the number of households of type k. The distribution terms represent the effects of the changing composition of families on aggregate consumption demands; ξ_t^d represents the aggregate total expenditure effect and ξ_t^L represents the effect due to different household types having different baskets when faced with the same prices. The k index is shorthand for the categories used in the consumption model as listed in table 3.5—the number of children (c), number of adults (z), region (d), location (u), sex of head (s), and race of head (r)—so that $n_k \equiv n_{czdrsu}$.

For the sample period the distribution terms, ξ_t^d and ξ_t^L, are obtained from the CEX data. These are functions of the total expenditure distribution and the distribution of household types. When we project these beyond the sample period we assume that the relative expenditures by type of households are fixed, that is, that the ratios m_{k_1} / m_{k_2} are fixed. We incorporate the population projections into the changing composition of household types.

To project the composition of the population by household types we first define the mean expenditure share of group K in the last year of the sample:

$$\overline{m}_K^0 = \frac{\overline{m}_{K,T=2006}}{M_{T=2006}}. \tag{6.5}$$

We then rewrite the income distribution term (6.3) by replacing m_{kt} / M_t with the base year share $\overline{m}_K^0$. To do this, we must first define a normalization term that uses the number of households in the current year (nf_{Kt}) as weights:

$$M_t^0 = \sum_K nf_{Kt} \overline{m}_K^0. \tag{6.6}$$

This term is equal to 1.0 in 2006, the last year of the sample. The ratio m_{kt} / M_t may thus be replaced by $\overline{m}_K^0$ / M_t^0 in the projection period. The distribution term (6.3) for a future year t is then written as

$$\xi_t^d = \left[\sum_k n_{kt} m_{kt} \ln m_{kt}\right] \Big/ M_t = \sum_k n_{kt} \frac{m_{kt}}{M_t} \ln \frac{m_{kt}}{M_t} + \ln M_t$$
$$= \sum\nolimits_K nf_{Kt} \frac{\bar{m}_K^0}{M_t^0} \ln \frac{\bar{m}_K^0}{M_t^0} + \ln M_t$$
$$= \xi_t^{dd} + \ln M_t \quad t = 2007, 2008, \ldots, 2016. \tag{6.7}$$

The distribution term for total expenditure effects consists of an exogenous component reflecting changes in the composition of the population, ξ_t^{dd}, and the endogenous level of full consumption expenditures, $M_t = PF_tF_t$. The second distribution term (6.4) is a vector consisting of 11 rows for the demographic categories explicitly included—1 child, 2 children, 3+ children, 2 adults, 3+ adults, Midwest, South, West, nonwhite, female, and rural. The omitted categories are 0 child, 1 adult, Northeast, white, male, and urban. The value of the jth term in the projection period is obtained by replacing the sample expenditure share with the base year share:

$$\xi_j^L = \sum_k nf_{kt} m_{kt} A_k(j) / M_t$$
$$= \sum_{all\ K \in j} nf_{Kt} \frac{\bar{m}_K^0}{M_t^0}. \tag{6.8}$$

The projection of ξ_t^{dd} and ξ_t^L requires a projection of the number of households of each type, n_{czdrsu}. We first construct a household bridge matrix (**B**) that links the distribution of household types to the population by 2 sexes, 20 age groups, and 2 races in the 2000 census. We use the federal census because it provides individual and household data for a relatively large sample, corresponding to 1% of the population. We then use the Census Bureau's projection of the population, $POP_{sar,t}$, to project n_{czdrsu}:

$$n_{czdrsu,t} = \mathbf{B}_{sar}^{czdrsu} POP_{sar,t}. \tag{6.9}$$

The projection of the income distribution term ξ_t^{dd} is plotted in figure 6.2. This falls from −18.83 in 2006 to −19.38 in 2050. The projections of the expenditure shares for households of various types are plotted in figure 6.3 to illustrate the magnitude of the changes. In 2006 16.5% of total expenditures were by households with exactly 1 child (ξ_{1child}^L), the rest have 0, 2, or 3+ children, but by 2050 this share has fallen to 14.7%. The nonwhite-headed households share ($\xi_{nonwhite}^L$) rises from 16.0% to 20.0% of all expenditures. The share going to households with exactly 2 adults also falls significantly, largely offset by the rise in 1-adult

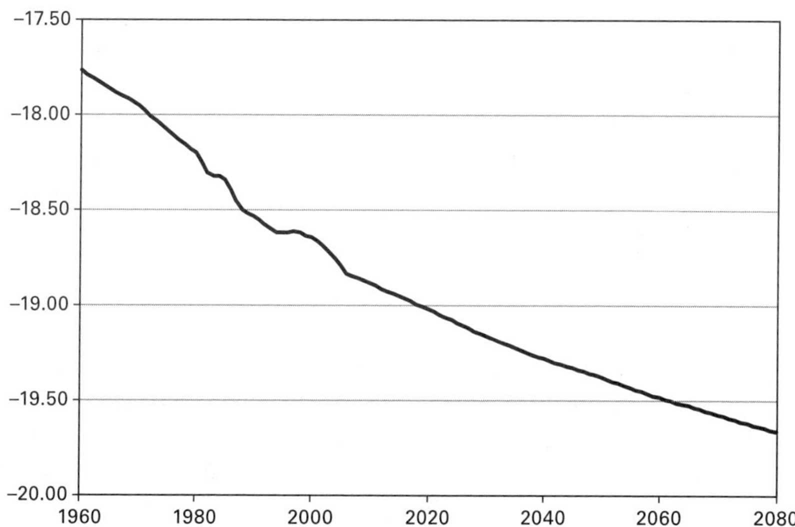

Figure 6.2
Projection of distribution term for income effects, ξ_t^{dd}.

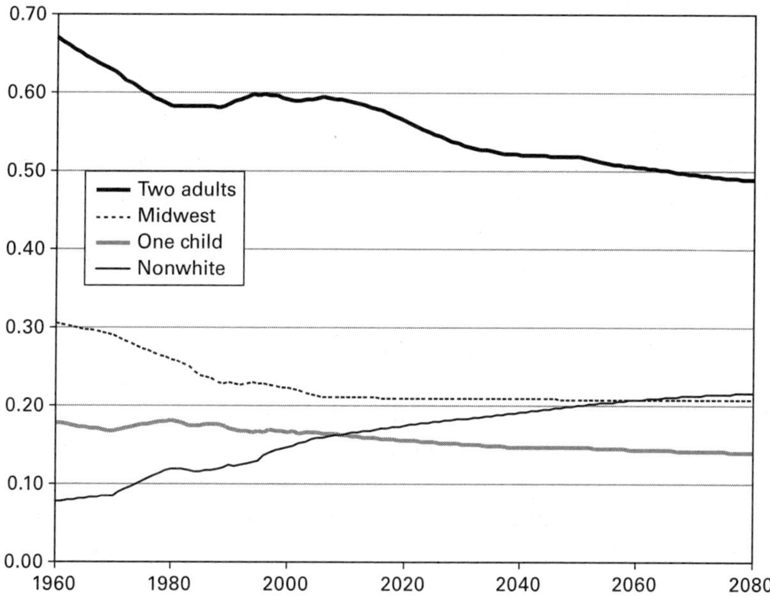

Figure 6.3
Projection of household types, share of total households.

households. We do not have an independent projection of regional distribution and so the share for "Midwest" is constant beyond the sample period.

The final exogenous variable related to population is the adjustment for business-cycle effects. In equation (2.90) we express the adjusted time endowment as the projected time endowment multiplied by a term to adjust for any unusual unemployment trends; this is repeated here:

$$LH_t^{adj} = (1 - u_t^{adj})LH_t. \tag{6.10}$$

In particular, this allows the model user to incorporate the widely projected below-trend employment rate and output for the years 2010–2015. To construct this adjustment we begin with the projected unemployment rate in CBO (2010, table E1). This series, u_t^{proj}, starts with a 10.1% rate in 2010 and falls gradually to 5.3% in 2014. The long-run unemployment rate is projected at 5.0% by CBO for 2017 and beyond.

We define the deviation from the long-run value as $du_t^{proj} = u_t^{proj} - 0.05$. The cyclical shift in the labor hours is set equal to this deviation, multiplied by the projected labor supply constructed from sample period employment rates:

$$dLS_t^{proj} = du_t^{proj} LS_t^{proj}. \tag{6.11}$$

The adjustment coefficient for time endowment is this cyclical change in work hours divided by the projected time endowment and scaled to the (total time: work time) ratio in the last year of the sample period:

$$u_t^{adj} = \frac{dLS_t^{proj}}{LH_t} \frac{LH_{2006}}{LS_{2006}}, \text{ t} = 2008, 2009, \ldots, 2016. \tag{6.12}$$

With the adjustment of the effective time endowment for the recession years, the projected endowment is below the trend time endowment. When this is multiplied by the leisure demand given by the household utility function, the household model generates leisure hours and labor supply that are lower than the trend levels. This, in turn, generates a level of output that is lower than trend output and closer to actual GDP during the years of the Great Recession.

6.2.2 *Current Account, World Prices, and Interest*

Two important assumptions that affect the composition of the economy are the government and current account deficits. A period with high twin deficits is associated with high consumption and low exports. In IGEM the transversality conditions require that government debt and foreign debt converge to stationary values. Since we impose zero productivity growth in the long run, the steady state is characterized by constant relative prices and constant quantities.

We have described in chapter 5 how we project the government deficits, beginning with the CBO medium-term projection for the federal budget. We assume that the deficit declines steadily to zero by 2060. This path of deficits cumulates into a stock of debt that converges to a constant value. We also assume that the current account deficit shrinks steadily, so that it too reaches a zero balance by 2060, and the stock of claims converges to a constant. These simplifying assumptions for the two deficits allow a smooth transition path to the steady state equilibrium.

For the current account there is no official counterpart to the CBO 10-year budget projection. We take the International Monetary Fund's *World Economic Outlook* projections of the U.S. current account balance as a starting point and assume that the balance gradually falls to zero by 2060.[5] The resulting projection is plotted in figure 6.4, where we give the government deficit for comparison. There is a sharp reduction of

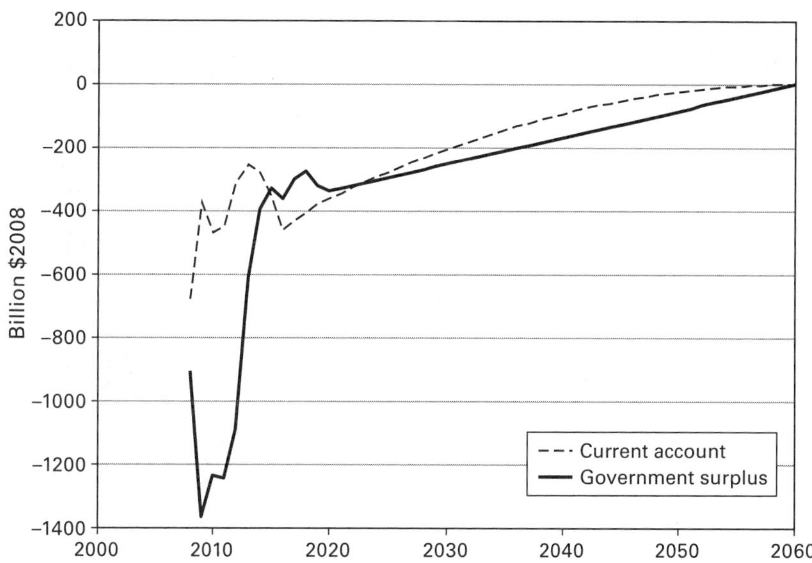

Figure 6.4
Government and current account deficits.

the U.S. current account deficit during the Great Recession of 2009–2010 and the IMF projects this lower path of deficits to continue, projecting it to be 3.5% of GDP by 2015.

The length of time for the transition to zero deficits obviously affects the base case path of the economy. We have allowed for a long transition period to allow the U.S. economy to adjust gradually to these two exogenous deficits. This gradual transition has only a modest impact on the size of the policy effects that the model simulates.

The import and export demands are functions of the world price, PM_{it}^* (equations 5.29 and 5.32). These prices must also be projected; since we do not have an explicit rest-of-the-world model, we assume that relative prices move in proportion to the autonomous productivity change projected for the U.S. industries as described in chapter 4, figure 4.25. That is, we assume:

$$\ln PM_{it}^* - \ln PM_{it-1}^* = f_t^i - f_{t-1}^i. \tag{6.13}$$

The exception to this is the imports of Oil and Gas Mining where we use the Energy Information Administration (EIA) projections of world oil prices from the *Annual Energy Outlook 2011*.[6] This projection is plotted in figure 6.5. After the fall in prices during the 2009 recession, world oil prices rose modestly back to $80 per barrel during the

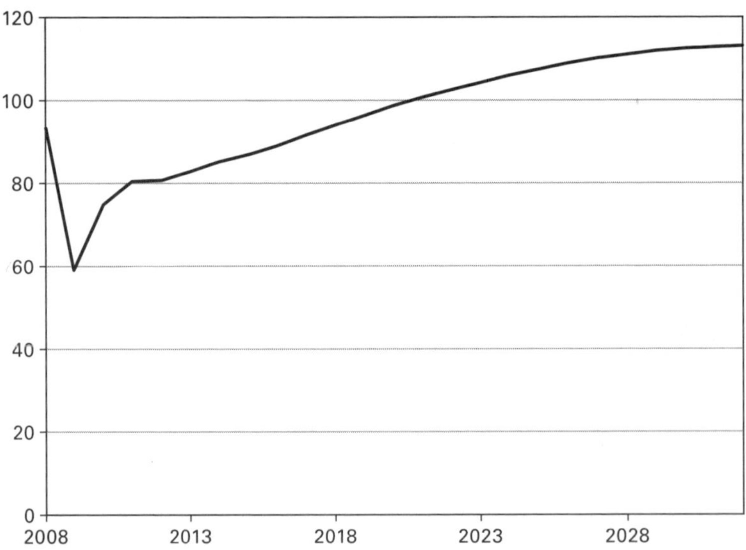

Figure 6.5
Projection of imported crude oil price ($2009 per barrel), *AEO 2011*.

expected recovery out to 2013, after which prices are projected to continue rising to \$114 per barrel in 2035.

6.2.3 *Calibration of Productivity Growth*

In the introduction we have noted that there are policies where the absolute size of the economy is central, for example, a numerical cap on greenhouse gas (GHG) emissions. The scale and details of the base case are also important when multiple models are employed in a single assessment. The recent Energy Modeling Forum multimodel study of climate change control scenarios (EMF 22) was such an exercise, and it included IGEM in the comparisons.[7] In these comparisons great care must be taken to craft a base case that is common to all models so that results can be reliably attributed to differing structures and parameters, as opposed to differing starting points and GDP growth rates.

Growth of total factor productivity (TFP) is one of the important determinants of economic growth in IGEM. This growth is mainly driven by the industry-level productivity growth described in chapter 4. Total factor productivity growth is highly uneven across industries, ranging from rapid growth in Electrical Machinery to negative growth in Construction. In order to align the long-run growth to the consensus forecasts embodied in the Social Security Trustees Report (SSA 2010) and CBO (2010b), we have added an adjustment term that raises TFP in all sectors equally. That is, the output price of industry j includes an A^{agg} term in addition to those described in equations (2.5) and (4.4):

$$\ln PO_j = \alpha_0^j + \alpha^{Pj'} \ln P^{Pj0} + \frac{1}{2} \ln P^{Pj0'} B^{Pj} \ln P^{Pj0} + \ln P^{Pj0'} f_t^{Pj} + f_t^j + \ln \lambda_j + \ln A^{agg}. \tag{6.14}$$

The projections in SSA (2010) assume that labor productivity over the 75-year horizon will be 1.7% per year with real GDP growing at 2.1% in the long run. The CBO long-term forecast is for a similar 2.0% growth in GDP. We choose the growth of aggregate productivity common to all industries ($\Delta \ln A_t^{agg}$) for each period during 2010–2085, so that the long-run GDP growth is 2.2% per year.

6.2.4 *Calibration of the Savings Rate*

The aggregate Euler equation for full consumption in equation (2.23) does not fit the historical rates of growth of full consumption closely, as is well known.[8] We first note that the rate of return used to estimate the rate of time preference in this equation is the average return over all assets as measured in the National Income and Product Accounts. These include risky assets as well as government bonds. In order to calibrate the growth path to the observed consumption share of GDP we modify the Euler equation (2.23) by introducing a risk-premium (r_t^{π}):

$$\frac{F_t}{F_{t-1}} = \frac{(1+n_t)(1+r_t)}{1+\rho+r_t^{\pi}} \frac{PF_{t-1}}{PF_t}. \tag{6.15}$$

The discount rate estimated using the detailed household model is about 0.015 as reported in table 3.14. When using the aggregate Euler equation (2.23) the estimated value of ρ is 0.026. In order to calibrate consumption rate (and hence the savings rate), we set the risk premium in the range of 0.003 to 0.01 in the first 20 years after the recovery from the Great Recession. In the first 3 years of the recovery we set r_t^{π} to 0.015. The calibration of other endogenous values to externally specified targets is discussed in section 6.3.

6.3 Base Case

We discuss two alternative base cases in this chapter. In this section we present an IGEM projection that is not calibrated to external targets. That is, the projected growth path of the U.S. economy depends only on the exogenous variables described in section 6.2. In section 6.4 we consider a base case projection that is calibrated to an externally set GDP growth rate.

We first describe the time path of the U.S. economy beginning in 2010. This is the time path we obtain by incorporating the exogenous variables described in section 6.2. We take the stock of capital and population at the end of 2009 as given. We follow the long-term projections by the CBO and the Census Bureau for 75 years and then allow the exogenous variables to converge rapidly to their long-run values. As described in chapter 2, we have approximated the steady state in 2130; this target date is chosen since the values of the endogenous variables calculated for 2130 were within the convergence tolerance of the separately calculated steady state that has identical values for the exogenous variables.

The entire transition path for capital and full consumption is plotted in figure 6.6 while the growth rates of key variables are given in

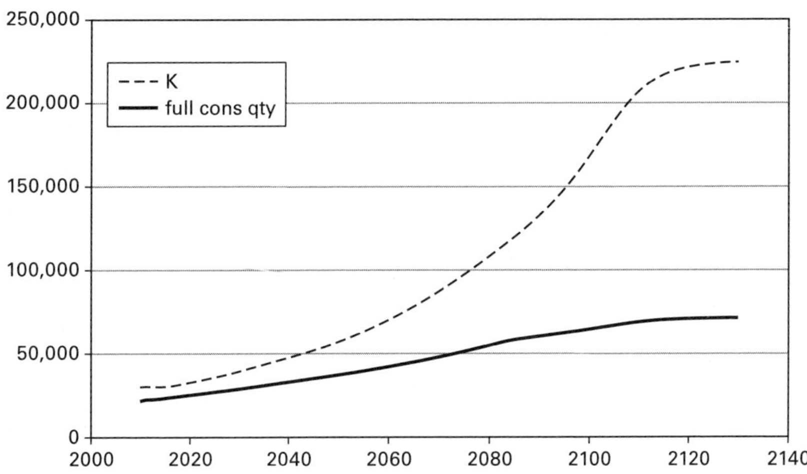

Figure 6.6
The base case path for capital stock and full consumption (billion $1996).

table 6.1 for the subperiods 2010–2035 and 2035–2085, that is, the first 25 years and the next 50 years. We are less concerned with the behavior of the U.S. economy after the 75-year horizon. Population growth and the government and current account deficits are assumed to be zero during the 2085–2130 transition period. In the medium-term the CBO projects a steady reduction in the unusually high unemployment rates seen during the Great Recession. We have incorporated this assumption in our unemployment adjustment (see equation [2.90]). To exclude this period of unusual adjustment, we also tabulate the growth rates for the period 2017–2035.

IGEM has rapid initial growth with high investment and smoothed consumption. These patterns are clear in the growth rates presented in table 6.1 and in the time paths charted in figures 6.6 through 6.8. Since the initial years, 2010–2016, are a period of unusual exogenous changes in unemployment rates that result in atypical consumption and investment patterns, we regard the 2017–2035 period as the first phase and 2035–2085 as the second phase. The share of investment in GDP is plotted in figure 6.7 and we can see that it falls from 21% in the late 2010s, to 19.4% in 2035, and to 18.2% by 2060. The share of consumption in GDP, after the period of recovery from the Great Recession, is close to 62% for all years. In the first phase GDP growth is 2.30% per year, decelerating to 2.19% in the next 50 years.

Table 6.1
Base case growth rates of key variables (% per year)

	2010–2035	2035–2085	Excluding Recovery 2017–2035	Excluding 1st Year (neg GDP) 2011–2035
Key macro variables				
Time endowment	1.07	0.74	1.03	1.08
Capital stock	1.48	2.03	1.88	1.50
GDP	2.16	2.19	2.30	2.39
Consumption	1.67	2.19	1.93	1.67
Investment	2.00	2.06	1.98	3.29
Government	1.47	1.51	1.80	1.59
Exports	4.17	2.74	4.09	4.41
Imports	1.71	2.59	2.46	2.44
Prices relative to labor numeraire				
Price of GDP	–0.69	–1.43	–1.07	–0.82
Price of consumption	–0.34	–1.43	–0.79	–0.44
Price of investment	–0.83	–1.48	–1.32	–1.02
World relative price (*e*)	0.96	–1.37	0.10	0.60
Growth accounting				
GDP	2.16	2.19	2.30	2.39
Capital input	1.90	2.38	2.29	1.92
Labor input	1.22	0.68	1.15	1.50
TFP	0.65	0.77	0.67	0.72
Energy and emissions				
Energy consumption (BTUs)	1.24	1.99	1.62	1.68
Electricity consumption	2.03	2.49	2.16	2.16
CO^2 emissions	1.58	2.05	1.74	1.94

Recall from equation (6.14) that the TFP growth is calibrated to deliver the projection of 2.2% growth over the latter part of the 75-year horizon. This results in somewhat different aggregate annual TFP growth rates for the different periods, 0.67% in the first 25 years and 0.77% in the next 50 years. If this growth rate had remained constant, the deceleration in GDP growth would be more noticeable. The first 25 years is the period when the government and trade deficits are substantially reduced. These deficits are gradually eliminated during

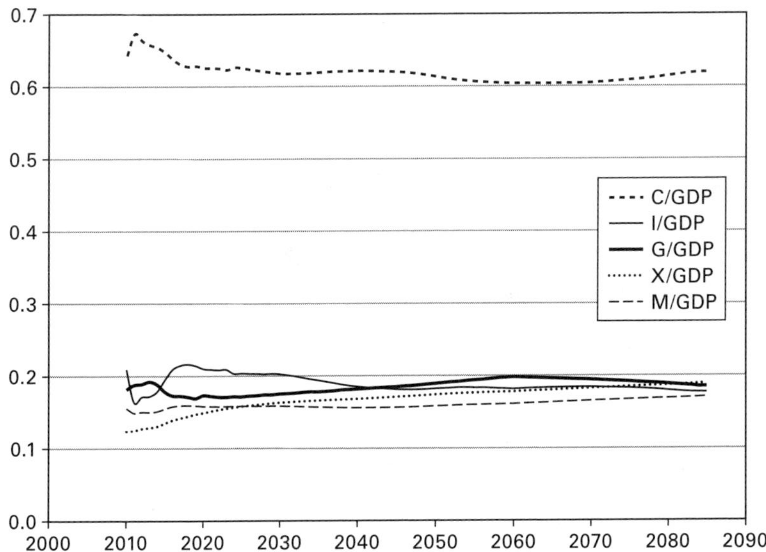

Figure 6.7
The base case GDP composition (shares of consumption, investment, government, exports, and imports).

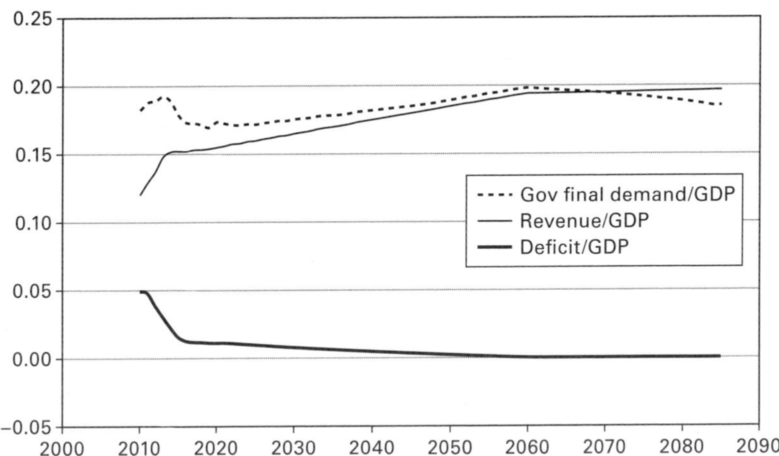

Figure 6.8
The base case government share of GDP.

the next 25 years as most other exogenous variables also converge to their steady-state levels. Factor biases and autonomous industry productivity trends stabilize together with foreign commodity prices as in equation (6.13).

The effect of these trends on the government share of the economy is plotted in figure 6.8. After some fluctuations in the first few years of the recovery from the Great Recession, government final purchases rise from about 17% of GDP to 19% in 2060 before falling slightly again. On the other hand, revenues rise significantly to meet the assumed decline in the deficit, from 15.3% of GDP in 2017 to 17.0% in 2035, and to 19.6% in 2085. These revenue shares include state and local expenditure but exclude the social insurance component, as explained in chapter 5.

With the assumed shrinkage of the trade deficit at a fairly rapid rate in the first 25 years, we see a fast growth of exports, 4.1% per year during 2017–2035 and a slow growth of imports at 2.5%. This closing of the deficit is induced by the real depreciation of the U.S. exchange rate, as plotted in figure 6.9. The world relative price, e_t, rises at 0.1% per year in the first phase. By contrast the growth of exports during 2035–2085 is similar to the growth of imports, about 2.7% per year. Given the difference between the elasticities in the import functions

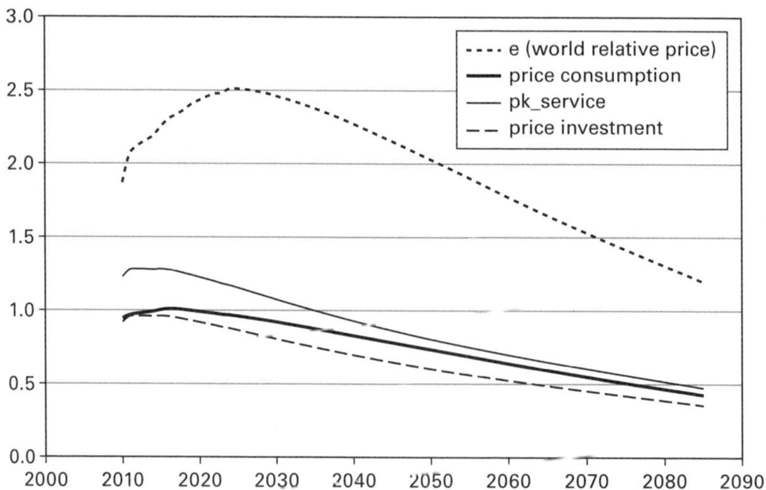

Figure 6.9
Prices in the base case transition path.

and those in the export functions, this common growth rate is accompanied by an appreciation of the world relative price e_t at a 1.4% rate.[9] In terms of shares of GDP in figure 6.7, the export share rises from 12.3% in 2010 to 16.6% in 2035 and to 17.8% in 2060. The import share is stable around 16% during the entire period.

The stable shares of consumption, government purchases and imports, the falling share of investment, and a rising share of exports result from the requirement that the paths of deficits satisfy transversality conditions. As shown in figure 6.7 the share of investment in GDP goes from 21.5% in 2017 to 19.4% in 2035, and to 18.2% in 2060. The result of the slowdown in investment is offset by the larger GDP and capital stock grows steadily as plotted in figure 6.6; the growth rate of capital is 1.9% per year during the first phase, and 2.4% during 2035–2085 (table 6.1).

6.3.1 *Aggregate Growth Accounting*

Aggregate output growth is generated by growth in capital input, labor input, and TFP in IGEM. The change in the growth rate of capital input is slightly smaller than the change of capital stock, from 2.3% during 2017–2035 to 2.4% during 2035–2085. This is due to the projected slowdown in the growth of capital quality, the aggregation index ψ_t^K in figure 5.7. The slowdown in labor input growth is much larger than the deceleration of capital input growth. Labor input is equal to labor supply. Labor supply in turn is given by the hours allocated to work, multiplied by an index of labor quality. Hours of work are given by the household leisure demand function. Leisure demand depends on the real wage, full consumption, and time endowment. The fall in the growth of time endowment is significant, from 1.07% per year during 2010–2035 to 0.74% during 2035–2085; however, the deceleration in the growth of labor input is even larger, from 1.2% to 0.68%.

Aggregate TFP growth is determined by the TFP growth in the individual industries and the reallocation of factors across sectors. The projected industry TFP growth rates decelerate over time, as explained in chapter 4, section 4.5. We have noted above that this deceleration, combined with a calibration adjustment, results in aggregate TFP growth at 0.67% per year during the 2017–2035 period, rising to 0.77% in the next 50 years. The slowdown in capital and labor input growth, together with this stable aggregate TFP growth leads to a GDP deceleration from 2.30% to 2.19%. Ignoring the first year of recovery, GDP growth in the first 11 years is 2.35% per annum.

6.3.2 *Growth at the Industry Level*

The change in the final demand composition of GDP and changes in prices lead to changes in the industry output structure. In figure 6.10 we plot the change in the price of industry output of all 35 industries.

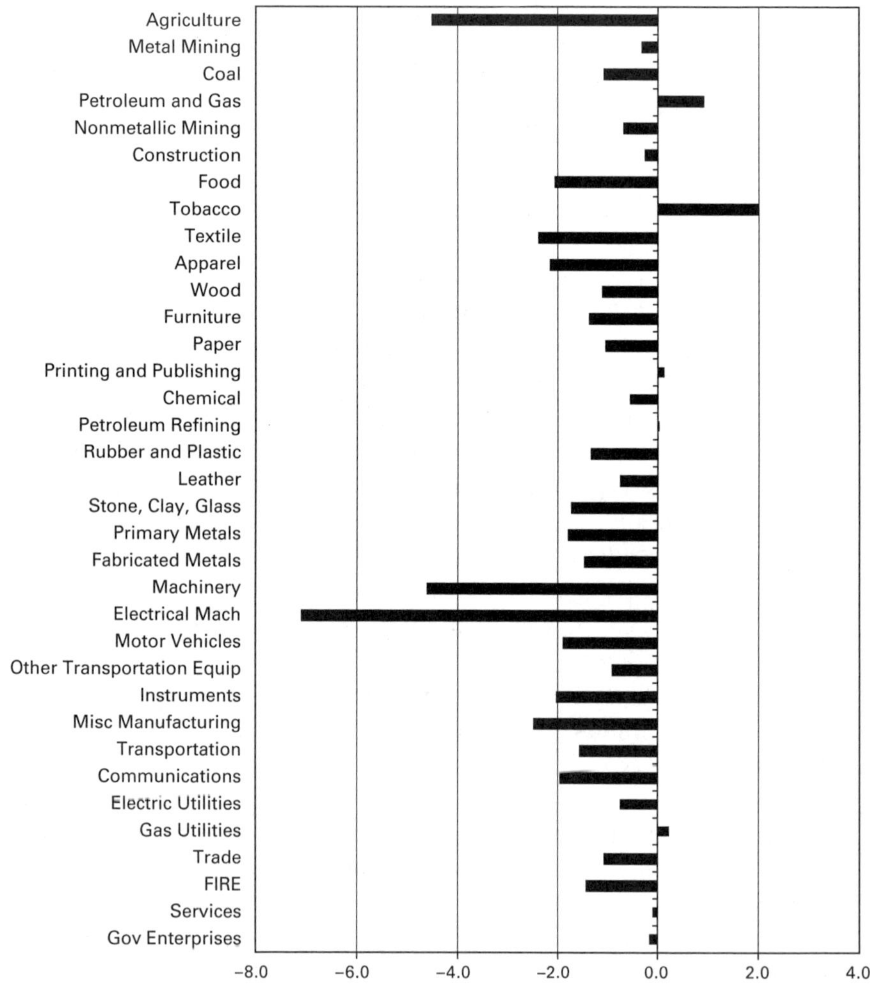

Figure 6.10
Base case industry output price, growth rate, 2017–2035.

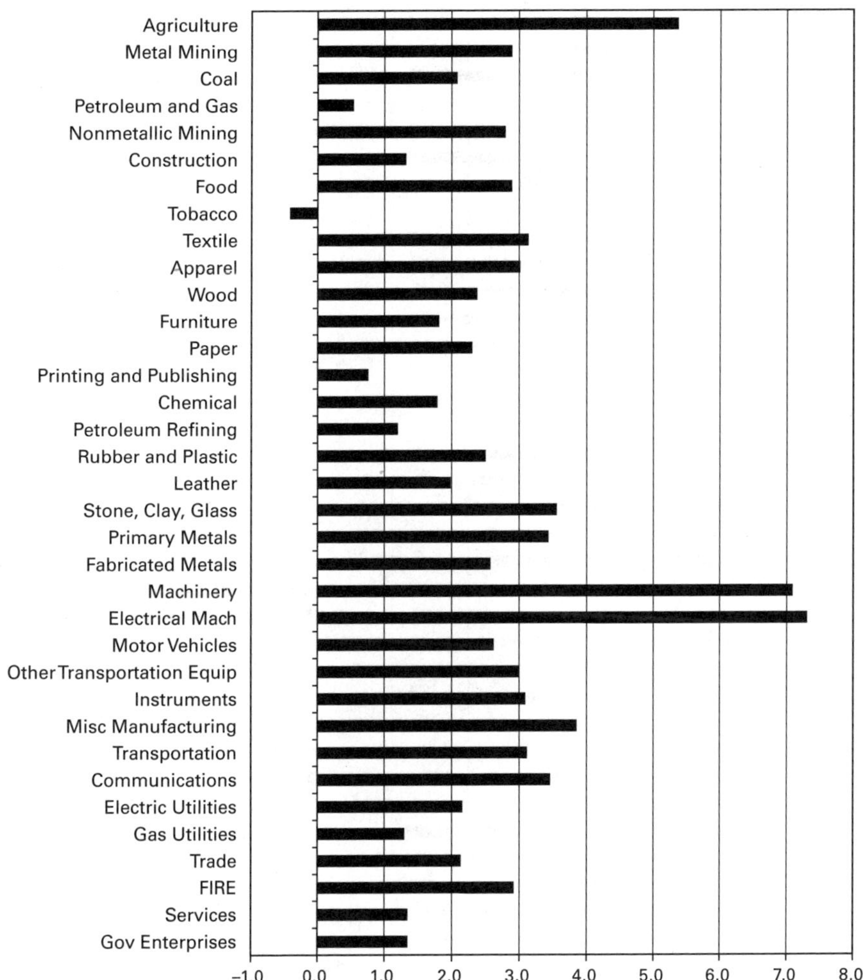

Figure 6.11
Base case industry output growth, 2017–2035 (% per annum).

In figures 6.11 and 6.12 we chart the growth rate of industry output, for the subperiods 2017–2035 and 2035–2085, respectively. We observe that the growth of industry output in almost all industries accelerates by contrast with the growth of GDP, which decelerates.

This phenomenon is due to the decline of intermediate input prices, relative to the price of labor, which induces a substitution away from labor and towards materials.

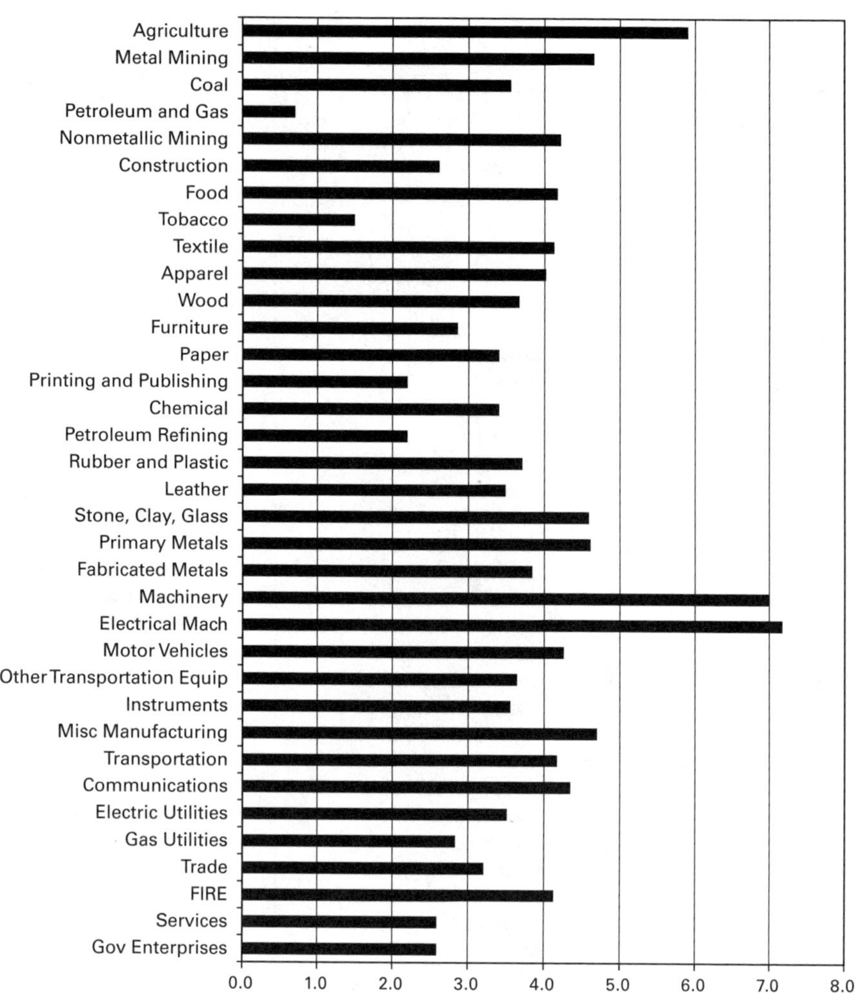

Figure 6.12
Base case industry output growth, 2035–2085 (% per annum).

Projections of the prices of consumption and investment goods, relative to the labor numeraire, are plotted in figure 6.9. We see a steady decline after the initial recovery period. Table 6.1 reports that the relative price of investment goods falls at a 1.3% rate in the first phase and at 1.5% in the next 50 years, while the fall in the price of consumption goods accelerates from 0.79% per year to 1.43%. In addition, there is also a slowdown in the material-saving technical change. A plurality of industries has material-saving change in the early part of the transition period, and all have essentially zero change during 2035–2085. This implies a larger shift towards material inputs during the latter years, resulting in industry output growth rates that exceed the GDP growth rate.

Although the growth rate of output in almost all industries accelerates, there is considerable dispersion across industries—dispersion in the growth rates during the first 25 years and dispersion in the rates of acceleration from the first phase to the second. During 2017–2035 the industries with the most rapid growth are the information technology—Machinery and Electrical Machinery—both growing faster than 7% per year. These industries are followed by Agriculture (5.4%); Miscellaneous Manufacturing (3.9%); Stone, Clay, and Glass (3.6%); and Communications (3.5%). At the other extreme the slow growth industries are Tobacco (–0.4%), Oil and Gas Mining (0.6%), and Printing and Publishing (0.8%). This pattern of growth is determined by two main factors: more rapid TFP growth in the fast growth sectors that lowers prices and stimulates consumption and rapid growth of exports and investment in some of the goods-producing industries in the 2017–2035 period. A third factor, the total expenditure effect on household demand, has a more modest impact.

The high TFP growth rate during the period 2010–2035 in Machinery, Electrical Machinery, and Agriculture generates the rapid decline of prices, as shown in figure 6.10, while the low or negative TFP growth in Tobacco, Petroleum and Gas Mining, Petroleum Refining and Gas Utilities leads to higher prices and corresponding slow growth of industry output. Among the commodities that have significant exports, the growth of exports is most rapid in Machinery, Electrical Machinery, Agriculture, Motor Vehicles, Transportation Services; and Finance, Insurance & Real Estate (FIRE).

Two opposing forces are acting on Construction; the low TFP growth gives rise to higher relative prices and a movement up the demand curve, while the growth in investment leads to an outward shift of the demand curve. The net effect is a relatively low growth rate in output. Similarly, for the largest sector, Services, the effect of high prices from low TFP growth dominates the total expenditure effect from household consumption driving up demand. This results in a low output growth rate.

Comparing the subperiod 2035–2085 to the first 25 years, the most notable feature is that the dispersion of growth rates is smaller. That is, the larger accelerations in growth rates are in the industries with low growth in the first 25 years—Petroleum Refining, Tobacco, Motor Vehicles, and Gas Utilities. This is due to the calibration process, which added a common rate of TFP growth to all industries to match the 2.2% GDP growth target. This reverses the large increase in relative prices during 2010–2035 and generates output growth patterns that are less dispersed. The highest growth rates during 2035–2085 are still in Machinery, Electrical Machinery, and Agriculture.

6.3.3 *Energy Utilization and Greenhouse Gas Emissions*

Turning to energy utilization, Coal Mining has relatively high projected TFP growth (see figure 4.25), a substantial reduction in prices, and thus a growth rate of output of 2.1% during 2017–2035. A part of the increase in coal output goes to higher exports; coal exports were a very small portion of total output in the sample period but rise significantly in the projection period, at 2.3% per year during 2017–2035 and 2.2% during 2035–2085. Petroleum and Gas Mining has the opposite price trend and has only a 0.56% growth rate. Domestic Petroleum Refining also has a negative projected TFP growth and output grows at a 1.2% rate during 2017–2035, with a similar slow growth of imported refined products (1.1% per year). The consumption of Gas Utilities rises at 1.5% per year. Electricity enjoys a strong TFP growth and sees output and consumption rising at 2.1% per year in the first phase.

As shown in the bottom section of table 6.1, total primary energy consumption rose at 1.62% during 2017–2035, a rate that is the average of the coal, oil, and gas growth rates. This is quite a bit slower than the GDP growth of 2.3% per year and reflects three factors: substitution away from more expensive oil, the energy-saving bias of technical change in most industries, and total factor productivity growth reducing input per unit output. The net result is that aggregate energy intensity falls at about 0.68% per year during 2017–2035. This is considerably slower than the 1.7% rate of improvement observed in the historical period 1990–2010. Electricity consumption growth, which benefits from a modest TFP improvement lowering electricity prices, is very close to GDP growth.

The estimation of greenhouse gas emissions is described in detail in chapter 7. We note that the emissions coefficients for the simulations are constant over time. The total CO_2 emissions, and the emissions per unit GDP, depend on both primary energy consumption and the composition of output. Total primary energy consumption is projected to grow at 1.6% in the first phase, as noted, and total CO_2 emissions growth is at 1.7% per year, giving a 0.56% annual rate of decrease in the aggregate emissions intensity. This fall in intensity is much slower than the 1.7% rate observed for 1990–2010.

Over the longer horizon when the growth rate of industry output is higher, the growth rate of energy consumption is also higher at 2.0% per year during 2035–2085. This corresponds to a slow 0.2% rate of fall in energy intensity. While coal consumption growth is slower compared to the first 25 years, oil consumption growth is much faster at 1.5% during 2035–2085. This is due in part to the assumed productivity growth in the oil sectors leading to a fall in relative prices compared to the earlier subperiod.

6.4 Calibrated Base Case

In the conduct of policy analysis, the scale and composition of output in the base case are important to simulation outcomes for many variables in level form. When multiple models are employed in a single assessment, great care needs to be taken in crafting a base case that is common to all models. The simulated outcomes can then be reliably attributed to differing model specifications and differing parameter estimates, as opposed to differing starting points and growth rates. The Energy Modeling Forum multimodel study of climate change control scenarios (EMF 22), in which IGEM participated, is an example of such an exercise. This is described in detail in Goettle and Fawcett (2009).

As we noted in chapter 1, IGEM was used in the analysis of climate change initiatives conducted by the EPA for the U.S. Congress during 2007–2011. These analyses also involved parallel applications of other models including the Applied Dynamic Analysis of the Global Economy (ADAGE) model from RTI, Inc.[10] For each legislative proposal, the two models were calibrated to the energy use projections made by the Energy Information Administration in the most recent *Annual Energy Outlook* (AEO). The EIA projections use the National Energy Model System (NEMS) and generally extend 25 to 30 years into the future. For example, the most recent *AEO 2012*, given in EIA (2012), covers the period 2011–2035. For the EPA policy exercises, the IGEM and ADAGE teams were also asked to use identical projections for GDP and energy use for the period through 2050.

IGEM was used to analyze five legislative proposals and each of these policy initiatives required a new base case. Updating the base cases was required in order to incorporate new releases of the AEO and new editions of EPA's *Inventory of U.S. Greenhouse Gas Emissions and Sinks* (*Inventory*). The latest *Inventory* for our purposes is given in EPA (2013). An updated *Inventory* required new starting points and trends for IGEM's emissions coefficients while a new set of AEO projections drove the trends in energy demand, emissions, and the overall economy against which the policy was compared.

Over the last several years, five IGEM calibrations were developed. Four of these support the five legislative analyses—the Climate Stewardship and Innovation Act of 2007 (Senate Bill S.280), the American Climate Security Acts of 2008 (S.2191 and its successor S.3036), the American Clean Energy and Security Act of 2009 (HR.2454), and the Senate's American Power Act (APA) of 2010.

The base cases for S.280 and S.2191 rely on the same *Inventory* (1990–2004) and *AEO 2006*. The base cases for S.3036, HR.2454, and the APA share a newer edition of the *Inventory* (1990–2006), but each is calibrated to a different AEO; S.3036 is calibrated to *AEO 2008*, HR.2454 to *AEO 2009*, and the APA to *AEO 2010*. Our analysis in chapter 8 of the *Handbook of Computable General Equilibrium Modeling*[11] does not employ a calibrated base case but does use EPA's *Inventory* (1990–2008). In this volume, we report base cases aligned with EPA's *Inventory* (1990–2010). Our carbon tax analysis of chapter 8 below is calibrated to *AEO 2011*.

After we develop starting-year emissions levels and emissions coefficients from the EPA's *Inventory*, five variables are targeted to grow at rates projected by the AEO. These variables are real GDP and total U.S. consumption of coal, oil, electricity, and natural gas. GDP growth is set exogenously so that the scale of the economy is comparable across models. The energy variables are chosen to have a common primary energy mix with corresponding levels of emissions, emissions growth, and changes in aggregate energy intensity and emissions intensity.

We calibrate IGEM quantities to the external targets by means of an iterative scheme involving TFP changes in the individual productivities of the four energy sectors and a TFP change in aggregate productivity affecting all sectors. Iteration begins with the energy targets and then cycles between the overall economy and energy until all of the target growth rates are achieved and convergence is completed. This back-and-forth iteration is required because the energy sector productivity changes influence the overall economy and the aggregate productivity change influences the details of energy consumption. For any given rate of overall economic growth, convergence to the energy growth targets requires relatively few iterations, while calibration of GDP growth involves comparatively larger effort.

The alignment to EPA's *Inventory* (1990–2010) and calibration to the projections in EIA's *Annual Energy Outlook 2011* are shown in table 6.2. Here we focus on the first phase of our base case projections, 2010–2035, and then through to 2050, the terminal year of policy interest. The growth rates for our uncalibrated base case are included for comparative purposes. We see that the GDP growth, 2010–2035, is projected at a higher rate in the AEO calibration, 2.66% versus our 2.16% per year. On the expenditure side, this results in higher rates of growth for all categories of final demand—consumption, investment, government, exports, and imports. On the supply side, while growth in the time endowment is identical, labor demand is stronger and results in a slightly faster growth of labor input, 1.36% versus 1.22%.

The higher rate of investment results in a faster growth of the capital stock; capital input grows at 2.29% annually versus 1.90% in the uncalibrated case. The net result of the changes in outputs and inputs is that aggregate TFP growth is faster, 2010–2035, in the calibrated base case, 0.90% per annum versus 0.65%. The faster growth of output and TFP is also manifested in the more rapid decline of prices of consumption goods and investment goods. There is less downward pressure on the dollar due in large measure to the reductions in relatively expensive energy imports.

After 2035 overall growth rates between the calibrated and uncalibrated base cases are broadly comparable. The main difference lies in the rate of capital accumulation. Investment in the calibrated case continues to grow at a faster rate, 2.18% versus 1.90%. The slowdown in economic growth, 2010–2035 to 2035–2050, in the calibrated case arises from a slowdown in the growth of labor input and TFP that is compensated by faster growth in capital input. In the uncalibrated case, labor input growth is the same, TFP growth is 0.12% faster per annum while capital growth is 0.41% slower to achieve nearly the same growth overall.

In the bottom section of table 6.2, we see more dramatic differences across the two base cases. The AEO growth rates of energy use are quite a bit lower than IGEM's uncalibrated base case. Annual electricity use grows in the 0.9% range compared to the 2.0% to 2.3% range, and total energy consumption grows at 0.40% (1.26%) compared to 1.24% (1.67%) over the period 2010–2035 (2035–2050). This results in a correspondingly slower annual growth of GHG emissions—1.40% versus 1.96% for the period 2010–2050.

The interindustry effects of calibration are displayed in figures 6.13 and 6.14 for the period 2010–2050. Figure 6.13 shows the price effects. By targeting GDP and energy consumption patterns through productivity changes, we are using IGEM's price system to achieve our growth targets. For the non-energy sectors and the economy as a whole, faster real growth implies that prices must fall faster or rise less rapidly relative to our labor price numeraire, as shown in figure 6.13. The aggregate productivity effect is even in evidence for the nontargeted crude oil and gas extraction sector, as its rate of relative price increase is less in the calibrated base case.

The effects of calibration are sharply different for the four targeted energy sectors—Coal Mining, Refined Petroleum, and Electric and Gas utilities. For Coal Mining and Electric Utilities the signs of relative price change actually reverse. In the uncalibrated case, these prices are declining relative to the numeraire, while calibration to lower growth rates requires relative coal and electricity prices to rise. For the Refined Petroleum and Gas Utility sectors, the relative price increases in the calibrated case must be larger than those in the uncalibrated case to achieve slower growth in their consumption.

Figure 6.14 shows the consequences for supplies from calibration, supply being defined as domestic commodity output plus imports. We note that targeting overall growth and the time paths of final energy consumption enhances the growth of all non-energy sectors or, in the case of tobacco, reduces its rate of decline. We also see improvements in domestic oil and gas production at the expense of imports. In relative terms, those sectors associated with the capital goods industries and their supply chains appear more heavily favored.

The growth differentials for Mining, Construction and the Wood, Metals, Machinery, and Equipment industries are larger than those for Agriculture, Food, Apparel, Paper and Printing, Chemicals and the non-energy Services sectors. This is consistent with the bias toward investment and capital formation reported above. Finally, we note the energy implications of targeting to *AEO 2011*. The growth in coal supply is reduced from 2.34% annually to 0.75%. Refined petroleum product growth is more than halved from 0.70% per annum to 0.32%. The growth in electricity and gas utility supplies is constrained to fall from 2.07% and 1.49% annually to 0.81% and 0.37%, respectively. The growth in GHG emissions reported in table 6.2 reflects not only the

Figure 6.13
Supply prices (growth 2010–2050); IGEM base vs. calibrated base relative to labor numeraire.

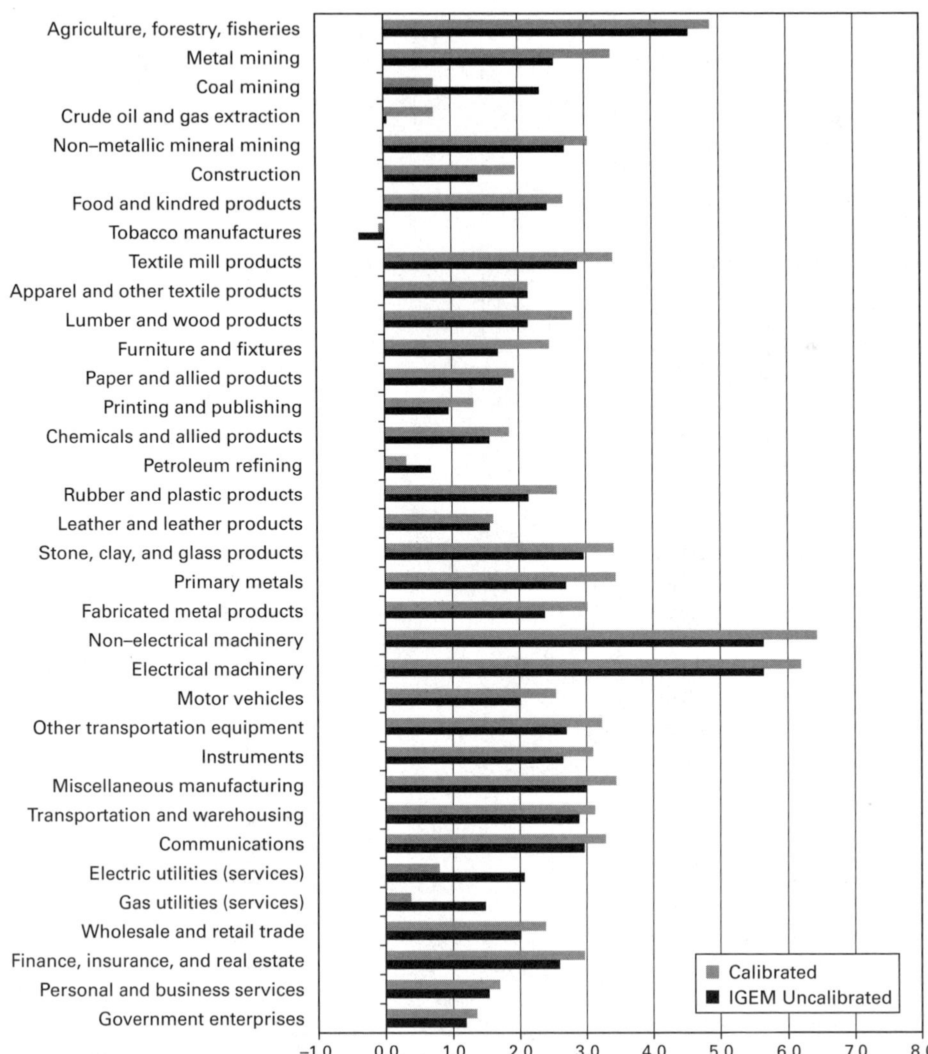

Figure 6.14
Output supplies (growth 2010–2050) IGEM base vs. calibrated base.

dramatic reductions occurring in these four energy sectors but also partially offsetting increases from the other nine emissions-generating sectors. In chapter 7 we turn to emissions accounting in IGEM.

6.5 Summary and Conclusion

In this chapter we have presented projections of the U.S. economy with no change in energy and environmental policies. The driving forces in U.S. economic growth are demography and technology. We incorporate population projections from the U.S. Bureau of the Census by age and sex and add our own projections of educational attainment. We project labor quality growth, defined as the growth of labor input per hour worked, on the basis of projections of the composition of the U.S. labor force. Our projection of the time endowment provides a summary measure of the potential growth of the time available for both work and leisure. Finally, we project the distribution of total expenditure over demographic groups required by our model of consumer behavior.

Our projections of technology are presented in chapter 4. We project the latent variables that describe the rate of productivity growth and changes in the composition of inputs for each of the 35 producing sectors of the U.S. economy. These variables combine to determine the overall rate of productivity growth and drive changes in the composition of economic activity. We also require projections of the government and rest-of-the-world sectors and derive these from the official projections of the Congressional Budget Office and the International Monetary Fund.

We project a slowdown of the overall rate of U.S. economic growth, due mainly to a declining growth rate of the labor force and slower growth of labor quality. As the economy slows, investment will decline relative to national output, but exports will rise to maintain the current account balance. The shares of consumption and imports in the national product will remain unchanged. We project supply prices and output levels for each of the 35 industrial sectors of the U.S. economy. Rapid productivity growth for high technology sectors will continue to generate declining prices and rising levels of output relative to GDP. Our base case projections reveal a continuing decline in energy intensity that will reduce the growth rate of greenhouse gas emissions.

Model comparisons are often required for the analysis of energy and environmental policies to provide broader coverage of the details that

Table 6.2
Base case calibrated to AEO: growth rates of key variables (% per year)

	Calibrated to *AEO 2011*		IGEM Uncalibrated Base Case	
	2010–2035	2035–2050	2010–2035	2035–2050
Key macro variables				
Time endowment	1.07	0.82	1.07	0.82
Capital stock	1.87	2.22	1.48	1.80
GDP	2.66	2.22	2.16	2.15
Consumption	1.88	1.94	1.67	1.99
Investment	3.12	2.18	2.00	1.90
Government	1.73	1.94	1.47	1.88
Exports	5.06	3.10	4.17	3.06
Imports	2.32	2.70	1.71	2.72
Prices relative to labor numeraire				
Price of GDP	–1.06	–1.28	–0.69	–1.26
Price of consumption	–0.63	–1.16	–0.34	–1.17
Price of investment	–1.18	–1.43	–0.83	–1.43
World relative price (*e*)	0.80	–0.92	0.96	–1.06
Growth accounting				
GDP	2.66	2.22	2.16	2.15
Capital input	2.29	2.61	1.90	2.20
Labor input	1.36	0.83	1.22	0.83
TFP	0.90	0.62	0.65	0.74
Energy and emissions				
Energy consumption (BTUs)	0.40	1.26	1.24	1.67
Electricity consumption	0.89	0.86	1.99	2.27
GHG emissions	1.44	1.33	1.69	2.41

Note: The "calibrated" case is set to match the GDP growth over the first 25 years in the *Annual Energy Outlook 2011*. The use of fossil fuels is also calibrated to the AEO projections.

are relevant for policy evaluation. To achieve consistency all models are calibrated to a common set of projections. We illustrate this by presenting an alternative base case for the U.S. economy that is calibrated to growth of national output and four energy sources from the *Annual Energy Outlook*, produced by the Energy Information

Administration. Table 6.2 compares this calibrated base case for IGEM with our uncalibrated base case.

In chapter 7 we discuss the integration of information on energy and environmental pollution into our projections. The data are taken from official sources, such as the Environmental Protection Agency's inventories of emissions of criterion air pollutants and greenhouse gases. We expand the scope of IGEM by including information from engineering studies of technologies for energy production and pollution control that are not in commercial use. Information about these technologies is summarized by marginal abatement cost schedules.

Notes

1. An example of an exception to this is a policy that consists of a numerical cap on emissions of CO_2 in a particular year in the future, to be enforced by an endogenous tax rate on emissions. A base case that projects a high growth of emissions under the no-policy scenario would require a higher tax rate than a base case that projects lower emissions. A higher tax rate will generate bigger changes between the base and policy cases. This aspect really emphasizes the need for a careful description and analysis of such a policy, i.e., a policy that is very sensitive to the level of economic activity.
2. The projections released in August 2008 may be found at the Census Bureau website: www.census.gov/population/projections/data/national/2008.html. We used the tables titled "Projected Population by Single Year of Age, Sex, Race, and Hispanic Origin for the United States: July 1, 2000 to July 1, 2050," which projects the "Resident Population." This is then used to project the broader concept of "resident plus armed forces overseas" that is given for the sample period.
3. The construction of our measures of labor input is described in more detail in Jorgenson, Ho, and Stiroh 2005, chapter 6.
4. The world population projection is from the U.S. Census Bureau's International Data Base, available at www.census.gov/ipc/www/idb/worldpoptotal.php.
5. The projections of the U.S. current account balance in the *World Economic Outlook 2010*, accessed August 2010: www.imf.org/external/pubs/ft/weo/2010/01/weodata/index.aspx.
6. The data is taken from the EIA's website, accessed March 2011, www.eia.doe.gov/oiaf/aeo, table Petroleum Products Prices, Reference Case, row Imported Crude Oil.
7. See Goettle and Fawcett (2009) and section 6.3.
8. See, for example, Flavin (1981) and Zeldes (1989).
9. The import share elasticities, β_{mm}, are in table 5.5 while the export β_{xx} are in table 5.6.
10. See Ross (2007) for a description of ADAGE.
11. See Jorgenson, Goettle, Ho, and Wilcoxen (2012).

7 Externalities

7.1 Introduction

The primary purpose of IGEM is to simulate the effects of changes in energy and environmental policies on changes in outcome variables. These include energy use and emissions of pollutants as well as changes in economic variables such as GDP and welfare. We described the determination of the economic variables in chapters 2 and 5. In this chapter we describe the energy and environmental variables in more detail and outline how they are determined in the simulations reported in chapter 8.

7.1.1 *Accounting for Externalities*

We first recall that IGEM defines 35 industry outputs (QI_{jt}) and 35 commodities where each commodity may be produced by several industries. The domestic output is QC_{it}, and this is combined with imports of M_i to produce the composite total supply, QS_i. The final demands for commodity i are C_i, I_i, G_i, X_i, and the intermediate demand by industry j is QP_{ij}.

In IGEM an externality is a quantity that is related to either the output of an industry or the consumption of a commodity. The externalities we report are emissions of EPA's six criterion air pollutants, such as sulfur dioxide, and emissions of greenhouse gases (GHGs) such as carbon dioxide. The emissions may be process related in that they arise from the production of a particular good or service; for example, carbon dioxide emissions may result from cement clinker production. Alternatively, emissions may be product related in that they arise from the use of a particular output or input, for example, sulfur dioxide emissions result from coal combustion. The terms *process emissions* and *combustion emissions* are often used to capture this distinction. However, the definition of an externality can be much broader. For example, we report the calorific content of fossil fuels, for example, the BTUs generated by combustion of fossil fuels or the kilowatt hours of electricity per unit of output of the Electric Utility sector.

We denote the quantity of an externality by E_{xt}, $x = SO_2, CO_2, CH_4$, BTU—the tonnes of sulfur dioxide, carbon dioxide, or methane emitted or the BTUs of energy used in the whole economy in year t. We denote the set of externalities by I_{EXT}. If the externality depends only on the level of commodity consumption, then the quantity of externality from commodity i is

$$XC_{ix}(QC_i - X_i) + XM_{ix}M_i \quad x \in I_{EXT}, \tag{7.1}$$

where XC_{ix} is the emission factor for the domestic commodity and XM_{ix} is the emission factor for imports.

For example, for SO_2 the coefficient $XC_{i,SO2}$ is tonnes of sulfur dioxide per billion dollars (constant \$2010) of output QC_i. We only count the commodities consumed domestically and exclude exports X_i. If the externality depends on the level of industry output, such as process emissions from agriculture, then the quantity from industry j is given similarly as the product of the emission factor and the level of output:

$$XP_{jx}QI_j. \tag{7.2}$$

The total emissions for the economy are the sum over all commodities and over all industries:

$$E_x = \sum_j XP_{jx}QI_j + \sum_i XC_{ix}(QC_i - X_i) + \sum_i XM_{ix}M_i \quad x \in I_{EXT}. \tag{7.3}$$

We account for emissions of greenhouse gases in terms of carbon dioxide-equivalents, CO_2e. That is, the emissions of the six main GHGs—carbon dioxide, methane, nitrous oxide (N_2O), hydrofluorocarbons (HFC), perfluorocarbons (PFC), and sulfur hexafluoride (SF_6)—are expressed in terms of the equivalent amount of carbon dioxide in terms of global warming potential. We compute one emission factor for any of the gases individually or in combination for any commodity or industry. These GHG emissions arise from combustion of fossil fuels, from industrial and mining processes, and from agricultural activities.

For simplicity the emissions of GHGs from combustion of fossil fuels are expressed as the emission factor for each fuel—coal, oil, gas—times the total domestic output plus the imported quantity of that fuel. Process emissions in these sectors also are included. We ignore the industry versus commodity distinction for these fuels since each of them is the product of a single industry. For oil and gas we only consider the combustion of the output of Refined Petroleum (industry 16) and the output of Gas Utilities (industry 31). The output of Oil and Gas Mining (industry 4) is not considered to contribute directly to combustion emissions, although it does contribute to process emissions, as does noncombustion in the Electric Utilities sector (industry 30).

Of the remaining industries in IGEM, eight currently produce process emissions. The largest among these are Agriculture (industry 1), Chemicals (industry 15), and Primary Metals (industry 20). There are thus a total of 13 industries with a positive emission factor, $XP_{j,GHG}$. The emissions of GHGs, in CO_2-equivalents from industry j and the corresponding imported commodity i are

$$E_{xj} = XP_{jx}QI_j + XM_{ix}M_i \quad x = GHGs. \tag{7.4}$$

Since little of the refined petroleum products is exported, we have ignored these exports in this equation. We subtract coal exports from the right-hand side of equation 7.4.

Process emissions of GHGs are generated from chemical processes, agriculture, and leakage from pipelines. These emissions are a function of total industry output, whether is it consumed domestically or exported. The economy-wide total GHG emissions in year t are thus the sum over all 35 sectors:

$$\begin{aligned} E_{GHG,t} &= \sum_j XP_{j,GHG,t}QI_{jt} + \sum_i XM_{i,GHG,t}M_{it} \\ &= E^{dom}_{GHG,t} + E^{imp}_{GHG,t}. \end{aligned} \tag{7.5}$$

In section 7.2 we describe how the emission factors are estimated and projected. Many of these coefficients are projected to change over time.

7.1.2 Emissions Intensity

Aggregate emission intensity and energy intensity are often used as summary indicators of the improvement in energy use or emission control. GHG emission intensity is defined as the emissions of CO_2-equivalents per unit of real GDP:

$$\sigma_t^{GHG} = \frac{E_{GHG,t}}{Y_t^{GDP}}. \tag{7.6}$$

The index of real GDP is a Tornqvist index of the major components of final demand as given in appendix A, equation (A.6.28).

To provide more insight into the sources of a change in aggregate intensity without all the details of energy consumption for each sector, we decompose the index (7.6) into changes in the industry-level intensity, changes in the industry composition of output, and changes in the structure of final demand. In the first step we decompose the change in aggregate intensity to a production component and to a final demand component:

$$\sigma_t^{GHG} = \frac{E_{GHG,t}^{prod} + E_{GHG,t}^{fd}}{Y_t^{GDP}}. \tag{7.7}$$

$E_{GHG,t}^{prod}$ is the emissions from domestic industries (combustion and process emissions), and $E_{GHG,t}^{fd}$ is the direct emissions from households and government. These include coal and gasoline combustion but exclude the emissions embodied in electricity use.

In order to define the production component of emissions we require more detail than the accounts given in section 7.1.1. We calculate the emissions from each industry j, taking into account both fuel combustion and process emissions. The combustion emissions from burning coal, oil, and gas in j are given by the quantity of the fuel multiplied by the emission coefficient:

$$XP_{xit} \frac{A_{i,j} PI_{it} QI_{it}}{PS_{it}}; x = CO_2, i = \text{coal, oil, gas } \{\text{commodities: } 3, 16, 31\}. \tag{7.8}$$

The quantity of fuel input is given by the input-output share A_{ij} multiplied by the output value and divided by the fuel price. The input demands are derived from the cost functions as explained in chapter 4, equation (4.30). The process emissions are given by the emission factor, multiplied by industry output, $XP_{xjt}QI_{jt}$.

The total production emissions from industry are the sum over the direct emissions of 32 business industries, excluding Coal Mining, Petroleum Refining, and Gas Utilities. The emissions from burning fossil fuels are given by (7.8) for the group of 32 non-fossil-fuel producers. We denote this group of 32 as *non-fossil*, and the productions emissions from the whole economy are

$$
\begin{aligned}
E_{xt}^{prod} &= \sum_{j \in nonfossil} E_{xjt}^{tot} \quad x = GHG \\
&= \sum_{j \in nonfossil} \left(XC_{x3t} \frac{A_{3,j} PI_{jt} QI_{jt}}{PS_{3t}} + XC_{x16t} \frac{A_{16,j} PI_{jt} QI_{jt}}{PS_{16t}} \right. \\
&\quad \left. + XC_{x31t} \frac{A_{31,j} PI_{jt} QI_{jt}}{PS_{31t}} + XP_{xjt} QI_{jt} \right). \qquad (7.9)
\end{aligned}
$$

The emissions from final demand (C, I, G, X) are the direct emissions from the use of fossil fuels. We do not count emissions due to fuels that are exported and ignore the small changes in inventories of fuels. The emissions from households and government are similarly given by the emission factor multiplied by the quantity of coal, oil, and gas consumption:

$$
\begin{aligned}
E_{GHG,t}^{fd} &= XC_{x3t}(C_{3t} + G_{3t}) + XC_{x16t}(C_{16t} + G_{16t}) \\
&\quad + XC_{x31t}(C_{31t} + G_{31t}); \; x = CO_2. \qquad (7.10)
\end{aligned}
$$

The change in aggregate intensity σ_t^{GHG} in equation (7.7) is given by the Tornqvist index over the production emissions and final demand emissions:

$$
\ln \frac{\sigma_t^{GHG}}{\sigma_{t-1}^{GHG}} = \bar{w}_t^{ind} \ln \frac{\sigma_{GHG,t}^{prod}}{\sigma_{GHG,t-1}^{prod}} + \bar{w}_t^{fd} \ln \frac{\sigma_{GHG,t}^{fd}}{\sigma_{GHG,t-1}^{fd}} + R_t^{GHG}, \qquad (7.11)
$$

where the weights are

$$
\bar{w}_t^{prod} = \frac{1}{2}(w_t^{prod} + w_{t-1}^{prod}); \quad w_t^{prod} = \frac{E_{GHG,t}^{prod}}{E_{GHG,t}}.
$$

There is an approximation residual term R_t^{GHG}. We refer to the first term as the contribution of production emissions to the change in intensity and to the second as the contribution of final demand emissions:

$$
\ln \frac{\sigma_t^{GHG}}{\sigma_{t-1}^{GHG}} = \Omega_{GHG,t}^{prod} + \Omega_{GHG,t}^{fd} + R_t^{GHG}. \qquad (7.11b)
$$

In the next step we decompose the change in the production intensity component to the changes in industry intensity and changes in the industry composition of output. The production intensity for $x = GHG$ is

$$
\begin{aligned}
\sigma_{xt}^{prod} &= \frac{E_{xt}^{prod}}{Y_t^{GDP}} = \sum_{j \in nonfossil} \frac{E_{xjt}^{tot}}{Y_t^{GDP}} \\
&= \sum_{j \in nonfossil} \frac{\sigma_{xjt}^{tot} QI_{jt}}{Y_t^{GDP}}. \qquad (7.12)
\end{aligned}
$$

where the industry j intensity is

$$\sigma_{xjt}^{tot} = E_{xjt}^{tot} / QI_{jt}. \tag{7.13}$$

The Tornqvist index for the change in production intensity is the sum of the industry intensity change and change in composition of industry output:

$$\begin{aligned} \ln \frac{\sigma_{xt}^{prod}}{\sigma_{x,t-1}^{prod}} &= \sum_{j \in nonfossil} \bar{w}_{jt} \ln \frac{\sigma_{xjt}^{tot}}{\sigma_{xjt-1}^{tot}} + \sum_{j \in nonfossil} \bar{w}_{jt} \ln \frac{QI_{jt}}{QI_{j,t-1}} + dR_t^{prod} \\ &= d\ln \Omega_t^{INT} + d\ln \Omega_t^{Q} + dR_t^{prod} \end{aligned} \tag{7.14}$$

where the weights are

$$\bar{w}_{jt} = \frac{1}{2}(w_{jt} + w_{jt-1}); \quad w_{jt} = \frac{E_{xjt}^{tot}}{\sum E_{xjt}^{tot}},$$

and R_t^{prod} is the approximation residual.

An alternative to the chained-weight Tornqvist index above is a fixed-weight index. In this case we write the change in "fixed-weight" production intensity as

$$\ln \frac{\sigma_{xt}^{prod,FIX}}{\sigma_{x,t-1}^{prod,FIX}} = \sum_{j \in nonfossil} \bar{w}_{j0} \ln \frac{\sigma_{xjt}^{tot}}{\sigma_{xjt-1}^{tot}} + \sum_{j \in nonfossil} \bar{w}_{j0} \ln \frac{QI_{jt}}{QI_{j,t-1}} \tag{7.15}$$

where the fixed weights are

$$w_{j0} = \frac{E_{xj0}^{tot}}{\sum E_{xj0}^{tot}}.$$

We can choose the period for the weights as the initial period, $w_{j0} = w_{j,T0}$, or the late period, $w_{j,T}$, or the middle of the time period of interest $(w_{j,\bar{T}})$.

We refer to the first term on the right-hand side of equation (7.14), Ω_t^{INT}, as the contribution of changes in industry intensity to changes in the aggregate production emission intensity. The second term, Ω_t^{Q}, is the contribution of changes in industry output composition. The first term is the growth rate of the economy-wide carbon intensity, correcting for changes in the composition of output.

7.2 Emissions Coefficients

In this section we describe how the emission factors described above are determined from data on emissions, output, and consumption. We also describe how they are projected for the future time periods. Earlier versions of IGEM have been used to discuss the control of sulfur dioxide in the Clean Air Act Amendments of 1990[1] and the control of greenhouse gases (GHGs).[2] Here we focus on GHG coefficients to illustrate the use of the environmental accounts.

A wide variety of GHG control policies have been considered by the U.S. Congress and by government agencies. These policies differ in the scope of economic activity covered by the policies and the types of gases included. A policy may exempt GHG emissions originating in agriculture or other activities in which measurement and monitoring are technically infeasible. For the assessment of the benefits and costs of climate change mitigation we consider four variables:

1. a composite of total greenhouse gas emissions in million metric tonnes of carbon dioxide equivalent ($MtCO_2$-e), covering all gases arising from all sources;
2. carbon emissions (the main GHG) in $MtCO_2$-e from all sources—fossil fuel combustion, industrial processes, agricultural processes, and mining processes;
3. greenhouse gas (GHG) emissions in $MtCO_2$-e arising from the economic activities covered by a particular policy initiative; and
4. emissions in $MtCO_2$-e not covered by the initiative, that is, the difference between (1) and (3) above.

We define five variables—one each for the four main categories of GHG—CO_2, CH_4, N_2O, and the High Global Warming Potential (HGWP) gases—and one for their total. In all cases our externality coefficients or emission factors are derived from detailed historical data appearing in the Environmental Protection Agency's *Inventory of U.S. Greenhouse Gas Emissions and Sinks*.[3] These data are sorted and aggregated to create the energy and emissions totals corresponding to the five externality variables defined above.

Table 7.1 shows how we relate the emissions given in the *Inventory* to the 35 IGEM sectors. For example, in 2010, we estimate that 96.0 million metric tonnes of CO_2 are generated by coal burning in the "industrial" sector, essentially the manufacturing industries. We allocate this to coal. The 8.7 $MtCO_2$-e from ammonia production in year 2010 is allocated to the Chemicals industry (industry 15), that is, process emissions due to production in industry 15. The 52.0 $MtCO_2$-e of methane gas (CH_4) from manure management is allocated as process

Table 7.1
Greenhouse gas (GHG) emissions by activity, sector, and gas (in million metric tonnes of carbon dioxide equivalent, $MmtCO_2$-e)

EPA Inventory—Source	Gas Source—Activity	IGEM	Gas	1990	2000	2010
Table 3-5	Coal—residential	**3**	CO_2	3.0	1.1	0.7
Table 3-5	Coal—commercial	**3**	CO_2	12.0	8.8	5.5
Table 3-5	Coal—industrial	**3**	CO_2	155.3	127.3	96.0
Table 3-5	Coal—electricity generation	**3**	CO_2	1547.6	1927.4	1827.3
Table 3-5	Coal—U.S. territories	**3**	CO_2	0.6	0.9	3.5
Table 3-5	Natural gas—residential	**31**	CO_2	238.0	270.7	267.1
Table 3-5	Natural gas—commercial	**31**	CO_2	142.1	172.5	172.4
Table 3-5	Natural gas—industrial	**31**	CO_2	409.9	457.3	402.3
Table 3-5	Natural gas—transportation	**31**	CO_2	36.0	35.6	36.0
Table 3-5	Natural gas—electricity generation	**31**	CO_2	175.3	280.8	399.4
Table 3-5	Natural gas—U.S. territories	**31**	CO_2		0.7	1.5
Table 3-5	Petroleum—residential	**16**	CO_2	97.4	98.8	81.8
Table 3-5	Petroleum—commercial	**16**	CO_2	64.9	49.6	50.8
Table 3-5	Petroleum—industrial	**16**	CO_2	284.9	269.0	293.8
Table 3-5	Petroleum—transportation	**16**	CO_2	1449.9	1773.9	1700.4
Table 3-5	Petroleum—electricity generation	**16**	CO_2	97.5	88.4	31.3
Table 3-5	Petroleum—U.S. territories	**16**	CO_2	27.2	34.2	36.7
Table 3-5	Geothermal	**30**	CO_2	0.4	0.4	0.4
Table 3-19/20	Industrial coking coal	**3**	CO_2	0.0	1.4	1.8
Table 3-19/20	Industrial other coal	**3**	CO_2	0.2	0.3	0.3
Table 3-19/20	Natural gas to chemical plants, other uses	**15**	CO_2	6.9	10.8	6.0
Table 3-19/20	Asphalt and road oil	**16**	CO_2	30.8	32.9	23.7
Table 3-19/20	LPG	**16**	CO_2	29.4	41.4	41.8
Table 3-19/20	Lubricants	**16**	CO_2	4.9	4.9	4.0
Table 3-19/20	Pentanes plus	**16**	CO_2	2.0	5.9	2.8
Table 3-19/20	Naphtha (<401°F)	**16**	CO_2	8.6	15.3	12.7
Table 3-19/20	Other oil (>401°F)	**16**	CO_2	17.4	13.8	10.9

Table 7.1 (continued)

EPA Inventory—Source	Gas Source—Activity	IGEM	Gas	1990	2000	2010
Table 3-19/20	Still gas	**16**	CO_2	0.6	0.3	4.0
Table 3-19/20	Petroleum coke	**16**	CO_2	0.7	0.2	0.1
Table 3-19/20	Special naphtha	**16**	CO_2	2.7	2.4	0.7
Table 3-19/20	Other (wax/misc.)	**16**	CO_2	0.0	0.0	0.0
Table 3-19/20	Distillate fuel oil	**16**	CO_2	0.2	0.3	0.5
Table 3-19/20	Waxes	**16**	CO_2	0.9	0.9	0.4
Table 3-19/20	Miscellaneous products	**16**	CO_2	3.6	3.1	4.3
Table 3-19/20	Lubricants	**16**	CO_2	4.6	4.6	3.8
Table 3-19/20	Lubricants	**16**	CO_2	0.0	0.1	0.0
Table 3-19/20	Other petroleum (misc. prod.)	**16**	CO_2	2.3	3.8	1.5
Table ES-2	Iron and steel production and metallurgical coke production	**20**	CO_2	99.6	86.0	54.3
Table 3-39	Field production	**4**	CO_2	9.7	6.4	10.8
Table 3-39	Processing	**4**	CO_2	27.8	23.3	21.3
Table 3-39	Transmission and storage	**28**	CO_2	0.1	0.1	0.1
Table 3-39	Distribution	**31**	CO_2			
Table ES-2	Cement production	**19**	CO_2	33.3	40.4	30.5
Table ES-2	Lime production	**19**	CO_2	11.5	14.1	13.2
Table ES-2	Incineration of waste	**30**	CO_2	8.0	11.1	12.1
Table ES-2	Limestone and dolomite use	**19**	CO_2	5.1	5.1	10.0
Table ES-2	Ammonia production	**15**	CO_2	13.0	12.2	8.7
Table ES-2	Cropland remaining cropland	**1**	CO_2	7.1	7.5	7.4
Table ES-2	Urea consumption for non-ag purposes	**15**	CO_2	3.8	4.2	4.4
Table ES-2	Soda ash production and consumption	**15**	CO_2	4.1	4.2	3.7
Table ES-2	Petrochemical production	**15**	CO_2	3.3	4.5	3.3
Table ES-2	Aluminum production	**20**	CO_2	6.8	6.1	3.0
Table ES-2	Carbon dioxide consumption	**15**	CO_2	1.4	1.4	2.2

(continued)

Table 7.1 (continued)

EPA Inventory—Source	Gas Source—Activity	IGEM	Gas	1990	2000	2010
Table ES-2	Titanium dioxide production	**15**	CO_2	1.2	1.8	1.9
Table ES-2	Ferroalloy production	**20**	CO_2	2.2	1.9	1.5
Table ES-2	Zinc production	**20**	CO_2	0.6	0.9	1.2
Table ES-2	Phosphoric acid production	**15**	CO_2	1.5	1.4	1.0
Table ES-2	Wetlands remaining wetlands	**1**	CO_2	1.0	1.2	1.0
Table ES-2	Lead production	**20**	CO_2	0.5	0.6	0.5
Table 3-44	Pneumatic device venting	**4**	CO_2	0.0	0.0	0.0
Table 3-44	Tank venting	**4**	CO_2	0.3	0.3	0.3
Table 3-44	Misc. venting and fugitives	**4**	CO_2	0.0	0.0	0.0
Table 3-44	Wellhead fugitives	**4**	CO_2	0.0	0.0	0.0
Table 3-44	Refining	**16**	CO_2	0.0	0.0	0.0
Table ES-2	Silicon carbide production and consumption	**23**	CO_2	0.4	0.2	0.2
Table ES-2	*Land use, land-use change, and forestry (sink)*		CO_2	*–809.7*	*–659.3*	*–1042.5*
Table 3-36	Production	**4**	CH_4	89.0	113.2	125.6
Table 3-36	Processing	**4**	CH_4	18.0	17.8	17.1
Table 3-36	Transmission and storage	**28**	CH_4	49.2	46.7	43.8
Table 3-36	Distribution	**31**	CH_4	33.4	31.4	28.5
Table ES-2	Enteric fermentation	**1**	CH_4	133.8	138.8	141.3
Table ES-2	Landfills	**34**	CH_4	147.7	111.1	107.8
Table ES-2	Coal mining	**3**	CH_4	84.1	60.4	72.6
Table ES-2	Manure management	**1**	CH_4	31.7	42.4	52.0
Table 3-42	Pneumatic device venting	**4**	CH_4	10.3	9.0	8.8
Table 3-42	Tank venting	**4**	CH_4	5.3	4.5	4.5
Table 3-42	Combustion and process upsets	**4**	CH_4	1.9	1.6	2.0
Table 3-42	Misc. venting and fugitives	**4**	CH_4	16.8	15.3	14.7
Table 3-42	Wellhead fugitives	**4**	CH_4	0.5	0.5	0.5

Table 7.1 (continued)

EPA Inventory—Source	Gas Source—Activity	IGEM	Gas	1990	2000	2010
Table 3-42	Crude oil transportation	**28**	**CH_4**	0.1	0.1	0.1
Table 3-42	Refining	**16**	**CH_4**	0.4	0.4	0.4
Table ES-2	Wastewater treatment	**34**	**CH_4**	15.9	17.2	16.3
Table ES-2	Rice cultivation	**1**	**CH_4**	7.1	7.5	8.6
Table 3-10	Electricity—coal	**3**	**CH_4**	0.3	0.3	0.3
Table 3-10	Electricity—fuel oil	**16**	**CH_4**	0.0	0.0	0.0
Table 3-10	Electricity—natural gas	**31**	**CH_4**	0.1	0.1	0.2
Table 3-10	Electricity—wood	**1**	**CH_4**	0.0	0.0	0.0
Table 3-10	Industrial—coal	**3**	**CH_4**	0.3	0.3	0.2
Table 3-10	Industrial—fuel oil	**16**	**CH_4**	0.2	0.1	0.1
Table 3-10	Industrial—natural gas	**31**	**CH_4**	0.2	0.2	0.2
Table 3-10	Industrial—wood	**1**	**CH_4**	0.9	1.0	0.9
Table 3-10	Commercial—coal	**3**	**CH_4**	0.0	0.0	0.0
Table 3-10	Commercial—fuel oil	**16**	**CH_4**	0.2	0.1	0.1
Table 3-10	Commercial—natural gas	**31**	**CH_4**	0.3	0.3	0.3
Table 3-10	Commercial—wood	**1**	**CH_4**	0.4	0.5	0.5
Table 3-10	Residential—coal	**3**	**CH_4**	0.2	0.1	0.0
Table 3-10	Residential—fuel oil	**16**	**CH_4**	0.3	0.3	0.3
Table 3-10	Residential—natural gas	**31**	**CH_4**	0.4	0.5	0.5
Table 3-10	Residential—wood	**1**	**CH_4**	3.7	2.7	2.7
Table 3-10	U.S. territories—coal	**3**	**CH_4**	0.0	0.0	0.0
Table 3-10	U.S. territories—fuel oil	**16**	**CH_4**	0.0	0.0	0.1
Table 3-10	U.S. territories—natural gas	**31**	**CH_4**	0.0	0.0	0.0
Table 3-10	U.S. territories—wood	**1**	**CH_4**	0.0	0.0	0.0
Table ES-2	Abandoned underground coal mines	**3**	**CH_4**	6.0	7.4	5.0
Table ES-2	Forest land remaining forest land	**1**	**CH_4**	2.5	11.6	4.8
Table ES-2	Mobile combustion	**16**	**CH_4**	4.7	3.4	2.0
Table ES-2	Composting	**1**	**CH_4**	0.3	1.3	1.6
Table ES-2	Petrochemical production	**15**	**CH_4**	0.9	1.2	0.9

(continued)

Table 7.1 (continued)

EPA Inventory—Source	Gas Source—Activity	IGEM	Gas	1990	2000	2010
Table ES-2	Iron, steel, and metallurgical coke production	**20**	CH_4	1.0	0.9	0.5
Table ES-2	Field burning of agricultural residues	**1**	CH_4	0.2	0.2	0.2
Table ES-2	Ferroalloy production	**20**	CH_4	0.0	0.0	0.0
Table ES-2	Silicon carbide production and consumption	**23**	CH_4	0.0	0.0	0.0
Table ES-2	Incineration of waste	**30**	CH_4	0.0	0.0	0.0
Table ES-2	Agricultural soil management	**1**	N_2O	211.7	225.7	223.8
Table ES-2	Mobile combustion	**16**	N_2O	43.9	53.2	23.9
Table 3-11	Electricity—coal	**3**	N_2O	6.3	7.7	12.5
Table 3-11	Electricity—fuel oil	**16**	N_2O	0.1	0.1	0.0
Table 3-11	Electricity—natural gas	**31**	N_2O	1.0	1.8	5.9
Table 3-11	Electricity—wood	**1**	N_2O	0.0	0.0	0.0
Table 3-11	Industrial—coal	**3**	N_2O	0.8	0.6	0.5
Table 3-11	Industrial—fuel oil	**16**	N_2O	0.5	0.4	0.4
Table 3-11	Industrial—natural gas	**31**	N_2O	0.2	0.3	0.2
Table 3-11	Industrial—wood	**1**	N_2O	1.8	2.0	1.7
Table 3-11	Commercial—coal	**3**	N_2O	0.1	0.0	0.0
Table 3-11	Commercial—fuel oil	**16**	N_2O	0.2	0.1	0.1
Table 3-11	Commercial—natural gas	**31**	N_2O	0.1	0.1	0.1
Table 3-11	Commercial—wood	**1**	N_2O	0.1	0.1	0.1
Table 3-11	Residential—coal	**3**	N_2O	0.0	0.0	0.0
Table 3-11	Residential—fuel oil	**16**	N_2O	0.3	0.3	0.2
Table 3-11	Residential—natural gas	**31**	N_2O	0.1	0.2	0.1
Table 3-11	Residential—wood	**1**	N_2O	0.7	0.5	0.5
Table 3-11	U.S. territories—coal	**3**	N_2O	0.0	0.0	0.0
Table 3-11	U.S. territories—fuel oil	**16**	N_2O	0.1	0.1	0.1
Table 3-11	U.S. territories—natural gas	**31**	N_2O	0.0	0.0	0.0
Table 3-11	U.S. territories—wood	**1**	N_2O	0.0	0.0	0.0
Table ES-2	Manure management	**1**	N_2O	14.8	17.4	18.3
Table ES-2	Nitric acid production	**15**	N_2O	17.4	19.1	16.7

Table 7.1 (continued)

EPA Inventory—Source	Gas Source—Activity	IGEM	Gas	1990	2000	2010
Table ES-2	Wastewater treatment	**34**	**N_2O**	3.5	4.3	5.0
Table ES-2	N_2O from product uses	**15**	**N_2O**	4.4	4.9	4.4
Table ES-2	Forest land remaining forest land	**1**	**N_2O**	2.1	9.9	4.3
Table ES-2	Adipic acid production	**15**	**N_2O**	15.8	5.5	2.8
Table ES-2	Composting	**1**	**N_2O**	0.4	1.4	1.7
Table ES-2	Settlements remaining settlements	**33**	**N_2O**	1.0	1.1	1.5
Table ES-2	Incineration of waste	**30**	**N_2O**	0.5	0.4	0.4
Table ES-2	Field burning of agricultural residues	**1**	**N_2O**	0.1	0.1	0.1
Table ES-2	Wetlands remaining wetlands	**1**	**N_2O**	0.0	0.0	0.0
Table ES-2	Substitution of ozone depleting substances	**15**	**HGWP**	0.5	119.7	208.9
Table ES-2	HCFC-22 production	**15**	**HGWP**	36.4	28.6	5.4
Table ES-2	Semiconductor manufacture	**23**	**HGWP**	0.3	0.4	0.5
Table ES-2	Semiconductor manufacture	**23**	**HGWP**	3.0	6.7	5.5
Table ES-2	Aluminum production	**20**	**HGWP**	18.4	8.6	1.6
Table ES-2	Electrical transmission and distribution	**30**	**HGWP**	44.5	25.2	19.7
Table ES-2	Magnesium production and processing	**15**	**HGWP**	5.4	3.0	1.1
Table ES-2	Semiconductor manufacture	**23**	**HGWP**	0.9	1.8	1.6
Total				6206.2	7176.3	6954.6
Net				5396.5	6517.0	5912.0

Table 7.2
GHG emissions by gas (in $MmtCO_2$-e)

Gas	1990	2000	2010
CO_2	5100.5	5974.7	5718.7
CH_4	668.3	650.4	666.2
N_2O	327.8	357.2	325.4
HGWP	109.5	193.9	244.2
Total	6206.2	7176.3	6954.6

Table 7.3
GHG emissions by sector (in $MmtCO_2$-e)

Gas Source	IGEM	1990	2000	2010
Agriculture, forestry, fisheries	**1**	420.5	471.8	471.7
Coal mining	**3**	1816.8	2143.9	2026.2
Crude oil and gas extraction	**4**	179.6	191.9	205.6
Chemicals and allied products	**15**	116.2	222.4	271.4
Petroleum refining	**16**	2181.5	2502.4	2333.7
Stone, clay, and glass products	**19**	49.9	59.5	53.7
Primary metals	**20**	129.1	105.0	62.6
Electrical machinery	**23**	4.6	9.2	7.8
Transportation and warehousing	**28**	49.4	46.9	44.0
Electric utilities (services)	**30**	53.4	37.0	32.5
Gas utilities (services)	**31**	1037.2	1252.5	1314.7
Finance, insurance, and real estate	**33**	1.0	1.1	1.5
Personal and business services	**34**	167.0	132.6	129.2
Total		6206.2	7176.3	6954.6

emissions in the Agriculture industry (industry 1) as is the 18.3 $MtCO_2$-e of nitrous oxide (N_2O) emissions. Tables 7.2 and 7.3 summarize these allocations by GHG and IGEM sector.

The externality coefficients are derived by dividing the total emissions of each gas by the level of output or commodity consumption in the sector to which the emissions are allocated. For example, the total of GHGs allocated to Agriculture in 2010 is 471.7 million tonnes with total output plus imports at $(1996)624.3 billion. The emission factor for that year is thus 0.756 tonnes of CH_4 per constant dollar. The

Table 7.4
Emissions coefficients (in MmtCO$_2$-e per constant dollar)

	1990	2000	2010
Agriculture, forestry, fisheries	1.364	1.142	0.756
Coal mining	59.634	66.398	51.690
Crude oil and gas extraction	1.100	0.882	1.074
Chemicals and allied products	0.397	0.669	0.807
Petroleum refining	13.047	8.935	9.338
Stone, clay, and glass products	0.748	0.639	0.580
Primary metals	0.984	0.661	0.437
Electrical machinery	0.016	0.012	0.010
Transportation and warehousing	0.121	0.084	0.061
Electric utilities (services)	0.255	0.158	0.112
Gas utilities (services)	14.150	17.839	13.027
Finance, insurance, and real estate	0.001	0.001	0.001
Personal and business services	0.093	0.050	0.041

emission coefficients for all the IGEM sectors implied by EPA's *2012 Inventory* are given in table 7.4.

The externality coefficients change over time due to changes in technology, changes in end-of-pipe treatments, and changes in the composition of output in each sector. Each sector in IGEM consists of various subsectors. For example, the Primary Metals industry produces different types of metals, including the iron and steel, magnesium, and aluminum. Any one of these will change the industry coefficient. The trends for total GHG intensity are illustrated in figures 7.1 and 7.2 for the energy and non-energy sectors, respectively. We can see that they are far from constant over time and are generally falling. We also see signs of convergence and greater stability in recent years.

In developing baseline projections we face four interrelated issues:

1. What weight should be attached to each of the detailed emission factors in table 7.1 when dealing with the aggregated sectors in IGEM?

2. How should emissions coefficients change over time to reflect compositional changes within a sector?

3. To what extent should historical trends be continued or abandoned in the projections? How should anticipated changes in policies be reflected in the future coefficients?

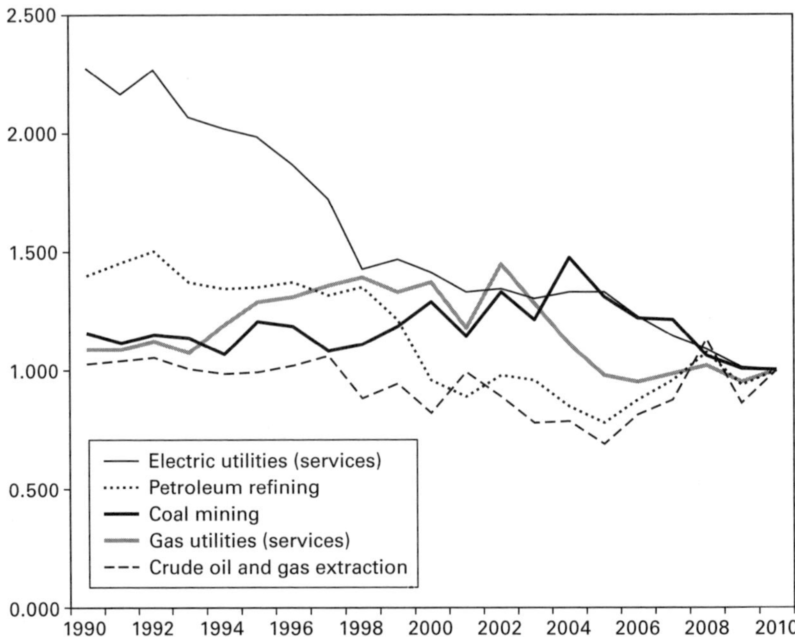

Figure 7.1
Emissions intensities—all GHG, energy sectors.

4. How should total externalities (emissions) be calibrated to official government projections?

Ideally, a separate analysis should be conducted for each gas and each economic activity listed in table 7.1. We could then project the trends for the detailed coefficients, simulate the level of output and consumption at the detailed level, and finally aggregate to the IGEM level. However, this would require a much more disaggregated model than IGEM and is not feasible. In IGEM we first aggregate the coefficients over the detailed items and then project the aggregated emission factors. The biases that this might introduce to the baseline emissions path can be examined by developing alternative base cases.

Changes in emissions intensities at the level of IGEM sectors result from both exogenous policy changes and responses to exogenous factors such as productivity growth. If a policy is treated as fixed, its projected impact on emissions coefficients should be included in both the base case and policy case. If a portion of the observed mitigation is due to the policy being assessed, the change in emission factors should

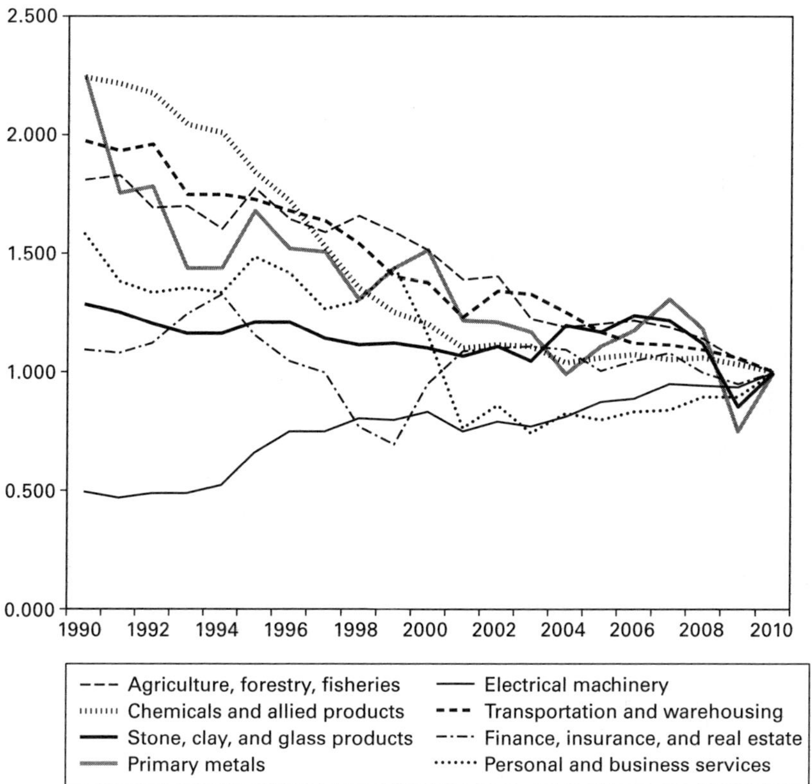

Figure 7.2
Emissions intensities—all GHG, non-energy sectors.

be separated when specifying the base case. Isolating the changes in emissions intensities due to changes in market conditions and policy changes is facilitated by using disaggregated data.

Calibration of emissions or emission intensities is sometimes required for policy analysis. A study may include projections of emission intensities, perhaps from a more specialized and detailed model. This is often the case in assessments involving a comparison of a variety of models. We calibrate IGEM's path of emissions to an exogenously specified series by calibrating the variables that drive emissions, or adjusting the emission coefficients, or both.

As an example, in simulations conducted for the EPA (2012a) we calibrated initial greenhouse gas emissions to match the historical levels in EPA's current *Inventory of U.S. Greenhouse Gas Emissions and*

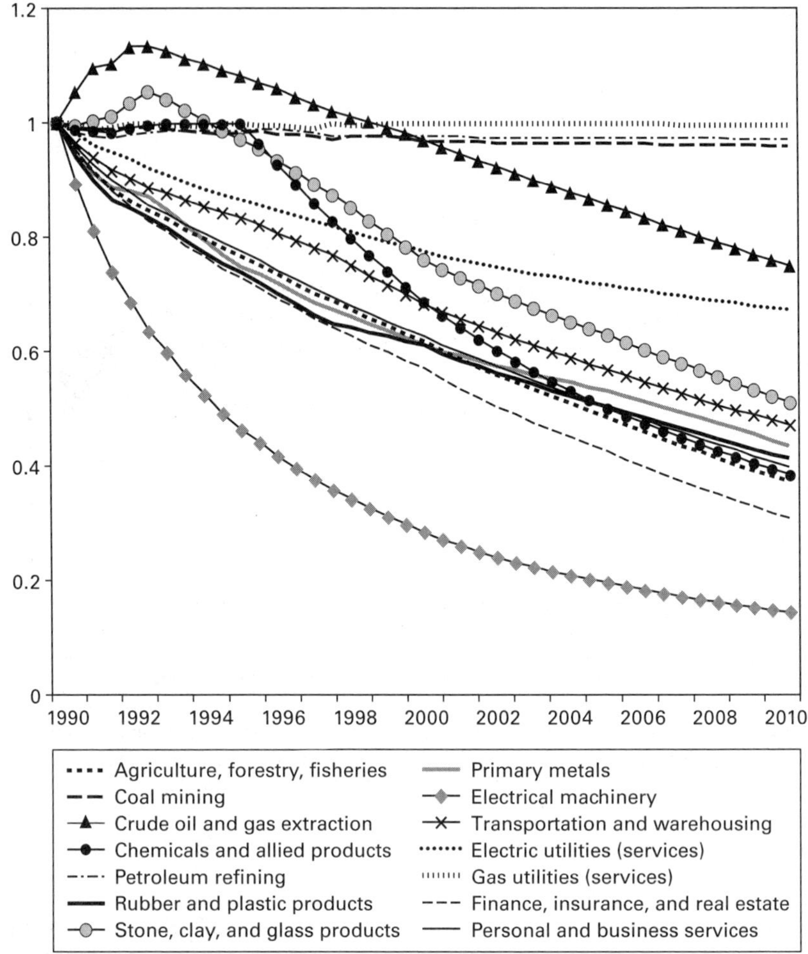

Figure 7.3
An example of autonomous changes in emissions intensities 2010 = 1.0.

Sinks. To project the future time path of emissions, the emissions coefficients for key sectors were adjusted to track a common set of projections from the Energy Information Administration's (EIA's) current *Annual Energy Outlook*. The remaining coefficients were projected by extrapolating historical trends through or beyond 2050 and then holding the coefficients constant at steady state values. Figure 7.3 displays the results.

Unraveling the influences on emissions intensities and their trends is a difficult task, so that holding them at their most recent level represents an attractive alternative. This is the procedure we follow in chapter 8. Holding the unobservable subsector technologies, end-of-pipe treatments, and their compositions constant, the analysis of outcomes focuses on supply and demand restructuring in response to price and productivity changes.

7.3 Marginal Abatement Costs

In this section we describe how more detailed information about technologies or market structures can be included in IGEM to provide a richer set of outcomes. Models, no matter how elaborate or detailed, cannot describe the full complexity of economic choices. One way to incorporate more information for example, data on corn ethanol production—is to include ethanol output in the Agriculture sector. An alternative approach is to summarize the information in a reduced-form equation.

As a concrete example, consider the option to capture and sequester emissions of carbon dioxide, a technology to mitigate the concentration of greenhouse gases that is not available commercially. Costs of sequestration could be included in the model to simulate the effects of the technology on the total costs of mitigating climate change. For this purpose we could specify equations for the production of sequestration services and the demand for them from power plants. Alternatively, we could construct a sequestration cost curve, using only information about the direct costs of deploying this technology. The external abatement cost curve can then be included in IGEM.

7.3.1 MAC Curves

Central to the analysis of climate change policy is the concept of marginal abatement cost (MAC). The marginal cost refers to diverting scarce resources to the elimination of an additional tonne of emissions. The marginal cost of abatement increases with the level of abatement, as often postulated in theory. The relationship between costs and quantities for a given greenhouse gas or a particular abatement source is summarized by a marginal abatement cost schedule.

Figure 7.4 illustrates common properties of the MAC schedules found in current GHG mitigation assessments. Curve A is the typical representation. At zero levels the marginal cost of abatement is also zero. Significant abatement is available at comparatively low unit cost.

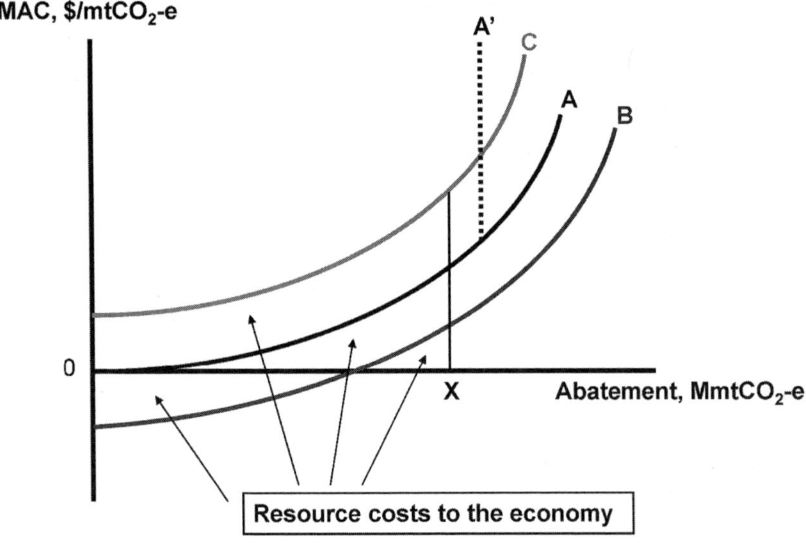

Figure 7.4
Marginal abatement cost schedules.

The MAC schedule rises but is initially relatively flat. However, as larger amounts of abatement are required, the MAC curve becomes more steeply sloped. Incremental emissions reductions become increasingly expensive in terms of their claims on the available resources. The vertical dotted line, A′, portrays a possible physical or regulatory limit on the availability of additional emissions reductions from this source; no additional abatement is to be had at any price.

Curve B shows some positive abatement at a negative cost, represented by the curve below the zero line. This represents abatement opportunities that are "profitable" in the sense of releasing resources to other uses while simultaneously reducing emissions. These opportunities arise most frequently for informational reasons; managers and traders are simply unaware of the realizable net benefits from their actions.[4] Eventually this option runs out and Curve B exhibits more typical behavior. Curve C depicts the situation where there is a fixed cost of starting abatement. In this case, abatement from this source is not economically justified until the benefit of abatement reaches some minimum threshold. A useful feature of the MAC schedule is that the cumulative area under the curve represents the opportunity cost of achieving a given level of abatement.

7.3.2 *Implementing External MACs in IGEM*

We next describe how to identify policy options not included in IGEM and how their MACs are included in IGEM through a reduced-form equation. We begin by examining each GHG and each economic activity in table 7.1. We identify the mitigation possibilities that are adequately represented in IGEM. These are considered to be internal to IGEM, as are the economic costs associated with implementation. All other mitigation possibilities are external to IGEM and require abatement cost schedules derived from outside sources. These include sequestration, international permit trading, biofuels, non-CO_2 gases, and other options.

The information embodied in marginal cost schedules is incorporated into the analysis using the following steps:

1. IGEM is simulated repeatedly over a wide range of allowance, or permit, prices to determine the model's response to a particular mitigation policy. This generates a family of marginal abatement cost (MAC) schedules that serves as the core of the reduced form. Specifically, we introduce a path of permit prices and observe the corresponding abatement.[5] The allowances or permits are auctioned by the government and the revenue is redistributed to achieve revenue and/or deficit neutrality. The resulting MACs show the abatement that is achievable in IGEM by year at various allowance prices and are denoted MAC_t^{IGEM}. An example is given in figure 7.5 on page 284.

2. For a given year, the marginal abatement cost schedule, MAC_t^{IGEM}, is summed horizontally with those cost schedules external to IGEM to create an aggregate marginal abatement cost schedule, MAC_t^{total}, for that year.

3. For a given CO_2-e allowance price, p_t^{CO2}, we read the total abatement from this MAC_t^{total} curve. The allocation of total abatement to IGEM and each of the external categories is determined from the component MACs, say $E_{at}^{lim,EXT}(p^{CO2})$, where {a = biofuels, sequestration, international trade, etc.}. The presence of these external abatement options lowers permit prices for each level of abatement. We also can reverse the process by reading the required abatement from MAC_t^{total} and determining the corresponding allowance price, p_t^{CO2} with allocation to follow.

4. After determining the level of abatement from each of the external sources, we calculate their economic costs by integrating the areas

under their MAC schedules. These total costs are then introduced into IGEM in the following manner:

i. International permit trading is treated as an additional term in the current account balance equation (5.34). Payments to foreigners for their emission permits are subtracted from the right side of (5.35); this means that higher net exports are required to hit the exogenous current account surplus.

ii. The costs associated with domestic sequestration are assumed to be borne entirely by IGEM's agriculture, forestry, and fisheries sector. The costs for reducing non-CO_2 GHGs are allocated to emissions-generating activities in proportion to their contributions to baseline GHG emissions. The costs of bioelectricity and carbon capture and storage (CCS) are borne by the electric sector. These costs are incorporated into IGEM by introducing a negative shock to productivity in industry j (λ_j in appendix A, equation A.2.2). For example, the costs of sequestering carbon are represented by requiring more inputs into Agriculture to generate the same level of output as in the base case.

5. We introduce into IGEM the allowance prices from step 3 and the costs for external abatement from step 4 to ascertain the economy-wide impacts from these reduced-form computations. To the extent that the simulated MACs in step 1 incorporate any and all direct effects that are driven by permit prices, we find there is no need to iterate. In other words, the MAC^{IGEM} that would result from iterating steps 2 through 4 matches nearly exactly the set of price-quantity points generated from the MAC_t^{IGEM}'s.

It is important to note that the MACs generated from IGEM are general equilibrium outcomes. Partial equilibrium schedules measure, for example, the direct costs of building and operating a carbon sequestration plant. By contrast the costs from IGEM's MACs are net of the cumulative substitution, restructuring, and price-induced productivity effects associated with achieving the levels of abatement. While these internal and external MACs can be combined to solve for an integrated time path of allowance prices, the associated costs are not comparable and cannot be combined.

Reduced-form equations are very convenient in representing climate policies. These policies include provisions for permit banking and borrowing, intricate rules governing the use of offsets, and an array of domestic and international abatement opportunities. Permit banking is the use of emission permits from earlier periods in qualifying for abatement, while borrowing is the reverse. Trading rules may take the form of time-varying constraints on the use of domestic and international offsets or discount future credits for the offsets.

Banking and borrowing, complex trading rules, and external offsets pose challenges for modeling climate policy. Banking and borrowing involve the addition of intertemporal trade-offs. Sophisticated trading rules vary over the life of the policy and are triggered endogenously, requiring reprogramming for each new policy initiative. One way of dealing with these difficulties is to use the reduced-form approach iteratively, allowing for quick determination of optimal allowance prices.

The iterative approach is used to determine the time path of allowance prices, abatement from sources explicitly identified in IGEM and from sources summarized in the MACs, and the cumulative costs for these sources. This can be reiterated to conform to the design of each policy initiative. This has the additional benefit of allowing a broader range of IGEM policy scenarios where the time path of allowance prices and the details of abatement are the only analytical objectives.

The procedure we have outlined is conceptually similar to the closed-form approach in the Emissions Prediction and Policy Analysis (EPPA) model of MIT's Joint Program on the Science and Policy of Climate Change.[6] Each external MAC curve is added to the equations of the model as an additional supply function. EPPA's final costs and levels of abatement are endogenously determined, even if these technologies are outside the boundaries of the primary model.

Our iterative process sacrifices the computational efficiency of this closed-form approach to gain fuller use of the information represented in the numerical MAC schedules, which may have kinks and jumps. Our numerical method allows us to capture precisely the curvature of the schedules and the points at which they become inelastic. We emphasize that both approaches incorporate the market and technological abatement opportunities.

7.4 Simulations Involving MACs

In our analysis of the American Clean Energy and Security Act of 2009, House Bill HR.2454 (EPA 2012a), the following external abatement options are considered:

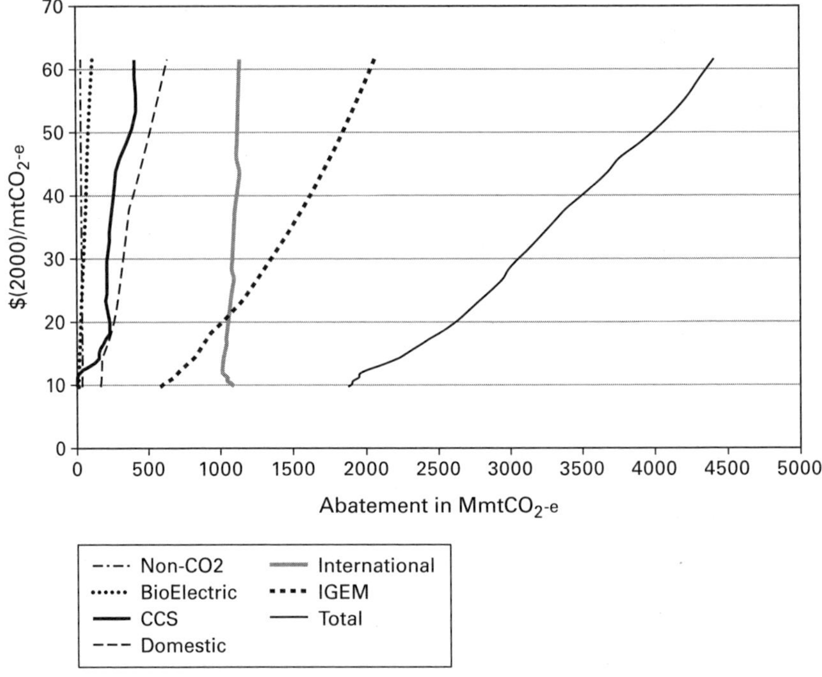

Figure 7.5
Sources of abatement, 2012–2050 House bill HR.2454 analysis.

i) non-CO_2 greenhouse gases (includes N_2O from adipic and nitric acid production, SF_6 from electric power systems, magnesium production and semiconductor manufacturing, PFC from semiconductor and aluminum production, and HFC-23 from HCFC-22 production, but excluding CH_4);

ii) coal-based carbon capture and storage (CCS) using different MACs for different build rates;

iii) electricity from a variety of biofuels (BioElectric);

iv) domestic offsets (in agriculture and forestry); and

v) international offsets (from all trading nations for a wide variety of CO_2 and non-CO_2 abatement options in agriculture and manufacturing)

Figure 7.5 shows the time paths of allowance prices and abatement, 2012–2050, arising from IGEM's reduced-form solution. Permit prices and abatement systematically increase from 2012 through 2050 and include the effects of allowance banking as well as technological and remedial subsidies. The MACs for non-CO_2 GHGs and for domestic and international offsets are aggregates of more detailed MACs underlying the analysis; for example, the non-CO_2 MAC sums over the component curves enumerated above. Also plotted in figure 7.5 is the locus of price-quantity points for GHG reductions from IGEM, with the curve to the far right as the total MAC or the horizontal sum of the six individual curves. Over the period 2012–2050, there is a total of 113.8 giga-tonnes (metric) of CO_2-e ($GtCO_2$-e) abatement representing 37.4% of total base case GHG emissions; of this, 48.0 $GtCO_2$-e comes from IGEM with 1.4 from non-CO_2 sources, 1.8 from bioelectricity, 8.2 from CCS, and 12.4 and 41.9 from domestic and international offsets, respectively.

The impetus for creating a new base case is provided by new releases of EPA's *Inventory of U.S. Greenhouse Gas Emissions and Sinks* (*Inventory*) and the EIA's *Annual Energy Outlook* (*AEO*). The base case may also change due to the differences in emissions coverage among the policy initiatives. The EPA's *Inventory* alters the starting points and trends in IGEM's emissions coefficients while the EIA's *AEO* projections drive the trends in energy demand and the overall economy. We should emphasize that the MACs generated for our reduced-form procedure are unique to each base case and not to a policy scenario.[7] This has a significant advantage in that our MACs hold for any policy initiative that is to be compared to a particular base case.

Examining the MAC schedules from IGEM for a range of base cases provides insights into the changing nature of these schedules. They also reveal behavioral characteristics that are unique to IGEM and have real-world implications for policy designs and outcomes. Table 7.5 summarizes the source data and emission coverage for five distinct base case–policy initiative combinations requested by the EPA. The base cases are those for the Climate Stewardship and Innovation Act of 2007 (Senate bill S.280), the American Climate Security Act of 2007 (S.2191), the Lieberman-Warner Climate Security Act of 2008 (S.3036), the American Clean Energy and Security Act of 2009 (HR.2454), and the Senate's American Power Act of 2010 (APA).[8] HR.2454 is also known as the Waxman-Markey bill.

The base cases for S.280 and S.2191 rely on the same EPA *Inventory (1990–2004)* and *AEO 2006*. The only differences lie in emissions-generating activities that are covered by policy. Coverage in S.280 is less than that in S.2191. Emissions reductions from a given allowance

Table 7.5
Policy influences on IGEM's marginal abatement cost schedules

	Policy				
	S.280	S.2191	S.3036	HR.2454	APA
EPA's *Emissions Inventory*	1990–2004	1990–2004	1990–2006	1990–2006	1990–2006
EIA's *Annual Energy Outlook*	2006	2006	2008	2009	2010
Cumulative GHG Emissions 2010–2050 in $GtCO_2$-e	386.5	386.5	333.7	318.0	310.6

price will usually be smaller since more substitutions toward uncovered activities will occur. The base cases for S.3036, HR.2454, and the APA differ in additional respects. They share the updated *Inventory (1990–2006)* but not the AEO assumptions. The base case for S.3036 is calibrated to *AEO 2008* while that for HR.2454 is calibrated to *AEO 2009*. The eventual coverage for S.3036 and HR.2454 is approximately the same but the latter is more generous in the very early years. The base case for the APA is calibrated to *AEO 2010* with similar coverage to HR.2454.

We note that the abatement achievable from a given allowance price depends critically on the baseline emission levels, which are driven by the EIA projections of fuel consumption in the AEO. Figure 7.6 shows the time paths of total greenhouse gas emissions under the assumptions of table 7.5. The more recent EPA *Inventory* (2006) results in slightly lower expected emissions in 2007 and somewhat slower emissions growth. The changes are more dramatic when we calibrate to different versions of the *Annual Energy Outlook*; the more recent projections give a much lower estimate of future emissions. These changes in the baseline emissions are driven primarily by the projections of slower economic growth, projected world oil prices, and policy-induced changes in energy demand in the successive AEO forecasts. The downward shift in the baselines in figure 7.6 has extremely important implications for climate change initiatives in that emissions abatement is achieved more easily with lower economic costs when the required abatement in absolute tonnes is reduced as a percentage of base year emissions.

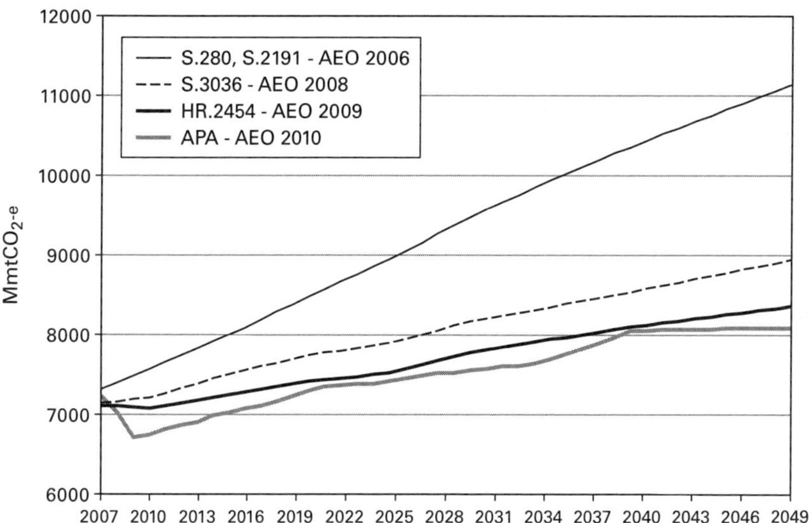

Figure 7.6
Total greenhouse gas emissions.

Figure 7.7 shows the simulated cost schedules for all five cases for 2050, the terminal policy year in each case. The first observation is that the extent of policy coverage matters. This is shown clearly by comparing S.2191 and S.280; these policies have the same base case projections, but S.2191 has a greater coverage. For a given price, the abatement secured is greater under the S.2191 family of MACs compared to the abatement under S.280.

The abatement achievable from a given allowance price diminishes as baseline emissions diminish, as shown by comparing the MACs of figure 7.7 according to their groupings in figure 7.6. The MAC for the American Power Act (APA) is the highest curve in figure 7.7 and has the lowest path of projected base case emissions in figure 7.6. In examining the progression from S.280 and S.2191, with the earlier projections from the AEO to S.3036, HR.2454, and the APA with their more recent AEO calibrations, it is clear that IGEM responds to price less elastically as energy use is calibrated to lower and lower levels.

The families of cost schedules for IGEM shift leftward with lower abatement in the moves from *AEO 2006* to *AEO 2008* and from *AEO 2008* to *AEO 2009* and *AEO 2010*. Furthermore, with constrained lower energy use, the 10-year gaps between successive MACs for the years 2010, 2020, 2030, 2040, and 2050 generally shrink over time. The MACs

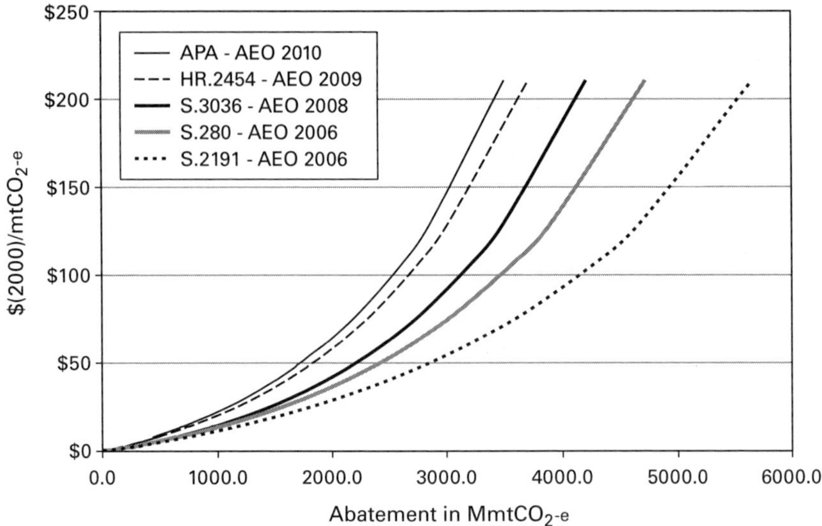

Figure 7.7
IGEM simulated MACs, 2050.

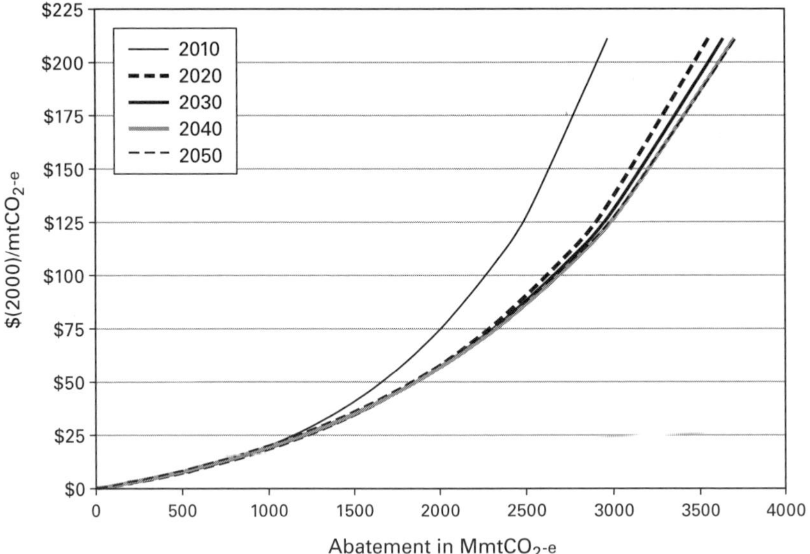

Figure 7.8
IGEM simulated MACs, 2010–2050 House bill HR.2454 analysis.

in the later years become virtually identical, as demonstrated in figure 7.8.

7.5 Uncalibrated and Calibrated Base Cases

We next explore IGEM's full GHG abatement potential. Climate change mitigation arises through output reductions, input and output restructuring, and induced technical change. As indicated above, the IGEM MACs generated in analyses of energy and environmental policy initiatives are limited in scope. The underlying coverage generally excludes emissions from agriculture and other costly and difficult-to-monitor activities. Substitutions from covered to noncovered sectors result in an understatement of the emissions reductions that are achievable in IGEM under more comprehensive treatments that leave fewer sectors uncovered.

In chapter 8 of the *Handbook of Computable General Equilibrium Modeling*,[9] we consider three cap-and-trade policies to control all greenhouse gas emissions in the United States, using an earlier version of IGEM with an uncalibrated base case. The caps refer to economy-wide emissions of GHG's—carbon dioxide, methane, nitrous oxide, and High Global Warming Potential gases. The least extreme of these three policies freezes total annual GHG emissions at the 2005 level of 7.2 metric giga-tonnes of carbon dioxide equivalent ($GtCO_2$-e) through 2050. The most extreme policy imposes a "cap," or cumulative emissions limit, on GHG of 205.4 $GtCO_2$-e over the period 2012–2050.

The trend reduction in emissions ultimately targets an emissions level in 2050 of 3.6 $GtCO_2$-e. This is 50% of the 7.2 $GtCO_2$-e of GHG emissions observed in 2005 and more than 40% below the 6.1 $GtCO_2$-e of 1990. Our central policy case lies halfway between these extremes. Specifically, cumulative emissions, 2012–2050, are capped at 241.4 $GtCO_2$-e with annual emissions tracking to 5.4 $GtCO_2$-e by 2050. After 2050 we opt for price rather than emissions certainty. We hold constant the allowance prices that are necessary to achieve the 2050 emissions target. In each case, the 2050 price is fixed indefinitely in terms of constant GDP purchasing power.

We plot in figure 7.9 the abatement possibilities from IGEM that arise as a consequence of implementing the three cap-and-trade policies. The vertical axis represents the present-value allowance or permit price, averaged over 2010–2050, based on IGEM's estimated annual social rate of time preference of 2.63%. Cumulative abatement of 78.3

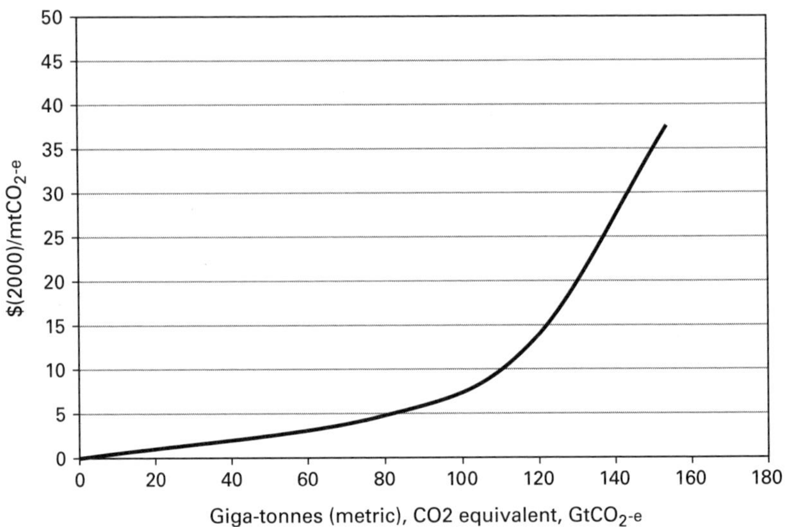

Figure 7.9
Cumulative emissions abatement, 2010–2050 cap-and-trade analysis.

$GtCO_2$-e, 2010–2050, occurs at an average present-value price of \$4.60 in 2005 dollars per $mtCO_2$-e. Over the period 2010–2050, total GHG emissions reductions of 117.8 and 153.9 $GtCO_2$-e occur at prices of \$12.89 and \$37.59, respectively.

The three climate policies are imposed on an uncalibrated base case under lump-sum redistributions of permit revenues and no borrowing or banking. In this base case, emissions are aligned to EPA's *Inventory* (1990–2008) and the only projections that are taken from the *AEO 2010* are the world prices for oil and gas. Not surprisingly, we find emissions reductions are less costly to achieve when coverage is broadened. However, MAC schedules steepen as caps tighten and more abatement is required. Abatement increases at a decreasing rate as allowance or permit prices rise.

Figure 7.10 shows the MACs for two uncalibrated base cases. We see broad similarity in the overall results and in the abatement opportunities at lower permit prices and tax rates. However, as these prices and tax rates increase, the base case aligned to earlier emissions (1990–2008) underachieves in comparison to the one aligned to more recent emissions (1990–2010). This arises from the revisions and updating of the series in table 7.1. To the extent that GHG emissions are more highly concentrated in those sectors that are more price-sensitive in the more

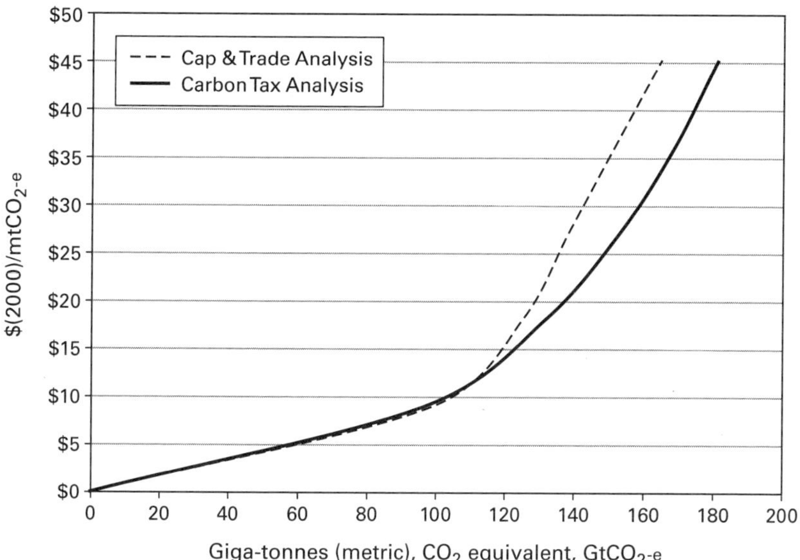

Figure 7.10
Cumulative emissions abatement, 2010–2050 uncalibrated base cases.

recent data, the newer base case secures more cumulative abatement for the same allowance price or tax rate.

A comparison of the MACs from the calibrated and uncalibrated cases is plotted in figure 7.11. The binding constraints on energy growth resulting from calibration lead to an economy that is significantly less responsive to climate policy. Using IGEM's price system to achieve the slower growth in energy use embodied in the AEO calibration, the model becomes less price elastic. For a given price, more abatement is possible from IGEM in the uncalibrated case than from the calibrated one; the uncalibrated curve in figure 7.11 is everywhere to the right of the calibrated curve.

Equivalently, to achieve a given level of abatement we require a higher price or tax in the calibrated case than in the uncalibrated one. Moreover, while the MACs maintain their traditional shape, the gap between abatement possibilities, calibrated versus uncalibrated, widens as permit prices or tax rates rise. At $9.10 per mt$CO_2$-e the gap is 43 Gt$CO_2$-e and increases to the 50 GtCO_2-e range at the higher prices. We must emphasize that this is merely an observation and not a concern for the conduct of policy analysis. In those base cases with slower energy growth, GHG emissions are lower and, thus, the abatement

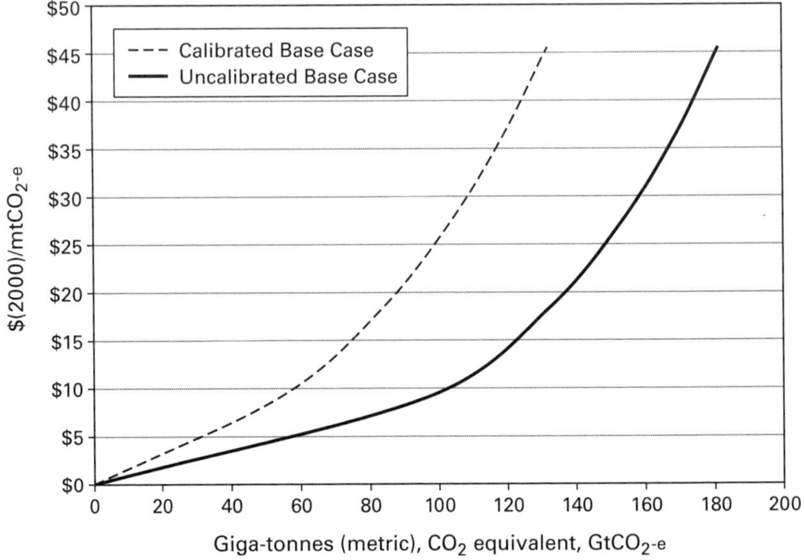

Figure 7.11
Cumulative emissions abatement, 2010–2050 carbon tax analysis.

necessary to comply with a given cap and their corresponding prices or tax rates are that much less.

7.6 Summary and Conclusion

In this chapter we have considered externalities or nonmarketed outputs that are essential for the evaluation of energy and environmental policies. We first describe the accounting framework for the outcomes of policy changes. We then consider emissions of greenhouse gases—carbon dioxide, methane, nitrous oxides, and High Global Warming Potential Gases. For convenience we express these in terms of equivalent amounts of carbon dioxide, the most important greenhouse gas. In earlier studies we have also considered emissions of EPA's criterion air pollutants, such as sulfur dioxide and particulates.

In order to incorporate externalities into IGEM we classify them into product and process emissions. We map the product emissions into outputs of the 35 industries included in IGEM. We classify process emissions by fossil fuel combustion and by industrial, agricultural, and mining processes and map these into the 35 commodities represented in IGEM. We summarize data on emissions from EPA's *Inventory of Greenhouse Gas Emissions and Sinks* by means of emissions coefficients for all the outputs and processes.

Marginal abatement cost schedules can be used to extend IGEM to include technologies that are well understood in engineering terms but are not in commercial use. Examples include carbon capture and storage and generation of electricity from biofuels. Marginal abatement cost schedules are also useful in describing offsets from agriculture and forestry and international offsets. We illustrate the application of marginal abatement cost schedules and emissions coefficients by the analysis of legislative initiatives considered in the U.S. Congress and analyzed by the Environmental Protection Agency. More detail is provided by EPA on its Climate Economics website.

In chapter 8 we turn to energy and environmental taxes, illustrated by a carbon tax that is levied on greenhouse gas emissions in proportion to the carbon dioxide equivalent in terms of global warming potential. We consider the impact of these taxes on emissions and economic variables such as GDP and individual and social welfare. We emphasize the recycling of carbon tax revenues through reductions in other taxes and financing of reductions in government deficits.

We analyze five carbon tax policies with rates of $10, $20, $30, $40, and $50 per metric tonne of carbon dioxide equivalent (mtCO_2-e) occurring in the year 2020 and expressed in 2005 dollars of GDP purchasing power. These 2020 tax rates are discounted backward to 2016 and compounded forward to 2050 at a 5% real rate of interest. After 2050 the carbon taxes are held at their 2050 levels in real terms. We impose the taxes on all emissions-generating processes and products, both domestic and imported, so there is complete coverage.

In chapter 8 we employ the calibrated base case of section 6.3 that is aligned to EPA's *Inventory* (1990–2010) and to *AEO 2011*'s GDP and energy growth.

Notes

1. Jorgenson and Wilcoxen (1993b).
2. Goettle and Fawcett (2009).
3. Here, we have employed EPA's *2012 Draft Inventory*.
4. See Ankvist et al. (2007), for example.

5. The permit price is relative to the GDP deflator. Recall that relative commodity prices change along the base case path even though there is no pure inflation in IGEM. The GDP deflator is thus not a constant relative to the labor price numeraire.
6. See Hyman et al. (2003).
7. This holds unless the policy under consideration includes any transfers that depend on allowance prices. In these situations, the simulated MACs used in our reduced form are wedded to both the base and policy simulations.
8. See EPA (2012a) for details on each of these IGEM base and policy cases.
9. See Jorgenson, Goettle, Ho, and Wilcoxen (2012).

8 Policy Evaluation

8.1 Introduction

Intense debates over measures to reduce the growth of the U.S. public debt have focused attention on fiscal reform to increase tax revenues and reduce government expenditures.[1]

Environmental taxes have been mentioned as potential sources of revenue, but few detailed proposals for fiscal reform involving environmental taxes have emerged.[2] This is in spite of the support of market-based approaches to environmental policy by many economists.[3] In this chapter we consider the economic and environmental impacts of taxes on emissions of greenhouse gases, expressed in terms of carbon dioxide equivalents. We refer to these as *carbon taxes*.[4]

We employed the IGEM model described in chapter 2 in analyzing alternative climate policies for the U.S. Environmental Protection Agency (EPA). These studies have focused primarily on cap-and-trade policies with complex trading rules, price triggers, safety valves, technology subsidies, sector rebates, and domestic and international offsets. The policies under consideration have stipulated emissions targets but have not provided estimates of the costs of abatement. Only limited attention has been given to the use of the government revenues generated by auctioning tradable permits.[5]

In this chapter we analyze the impacts of five levels of carbon tax rates—\$10, \$20, \$30, \$40, and \$50 per metric tonne of carbon dioxide equivalent (mtCO_2-e). These rates are expressed in 2005 dollars and imposed in the year 2020. The 2020 tax rates are discounted back to 2016 and compounded forward to 2050 at a 5% real rate of interest, so that we arrive at five distinct time paths for carbon taxes. By 2050 these five trajectories lead to tax rates of \$43, \$86, \$130, \$173, and \$216 per mtCO_2-e, respectively. After 2050 the carbon tax rates are held at 2050

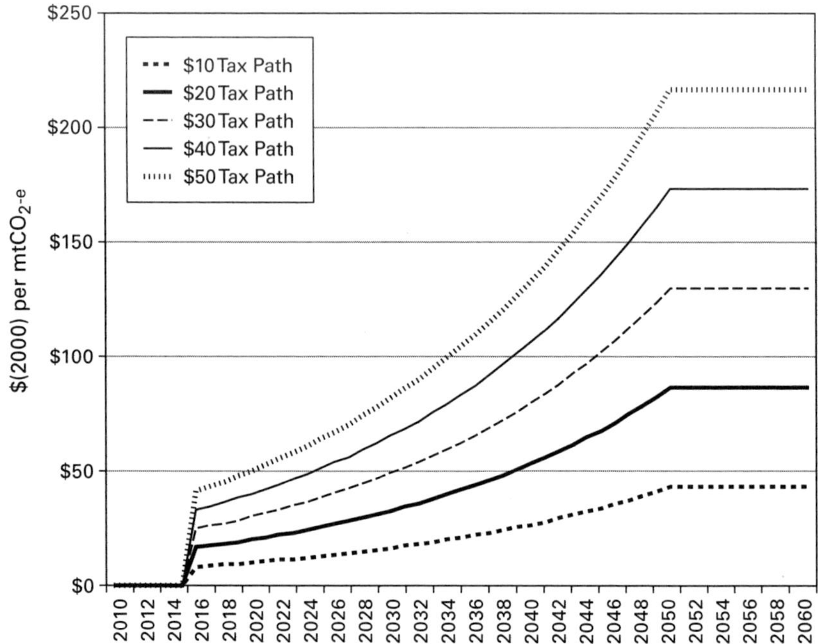

Figure 8.1
Carbon taxes.

levels, relative to the GDP deflator. Figure 8.1 displays the results of these assumptions.[6]

Substitution of carbon taxes for other sources of revenue is the key to integration of carbon taxes with proposals for fiscal reform. We explore the response of the U.S. economy to different carbon tax rates and the different uses of carbon tax revenues.

We consider four options for utilizing the carbon tax revenues: (1) reducing capital tax rates, (2) proportionally reducing capital and labor tax rates, (3) reducing labor tax rates, and (4) redistributing the revenues through lump sum transfers to households. We refer to these options for using carbon tax proceeds as *revenue recycling*.[7]

The purpose of imposing a carbon tax is to reduce U.S. emissions of greenhouse gases. This would be the U.S. contribution to an international effort to moderate changes in the climate. In section 8.2 we consider the impacts of alternative carbon tax policies on emissions of greenhouse gases. We first consider the overall impact of these policies on emissions expressed in terms of carbon dioxide equivalents. We then analyze the impact of carbon taxes on emissions of carbon dioxide, methane, nitrogen oxide, and the remaining greenhouse gases, grouped as the High Global Warming Potential gases.

In section 8.3 we turn to economic impacts of imposing carbon taxes, beginning with the impacts on supply prices of all commodities. This reflects the fact that carbon taxes with the various options for recycling the tax revenues work through the price system. We next consider the impacts of carbon taxes on economic performance, including the components of final demand—consumption, investment, government purchases, exports, and imports—and the supplies of capital and labor services as well as the demand for leisure. In section 8.4 we analyze the contribution of endogenous technical change to the economic responses to a carbon tax regime.

Our final objective is to evaluate the economic impacts of energy and environmental policies. For this purpose we employ the measures of individual and social welfare presented in sections 3.7 and 3.8. Our representations of individual welfare are derived from the model of consumer behavior discussed in chapter 3. In section 8.5 we present distributions of the changes in individual welfare that result from carbon tax policies. Under the Pareto principle a policy change can be recommended if measures of individual welfare are at least as large for all households and these measures are larger for some households.[8]

In section 8.6 we employ social welfare functions to combine measures of individual welfare. A social welfare function enables us to rank policy changes in terms of their impacts on social welfare. Measures of social welfare depend on value judgments about horizontal and vertical equity as well as the preferences of individuals. To illustrate the role of value judgments, we present changes in social welfare corresponding to different social welfare functions, ranging from highly egalitarian to least egalitarian.

Finally, changes in our measures of social welfare can be decomposed into changes in efficiency and changes in equity. Changes in efficiency reflect the impacts of alternative policies under the assumption that changes in full wealth are redistributed to maximize social welfare. Efficiency changes are the same for the different social welfare functions we consider. Changes in social welfare depend on the actual distribution of the changes in full wealth and reflect value judgments about equity. Changes in equity are the differences between efficiency changes and changes in social welfare. Since we do not consider the distribution of benefits of government purchases, we evaluate only the options for recycling carbon tax revenues that hold government purchases constant in terms of social welfare.

Recycling carbon tax revenues through reductions of capital income tax rates provides the largest margins of economic benefits over the costs of emissions control. This tax substitution produces a gain in efficiency that greatly outweighs the modest losses in equity, however these are measured. Recycling revenues by reducing capital tax rates mitigates the costs of greenhouse gas reduction by lowering the cost of capital services and increasing the rate of capital formation. This mechanism provides a dramatic illustration of the usefulness of intertemporal general equilibrium modeling in the design of new energy and environmental policies for the United States.

Section 8.7 summarizes and concludes the chapter. We find that levels of emissions control increase with carbon tax levels but at diminishing rates that reflect rising marginal costs of abatement. However, levels of emissions control for a given carbon tax level are very similar for different revenue recycling policies. We provide impacts on social welfare of carbon tax policies with revenue recycling by tax substitution. We decompose the results into efficiency and equity impacts. In addition, we provide measures of the economic impacts of carbon tax policies on production, consumption, and the industry structure of the U.S. economy. We conclude that substitution of carbon taxes for capital income taxes is a new policy option that can be integrated with proposals for fiscal reform.

8.2 Emissions Impacts

Figure 8.2 illustrates the potential for emissions abatement associated with carbon taxes. We simplify this representation by giving results only for lump sum redistributions of the tax revenues. For the $10 carbon tax trajectory there is an immediate emissions reduction of over 10% in 2016, rising to more than 20% by 2050. In the $20 carbon tax scenario, the reductions are almost 20% in 2016 and over 30% in 2050. For the remaining three tax levels, the emissions reductions in 2016 are in the 20% to 30% range, while those by 2050 are in the 40% to 50% range. Emissions abatement increases with rising taxes but at diminishing rates.

For concise comparisons of emissions abatement among the four options for recycling carbon tax revenues, we focus on cumulative emissions of greenhouse gases over the period 2010–2050 instead of

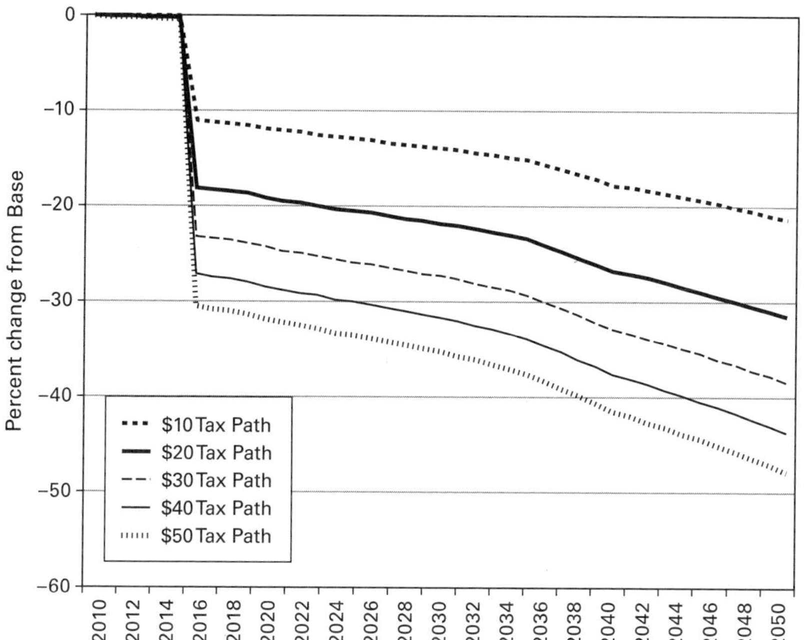

Figure 8.2
Total GHG emissions abatement under lump sum redistribution.

discussing annual changes. These are shown in table 8.1 and reflect the steepening marginal abatement cost schedules. There is remarkable uniformity in the levels of emissions abatement. Averaging across the different tax treatments, the cumulative reductions in greenhouse gas emissions for 2010–2050, for each of the five tax trajectories, are 53, 82, 101, 117, and 129 metric giga-tonnes in carbon dioxide equivalents (GtCO_2-e), respectively. Emissions levels are reduced, on average from 387 GtCO_2-e in the IGEM base case to 334, 306, 286, 271, and 258 GtCO_2-e under the five tax scenarios. For a $50 tax, deviations in abatement from the average are in the 2% range across the four recycling options. Deviations in abatement from the average are in the 1% to 2% range.[9]

Table 8.2 shows the composition of greenhouse gas emissions—carbon dioxide (CO_2), methane (CH_4), nitrogen oxide (N_2O), and the High Global Warming Potential (HGWP) gases—across the four recycling policies. We provide details for the base case and the $20 and $50 tax schedules. For each tax trajectory, the levels and compositions of

Table 8.1
Cumulative emissions under alternative recycling scenarios, 2010–2050 (Emissions in $GtCO_2$-e)

	Capital Rates	All Rates	Labor Rates	Lump Sum
Levels				
Base case	387.4	387.4	387.4	387.4
$10 tax path	335.3	335.6	335.7	333.0
$20 tax path	307.4	307.8	307.9	303.9
$30 tax path	287.9	288.3	288.4	283.6
$40 tax path	272.7	273.1	273.1	267.9
$50 tax path	260.2	260.5	260.5	255.1
Abatement				
$10 tax path	52.0	51.7	51.6	54.4
$20 tax path	79.9	79.5	79.4	83.5
$30 tax path	99.4	99.1	99.0	103.7
$40 tax path	114.6	114.3	114.2	119.4
$50 tax path	127.1	126.8	126.8	132.3
Marginal abatement				
$10 tax path	52.0	51.7	51.6	54.4
$20 tax path	27.9	27.8	27.8	29.1
$30 tax path	19.5	19.5	19.5	20.3
$40 tax path	15.2	15.2	15.3	15.7
$50 tax path	12.5	12.5	12.6	12.8
Percentage reductions				
$10 tax path	13.4%	13.4%	13.3%	14.0%
$20 tax path	20.6%	20.5%	20.5%	21.6%
$30 tax path	25.7%	25.6%	25.6%	26.8%
$40 tax path	29.6%	29.5%	29.5%	30.8%
$50 tax path	32.8%	32.7%	32.7%	34.1%

emissions are broadly similar for the four policies for revenue recycling.

For the $20 tax regime CO_2 emissions decline from 71.2% of the total to 68.4%, while the relative importance of the other greenhouse gases increases—CH_4 from 14.2% to 15.5%, N_2O from 10.5% to 11.1%, and the HGWPs from 4.15% to 5.0%. These results suggest that CO_2-generating activities, mostly fossil fuel combustion, are more price-responsive than those generating CH_4, N_2O, and the HGWPs (mostly agriculture and chemical manufacturing), at least initially. For the $50 tax scenario,

Table 8.2
Cumulative emissions of alternative recycling scenarios, 2010–2050, by types of GHG (Emissions in $GtCO_2$-e)

Levels	Capital Rates	All Rates	Labor Rates	Lump Sum
Base case				
All GHG	387.4	387.4	387.4	387.4
CO_2	275.8	275.8	275.8	275.8
CH_4	55.1	55.1	55.1	55.1
N_2O	40.6	40.6	40.6	40.6
HGWP	16.0	16.0	16.0	16.0
Composition				
All GHG	100.0%	100.0%	100.0%	100.0%
CO_2	71.2%	71.2%	71.2%	71.2%
CH_4	14.2%	14.2%	14.2%	14.2%
N_2O	10.5%	10.5%	10.5%	10.5%
HGWP	4.1%	4.1%	4.1%	4.1%
$20 tax path				
All GHG	307.4	307.8	307.9	303.9
CO_2	210.0	210.2	210.2	207.9
CH_4	47.6	47.8	47.8	47.0
N_2O	34.3	34.4	34.4	33.8
HGWP	15.5	15.5	15.5	15.2
Composition				
All GHG	100.0%	100.0%	100.0%	100.0%
CO_2	68.3%	68.3%	68.3%	68.4%
CH_4	15.5%	15.5%	15.5%	15.5%
N_2O	11.2%	11.2%	11.2%	11.1%
HGWP	5.0%	5.0%	5.0%	5.0%
$50 tax path				
All GHG	260.2	260.5	260.5	255.1
CO_2	175.3	175.4	175.3	172.3
CH_4	41.6	41.8	41.8	40.7
N_2O	28.5	28.5	28.5	27.7
HGWP	14.8	14.8	14.8	14.3
Composition				
All GHG	100.0%	100.0%	100.0%	100.0%
CO_2	67.4%	67.3%	67.3%	67.6%
CH_4	16.0%	16.0%	16.1%	15.9%
N_2O	10.9%	10.9%	10.9%	10.9%
HGWP	5.7%	5.7%	5.7%	5.6%

the share of CO_2 falls from 68.4% to 67.5%, the share of CH_4 continues to rise from 15.5% to 16.0%, the share of N_2O falls from 11.1% to 10.9%, and the share of the HGWPs increases from 5.0% to 5.7%.

As tax rates rise, emissions abatement continues to increase for all four categories of greenhouse gases but at diminishing rates. Emissions of CO_2 are relatively more price-sensitive and the CO_2 share continues to fall. The N_2O share is also marginally lower. The shares of CH_4 and HGWP increase, demonstrating that these emissions are less price-responsive.

8.3 Economic Impacts

We next examine the economic impacts of carbon taxes by considering the average adjustments of economic activity over the period 2010–2050. The driving force behind these changes is that prices rise for almost all commodity groups relative to the leisure price numeraire, so that market participants must adjust to higher prices. However, these adjustments differ substantially among different methods for utilizing the tax revenues, reflecting differences in the mechanisms for responding to changes in relative prices.

We present the impacts of alternative policies for emissions control on prices in tables 8.3 and 8.4. Table 8.3 shows the effects of the five tax regimes on commodity supply prices under lump sum redistributions of tax revenues. Table 8.4 shows these outcomes for the $20 tax trajectory for the four recycling scenarios. The price impacts of the other tax trajectories differ mainly in the scale of the economic responses.

8.3.1 Lump Sum Recycling

Energy prices—coal, oil, gas, and electricity—are strongly affected by carbon taxes with the greatest impact on coal prices. This is not surprising in that 82% of greenhouse gas emissions for 2010 are fossil-fuel-related—the production and use of coal (29%), refined petroleum (34%), and gas (19%). Coal has the highest carbon content among the fossil fuels and is used extensively along with gas in the generation of electricity in the United States, hence the shock to the electricity price.

We assume that the stock of capital is fixed in the oil and gas mining sector. This leads to an upward-sloping oil and gas supply curve. With the reduced demand for crude from Petroleum Refining due to the

Table 8.3
Impacts on commodity supply prices in lump sum redistribution case: Average percent change from base, 2010–2050

Lump Sum Redistribution	$10 Tax Path	$20 Tax Path	$30 Tax Path	$40 Tax Path	$50 Tax Path
Agriculture, Forestry, Fisheries	5.06	10.00	14.84	19.61	24.33
Metal Mining	0.79	1.43	2.00	2.52	3.02
Coal Mining	57.65	114.49	170.90	227.05	283.03
Crude Oil and Gas Extraction	–1.01	–1.93	–2.76	–3.49	–4.13
Nonmetallic Mineral Mining	1.22	2.26	3.20	4.08	4.91
Construction	0.47	0.90	1.30	1.68	2.06
Food and Kindred Products	1.54	2.93	4.22	5.44	6.61
Tobacco Manufactures	0.73	1.40	2.01	2.59	3.15
Textile Mill Products	0.75	1.41	2.03	2.62	3.19
Apparel and Other Textile Products	0.33	0.58	0.80	1.00	1.20
Lumber and Wood Products	0.76	1.43	2.04	2.62	3.18
Furniture and Fixtures	0.45	0.82	1.14	1.45	1.74
Paper and Allied Products	0.50	0.87	1.19	1.49	1.77
Printing and Publishing	0.29	0.54	0.76	0.97	1.17
Chemicals and Allied Products	1.17	2.25	3.28	4.29	5.28
Petroleum Refining	4.26	8.39	12.45	16.48	20.48
Rubber and Plastic Products	0.53	0.98	1.39	1.78	2.16
Leather and Leather Products	0.37	0.66	0.91	1.14	1.36
Stone, Clay, and Glass Products	0.51	1.32	2.24	3.21	4.21
Primary Metals	1.74	3.09	4.26	5.34	6.37
Fabricated Metal Products	0.78	1.40	1.95	2.46	2.94
Nonelectrical Machinery	0.36	0.64	0.89	1.12	1.34
Electrical Machinery	0.36	0.65	0.91	1.16	1.41
Motor Vehicles	0.34	0.60	0.81	1.01	1.21
Other Transportation Equipment	0.33	0.60	0.84	1.05	1.26
Instruments	0.24	0.42	0.56	0.70	0.84
Miscellaneous Manufacturing	0.34	0.59	0.80	1.01	1.20
Transportation and Warehousing	0.77	1.47	2.13	2.77	3.39
Communications	0.29	0.54	0.77	0.97	1.18
Electric Utilities (Services)	2.84	4.90	6.58	8.04	9.36
Gas Utilities (Services)	3.99	7.73	11.34	14.88	18.36
Wholesale and Retail Trade	0.45	0.83	1.17	1.49	1.80
Finance, Insurance, and Real Estate	0.36	0.67	0.95	1.20	1.46
Personal and Business Services	0.36	0.68	0.97	1.24	1.50
Government Enterprises	0.53	1.00	1.43	1.84	2.24

Table 8.4
Impacts on commodity supply prices under alternative recycling scenarios: Average percent change from base, 2010–2050

$20 Tax Path	Capital Rates	All Rates	Labor Rates	Lump Sum
Agriculture, Forestry, Fisheries	9.09	8.01	7.52	10.00
Metal Mining	0.61	–0.50	–0.99	1.43
Coal Mining	113.06	112.38	112.08	114.49
Crude Oil and Gas Extraction	–1.39	–2.90	–3.61	–1.93
Nonmetallic Mineral Mining	1.11	0.25	–0.12	2.26
Construction	0.32	–1.10	–1.74	0.90
Food and Kindred Products	2.05	0.92	0.42	2.93
Tobacco Manufactures	0.34	–0.64	–1.07	1.40
Textile Mill Products	0.55	–0.63	–1.15	1.41
Apparel and Other Textile Products	0.19	–1.28	–1.94	0.58
Lumber and Wood Products	0.69	–0.54	–1.10	1.43
Furniture and Fixtures	0.26	–1.14	–1.77	0.82
Paper and Allied Products	0.41	–0.98	–1.61	0.87
Printing and Publishing	–0.17	–1.48	–2.07	0.54
Chemicals and Allied Products	1.48	0.32	–0.20	2.25
Petroleum Refining	8.42	7.03	6.39	8.39
Rubber and Plastic Products	0.42	–0.93	–1.54	0.98
Leather and Leather Products	0.25	–1.18	–1.82	0.66
Stone, Clay, and Glass Products	0.61	–0.59	–1.13	1.32
Primary Metals	2.48	1.16	0.56	3.09
Fabricated Metal Products	0.59	–0.61	–1.14	1.40
Nonelectrical Machinery	0.12	–1.29	–1.92	0.64
Electrical Machinery	0.28	–1.17	–1.82	0.65
Motor Vehicles	0.23	–1.22	–1.88	0.60
Other Transportation Equipment	0.13	–1.38	–2.06	0.60
Instruments	0.13	–1.45	–2.17	0.42
Miscellaneous Manufacturing	0.14	–1.26	–1.89	0.59
Transportation and Warehousing	0.78	–0.49	–1.06	1.47
Communications	–0.60	–1.52	–1.93	0.54
Electric Utilities (Services)	3.43	2.85	2.60	4.90
Gas Utilities (Services)	6.90	5.98	5.57	7.73
Wholesale and Retail Trade	0.10	–1.21	–1.80	0.83
Finance, Insurance, and Real Estate	–0.81	–1.44	–1.70	0.67
Personal and Business Services	0.06	–1.35	–1.98	0.68
Government Enterprises	0.06	–1.02	–1.51	1.00

carbon tax, the output of this sector falls, lowering the cost of capital and thus lowering prices for domestic crude oil and gas extraction.

All non-energy prices increase relative to the price of labor under lump sum recycling. Agriculture; Chemicals; Stone, Clay, and Glass; Primary Metals; Electrical Machinery (semiconductors); Transportation (pipelines); and Services (waste management) generate emissions covered by the carbon tax policies, as shown in table 7.3. In addition to the direct carbon tax, prices in these sectors are also affected by increases in energy input prices. Prices for Food, Apparel, Paper, Plastics, Motor Vehicles, Communications, and Trade are affected only indirectly via higher input costs.

We next consider the impacts of price changes on economic performance. Table 8.5 shows the impacts on final demand (GDP) and its components, while table 8.6 presents the outcomes for the capital stock, labor demand and supply, leisure demand, and full consumption. While these tables summarize all five tax scenarios and all four recycling options, our initial focus is on lump sum redistributions. We then discuss the alternative recycling options.

Among the combinations of carbon tax levels and fiscal reforms, lump sum redistributions result in the largest negative impact on both the demand and supply sides of the U.S. economy. Losses in GDP from base case levels, averaged over 2010–2050, range from 1.0% to 3.7% as carbon tax rates increase. Losses in consumer spending average less than half these amounts while investment and trade, especially exports, experience more significant reductions.

The declines in investment adversely affect capital formation, so that the capital stock averages anywhere from 0.8% to 2.9% lower, depending on the tax trajectory. In addition, lump sum redistributions lead to reductions in labor supply and demand. These losses average from 0.6% to 2.1% as taxes rise from $10 to $50. An important benefit in these outcomes is the increase in leisure that reflects the decline in labor supply. These gains range from 0.2% to 0.8%, depending on the tax trajectory, and partially compensate households in terms of full consumption for losses in personal consumption expenditures on goods and services.

The economic impacts of carbon taxes on the U.S. economy are dominated by the decisions of households. Household decisions begin with the allocation of full wealth among levels of full consumption in different time periods, including expenditures on goods and services and leisure. Anticipating price increases from rising carbon taxes,

Table 8.5
Impacts on final demand quantities: Average percent change from base, 2010–2050

	Capital Rates	All Rates	Labor Rates	Lump Sum
$10 tax path				
GDP	0.23	0.00	−0.13	−0.97
Consumption	−0.01	0.33	0.48	−0.47
Investment	1.69	0.25	−0.47	−1.49
Government	0.00	0.00	0.00	0.00
Exports	−0.53	−1.18	−1.49	−2.30
Imports	−0.08	−0.50	−0.71	−1.47
$20 tax path				
GDP	0.35	−0.04	−0.26	−1.79
Consumption	−0.05	0.56	0.84	−0.89
Investment	2.98	0.47	−0.82	−2.66
Government	0.00	0.00	0.00	0.00
Exports	−1.11	−2.24	−2.81	−4.22
Imports	−0.18	−0.90	−1.28	−2.64
$30 tax path				
GDP	0.40	−0.10	−0.41	−2.50
Consumption	−0.13	0.74	1.12	−1.27
Investment	4.01	0.65	−1.12	−3.65
Government	0.00	0.00	0.00	0.00
Exports	−1.70	−3.22	−4.01	−5.90
Imports	−0.33	−1.28	−1.80	−3.65
$40 tax path				
GDP	0.40	−0.18	−0.56	−3.15
Consumption	−0.23	0.87	1.35	−1.63
Investment	4.86	0.79	−1.39	−4.52
Government	0.00	0.00	0.00	0.00
Exports	−2.28	−4.14	−5.14	−7.40
Imports	−0.50	−1.64	−2.28	−4.55
$50 tax path				
GDP	0.37	−0.27	−0.71	−3.74
Consumption	−0.34	0.99	1.53	−1.98
Investment	5.56	0.92	−1.64	−5.33
Government	0.00	0.00	0.00	0.00
Exports	−2.85	−5.00	−6.18	−8.79
Imports	−0.69	−1.98	−2.7	−5.38

Table 8.6
Impacts on capital, labor, leisure, and full consumption: Average percent change from base, 2010–2050

	Capital Rates	All Rates	Labor Rates	Lump Sum
$10 tax path				
Capital stock	1.02	0.16	–0.24	–0.79
Labor demand and supply	–0.15	0.26	0.45	–0.59
Leisure demand	0.06	–0.11	–0.18	0.23
Full consumption	0.11	0.04	0.02	0.00
$20 tax path				
Capital stock	1.82	0.31	–0.43	–1.43
Labor demand and supply	–0.28	0.48	0.82	–1.05
Leisure demand	0.12	–0.19	–0.33	0.42
Full consumption	0.18	0.07	0.01	–0.03
$30 tax path				
Capital stock	2.48	0.44	–0.59	–1.97
Labor demand and supply	–0.41	0.67	1.15	–1.44
Leisure demand	0.17	–0.27	–0.46	0.58
Full consumption	0.23	0.08	0.00	–0.05
$40 tax path				
Capital stock	3.03	0.56	–0.73	–2.45
Labor demand and supply	–0.52	0.83	1.44	–1.79
Leisure demand	0.21	–0.33	–0.58	0.72
Full consumption	0.27	0.09	–0.01	–0.08
$50 tax path				
Capital stock	3.52	0.68	–0.85	–2.91
Labor demand and supply	–0.63	0.98	1.70	–2.08
Leisure demand	0.26	–0.39	–0.68	0.83
Full consumption	0.30	0.09	–0.03	–0.13

households shift full consumption toward the present and away from the future. This reduces saving for future consumption and lowers the rate of capital formation.

Households next choose the allocation of full consumption among goods, services, and leisure. Since carbon taxes make consumer goods and services more expensive relative to the leisure numeraire, the overall price of leisure is lower and households substitute leisure for goods and services. Although full consumption rises in the near term, consumption of goods and services declines because the increase in nominal consumer spending is proportionally smaller than the increase in consumer prices.

In addition to reducing personal consumption expenditures, the shift to leisure by households in response to the decrease in real wages means a fall in labor supply. Increased leisure improves household welfare, while reducing personal consumption expenditures reduces welfare. However, the reduction in labor supply leads to a reduction in the output of the economy, as measured by the GDP. We evaluate the impacts of alternative carbon tax policies in terms of their impacts on the welfare of individual households and the level of social welfare rather than in terms of production.

The third set of decisions by households is to allocate the reduced level of household spending among the 35 commodities and capital services. Personal consumption expenditures are redirected from goods and services with large price increases toward those with smaller price increases. Since household spending is a large fraction of final demand, the decisions of households influence the structure of real GDP and the domestic production activity that supports it.

The production side of the economy is affected adversely by the fall in labor and capital supply due to the carbon taxes. All industries experience declines in output. Industries subject to the carbon tax are especially hard hit. The changes in industry output for the lump sum case are given for all tax rates in table 8.7 and for all recycling scenarios in the $20 tax case in table 8.8. We see comparatively large reductions in output in Agriculture, Coal Mining, Chemicals, Petroleum Refining, Primary Metals, Transportation, and Electric and Gas Utilities—the dominant contributors of greenhouse gas emissions in table 7.3.

Negative industry output effects result not only from higher prices, as shown in table 8.9, and declining demands throughout the economy but also from reductions in the availability of capital and labor inputs. Facing reduced demands for output and more limited factor supplies,

Table 8.7
Impacts on domestic output quantities: Average percent change from base, 2010–2050

Lump Sum Redistribution	$10 Tax Path	$20 Tax Path	$30 Tax Path	$40 Tax Path	$50 Tax Path
Agriculture, Forestry, Fisheries	–6.80	–12.30	–16.90	–20.83	–24.26
Metal Mining	–2.27	–4.46	–6.49	–8.37	–10.13
Coal Mining	–37.43	–52.41	–60.52	–65.60	–69.07
Crude Oil and Gas Extraction	–0.92	–1.80	–2.65	–3.46	–4.25
Nonmetallic Mineral Mining	–2.92	–5.42	–7.62	–9.61	–11.43
Construction	–1.06	–1.93	–2.68	–3.36	–3.97
Food and Kindred Products	–1.94	–3.60	–5.07	–6.39	–7.62
Tobacco Manufactures	–1.20	–2.27	–3.25	–4.16	–5.02
Textile Mill Products	–1.47	–2.68	–3.74	–4.70	–5.62
Apparel and Other Textile Products	–0.04	–0.05	–0.05	–0.06	–0.09
Lumber and Wood Products	–1.46	–2.66	–3.71	–4.65	–5.52
Furniture and Fixtures	–1.21	–2.15	–2.94	–3.65	–4.30
Paper and Allied Products	–1.37	–2.46	–3.39	–4.23	–5.01
Printing and Publishing	–0.87	–1.60	–2.25	–2.84	–3.39
Chemicals and Allied Products	–2.56	–4.75	–6.70	–8.49	–10.14
Petroleum Refining	–5.89	–10.83	–15.10	–18.85	–22.18
Rubber and Plastic Products	–1.59	–2.75	–3.69	–4.50	–5.22
Leather and Leather Products	–0.67	–1.20	–1.67	–2.10	–2.52
Stone, Clay, and Glass Products	–1.63	–3.49	–5.33	–7.11	–8.82
Primary Metals	–3.85	–6.84	–9.38	–11.62	–13.65
Fabricated Metal Products	–2.01	–3.56	–4.88	–6.05	–7.12
Nonelectrical Machinery	–1.74	–3.07	–4.19	–5.17	–6.07
Electrical Machinery	–1.28	–2.34	–3.25	–4.09	–4.86
Motor Vehicles	–1.47	–2.58	–3.51	–4.34	–5.10
Other Transportation Equipment	–0.60	–1.11	–1.54	–1.92	–2.24
Instruments	–1.03	–1.87	–2.60	–3.24	–3.83
Miscellaneous Manufacturing	–1.28	–2.37	–3.34	–4.21	–5.03
Transportation and Warehousing	–2.02	–3.73	–5.25	–6.63	–7.91
Communications	–0.81	–1.48	–2.08	–2.61	–3.12
Electric Utilities (Services)	–2.30	–3.87	–5.09	–6.12	–7.03
Gas Utilities (Services)	–5.73	–10.80	–15.25	–19.18	–22.66
Wholesale and Retail Trade	–1.07	–1.94	–2.68	–3.35	–3.97
Finance, Insurance, and Real Estate	–0.98	–1.79	–2.49	–3.13	–3.72
Personal and Business Services	–0.78	–1.44	–2.03	–2.57	–3.08
Government Enterprises	–1.12	–2.08	–2.95	–3.74	–4.49

Table 8.8
Impacts on domestic output quantities: Average percent change from base, 2010–2050

$20 Tax Path	Capital Rates	All Rates	Labor Rates	Lump Sum
Agriculture, Forestry, Fisheries	–11.13	–11.01	–10.97	–12.30
Metal Mining	0.20	–2.05	–3.18	–4.46
Coal Mining	–51.84	–52.14	–52.28	–52.41
Crude Oil and Gas Extraction	–1.32	–1.31	–1.31	–1.80
Nonmetallic Mineral Mining	–1.81	–3.56	–4.43	–5.42
Construction	1.12	0.06	–0.50	–1.93
Food and Kindred Products	–2.70	–1.89	–1.53	–3.60
Tobacco Manufactures	–1.40	–0.37	0.10	–2.27
Textile Mill Products	0.74	–0.34	–0.91	–2.68
Apparel and Other Textile Products	–0.08	1.62	2.41	–0.05
Lumber and Wood Products	1.02	–0.51	–1.30	–2.66
Furniture and Fixtures	2.76	0.63	–0.47	–2.15
Paper and Allied Products	–0.95	–0.72	–0.64	–2.46
Printing and Publishing	–0.06	0.22	0.33	–1.60
Chemicals and Allied Products	–3.19	–3.14	–3.14	–4.75
Petroleum Refining	–10.14	–9.96	–9.89	–10.83
Rubber and Plastic Products	–0.26	–0.78	–1.07	–2.75
Leather and Leather Products	–0.81	0.41	0.97	–1.20
Stone, Clay, and Glass Products	–0.30	–1.61	–2.28	–3.49
Primary Metals	–2.94	–4.73	–5.63	–6.84
Fabricated Metal Products	–0.10	–1.51	–2.24	–3.56
Nonelectrical Machinery	1.67	–0.27	–1.27	–3.07
Electrical Machinery	0.90	–0.28	–0.89	–2.34
Motor Vehicles	1.03	–0.35	–1.07	–2.58
Other Transportation Equipment	0.43	–0.14	–0.45	–1.11
Instruments	0.96	0.20	–0.22	–1.87
Miscellaneous Manufacturing	1.02	–0.01	–0.55	–2.37
Transportation and Warehousing	–2.59	–2.34	–2.24	–3.73
Communications	–0.28	–0.05	0.03	–1.48
Electric Utilities (Services)	–2.19	–2.23	–2.28	–3.87
Gas Utilities (Services)	–10.33	–9.65	–9.34	–10.80
Wholesale and Retail Trade	0.49	0.39	0.30	–1.94
Finance, Insurance, and Real Estate	0.13	–0.20	–0.39	–1.79
Personal and Business Services	–0.96	–0.06	0.35	–1.44
Government Enterprises	–1.08	–0.68	–0.52	–2.08

Table 8.9
Impacts on selected final demand prices: Average percent change from base, 2010–2050

	Capital Rates	All Rates	Labor Rates	Lump Sum
$10 tax path				
Consumption	–0.05	–0.52	–0.73	0.61
Investment	0.05	–0.68	–1.02	0.38
Government	0.16	–0.77	–1.20	0.33
$20 tax path				
Consumption	–0.05	–0.90	–1.28	1.15
Investment	0.11	–1.23	–1.83	0.71
Government	0.30	–1.38	–2.15	0.61
$30 tax path				
Consumption	–0.01	–1.22	–1.74	1.63
Investment	0.19	–1.68	–2.52	1.00
Government	0.45	–1.90	–2.95	0.86
$40 tax path				
Consumption	0.05	–1.47	–2.12	2.09
Investment	0.28	–2.06	–3.11	1.28
Government	0.59	–2.34	–3.65	1.10
$50 tax path				
Consumption	0.13	–1.69	–2.44	2.53
Investment	0.39	–2.40	–3.62	1.55
Government	0.73	–2.73	–4.27	1.33

producers are forced to raise prices in order to cover the increase in costs. Producers do their best to insulate their prices from the impacts of more expensive energy inputs. Substitutions from more costly energy toward relatively cheaper materials, labor, and capital inputs help to mitigate the adverse effects.

The reduction in labor income from the households' reduced labor supply combines with lower capital income from businesses to yield a reduction in the nominal GDP. Personal consumption declines with a lump sum redistribution of tax revenues to households. Private saving also declines. The reduction in saving is accompanied by a corresponding reduction in private investment. With higher prices for investment goods, the available investment funding buys fewer capital goods and leads to a lower capital stock and diminished availability of capital inputs. Reduced capital and labor inputs limit the economy's domestic supply, following the imposition of carbon taxes.

IGEM's savings-investment balance, given in equation 2.91 in chapter 2, summarizes the net flow of funds available for investment. Domestic saving must satisfy two important claims before flowing through to investment. The first claim on saving is the combined deficits of the government sectors. The second claim arises from the nation's interactions with the rest of the world. A surplus in the current account balance is the excess of the value of exports over the value of imports and must be financed by net foreign investment. The funds available for private investment are equal to those remaining from private saving after financing government deficits and net foreign investment. The current account deficits that are projected for the United States in the near term imply that domestic saving is augmented by foreign saving in financing U.S. investment.

In order to capture the impacts of declines in saving we eliminate the direct effects of governments on investment spending. Our scenarios for recycling of government revenues through lump sum redistributions, as well as recycling through reductions of capital and labor tax rates, assume no change in the deficits of the government sectors or the levels of government purchases. Under this assumption the time path of public debt is unaffected by the choice of methods for revenue recycling.

All scenarios for recycling carbon tax revenues hold constant the current account balance and net foreign indebtedness. The current account balance is maintained by adjusting the exchange rate. The prices of U.S.-made goods rise relative to world prices in the initial stage of the carbon tax. Since we estimate that supplies of exports are price-elastic, export volumes fall more than export prices rise and the value of exports declines.

The change in imports is more complicated in that we have both income and price effects. Lower real household income reduces lifetime consumption, although consumption in different phases of the transition may rise temporarily, as discussed above. The lower lifetime consumption also means lower aggregate consumption of imported goods in the long run. Initially, untaxed domestic-goods prices rise relative to world prices as a result of the carbon tax, inducing a substitution toward imported varieties. For fossil fuels and other commodities subject to a carbon tax, the imports are similarly taxed and demand falls.

The opposing income and price effects result in a reduction in aggregate import demand that is smaller than the reduction in exports in the long run. To maintain the current account balance at base case levels, market equilibrium requires a long-run depreciation of the exchange rate. With consumption pulled forward, there is a positive impact on import demand. This requires a short-term appreciation of the exchange rate to maintain the current account balance.

In revenue recycling, such as the lump sum redistribution case just discussed, the government deficit, and hence the debt, is held unchanged at base case levels. When carbon tax revenues are recycled as tax cuts, the higher (nominal) incomes are used to partly offset the higher consumer prices, and real saving and investment may be higher or lower than in the base case, depending on the period. In the lump sum recycling case, real investment is lower in all periods.

8.3.2 *Cutting Taxes on Labor and Capital*

We now turn to revenue recycling by reducing tax rates, beginning with labor income tax rates. As before, the taxes levied on emissions of greenhouse gases raise prices to producers and consumers. The increases in carbon tax revenues are returned to households through reductions in the average and marginal tax rates on labor income. For the $10 carbon tax trajectory, these rate reductions average 5.2% from 2016, the initial tax year, through 2050. The $20, $30, $40, and $50 tax trajectories permit corresponding reductions that average 9.4%, 13.2%, 16.7%, and 19.8%, respectively.

The labor tax rate reductions raise the opportunity cost of consuming leisure. Households substitute toward consumption and away from leisure. Labor supply increases at reduced pretax wages. Producers absorb this additional labor, restructuring inputs toward labor and away from emissions-generating activities and capital. With the numeraire as the leisure price, the changes in the labor tax rate imply a lower labor input price to employers. Unit production costs and commodity prices in terms of the numeraire fall relative to the base case and the other recycling options.

Labor tax rate reductions favor consumption over saving and investment. Income rises from greater labor supply, but this is more than offset by a decline in capital income due to a lower capital stock. Given the intertemporal preferences we have estimated and the time profile of real wages, the reduction in lifetime full income is optimized by having higher full consumption in the near term before the carbon tax is imposed and lower full consumption in the longer term. Higher full consumption in the near term combined with higher labor supply means higher goods consumption and reduced saving. Reduced saving leads to reductions in investment and a lower rate of capital formation even with lower prices for investment goods.

The favorable price effects from labor tax recycling at the commodity level, relative to the leisure price numeraire, are shown in table 8.4. In the columns for Capital Rates and Lump Sum we see price increases with just a few exceptions; under labor tax recycling we see price decreases for most commodities and only moderate price increases for the more carbon-intensive commodities. These changes in commodity prices are reflected in the final demand prices shown in table 8.9; the prices of consumption, investment, and government purchases decline in the range of 0.7 to 1.2% for the $10 tax trajectory and 2.4% to 4.3% in the $50 case. No other recycling option delivers this price effect.

In tables 8.5 and 8.6 labor tax recycling promotes consumption over investment and labor over leisure. Over the five tax trajectories, average increases in consumption range from 0.5% to 1.5% with broadly similar average increases in labor supply. The consumption-leisure effects are largely offsetting, leaving full consumption virtually unaffected. The declines in investment are modest in comparison to those in the lump sum case and yield corresponding declines in the capital stock. This is partially offset by increased labor services, resulting in the smallest losses in GDP discussed so far, averaging just under 0.1% in the $10 carbon tax trajectory and just under 0.7% in the $50 trajectory.

We next consider the substitution of carbon taxes for capital income taxes. We hold government purchases, deficits, and debt at base case levels. As before, carbon tax policy raises prices to producers and consumers. Under the $10 carbon tax trajectory capital tax rates average 11.1% lower than in the base case over the period 2016–2050. In the $20, $30, $40, and $50 trajectories the corresponding reductions average 19.9%, 27.5%, 34.3%, and 40.3%, respectively. For broadly similar carbon tax revenues, the differences in tax bases and tax rates imply that capital tax reductions must be proportionally more than twice as large as labor tax reductions to achieve deficit neutrality.

Recycling carbon tax revenues through lower tax rates on capital reduces the rental price of capital services and raises the returns on saving and investment. Referring to tables 8.5 and 8.6, this policy favors capital formation over consumption but enhances the possibilities for reducing losses in consumption or even increasing consumption in the longer term. The increased availability of capital—averaging from 1.0% to 3.5% as carbon tax rates increase—helps insulate the U.S. economy from higher prices.

Greater capital formation dampens, but does not eliminate, the substitution of leisure for the consumption of goods and services. The increases in leisure complement the losses in consumption, leading to increases in full consumption from 0.1% to 0.3%, depending on the carbon tax trajectory. With trade effects further moderated compared to the lump sum case, real GDP increases as a result of increased investment and a larger capital stock. These increases, ranging from 0.2% to 0.4% under the various tax trajectories, are only partially offset by the price-induced withdrawal of labor services by households.

Proportionally reducing both capital and labor tax rates blends the effects from labor and capital tax recycling. Average losses in GDP, 2010–2050, range from nothing in the $10 carbon tax trajectory to 0.27% in the $50 trajectory. The effects for other key measures—consumption, investment, the capital stock, labor, leisure, and full consumption—also are composites of the pure labor and capital tax scenarios. Over the five carbon tax trajectories, the labor tax effects are dominant in the mix. This is not surprising since labor is the largest component of value added.

For lower carbon tax trajectories of $10 and $20 in the combined tax reduction case, capital tax recycling accounts for approximately 36% of the average impacts on GDP with labor tax reductions providing the remainder. However, as capital becomes relatively more important, the importance of the capital tax in the combined recycling option increases. Under the $30, $40, and $50 carbon tax trajectories, the contributions from capital tax recycling to the GDP rise from 36% to 38%, 40%, and 41%, respectively.

8.4 Impacts of Technical Change

The role of endogenous or price-induced technical change (ITC) is widely discussed in analyzing the impact of environmental policy.[10] In addition to substitution in response to higher energy prices, there may be changes in technology. These induced changes in technology may lead to reduced emissions and help to offset the higher costs of energy, thus lowering the economic cost of achieving a given environmental target or allowing more aggressive emission reductions.

In chapter 4 we have shown how IGEM captures the impact of induced technical change along with substitution among inputs in response to input price changes for each of the 35 industries that comprise the U.S. economy. The first step is to characterize biases of technical change for inputs of capital, labor, energy, and materials. The rate of technical change then contains two components, an endogenous component induced by changes in relative input prices and an autonomous component that is unaffected by price changes.

In this section our objective is to analyze the contribution of induced technical change to the outcomes of changes in carbon tax policies. An environmental policy change introduced into IGEM alters relative prices and induces changes in rates of productivity growth through policy-invariant patterns of technical change. The full measure of the effects of ITC depends on the projected trends in these patterns. In chapter 5 we have discussed the methodology for making these projections.

To illustrate the impacts of price-induced technical change, we present four model simulations—the \$20 tax trajectory with capital tax recycling, labor tax recycling, and lump sum redistributions to households and the \$50 tax scenario with lump sum redistributions. Under each scenario we compute the impacts of induced technical change and compare these with the overall impacts of changes in carbon tax policy; that is, we compute the $\sum_i \ln p_{it} f_{it}^{Pj}$ term in equations 4.4 and 4.7 and compare it to the changes in domestic output, QI_{jt}. The economy-wide contribution of the ITC effect is the weighted sum over all industries of this term, where the weights are the gross output value share. The economy-wide output loss is the weighted sum of the percent change in QI_{jt} due to the policy, where the weights are the industry output quantities.

Table 8.10 shows the economy-wide contributions of ITC for the years 2030 and 2050 along with corresponding losses in domestic industry output for these four cases. We note first that the induced productivity effects are cumulative, so that the impacts of ITC in 2050 are more than three times those we observe in 2030. We also find that the effects of ITC increase with more aggressive tax policies.

Under lump sum recycling of carbon tax revenues, the \$20 tax trajectory elicits annual benefits of 0.16% and 0.53% in 2030 and 2050, respectively, while in the \$50 tax scenario these contributions rise to 0.35% and 1.11%. Aside from capital tax recycling, there is a remarkable

Table 8.10
The economy-wide contribution of price-induced technical change (percent change from the base case)

	Technical Change		Output Loss	
	2030	2050	2030	2050
$20 tax path				
Capital rates	0.13	0.44	–0.47	–2.78
Labor rates	0.15	0.52	–1.22	–3.09
Lump sum	0.16	0.53	–3.03	–6.72
$50 tax path				
Lump sum	0.35	1.11	–6.36	–13.22

similarity in ITC magnitude across the other $20 cases with each recycling option in the range of 0.15% to 0.16% for 2030 and 0.51% to 0.53% for 2050. We attribute the smaller effects under capital tax recycling to the benefits of greater capital availability. For the same carbon tax regime the presence of a larger capital stock slightly diminishes the rate and role of price-induced technical change.

For lump sum recycling of carbon tax revenues, the impacts of induced technical change are small in comparison to the observed output losses. These impacts range from about 5% in 2030 to about 8% in 2050 with slightly higher percentages under higher carbon taxes. With significantly smaller output losses under labor tax recycling, the relative impacts of induced technical change increase even further. The impacts range from 12% for 2030 to 16% for 2050. Under capital tax recycling we see even more dramatic reductions in the output losses. In 2030 the impacts of induced technical change are 28% of the output effects. In 2050 this number falls to about 16% and is comparable to the 2050 figure for labor tax recycling. For recycling through capital tax reductions the relative importance of the impacts of price-induced technical change diminishes over time as more capital accumulation takes place.

The economy-wide effects we have described are aggregates of the industry patterns of technical change. Figures 8.3 through 8.6 show the contributions to total technical change for the four simulations reported in table 8.10. Given the biases of technical change that we report in chapter 4, we find in all these four cases sectors that undergo more

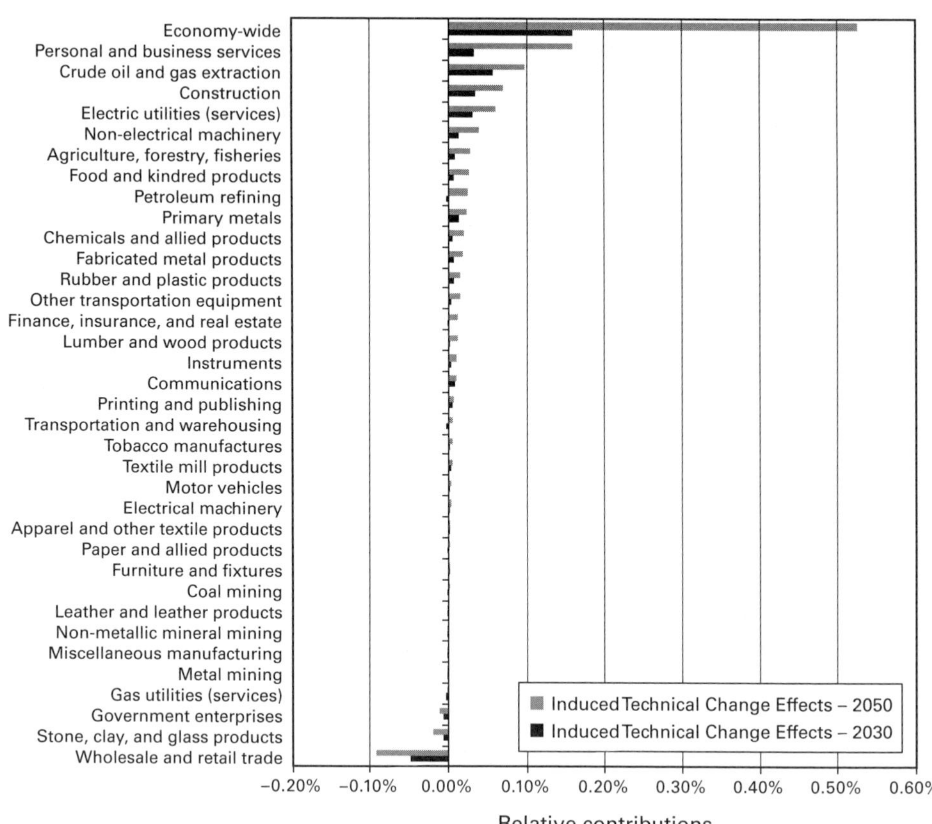

Figure 8.3
Price-induced technical change—$20 lump sum case.

rapid technical changes, sectors that experience slower changes, and sectors that are essentially unaffected by induced technical change.

Revenue recycling with lump sum redistributions results in minor variations in the ordering of impacts on production between the $20 and $50 tax trajectories given in figures 8.3 and 8.4. Services, Crude Oil and Gas, Construction, Electric Utilities, Non-electric Machinery, Agriculture, Food, and Petroleum Refining undergo positive price-induced technical change. Gas Utilities; Government Enterprises; Stone, Clay, and Glass; and Trade experience negative induced technical change.

In mitigating the negative impacts of carbon tax policies, price-induced technical change has effects that are offsetting. For example, ITC in the Electric Utilities sector plays an important role in the overall

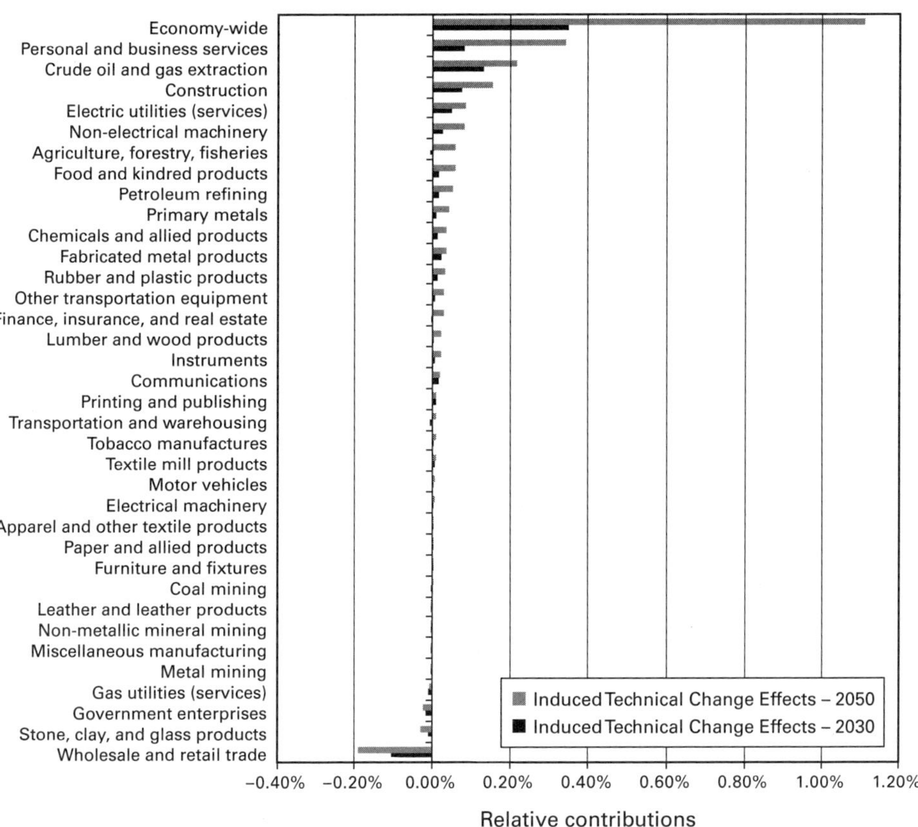

Figure 8.4
Price-induced technical change—$50 lump sum case.

impact of ITC. Electricity prices are lower and demand is higher than without ITC. Since ITC helps to lower electricity prices, energy use and emissions are higher, which implies that tax rates would have to be higher to achieve a given emissions reduction.

On the other hand, price-induced technical change in Services has very different implications. The ITC effect calculated for Services works to lower service prices. This is beneficial to Service sector growth and growth in the overall economy. However, the Service sector is not energy- or emissions-intensive. The shift toward services that accompanies ITC results in an economy that is less energy- and emissions-intensive, so that the tax rates required to achieve a given emissions target are modestly lower as a result.

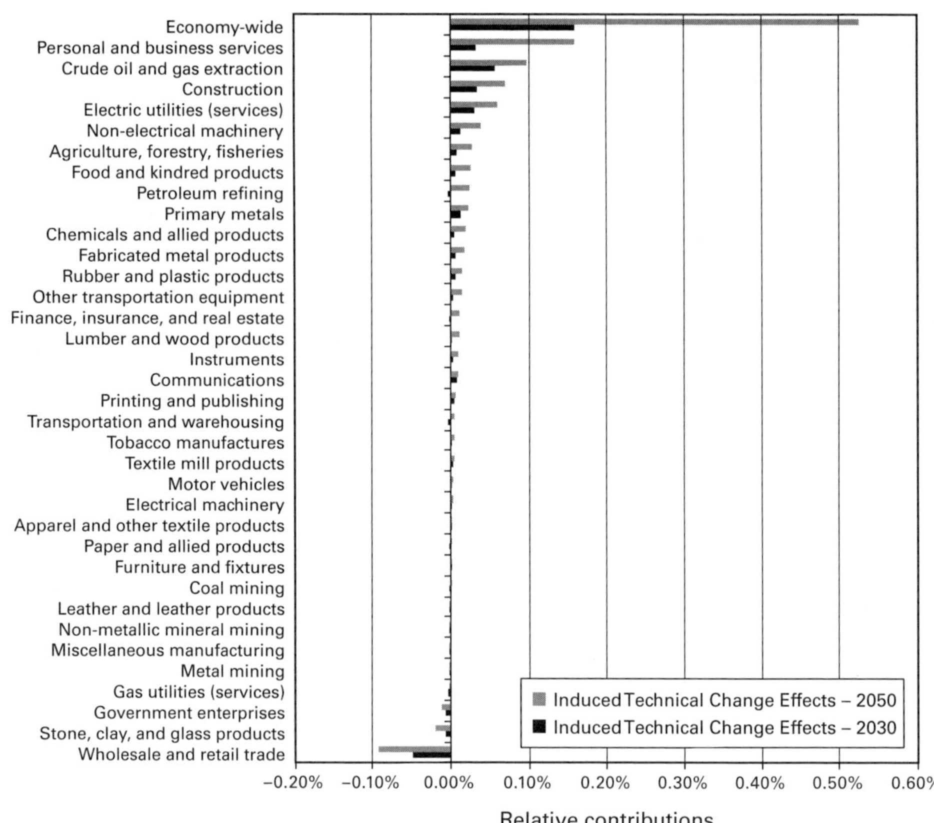

Figure 8.5
Price-induced technical change—$20 labor tax case.

The economy-wide impacts of ITC are similar for revenue recycling by means of lump sum distributions to households and reductions in labor tax rates, as shown in figures 8.3 and 8.5. However, there are important differences in the industry composition of these impacts. For Petroleum Refining the change in recycling policies from lump sum to labor tax reductions changes the sign of the impacts. Several industries move up in their relative importance, becoming more positive or less negative. Primary Metals, Electrical Machinery, and the Non-energy Extraction industries are among these industries.

The changes in industry composition are even more striking for the switch from lump sum distributions to capital tax rate reductions in figures 8.3 and 8.6. Electricity, Crude Oil and Gas, and Food increase in relative importance, becoming the largest contributors to

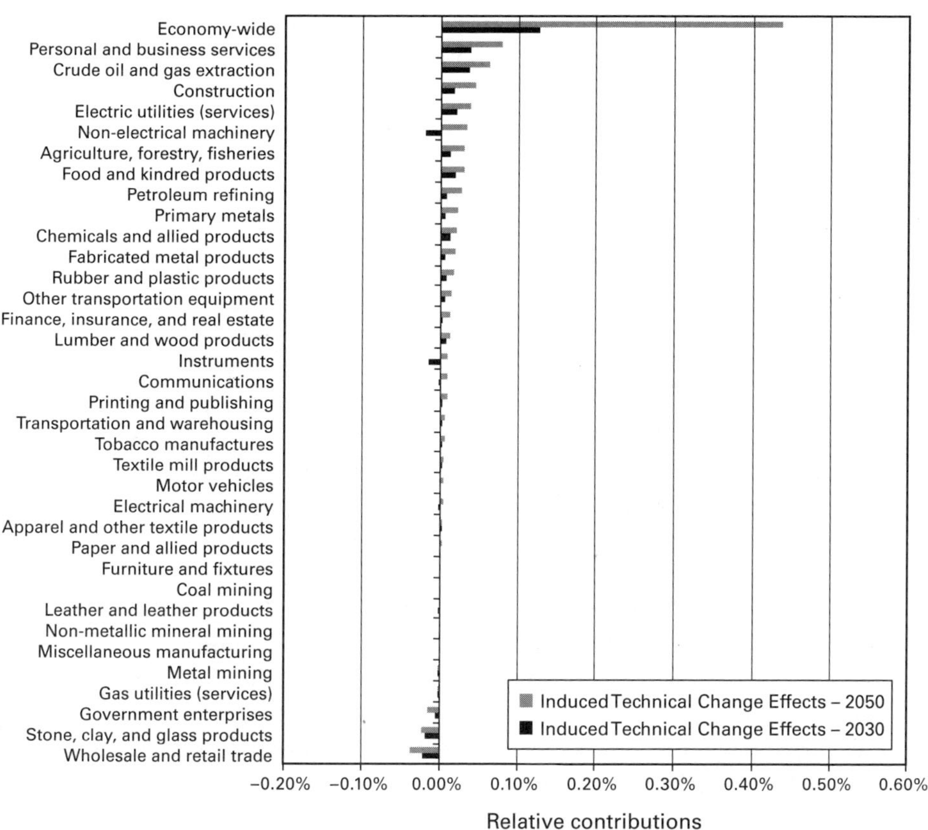

Figure 8.6
Price-induced technical change—$20 capital tax case.

price-induced technical change. The Services sector not only diminishes as a top contributor in 2050 but reduces overall ITC in 2030. Under capital tax recycling, both Gas Utilities and Coal Mining eventually contribute to economy-wide ITC. Finally, the Finance sector, neutral or positive under lump sum and labor tax recycling, becomes second only to Trade in reinforcing the adverse price effects of carbon tax policy.

8.5 Individual Welfare Impacts

In section 3.7 we established the link between our model of consumer behavior and the measurement of individual welfare. Measures of individual welfare depend on the demographic characteristics of households: size (numbers of children—0, 1, 2, or 3 or more—and adults—1,

2, or 3 or more), region of residence, (Northeast, Midwest, South, West), race and gender of head (white, nonwhite, male, female), and location (urban, rural). These combinations yield 384 possible household types, of which only 244 are represented in the Consumer Expenditure Survey (CEX).

For each household type we derive an expenditure function that depends on prices and full wealth, defined as tangible assets plus household time endowments. We calculate the welfare impact of an energy and environmental policy as its impact on the equivalent variation in full wealth (equation 3.52). This answers the question, how much would full wealth have to increase at base case prices in order to generate the same increase in household welfare as a given change in policy?

Since our utility function is non-homothetic, the income elasticities differ from one. We present equivalent variations for three possible levels of full wealth for each demographic type—the mean, half the mean, and twice the mean. Combining these three levels of full wealth with the 244 household types, we present a total of 732 equivalent variations in response to each change in energy and environmental policy.

The characteristics of our household sample provide a useful perspective for the results that follow. The lowest level of lifetime full wealth that we consider is $0.8 million in 2005 dollars, while the highest is $32.8 million. For comparative purposes these are our "poorest" and "richest" households. We use the term "mean full wealth" to refer to the mean over all households in each of the 244 types. The population-weighted average mean full wealth is $6.6 million, averaged over the 244 types, while the averages at half and twice mean full wealth are $3.3 million and $13.2 million, respectively.

Almost two-thirds of the households in this sample have no children—29.5% are single-adult households, 28.8% are two-adult households, and 7.6% have three or more adults. Of the 34.2% of households with children, more than 80% have only one or two (27.6% of all households), leaving 6.6% with three or more children. Regionally, 18.9% of the households reside in the Northeast, 23.0% reside in the Midwest, 36.5% reside in the South, and 21.6% reside in the West. On race and gender, 7.4% of the sample households are headed by nonwhite females, 22.5% are headed by white females, 10.3% are headed by nonwhite males, and 59.8% are headed by white males. Finally, 92.1% of the sample households are located in urban areas with the remaining 7.9% residing in rural locations.

Table 8.11
Household welfare effects, reference households: Equivalent variations in 2005 dollars and as percentages of full wealth

	Poorest Household[1]		Richest Household[2]	
	$2005	% of Wealth	$2005	% of Wealth
$10 tax path				
Capital	$362	0.045	$43,926	0.134
Labor	–$161	–0.020	–$36,133	–0.110
Lump sum	–$1,296	–0.161	$34,120	0.104
$50 tax path				
Capital	–$495	–0.062	$131,852	0.403
Labor	–$2,057	–0.256	–$144,855	–0.442
Lump sum	–$5,891	–0.734	$99,379	0.303

[1] Female-headed, nonwhite household with 1 child living in the rural South with lifetime full wealth of $0.8 million.
[2] Male-headed, nonwhite household with 3 or more each of adults and children living in the urban West with lifetime full wealth of $32.8 million.

We derive household welfare measures for the five carbon tax scenarios and four revenue recycling options—capital tax rate recycling, combined capital and labor tax rate recycling, labor tax rate recycling, and lump sum redistributions to households. To simplify comparisons among household types, we focus on the extremes under the revenue recycling options. In table 8.11 we show the welfare changes in 2005 dollars and as a percentage of full wealth for two reference households—the poorest and richest, as described above. The former is a female-headed, nonwhite household with one child living in the rural South with lifetime full wealth of $0.8 million. The latter is a male-headed, nonwhite household with three or more each of adults and children living in the urban West with lifetime full wealth of $32.8 million.

For the poorest household we observe small welfare gains, measured in dollars and as a percentage of full wealth, under capital tax rate recycling and low carbon tax rates. As carbon tax rates rise, these small gains become small losses (from 0.045% of full wealth to –0.062%) as the benefits from recycling are outweighed by the costs of the higher carbon taxes. For the richest household type, the capital tax rate policy yields a larger absolute and proportional benefit that increases with rising carbon taxes. The changes are very small shares of full wealth;

indeed, there is no change in any direction under any policy combination that exceeds 0.9% of lifetime full wealth.

The poorest households experience welfare losses under both labor tax rate and lump sum recycling, but reductions in labor tax rates are preferable. Lump sum redistributions offer welfare benefits for the richest households under all carbon tax regimes, benefits which approach those of capital tax reductions. Larger and richer households demand more leisure, which has become more expensive in the policy case. Reductions in labor tax rates encourage increases in labor supply and corresponding decreases in leisure demand. For these households, the gains in consumption are insufficient to compensate the losses in leisure. For the wealthier households, labor tax rate recycling is welfare-reducing while lump sum transfers, which are proportional to expenditures, are welfare-enhancing.

We show the largest and smallest welfare changes across all 732 possible policy combinations in table 8.12. We present gains and losses both in dollars and as percentages of full wealth. Unlike table 8.11, which gives the welfare impacts for the same household type in adjacent columns, in table 8.12 the underlying household characteristics for

Table 8.12
Household welfare effects, largest and smallest: Equivalent variations in 2005 dollars and in percentages of full wealth

	Impact	$2005	% of Wealth[1]
$10 tax path			
Capital	Largest	$45,985	0.204
	Smallest	$111	0.005
Labor	Largest	$1,297	0.020
	Smallest	–$36,133	–0.118
Lump sum	Largest	$35,054	0.136
	Smallest	–$6,509	–0.202
$50 tax path			
Capital	Largest	$139,978	0.574
	Smallest	–$5,740	–0.137
Labor	Largest	–$1,733	–0.074
	Smallest	–$144,855	–0.515
Lump sum	Largest	$110,314	0.429
	Smallest	–$36,554	–0.893

[1] Household characteristics often do not correspond to those represented in the adjacent $2005 column.

the measures in dollars can differ from those for percentages. Our goal is to document the extremes without respect to the household type in which they occur.

We observe the largest gain to be around $140,000 in 2005 dollars and the largest loss around $145,000. Not surprisingly, these occur under the highest carbon tax rates. The gains seem large but are less striking when expressed as proportions of full wealth. The largest percentage gain is 0.6% of full wealth and the largest percentage loss is 0.9%.

Under low carbon tax rate trajectories and capital tax rate recycling, all households experience an increase in welfare, so that these policies would be preferred to no change in policy by the Pareto principle. As the carbon tax trajectories become more aggressive, some households gain while other types begin to suffer welfare losses. The recycling benefits outrun the adverse price and tax effects for some households; for others, it is the reverse.

For labor tax rate recycling there are small welfare gains and relatively large welfare losses under the lowest tax trajectory. As carbon tax rates increase, the gains give way to losses and the losses magnify to the point where there are no winners. Under lump sum redistribution, we see both winners and losers at the $10 tax rates. The gains are not as large as those for capital tax recycling, but the losses are substantially smaller than those for labor tax recycling. As tax rates increase, the welfare gains and losses also increase.

To explore the comparison between labor tax rate recycling and lump sum redistributions, we consider the differences in the percentages of equivalent variations of full wealth among all household types for the three measures of full wealth—half mean, mean, and twice mean. That is, we show $\%EV_d^{LaborTax}(W_d) - \%EV_d^{LumpSum}(W_d)$ in figure 8.7 for the $20 case, sorted from the most negative difference to the most positive, for the three values of W_d = mean, half mean, and twice mean full wealth. As full wealth increases, due either to more persons per household or more expensive leisure per household, the difference becomes more negative; that is, lump sum recycling is the more beneficial alternative for them since the lump sum payment is proportional to the total expenditures.

To summarize the demographic distributions of changes in household welfare, we compute population-weighted averages for each combination of the household characteristics. These are shown in tables 8.13 through 8.16 for the $20 carbon tax trajectory and the four revenue

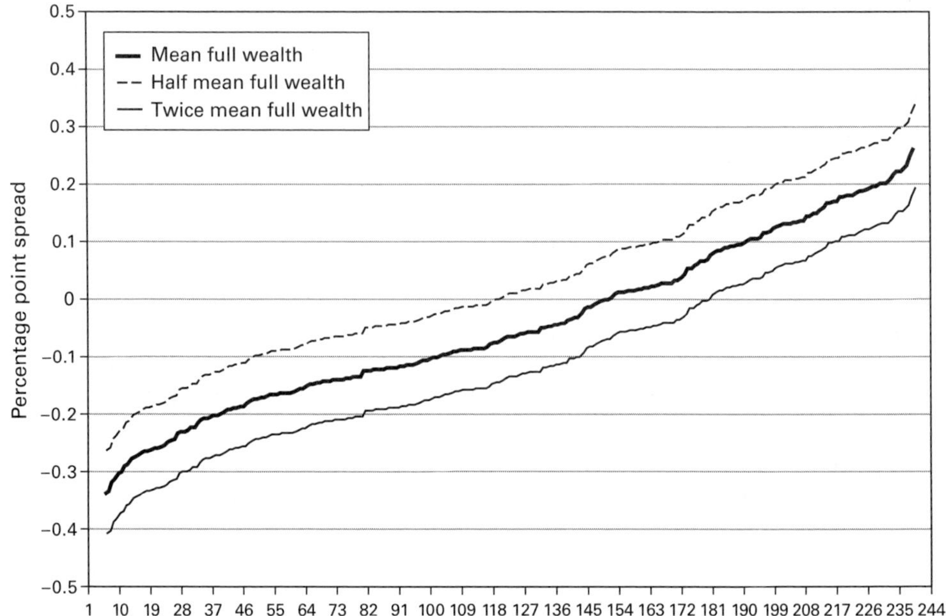

Figure 8.7
Equivalent variations—labor tax less lump sum.

recycling options—capital rate recycling only (8.13), combined capital and labor rate recycling (8.14), labor rate recycling (8.15), and lump sum redistributions (8.16). The findings are robust to changes in the carbon tax rates. It is important not to misinterpret these summary measures as indicators of social welfare, which are discussed in the next section.

In the top section of these tables, under "Children, adults per household," the row heading number pair should be read as "number of children, number of adults." Under capital rate reductions, combined tax rate reductions, and labor tax reductions we find that households with fewer adults improve in average individual welfare (going from row 1 to row 5 to row 9). For lump sum recycling (table 8.16), we find that households with more adults improve in welfare. For a given number of adults, those with fewer children fare better (e.g., going from row 1 through row 4). For capital rate reductions, combined tax rate reductions, and lump sum recycling, the West is the most favorably affected region, followed by the Northeast, Midwest, and South. With labor tax reductions, the regional ranking is Midwest, West, South, and

Table 8.13
Household welfare effects, $20 carbon tax, capital tax case: Population weighted-average equivalent variations as a percentage of full wealth

	Full Wealth		
	Mean	Half Mean	Twice Mean
Children, adults per household			
3+, 3+	0.144	0.108	0.179
2, 3+	0.159	0.124	0.195
1, 3+	0.172	0.136	0.207
0, 3+	0.197	0.161	0.232
3+, 2	0.170	0.134	0.205
2, 2	0.192	0.156	0.227
1, 2	0.198	0.163	0.234
0, 2	0.219	0.184	0.255
3+, 1	0.184	0.148	0.219
2, 1	0.210	0.175	0.246
1, 1	0.225	0.190	0.261
0, 1	0.251	0.216	0.287
Region of household			
Northeast	0.243	0.208	0.279
Midwest	0.203	0.168	0.239
South	0.187	0.151	0.222
West	0.256	0.221	0.292
Race and gender of household head			
Nonwhite female	0.212	0.177	0.248
White female	0.232	0.197	0.267
Nonwhite male	0.206	0.171	0.241
White male	0.213	0.177	0.248
Location of household			
Urban	0.225	0.190	0.260
Rural	0.115	0.079	0.150
Overall	0.216	0.181	0.252

Table 8.14
Household welfare effects, $20 carbon tax, all tax cases: Population weighted-average equivalent variations as a percentage of full wealth

	Full Wealth		
	Mean	Half Mean	Twice Mean
Children, adults per household			
3+, 3+	–0.067	–0.078	–0.056
2, 3+	–0.047	–0.058	–0.036
1, 3+	–0.047	–0.058	–0.036
0, 3+	–0.041	–0.052	–0.030
3+, 2	–0.017	–0.028	–0.006
2, 2	0.004	–0.007	0.015
1, 2	0.003	–0.008	0.014
0, 2	0.009	–0.002	0.020
3+, 1	0.040	0.029	0.051
2, 1	0.067	0.056	0.078
1, 1	0.068	0.057	0.079
0, 1	0.078	0.067	0.089
Region of household			
Northeast	0.028	0.017	0.039
Midwest	0.020	0.009	0.031
South	0.013	0.002	0.024
West	0.036	0.025	0.047
Race and gender of household head			
Nonwhite female	0.020	0.009	0.031
White female	0.059	0.048	0.070
Nonwhite male	–0.015	–0.026	–0.004
White male	0.015	0.004	0.026
Location of household			
Urban	0.026	0.015	0.037
Rural	–0.024	–0.035	–0.013
Overall	0.022	0.011	0.033

Table 8.15
Household welfare effects, $20 carbon tax, labor tax case: Population weighted-average equivalent variations as a percentage of full wealth

	Full Wealth		
	Mean	Half Mean	Twice Mean
Children, adults per household			
3+, 3+	–0.175	–0.175	–0.176
2, 3+	–0.153	–0.153	–0.153
1, 3+	–0.159	–0.159	–0.159
0, 3+	–0.162	–0.161	–0.162
3+, 2	–0.115	–0.115	–0.115
2, 2	–0.095	–0.095	–0.095
1, 2	–0.099	–0.099	–0.099
0, 2	–0.100	–0.100	–0.100
3+, 1	–0.040	–0.040	–0.040
2, 1	–0.013	–0.013	–0.013
1, 1	–0.018	–0.018	–0.018
0, 1	–0.016	–0.015	–0.016
Region of household			
Northeast	–0.085	–0.085	–0.085
Midwest	–0.077	–0.077	–0.077
South	–0.079	–0.079	–0.079
West	–0.078	–0.078	–0.079
Race and gender of household head			
Nonwhite female	–0.081	–0.081	–0.081
White female	–0.034	–0.034	–0.034
Nonwhite male	–0.129	–0.129	–0.129
White male	–0.088	–0.088	–0.088
Location of household			
Urban	–0.078	–0.078	–0.078
Rural	–0.099	–0.099	–0.099
Overall	–0.080	–0.079	–0.080

Table 8.16
Household welfare effects, $20 carbon tax, lump sum case: Population weighted-average equivalent variations as a percentage of full wealth

	Full Wealth		
	Mean	Half Mean	Twice Mean
Children, adults per household			
3+, 3+	0.001	–0.074	0.077
2, 3+	–0.002	–0.077	0.074
1, 3+	0.030	–0.046	0.105
0, 3+	0.081	0.006	0.157
3+, 2	–0.067	–0.142	0.008
2, 2	–0.060	–0.136	0.015
1, 2	–0.040	–0.115	0.036
0, 2	0.004	–0.072	0.079
3+, 1	–0.196	–0.271	–0.120
2, 1	–0.191	–0.267	–0.116
1, 1	–0.163	–0.238	–0.087
0, 1	–0.128	–0.203	–0.052
Region of household			
Northeast	–0.032	–0.107	0.044
Midwest	–0.064	–0.139	0.012
South	–0.068	–0.143	0.008
West	–0.026	–0.102	0.049
Race and gender of household head			
Nonwhite female	–0.058	–0.134	0.017
White female	–0.104	–0.179	–0.028
Nonwhite male	0.008	–0.067	0.084
White male	–0.041	–0.116	0.035
Location of household			
Urban	–0.046	–0.122	0.029
Rural	–0.106	–0.181	–0.030
Overall	–0.051	–0.127	0.024

Northeast. With capital, combined, and labor tax policies, households headed by females or whites fare better than those headed by males or nonwhites; under the lump sum arrangement, this reverses. In all cases, households located in urban areas are better off under a carbon tax than those located in rural areas.

Under capital tax rate recycling, the population-weighted average welfare benefit increases from 0.181% to 0.216% to 0.252% of full wealth as full wealth increases from half mean to mean to twice mean. Under combined tax rate reductions, these average benefits are much smaller—0.011%, 0.022%, and 0.033%, respectively—but increase as wealth increases. With pure labor tax rate recycling, there are only average welfare losses and these are virtually identical at 0.080% of full wealth over the three mean wealth levels. Under lump sum redistribution, there are losses as a percentage of full wealth at lower levels of full wealth—0.127% at half mean, 0.051% at mean—and a small gain of 0.024% at twice mean.

8.6 Social Welfare Impacts

Jorgenson, Slesnick, and Wilcoxen (1992) present money-metric measures of policy impacts based on social welfare functions. These reflect varying degrees of society's aversion to inequality. We present similar social welfare measures for the carbon tax recycling options reported above. We compute social welfare for two extreme assumptions about society's aversion to inequality. The egalitarian view gives the greatest weight to equity while the utilitarian view gives the least weight to equity.

The egalitarian and utilitarian measures for social welfare are presented graphically in figures 8.8 and 8.9, respectively. We decompose welfare change between equity and efficiency changes. We define efficiency change as the change in social welfare under a perfectly egalitarian distribution of full wealth. This is the maximum change in welfare for a given policy and is independent of the actual distribution of full wealth among households as well as society's aversion to inequality. The change due to equity is the difference between the efficiency change and the actual change in social welfare. Changes in social welfare and in equity depend on the social welfare function.

Capital tax rate recycling emerges as the clear winner in our social welfare comparisons. This recycling option is welfare-improving under both views of social welfare. Moreover, the improvements

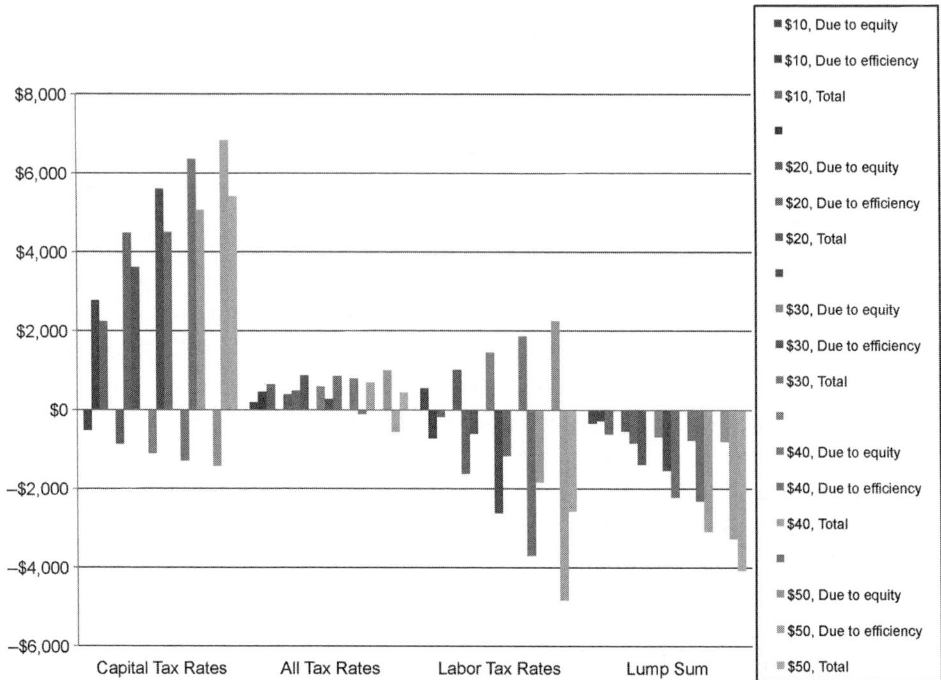

Figure 8.8
Social welfare changes, egalitarian view (bil. $2005).

in social welfare increase with increasingly aggressive carbon tax structures—from $2.2 trillion in the $10 case to $5.4 trillion in the $50 case in the egalitarian system and from $2.6 to $6.5 trillion in the utilitarian system. These are large in absolute terms but, like their household counterparts, are small proportions of full wealth, in the range of 0.2% to 0.4%. The benefits from this recycling option more than compensate for the economic costs of the carbon taxes.

Combining capital and labor tax rate reductions is also welfare-improving under both views of inequality. There are rising efficiency gains for the two lowest carbon tax trajectories, but these begin to erode under the $30 tax trajectory and become efficiency losses for the higher two trajectories. This recycling policy is progressive in the sense defined in chapter 3, both absolutely and relatively. Absolute progressivity corresponds to a gain in our measure of equity. Relative progressivity corresponds to a gain in the ratio of actual welfare to efficiency. The equity change is more highly valued in the egalitarian case, leading to larger offsets to declining efficiency.

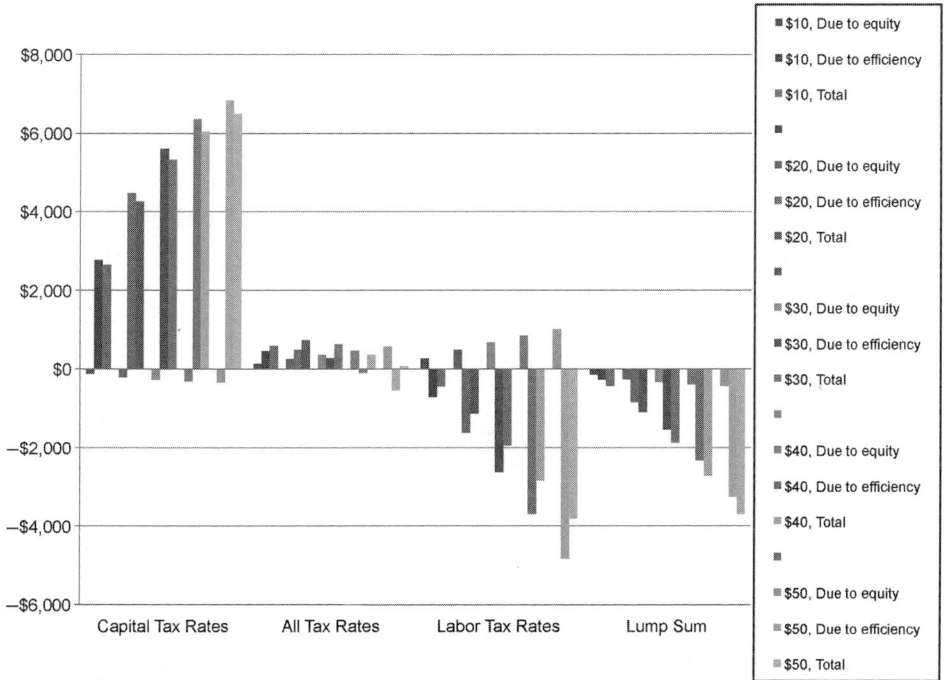

Figure 8.9
Social welfare changes, utilitarian view (bil. $2005).

Labor tax rate recycling unambiguously involves social welfare losses—$0.2 to $2.6 trillion in the egalitarian system and $0.5 to $3.8 trillion in the utilitarian. The ranking of the carbon tax recycling options under the egalitarian view are capital rate reduction first, followed by combined rate reduction, labor rate reduction, and lump sum redistribution. Capital tax rate recycling is regressive in the absolute sense but progressive in the relative sense. The gains in social welfare are not as large under the egalitarian view as under the utilitarian view. Society's aversion to inequality weights the adverse equity effects more heavily under the egalitarian view.

Labor tax recycling is progressive in both the absolute and relative senses. For the combined tax rate reductions, there is a large equity boost in welfare under the egalitarian view, offsetting the large efficiency losses, but only a small equity change under the utilitarian view. As a result, the labor tax rate reduction appears slightly inferior to lump sum distributions in the utilitarian view and the ranking differs from that under the egalitarian view.

Under lump sum redistribution, the efficiency losses in welfare are smaller than those in the labor tax rate reduction. Losses in consumption are partially compensated by gains in leisure. Lump sum recycling is regressive in both the absolute and relative senses. The efficiency losses are reinforced by equity changes, more so under egalitarianism and less so under utilitarianism. In the end, the overall losses in welfare compared to those of labor tax recycling are much larger under the egalitarian rule—3.5 to 1.5 times as tax schedules rise—and slightly smaller under the utilitarian rule.

8.7 Summary and Conclusion

In this chapter we explored the U.S. economy's response to different choices on the use of carbon tax revenues. We analyzed five trajectories for carbon tax rates—\$10, \$20, \$30, \$40, and \$50 in 2005 dollars per metric tonne of carbon dioxide equivalent (mtCO_2-e). We considered four options for the use of this tax revenue: (1) reducing capital tax rates, (2) proportionally reducing capital and labor tax rates, (3) reducing labor tax rates, and (4) lump sum redistribution to households.

There are significant differences in impact across IGEM's 35 producing sectors, depending on the choice of recycling mechanism. However, there is remarkable uniformity in the changes for those 13 sectors responsible for greenhouse gas (GHG) emissions. As the carbon tax rates increase, we find cumulative abatement increasing at a decreasing rate.

Finally, we provide measures of individual and social welfare for capital and labor tax rate reductions and lump sum distribution. For alternative tax rate trajectories and recycling options, we usually find both welfare improvements and welfare losses among households, so that the Pareto principle does not provide a welfare ordering. At low carbon tax rates, all household types gain in welfare under capital tax rate recycling while at higher tax rates there are only losers under labor rate tax recycling. Lump sum distributions are not unambiguously the worst recycling option for carbon tax revenues, contrary to much conventional wisdom.

Reductions in capital tax rates are unambiguously the best option for recycling carbon tax revenues. The welfare benefits substantially exceed the costs of emissions control. For both egalitarian and utilitarian social welfare functions, gains in efficiency from capital tax rate reductions greatly exceed the relatively modest costs in lost equity.

While this recycling option is regressive in absolute terms, reflecting losses in equity, it is progressive in relative terms when welfare is expressed relative to efficiency.

On a proportionate scale the gains and losses from carbon taxes are small. For households, the gains or losses are in the tens of thousands of dollars relative to millions in lifetime full wealth. Maximum individual gains or losses are in the range of 0.6% to 0.9% of lifetime full wealth. Urban households fare better than rural ones. Beyond this, we find no invariant pattern. For a given number of adults in a household, having fewer children is generally welfare-improving. Under lump sum recycling, households with more adults, headed by nonwhites or headed by males fare better, whereas we find the opposite under the three tax rate reduction alternatives.

We have provided measures of the impacts of carbon taxes on individual and social welfare. These can serve as a guide to the trade-offs between carbon taxes and other changes in government revenues associated with fiscal reforms. We have provided a menu of possibilities for increasing the role of energy and environmental taxes in fiscal reform. The results demonstrate the substantial margin of benefits over costs made feasible by appropriate policy design, even without incorporating the benefits of emissions abatement.

Our final conclusion is that capital tax rate reductions provide the greatest improvements in social welfare for all carbon tax rate trajectories. Substantial emissions reduction is accompanied by welfare gains from capital tax rate reductions, providing a double dividend from carbon tax policies. Cuts in capital income tax rates reduce the cost of capital and increase the rate of capital formation, mitigating the costs of GHG control. This mechanism is a striking implication of the intertemporal approach to general equilibrium modeling embodied in IGEM. The substitution of carbon taxes for reductions in capital income tax rates is a promising new approach to energy and environmental policies in the United States.

Notes

1. See, for example, National Commission on Fiscal Responsibility and Reform (2010), www.fiscalcommission.gov/news/moment-truth-report-national-commission-fiscal-responsibility-and-reform. Bowles and Simpson (2013), cochairs of the National Commission, have recently released a revised version of their report: www.momentoftruthproject.org/news/bowles-and-simpson-release-new-deficit-reduction-framework.

2. For example, the Congressional Budget Office (2012) includes a "price on emissions of greenhouse gases" as a potential revenue source. See table 5, p. 19, in www.cbo.gov/publication/43692. Dinan (2012) discusses options for reducing the impacts of a carbon tax on low-income households. Marron and Toder (2013) consider the potential role of carbon taxes in corporate tax reform. See www.taxpolicycenter.org/UploadedPDF/412744-Carbon-Taxes-and-Corporate-Tax-Reform.pdf.
3. Fullerton and Wolfram (2012) provide a recent collection of papers on the economics of climate policy.
4. McKibbin, Morris, Wilcoxen, and Cai (2012) have used the G-cubed model of the world economy to analyze the impact of a U.S. carbon tax. The model is described in more detail in McKibbin and Wilcoxen (2012). The impacts of a carbon tax have been analyzed by NERA Economic Consulting (2013). This study uses a macroeconomic model of the U.S. economy integrated with an energy model with plant-level detail on the electricity sector.
5. See www.epa.gov/climatechange/EPAactivities/economics/modeling.html. The results of these studies are summarized by Jorgenson, Goettle, Ho, and Wilcoxen (2012). Goulder (2013) provides a recent survey of economic literature on tradable permits. Newell, Pizer, and Railmi (2013) discuss the role of markets for permits to emit carbon.
6. The $20 and $30 carbon tax trajectories correspond to tax rates in the range of the prices of tradable permits that we have determined in analyzing cap-and-trade policies for the U.S. Environmental Protection Agency (EPA 2012a). The $10 trajectory is closest to the tax rates proposed by Nordhaus (2010).
7. Jorgenson and Wilcoxen (1993b) have shown that substitution of a carbon tax for a capital income tax in the United States could stabilize emissions while increasing GDP. Surveys of the literature on the double dividend are presented by Goulder (1995), Bovenberg (1999), and Agnar Sandmo (2000). Goulder (2002) provides a collection of papers on substitutions between environmental taxes and other taxes. Recycling the revenues from a carbon tax has been discussed more recently by McKibbin, Morris, Wilcoxen, and Cai (2012) and NERA Economic Consulting (2013).
8. Rausch and Reilly (2012) have analyzed the welfare impacts of a similar menu of carbon tax recycling policies using USREP, a static general equilibrium model of the United States with individual household data from the Consumer Expenditure Survey for 2006. Details on the model are provided by Rausch, Metcalf, Reilly, and Paltsev (2010).
9. The cumulative emissions of 258 Gt in our highest tax case are well above the quantity targets in the legislative proposals of the past decade; that is, the emission reductions seem to be much smaller at this high price. This is due to the absence of abatement opportunities external to IGEM included in these proposals and discussed in chapter 7, such as sequestration and international trading.
10. A comprehensive survey of the literature on the role of induced technical change in climate policy is provided by Nordhaus (2002). Recent surveys are provided by Goulder (2004) and Gillingham, Newell, and Pizer (2008).

9 Confidence Intervals

9.1 Introduction

A distinguishing feature of the Intertemporal General Equilibrium Model (IGEM) presented in chapter 2 is that the parameters are estimated econometrically. The models of consumer behavior in chapter 3 are estimated from more than 150,000 observations for individual households from the Consumer Expenditure Survey (CEX). The models of producer behavior in chapter 4 are estimated from extensive time series data. Econometric estimates for the parameters of our models of government, investment, and the rest of the world are given in chapter 5. Covariance matrices for all these parameter estimates provide measures of uncertainty. In this chapter we use these measures of uncertainty to derive confidence regions for the base case projections of the U.S. economy in chapter 6 and the outcomes of alternative energy and environmental policies in chapter 8, including the effects of those policies on social welfare.

Our confidence regions are based on the *delta method* introduced by Tuladhar and Wilcoxen (1999) and Tuladhar (2003).[1] In section 9.2 we derive distributions for model projections, policy outcomes, and social welfare from the distributions of the parameter estimates presented in earlier chapters.[2] To assess the validity of the delta method we compare the results with a Monte Carlo simulation that involves sampling from the estimated distribution of the parameter values and solving IGEM repeatedly to derive a sampling distribution for the projections and the policy outcomes. We find that the two approaches generate very similar results.

In section 9.3 we quantify the uncertainties in the IGEM base case projections of the U.S. economy by means of confidence regions. We first solve IGEM to obtain the base case projections, as outlined in chapters 2 and 6. We employ the delta method to derive the distribution of base case projections of consumption, production, prices, and other economic variables from the distribution of the parameter estimates. The econometric approach to general equilibrium modeling was introduced by Hudson and Jorgenson (1974) and greatly extended in the original version of IGEM presented by Jorgenson and Wilcoxen (1990).[3] Confidence regions for model outcomes based on econometric estimates for Version 16 of IGEM are presented by Jorgenson, Jin, Slesnick, and Wilcoxen (2012).

An alternative approach to deriving measures of uncertainty for our base case projections is to use the Monte Carlo method. In section 9.3 we use Monte Carlo simulations to sample from the distributions of our parameter estimates. We derive the distributions of production, consumption, and the other variables determined by our base case projection of IGEM from 10,000 solutions of IGEM for different values of our parameter estimates. The resulting distributions produce confidence regions that are very similar to those generated by the delta method. However, the delta method requires far less computer time. Furthermore, it is scalable and can be carried out easily for models that involve a large number of parameters like IGEM.

In section 9.4 we use the delta method to generate confidence regions for the outcomes of energy and environmental policies presented in chapter 8. Policy evaluations are frequently presented as point estimates of model outcomes without an accompanying measure of uncertainty. The delta method provides a straightforward approach to characterizing the uncertainty. We illustrate this with the most promising energy and environmental policy that we have identified in chapter 8. This is the use of revenues from a carbon tax to reduce rates of taxation for capital income. The outcomes of this policy are substantial gains in economic performance accompanied by considerable pollution abatement. We also show that the similarity between the confidence regions produced by the delta method and Monte Carlo analysis for base case variables carries over to these policy changes: the delta method generated results are very similar to those from Monte Carlo simulation.

In section 9.5 we recommend that econometric estimates for the parameters of general equilibrium models be provided along with measures of uncertainty based on estimates of the covariance matrices. The crucial advantage of econometric methods for determining the parameters is that these measures of uncertainty are routinely calculated along with the estimates themselves. Our second recommendation is that confidence regions for projections and policy outcomes be derived from the distributions of parameter estimates by means of the delta method presented in this chapter. These confidence regions are essential for characterizing the uncertainty in energy and environmental policies, such as the carbon taxes and revenue recycling options that we have analyzed in chapter 8.

An alternative approach for characterizing the uncertainty associated with projections and model outcomes has been developed under the rubric of Systematic Sensitivity Analysis.[4] Hertel, Hummels, Ivanic, and Keeney (2007) provide an example based on a model of international trade. They present econometric estimates of elasticities of substitution among imports from various countries for 40 commodity groups.[5] They compare these estimates with parameter estimates reported in the literature. The 40 econometric estimates are assumed to be uncorrelated, so that the covariance matrix for these estimates is diagonal. Hertel et al. (2007) use the Gaussian quadrature method proposed by DeVuyst and Preckel (1997) for approximating the distribution of the parameter estimates. They sample from this approximate distribution to derive confidence intervals for model outcomes. This approach to Systematic Sensitivity Analysis has been generalized to a known, positive definite, covariance matrix by Horridge and Pearson (2011).

9.2 Methodology

The basis for the delta method introduced by Tuladhar and Wilcoxen (1999) is a first-order Taylor series approximation to a general equilibrium model. This allows the prediction errors for the endogenous variables to be expressed as a linear function of the parameter estimates and disturbances. We let Y be a vector of endogenous variables that depends on a vector of exogenous variables X and a vector of parameters β through the vector-valued function F:

$$Y = F(X, \beta). \tag{9.1}$$

Suppose that the vector β is estimated by adding a vector of stochastic disturbances ϵ to the system of equations and let the vector of estimates be $\hat{\beta}$. The predicted vector of endogenous variables will be $\hat{Y}$, so that

$$\hat{Y} = F(X, \hat{\beta}, 0), \tag{9.2}$$

where the stochastic disturbances ϵ are equal to zero. The vector of prediction errors e will be given by the following expression:

$$e = Y - \hat{Y} = F(X, \beta, \epsilon) - F(X, \hat{\beta}, 0). \tag{9.3}$$

In general, the vector-valued function F will be nonlinear. However, this function can be approximated by means of a first-order Taylor series expansion. Expanding F in Taylor series,

$$F\left(X, \hat{\beta}, 0\right) \approx F(X, \beta, \epsilon) + J_\beta\left(\hat{\beta} - \beta\right) - J_\epsilon \epsilon, \tag{9.4}$$

where J_β and J_ϵ denote the Jacobian matrices of partial derivatives of F with respect to the vectors β and ϵ.

9.2.1 *Confidence Intervals for Projections*

The vector of prediction errors can be approximated by a linear function of the parameter estimates and the disturbance vector, as follows:

$$e \approx -J_\beta\left(\hat{\beta} - \beta\right) + J_\epsilon \epsilon. \tag{9.5}$$

The approximation is unbiased. Taking the expectation of the prediction error e,

$$E(e) \approx -J_\beta E\left(\hat{\beta} - \beta\right) + J_\epsilon E(\epsilon) = 0. \tag{9.6}$$

If the covariance matrix for $\hat{\beta}$ is Σ_β and the covariance matrix of ϵ is Σ_ϵ, the covariance of e, Σ_Y, can be written

$$\Sigma_Y \approx J_\beta \Sigma_\beta J'_\beta + J_\epsilon \Sigma_\epsilon J'_\epsilon. \tag{9.7}$$

This equation is the core of the delta method discussed by Oehlert (1992).

The first term on the right-hand side of (9.7) is the covariance matrix for the vector of predicted endogenous variables. Denoting this $\Sigma_{\bar{Y}}$,

$$\Sigma_{\bar{Y}} = J_\beta \Sigma_\beta J'_\beta. \tag{9.8}$$

For general equilibrium modeling $\Sigma_{\bar{Y}}$ is of more interest than Σ_Y because the usual goal is to characterize the distribution of the mean values of particular variables (or changes in the means) rather than to compute the full range of possible outcomes.

The diagonal elements of $\Sigma_{\bar{Y}}$ are the variances of the mean values of the model's endogenous variables and can be used to compute confidence regions. In scalar notation, the variance of endogenous variable i is given by the following equation, where σ_{jk}^2 is the element of Σ_β at row j, column k:

$$\sigma_i^2 = \sum_j \sum_k \frac{\partial F_i}{\partial \beta_j} \sigma_{jk}^2 \frac{\partial F_i}{\partial \beta_k}. \tag{9.9}$$

Computing $\Sigma_{\bar{Y}}$ thus requires two matrices: the Jacobian matrix, J_β, and the parameter covariance matrix, Σ_β. Obtaining Σ_β is straightforward since it is usually calculated in the course of estimating the parameters. The Jacobian matrix, however, must be computed by symbolic or numeric differentiation of the model.

9.2.2 *Confidence Intervals for Policy Evaluation*

The delta method can be extended to the most common application of general equilibrium models, namely, the evaluation of economic policies. Policy evaluation focuses on determining the response of the model's endogenous variables to changes in taxes and other policy variables. For example, in chapter 8 we considered changes in economic variables and environmental outcomes with respect to changes in energy and environmental taxes, accompanied by recycling the tax revenues. This involves two solutions of the model: a base case with exogenous variables taken as given and a policy case with one or more of the exogenous variables changed by policy.

If the values of a general equilibrium model's exogenous variables under the base and policy cases are X_b and X_p, the resulting policy response in the endogenous variables, ΔY, will be

$$\Delta Y = Y_p - Y_b = F(X_p, \beta) - F(X_b, \beta). \tag{9.10}$$

The prediction error for ΔY, $e\Delta Y$, will be

$$e\Delta Y = (Y_p - Y_b) - (\hat{Y}_p - \hat{Y}_b) = (Y_p - \hat{Y}_p) - (Y_b - \hat{Y}_b) = e_p - e_b. \tag{9.11}$$

That is, the prediction error for the policy response is the difference between the prediction errors for the base case and policy simulations.

Each prediction error can be approximated as follows, where the two Jacobian matrices are evaluated at the vectors of exogenous variables corresponding to the base case, X_b, or the policy case X_p:

$$e_i \approx -J_\beta|_{Xi}(\hat{\beta} - \beta) + J_\epsilon|_{Xi}\,\epsilon. \tag{9.12}$$

For example, for e_p the Jacobian J_β would be evaluated at X_p. For convenience, define ΔJ_β and ΔJ_ϵ as follows:

$$\Delta J_\beta = J_\beta|_{Xp} - J_\beta|_{Xb}. \tag{9.13}$$

$$\Delta J_\epsilon = J_\epsilon|_{Xp} - J_\epsilon|_{Xb}. \tag{9.14}$$

Since the error terms are additive, ΔJ_ϵ will be zero. That is, to a first-order approximation the disturbance uncertainty does not contribute to the uncertainty in the model's predicted response. This differentiates the uncertainty in policy evaluation from the uncertainty in base case projections.

Using equations (9.12), (9.13), and the zero value for ΔJ_ϵ, the prediction error for the policy response can be expressed as

$$e\Delta Y \approx -\Delta J_\beta\left(\hat{\beta} - \beta\right). \tag{9.15}$$

The expected value and covariance matrix for $e\Delta Y$ are

$$E(e\Delta Y) = 0. \tag{9.16}$$

$$\Sigma_{\Delta Y} \approx \Delta J_\beta \Sigma_\beta \Delta J'_\beta. \tag{9.17}$$

The variance of the policy response in endogenous variable i for a small change in exogenous variable m will be in scalar notation:

$$\sigma_i^2 = \sum_j \sum_k \frac{\partial^2 F_i}{\partial \beta_j \partial X_m} \sigma_{jk}^2 \frac{\partial^2 F_i}{\partial \beta_k \partial X_m}. \tag{9.18}$$

9.2.3 *Confidence Intervals for Social Welfare*

Finally, it is also possible to use the delta method to construct confidence intervals for measures of changes in social welfare. The process is conceptually similar to the approach used in previous sections but somewhat more complex because the welfare measures we use are nonlinear functions of the household parameters and two sets of simulation results: the base and policy cases. We present the approach in detail in the remainder of this section.

As shown in chapter 3, the social expenditure function can be used to compute an equivalent variation for a policy that depends on the set of household parameters, a vector of base case prices, and the welfare levels achieved in the base and policy cases. Let $EV = G(Y_b, Y_p, \theta)$ represent the social equivalent variation as a share of base case wealth, where Y_b and Y_p are endogenous variables from the base and policy cases (including the achieved levels of welfare) and θ is a vector of household parameters. Vectors Y_b and Y_p, in turn, are functions of the model's exogenous variables and the full set of parameters. Using ϕ to represent the set of production parameters (that is, all parameters other than θ) and following the notation used in previous sections, the endogenous variables in the base and policy cases will be given by $Y_b = F(X_b,\phi,\theta)$ and $Y_p = F(X_p,\phi,\theta)$. Using these expressions allows EV to be written as follows:

$$EV = G[(F(X_b,\phi,\theta), F(X_p,\phi,\theta),\theta)]. \tag{9.19}$$

The confidence interval for EV arises from uncertainty in ϕ and θ. To first order, the sensitivity of EV with respect to perturbations in the parameters can be written in terms of the partial derivatives of G and F as follows:

$$\Delta EV = G_b F_\phi^b \Delta\phi + G_p F_\phi^p \Delta\phi + G_b F_\theta^b \Delta\theta + G_p F_\theta^p \Delta\theta + G_\theta \Delta\theta, \tag{9.20}$$

where F_ϕ^b is the matrix of partial derivatives of F with respect to ϕ evaluated at the exogenous variable vector X_b (that is, it is the Jacobian of F with respect to ϕ evaluated at X_b). The remaining terms are defined in similar fashion.

For convenience, define two composite matrices, Γ_ϕ and Γ_θ, as follows:

$$\Gamma_\phi = G_b F_\phi^b + G_p F_\phi^p. \tag{9.21}$$

$$\Gamma_\theta = G_b F_\theta^b + G_p F_\theta^p + G_\theta. \tag{9.22}$$

Equation (9.21) gives the overall Jacobian matrix for the equivalent variation with respect to the set of production parameters in ϕ. Equation (9.22) is similar but for the household parameters. Equation (9.22) emphasizes that the household parameters affect the equivalent variation through an additional channel beyond those that apply to the production parameters: the last term, G_θ, captures the effect of the household parameters on the social expenditure function itself.

Using (9.21) and (9.22) to rewrite (9.20) allows the sensitivity of the equivalent variation to changes in the parameters to be expressed as

$$\Delta EV = \Gamma_\phi \Delta\phi + \Gamma_\theta \Delta\theta. \tag{9.23}$$

The covariance of EV is the expectation of the square of (9.23). However, the covariance between the estimates in ϕ and θ is zero since the industry and household submodels are estimated independently. This allows the covariance of EV, Σ_{EV}, to be written in terms of the parameter covariance matrices Σ_ϕ and Σ_θ as follows:

$$\Sigma_{EV} = \Gamma'_\phi \Sigma_\phi \Gamma_\phi + \Gamma'_\theta \Sigma_\theta \Gamma_\theta. \tag{9.24}$$

In summary the delta method allows the covariance of the projected values of a model's endogenous variables to be approximated by means of equation (9.8), the covariance of predicted policy responses to be approximated using equation (9.17), and the covariance of social welfare results to be approximated using equation (9.24). Given the covariance matrix, it is possible to construct confidence intervals for individual variables by using the diagonal elements of the matrix. Finally, confidence regions for vectors of endogenous variables can be constructed from the full matrix of variances and covariances.

9.3 Application to the Base Case

In this section we show how the delta method presented in section 9.2 is used to characterize the uncertainty of IGEM's steady state solution due to uncertainties in the estimates of key parameters in the models of producer and consumer behavior. Table 9.1 shows the steady state values for the IGEM base case used in chapter 8 for 25 selected variables in the model. Five variables summarize macroeconomic conditions in the model—the real value of private consumption, the capital stock, gross domestic product, the amount of leisure consumed by households, and the total amount of greenhouse gases emitted each year, expressed as equivalent amounts of carbon dioxide. The next 10 variables show industry outputs in 5 energy sectors and 5 important non-energy sectors. The remaining 10 variables show the corresponding supply prices.

We examine the confidence intervals for the endogenous variables that result from uncertainty in two sets of parameters. The first set consists of 42 parameters in the top tier of the household demand model that allocates full expenditure among leisure and goods and services. We refer to this as the household parameter set, although, strictly speaking, it is a subset of the household parameters. The second set consists of 10 parameters from the top tier of each of the 35 industry price functions in IGEM for a total of 350 parameters. We will refer to this as the production parameter set, although it is also a subset.

Table 9.2 shows some of the household parameters and their standard errors; a complete list is given in chapter 3. On the whole, the

Table 9.1
Base case results for selected variables

Variable	Base Case
Macroeconomic conditions	
Consumption	13294
GDP	20747
Capital	104352
Leisure	29362
Carbon	14588
Industry output	
Coal	55
Crude Oil	121
Refining	219
Electric Utilities	489
Gas Utilities	104
Agriculture	6990
Nonelectric Machinery	27958
Electric Machinery	12702
Vehicles	406
Services	7433
Supply prices	
Coal	1.01
Crude Oil	2.62
Refining	3.72
Electric Utilities	1.86
Gas Utilities	3.32
Agriculture	0.10
Nonelectric Machinery	0.07
Electric Machinery	0.05
Vehicles	0.44
Services	0.86

Table 9.2
Selected household parameters

Parameter	Value	Standard Error
α_1^p	−0.5299	0.0028
α_2^p	−0.2559	0.0043
α_3^p	−0.0165	0.0032
β_{11}^{pp}	−0.0158	0.0014
β_{12}^{pp}	−0.0237	0.0013
β_{13}^{pp}	0.0502	0.0009
…	…	…
β_2^{hm}	−0.0087	0.0004
β_3^{hm}	0.0051	0.0003

Table 9.3
Covariance matrix for selected household parameters

	α_1^p	α_2^p	α_3^p	β_{11}^{pp}	β_{12}^{pp}	β_{13}^{pp}	…	β_3^m
α_1^p	7.92E-06	1.30E-06	1.78E-06	−8.24E-07	−3.47E-07	4.21E-08	…	−1.54E-07
α_2^p		1.87E-05	7.43E-07	1.25E-07	−4.38E-07	6.78E-08	…	−6.03E-08
α_3^p			1.02E-05	−6.15E-08	7.96E-08	−2.48E-07	…	−8.80E-07
β_{11}^{pp}				1.97E-06	−2.30E-07	1.75E-07	…	−1.71E-09
β_{12}^{pp}					1.58E-06	−2.78E-07	…	−3.78E-09
β_{13}^{pp}						7.98E-07	…	−1.07E-08
…							…	…
β_3^m								8.20E-08

estimates are fairly precise. The standard errors are typically about 5% of each coefficient estimate. We denote the corresponding covariance matrix Σ_β^h and its upper triangular portion is shown in table 9.3. The diagonal terms tend to be somewhat larger than the off-diagonal terms. In table 9.3 the difference is sometimes two orders of magnitude. This might suggest that it would be adequate to approximate the full covariance matrix with its diagonal. However, we show below that off-diagonal elements play a pivotal role in determining the confidence intervals of the model's endogenous variables; omitting them can bias confidence intervals downward by as much as 50%.

Selected parameter estimates for the production model and their standard errors are given in table 9.4 for three of the 35 industries in IGEM. The corresponding upper triangular covariance matrices are shown in tables 9.5 through 9.7. The production parameters tend to be

Table 9.4
Selected production parameters

Parameter	Industry 1: Agriculture		Industry 3: Coal		Industry 4: Crude Oil	
	Value	SE	Value	SE	Value	SE
α^p	−0.2245	0.0106	−0.1857	0.0857	0.1487	0.0806
α^p_K	0.2032	0.0033	0.2677	0.0296	0.4439	0.0247
α^p_L	0.2283	0.0166	0.3327	0.0535	0.1411	0.0111
α^p_E	0.0402	0.0085	0.1412	0.0593	0.1850	0.0344
β^{pp}_{KK}	0.1130	0.0137	0.0172	0.0096	0.1188	0.0173
β^{pp}_{KL}	−0.0394	0.0065	−0.0137	0.0105	0.0091	0.0171
β^{pp}_{KE}	−0.0017	0.0171	−0.0198	0.0348	−0.0152	0.0137
β^{pp}_{LL}	0.0363	0.0168	−0.2068	0.0204	0.0222	0.0048
β^{pp}_{LE}	−0.0262	0.0116	0.0868	0.0402	−0.0299	0.0102
β^{pp}_{EE}	−0.0039	0.0158	0.0100	0.0246	0.0055	0.0175

less precisely estimated than the household parameters. In addition, the estimates of some parameters in some sectors, such as β^{pp}_{KE} and β^{pp}_{EE} for the sectors in tables 9.5 through 9.7, are close to zero in magnitude. We refer to the covariance matrix for all the production sectors together as Σ^p_β. Since the sectors are estimated independently, Σ^p_β will be block diagonal with one block per sector. We will refer to the block for production sector n as Σ^{pn}_β. On the whole, the diagonal and off-diagonal terms in Σ^{pn}_β are closer in magnitude for most production sectors than they were for the household parameters. In other words, the correlations between production parameter estimates are larger.

9.3.1 *Confidence Intervals for Base Case Values*

To construct standard errors for the mean values of the model's endogenous variables, we use numerical differentiation to obtain the Jacobian J_β for both the household and production parameters. Following the notation used for covariance matrices, we use J^h_β to represent the matrix of derivatives of endogenous variables with respect to the household parameters, J^{pi}_β for derivatives with respect to production parameters in industry i, and J^p_β for combined set of derivatives for all production parameters. The total number of solutions of IGEM required to construct the Jacobian matrices is 393: 1 for an unperturbed solution, 42 for perturbations to construct the household matrix J^h_β, and 350 for perturbations to construct the production matrices J^{pi}_β.

Table 9.5
Covariance matrix for parameters in Agriculture

	α^p	α^p_K	α^p_L	α^p_E	β^{pp}_{KK}	β^{pp}_{KL}	β^{pp}_{KE}	β^{pp}_{LL}	β^{pp}_{LE}	β^{pp}_{EE}
α^p	0.00011	0.00003	0.00018	0.00009	–0.00014	–0.00007	0.00018	0.00018	0.00012	0.00016
α^p_K		0.00001	0.00005	0.00003	–0.00004	–0.00002	0.00006	0.00006	0.00004	0.00005
α^p_L			0.00027	0.00014	–0.00023	–0.00011	0.00028	0.00028	0.00019	0.00026
α^p_E				0.00007	–0.00011	–0.00006	0.00014	0.00014	0.00010	0.00013
β^{pp}_{KK}					0.00019	0.00009	–0.00023	–0.00023	–0.00016	–0.00021
β^{pp}_{KL}						0.00004	–0.00011	–0.00011	–0.00007	–0.00010
β^{pp}_{KE}							0.00029	0.00028	0.00020	0.00026
β^{pp}_{LL}								0.00028	0.00019	0.00026
β^{pp}_{LE}									0.00013	0.00018
β^{pp}_{EE}										0.00025

Table 9.6
Covariance matrix for parameters in Coal Mining

	α^p	α_K^p	α_L^p	α_E^p	β_{KK}^{pp}	β_{KL}^{pp}	β_{KE}^{pp}	β_{LL}^{pp}	β_{LE}^{pp}	β_{EE}^{pp}
α^p	0.00735	–0.00252	–0.00416	0.00457	–0.00052	0.00004	–0.00268	–0.00147	0.00326	0.00189
α_K^p		0.00087	0.00144	–0.00157	0.00018	0.00000	0.00092	0.00050	–0.00113	–0.00065
α_L^p			0.00287	–0.00202	0.00021	–0.00010	0.00159	0.00101	–0.00197	–0.00112
α_E^p				0.00351	–0.00041	–0.00012	–0.00153	–0.00073	0.00194	0.00113
β_{KK}^{pp}					0.00009	–0.00003	0.00025	0.00007	–0.00026	–0.00018
β_{KL}^{pp}						0.00011	–0.00015	–0.00003	0.00005	0.00006
β_{KE}^{pp}							0.00121	0.00056	–0.00129	–0.00081
β_{LL}^{pp}								0.00041	–0.00073	–0.00040
β_{LE}^{pp}									0.00161	0.00094
β_{EE}^{pp}										0.00060

Table 9.7

Covariance matrix for parameters in Crude Oil and Gas

	α^o	α^p_K	α^p_L	α^p_E	β^{pp}_{KK}	β^{pp}_{KL}	β^{pp}_{KE}	β^{pp}_{LL}	β^{pp}_{LE}	β^{pp}_{EE}
α^o	0.00650	0.00198	0.00077	0.00277	0.00138	−0.00104	0.00110	−0.00036	0.00075	0.00134
α^p_K		0.00061	0.00024	0.00085	0.00042	−0.00031	0.00034	−0.00011	0.00023	0.00042
α^p_L			0.00012	0.00034	0.00015	−0.00006	0.00014	−0.00004	0.00006	0.00019
α^p_E				0.00118	0.00059	−0.00042	0.00047	−0.00015	0.00031	0.00058
β^{pp}_{KK}					0.00030	−0.00024	0.00023	−0.00008	0.00017	0.00028
β^{pp}_{KL}						0.00029	−0.00016	0.00007	−0.00017	−0.00016
β^{pp}_{KE}							0.00019	−0.00006	0.00012	0.00024
β^{pp}_{LL}								0.00002	−0.00005	−0.00007
β^{pp}_{LE}									0.00010	0.00013
β^{pp}_{EE}										0.00031

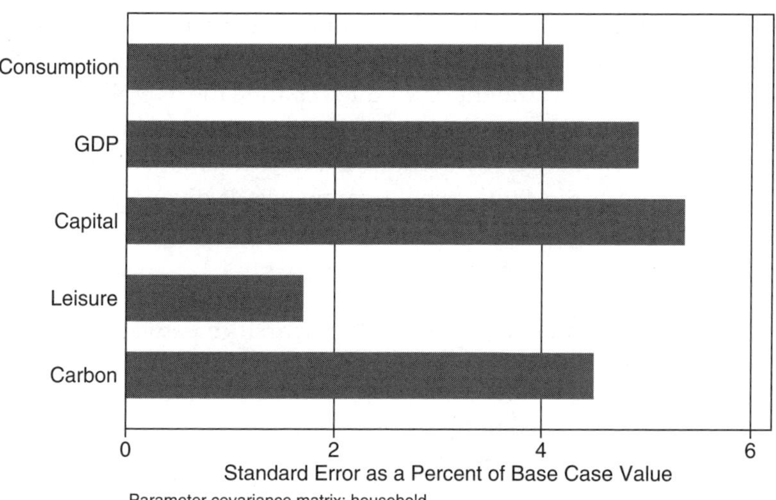

Figure 9.1
Base case uncertainties from household parameters: Key macroeconomic variables.

We next examine the uncertainties induced in the endogenous variables by the covariances among the household parameter estimates. Due to the household parameters alone, the covariance matrix for the mean values of the endogenous variables is $\Sigma^h_{\bar{Y}}$, which can be computed as follows:

$$\Sigma^h_{\bar{Y}} = J^h_\beta \Sigma^h_\beta J^{h\prime}_\beta . \tag{9.25}$$

Figure 9.1 presents the result of this calculation for key endogenous variables representing the overall state of the economy. The results are standard errors expressed as percentages of the corresponding variable's base case value.

For example, figure 9.1 shows that uncertainty in the household parameters leads to a standard error in the predicted value of real consumption expenditure of just over 4%. The 95% confidence interval for consumption is thus 92% to 108% of the model's reported value. The standard error for the capital stock, again resulting from uncertainty in the household parameters, is somewhat larger—about 5%—while the standard error for leisure is considerably smaller: less than 2% of the predicted value. The final bar shows that the standard error in carbon emissions induced by uncertainty in the household parameters is about 4.5%.

As noted above, an additional benefit of the delta method is that it allows detailed analysis of the sources of uncertainty in any given variable. In particular, it is straightforward to separate the overall variance of a variable into components associated with specific parameter estimates and their estimated covariances. In scalar notation, the variance of variable i due to the 42 household parameters is given by

$$\sigma_i^2 = \sum_{j=1}^{42} \sum_{k=1}^{42} J_{ik}^h \Sigma_{kj}^h J_{ji}^h. \tag{9.26}$$

The relative contribution of term kj—the covariance between parameters k and j—to σ_i^2 can be summarized by computing its share, ω_{ijk}, in the overall variance:

$$\omega_{ijk} = \frac{J_{ik}^h \Sigma_{kj}^h J_{ji}^h}{\sigma_i^2}. \tag{9.27}$$

Figure 9.2 shows the six largest values of ω_{ijk} for real consumption. They are expressed as percentages and listed in order of importance. Each term is weighted appropriately for the number of times the underlying covariance term occurs in the sum (9.27), once for diagonal elements of Σ_Y^h and twice for off-diagonal terms. Finally, each bar is labeled with the names of the parameters corresponding to row k and column j of the parameter covariance matrix; for variances, the two labels will be identical.

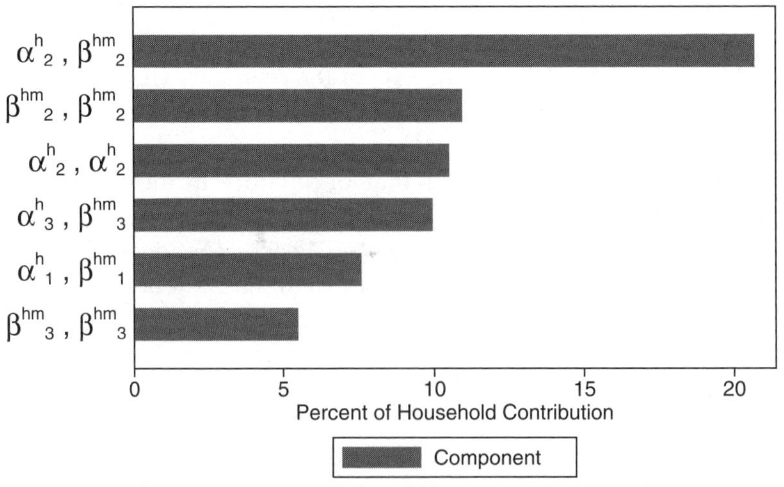

Figure 9.2
Decomposition of uncertainty in consumption: Components.

The largest single effect in figure 9.2 is due to the covariance between α_2^h and β_2^{hm}. This alone accounts for about 21% of the overall variance in consumption. The next three terms each contribute about 10% of the variance and subsequent terms contribute much smaller percentages. Figure 9.2 illustrates an important advantage of the delta method over Systematic Sensitivity Analysis based on an assumed diagonal covariance matrix. A diagonal covariance matrix cannot capture effects associated with covariances. Only half of the terms in figure 9.2 arise from the variance in a single parameter (the second, third, and sixth terms) and those terms are not necessarily the most important. The other components would be omitted by disregarding the covariances.

Each of the ω_{ijk} terms can be further decomposed to determine whether the underlying uncertainty is due to imprecision in the estimates, that is, a large value of Σ_{kj}^h, or to unusually high sensitivity of the model to those terms, large values of J_{ik}^h or J_{ji}^h. For example, the first term in figure 9.2 is the product of the partial derivative of consumption with respect to α_2^h (J_{ik}^h), the covariance between α_2^h and β_2^{hm} (Σ_{kj}^h), and the partial derivative of consumption with respect to β_2^{hm} (J_{ji}^h).

Figure 9.3 presents the Jacobian terms corresponding to figure 9.2. Each is expressed as a partial elasticity: the percentage change in consumption for a unit change in the parameter. The two terms for each variance component are grouped together. For example, the first bar in

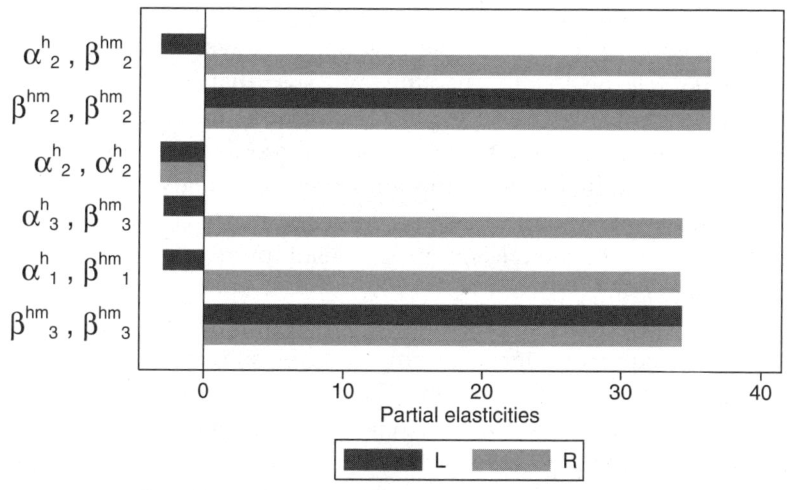

Figure 9.3
Decomposition of uncertainty in consumption: Jacobian terms.

the first pair shows that a unit increase in α_2^h would lower consumption by a factor of three. The second bar in the first pair, in contrast, shows that a unit increase in β_2^{hm}, which is related to the income elasticity of demand for capital, would raise consumption by about a factor of 35.

To interpret the elasticities in figure 9.3, note that the standard errors of the parameters, shown in table 9.2, are quite small—0.0043 for α_2^h and 0.0004 for β_2^{hm}. As a result, relevant perturbations in the parameters are small and produce modest changes in consumption despite the large elasticities. For example, a perturbation of α_2^h by one standard error would lower consumption by 1.3% while a perturbation in β_2^{hm} by one standard error would lower it by 1.4%. The fact that the Jacobian terms have opposite signs, which is also true for two other pairs of parameters in the figure, implies that positively correlated uncertainties in the parameters would tend to cancel each other out.

Moving further down figure 9.3, the bars in the second pair are both associated with β_2^{hm} and are equal to each other and to the second bar from the first pair. All are based on the same partial derivative. Moreover, they are large in magnitude, and the overall contribution of β_2^{hm} depends on their product, so the uncertainty in consumption will be very sensitive to uncertainty in β_2^{hm}. Moving further down the chart, the next pair of bars shows the effect of α_2^h, which is equal to the first bar in the first pair. Subsequent pairs show qualitatively similar effects but with gradually diminishing magnitudes.

Figure 9.4 completes the decomposition by showing the covariances of the six terms in figure 9.2. The covariance between α_2^h and β_2^{hm} is negative. If the Jacobian terms had the same sign, that is, if both parameters tended to increase or decrease consumption, the uncertainties in the parameters would tend to cancel out and would play little role in the overall uncertainty in consumption. However, as noted above, the Jacobian terms are of opposite signs. As a result, the covariance contributes positively to the uncertainty in consumption and is the largest single component.

Moving down figure 9.4, the second bar shows that the variance of β_2^{hm} is very small. However, the Jacobian terms show that β_2^{hm} plays a very important role in determining consumption. Taken together the overall contribution of β_2^{hm}, as shown in figure 9.2, is second in importance even though the parameter itself is very precisely estimated. The situation is reversed for α_2^h. Its Jacobian term indicates that it is much less important in the overall level of consumption, but it contributes

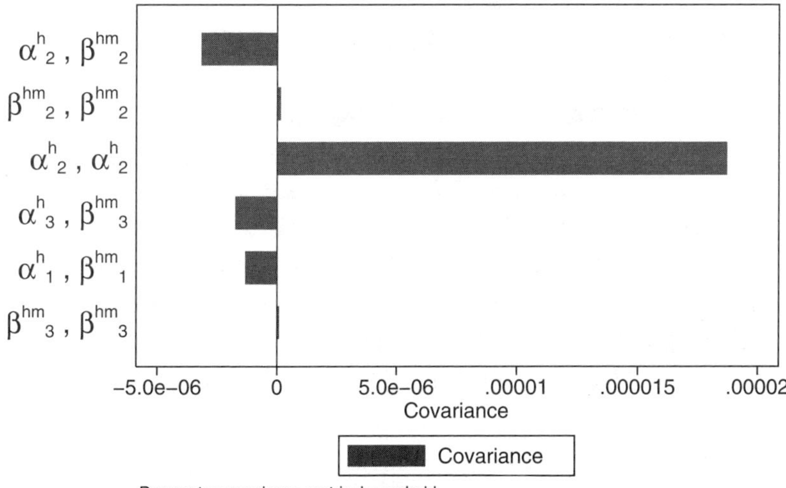

Figure 9.4
Decomposition of uncertainty in consumption: Covariances.

significantly to the overall uncertainty because it is much less precisely estimated.

Returning to the overall assessment of the effect of uncertainties in estimates of the household parameters, figure 9.5 gives the corresponding standard errors for the levels of output for selected industries. As with figure 9.1, they result from only uncertainties in the household parameters. The first five industries are the energy sectors: Coal Mining, Crude Oil and Gas, Petroleum Refining, Electric Utilities, and Gas Utilities. The remaining five industries—Agriculture, Nonelectrical Machinery, Electrical Machinery, Motor Vehicles, and Services—were chosen to represent the range of effects occurring in the 30 non-energy sectors.

For most industries, uncertainty in the household parameters leads to a standard error in the level of output of about 4% to 5%. The notable exception is Crude Oil and Gas production, where household parameters contribute very little to the standard error in the industry's output. The underlying reason is that crude oil is not directly demanded by households and the Jacobian terms linking household parameters to the industry's output are relatively small. For example, the Jacobian terms for Refined Petroleum are five times larger, and those for Services are nine times larger.

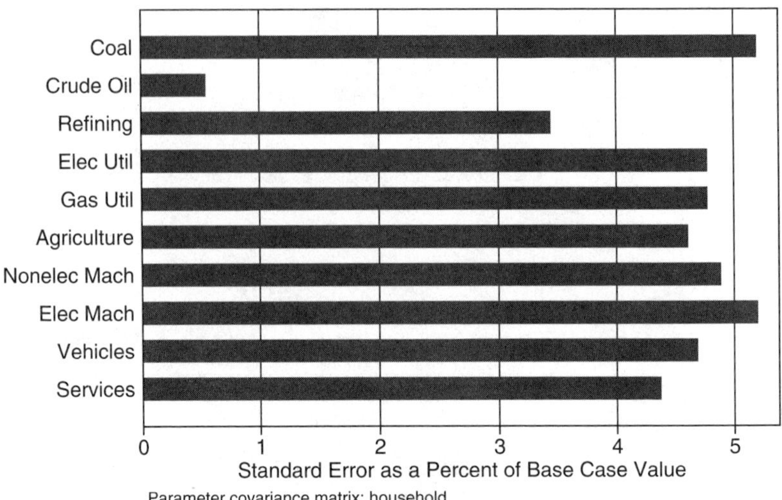

Figure 9.5
Base case uncertainties from household parameters: Industry output.

The contribution of the household parameters to uncertainty in steady state prices is shown in figure 9.6. In most cases, the household parameters induce very little uncertainty in industry prices: the standard errors are generally less than 0.5%. Even the largest standard errors, for Crude Oil and Refined Petroleum, are 2% or less. It is not surprising that household parameters contribute little uncertainty to industry prices, since these prices are largely determined by the industry parameters, as we discuss in detail below. The main link between household parameters and industry prices operates through the supplies of primary factors of production, so the uncertainties in industry prices will be related to the uncertainties in the supplies of capital and labor inputs but attenuated due to the presence of other inputs.

9.3.2 *The Delta Method versus Monte Carlo Simulation*

To confirm that the delta method closely approximates the standard errors of the endogenous variables of IGEM, we carried out a Monte Carlo simulation, using 10,000 draws from the joint distribution of the household parameters. We solved IGEM for each draw and tabulated the values of the key results. The resulting standard error for each variable is shown by the second bar in each pair in figures 9.7 through 9.9. For reference, the delta method results from figures 9.1, 9.5, and 9.6 are

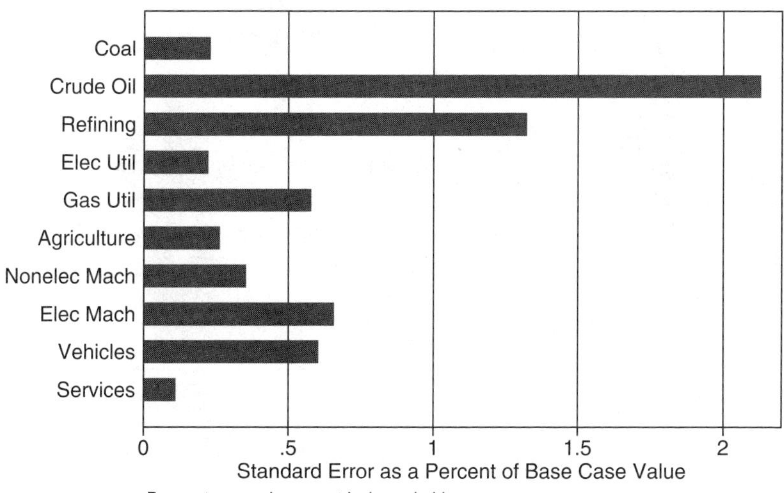

Figure 9.6
Base case uncertainties from household parameters: Industry prices.

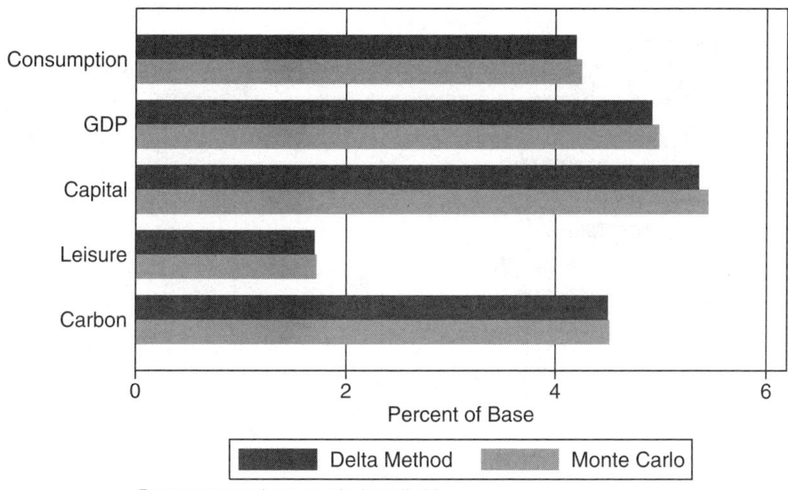

Figure 9.7
Results of delta versus Monte Carlo methods: Key macroeconomic variables.

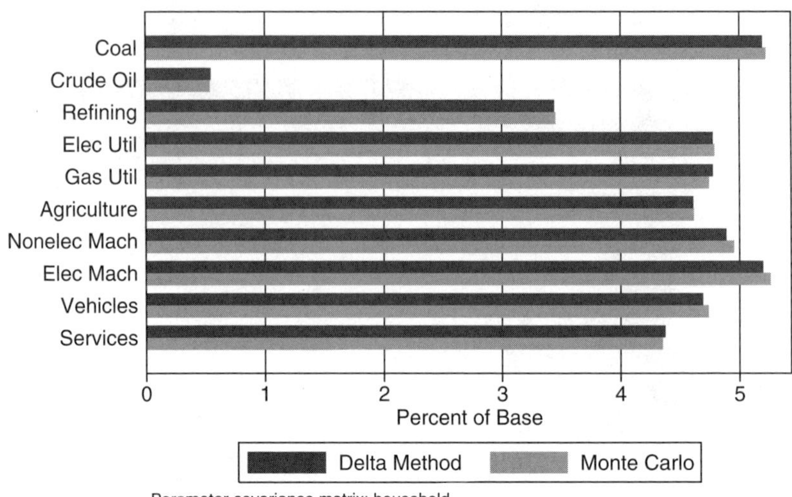

Figure 9.8
Results of delta versus Monte Carlo methods: Industry output.

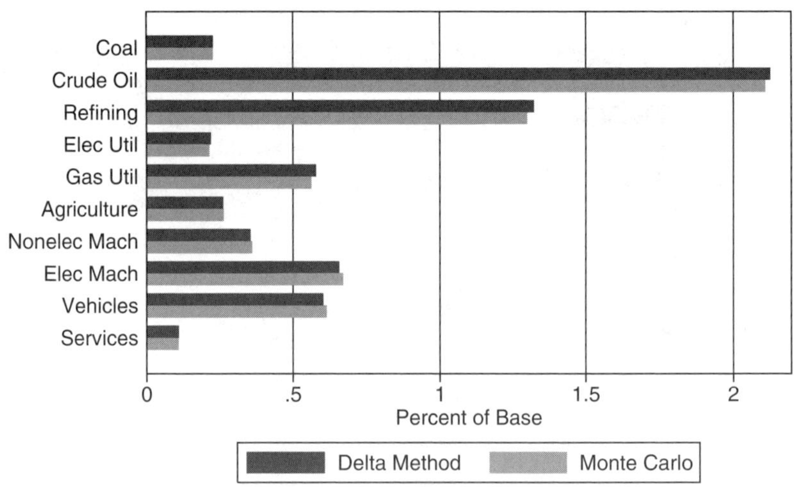

Figure 9.9
Results of delta versus Monte Carlo methods: Industry prices.

shown by the first bar in each pair. The results for the two methods are nearly identical in all three figures. However, the number of simulations needed for the delta method is equal to the number of parameters plus one, one unperturbed solution, and 42 perturbations in this example. The number of runs required for the Monte Carlo simulation is orders of magnitude higher, 10,000 in this example.

Turning to the production side of IGEM, uncertainties in the production parameter estimates induce covariances $\Sigma_{\bar{Y}}^{p}$ in the mean values of the endogenous variables, where $\Sigma_{\bar{Y}}^{p}$ is given by

$$\Sigma_{\bar{Y}}^{p} = J_{\beta}^{p} \Sigma_{\beta}^{p} J_{\beta}^{p\prime}. \tag{9.28}$$

The standard errors resulting from this calculation are shown in figures 9.10 through 9.12 and are sharply different from the uncertainties induced by the household parameters. The standard errors in consumption and GDP due to the production parameters are considerably less than 1% while both were more than 4% for the household parameters.

As would be expected, the standard error in leisure induced by the production parameters is much smaller that it was for the household parameters. By contrast, the production parameters contribute much more to uncertainty in carbon emissions than the household parameters. The standard error in figure 9.10 is more than 12% while the

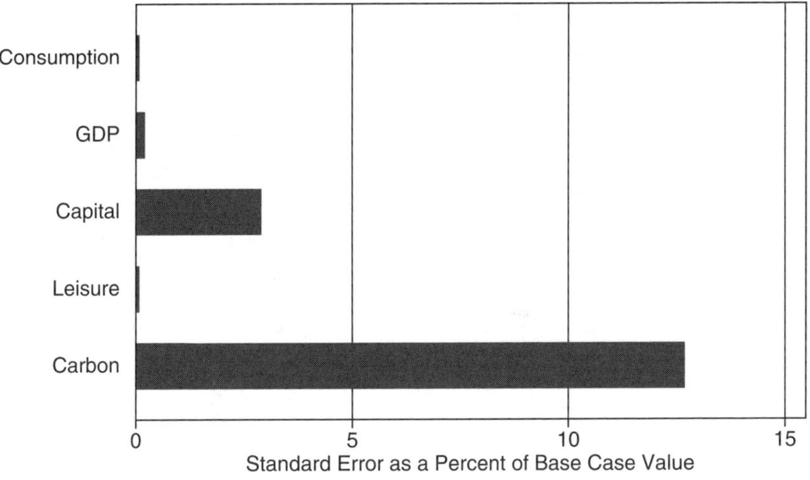

Figure 9.10
Base case uncertainties from production parameters: Key macroeconomic variables.

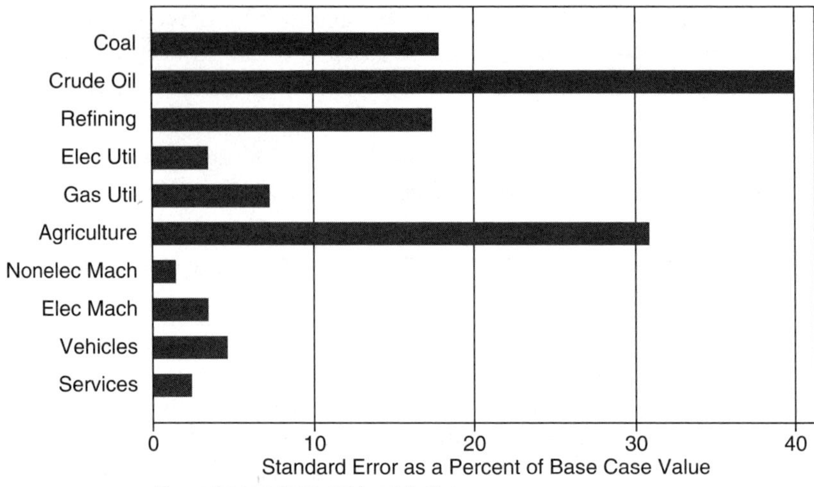

Figure 9.11
Base case uncertainties from production parameters: Industry output.

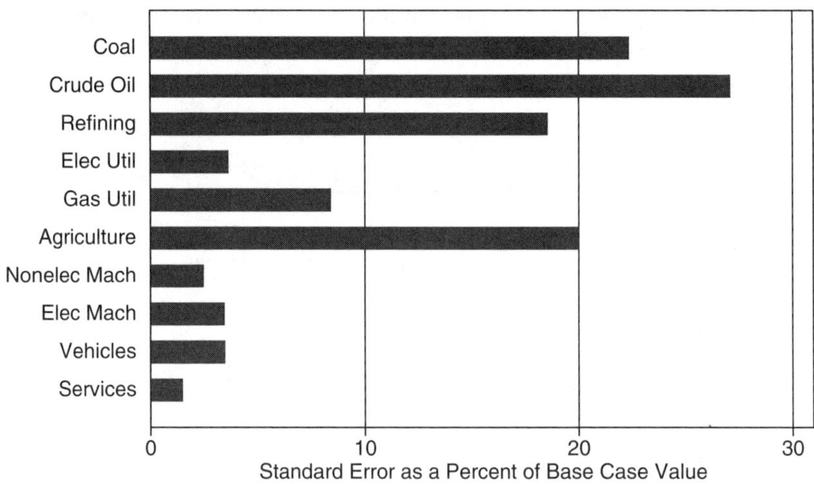

Figure 9.12
Base case uncertainties from production parameters: Industry prices.

corresponding value for the household parameters was just above 4%. Finally, the standard error for the capital stock is slightly smaller for the production parameters than it was for the household parameters.

Uncertainties in the production parameters are far more important for industry output and prices than were the uncertainties in the household parameters. In figure 9.11 the standard errors in output range from less than 10% to as much as 40% for Crude Oil and Natural Gas extraction. Most sectors have relatively small standard errors but four exceed 15%: those for Coal Mining, Crude Oil and Natural Gas Extraction, Refined Petroleum, and Agriculture.

Standard errors for industry prices are shown in figure 9.12. The results are qualitatively similar to those for output. Most sectors have small standard errors but there are four exceptions: Coal Mining, Crude Oil and Natural Gas, Petroleum Refining, and Agriculture. However, the standard errors for those prices are more similar to one another, about 20%, than were the corresponding standard errors for output, ranging from about 18% to 40%.

The decomposition technique described above can also be used to determine which sets of industry parameters contribute most to the uncertainties in the endogenous variables. The variance of endogenous variable i due to the full set of 350 production parameters is given by

$$\sigma_i^2 = \sum_{j=1}^{350}\sum_{k=1}^{350} J_{ik}^p \Sigma_{kj}^p J_{ji}^p. \tag{9.29}$$

Since Σ^p is block diagonal, equation (9.29) can be rewritten in terms of its 35 Σ_{kj}^{pn} components as follows:

$$\sigma_i^2 = \sum_{n=1}^{35}\sum_{j=1}^{10}\sum_{k=1}^{10} J_{ik}^p \Sigma_{kj}^{pn} J_{ji}^p. \tag{9.30}$$

For convenience we define σ_{in}^2 to be the variance in endogenous variable i associated with the covariance Σ^{pn} in industry n's parameters:

$$\sigma_{in}^2 = \sum_{j=1}^{10}\sum_{k=1}^{10} J_{ik}^p \Sigma_{kj}^{pn} J_{ji}^p. \tag{9.31}$$

This allows the overall variance in variable i to be written

$$\sigma_i^2 = \sum_{n=1}^{35} \sigma_{in}^2. \tag{9.32}$$

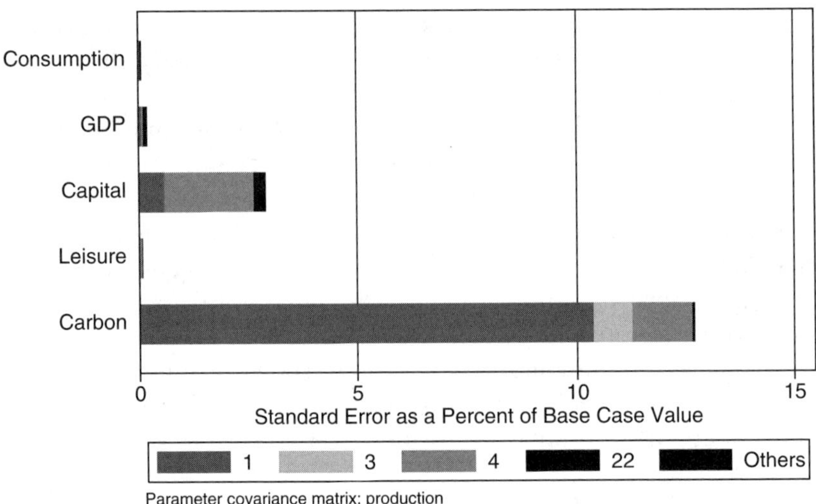

Figure 9.13
Decomposition of uncertainties by industry: Key macroeconomic variables.

The share of σ_i^2 contributed by industry n is thus

$$\omega_{in} = \frac{\sigma_{in}^2}{\sigma_i^2}. \tag{9.33}$$

Applying equation (9.33) to the representative set of endogenous variables, we produce the decomposition shown in figures 9.13 through 9.15. The length of each bar shows the overall standard error in the corresponding variable originating from the production parameters and matches figures 9.10 through 9.12. The bars are shaded according to the fraction of each variable's variance that originates with the parameters in a given industry. Four industries are the dominant sources of production-parameter uncertainty for the variables in the figures: Agriculture (sector 1), Coal Mining (sector 3), Oil and Gas Extraction (sector 4), and Nonelectrical Machinery (sector 22). The remaining variance is associated with the other 31 industries and is shown as a grey segment with the legend "Others."

In figure 9.13, the key production-side uncertainties for the capital stock are in Agriculture (sector 1) and Oil and Gas Extraction (sector 3). All remaining sectors together contribute only a small additional degree of uncertainty. For carbon emissions, the dominant source of uncertainty is Agriculture, which we discuss in more detail below. In figures 9.14 and 9.15 uncertainties in Oil and Gas Extraction is the

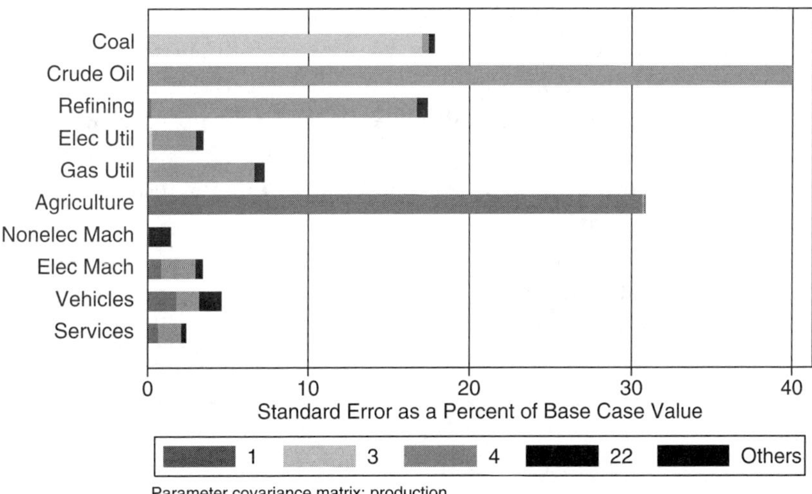

Figure 9.14
Decomposition of uncertainties by industry: Industry output.

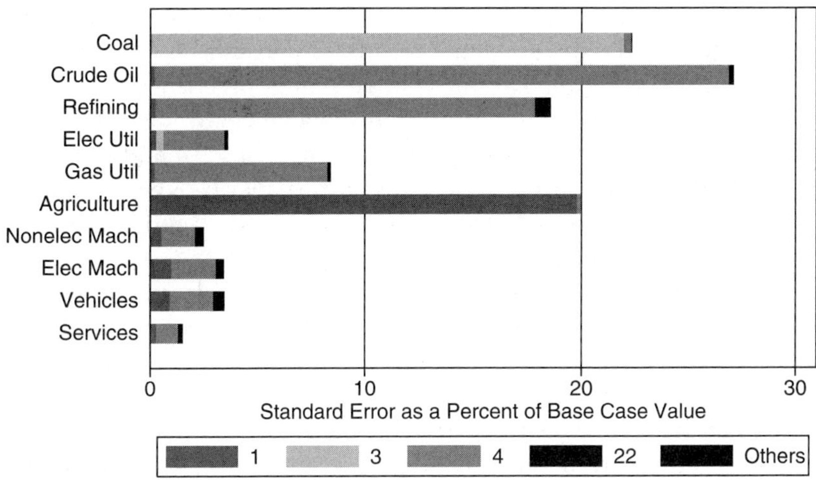

Figure 9.15
Decomposition of uncertainties by industry: Industry prices.

major component of the uncertainties in industry outputs and prices. For example, uncertainties in the parameter estimates for Oil and Gas Extraction are more important for the uncertainties in Refined Petroleum, Electric Utilities, Natural Gas Utilities, Electrical Machinery, and Services than each industry's own parameter estimates. However, for Coal, Agriculture, and Nonelectrical Machinery, the industry's own parameters dominate.

Further decomposition can be used to determine which parameters within an industry are most important for the uncertainty in a given endogenous variable and to understand precisely why those parameters are important. Industry n's contribution to the variance in endogenous variable i, σ_{in}^2, can be decomposed into components associated with covariances between specific parameters. The share of σ_{in}^2 resulting from the covariance between parameters l and m will be ω_{inlm}

$$\omega_{inlm} = \frac{J_{il}^{p} \Sigma_{lm}^{pn} J_{mi}^{p}}{\sigma_{in}^{2}}. \tag{9.34}$$

Applying equation (9.34) to the variance in the capital stock due to parameters in Oil and Gas Extraction (sector 4), selecting the six largest components, and expressing the results as percentages, we produce panel A in figure 9.16. The most important component arises from the covariance between α^0 and α_E^p, which alone contributes about 8% of σ_{in}^2. Panels B and C are similar to figures 9.3 and 9.4 and show the relative magnitudes of each Jacobian term (panel B, where L and R indicate the left and right parameters of the pair) and covariance between the parameters (panel C).

For the first term the Jacobian terms are relatively small and the covariance is large. Thus the first component is explained by the inherent uncertainty in the parameter estimates rather than by a particularly strong link between either of the parameter estimates and the capital stock. For the second component, which is associated with α_E^p and β_{KE}^p, the effects are reversed. The covariance is relatively small but the partial elasticity of the capital stock with respect to β_{KE}^p is relatively large. The parameter β_{KE}^p also contributes to the third and sixth components.

Intuitively, it makes sense that uncertainty in the parameter estimate for β_{KE}^p for Oil and Gas Extraction is important for the overall capital stock. This is the change in the industry's share of capital in total costs in response to a percentage change in the relative price of energy. Thus the parameter is a key determinant of the industry's capital stock and hence the capital stock for the U.S. economy as a whole. Figure 9.16

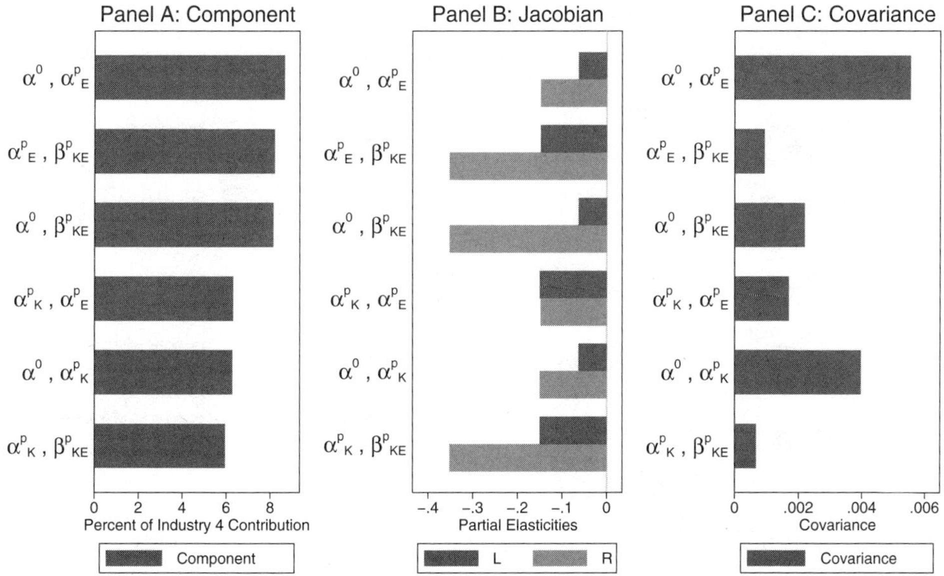

Figure 9.16
Capital stock uncertainty due to crude oil parameters.

emphasizes another benefit of the delta method mentioned earlier, namely, that it captures the uncertainties associated with the covariances. In this case, none of the top six components arise from the variance of a single parameter estimate.

Figure 9.17 is structurally similar to figure 9.16 but decomposes the uncertainty in a different variable, carbon emissions, resulting from the parameter estimates in a different industry, Agriculture. The largest component arises from the covariance between β^p_{LE} and β^p_{EE}. Panel B shows that the overall level of carbon emissions is quite sensitive to both parameters. Particularly important is β^p_{LE}, the change in the share of labor in response to a percentage change in energy prices. The partial elasticity of carbon emissions with respect to this parameter estimate is large, greater than 2.5 in magnitude, and it contributes to four of the top six components.

Partial elasticities for both parameters are large because base case productivity growth in Agriculture is strong and base case output in the Coal sector grows very slowly. Taken together these productivity terms cause Agricultural emissions of greenhouse gases to rise as a share of the total, eventually accounting for about 39% of emissions in

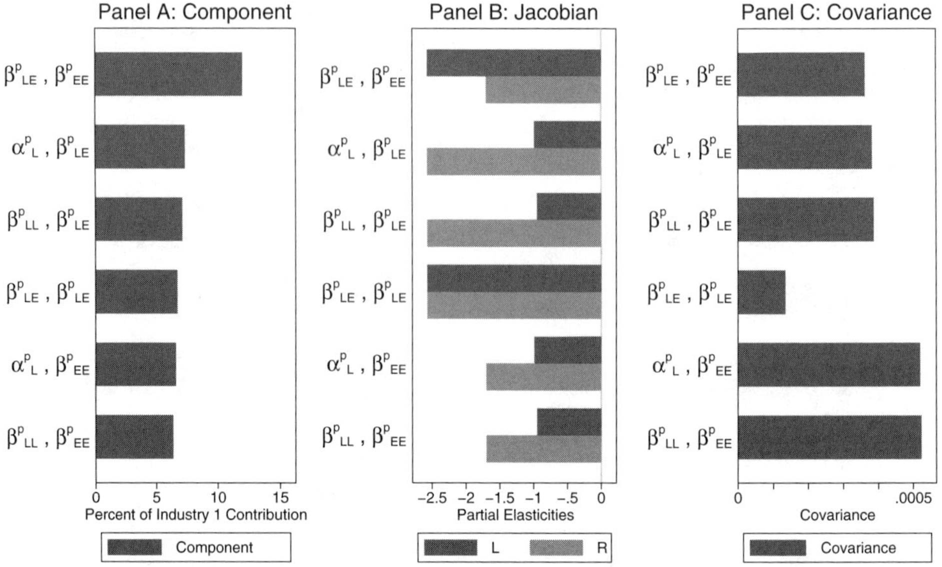

Figure 9.17
Carbon uncertainty due to agriculture parameters.

the steady state. For the same reason, the elasticities of carbon emissions with respect to the Coal Mining sector (industry 3), shown in figure 9.18, panel B, are relatively small. As a result, uncertainty in the Coal Mining sector parameters contributes much less to the overall uncertainty in carbon emissions, even though the covariances in panel C are considerably larger than the corresponding values in figure 9.17.

A second important feature of figure 9.18 is that the contribution of the fourth term is negative. This tends to reduce the overall uncertainty in carbon emissions. The cause is the negative covariance in α^0 and α^p_L shown in panel C. Since both elasticities in panel B have the same sign, negative in this case, the negative covariance causes the overall contribution to the variance to be negative. For carbon emissions, in other words, errors in one of the parameters are associated with offsetting errors in the other parameter.

Figures 9.19 through 9.21 show the overall standard errors resulting from the household and production parameters together. In all three figures, the bars are shaded based on the shares of each variable's overall variance that can be attributed to each set of parameters. Figure 9.19 emphasizes a point made earlier. Uncertainty in the household

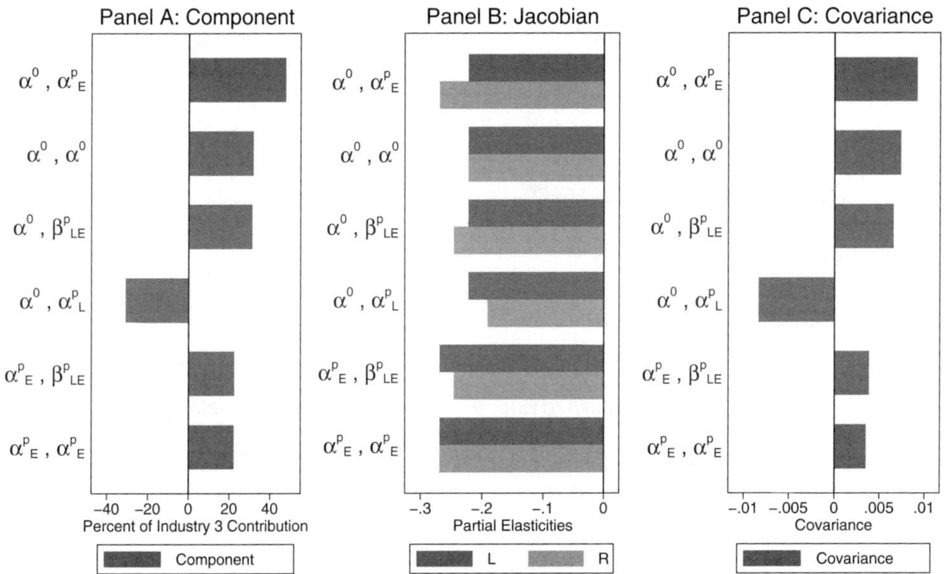

Figure 9.18
Carbon uncertainty due to coal sector parameters.

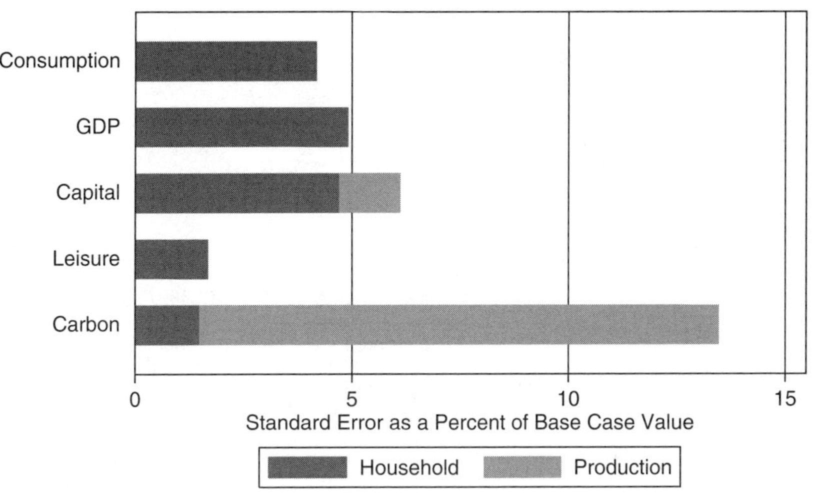

Figure 9.19
Overall base case uncertainties: Key macroeconomic variables.

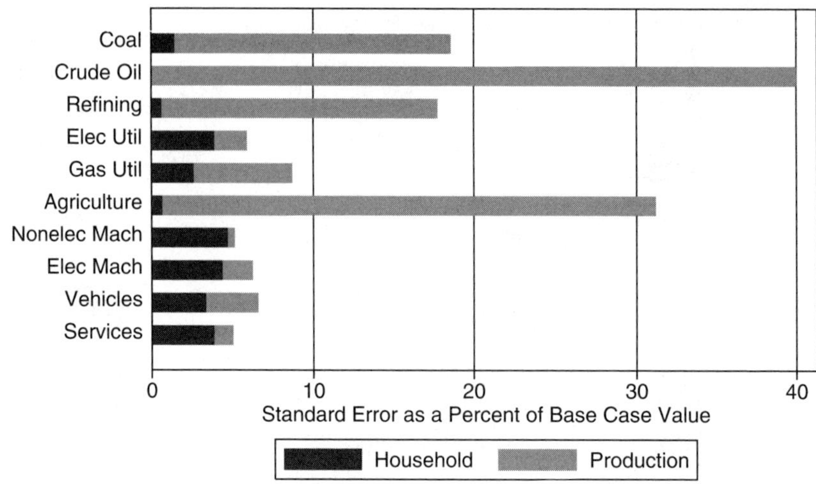

Figure 9.20
Overall base case uncertainties: Industry output.

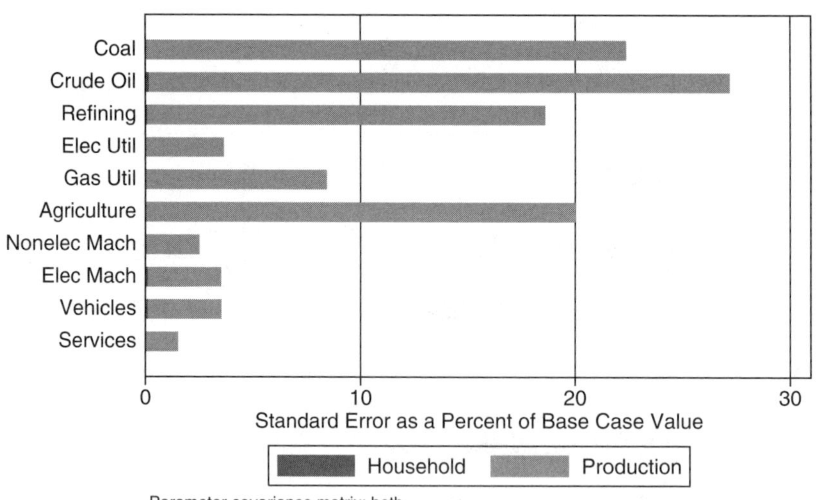

Figure 9.21
Overall base case uncertainties: Industry prices.

parameters is far more important for most economy-wide variables than uncertainty in the entire set of production parameters, carbon emissions being the exception. By contrast, for industry output both sets of parameters are important while for industry prices only uncertainties in the production parameters matter.

9.3.3 *Relationship to Systematic Sensitivity Analysis*

We have combined econometric estimates of the parameters of IGEM and the delta method for characterizing the uncertainty for the variables of the IGEM base case and outcomes of policy evaluations. This approach has important advantages over Systematic Sensitivity Analysis. The delta method scales easily, since it depends on covariance matrices for the parameter estimates that are calculated as part of the estimation of the parameters. By contrast, Systematic Sensitivity Analysis relies on the assumption that the covariance matrices are diagonal or are otherwise simplified. This runs a serious risk of missing key sources of uncertainty in the parameter estimates.

Correctly accounting for covariances among parameter estimates is particularly important because parameter estimates within a subsection of a model—such as the representation of producer behavior in a given sector—are usually highly correlated. In Systematic Sensitivity Analysis these covariances are set equal to zero or to assumed values. Failing to use econometric estimates of the covariances can produce misleading results because these covariances may contribute positively or negatively to the uncertainties of model outcomes.

For example, consider the relationship between α_2^h and β_2^{hm} discussed above in relation to the uncertainty in consumption. Setting aside the other household parameters, if there were no correlation between α_2^h and β_2^{hm} the joint distribution of α_2^h and β_2^{hm} would produce the 95% confidence ellipse shown in figure 9.22. However, as noted in figure 9.23, the covariance between α_2^h and β_2^{hm} is actually negative. In fact, the relationship between the parameters is quite strong: the correlation coefficient between the two is –0.96. The actual joint distribution of α_2^h and β_2^{hm}, again setting aside the remaining household parameters, produces the 95% confidence ellipse shown in figure 9.23. As expected from the correlation coefficient, it is quite narrow.

Capturing perturbations toward the upper left or lower right in figure 9.23 is particularly important because α_2^h and β_2^{hm} move

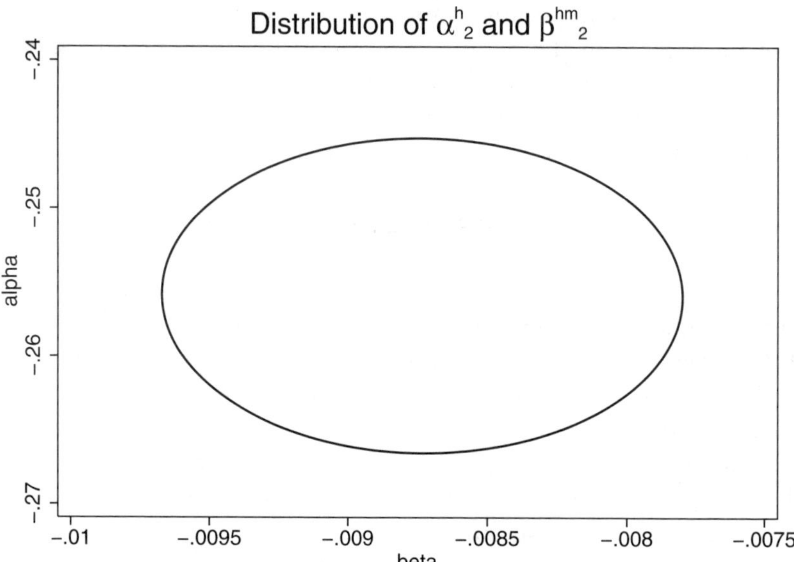

Figure 9.22
95% Confidence ellipse if α_2^h and β_2^{hm} were uncorrelated.

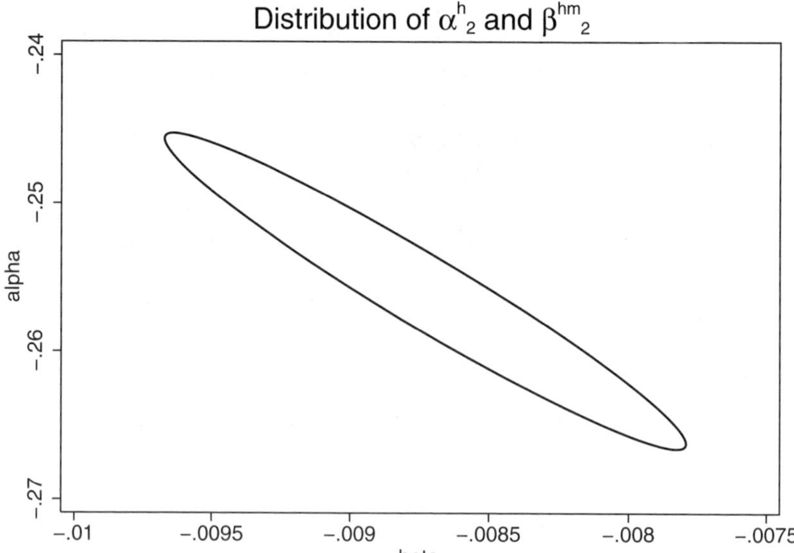

Figure 9.23
95% True confidence ellipse for α_2^h and β_2^{hm}.

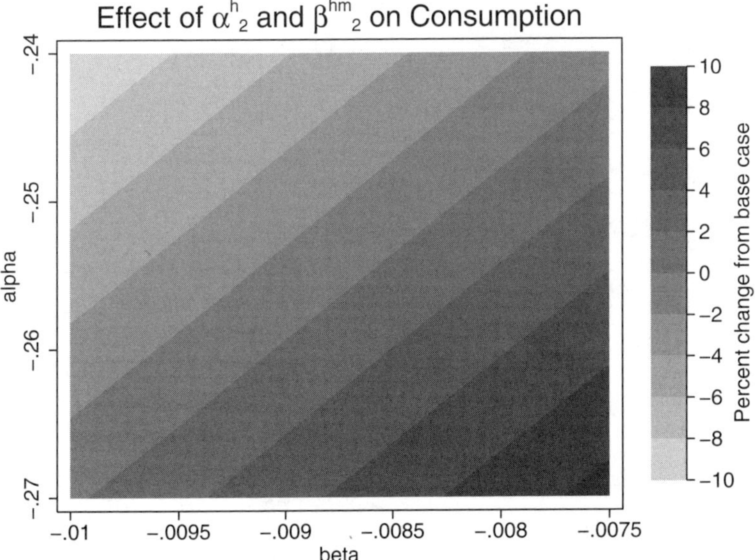

Figure 9.24
Effect of α_2^h and β_2^{hm} on consumption.

consumption in opposite directions. Figure 9.24 is a contour plot showing the result of applying the partial elasticities shown in figure 9.3 to the parameter space in figure 9.23. Consumption varies most from the upper left to the lower right—very closely aligned with the major axis of the ellipse in figure 9.23. Parameter combinations at the upper left would lower steady state consumption by 10% while those at the lower right would raise it by a similar amount. Confidence regions based on econometric estimates and the delta method fully account for the covariances.

To assess the broader importance of the off-diagonal terms we computed standard errors using only the diagonal terms in the household and production parameter covariances. The results for key macroeconomic variables and industry output are shown in figures 9.25 and 9.26. Overall, the off-diagonal terms are very important: failing to include them would lead to downward bias in the standard errors of the endogenous variables and thus overstatement of the precision of the results. In some cases, such as Crude Oil or the output of Agriculture, the understatement is more than 50%.

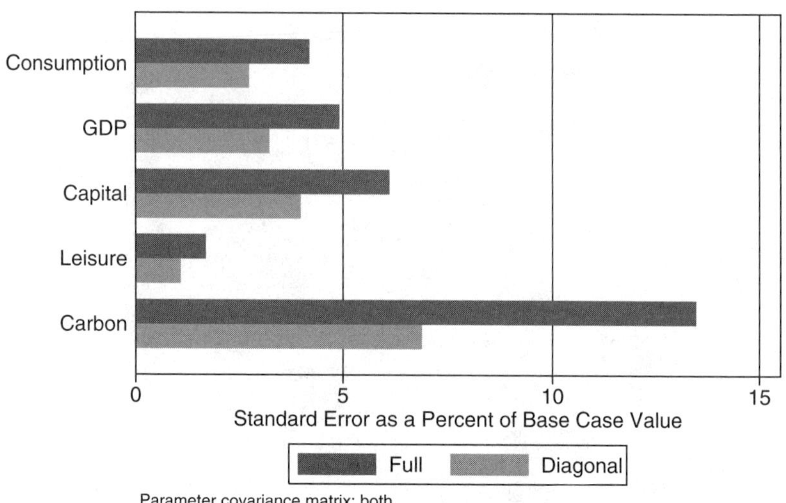

Figure 9.25
Diagonal versus full covariance matrix: Key macroeconomic variables.

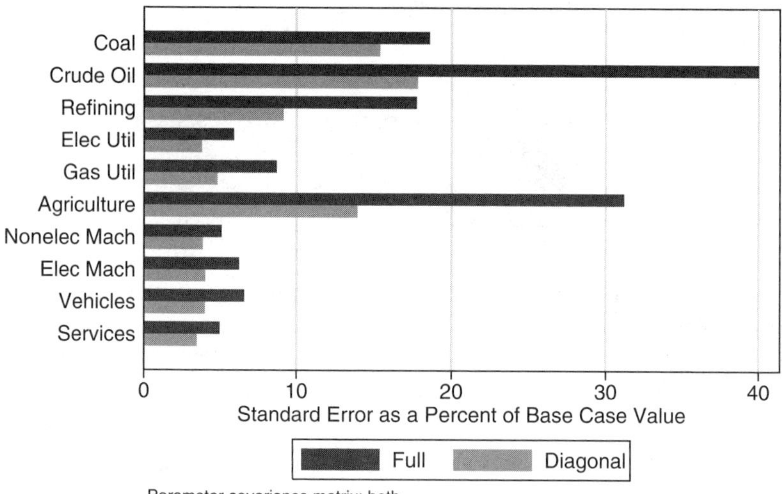

Figure 9.26
Diagonal versus full covariance matrix: Industry output.

9.4 Application to Environmental Policy

We next consider the application of the delta method to evaluating the uncertainties in the model's response to a policy experiment. In particular, we compare the IGEM base case with a policy case consisting of a \$10 carbon tax with revenue recycled via a reduction in the capital tax rate. Results for the simulation are shown in table 9.8 with an additional column showing the change in each variable from its base case value. Paralleling the approach outlined in section 9.3, we begin by computing the confidence intervals associated with the household parameters alone and comparing the delta method with a Monte Carlo simulation. We then present the overall confidence intervals including both household and production parameters.

To compute confidence intervals induced by the household parameters we apply equation (9.17) with Σ_β^h inserted for Σ_β. The results for key macroeconomic variables are given in figure 9.27. The percentage change in each variable produced by the policy from table 9.8 is shown by a shaded bar. At the end of each bar are two smaller bars with the 95% confidence interval computed by the delta method shown by the bottom bar and by Monte Carlo simulation by the top bar.

Three facts are immediately apparent. First, the close alignment between the delta method and the Monte Carlo results observed for

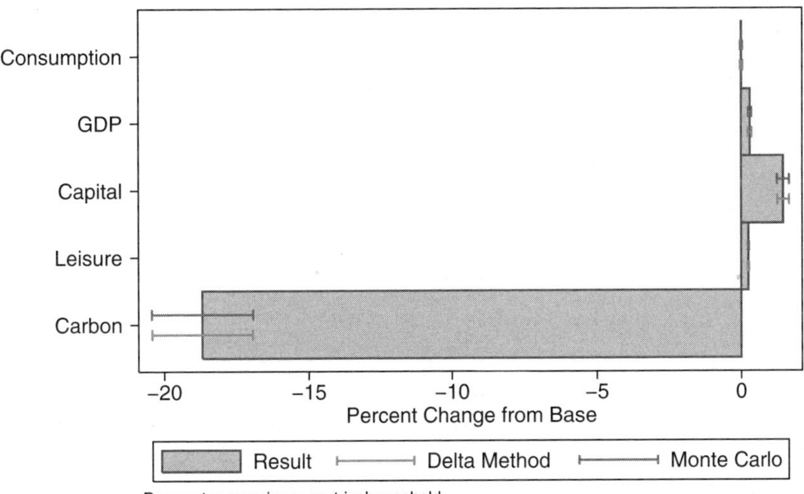

Figure 9.27
Confidence intervals due to household parameters: Key macroeconomic variables.

Table 9.8
Carbon tax results for selected variables

Variable	Carbon Tax	Percentage Change
Macroeconomic conditions		
Consumption	13295	0.01
GDP	20810	0.30
Capital	105909	1.49
Leisure	29438	0.26
Carbon	11863	–18.68
Industry output		
Coal	27	–50.19
Crude Oil	121	–0.40
Refining	206	–5.95
Electric Utilities	476	–2.48
Gas Utilities	98	–5.53
Agriculture	5685	–18.67
Nonelectric Machinery	28068	0.39
Electric Machinery	12586	–0.91
Vehicles	405	–0.37
Services	7346	–1.17
Supply prices		
Coal	1.84	83.30
Crude Oil	2.60	–0.85
Refining	3.88	4.27
Electric Utilities	1.91	2.53
Gas Utilities	3.45	3.97
Agriculture	0.11	15.70
Nonelectric Machinery	0.07	0.16
Electric Machinery	0.05	0.60
Vehicles	0.44	0.20
Services	0.86	0.10

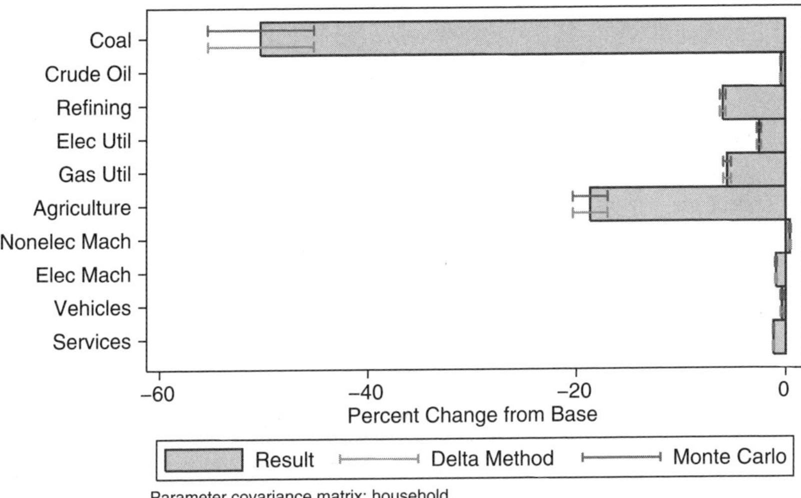

Figure 9.28
Confidence intervals due to household parameters: Industry output.

the IGEM base case in section 9.3 carries over to policy outcomes. The confidence intervals are nearly indistinguishable. Second, the policy results are all significant with respect to the household parameters; that is, none of the confidence intervals includes zero. Third, the confidence intervals for policy deviations are narrower than those for the IGEM base case projections.

For example, the household parameters induce standard errors of more than 4% in both consumption and carbon emissions (see figure 9.1). The 95% confidence intervals for the base case values of those variables would thus be plus or minus 8% or 16% overall. However, the two confidence intervals for the policy deviations are quite narrow, vanishingly small for consumption and 4% for carbon. They differ from those for the IGEM base case because the parameter covariance matrix is weighted by the change in the Jacobian, ΔJ_β, rather than the Jacobian itself. For this experiment in IGEM, most of the terms in ΔJ_β (87%) are considerably smaller in magnitude than the corresponding values in J_β. As a result, the confidence intervals for policy deviations are considerably narrower than those for the base case.

The uncertainties induced by the household parameters in industry output and prices are shown in figures 9.28 and 9.29. Because the household parameters contribute little to the base case industry uncertainties (see figures 9.5 and 9.6), the confidence intervals they induce

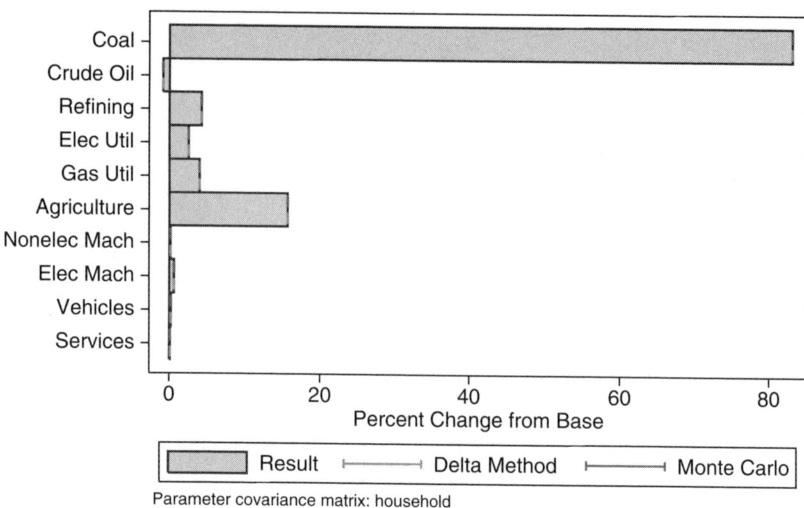

Figure 9.29
Confidence intervals due to household parameters: Industry prices.

in the policy deviations are small for industry output and especially small for industry prices. However, it is important to keep in mind that figures 9.28 and 9.29 do not include uncertainty in the production parameters: the full confidence intervals discussed below are larger.

Accounting for both household and production parameter uncertainty produces the confidence intervals shown in figures 9.30 through 9.32. Because the production parameters have little effect on consumption, GDP, or leisure, those confidence intervals are essentially unchanged from figure 9.27. However, as shown in figure 9.13, the production parameters do play an important role in the standard errors of the capital stock and carbon emissions. As a result, the confidence intervals for those variables in figure 9.30 are considerably larger than they were in figure 9.27. However, the changes in both variables are significant. The mean increase in the capital stock is 1.5% (of its base case value) and its 95% confidence interval runs from 0.8 to 2.2%. The mean decrease in carbon emissions is 19% and its confidence interval runs from –28 to –10%.

Turning to industry output, figure 9.31 shows that the reductions in the output of the energy sectors other than Crude Oil are all significant: the confidence intervals for Coal, Refined Petroleum, Electric Utilities, and Gas Utilities all exclude zero change. The effect on Agriculture, in

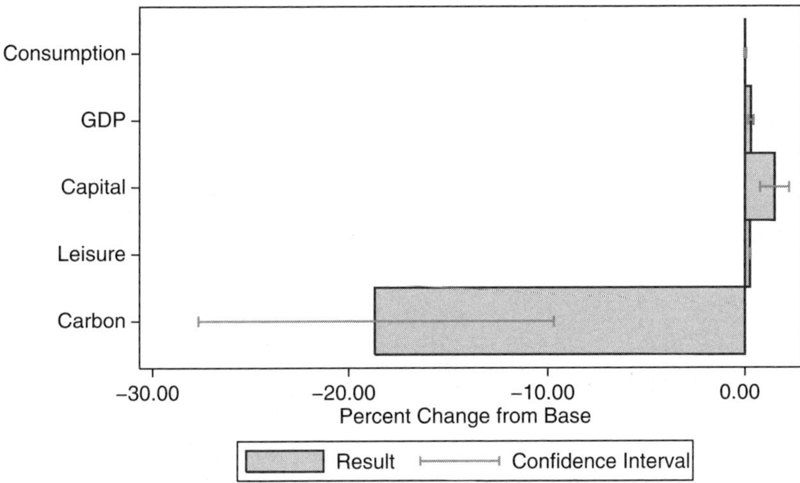

Figure 9.30
Confidence intervals: Key macroeconomic variables.

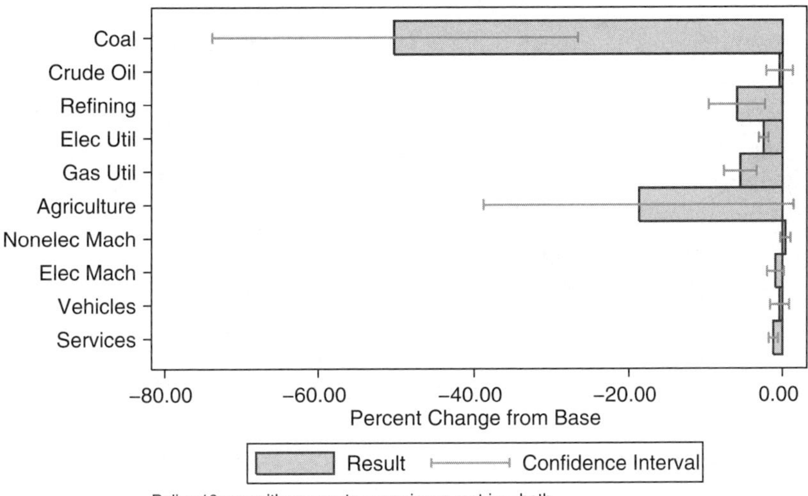

Figure 9.31
Confidence intervals: Industry output.

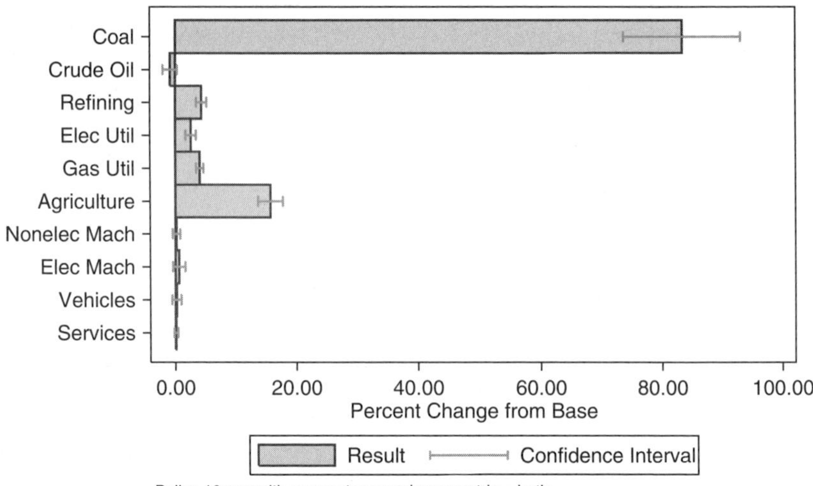

Figure 9.32
Confidence intervals: Industry prices.

contrast, is less clear due to the large underlying uncertainties shown in figure 9.20. The expected effect is a drop of 20% relative to the base case but the confidence interval ranges from a drop of more than 40% to a slight increase in output. Finally, the effect of the carbon tax on the remaining sectors is both small and insignificant.

Figure 9.32 shows confidence intervals for industry prices. The results generally parallel figure 9.31. The confidence intervals are largest for Coal and Agriculture, but both price changes are significant; the energy sectors other than Coal have much more modest increases in prices that are also significant; and the non-energy sectors other than Agriculture have very small price changes that are insignificant. Both Coal Mining and Agriculture are strongly affected by the tax so it is not surprising that their price changes are significant.

Figure 9.33 shows the effects of the carbon tax policy on the egalitarian measure of social welfare and its efficiency and equity components. All three results are equivalent variations expressed as percentages of base case wealth. The error bars show the 95% confidence interval for each result. The total effect and both components are all significant: none of the confidence intervals includes zero.

Uncertainty in the efficiency effect is much larger than the uncertainty in the equity effect, and the two are strongly and negatively correlated, as shown by the 95% confidence ellipse in figure 9.34. Since

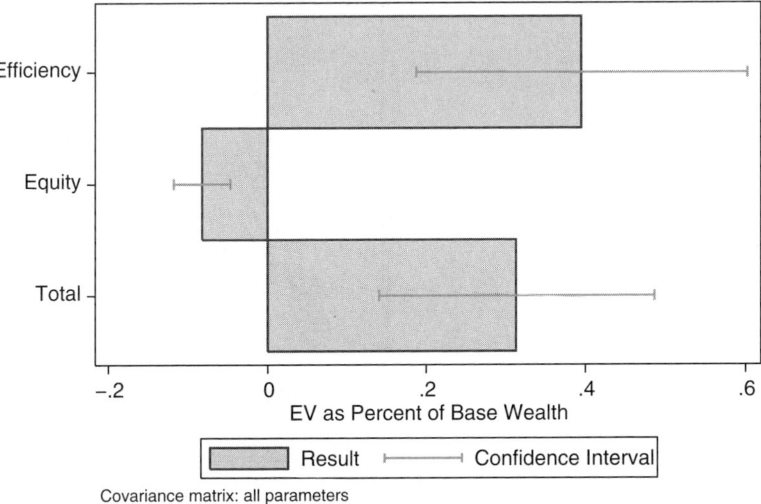

Figure 9.33
Carbon tax effects under the egalitarian measure of social welfare.

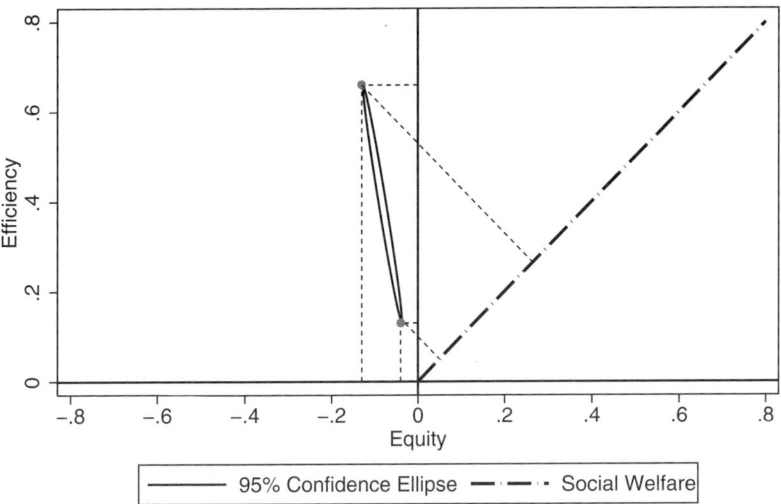

Figure 9.34
Confidence ellipse for the egalitarian measure of social welfare.

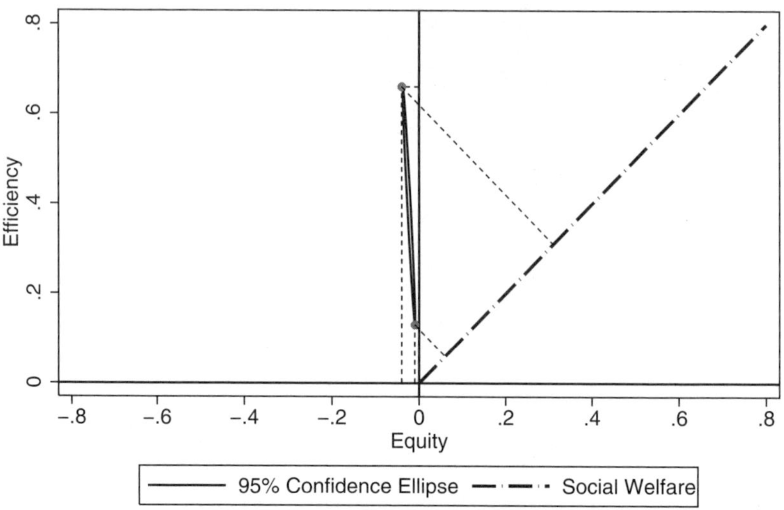

Figure 9.35
Confidence ellipse for the utilitarian measure of social welfare.

overall social welfare is the sum of the efficiency and equity components, it can be measured along the 45 degree line shown in the diagram. The dashed lines in the figure show projections of the ellipse onto both axes and the 45 degree line for social welfare. The origin lies outside all three projected intervals, indicating that all three effects are jointly significant at the 5% level.

Figure 9.35 shows a similar ellipse for the utilitarian measure of social welfare. The efficiency effect is the same as in the egalitarian case, but the equity effect is much smaller. As a result, the confidence interval for social welfare shifts further away from the origin along the 45 degree line. The welfare effects are dominated by the efficiency component, which is clearly positive.

The relative precision of the two components under the egalitarian measure is shown in figure 9.36, where each standard error has been plotted as a percentage of the magnitude of the corresponding effect. For example, the efficiency effect is equal to 0.40% of base case wealth and its standard error is 0.11%, so the standard error is about 27% of the value itself. From the figure, it is clear that the efficiency component is less precisely determined than the equity component: the standard error of the equity component is 22%.

The standard errors in figure 9.36 can be decomposed to determine the key factors driving each result. Figure 9.37 shows the two bars

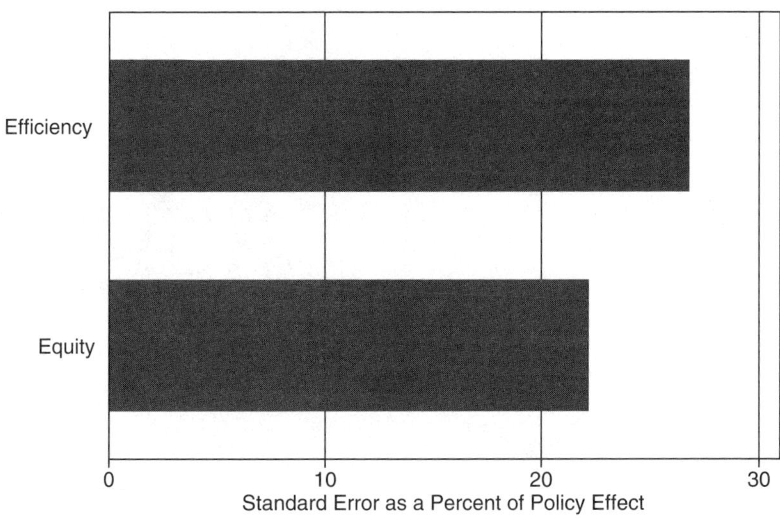

Figure 9.36
Standard errors as percentages of corresponding welfare effects.

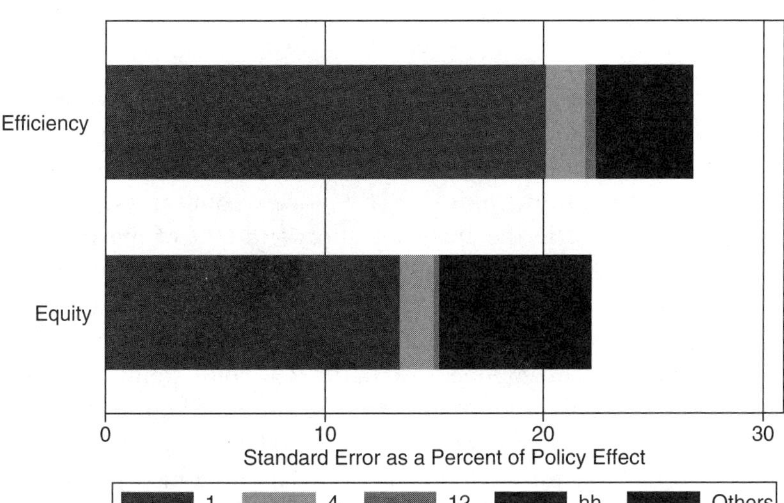

Figure 9.37
Decomposition of standard errors in social welfare components.

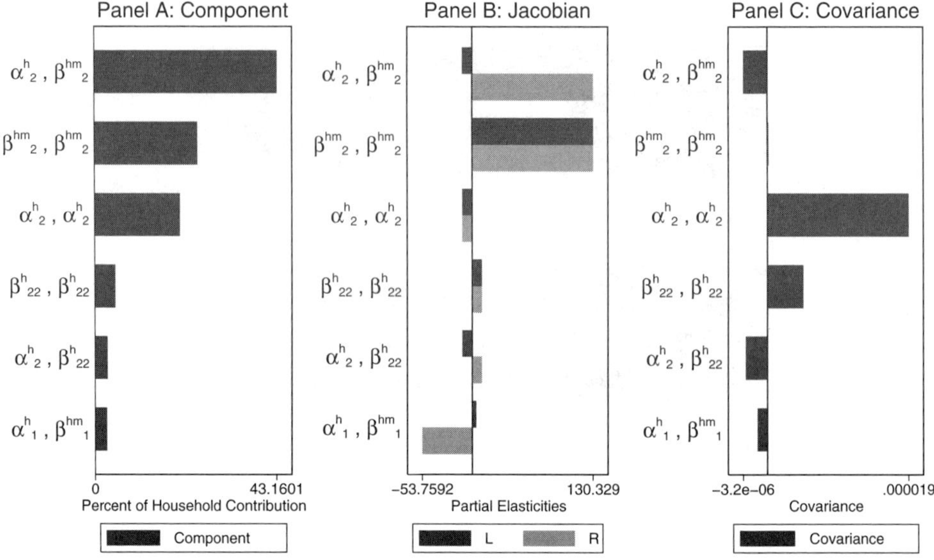

Figure 9.38
Uncertainty in social welfare due to household parameters.

shaded in proportion to the shares of the corresponding variances attributable to the parameters from key industries or the household sector. The largest component is associated with uncertainties in the parameters of Agriculture (industry 1): it alone accounts for about 75% of the standard error in the efficiency effect and 60% of the standard error in the equity effect. Agriculture is an important determinant of the equivalent variation because (as discussed above) its parameters are among the most important in determining the effect of carbon tax.

The second largest components in figure 9.37 come from the household parameters (shown as "hh" in the figure): household parameters account for 14% of the standard error in the efficiency effect and 30% of the error in the equity effect. The third largest component comes from the parameters of the Crude Oil and Gas Extraction sector (industry 4): it accounts for about 7% of each standard error. The remaining industries together contribute very little.

The standard errors for the components of welfare can be further decomposed into components associated with particular parameter covariances. Figure 9.38 shows the six household covariances that contribute most to the uncertainty in social welfare. Panel A shows the magnitude of each contribution as a percentage of the contribution of

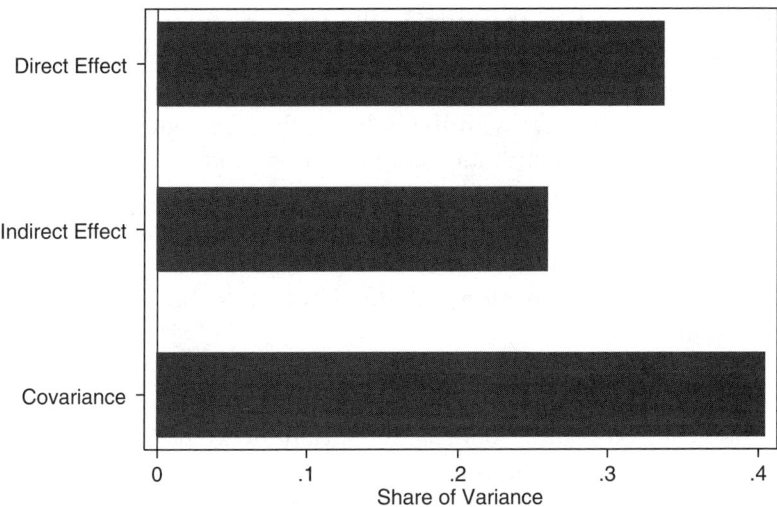

Figure 9.39
Direct and indirect effects of household parameters on efficiency.

the household parameters to the standard error in social welfare. More than 40% is due to one covariance alone: that between α_2^h and β_2^{hm}. As shown in panel B, it is due primarily to a very large Jacobian term (partial elasticity) between welfare and parameter β_2^{hm}.

Finally, as indicated by equations (9.20) and (9.22), the household parameters contribute to the uncertainty in the welfare results through two channels: their direct effect on the expenditure function and their indirect effects through the uncertainties they induce in the model's endogenous variables. Figure 9.39 decomposes the household contribution into these two components. The direct effect of the parameters on the expenditure function accounts for about 35% of the overall variance contributed by the household parameters to social welfare. The indirect effect in isolation (that is, the effect of the household parameters on welfare through their effect on the model's endogenous variables alone) contributes about 25% of the variance. The covariance between the direct and indirect effects contributes the remaining 40%.

Thus, the principal sources of uncertainty in the welfare results are the base and policy case simulation results.

9.5 Summary and Conclusion

In this chapter we have shown that a key advantage of the econometric estimation of the parameters of IGEM is that it provides the information needed to characterize the uncertainty of IGEM's base case projections and outcomes of policy simulations. We have combined information on the distributions of the parameter estimates given in earlier chapters with the delta method presented in section 9.2 to determine the distributions of projections and policy outcomes. The delta method involves straightforward calculations that are fast, scalable, and easily decomposed to obtain information about the determinants of model outcomes. Furthermore, the results coincide closely with those from Monte Carlo simulations that are far more burdensome.

Given the distributions of model results, we can determine confidence regions for the IGEM base case projections given in chapter 6 and the policy outcomes from chapter 8. Confidence regions are valuable because they provide concise and transparent summaries of the uncertainties for the projections and the model outcomes. This information is a valuable complement to the IGEM simulation results and will greatly aid in the design of energy and environmental policies for the United States. The leading illustration of the value of confidence regions is the double dividend that results from combining a carbon tax with recycling the revenues to reduce capital income tax rates. This produces reductions in greenhouse gas emissions with a narrow range of uncertainty along with improvements in economic performance with a range of uncertainty that is also very narrow.

The delta method is a standard technique in econometrics and statistics that has been adapted for general equilibrium modeling by Tuladhar and Wilcoxen (1999). The key idea is to represent IGEM by a Taylor series approximation that depends on the parameter estimates and the disturbances from the behavioral equations. We employ the covariance matrix of the parameter estimates to characterize the uncertainty in these estimates and derive the covariance matrix of the model outcomes by means of the delta method. Application of this method requires calculation of Jacobian matrices representing the derivatives of the model outcomes with respect to the parameter estimates and the disturbances. This calculation requires a number of solutions of IGEM equal to the number of unknown parameters and disturbances plus one for the base case projection of the model.

In section 9.3 we have illustrated the application of the delta method for deriving confidence regions for the base case projections of IGEM. We have incorporated information about estimates of the parameters of both household and production submodels of IGEM. We have shown how confidence regions for the model outcomes can be decomposed to provide information about the sources of the uncertainty. We also show that information about the covariances of the parameter estimates is essential to avoid misleading results. Ignoring these covariances by assuming their values to take a specified value such as zero could lead to overestimation or underestimation of the degree of uncertainty.

Deriving confidence regions for the outcomes of energy and environmental policies in section 9.4 is simpler and more straightforward than for base case projections. Policy evaluations are based on comparisons between base case and policy case projections of IGEM. Since the disturbances are the same in both sets of projections, they are not a source of uncertainty in the policy evaluations. We illustrate this with the double dividend policy considered in chapter 8. We derive confidence for measures of economic performance, pollution abatement, and social welfare. We find that all three are determined within a narrow range of uncertainty, so that we can recommend the policy of recycling revenues from a carbon tax by reducing tax rates for capital income with a high degree of confidence.

Our first conclusion is that econometric estimation of the unknown parameters of general equilibrium models has enormous advantages over methods for parameter determination that are not accompanied by measures of uncertainty. This conclusion is supported by the analysis of Hertel et al. (2007), using Systematic Sensitivity Analysis to characterize the uncertainties in outcomes of a trade model derived from estimates of elasticities of substitution among commodities from different sources. Econometric methods for estimating the parameters of general equilibrium models have been surveyed by Jorgenson, Jin, Slesnick, and Wilcoxen (2012) and Hillberry and Hummels (2012).

Our second conclusion is that the delta method provides a straightforward and powerful method for deriving measures of uncertainty for model outcomes, like the base case projections of IGEM analyzed in section 9.3 and the policy evaluation for environmental taxes discussed in section 9.4. This method is routinely applied on statistics and econometrics and has been adapted to general equilibrium modeling by Tuladhar and Wilcoxen (1999). In this chapter we have shown that the results are similar to the far more burdensome technique of Monte Carlo simulation. The delta method is based on a linear approximation to a general equilibrium model, so that standard techniques for model solution can be adapted for applications of the method.

Notes

1. See Tuladhar and Wilcoxen (1999) and Tuladhar (2003).
2. A concise exposition of the delta method is provided by Oehlert (1992).
3. See also Jorgenson (1998a) and (1998b)
4. See Hertel (2012), pp. 840–841, and the references given there.
5. See Hertel, Hummels, Ivanic, and Keeney (2007). Hillberry and Hummels (2012) have surveyed econometric methods for estimating trade elasticities.

10 Epilogue

The design of new energy and environmental policies for the United States requires a market-based approach for internalizing the health costs and environmental damages from using energy. The goal of environmental policy is to assure that all market participants face the incremental costs of energy use, so that these costs are incorporated into economic decisions. Market-based approaches like environmental taxes and tradable permits are cost-effective, since all market participants face the same prices for energy. Other approaches leave opportunities to reduce the cost of pollution abatement unexploited and impose undue burdens on economic activity.

Market-based approaches to environmental policy could generate substantial government revenues, so that integration of these revenues into government budgets is an essential part of policy design. In chapter 8 we have shown how revenues from environmental taxes can reduce other taxes, improve economic performance, and enhance environmental quality. However, there can be no presumption that market-based policies will abate pollution or improve economic performance. The environmental and economic impacts of these policies must be assessed empirically in every policy evaluation.

Finally, market-based environmental policies affect the decisions of millions of individual firms and households. We have evaluated these policies in terms of their effects on individual and social welfare. For this purpose we translate the decisions of households into measures of individual welfare that are distributed over the entire U.S. population. We combine measures of individual welfare with value judgments about horizontal and vertical equity to obtain a measure of social welfare. In chapter 8 we rank alternative environmental policies in terms of their impacts on social welfare.

The design of new energy and environmental policies for the United States requires a new analytical framework to capture policy impacts on all markets in every period of time. These markets are equilibrated by the intertemporal price system that we discuss in chapter 1. The most important innovation in our framework is to link markets in different time periods through markets for capital services and investment goods in each period. The prices determined in these markets summarize the expectations of future prices needed for current decisions.

In chapter 2 we capture the key features of our analytical framework in the Intertemporal General Equilibrium Model (IGEM). In chapter 8 we illustrate the power of the new approach to policy design embodied in IGEM. We consider a policy that involves using the revenues from a carbon tax to reduce tax rates on capital income. This reduces the cost of capital, determined in the market for capital services, and stimulates capital formation, determined in the market for investment goods. The increase in future capital input offsets the costs of pollution abatement and improves the performance of the U.S. economy. We refer to this outcome as a double dividend.

To analyze energy markets, we have modeled the behavior of individual households in chapter 3. Substitution among goods and services and leisure time is the key to understanding consumer behavior. Our main innovation is to capture the heterogeneity of household behavior by including the demographic characteristics of individual households, together with prices and total expenditure, as determinants of consumer demand. We combine survey data on households with price data that vary over time and across the thousands of households that we consider at each point of time.

The new model of consumer behavior we present in chapter 3 is essential for capturing heterogeneity of individual households. We represent consumer behavior in IGEM by summing demands over all households. To measure the impact of energy and environmental policies on the welfare of individuals, our most important innovation is to recover models of individual consumer behavior from our aggregate model. By exploiting the consumer demand functions at the household level, we are able to construct a measure of welfare for each household.

A major innovation in chapter 3 is to combine measures of individual welfare into a measure of social welfare. Our measure of social welfare rests on value judgments rooted in the well-established principles of horizontal and vertical equity. We are able to evaluate the impacts of alternative energy and environmental policies on the basis of equity as well as efficiency. Our measure of social welfare leads to a complete ordering of alternative policies and produces clear-cut policy recommendations.

In chapter 4 we incorporate models of producer behavior for 35 individual industries into IGEM, including 5 industries that comprise the energy sector of the U.S. economy. The remaining industries include Agriculture and Mining, Manufacturing, Services, and Trade. For each industry, we consider substitution among inputs of Capital Services, Labor Services, Energy, and Materials in response to changes in the prices of these inputs. Our most significant innovation in chapter 4 is to distinguish input substitution from changes in technology induced by price changes. We have quantified the importance of price-induced changes in technology in the policy simulations of chapter 8.

In chapter 5 we incorporate demands by the government sector, investment demands, and imports and exports from the rest of the world into IGEM. The government budget includes revenues and expenditures. The budget also incorporates a complete representation of the U.S. tax system, providing a role for the energy and environmental taxes that we consider. Our most important innovation in this chapter is to integrate energy and environmental policies into the government budget. This provides the basis for the base case projections of the U.S. economy presented in chapter 6 and the policy cases considered in chapter 8.

Chapter 7 describes the role of environmental variables in the impacts of alternative energy and environmental policies. The environmental variables are based on official inventories published by the Environmental Protection Agency and energy variables are obtained from the Energy Information Agency. Our most significant innovation in this chapter is to include technologies that are not reflected in the U.S. national accounts and other economic reports. This greatly broadens the scope of environmental impacts encompassed by IGEM.

The distinguishing feature of our approach for designing energy and environmental policies for the United States is to estimate the parameters of IGEM econometrically. The estimates presented in chapters 3, 4, and 5 are accompanied by measures of uncertainty. Our final innovation is to employ the delta method introduced by Tuladhar and Wilcoxen (1999) to derive measures of uncertainty for the IGEM base case projection of the U.S. economy. We derive similar measures of uncertainty for policy evaluations that compare the base case with policy cases. In chapter 9 we express these measures of uncertainty through confidence intervals with associated probabilities.

The innovations presented in this book, taken together, constitute a new approach for designing energy and environmental policies for the United States. We have emphasized environmental taxes, following a long line of economists since Pigou (1920). However, we integrate these taxes into the government budget, following more recent literature on the double dividend. We analyze the impacts of energy and environmental policies by means of the intertemporal price system modeled by IGEM. Finally, we evaluate these policy impacts in terms of empirical measures of individual and social welfare.

Very few analytic results are available for choosing among alternative energy and environmental policies. This is the primary reason that the U.S. Environmental Protection Agency (2000, 2010a) emphasizes general equilibrium models in its *Guidelines for Preparing Economic Analyses*. Econometric general equilibrium modeling is essential for exploiting the vast range of economic data required for evaluating energy and environmental policies and providing sound policy advice.

Although much of the economic literature on energy and environmental policies focuses on market-based approaches like those discussed in this book, these policies are rarely integrated into fiscal reform, as proposed in our subtitle. This has been a major barrier to widespread adoption of market-based policies. Energy and environmental policies that do not use energy markets may not be cost-effective and may impose unnecessary burdens on the U.S. economy. These policies may also fail to cope with the hidden costs of energy, the key policy objective.

In this book our objective is to design policies that are sufficiently stringent to achieve environmental objectives and, at the same time, enhance economic performance. This is no longer the impossible dream that it seemed in 1990 when we constructed the first version of IGEM. The innovations presented in this book make it possible to incorporate the wide range of information on policy impacts that is now available and evaluate these impacts in terms of individual and social welfare. While this is very demanding, our goal from the beginning has been to improve both environmental quality and economic performance, in short, to achieve a double dividend.

A Equations and Glossary

A.0 Notation

Time

$t \in I_T$ — $I_T = \{1,2,\ldots, T, \ldots\}$

Industry/producer

$j \in I_{IND}$ — $I_{IND} = \{1,2, \ldots, 35\}$

Legal form of organization

$c \in I_{LEGAL}$ — $I_{LEGAL} = \{\text{corporate, noncorporate}\}$

IO commodities

$i \in I_{COM}$ — $I_{COM} \in \{1,2, \ldots, 35\}$

Industry inputs

$i \in I_{INP}$ — $I_{INP} \in \{1,2, \ldots, 35, NCI, K, L\}$

NIPA PCE commodities

$n \in I_{PCE}$ — $I_{PCE} = \{1,2, \ldots, 38\}$

Purchasers of domestic output

$j \in I_{BUY}$ — $I_{BUY} = \{1,2, \ldots, 35, C, I, G, X\}$

Households

$k \in I_{POP}$

Nodes of production function

$m \in I_{PNODE}$ — $I_{PNODE} = \{E, M, \ldots, EQ\}$

$i \in I_{PNODEm}$ — I_{PNODEm} in table 2.2

Nodes of consumption function

$m \in I_{CNODE}$ — $I_{CNODE} = \{ND, EN, \ldots, RC\}$

$i \in I_{CNODEm}$ — I_{CNODEm} in table 2.4

Nodes of investment function

$m \in I_{INV}$ $I_{\text{INV}} = \{\text{fixed}, \ldots, \text{mining}\}$

$i \in I_{INVm}$ I_{INVm} in table 5.4

Nodes of capital demand function

$s \in I_{ASSET}$ $I_{ASSET} = \{\text{short-lived,long-lived}\}$

Levels of government

$f \in I_{GOV}$ $I_{\text{GOV}} = \{\text{federal, state, \& local}\}$

Externalities

$x \in I_{EXT}$ $I_{EXT} = \{1,2,3,4\} = \{CO_2, SO_2, \ldots\}$

Vector of 1's

ι

Transpose of matrix A

A'

Diagonal matrix of a vector v

$\text{Diag}(v)$

A.1 Household Sector

Household First-Stage Decision, Euler Equation

$$\text{Max} \sum_{t=1}^{\infty} \frac{N_t^{eq}}{(1+\rho)^t} \left(F_t / N_t^{eq}\right)^{1-\frac{1}{\sigma}} \quad \text{given } K_0, \{\bar{L}_t\}, \tag{A.1.1}$$

subject to

$$WF \equiv PK_0 K_0 + BG_0 + BF_0 + \sum_{t=1}^{\infty} \frac{Y_t^{full}}{\prod_{s=1}^{t} 1+r_s} \geq \sum_{t=1}^{\infty} \frac{PF_t F_t}{\prod_{s=1}^{t} 1+r_s}. \tag{A.1.2}$$

$$Y^{full} = P^h \bar{L} + G^{TRAN} - twW_{t-1} - TLUMP - H^{row} - R^N. \tag{A.1.3}$$

$$\left[\frac{F_t / N_t^{\text{eq}}}{F_{t-1} / N_{t-1}^{\text{eq}}}\right]^{1/\sigma} = \frac{1+r_t}{1+\rho} \frac{PF_{t-1}}{PF_t}. \tag{A.1.4}$$

Wealth, Private Income, and Savings

$$W_t \equiv PK_t K_t + BG_t + BF_t. \tag{A.1.5}$$

$$YF_t = YK_t^{net} + P^h\bar{L} + G^{tran} - TLUMP_t - twW_{t-1} + G_t^{Ktran} + R\_CON^{reb}. \quad \text{(A.1.6)}$$

$$Y_t = YK_t^{net} + YL_t + G^{tran} - TLUMP_t - twW_{t-1} + G_t^{Ktran} + R\_CON^{reb}$$
$$= YF_t - p_t^{leis}L_t^{leis} = YF_t - w_t\psi_C^R C_R^N \quad \text{(A.1.7)}$$

$$YL = P^h LS\frac{1-tl^a}{1-tl^m} = (1-tl^a)YL^{gross} = (1-tl^a)\sum_j PLD_j LD_j. \quad \text{(A.1.8)}$$

YK^{net} is equation A.3.15.

$$S_t = YF_t - PF_tF_t - H_t^{row} - R_t^N - R\_ITC$$
$$= YF_t - w_t\psi_C^R C_R^N - P_t^C C_t - H_t^{row} - R_t^N - R\_ITC \quad \text{(A.1.9)}$$
$$= Y_t - P_t^C C_t - H_t^{row} - R_t^N - R\_ITC. \quad \text{(A.1.10)}$$

Household and business net transfers to foreigners set exogenous in levels, or as fixed shares of GDP:

$$\bar{H}^{row} \quad \text{(A.1.11a)}$$

$$H^{row} = \alpha^{H\_row}GDP \quad \text{(A.1.11b)}$$

Household Second-Stage Decision, Goods, and Leisure Choice

Rank two model estimated for household k from CEX data, the indirect utility function:

$$\ln V_k = \alpha_0 + \alpha^H \ln\frac{\rho_r}{m_k} + \frac{1}{2}\ln\frac{\rho_r}{m_k}'\mathbf{B}^H \ln\frac{\rho_r}{m_k} + \ln\frac{\rho_r}{m_k}'\mathbf{B}_{pA}A_k. \quad \text{(A.1.12)}$$

$\mathbf{c}_k^X = (C_{NDk}^X, C_{Kk}^X, C_{CSk}^X, C_{Rk}^X)'$ consumption vector.

$\boldsymbol{\rho}_r = (p_{ND}^r, p_K^r, p_{SV}^r, p_R^r)'$ price vector indexed by region.

$$m_k = p_{ND}^r C_{NDk}^X + p_K^r C_{LKk}^X, p_{CS}^r C_{CSk}^X + p_R^r C_{Rk}^X. \quad \text{(A.1.13)}$$

$$C_{Rk}^X = \sum_{m\ adults} q_{kt}^m(5110 - hoursworked_{kt}^m); \quad q_{kt}^m = p_{Rt}^m / p_{Rt}^r. \quad \text{(A.1.14)}$$

A_k = (0,1) dummies for {1 child, 2 children, 3+ children, 2 adults, 3+ adults, Midwest, South, West, nonwhite, female, rural} (left out groups: 0 children, 1 adult, Northeast, white, male, urban)

e.g., (1,1,0,1,0,0) for "1 child, 2 adults, Northeast, nonwhite, male, urban"

The household demand vector in share form:

$$w_k = \frac{1}{D(p_k)}\left(\alpha_p + B_{pp}\ln\frac{p_k}{M_k} + B_{pA}A_k\right). \tag{A.1.15}$$

$$D(p_k) = -1 + \iota' B_{pp}\ln p_k.$$

Summing over households gives the aggregate demand vector:

$$w = \frac{1}{D(p)}\left[\alpha_p + B_{pp}\ln p - \iota' B_{pp}\frac{\sum_k m_k \ln m_k}{M} + B_{pA}\frac{\sum_k m_k A_k}{M}\right]. \tag{A.1.16}$$

This is modified for use beyond the sample period using exogenous distribution terms expressed as function of the number of households of type k, nf_k:

$$PFF = M = \sum_k m_k = \sum_K nf_K \bar{m}_K. \tag{A.1.17}$$

$$\bar{m}_K^0 = \frac{\bar{m}_{K,baseyear}}{M_{baseyear}} \quad M_t^0 = \sum_K nf_{Kt}\bar{m}_K^0. \tag{A.1.18}$$

$$\begin{aligned} w_t &= \frac{1}{D(p)}\left[\alpha_p + B_{pp}\ln p_t - \iota' B_{pp}\frac{\sum_K nf_{Kt}\bar{m}_K \ln \bar{m}_K}{M} + B_{pA}\frac{\sum_k m_k A_k}{M}\right] \\ &= \frac{1}{D(p)}\left[\alpha_p + B_{pp}\ln p_t - \iota' B_{pp}\xi_t^d + B_{pA}\xi_t^L\right]. \end{aligned} \tag{A.1.19}$$

We replace $\sum_K nf_{Kt}\bar{m}_K \ln \bar{m}_K / M = \sum_K nf_{Kt}\frac{\bar{m}_K}{M}\ln\frac{\bar{m}_K}{M} + \ln M$ with

$$\begin{aligned} \xi_t^d &= \sum_K nf_{Kt}\frac{\bar{m}_K^0}{M_t^0}\ln\frac{\bar{m}_K^0}{M_t^0} + \ln M_t = \xi_t^{dd} + \ln PFF_t \\ \xi_t^{dd} &= \sum_K nf_{Kt}\frac{\bar{m}_K^0}{M_t^0}\ln\frac{\bar{m}_K^0}{M_t^0}; \end{aligned} \tag{A.1.20}$$

and replace the vector $\sum_k m_k A_k / M$ with

$$\xi^L = (\xi_{1child}^L, \ldots \xi_j^L, \ldots, \xi_{rural}^L)' \quad j = \{1\text{ child}, \ldots, \text{female}, \text{rural}\}$$

$$\xi_j^L = \sum_{all\ K\in j} nf_{Kt}\frac{\bar{m}_K^0}{M_t^0} = j^{\text{th}} \text{ row of } \sum_k \frac{m_k A_k}{M}. \tag{A.1.21}$$

The demand shares on the CEX basis is

$$SC^X = \frac{\alpha^H + B^H \ln P^{H1} - B^H \iota \xi^d + B_{pA}\xi^L}{D(p)}. \tag{A.1.22}$$

$$SC^X \equiv \left(\frac{PC^X_{ND} C^X_{ND}}{MF^X}, \frac{PC^X_K C^X_K}{MF^X}, \frac{PC^X_{CS} C^X_{CS}}{MF^X}, \frac{PC^X_R C^X_R}{MF^X} \right),$$

$$D(p) = -1 + \iota' B^H \ln P^{H1}. \tag{A.1.23}$$

$$\ln P^{H1} = (\ln PC^X_{ND}, \ln PC^X_K, \ln PC^X_{CS}, \ln PC^X_R).$$

Exogenous bridge equation between CEX units and NIPA units:

$$\Delta SC_{it} = SC^N_{it} - SC^X_{it} \quad i = \{\text{ND,K,CS,R}\}. \tag{A.1.24}$$

$$\Delta SC_{it} = \alpha + \beta \Delta SC_{it} + \varepsilon_{it} \quad \varepsilon_{it} = \rho \varepsilon_{it} + u_{it}. \tag{A.1.25}$$

$$SC^N \equiv \left(\frac{PN^{ND} N^{ND}}{MF^N}, \frac{PN^K N^K}{MF^N}, \frac{PN^{CS} N^{CS}}{MF^N}, \frac{PN^R N^R}{MF^N} \right)'$$

$$PC^X_{ND} = PN^{ND}. \tag{A.1.26}$$

$$PC^X_{CS} = PN^{CS}.$$

$$PC^X_K = PN^K = PKD_C.$$

$$PC^X_R = PN^R = \psi^R_C P^h.$$

$$MF^N = PF \cdot F = PCC \cdot CC + PN^R N^R. \tag{A.1.27}$$

$$VCC = PCC \cdot CC = PN^{ND} N^{ND} + PN^K N^K + PN^{CS} N^{CS}. \tag{A.1.28}$$

Time Endowment, Labor Supply, Leisure, Price of Hours, Price of Leisure

$$P^h \bar{L} = P^h LS + PN^R N^R. \tag{A.1.29}$$

$$LS = \bar{L} - \psi^R_C N^R. \tag{A.1.30}$$

$$d \ln \bar{L}_t = \sum_k \frac{1}{2} (v^L_{kt} + v^L_{kt-1}) d \ln(14 \cdot 365 \cdot POP_{kt}); \; v^L_{kt} = (1 - tl^m_t) P^L_{kt}. \tag{A.1.31}$$

Household Third-stage Decision, Allocation of Detailed PCE

NESTED STRUCTURE OF CONSUMPTION (A.1.32)

1	$F = F(N^{ND}, N_K, N^{CS}, N_R)$.	Aggregate full consumption
2	$N^{ND} = N^{ND}(N^{EN}, N^F, N^{CG})$.	Nondurables
3	$N^{EN} = N^{EN}(N_6, N^{FC}, N_{18}, N_{19})$.	Energy
4	$N^F = N^F(N_1, N_2, N_3, N_9)$.	Food
5	$N^{CG} = N^{CG}(N^{CL}, N^{HA}, N_{12}, N^{MS})$.	Consumer goods

6	$N^{CS} = N^{CS}(N_{34}, N^{HO}, N^{TR}, N^{MD}, N^{MI})$.	Consumer services
7	$N^{FC} = N^{FC}(N_7, N_8)$.	Fuel and coal
8	$N^{CL} = N^{CL}(N_4, N_5)$.	Clothing and shoes
9	$N^{HA} = N^{HA}(N_{10}, N_{11})$.	Household articles
10	$N^{MS} = N^{MS}(N_{13}, N_{14}, N_{15}, N_{16})$.	Miscellaneous nondurables
11	$N^{K} = N^{K}(N_{35}, N_{17})$.	Capital services
12	$N^{HO} = N^{HO}(N_{20}, N_{21}, N_{22}, N_{23})$.	Household operation
13	$N^{TR} = N^{TR}(N_{24}, N_{25})$.	Transportation
14	$N^{MD} = N^{MD}(N_{26}, N_{27})$.	Medical
15	$N^{MI} = N^{MI}(N_{28}, N^{BU}, N^{RC}, N_{32})$.	Miscellaneous services
16	$N^{BU} = N^{BU}(N_{29}, N_{30})$.	Business services
17	$N^{RC} = N^{RC}(N_{31}, N_{33})$.	Recreation
	subscripts $\in I_{PCE}$	

Price dual of **lower** tiers consumption demands $N^m(\ldots)$:

$$\ln PN^m = \alpha^{Hm\prime} \ln P^{Hm} + \frac{1}{2} \ln P^{Hm\prime} B^{Hm} \ln P^{Hm} + \ln P^{Hm\prime} f^{Hm} \quad m \in I_{\text{CNODE}}. \tag{A.1.33}$$

$$\ln P^{Hm} \equiv (\ln PN_{m1}, \ldots, \ln PN_{mi}, \ldots, \ln PN_{m,im})' \quad i \in I_{\text{CNODE}m} \tag{A.1.34}$$

$$f_t^{Hm} = F^{Hm} f_{t-1}^{Hm} + v_t^{Hm} \tag{A.1.35}$$

$$SN^m = \begin{bmatrix} PN_{m1} N_{m1} / PN^m N^m \\ \cdots \\ PN_{m,im} N_{m,im} / PN^m N^m \end{bmatrix} = \alpha^{Hm} + B^{Hm} \ln PN^{Hm} + f^{Hm} \tag{A.1.36}$$

$$\begin{aligned} PN_{mi} &\in \{PN_1, \ldots, PN_{34}, PN^{ND}, \ldots, PN^{RC}\} \\ N_{mi} &\in \{N_1, \ldots, N_{34}, N^{ND}, \ldots, N^{RC}\} \\ PN_1 N_1 &= s_1^{con} PF \cdot F = SN_1^F \cdot SN_2^{ND} \cdot SN_1^{\text{TOP}} \cdot PF \cdot F \\ PN_2 N_2 &= s_2^{con} PF \cdot F = SN_2^F \cdot SN_2^{ND} \cdot SN_1^{\text{TOP}} \cdot PF \cdot F \\ &\cdots \end{aligned} \tag{A.1.37}$$

$$PN_{34} N_{34} = s_{34}^{con} PF \cdot F = SN_2^H \cdot SN_1^{CS} \cdot SN_3^{\text{TOP}} \cdot PF \cdot F$$

$$VN \equiv (PN_1 N_1, \ldots, PN_{34} N_{34} PKD_C KD_C)'.$$

$$PN = \mathbf{H}' PS^C \quad \text{where the components of } PS^C: \tag{A.1.38}$$

$$PS_i^C = (1 + tc_i)PS_i \quad i \in I_{COM} \tag{A.1.39}$$

$$\begin{aligned} PS_N^C &= (1 + tc_N)PNCI_C \\ PS_K^C &= (1 + tc_K)PKD_C \\ PS_L^C &= (1 + tc_L)PLD_C \end{aligned} \tag{A.1.40}$$

Converting from NIPA Categories to IO Categories

$$\begin{aligned} VC &\equiv (PS_1C_1, \ldots, PS_{35}C_{35}, \ldots, PLD_CLD_C)' \\ &= \mathbf{H}VN \end{aligned} \tag{A.1.41}$$

$$C_i = VC_i / PS_i \quad i \in I_{INP} \tag{A.1.42}$$

$$\begin{aligned} C^P &\equiv (C_1, C_2, \ldots, C_{35})' \\ C &\equiv (C_1, \ldots, C_{35}, NCI_C, KD_C, LD_C)'. \end{aligned}$$

Simple Cobb-Douglas price index of consumption:

$$\ln PCC = \sum_{i=1}^{I_{INP}} \frac{VC_i}{VCC} \log PS_i. \tag{A.1.43}$$

$$CC = VCC / PCC. \tag{A.1.44}$$

A.2 Producer Model

NESTED STRUCTURE OF PRODUCTION (A.2.1)

$QI_j = QI^j\,(KD_j, LD_j, QP^{jE}, QP^{jM}).$ Industry output

$QP^{jE} = QP^E(QP_3^j, QP_4^j, QP_{16}^j, QP_{30}^j, QP_{31}^j)\cdot$ Energy aggregate

$QP^{jM} = QP^M(QP_6^j, QP^{jMA}, QP^{jME}, QP^{jMN}, QP^{jMS})\cdot$ Material aggregate

$QP^{jMA} = QP^{AG}(QP_1^j, QP_7^j, QP_8^j, QP^{jTX}, QP^{jWP})\cdot$ Agriculture Materials

$QP^{jMM} = QP^{MM}\,(QP^{jFM}, QP^{jMC}, QP^{jEQ}).$ Metallic Materials

$QP^{jMN} = QP^{MN}(QP_5^j, QP_{15}^j, QP_{17}^j, QP_{19}^j, QP_{27}^j)\cdot$ Nonmetallic Materials

$QP^{jMS} = QP^{MS}(QP_{28}^j, QP_{32}^j, QP_{33}^j, QP_{34}^j, QP^{jOS})\cdot$ Service Materials

$QP^{jTA} = QP^{TA}(QP_9^j, QP_{10}^j, QP_{18}^j)\cdot$ Textile-Apparel

$QP^{jWP} = QP^{WP}(QP_{11}^j, QP_{12}^j, QP_{13}^j, QP_{14}^j)\cdot$ Wood and Paper aggregate

$QP^{jOS} = QP^{OS}(QP_{29}^j, QP_{35}^j, QP_{NCI}^j)\cdot$ Miscellaneous Services

$QP^{jFM} = QP^{FM}(QP_2^j, QP_{20}^j, QP_{21}^j)$ · Fabricated-Other Metal

$QP^{jMC} = QP^{MC}(QP_{22}^j, QP_{23}^j)$ · Machinery aggregate

$QP^{jEQ} = QP^{EQ}(QP_{24}^j, QP_{25}^j, QP_{26}^j)$ · Equipment aggregate

Price dual of top tier of production function $QI_j = QI\ (\ldots)$:

$$PO_j = PO^j(PKD_j, PLD_j, PP^{jE}, PP^{jM}, t; \lambda_j, A^{agg}) \quad j \in I_{IND}$$
$$A_t^{agg} = (1 - \Delta A^{agg})A_{t-1}^{agg}. \tag{A.2.2}$$

λ_j exogenous productivity shock in industry j

ΔA^{agg} exogenous aggregate productivity shock, common to all

Option "logistic_gt"

$$\ln PO_j = \alpha_0^j + \alpha^{Pj'} \ln P^{Pj0} + \frac{1}{2} \ln P^{Pj0'} B^{Pj} \ln P^{Pj0} + \ln P^{Pj0'} B_{pt}^j g(t)$$
$$+ \alpha_t^j g(t) + \frac{1}{2} \beta_{tt}^j g(t)^2 + \ln \lambda_j + \ln A^{agg} \tag{A.2.3}$$

$$\text{where } g(t) = \frac{1}{1 + \exp[-\mu^j (t - \tau^j)]}. \tag{A.2.4}$$

$$A_j^{TFP} = \ln P^{Pj0'} B_{pt}^j g(t) + \alpha_t^j g(t) + \frac{1}{2} \beta_{tt}^j g(t)^2 + \ln \lambda_j + \ln A^{agg}.$$
$$\ln P^{Pj0} \equiv (\ln PKD_j, \ln PLD_j, \ln PP^{jEN}, \ln PP^{jM})'. \tag{A.2.5}$$

$$SP^{jTOP} = \begin{bmatrix} PKD_j KD_j / PQ_j QI_j \\ \ldots \\ PP^{jM} QP^{jM} / PO_j QI_j \end{bmatrix} = \alpha^{Pj} + B^{Pj} \ln P^{Pj0} + B_{pt}^j g(t). \tag{A.2.6}$$

Option "kalman"

$$\ln PO_j = \alpha_0^j + \alpha^{Pj'} \ln P^{Pj0} + \frac{1}{2} \ln P^{Pj0'} B^{Pj} \ln P^{Pj0} + \ln P^{Pj0'} f_t^{Pj}$$
$$+ f_t^j + \ln \lambda_j + \ln A^{agg}. \tag{A.2.7}$$

$$\xi_t^{Pj} = F^{Pj} \xi_{t-1}^{Pj} + v_t^{Pj}.$$
$$\xi_t^{Pj} = (1, f_{Kt}^{Pj}, f_{Lt}^{Pj}, f_{Et}^{Pj}, f_{Mt}^{Pj}, \Delta f_t^j)'. \tag{A.2.8}$$

$$A_j^{TFP} = \ln P^{Pj0'} f_t^{Pj} + f_t^j + \ln \lambda_j + \ln A^{agg}. \tag{A.2.9}$$

$$SP^{j\text{TOP}} = \begin{bmatrix} s_j^K \\ s_j^L \\ s_j^E \\ s_j^M \end{bmatrix} = \begin{bmatrix} PKD_j KD_j / PQ_j QI_j \\ \dots \\ PP^{jM} QP^{jM} / PO_j QI_j \end{bmatrix} = \alpha^{Pj} + B^{Pj} \ln P^{Pj0} + f_t^{Pj}. \qquad \text{(A.2.10)}$$

Price dual of lower tiers of production functions $QP^{jm} = QP(\dots)$:

$\ln P^{Pjm} \equiv (\ln PP_{m1}^j, \dots, \ln PP_{mi}^j, \dots, \ln PP_{m,im}^j)' \quad i \in I_{PNODEm}.$

Option "lowertier_std"

$$\ln PP^{jm} = \alpha_0^{jm} + \alpha^{Pjm'} \ln P^{Pjm} + \frac{1}{2} \ln P^{Pjm'} B^{Pjm} \ln P^{Pjm} \quad m \in I_{\text{PNODE}}. \qquad \text{(A.2.11)}$$

$$SP^{j\text{m}} = \begin{bmatrix} PP_{m1}^j QP_{m1}^j / PQ^{jm} QP^{jm} \\ \dots \\ PP_{m,im}^j QP_{m,im}^j / PP^{jm} QP^{jm} \end{bmatrix} = \alpha^{Pjm} + B^{Pjm} \ln P^{Pjm}. \qquad \text{(A.2.12)}$$

Option "lowertier_kalman"

$$\ln PP^{jm} = \alpha_0^{jm} + \alpha^{Pjm'} \ln P^{Pjm} + \frac{1}{2} \ln P^{Pjm'} B^{Pjm} \ln P^{Pjm} + \ln P^{Pjm'} f_t^{Pjm} \quad m \in I_{\text{PNODE}}. \qquad \text{(A.2.13)}$$

$$f_t^{Pjm} = F^{Pjm} f_{t-1}^{Pjm} + v_t^{Pjm}. \qquad \text{(A.2.14)}$$

$$SP^{j\text{m}} = \begin{bmatrix} PP_{m1}^j QP_{m1}^j / PQ^{jm} QP^{jm} \\ \dots \\ PP_{m,im}^j QP_{m,im}^j / PP^{jm} QP^{jm} \end{bmatrix} = \alpha^{Pjm} + B^{Pjm} \ln P^{Pjm} + f_t^{Pjm}. \qquad \text{(A.2.15)}$$

$PP_{mi}^j \in \{PS_1, \dots, PS_{35}, PNCI_j, PP^{jMA}, \dots, PP^{jOS}\}.$

$QP_{mi}^j \in \{QP_1^j, \dots, QP_{35}^j, NCI_j, QP^{jMA}, \dots, QP^{jOS}\}.$

Vectors for use in formulas below:

$V^{QI} \equiv (PO_1 QI_1, \dots, PO_{35} QI_{35})'.$

Taxes (Net vs. Gross Output)

$$\begin{aligned} PI_j &= \left(1 + tt_j + tx_j^v\right) PO_j + tu_j + tx_j^u \quad j \in I_{\text{IND}} \\ &= \left(1 + tt_j^{full}\right) PO_j \end{aligned} \qquad \text{(A.2.16)}$$

$$VT^{QI} \equiv (PI_1QI_1, \ldots, PI_{35}QI_{35})'$$
$$= Diag(\iota + tt^{full})V^{QI} \quad \text{(A.2.17)}$$

Commodities from Industry Outputs

$$\mathbf{M} = [M_{ji}] = \text{value of commodity } i \text{ made by industry } j. \quad \text{(A.2.18)}$$

$$m_{ji}^{col} = \frac{M_{ji}}{\sum_k M_{ki}}; \quad m_{ji}^{row} = \frac{M_{ji}}{\sum_k M_{jk}}. \quad \text{(A.2.19)}$$

$$\ln PC = \mathbf{m}^{\mathbf{col}'} \ln PI. \quad \text{(A.2.20)}$$

$$V^{QC} \equiv (PC_1QC_1, \ldots, PC_{35}QC_{35})'$$
$$= \mathbf{m}^{\mathbf{row}'} VT^{QI} \quad \text{(A.2.21)}$$

$$QC_i = V_i^{QC} / PC_i \quad i \in I_{\text{COM}}. \quad \text{(A.2.22)}$$

The Input-Output USE Matrix

In share terms, used in equation A.6.4:

$$A_{1j} = SP_1^{jAG} \cdot SP_2^{jM} \cdot SP_4^{jTOP}$$
$$A_{2j} = SP_1^{jFM} \cdot SP_1^{jMM} \cdot SP_3^{jM} \cdot SP_4^{jTOP}$$
$$\cdots\cdots\cdots\cdots \quad \text{(A.2.23)}$$
$$A_{35j} = SP_2^{jOS} \cdot SP_5^{jMS} \cdot SP_5^{jM} \cdot SP_4^{jTOP}$$

$$A_j \equiv (A_{1j}, A_{2j}, \ldots, A_{35j})' \quad j \in I_{\text{IND}}. \quad \text{(A.2.24)}$$

$$\mathbf{A} \equiv [A_1, A_2, \ldots, A_{35}]'. \quad \text{(A.2.24b)}$$

$$PS_iQP_i^j = A_{ij}VQI_j \quad \text{(A.2.25)}$$

$$PNCI_jNCI_j = SP_3^{jOS} \cdot SP_5^{jMS} \cdot SP_5^{jM} \cdot SP_4^{jTOP} \cdot PO_j \cdot QI_j \quad \text{(A.2.26)}$$

$$PKD_jKD_j = SP_1^{jTOP} \cdot PO_j \cdot QI_j. \quad \text{(A.2.27)}$$

$$PLD_jLD_j = SP_2^{jTOP} \cdot PO_j \cdot QI_j. \quad \text{(A.2.28)}$$

For j = oil mining; the fixed capital option:

$$KD_4 = \overline{KD}_4 \quad \text{(oil sector)} \quad \text{(A.2.29)}$$

PKD_4 independent endogenous variable

The mobile capital option:

$$PKD_4 = \psi_4^K PKD. \tag{A.2.30}$$

A.3 Capital and Investment

The Owner of Private Aggregate Capital

$$\text{Max}\sum_{t=u}^{\infty}\frac{(1-tk)(PKD_t\psi^K K_{t-1} - tpPK_{t-1}) - (1-t^{ITC})PII_t I_t^a}{\prod_{s=u}^{t} 1+r_s} \tag{A.3.1}$$

subject to

$$K_t = (1-\delta)K_{t-1} + \psi^I \varepsilon^I I_t^a \tag{A.3.2}$$

ε_t^I investment productivity shock

Hamiltonian

$$\frac{(1-tk)(PKD_t\psi^K K_{t-1} - tpPK_{t-1}\text{K}_{t-1}) - (1-t^{ITC})PII_t I_t^a}{\prod_{s=u}^{t} 1+r_s} + \frac{\lambda_t}{\prod_{s=u}^{t} 1+r_s}\left((1-\delta)K_{t-1} + \psi^I \varepsilon^I I_t^a - K_t\right) \tag{A.3.3}$$

Euler Equation

$$(1+r_t)\frac{PII_{t-1}}{\psi_{t-1}^I \varepsilon_{t-1}^I} = \frac{1-tk}{1-t^{ITC}}(PKD_t\psi_t^K - tpPK_{t-1}) + (1-\delta)\frac{PII_t}{\psi_t^I \varepsilon_t^I}. \tag{A.3.4}$$

Aggregation Relationships

$$PK_t = \psi_t^{PK} PII_t(1-t^{ITC}). \tag{A.3.5}$$

$$KD_t = \psi_t^K K_{t-1}. \tag{A.3.6}$$

In the projection period,

$$\psi_t^K = \psi_{t-1}^K + \Delta\psi_t^K. \tag{A.3.7}$$

$$\Delta\psi_t^K = \alpha_0^{\psi K} + \alpha_1^{\psi K}\Delta\psi_{t-1}^K + \alpha_2^{\psi K}\Delta\psi_{t-2}^K + v_t^{\psi K} \tag{A.3.8a}$$

$$\Delta\psi_t^I = \alpha_0^{\psi I} + \alpha_1^{\psi I}\Delta\psi_{t-1}^I + \alpha_2^{\psi I}\Delta\psi_{t-2}^I + v_t^{\psi I} \tag{A.3.8b}$$

$$\Delta\psi_t^{PK} = \alpha_0^{PK} + \alpha_1^{PK}\Delta\psi_{t-1}^{PK} + \alpha_2^{PK}\Delta\psi_{t-2}^{PK} + v_t^{PK}. \tag{A.3.8c}$$

$$VII = PII.I^a. \tag{A.3.9}$$

Standard Version with No Corporate-Noncorporate Distinction

$$PK^{gain} = \left(\frac{PK_t - PK_{t-1}}{PK_{t-1}} - \delta\right). \tag{A.3.10}$$

$$VK^{gain} = \left(\frac{PK_t - PK_{t-1}}{PK_{t-1}} - \delta\right)PK_{t-1}K_{t-1}. \tag{A.3.11}$$

$$Y^I = r(BG + BF). \tag{A.3.12}$$

$$YK^{gov} = (1 - tk)PKD_{35}KD_{35}. \tag{A.3.13}$$

$$YK = \sum_{j=1}^{36} PKD_j KD_j - R\_K^{hh}. \tag{A.3.14}$$

$$YK^{net} = DIV - YK^{gov} + Y^I + (1 - tk)(GINT^{adj} + Y^{ROW,adj}). \tag{A.3.15}$$

Option exogenous interest, this simplifies to

$$YK^{net} = DIV - YK^{gov} + (1 - tk)\left(\overline{GINT}^{hh} + \overline{GINT}^{ss} - R\_SS + \bar{Y}^{row}\right). \tag{A.3.15a}$$

Option endogenous interest, this simplifies to

$$YK^{net} = DIV - YK^{gov} + Y^I - (1 - tk)R\_SS. \tag{A.3.15b}$$

$$DIV = (1 - tk)[YK - tpPK_{t-1}K_{t-1}]. \tag{A.3.16}$$

$$\alpha^{div} = DIV / PK_{t-1}K_{t-1}. \tag{A.3.16b}$$

$GINT^{adj}$ given in (A.4.35) and (A.4.37)
$Y^{ROW,adj}$ given in (A.5.26)

$$r_t = \alpha^{div} + PK^{gain} \tag{A.3.17}$$

equivalent to

$$r_t PK_{t-1}K_{t-1} = (1 - tk)[YK - tpPK_{t-1}K_{t-1}] + (PK_t - PK_{t-1})K_{t-1} - \delta PK_{t-1}K_{t-1}.$$

Programming note: In the IGEM code, kap_income_net = $YK^{net} - twW_{t-1}$.

In section 6 we have the rental cost for industry j:

$$PKD_j = \psi_j^K PKD \quad j \in I_{BUY} \tag{A.6.8a}$$

Household capital equation for special treatment of mortgage deductions, etc.:

$PKD_{j=36} = (1+tk_t^{hh})\psi_{36}^{K} PKD \quad j = 36$ denotes household sector.

$PKD_{hh}^{net} = PKD_{36} / (1+tk^{hh}).$

$R\_K^{hh} = PKD_{hh}^{net} KD_{36} tk^{hh}.$

NESTED STRUCTURE OF INVESTMENT

$I^a = I^a\ (I^{\text{fixed}}, I^{\text{inventory}}).$	Aggregate investment
$I^{\text{fixed}} = I^{FX}\ (I^{\text{long}}, I^{\text{short}}).$	Fixed investment aggregate
$I^{\text{inventory}} = I^{IY}.$	Change in business inventories
$I^{\text{long}} = I^{LG}\ (I_6, I_{33}).$	Long-lived investment aggregate
$I^{\text{short}} = I^{SH}\ (I^{\text{vehicles}}, I^{\text{machinery}}, I^{\text{services}}).$	Short-lived investment aggregate
$I^{\text{vehicles}} = I^{VE}\ (I_{24}, I_{25}).$	Vehicle aggregate
$I^{\text{machinery}} = I^{MC}\ (I_{22}, I_{23}, I^{\text{other}-m}).$	Machinery aggregate
$I^{\text{services}} = I^{SV}\ (I_{32}, I^{\text{other}-s}).$	Service aggregate
$I^{\text{other}-m} = I^{MO}\ (I^{\text{gadgets}}, I^{\text{wood}}, I^{\text{nonmetal}}, I^{\text{misc}}).$	Other Machinery aggregate
$I^{\text{other}-s} = I^{SO}\ (I_{34}, I^{\text{movers}}).$	Other Services aggregate
$I^{\text{gadgets}} = I^{GD}\ (I_{20}, I_{21}, I_{26},).$	Metals and Instruments aggregate
$I^{\text{wood}} = I^{WD}\ (I_{11}, I_{12},).$	Wood Products aggregate
$I^{\text{nonmetal}} = I^{MN}\ (I_{15}, I_{17}, I_{29}, I_{27}).$	Nonmetallic products aggregate
$I^{\text{misc}} = I^{OO}\ (I^{\text{textile}}, I_{13}, I^{\text{mining}}).$	Miscellaneous aggregate
$I^{\text{mover}} = I^{TC}\ (I_{28}, I^{29}).$	Transportation and Communicating aggregate
$I^{\text{textile}} = I^{TX}\ (I_9, I_{10}, I_{18}, I_{NCI}).$	Textile aggregate
$I^{\text{mining}} = I^{MG}\ (I_2, I_4).$	Minerals aggregate

At top tier of investment functions $I = I(\ldots)$:

$$VII = VII^{\text{fixed}} + VII^{\text{invy}}. \tag{A.3.18}$$

$$\frac{VII^{\text{invy}}}{VII} = \alpha^{IY}. \tag{A.3.19}$$

$$VII_{\text{i}}^{\text{invy}} = \alpha_i^{IY} VII^{\text{invy}} \quad i \in I_{\text{COM}}. \tag{A.3.20}$$

Price dual of fixed investment demand tiers $I^m = I^m(\ldots)$:

$$\ln PII^m = \alpha^{Im} \ln P^{Im} + \frac{1}{2} \ln P^{Im\prime} B^{Im} \ln P^{Im} + \ln P^{Im\prime} f_t^{Im} + \log \lambda^I \quad \mathrm{m} \in \mathrm{I_{INV}}. \tag{A.3.21}$$

$$f_t^{Im} = F^{Im} f_{t-1}^{Im} + v_t^{Im}. \tag{A.3.22}$$

$$\ln P^{Im} \equiv (\ln PII_{m1}, \ldots, \ln PII_{mi}, \ldots, \ln PII_{m,im}) \quad i \in I_{INVm}.$$

$$SI^{\mathrm{m}} = \begin{bmatrix} PII_{m1} I_{m1}^f / PII^m I^m \\ \ldots \\ PII_{m,im} I_{m,im}^f / PII^m I^m \end{bmatrix} = \alpha^{Im} + B^{Im} \ln PII^{Im} + f_t^{Im} \quad \begin{matrix} \mathrm{m} \in \mathrm{I_{INV}} \\ \mathrm{mi} \in \mathrm{I_{INVm}} \end{matrix}. \tag{A.3.23}$$

$$PII_{mi} \in \{PS_1, \ldots, PS_{35}, PII^{\mathrm{fixed}}, \ldots, PII^{\mathrm{mining}}\}.$$

$$I_{mi} \in \{I_1^f, \ldots, I_{35}^f, I^{\mathrm{fixed}}, \ldots, I^{\mathrm{mining}}\}.$$

Share demands under Cobb-Douglas option:

$$SI = \begin{bmatrix} PS_1 I_1^f / VII \\ \ldots \\ PS_{NINP} I_{NINP}^f / VII \end{bmatrix} = \alpha^{CD,Im}. \tag{A.3.23b}$$

Values of Individual Commodities Making Up Aggregate Investment Demand

$$VI_i = VI_i^{fixed} + VI_i^{inventory}:$$

$$\begin{aligned} VI_1 &= 0 + VI_1^{\mathrm{invy}} \\ VI_2 &= SI_1^{MG} \cdot SI_3^{OO} \cdot SI_4^{MO} \cdot SI_3^{MC} \cdot SI_2^{SH} \cdot SI_2^{FX} VII^{\mathrm{fixed}} + VI_2^{\mathrm{invy}} \\ &\ldots\ldots\ldots\ldots\ldots\ldots \\ VI_{34} &= SI_1^{SO} \cdot SI_2^{SV} \cdot SI_3^{SH} \cdot SI_2^{FX} VII^{\mathrm{fixed}} + VI_{343}^{\mathrm{invy}} \\ VI_{35} &= 0 \end{aligned} \tag{A.3.24}$$

$$I_i = VI_i / PS_i. \tag{A.3.25}$$

Vectors used in A.6.2:

$VI \equiv (PS_1 I_1, \ldots, PS_{35} I_{35}, PNCI_I NCI_I)'$.

$I^P \equiv (I_1, \ldots, I_{35})'$.

$I \equiv (I_1, \ldots, I_{35}, NCI_1)'$.

Disaggregated Capital Version

$$YK_t = \sum_{j-1}^{34} PKD_j KD_j + PKD_h KD_h + \left(i_t BF_{t-1} + Y_t^{row,adj} + i_t BG_{t-1} + GINT_t^{adj}\right) \tag{A.3.26}$$

cash_flow, CF_j is (A.3.64); BH is (A.3.67).

$$YK_t^{net} = \sum_{j-1}^{34} CF_j + PKD_h KD_h - t_h^e BH - t_h^p PII_t K_{ht-1} + (1-t_n^e)\left(i_t BF_{t-1} + Y_t^{row,adj} + i_t BG_{t-1} + GINT_t^{adj}\right) \tag{A.3.27}$$

Capital Services

$$KD = KD_1 + \cdots + KD_{35} + KD_h. \tag{A.3.28}$$

$$KD_j = KD^j(KD_{jc}, KD_{jn}) \quad \text{corporate} + \text{noncorporate} \quad j \in I_{IND}. \tag{A.3.29}$$

$$KD_{jc} = KD(KD_{jcs}, KD_{jcl}) \quad \text{short-lived} + \text{long-lived} \quad c \in I_{LEGAL}. \tag{A.3.30}$$

$$VKD_{jcst} = PKD_{jcst} KD_{jcst} \quad s \in I_{ASSET}. \tag{A.3.31}$$

Total Industry Capital

$$\ln PKD_j = \alpha_{KD0}^j + \alpha_{KD}^j \ln P + \frac{1}{2} \ln P' B_{KD}^j \ln P, \quad \ln P = (\ln PKD_{jc}, \ln PKD_{jn})' \tag{A.3.32}$$

$$\begin{bmatrix} PKD_{jc} KD_{jc} / VKD_j \\ PKD_{jn} KD_{jn} / VKD_j \end{bmatrix} = \alpha_{KD}^j + B \ln P, \tag{A.3.33}$$

Corporate Capital

$$\ln PKD_{jc} = \alpha_{KD0}^c + \alpha_{KD}^{jc\prime} \ln P + \frac{1}{2} \ln P' B_{KD}^{jc} \ln P, \quad \ln P = (\ln PKD_{jcs}, \ln PKD_{jnl})' \tag{A.3.34}$$

$$\begin{bmatrix} PKD_{jcs} KD_{jcs} / VKD_j \\ PKD_{jcl} KD_{jcl} / VKD_j \end{bmatrix} = \alpha_{KD}^{jc} + B_{KD}^{jc} \ln P, \tag{A.3.35}$$

$$PKD_{jcst} = \left\{ \frac{1 - t_{cs}^{ITC} - t_c z_{cs}}{1 - t_c} [r_{jc} + (1+\pi)\delta_{cs}] + \gamma_c^p t_c^p \right\} PK_{t-1} \quad s \in I_{ASSET}, \tag{A.3.36}$$

$$\text{where} \quad r_{csj}^{net} = r_{jc} + (1+\pi)\delta_{cs}. \tag{A.3.37}$$

Note: We do not index *PK* by PK_{jcs} or PK_{jns} but have a common price of capital goods for all buyers. Similarly, π is common to all equations.

$$r_{jc} = (1-\beta_{jc})r_{ce}^{equ} + \beta_{jc}\{[1-(1-\gamma_c^i)t_c]i_t - \pi\}, \tag{A.3.38}$$

$$\text{where} \quad r_c^{equ} = \frac{\rho^e - \pi\left[1-\left(1-\gamma_c^g\right)t_c^g\right]}{1-t_c^{earn}}\left(1-\alpha^{DIV}\gamma_c^d t_c\right), \tag{A.3.38b}$$

$$\text{where} \quad t_c^{earn} = \alpha^{DIV} t_c^e + (1-\alpha^{DIV})t_c^g. \tag{A.3.38c}$$

Noncorporate Capital

$$\begin{aligned} \ln PKD_{jn} &= \alpha_{KD0}^{jn} + \alpha_{KD}^{jn} \ln P + \frac{1}{2}\ln P' B_{KD}^{jn} \ln P \\ \ln P &= (\ln PKD_{jns}, \ln PKD_{jnl})' \end{aligned} \tag{A.3.39}$$

$$PKD_{jns} = \left\{\frac{1-t_{ns}^{ITC} - t_n^e z_{ns}}{1-t_n^e}[r_{jn} + (1+\pi)\delta_{ns}] + \gamma_n t_n^p\right\} PK_{t-1} \quad s = s, l \tag{A.3.40}$$

$$\text{where} \quad r_{nsj}^{net} = r_{jn} + (1+\pi)\delta_{ns}. \tag{A.3.40b}$$

$$\begin{bmatrix} PKD_{ns}KD_{ns} / VND_j \\ PKD_{nl}KD_{nl} / VND_j \end{bmatrix} = \alpha_{KD}^{jn} + B_{KD}^{jn} \ln P, \tag{A.3.41}$$

$$r_{jn} = \left(1-\beta_{jn}\right)\left(r_n^{equ}\right) + \beta_{jn}\left(1-\left(1-\gamma_n^i\right)t_n^e\right)i_t - \pi \tag{A.3.42}$$

$$r_n^{equ} = \rho^e - \pi\left[1-\left(1-\gamma_n^g\right)t_n^g\right] \tag{A.3.43}$$

Household Capital

$$PKD_{hs} = [r_h + (1+\pi)\delta_{hs} + (1-\gamma_h^p)t_{hs}^p]PK_{t-1} \quad s = s, l, \tag{A.3.44}$$

$$\text{where} \quad r_{hs}^{net} = r_h + (1+\pi)\delta_{hs}. \tag{A.3.45}$$

$$\begin{aligned} \ln PKD_h &= \alpha_{KD0}^h + \alpha_{KD}^h \ln P + \frac{1}{2}\ln P' B_{KD}^h \ln P, \\ \ln P &= (\ln PKD_{hs}, \ln PKD_{hl})' \end{aligned} \tag{A.3.46}$$

$$\begin{bmatrix} PKD_{hs}KD_{hs} / VHD \\ PKD_{hl}KD_{hl} / VHD \end{bmatrix} = \alpha_{KD}^h + B_{KD}^h \ln P, \tag{A.3.47}$$

$$r_h = (1-\beta_h)r_h^{equ} + \beta_h[1-(1-\gamma_h^i)t_h^e(1-dhi)]i_t - \pi, \tag{A.3.48}$$

$$\text{where} \quad r_h^{equ} = \rho^e - \pi\left[1-\left(1-\gamma_n^g\right)t_h^g\right]. \tag{A.3.49}$$

$$t_c = t_c^f(1-t_c^s)+t_c^s. \tag{A.3.50}$$

Replacement cost

$$VK_j^{rep} = \sum_{cs}(1-t_{cs}^{ITC}-t_c z_{cs})PK_{t-1}K_{jcst-1}. \tag{A.3.51}$$

Value of Depreciation Deductions and Property Tax

$$D_{jc} = \sum_{s,I} z_{cs}(r_c+(1+\pi)\delta_{cs})(1-t_{cs}^{ITC}-t_c z_{cs})PK_{t-1}K_{jcst-1}. \tag{A3.52}$$

$$D_{jn} = \sum_{s,I} z_{ns}(r_n+(1+\pi)\delta_{ns})(1-t_{ns}^{ITC}-t_n z_{ns})PK_{t-1}K_{jnst-1}. \tag{A.3.53}$$

$$R_{jc}^p = t_c^p(1-t_{cs}^{ITC}-t_c z_{cs})PK_{t-1}K_{jcst-1} \quad c=c,n \quad j=1\in I_{IND}. \tag{A.3.54}$$

Interest Cost

$$IC_{cj} = \beta_{jc}\sum_{s,I}(1-t_{cs}^{ITC}-t_c z_{cs})PK_{t-1}K_{jcst-1}\mathrm{i}_t \quad c=c,n \quad j=1\in I_{IND}. \tag{A.3.55}$$

Corporate Income Tax Base; Corporate Tax Revenue

$$BQ_j = PKD_{jc}KD_{jc}-D_{jc}-IC_{jc}-R_{jc}^p. \tag{A.3.56}$$

$$R_{jc}^f = t_c^f(1-t_c^s)BQ_j. \tag{A.3.57}$$

$$R_{jc}^s = t_c^s BQ_j. \tag{A.3.58}$$

Noncorporate Income Tax Base

$$BN_j = PKD_{jn}KD_{jn}-D_{jn}-IC_{nj}-R_{jn}^p. \tag{A.3.59}$$

Individual Capital Income Tax Base

$$B_j^{IDV} = BQ_j - t_c BQ_j + BN_j + IC_{jc} + IC_{jn}. \tag{A.3.60}$$

Individual Capital Income Tax Revenue from Industry* j*; Cash Flow

$$t_c^{earn} = \left[\alpha^{DIV}t_c^e + (1-\alpha^{DIV})t_c^g\right]. \tag{A.3.61}$$

$$R_j^{If} = \left[\alpha^{DIV}t_c^{ef}+(1-\alpha^{DIV})t_c^{gf}\right](BQ_j-R_{jc}^f)+t_n^{ef}BN_j+t_n^{ef}(IC_{jc}+IC_{jn}). \tag{A.3.62}$$

$$R_j^{Is} = \left[\alpha^{DIV}t_c^{es}+(1-\alpha^{DIV})t_c^{gs}\right](BQ_j-R_{jc}^s)+t_c^{es}BN_j+t_c^{es}(IC_{jc}+IC_{jn}). \tag{A.3.63}$$

$$
\begin{aligned}
CF_j &= B_j^{IDV} - R_j^{If} - R_j^{Is} + DC_j + DN_j \\
&= (1-t_c)(PKD_{jc}KD_{jc} - D_{jc} - IC_{jc} - R_{jc}^{p}) + IC_{jc} + D_{jc} \\
&\quad + PKD_{jn}KD_{jn} - R_{jn}^{p} - R_j^{If} - R_j^{Is}
\end{aligned}
\tag{A.3.64}
$$

Household Property Taxes

$$R_h^p = t_h^p PK_{t-1}(K_{hst-1} + K_{hlt-1}) \tag{A.3.65}$$

$$\text{debt}_h = \beta_h PK_{t-1}(K_{hst-1} + K_{hlt-1}) \tag{A.3.66}$$

$$BH = 0 - R_h^p - debt_h i_t \left(1 - \frac{PKD_{h,short}KD_{h,short}}{PKD_h KD_h}\right). \tag{A.3.67}$$

$$RKH^{eq} = \sum_j (R_j^{If} + R_j^{Is}). \tag{A.3.68}$$

$$RKH^{hh} = t_h^e BH. \tag{A.3.69}$$

$$RKH^{int} = t_n^e (GINT^p + Y^{row}). \tag{A.3.70}$$

$$RKH = RKH^{eq} + RKH^{hh} + RKH^{int}. \tag{A.3.71}$$

$$RP = \sum_j^{N_{IND}} R_{jc}^p + R_{jn}^p + R_h^p. \tag{A.3.72}$$

$$
\begin{aligned}
RK^f = &\sum_j^{N_{IND}} R_{jc}^f + R_j^{If} + BHt_h^{ef} \\
&+ \frac{tk^f}{1-tk}(rBG + rBF) + tk^f\left(GINT^p + Y^{row}\right) + \left(1 - tk^f\right)PKD_{35}KD_{35}
\end{aligned}
\tag{A.3.73}
$$

$$
\begin{aligned}
RK^s = &\sum_j^{N_{IND}} R_{jc}^s + R_j^{Is} + BHt_h^{es} \\
&+ \frac{tk^s}{1-tk}(rBG + rBF) + tk^s\left(GINT^p + Y^{row}\right) + \left(1 - tk^s\right)PKD_{35}KD_{35}
\end{aligned}
\tag{A.3.74}
$$

$$
\begin{aligned}
RW^f = tw^f \Bigg[&\sum_{j=1}^{NIND} \sum_{s,l} (1 - ITC_{cs} - t_c z_{cs}) PK_{t-1} K_{jcst-1} \\
&+ (1 - ITC_{ns} - t_n z_{ns}) PK_{t-1} K_{jnst-1} + BG_t + BF_t \Bigg] \quad f = f, s.
\end{aligned}
\tag{A.3.75}
$$

$$Y^I = \sum_j^{N_{IND}} IC_{jc} + IC_{jn} + debt_h i_t. \tag{A.3.76}$$

$$YK = \sum_j PKD_j KD_j. \tag{A.3.77}$$

$$YK^{gov} = PKD_{35}KD_{35} - R_{35}^p - R_{35c} - R_{35}^I. \tag{A.3.78}$$

$$YK^{bus} = YK - PKD_{35}KD_{35} - PKD_{36}KD_{36}. \tag{A.3.79}$$

$$DEP^{tot} = \sum_j D_{jc} + D_{jn}. \tag{A.3.80}$$

End of disaggregated capital version.

A.4 The Government and Pollution Externalities

Tax Rates

$$tc_i = tc + tc^g \quad i \in I_{\text{COM}} \tag{A.4.1}$$

$$tc_N = tc + tc^N \tag{A.4.2}$$

$$tc_K = tc + tc^K \tag{A.4.3}$$

$$tc_L = tc + tc^L \tag{A.4.4}$$

$$tx_i^v = \sum_{x=1} tx_x^{Xv} XP_{ix} \quad i \in I_{IND} \quad \text{x} \in I_{EXT} \tag{A.4.5}$$

$$tx_i^u = \sum_{x=1} tx_x^{Xu} XP_{ix} \tag{A.4.6}$$

$$tx_i^{rv} = \sum_{x=1} tx_x^{Xv} XM_{ix} \tag{A.4.7}$$

$$tx_i^{ru} = \sum_{x=1} tx_x^{Xu} XM_{ix} \tag{A.4.8}$$

$$tt_i^{\text{full}} = tt_i + tx_i^v + \frac{tu_i + tx_i^u}{PO_i} \tag{A.4.9}$$

$$tl^0 = \sum_j PLD_j LD_j \left(1 - \frac{tl^a}{tl^m}\right) \tag{A.4.10}$$

Stock-Flow Relations

$$BG_t = BG_{t-1} + \Delta G + GFI + \Delta P_t^{BGF} + BG^{disc}. \tag{A.4.11}$$

$$BG_t^* = BG_{t-1}^* - GFI - \Delta P_t^{BGF*}. \tag{A.4.12}$$

Revenues and Expenditures

$$\begin{aligned} R\_TOTAL = R\_SALES + R\_TARIFF + R\_P + R\_K + RK^{hh} + R\_L \\ + R\_W + R^N + R\_UNIT + R\_EXT + R\_ITC + VG_{GK} + YK^{gov} \\ + R\_CON - R\_CON^{reb} + R\_CON^{gov} + TLUMP \end{aligned} \tag{A.4.13}$$

Coding note: rev_total +YK^{gov} = R_TOTAL

$$R\_GROSS = R\_TOTAL + R\_SS \tag{A.4.14}$$

$$R\_SALES = \sum_j tt_j PO_j QI_j \tag{A.4.15}$$

$$R\_TARIFF = \sum_i tr_i PM_i M_i \tag{A.4.16}$$

$$R\_P = tpPK_{t-1}K_{t-1} \tag{A.4.17}$$

$$R\_K = tk(YK - R\_P) + \frac{tk}{1-tk} r(BG_{t-1} + BF_{t-1}) + tkGINT^{adj} + tkY^{ROW,adj} \tag{A.4.18}$$

$YK = \sum_{j=1}^{36} PKD_j KD_j - R\_K^{hh}$ was given in A.3.14

Option exogenous interest, this simplifies to

$$R\_K = tk(YK - R\_P) + tk(\overline{GINT}^{hh} + \overline{GINT}^{ss} - R\_SS) + tk\overline{Y}^{ROW} \tag{A.4.18a}$$

Option endogenous interest, this simplifies to

$$R\_K = tk(YK - R\_P) + \frac{tk}{1-tk} r(BG_{t-1} + BF_{t-1}) - tkR\_SS. \tag{A.4.18b}$$

$$RK^{hh} = \frac{tk^{hh}}{1-tk^{hh}} PKD_{36} KD_{36}. \tag{A.4.19}$$

$$R\_L = tl^a P^h LS / (1 - tl^m) = tl^a \sum_j PLD_j LD_j. \tag{A.4.20}$$

$$R\_W = tw(PK.K + BG + BF). \tag{A.4.21}$$

$$R\_UNIT = \sum_j tu_j QI_j. \tag{A.4.22}$$

$$R\_EXT = \sum_j tx_j^v PI_j QI_j + \sum_i tx_i^{rv} PM_i M_i + \sum_j tx_j^u QI_j + \sum_i tx_i^{ru} M_i. \tag{A.4.23}$$

$$R\_ITC = -t^{ITC} PII_t I_t^a. \tag{A.4.24}$$

$$R\_CON^{marg} = \sum_{I_{COM}} tc_i PS_i C_i + RCON^{hk}. \tag{A.4.25}$$

$$R\_CON^{hk} = (tc + tc^K) \frac{\psi_{36}^K KD_{36}}{KD} PII_t I_t^a. \tag{A.4.26}$$

$$R\_CON^{reb} = tcVCC^{exempt}. \tag{A.4.27}$$

$$R\_CON^{gov} = \frac{tc^G}{1+tc^G} VGG. \tag{A.4.28}$$

$$R\_CON^{net} = R\_CON^{marg} - R\_CON^{reb}. \tag{A.4.29}$$

VG_{GK} given in (A.4.39c), YK^{gov} given in (A.3.13)

The following revenue and expenditure variables may be set exogenously.

R^N	nontax receipts
GFI	government foreign net investment
$GINT^{row}$	government net interest payments to foreigners
G^{tran}	government transfer payments to households (excluding social insurance)
$G^{tran,row}$	government transfer payments to foreigners
$\overline{GINT}^{hh}$	government interest payments to private bond holders
$GINT^{ss}$	investment income of social insurance funds
R_SS	transfers to government from social insurance funds for administration expenses
ΔG	government deficit

or, as shares of GDP:

$$\begin{aligned} R^N &= \alpha^{nontax} GDP. \\ G^{tran} &= \alpha^{GTRAN} GDP. \\ G^{tran.row} &= \alpha^{GTR\_R} GDP. \\ R\_SS &= \alpha^{R\_SS} GDP. \end{aligned} \tag{A.4.30}$$

$$EXP^{gengov} = VGG + G^{tran} + G^{tran,row} + G^{Ktran} + G^{Ktran,row} + GINT^{hh} + GINT^{row}. \tag{A.4.31}$$

$$EXPEND = EXP^{gengov} + GINT^{ss}. \tag{A.4.31b}$$

$$G\_SS = GINT^{ss} - R\_SS. \tag{A.4.32}$$

$$\Delta G = EXPEND - R\_TOTAL. \tag{A.4.33}$$

$$GINT = GINT^{hh} + GINT^{ss} = \frac{r}{1-tk} BG. \tag{A.4.34}$$

Option "exogenous interest payments":

$$GINT^{adj} = \overline{GINT}^{hh} + \overline{GINT}^{ss} - R\_SS - \frac{r}{1-tk} BG_{t-1}. \tag{A.4.35}$$

$$VGG = \Delta G + R\_TOTAL - GINT - GINT^{adj} - GINT^{row} - G^{TRAN} - G^{tran.row} - G^{Ktran} - G^{Ktran,row}$$
$$= \Delta G + R\_TOTAL + R\_SS - \overline{GINT}^{hh} - \overline{GINT}^{ss} - GINT^{row} - G^{TRAN} - G^{tran.row} - G^{Ktran} - G^{Ktran,row} \quad \text{(A.4.36)}$$

Option "endogenous interest payments":

$$GINT^{adj} = -R\_SS. \quad \text{(A.4.37)}$$

$$VGG = \Delta G + R\_TOTAL + R\_SS - GINT - GINT^{row} - G^{TRAN} - G^{tran.row} - G^{Ktran} - G^{Ktran,row}. \quad \text{(A.4.38)}$$

$$VG_i = \alpha_i^G VGG \quad i \in I_{INP} \quad \text{(A.4.39)}$$

$$PLD_{Gt} LD_{Gt} = \alpha_L^G VGG_t \quad \text{(A.4.39b)}$$

$$VG_K = 0 \qquad \text{(private capital)}$$
$$VG_{GK} = \alpha_{GK}^G VGG \quad \text{(government capital)} \quad \text{(A.4.39c)}$$

$$G_i = VG_i / PS_i$$
$$KD_{Gt} = 0 \quad \text{(A.4.40)}$$

Vectors for use in A.6.2 below:

$$VG \equiv (PS_1 G_1, \ldots, PS_{35} G_{35})'$$
$$G^P \equiv (G_1, \ldots, G_{35})' \quad \text{(A.4.41)}$$
$$G \equiv (G_1, \ldots, G_{35}, NCI_G, KD_G, LD_G)'$$

$$PGG = \prod_i PS_i^{\alpha_i^G} \quad \text{(A.4.42)}$$

$$GG = VGG / PGG \quad \text{(A.4.43)}$$

Government closure options:

$$VGG_t = \begin{cases} R\_TOTAL + \Delta G + \ldots & \text{'resid'} \\ \gamma_t^{VGG} GDP_t & \text{'propr'} \end{cases} \quad \text{(A.4.44)}$$

$$g^{GDP} = \frac{VGG}{GDP} \quad \text{(A.4.45)}$$

Externalities

$$E_x = \sum_j XP_{jx} QI_j + \sum_j XM_{ix} M_i \quad x \in I_{EXT} \quad \text{(A.4.46)}$$

$$\sigma_t^{GHC} = \frac{E_{GHG,t}}{Y_t^{GDP}} \tag{A.4.47}$$

A.5 The Rest of the World

Noncompetitive Imports

$$PNCI_j = e(1+tr_j^n)PNCI_j^* \quad j=1,\dots,35,C,I,G \tag{A.5.1}$$

$$PNCI_i^{land} = ePNCI_j^* \tag{A.5.2}$$

Competitive imports and domestic output making up total supply:

$$QS_i = QS(QC_i, M_i) \quad i \in I_{COM} \tag{A.5.3}$$

$$\begin{aligned} \ln PS_{it} &= \alpha_{ct}\ln PC_{it} + \alpha_{mt}\ln PM_{it} + \frac{1}{2}(\beta_{cc}\ln^2 PC_{it} + 2\beta_{cm}\ln PC_{it}\ln PM_{it} \\ &\quad + \beta_{mm}\ln^2 PM_{it}) + f_{ct}^M \ln PC_{it} + f_{mt}^M \ln PM_{it} \\ &\equiv a^M \ln P^{M_i} + \ln P^{M_i\prime} B^{M_i} \ln P^{M_i} + \ln P^{M_i\prime} f_t^M \end{aligned} \tag{A.5.4}$$

$$\begin{aligned} &\ln P^{M_i} \equiv (\ln PC_i, \ln PM_i)' \\ &PM_i = e(1+tr_i+tx_i^{rv})PM_i^* + tx_i^{ru} \quad i \in I_{COM} \end{aligned} \tag{A.5.5}$$

$$PM_i^{land} = ePM_i^* \tag{A.5.6}$$

$$SD^i \equiv \begin{bmatrix} PC_iQC_i / PS_iQS_i \\ PM_iM_i / PS_iQS_i \end{bmatrix} = \alpha^{M_i} + B^{M_i}\ln P^{M_i} + f_t^{Mi} \tag{A.5.7}$$

Cobb-Douglas option:

$$SD^i \equiv \begin{bmatrix} PC_iQC_i / PS_iQS_i \\ PM_iM_i / PS_iQS_i \end{bmatrix} = \alpha^{CD,M_i} \tag{A.5.7b}$$

$$PS_iQS_i = PC_iQC_i + PM_iM_i \quad i \in I_{COM} \tag{A.5.8}$$

Vectors for use in A.6.5:

$$\begin{aligned} VQS &\equiv (PS_1QS_1,\dots,PS_{35}QS_{35})'. \\ VM &\equiv (PM_1M_1,\dots,PM_{35}M_{35})'. \\ SM &\equiv (SD_2^1, SD_2^2,\dots,SD_2^{35})'. \\ M &\equiv (M_1, M_2,\dots,M_{35})'. \end{aligned} \tag{A.5.9}$$

$$PS_i^C = (1+tc_i)PS_i \quad i \in I_{COM} \tag{A.5.10}$$

$$PS_N^C = (1 + tc_N)PNCI_C$$
$$PS_K^C = (1 + tc_K)PKD_C \qquad (A.5.11)$$
$$PS_L^C = (1 + tc_L)PLD_C$$

$$\Delta \ln PM_{it}^* = \Delta f_{it}^p \quad t > 2005; \quad PM_{it}^* = \text{data for } t = ..,2004,2005. \qquad (A.5.12)$$

Exports

$$SX^i \equiv \frac{PC_i X_i}{PC_i QS_i} = \alpha^{X_i} + B^{X_i} \ln P^{X_i} + f_t^{Xi}$$
$$\ln P^{X_i} \equiv (\ln e_t PM_{it}^*, \ln PC_{it})' \qquad (A.5.13)$$

Vectors used in A.6.2:

$$X \equiv (X_1, \dots, X_{35})'.$$
$$VX \equiv (PC_1 X_1, \dots, PC_{35} X_{35})'. \qquad (A.5.14)$$

Current Account and Net Foreign Assets

$$V^{IMP} = \sum_i ePM_i^* M_i. \qquad (A.5.15)$$

$$V^{NCI} = \sum_j ePNCI_j^* NCI_j. \qquad (A.5.16)$$

$$V^{EX} = \sum_i PC_i X_i. \qquad (A.5.17)$$

$$TB = V^{EX} - V^{IMP} - V^{NCI}. \qquad (A.5.18)$$

$$TB^* = TB / e. \qquad (A.5.19)$$

$$CA = TB + \overline{Y}^{row} - GINT^{row} - G^{tran,row} - G^{Ktran,row} - H^{row} \qquad (A.5.20)$$

$$= TB + \frac{r}{1 - tk} BF + Y^{row,adj} - GINT^{row} - G^{tran,row} - G^{Ktran,row} - H^{row}.$$
(A.5.20b)

$$CA^* = CA / e. \qquad (A.5.21)$$

$$Y^{ROW,adj} = \overline{Y}^{ROW} - \frac{r}{1 - tk} BF. \qquad (A.5.22)$$

Stock-flow relation:

$$BF_t = BF_{t-1} + CA_t - GFI + BF^{disc} + \Delta P^{BF}. \qquad (A.5.23)$$

CA current account surplus of the United States

Y^{row} net private factor income from the rest of world

A.6 Markets, Numeraire, and National Accounting

Final Demands

$$VFD_i = PS_i(C_i^P + I_i^P + G_i^P) + PC_iX_i \quad i \in I_{COM}. \tag{A.6.1}$$

$$\begin{aligned} VFD &\equiv (VFD_1, \ldots, VFD_{35})' \\ &= VC + VI + VG + VX. \end{aligned} \tag{A.6.2}$$

Supply Equal Demand for Commodities

$$\begin{aligned} PS_iQS_i &= \sum_{j=1}^{35} PS_iQP_i^j + VFD_i \\ &= \sum_{j=1}^{35} A_{ij}VQI_j + VFD_i \end{aligned} \quad i \in I_{COM} \tag{A.6.3}$$

$$VQS = \mathbf{A}\, VQI + VFD. \tag{A.6.4}$$

$$VQC = \text{Diag}(SM)VQS. \quad VQS = \text{Diag}(1/SM)VQC. \tag{A.6.5}$$

$$\begin{aligned} &\text{Diag}(1/SM)VQC - \mathbf{A}\, VQI = VFD. \\ &\text{Diag}(1/SM)\mathbf{M}'\text{Diag}(\iota + tt^{\text{full}})VQI - \mathbf{A}\, VQI = VFD. \\ &[\text{Diag}(1/SM)\mathbf{M}'\text{Diag}(\iota + tt^{\text{full}}) - \mathbf{A}]VQI = VFD. \end{aligned} \tag{A.6.6}$$

Saving-Investment Balance

$$\begin{aligned} VII &= S - \left(BG_t - BG_{t-1} - \Delta P_t^{BGF} - BG^{disc}\right) - \left(BF_t - BF_{t-1} - BF^{disc} - \Delta P^{BF}\right) \\ &= S - (\Delta G + GFI) - (CA - GFI) \\ &= S - \Delta G - CA \end{aligned} \tag{A.6.7}$$

Demand Equal Supply of Private Capital

Option "free oil mining capital":

$$PKD_j = \psi_j^K PKD \quad j \in I_{BUY}. \tag{A.6.8a}$$

Option "fixed oil mining capital":

$$\begin{aligned} &PKD_j = \psi_j^K PKD \quad j \in I_{BUY\setminus 4}. \\ &KD_{j=4} = \overline{KD}^{oil}; \quad \text{endogenous } PKD_{j=oil}. \end{aligned} \tag{A.6.8b}$$

$$\sum_{j=1}^{C} PKD_j KD_j = PKD.KD. \tag{A.6.9}$$

$$\sum_{j=1}^{C} \psi_j^K KD_j = KD = \psi^K K_{t-1}. \tag{A.6.10}$$

Demand Equal Supply of Government Capital

$$VG_{GK} = P^{KG} K_{t-1}^G. \tag{A.6.10b}$$

Demand Equal Supply of Labor

$$PLD_j = \psi_j^L \frac{P^h}{(1-tl^m)} \quad j \in I_{\text{BUY}}. \tag{A.6.11}$$

$$PN^R = \psi_C^R P^h. \tag{A.6.12}$$

$$YL^{gross} = VLD = \sum PLD_j LD_j. \tag{A.6.13}$$

$$(1-tl^m)YL^{gross} = P^h LS = P^h(\overline{L}^{ua} - \psi_C^r N^R). \tag{A.6.14}$$

$$\sum_{j=1}^{G} \psi_j^L LD_j = LS. \tag{A.6.15}$$

Business Cycle Adjustment for Large Changes in Unemployment

$$\overline{L}^{ua} = (1-u)\overline{L}. \tag{A.6.16}$$

Disaggregated Capital Version: Arbitrage Between Different Assets

$$i = \rho^{eq} - \pi^{eq} \tag{A.6.17}$$

$$\rho^e = \overline{r}_0 PKD + \pi \tag{A.6.18}$$

$$\pi^{eq} = i(BAA) - \rho^e \tag{A.6.19}$$

$\overline{r}_0$ from model simulation trials. (A.6.20)

National Accounting

$$GDP = VCC + VII + VGG + V^{EX} - V^{IMP} - V^{NCI}. \tag{A.6.21}$$

$$GNP = GDP + Y^{ROW} - GINT^{row} - G^{tran,row} - H^{row}. \tag{A.6.22}$$

$$CC^{div} = divisia(C_i; PS_i^C). \tag{A.6.23}$$

$$II^{div} = divisia(I_i;PS_i). \tag{A.6.24}$$

$$GG^{div} = divisia(G_i;PS_i). \tag{A.6.25}$$

$$X^{div} = divisia(X_i;PC_i). \tag{A.6.26}$$

$$M^{div} = divisia(M_i,NCI_j). \tag{A.6.27}$$

$$Y^{GDP} = divisia(CC^{div},II^{div},GG^{div},X^{div}) - M^{div}. \tag{A.6.28}$$

Formula for $Q = divisia(q_i;p_i)$:

$$\ln\frac{Q_t}{Q_{t-1}} = \sum_{i=1}^{n}\frac{1}{2}\left(\frac{p_{it}q_{it}}{V_t}+\frac{p_{i,t-1}q_{i,t-1}}{V_{t-1}}\right)\ln\frac{q_{it}}{q_{i,t-1}}; \quad V_t = \sum_{i=1}^{n}p_{it}q_{it}. \tag{A.6.29}$$

Numeraire

$$P_t^h = \overline{P}_t^h. \tag{A.6.30}$$

Walras Law Check

$$wal = [P^h\overline{L} - (1-tl^m)YL^{gross} - P^{leis}L^{leis}] / P^h\overline{L}. \tag{A.6.31}$$

Household Welfare and Social Welfare

$$\begin{aligned}\ln V_{dt} &= \alpha_p'\ln p_t + \frac{1}{2}\ln p_t' B_{pp}\ln p_t - D(p)\ln\frac{M_{dt}}{N_{dt}}.\\ &= \frac{D_t}{D_0}\ln V_{d0} + D_t\ln\left(\frac{D_0\gamma_t N_{dt}P_t}{\delta^t D_t N_{d0}P_0}\right).\end{aligned} \tag{A.6.32}$$

$$\begin{aligned}\ln N_{dt} &= \frac{1}{D(p_t)}\ln p_t B_A A_d.\\ \ln P_t &= \frac{\alpha_p'\ln p_t + \frac{1}{2}\ln p_t' B_{pp}\ln p_t}{D_t}.\end{aligned} \tag{A.6.33}$$

$$V_d = \sum_{t=0}^{\infty}\delta^t\ln V_{dt} \quad \delta = \frac{1}{1+\rho}. \tag{A.6.34}$$

$$\Omega_d = \sum_{t=0}^{\infty}\gamma_t M_{dt}(p_t,V_{dt},A_d) \quad \gamma_t = \prod_{s=0}^{t}\frac{1}{1+r_s}. \tag{A.6.35}$$

$$\ln\Omega_d(\{p_t\},\{\gamma_t\},V_d) = \frac{1}{S}\left[S\ln R + \sum_{t=0}^{\infty}\delta^t D_t\ln\left(\frac{D_0\gamma_t N_{dt}P_t}{\delta^t D_t P_0}\right) - V_d\right]. \tag{A.6.36}$$

$$\Delta W_d = \Omega_d(\{p_t^0\},\{\gamma_t^0\},V_d^1) - \Omega_d(\{p_t^0\},\{\gamma_t^0\},V_d^0). \tag{A.6.37}$$

A.7 Intertemporal Equilibrium and Steady State

The intertemporal equations for any $t - 1$ and $t < T$:

$$\left[\frac{F_t / N_t^{\text{eq}}}{F_{t-1} / N_{t-1}^{\text{eq}}}\right]^{1/\sigma} = \frac{1+r_t^{net}}{1+\rho}\frac{PF_{t-1}}{PF_t}. \tag{A.1.4}$$

$$(1+r_t)\frac{PII_{t-1}}{\psi_{t-1}^I \varepsilon_{t-1}^I} = \frac{1-tk}{1-t^{ITC}}(PKD_t\psi_t^K - tpPK_{t-1}) + (1-\delta)\frac{PII_t}{\psi_t^I \varepsilon_t^I}. \tag{A.3.4}$$

$$r_t^{net} = r_t - \rho_t^{risk}. \tag{A.7.1}$$

ρ_t^{risk} exogenous risk premium for calibration purposes

Steady State

T denotes the terminal period that approximates the steady state. The additional equations that hold at T (and do not hold at $t < T$):

$$\text{Prices}_T - \text{Prices}_{T-1} < tol. \tag{A.7.2}$$

$$\text{Quantities}_T - \text{Quantities}_{T-1} < tol. \tag{A.7.3}$$

$$\Delta G_T = 0. \tag{A.7.4}$$

$$CA_T = 0. \tag{A.7.5}$$

$$r_t = \rho. \tag{A.7.6}$$

$$\psi^I I_T^a = \delta K^T. \tag{A.7.7}$$

A.8 Glossary

A.8.1 Values

A		IO Use matrix; the use of commodities by each industry
A_j	$j \in I_{IND}$	Columns of A
A_{ij}	$j \in I_{COM}$ $\quad j \in I_{IND}$	Share of input i in producing output j
BB^{flat}		Business tax base (flat tax)

BF		Net U.S. private sector claims on rest-of-world
BF^{disc}		Stock-flow discrepancy in the U.S. external accounts
BG		Government debt to domestic households
BG^{disc}		Stock-flow discrepancy in the U.S. government accounts
BG^*		Government debt to rest-of-world
BN_j	$j \in I_{IND}$	Tax base of noncorporate portion of capital income
BQ_j	$j \in I_{IND}$	Tax base of corporate portion of capital income
CA		Current account surplus of the United States
CF_j	$j \in I_{IND}$	Cash flow of industry j (version 9)
D_{jc}	$j \in I_{IND} \quad c \in I_{LEGAL}$	Depreciation deductions
$debt_h$	`	Debt financed portion of household capital
DEP^{tot}		Value of total depreciation
DIV		"Dividends"; after-tax capital income
EXP^{gengov}		Total expenditures of general government
$EXPEND$		Total expenditures of government
G^{Ktran}		Capital transfers from government to households
$G^{Ktran,row}$		Capital transfers from government to rest-of-world
G^{tran}		Government transfers to households
$G^{tran,row}$		Government transfers to rest-of-world
$G^{tran,SS}$		Transfers from general government to Social Insurance Trust Fund

GDP		Value of gross domestic product
GFI		Government net foreign investment
$GINT$		Government interest payments on public debt to households (including social insurance funds)
$GINT^{adj}$		Arbitrage adjustment for interest income on government bonds
$GINT^{endog}$		Government interest payments in the endogenous option
$GINT^{hh}$		Government interest payments on public debt to households (excluding social insurance funds)
$GINT^{p}$		Government interest payments on all debt to residents (including social insurance funds)
$GINT^{row}$		Government interest payments to rest-of-world
$GINT^{ss}$		Government interest payments on public debt to social insurance funds
GNP		Value of gross national product
GM		Government net imports
G_SS		Net general government payments to Social Insurance Trust Funds
H^{row}		Household transfers to rest-of-world
IC_{jc}	$j \in I_{IND} \quad c \in I_{LEGAL}$	Interest cost of industry debt
$\mathbf{M}$		Input-output make matrix
M_k		Expenditures by household k
MF^X		Full expenditures (including leisure), CEX basis
MF^N		Full expenditures (including leisure), NIPA basis
R^f_{jc}	$j \in I_{IND}; f \in I_{GOV}$	Corporate income tax revenue from j; {federal, S&L}

R_j^{If}	$f \in I_{GOV}$	Individual capital income tax revenue from industry j
R_{jc}^p	$j \in I_{IND} \quad c \in I_{LEGAL}$	Property tax revenue from j; {corporate, noncorporate}
R_h^p		Property tax revenue from household
$R^{gengov,TOT}$		Total tax revenues of general government
R^N		Non-tax receipts of the government
RHK		Revenue from individual capital taxes; total
RK^{hh}		Revenue from household capital services tax
RKH^{eq}		Revenue from individual capital cap taxes on equity
RKH^{hh}		Revenue from individual capital taxes on HH capital
RKH^{int}		Revenue from individual capital taxes on HH claims on government and ROW
R_CON^{gov}		Revenue from consumption taxes on government spending
R_CON^{hk}		Revenue from consumption taxes on household capital
R_CON^{marg}		Notional revenue from consumption taxes (ignoring the exemption/rebate)
R_CON^{net}		Revenue from consumption taxes
R_CON^{reb}		Rebate for consumption taxes
R_EXT		Revenue from externality taxes
R_FLAT		Revenue from flat taxes
R_FLAT^{bus}		Revenue from business flat tax
R_FLAT^{hh}		Revenue from household flat tax
R_ITC		Negative revenue from investment tax credit

R_K		Capital tax revenue
R_K^{hh}		Revenue from taxes on household capital
R_P		Revenue from property taxes
R_SALES		Revenue from sales taxes
R_SS		Transfers from Social Insurance for administration expenses
R_TARIFF		Revenue from tariffs on imports
R_TOTAL		Total revenues of government
R_UNIT		Revenue from new taxes on unit of output
R_W		Revenue from taxes on wealth (estate tax)
S		Private savings
$TLUMP$		Lump sum tax
TB		Trade balance
TB^*		Trade balance in foreign prices
V^{EX}		Total value of exports
V^{IMP}		Total value of competitive imports
V^{NCI}		Total value of noncomparable imports
V^{QC}		Vector of values of domestic commodity output
V^{QI}		Vector of values (to producer) of domestic industry output
VC		Vector of values of household purchases of commodities
VCC		Value of aggregate consumption (PCE)
VCC^{exempt}		Consumption tax exemption base
VFD		Vector of values of final demand for commodities
VG_i (VG)	$i \in I_{NCOM}$	Value of government demand for commodity i (vector)
VG_{GK}		Value of government capital consumption

VGG		Government spending on goods and services
VI		Vector of values of investment inputs
VII		Value of domestic private investment
VII^{bus}		Value of business investment (flat tax)
VII^{invy}		Value of inventory investment
VII^{fixed}		Value of fixed private investment
VK^{gain}		Value of aggregate capital gains
VK_j^{rep}	$j \in I_{IND}$	Replacement cost of capital stock
VN		Vector of values of household purchases of NIPA commodities
VP^j	$j \in I_{IND}$	Vector of values of input into industry j
VT^{QI}		Vector of values of domestic industry output inclusive of sales tax
VQS		Vector of values of total commodity supply
VX		Vector of values of commodity exports
W		Tangible wealth of private sector (households)
wal		percentage error in Walras Law check
WF		Full wealth of private sector (households)
XR		Travel exports: Expenditures by foreign tourists in United States
Y		Private income
Y^I		Interest from debt portion of claims on all capital
Y^*		Exogenous projected rest-of-world income

Y^{row}		Net income from rest-of-world
$Y^{row,adj}$		Arbitrage adjustment for income from rest-of-world
YF		Full private income (including imputations on leisure)
YK		Gross private capital income
YK^{bus}		Capital income from private business (flat tax)
YK^{gov}		Capital income from government enterprises
YK^{net}		Private capital income after tax
YL		Labor income after tax
YL^{gross}		Value of labor income
ΔA_j^{TFP}	$j \in I_{IND}$	Total technical change in industry j
ΔG		Government deficit
ΔP^{BF}		Capital gains on net foreign assets
ΔP^{BG}		Capital gains on government bonds
ΔP^{BG*}		Capital gains on government liabilities to ROW
ΔSC_i	$i \in I_{CNODE=top}$	Difference in cons shares, CEX vs. NIPA basis

A.8.2 *Quantities*

A^{agg}		Productivity shift term that applies to all industries
A_j^{TFP}	$j \in I_{IND}$	Productivity in industry j due to both exogenous and induced components; and shocks
C^P		Vector of quantities of consumption of produced commodities
C		Vector of consumption, commodities and nonproduced goods
C_i	$i \in I_{INP}$	Consumption of IO commodity i

C_i^X	$i \in I_{CNODE=top}$	Consumption CEX basis, top node item i
CC		Aggregate real consumption (from simple Cobb-Douglas index)
CC^{div}		Divisia index of real consumption
EX_{it}^0	$i \in I_{NCOM}$	Exogenously projected portion of export function
EXT_x	$x \in I_{EXT}$	Quantity of externality of type x
F		Full consumption (commodities and leisure)
G^P		Vector of government purchases of commodities
G		Vector of government purchases, commodities, and nonproduced goods
G_i	$i \in I_{NCOM}$	Government purchases of commodity i
GG		Real government final purchases (from CD index)
GG^{div}		Divisia index of real government final purchases
I^a		Aggregate investment in domestic capital stock
I		Vector of commodities used in aggregate investment
I^m	$m \in I_{INV}$	Investment aggregate m
I_i^f	$i \in I_{NCOM}$	Investment of commodity i in fixed investment
I_i	$i \in I_{NCOM}$	Investment of commodity i in domestic capital stock
II^{div}		Divisia index of real aggregate investment
K		Aggregate private domestic capital stock
$K_{4(oil)}$		Capital stock in "oil and gas mining"
KD		Quantity of aggregate capital input normalized such that its rental price is one

KD_j	$j \in I_{NBUY}$	Quantity of capital input into sector j
KD_{jcs}	$j \in I_{NBUY}$ $c = \{c,n,h\}$ $s \in I_{ASSET}$	Quantity of capital input into sector j, {corporate, noncorporate}, {short asset, long asset}
$\bar{L}$		Time endowment of economy
$\bar{L}^{ua}$		Time endowment with unemployment adjustment
LD_j	$j \in I_{NBUY}$	Quantity of labor input into sector j
LS		Labor supply
M		Vector of competitive imports
M_i	$i \in I_{COM}$	Imports of (competitive) commodities
M^{div}		Divisia index of real imports (competitive and noncompetitive imports)
N^{eq}		Number of household equivalent members in economy
N^m	$m \in I_{CNODE}$	Consumption of NIPA aggregate m
N^R		Leisure quantity (NIPA units)
N_i	$i \in I_{PCE}$	Consumption of NIPA commodities
NCI_j	$j \in I_{NBUY}$	Noncompetitive imports into sector j
QC_i	$i \in I_{COM}$	Total domestic output of commodity i
QI_j	$j \in I_{IND}$	Output industry j
QP^{jm}	$j \in I_{IND}$ $m \in I_{PNODE}$	Aggregate input m into industry j
QP_i^j	$i \in I_{COM}$ $j \in I_{IND}$	Input of commodity i into industry j
QS_i	$i \in I_{COM}$	Total supply of commodity i
$rGDP$		Divisia index of real GDP
X		Vector of exports
X_i	$i \in I_{COM}$	Exports of commodity i
X_i^{IDEN}	$i \in I_{COM}$	Exports that are explicitly identified in IO
X_i^{tr}		Travel exports of commodity i
X^{div}		Divisia index of real exports

A.8.3 Prices

e		"Exchange rate"
i^*		Interest rate on private U.S.-owned foreign assets
i		Cost of capital return to debt
P^h		Price of total hours (work and leisure)
P^{Hm}	$m \in I_{CNODE}$	Vector of prices at node m of consumption function
P^{Im}	$m \in I_{INV}$	Vector of prices at node m of investment function
P^{Pjm}	$j \in I_{IND}$; $m \in I_{PNODE}$	Vector of prices at node m of industry j's production function
PC_i	$i \in I_{COM}$	Price of domestically produced commodities
PC_i^X	$i \in I_{CNODE=top}$	Price of consumption CEX basis
PC_R^X		Price of leisure on CEX basis
PCC		Price of aggregate commodity consumption from simple Cobb-Douglas index
PF		Price of full consumption
PGG		Price of aggregate government consumption (Cobb-Douglas index)
PI_j	$j \in I_{IND}$	Price of industry output paid by buyers
PII		Price of aggregate investment goods
PII^m	$m \in I_{INV}$	Price of investment aggregate m
PII_{mi}	$mi \in I_{INVm}$	Union of above-aggregate investment prices and supply prices
PK		Price of capital stock
PK^{gain}		Capital gain rate for aggregate capital
PKD		Rental price of aggregate capital
PKD_j	$j \in I_{BUY}$	Rental price of capital paid by producer

PKD_{oil}		Rental price of capital of "oil and gas mining"
PKD_{hs}	$s \in I_{ASSET}$	Rental price of household capital; short- and long-lived
PKD_{jc}	$c \in I_{LEGAL}$	Rental price of capital; corporate and noncorporate
PKD_{jcs}	$s \in I_{ASSET}$	Rental price of capital; short- and long-lived
PLD_j	$j \in I_{BUY}$	Price of labor paid by employers
PM_i	$i \in I_{COM}$	Price of competitive imports paid by importers
PM_i^*	$i \in I_{COM}$	World price of competitive imports
PM_i^{land}	$i \in I_{COM}$	Landed price of imports before tariffs
PN_n	$n \in I_{NIPA}$	Price of NIPA PCE commodity
PN^m	$m \in I_{CNODE}$	Price of consumption aggregate m
PN_{mi}	$mi \in I_{CNODEm}$	Union of above 2 sets of consumption prices
PN^R		Price of leisure (NIPA basis)
$PNCI_j^*$	$j \in I_{BUY}$	World price of noncompetitive imports
$PNCI_j$	$j \in I_{BUY}$	Price of noncompetitive imports paid by importers
$PNCI_j^{land}$	$j \in I_{BUY}$	Landed price of noncompetitive imports before tariffs
PO_j	$j \in I_{IND}$	Price of industry output received by producer
PP^{jm}	$j \in I_{IND}$ $m \in I_{PNODE}$	Price of aggregate input m into industry j
PP_{mi}^j	$mi \in I_{PNODEm}$	Union of above set of aggregate production prices and prices of inputs
PS		Vector of supply prices
PS_i	$i \in I_{COM}$	Price of commodities to buyers
PS_i^C	$i \in I_{COM}$	Price of commodities paid by the household sector (after consumption taxes)

r		After-tax interest rate used in Euler equation
r_{jc}	$j \in I_{IND}\ c \in I_{LEGAL}$	Weighted (equity and debt) rate of return, corporate and noncorporate
r_h		Weighted (equity and debt) rate of return to household capital
r_{csj}^{net}	$j \in I_{IND}; c \in \{c, n, h\}$ $s \in I_{ASSET}$	Net return on capital, {corporate, noncorporate, household}, {short, long}
r_c^{equ}	$c = \{c,n,h\}$	Rate of return to equity; {corporate, noncorporate, household}
π		Inflation rate in cost of capital formula (version 9)
π^{eq}		Equity premium (over debt)
ρ^e		Cost of capital return to equity

A.8.4 Shares and Probabilities

g^{GDP}		Government purchases share of GDP
m_{ji}^{col}	$i \in I_{COM}$	Share of national commodity *i* made by industry j
m_{ji}^{row}	$j \in I_{IND}$	Share of industry *j*'s output going to commodity *i*
H		Matrix converting NIPA PCE classification to IO commodity classification
s_i^{con}	$i \in I_{PCE}$	NIPA commodity shares of consumption
s_j^m	$j \in I_{IND}$; m=K,L,E,M	{capital, labor, energy, material} input cost shares for industry *j*
SC_i^N	$i \in I_{CNODE=top}$	Shares of household demand, top tier, NIPA basis
SC_i^X	$i \in I_{CNODE=top}$	Shares of household demand, top tier, CEX basis
SD^i	$i \in I_{COM}$	Shares of domestic output, imports in total supply of *i*
SF		Vector of shares of commodities and leisure in full consumption

SI^M	$m \in I_{INV}$	Shares of investment at node *m*
SM		Vector of shares of imports in total supply
SN^m	$m \in I_{CNODE}$	Shares of consumption at node *m*
SP^{jm}	$j \in I_{IND}$ $m \in I_{PNODE}$	Shares of production at node *m* of industry *i*
SX^i	$i \in I_{COM}$	Shares of total supply of *i* exported

A.8.5 Parameters of Behavioral Equations, Kalman Filter Terms

Household Functions

ρ		Pure rate of time preference
σ		Household intertemporal elasticity of substitution
α^{Hm}	$m \in I_{CNODE}$	Shares (at unit prices) of consumption at node *m*
B^{Hm}		Share elasticity of consumption (w.r.t. prices) at node *m*
B_{pA}		Coefficients on demographic characteristics of CC function
ξ^{dd}		Distribution coefficient in top-tier household demand function
ξ^L		Coefficients of demographic terms in top-tier household demand function
f_t^{Hm}	$mf \in I_{CNODE}$	Latent variable for bias of consumption change, lower tiers
ψ_C^R		Aggregation constant of leisure
H		Bridge matrix linking NIPA "Personal Constant Expenditures" commodities to IO commodities

Production and Commodity Functions

α_0^j	$j \in I_{IND}$	Cost function constant
α^{Pjm}	$j \in I_{IND}$; $m \in I_{PNODE}$	Shares (at unit prices) of inputs into industry *j* at node *m*
B^{Pjm}	$j \in I_{IND}$	Share elasticity of input demands (w.r.t.) at node *m*

B_{pt}^{j}	$j \in I_{IND}$	Biases of technical change
f_t^{Pj}	$j \in I_{IND}$	Latent variable for bias of technical change, top tier
f_t^{j}	$j \in I_{IND}$	Latent variable for technical change, top tier
f_t^{Pjm}	$j \in I_{IND}$ $m \in I_{PNODE}$	Latent variable for bias of technical change, lower tiers
A^{agg}	$j \in I_{IND}$	Index of aggregate technology shock
ΔA^{agg}		Aggregate technology improvement
λ_j	$j \in I_{IND}$	Industry technology shock
$\mathbf{M}$		IO Make matrix; the contribution of each industry to each commodity
m^{row}		Row shares of make matrix
m^{col}		Column shares of make matrix
δ		Depreciation rate (aggregate capital)

Capital Input and Cost of Capital Functions

α_{KD0}^{j}	$j \in I_{IND}$	Constant of industry capital input price function
α_{KD}^{j}	$j \in I_{IND}$	Shares (at unit prices) of inputs of industry capital input
B_{KD}^{j}	$j \in I_{IND}$	Share elasticity of components of industry capital input
α_{KD}^{jc}	$j \in I_{IND}$	Shares (at $p = 1$) of components of industry corporate capital input
B_{KD}^{jc}	$j \in I_{IND}$	Share elasticity of components of industry corporate capital input
α_{KD}^{jn}	$j \in I_{IND}$	Shares (at $p = 1$) of components of industry noncorporate capital input
B_{KD}^{jn}	$j \in I_{IND}$	Share elasticity of components of industry noncorporate capital input
α_{KD0}^{h}		Constant of household capital input price function
α_{KD}^{h}		Shares (at $p = 1$) of components of household capital input

B_{KD}^{h}		Shares of components of household capital input
δ		Depreciation rate (aggregate capital)
δ_{cs}	$c = c,n,h$	Rate of depreciation of short-lived capital stock
δ_{cl}	$c = c,n,h$	Rate of depreciation of long-lived capital stock
β_{jc}	$j \in I_{IND}$	Corporate debt-equity ratio, industry j
β_{jn}	$j \in I_{IND}$	Noncorporate debt-equity ratio, industry j
β_{h}		Debt-equity ratio, household
α^{DIV}		Dividend-payout ratio

Investment Functions and Capital Stock Functions

α^{IY}		Share of inventory investment in total investment
α_{i}^{IY}	$i \in I_{COM}$	Share of inventory investment going to commodity i
α^{Im}	$m \in I_{INV}$	Shares (at unit prices) of commodities at investment node m
B^{Im}	$m \in I_{INV}$	Shares elasticity of components of total investment at node m
λ^{I}		Shocks to investment cost function
ε^{I}		Shock to rate of capital formation
f_{t}^{Im}	$m \in I_{INODE}$	Latent variable for bias of investment change, lower tiers
ψ^{K}		Aggregation constant of capital services
ψ_{j}^{K}	$j \in I_{BUY}$	Aggregation constant of capital
ψ^{I}		Aggregation constant of investment goods
ψ^{PK}		Aggregation constant of price of capital stock

Trade Functions

α^{Mi}	$i \in I_{COM}$	Shares (at unit prices) of domestic commodities and imports in total supply
B^{Mi}	$i \in I_{COM}$	Shares elasticity of components of total supply
f^{Mi}		Latent variable for bias of import change

η^i	$i \in I_{COM}$	Export price elasticities
α^{Xi}	$i \in I_{COM}$	Shares of exports in total supply
B^{Xi}	$i \in I_{COM}$	Shares elasticity of components of exports
f^{Xi}		Latent variable for bias of export change

Government Functions

α_i^G	$i \in I_{INP}$	Share of government expenditures on *i*

Labor Functions

ψ_j^L	$j \in I_{BUY}$	Aggregation constant of labor
ψ_C^R		Aggregation constant for aggregate leisure

Externalities Functions

XP_{jx}	$j \in I_{IND}$	$x \in I_{EXT}$	Production externalities
XM_{jx}	$i \in I_{COM}$	$x \in I_{EXT}$	Import externalities

A.8.6 Tax Rates, Tax Parameters, Government and Funds Spending Rates

γ_c^p	$c = c,n,h$	Deduction of property taxes (=1 in version 9)
γ_c^i	$c = c,n,h$	Proportion of interest payments deducted before tax
γ_c^d		Proportion of dividends deducted before tax on corporations
γ_c^g	$c \in I_{LEGAL}$	Proportion of capital gains on corporate equities excluded from individual income for tax purposes
γ^{VGG}		Parameter for setting government purchases as share of GDP
dhi		Proportion of inflation premium in interest determined by indexing rule of household interest expense
t_c		Tax rate on corporate capital income (federal + S&L)
t_c^e	$c = c,n,h$	Tax on equity income (corporate, noncorporate, household)

t_c^{earn}		Average tax on personal corporate capital income
t_c^f	$f = f,s$	Statutory tax rate on corporate capital income; federal, S&L
t_c^g	$c = c,n,h$	Capital gains tax (corporate, noncorporate, household)
t_c^p	$c = c,n,h$	Property tax rate (corporate, noncorporate, household)
t_{cs}^{ITC}	$c \in I_{LEGAL}$ $s \in I_{ASSET}$	Rate of investment tax credit
t_h		Tax rate on household income used to adjust deductions
tc_i	$i \in I_{COM}$	Total tax rate on consumption commodity
tc		Consumption tax rate
tc^g		Consumption tax on goods only
tc^G		Consumption tax on government spending
tc^K		Consumption tax on household capital input
tc^L		Consumption tax on private household labor
tc^N		Consumption tax on imports only (NCI)
tl^a		Average tax rate on labor income
tl^{af}	$f = f,s$	Average tax rate on labor income; federal, state
tl^{flat}		Flat tax rate on income
tl^m		Marginal tax rate on labor income
tl^{mf}	$f = f,s$	Marginal tax rate on labor income; federal, state
tl^0		Implied tax rate on labor income at zero income
tk		Tax rate on aggregate capital income (version 8)
tk^{hh}		Tax rate on household capital input (version 8)
tp		Tax rate on aggregate property (version 8)
tr_i	$i \in I_{COM}$	Tariff rate on competitive imports
tr_i^n	$i \in I_{BUY}$	Tariff rate on noncompetitive imports
tr_i^*	$i \in I_{COM}$	World tariff rate on U.S. exports
tt_j	$j \in I_{IND}$	Indirect business tax (sales tax)

tt_j^f	$f = f,s$	Indirect business tax; federal, state, & local
tt_j^{full}	$j \in I_{IND}$	The full tax rate on sales
tu_i	$i \in I_{IND}$	Unit tax on quantities sold
tx_i^u	$i \in I_{IND}$	Total unit externalities tax on quantities sold
tx_i^v	$i \in I_{IND}$	Total externalities tax on sales
tx_i^{ru}	$i \in I_{COM}$	Total unit externalities tax on quantities imported
tx_i^{rv}	$i \in I_{COM}$	Total externalities tax on imports
tx_x^{Xu}	$x \in I_{EXT}$	Tax on one unit of externality x
tx_x^{Xv}	$x \in I_{EXT}$	Tax on \$1 of externality x
tw		Wealth tax rate (estate taxes)
tw^f	$f = f,s$	Wealth tax rate (estate taxes); {federal, state, and local}
z_{cs}	$c \in I_{LEGAL}$ $s \in I_{ASSET}$	Depreciation allowances for \$1 of investment

B Accounts for General Equilibrium Modeling

B.1 Introduction

The econometric approach to general equilibrium modeling employed in IGEM is based on a new system of national accounts for the United States. The distinctive feature of these accounts is that demands and supplies of commodities and factors of production are presented in both current and constant prices. Traditional systems of accounts give the final demands that make up the gross domestic product (GDP) in current and constant prices. The factor supplies that generate gross domestic income (GDI) are presented only in current prices.

Before the introduction of the econometric approach to general equilibrium modeling summarized by Jorgenson (1998a), macroeconometric modeling was essentially limited to the demand side of the economy. As we have emphasized in chapter 1, parameters required for supply-side modeling in computable general equilibrium models were chosen largely by calibration to a single data point, following Johansen (1960). These modeling strategies were the consequence of the limitations of official systems of national accounts.

The new architecture for the U.S. national accounts presented by Jorgenson and Landefeld (2006) and updated by Jorgenson (2009b) provides data on the price and quantity of capital services for all assets in the U.S. economy. This is essential for intertemporal general equilibrium modeling. The accumulation equation that relates investment and capital stock provides the backward-looking dynamics in IGEM. The cost of capital equation that relates the price of capital services to the price of capital assets imparts forward-looking dynamics to IGEM.

The new system of national accounts employed in IGEM is outlined in chapter 2. The demand side coincides with the U.S. National Income and Product Accounts (NIPAs), the official system of national accounts prepared by the Bureau of Economic Analysis (BEA). The supply side includes an industry-level production account with outputs and inputs for the individual industries included in IGEM in current and constant prices. These data are used in modeling producer behavior in chapter 4.

We have combined time series data on final demands for Personal Consumption Expenditures (PCE) from the NIPAs with microeconomic data in modeling consumer behavior in chapter 3. The Consumer Expenditure Survey (CEX) by the Bureau of Labor Statistics (BLS) reflects the enormous heterogeneity of individual households that is typical of microeconomic data sets. The CEX provides the information needed to incorporate the demographic characteristics of households into our model of consumer behavior.

In modeling the behavior of the government sector in chapter 5, we have employed data on final demands by governments from the NIPAs. Similarly, our model of investment expenditures incorporates demand-side data on Gross Private Domestic Investment (GPDI) from the NIPAs. Finally, our models of the demand for imports and the supply of exports are based on time series data on imports and exports in current and constant prices. Models of this type can be found in macroeconometric models, as well as computable general equilibrium models.

Data appropriate for econometric modeling of producer behavior were generated for the United States by Jorgenson, Gollop, and Fraumeni (1987). These data provided the empirical basis for the econometric models of production employed by Jorgenson and Wilcoxen (1990). For the new version of IGEM presented in this book the U.S. data cover the time period 1960–2005 and are based on those of Jorgenson, Ho, and Stiroh (2005, henceforward JHS) and Jorgenson, Ho, Samuels, and Stiroh (2007).

Industry-level production accounts like those constructed for the United States by Jorgenson, Gollop, and Fraumeni have been incorporated into the methodology for productivity measurement presented in Schreyer's (2001) OECD productivity manual. The methods for compiling the capital data required for intertemporal general equilibrium modeling are presented in Schreyer's (2009) OECD manual on capital measurement. Jorgenson and Schreyer (2013) show that the methodology presented in these two OECD manuals is consistent with the new United Nations' (2009) *2008 System of National Accounts*.

Fortunately, industry-level production accounts are now available for a wide range of advanced countries, as a result of the completion of the EU KLEMS project in 2008. In addition to accounts for 25 of the 27 EU members, these accounts have been constructed for Australia, Canada, Japan, and Korea, as well as the United States, following the methodology of Jorgenson, Ho, and Stiroh (2005). These accounts will be extended to many emerging economies through the World KLEMS Initiative established in 2010.

In this appendix we present the industry-level production accounts that underlie our econometric models of producer behavior in more detail. Our presentation follows Jorgenson, Ho, and Stiroh (2005). We give production accounts for the 35 industrial sectors employed in IGEM, as well as the government and household sectors that complete the model. Section B.2 presents the methodology and data sources for output and intermediate inputs, Section B.3 for labor inputs, and Section B.4 for capital inputs. We describe the population data in B.5 and provide details of the government accounts in B.6.

B.2 Output and Intermediate Inputs

In this section we present measures of industry output and intermediate inputs. Our methodology and data sources are given in more detail in chapter 4 of Jorgenson, Ho, and Stiroh (2005, henceforward JHS). The industry classification in JHS (2005) was chosen to illuminate the role of the information technology–producing industries. For IGEM we focus on the energy-producing sectors and sectors that are intensive users of energy. Table B.1 gives the output and inputs for the 35 market industries, as well as household and government sectors.

Section B.2.5 describes the data sources and our adjustments to them. The results are reported in section B.2.6 for the energy producers and in Section B.2.7 for the remaining industries. Our methodology for measuring industry output, intermediate inputs, and value added is based on a time series of input-output tables. This gives the flows of all commodities in the economy, as well as payments for capital and labor services, in current and constant prices. We account for the supply of every commodity, whether produced domestically or imported. We also describe the use of every commodity, whether consumed as an intermediate input or allocated to final demand.

Although current information on industry outputs in the NIPAs uses the North American Industrial Classification System (NAICS), our time series of input-output tables requires detailed historical data that are not yet available in NAICS. Table 2.1 in chapter 2 provides the list of

Table B.1
IGEM industry output and inputs, 2005 (bil. $)

			Input		
	Industry Name	Output	Energy	Material	Value-Added
1	Agriculture	424.0	18.7	221.6	183.6
2	Metal Mining	25.0	2.5	13.3	9.3
3	Coal Mining	25.5	3.2	8.0	14.3
4	Petroleum and Gas	259.6	19.7	56.7	183.2
5	Nonmetallic Mining	23.5	2.9	7.5	13.1
6	Construction	1355.7	36.5	736.2	583.0
7	Food Products	595.4	10.5	390.3	194.7
8	Tobacco Products	31.0	0.2	22.3	8.5
9	Textile Mill Products	60.2	1.9	36.5	21.7
10	Apparel and Textiles	36.0	0.5	20.4	15.0
11	Lumber and Wood	129.5	3.7	77.6	48.2
12	Furniture and Fixtures	101.3	2.0	53.9	45.4
13	Paper Products	168.0	7.4	88.1	72.5
14	Printing and Publishing	229.7	2.6	84.8	142.3
15	Chemical Products	521.4	25.6	263.3	232.6
16	Petroleum Refining	418.8	214.7	67.1	137.1
17	Rubber and Plastic	187.9	4.6	98.6	84.6
18	Leather Products	6.3	0.2	3.9	2.3
19	Stone, Clay, and Glass	129.4	7.7	58.7	63.0
20	Primary Metals	251.1	12.8	161.4	77.0
21	Fabricated Metals	296.5	6.4	161.1	128.9
22	Industrial Machinery	424.0	5.4	234.4	184.2
23	Electronic and Electric Equipment	330.5	4.5	172.0	154.0
24	Motor Vehicles	442.2	3.8	352.2	86.2
25	Other Transportation Equipment	227.5	2.9	112.3	112.3
26	Instruments	207.4	2.1	85.8	119.5
27	Miscellaneous Manufacturing	60.5	1.1	33.7	25.7
28	Transport and Warehouse	667.8	87.5	268.1	312.3
29	Communications	527.9	4.0	231.6	292.3
30	Electric Utilities	373.0	52.9	77.4	242.8
31	Gas Utilities	77.4	42.6	11.9	23.0
32	Trade	2487.9	79.1	896.5	1512.3
33	FIRE	2752.3	33.8	927.8	1790.7
34	Services	4353.6	74.2	1482.2	2797.2
35	Government Enterprises	327.5	25.5	86.1	215.9
36	Private Households	1911.1			1911.1
38	General Government	1572.7			1572.7

the 35 business industries in IGEM, together with definitions from the 1987 Standard Industrial Classification (SIC) codes. Households include the rental flow of capital services from owner-occupied housing and consumer durables. General Government, excluding government enterprises, employs labor services and public capital.

In the NIPAs, Government Enterprises include electric utilities. In IGEM electric utilities, both private and public, are consolidated into a single Electric Utilities industry, while the Government Enterprises sector excludes the electric utilities. The NIPAs also provide separate accounts for government producers. For example, private hospitals and private universities are in Services, while government hospitals and universities are in General Government. In IGEM the inputs General Government industry in the official BEA accounts are included in the final demands of the Government sector.

Table B.1 provides output, energy, and non-energy materials inputs, and value added for all sectors in 2005. These are discussed in detail below. We refer to the 35 market industries in IGEM as the business sector, since we exclude General Government and Households. The capital services of the Households sector include the service flow from consumer durables, which is excluded from the official definition of GDP. Accordingly, value added for the IGEM industries exceeds the official GDP.

B.2.1 Notation

Models of producer behavior for domestic industries in IGEM are presented in chapter 4. For convenience we repeat the definitions of key variables that describe the outputs, the inter-industry flows of goods and services, and the flows of capital and labor services. The subscript i refers to commodities, while j refers to industries. The variables are

i index for commodity, $i = 1, \dots , M, M + 1$

j index for industry, $j = 1, \dots , M$

t index for time, $t = 1960, 1978, \dots , 2005$

QI_j quantity of gross output of industry j

VQI_j nominal value of gross output of industry j

PO_j price of gross output to producers in industry j

PI_i price of gross output to purchasers from industry j

QP_i^j	quantity of commodity input i into industry j
PS_i	price of commodity i to buyers
KD_j	quantity of capital input in industry j
LD_j	quantity of labor input in industry j
E_j	index of energy intermediate input into j
M_j	index of total non-energy intermediate input into j
$P_{E,j}$	price of energy intermediate input into j
$P_{M,j}$	price of total non-energy intermediate input into j
PKD_j	price of total capital input to industry j
PLD_j	price of total labor input to industry j
QC_i	quantity of domestically produced commodity i
PC_i	price of domestically produced commodity i
M_i	quantity of comparable imports of commodity i
PM_i	price of imported commodity i
QS_i	quantity of total supply of commodity i
$M_{j,i}$	Make matrix; value of commodity i made by industry j

B.2.2 Prices and Quantity Indexes

Our industry models of production are based on production functions with industry outputs expressed as functions of capital, labor, and intermediate inputs. Each industry, indexed by j, has its own production function and purchases M distinct intermediate inputs and noncomparable imports for a total of $M + 1$ intermediate inputs. The noncomparable imports, denoted NCE, are distinct from competitive imports included in the M intermediate inputs. The official input-output tables classify imports as noncomparable if they are judged to have no close domestic substitutes.

We group intermediate inputs into energy and non-energy aggregates. Production functions are assumed to be separable in these groups and may be written

$$\begin{aligned} &QI_j = f(KD_j, LD_j, E_j, M_j, t); \\ &\quad E_j = E(QP_3^j \ldots); \quad M_j = M(QP_1^j, \ldots) \end{aligned} \tag{B.1}$$

where KD is capital services, LD is labor services, E is an index of energy intermediate inputs—Coal Mining, Oil and Gas Mining, Petroleum Refining, Electric Utilities, and Gas Utilities—and M is an index of non-energy materials inputs, comprising the 30 non-energy commodities and noncomparable imports.

The production model (B.1) is used for the 35 market industries. The remaining two industries, Households and General Government, have no intermediate inputs. The production functions for these industries are described at the end of this section. The M commodity inputs correspond to the primary products of the 35 market industries.

Under the assumptions of constant returns to scale and competitive markets, the value of output is equal to the value of all inputs:

$$\begin{aligned} &PO_{jt}QI_{jt} = VQI_{jt} = PKD_{jt}KD_{jt} + PLD_{jt}LD_{jt} + P_{Ejt}E_{jt} + P_{Mjt}M_{jt} \\ &P_{Ejt}E_{jt} = PS_{3t}QP^j_{3t} + PS_{4t}QP^j_{4t} + \ldots + PS_{31t}QP^j_{31t} \\ &P_{Mjt}M_{jt} = PS_{1t}QP^j_{1t} + PS_{2t}QP^j_{2t} + \ldots + PS_{NCI,t}QP^j_{NCI,t} \end{aligned} \tag{B.2}$$

where PO_j denotes the price of output, PS_i denotes the price of each commodity and the time subscript has been dropped for brevity. The price of industry capital services, PKD_j, is defined as a residual, so that (B.2) holds as an accounting identity. The price of labor services PLD_j is discussed in section B.3 and the price of capital services in section B.4.

We assume that the price of the ith intermediate input PS_i is the same for all purchasing sectors. Each of the IGEM industries is an aggregate with many components. Therefore, each input QP_i^j is a commodity bundle consisting of these components. Even if the prices of all of the components were the same for all purchasers, differences in the composition of inputs among industries would generate a different input price PS_i for each purchasing industry.

Our aggregation over industries is based on the Tornqvist quantity index, which provides a close approximation to the Fisher ideal index currently employed in the NIPAs. The Tornqvist quantity index is an exact index number that replicates the translog model used in IGEM.[1] The energy index for industry j is

$$\Delta \ln E_{jt} = \sum_{i=3,4,16,30,31} \bar{v}_{ijt} \Delta \ln QP^j_{it}, \tag{B.3}$$

where $\Delta \ln Xt \equiv \ln Xt - \ln X_{t-1}$ is the growth rate.

The weights in the Tornqvist quantity index are shares of the component in the total value of the industry's energy inputs defined as[2]

$$v_{ijt} = \frac{PS_{it}QP^j_{it}}{\sum_{i=3,4,16,30,31} PS_{it}QP^j_{it}}. \tag{B.4}$$

The two-period average value share is

$$\overline{v}_{ijt} = \frac{1}{2}(v_{ijt} + v_{ijt-1}). \tag{B.5}$$

The *price index of aggregate energy input*, P_{Ej}, is defined implicitly to make the following value identity hold:

$$P_{Ej}E_j = \sum_{i=3,4,16,30,31} PS_i QP_i^j. \tag{B.6}$$

We construct a similar set of index numbers for non-energy input defined over the set $I_{Mat} = \{1,2,5, \ldots 35, nci\}$:

$$\Delta \ln M_{jt} = \sum_{i=I_{Mat}} \overline{v}_{ijt} \Delta \ln QP_{it}^j. \tag{B.7}$$

$$P_{Mj}M_j = \sum_{i=I_{Mat}} PS_i QP_i^j.$$

Equations (B.3) and (B.7) represent growth rates of energy and non-energy inputs, so that we normalize prices at unity in the base year,

$$P_{Ej,t=base} = P_{Mj,t=base} = 1.0.$$

We emphasize that the prices of energy and non-energy inputs are specific to each industry, even though prices of the component inputs are the same for all industries. This reflects differences in the shares of intermediate inputs in the value of output among industries.

We distinguish between purchasers' and producers' prices; the value to the purchaser is the value of output to the producer, plus output taxes paid on j's output T_j:

$$VQI_j = PI_j QI_j = PO_j QI_j + T_j. \tag{B.8}$$

The purchaser's price PI is defined in equation (2.12).

Value added, inclusive of taxes, of industry j is the sum of payments for capital, labor, and indirect taxes:

$$VA_{jt}^T = PKD_{jt}KD_{jt} + PLD_{jt}LD_{jt} + T_{jt}. \tag{B.9}$$

Gross domestic product (GDP) in nominal terms is then given by the sum of value added over all sectors, including the government and households:

$$GDP = \sum_j VA_{jt}^T. \tag{B.10}$$

B.2.3 *Inter-Industry Accounts*

The basic building block for our measures of output and intermediate inputs is a time series of inter-industry transactions tables. These tables describe the industries that produce each product and the industries that use them. The Use table, presented in figure 2.1, allocates the supply of each commodity among the categories of intermediate input and final demand. The Make table, given in figure 2.2, shows how each commodity is supplied or made by the various industries. Each industry produces a primary commodity and, possibly, some secondary commodities. Each commodity is produced by one or more industries.

The inter-industry transactions tables for our industry classification have dimension 35 × 35. To illustrate the concepts that underlie our industry-level production accounts, we give a condensed three-sector Use table for year 2005 in table B.2a, and a Make table for 2005 in table B.2b. The three industries are Mining (including oil, gas, coal, and other mining), Secondary Energy (utilities and refining), and Non-energy (all other industries). The final demanders are household consumption (C), general government (G), Investment (I), and Exports (X). The supply from Imports (M) is entered as a negative number.

A key consistency requirement for IGEM is that the output of a given commodity by all industries must be equal to the use of this commodity by other industries and final demanders. On the input side, the jth column of the Use table represents the inputs of that industry. Equations (B.2) and (B.8) may be combined to express the constraint that the sum of inputs is equal to the value of industry output to the purchaser:

$$PI_jQI_j = \sum_i PS_iQP_i^j + PKD_{jt}KD_{jt} + PLD_{jt}LD_{jt} + T_j. \tag{B.11}$$

On the output side, each industry produces many commodities and the exact composition is given by the Make table. The jth row of the Make table gives the values of the various commodities produced by industry j, and the row total is the industry output:

$$PI_jQI_j = \sum_i M_{j,i}. \tag{B.12}$$

The ith column of the Make table gives the contributions of each industry to the domestic output of the ith commodity. Let QC_i denote the quantity of domestically produced commodity i, PC_i the price, and VC_i the value. The Make column total is the value of total

Table B.2a
Three-sector U.S. USE table, 2000 (bil. $)

	Business Sectors			Final Demand					
	Primary Energy	Secondary Energy	Nonenergy	C	I	G	X	M	Total: Commodity
Primary energy	19.5	173.7	7.9	0.1	35.5	0.2	3.6	–94.7	145
Secondary energy	6.1	77.9	327.6	247.0	7.1	61.5	21.3	–80.6	668
Nonenergy	45.0	107.2	6238.0	5005.7	2544.6	669.6	1078.0	–1126.3	14562
nci	2.3	1.0	98.1	51.2	0.0	12.6	0.0	–165.3	0
Capital	58.6	165.3	2550.6	1394.4		330.6			4499
Labor	20.0	75.6	4991.6			889.9			5977
Tax	1.6	12.6	395.0						409
Total:									
Industry output	153	613	14609	6698	2587	1964	1103	–1467	
	Gross output =		15375		GDP =	10886			

Note: The definition of income and expenditures (GDP) is larger than the official definition due to the treatment of durables and methods of imputing rentals. "C" is consumption of nondurables and services; "I" includes consumer durables.

Table B.2b
Three-sector U.S. MAKE (Supply) table, 2000 (bil. $)

	Business Sectors			
	Primary Energy	Secondary Energy	Non-energy	Total: Industry
Primary Energy	145.5	6.9	0.6	153
Secondary Energy	0.0	599.5	12.7	612
Non-energy	0.0	61.4	14548.2	14610
Total: Commodity	145	668	14562	

domestic output of each commodity, summed over all the supplying industries:

$$VC_i = PC_i QC_i = \sum_j M_{j,i}. \tag{B.13}$$

We explain the division of the value into price and quantity later in equation (B.20).

These concepts are illustrated in table B.2. The Primary Energy industry is represented by the *Pri. Energy* column in the Use table and the *Pri. Energy* row in the Make table; the *Primary Energy* commodity is in the corresponding row of the Use table and column of the Make table. The Primary Energy industry output is $PI_{i=P.E.} QI_{j=P.E.} = 153$ billion dollars, and the value of domestically produced Primary Energy commodity is $PC_{i=P.E} QC_{i=P.E.} = 145$ billion dollars. The value added of the industry is $VA^T_{j=P.E.} = 80.2$ billion dollars. The value of Primary Energy commodities as intermediate inputs into the Secondary Energy industry is

$$PS_1 QP_1^{j=2} = 173.7 \text{ billion dollars.}$$

The Use table also includes the familiar breakdown of sales to final demand—consumption, investment, government, exports, and imports. In the summary Use table B.2, these are the columns marked C, I, G, X, and M. The official U.S. Interindustry Transactions Accounts distinguish two types of imports—comparable and noncomparable. In the IGEM import column (M), commodities 1 through 35 are comparable imports, and we denote them M_i. This implies that the commodity is produced domestically and imported from abroad. By contrast, imports that are not produced domestically, the noncomparable imports, are in the *nci* row, where $P_j^{NCI} QP_{NCI}^j$ is the value of NCI input into industry j.

Total imports equal the sum of comparable and noncomparable imports.[3]

The sum of all the elements in row i of the Use table equals the value of deliveries of the ith commodity to all users—intermediate inputs to other industries and final demand. Thus, the supply-demand balance for domestic commodity i in value terms is

$$PC_iQC_i = \sum_j PS_iQP_i^j + PS_i(c_i + i_i + g_i + x_i) - PM_iM_i. \tag{B.14}$$

The domestic commodity totals are given in the right-most column of table B.2a. It is more intuitive, however, to rewrite this as the total supply from domestic suppliers and competitive imports, equal to total demand:

$$PC_iQC_i + PM_iM_i = \sum_j PS_iQP_i^j + PS_i(c_i + i_i + g_i + x_i). \tag{B.15}$$

Relating equation (B.15) to table B.2.a we see that in the Primary Energy row of the Use table the \$245 billion of the domestic commodity is augmented by imports of \$94.7 billion, giving a total supply of \$588 billion. Excluding exports of \$3.6 billion, the total supply of \$240 billion to the domestic market is divided among \$201.1 billion for intermediate demand and \$35.5 for Investment. In terms of the notation of chapter 2, sections 2.1 and 2.5,

$$PC_{i=P.E.}QC_{i=P.E.} = 145.$$

$$PM_{i=P.E.}M_{i=P.E.} = 94.7.$$

The key assumption necessary for a quantity version of (B.15) to hold is that all industries and final demand categories purchase the same commodity bundle of commodity i with the same share of the imported variety. Let QS_i denote the quantity of total supply of commodity i and PS_i the price. The total value of supply for each commodity is then

$$PS_iQS_i = VS_i = PC_iQC_i + PM_iM_i. \tag{B.16}$$

The quantity of the total supply of commodity i is a Tornqvist index of the domestic and imported varieties:

$$\Delta \ln QS_i = (1 - \overline{v}_m)\Delta \ln QC_i + \overline{v}_m \Delta \ln M_i, \tag{B.17}$$

where the weights are (averaged) value shares:

$$v_{mt} = \frac{PM_{it}M_{it}}{VS_{it}}. \tag{B.18}$$

The price PS_i is defined implicitly from the total supply and the quantity index in equation (B.17):

$$PS_i = \frac{VS_i}{QS_i}. \tag{B.19}$$

We have now completed the circle in the inter-industry flow of goods. The price PS_i of commodity i is the price paid by producers for their input in B.2, which was introduced at the beginning of our description of the input-output system. In other words, the input of commodity i bought by industry j, denoted QP_i^j in B.2 and B.3, is a composite good made up of imports M_i and the domestic variety QC_i, which is in turn composed of output from domestic industries through (B.13).

Finally, we note that the Bureau of Economic Analysis does not produce an official input-output table in constant dollars. The final demands—C, I, G, X, and M—are based on purchasers' prices, where components of final demand are made up of many input-output commodities.[4] However, purchasers' prices for the components of final demand are not linked to the producers' prices. Our accounting system, involving the price indexes *PO*, *PI*, *PC*, and *PS*, is not used by the BEA in estimating the real GDP.

In the growth accounting methodology used in IGEM, we take the industry output quantities and prices to be primary data. Each commodity is regarded as a Cobb-Douglas aggregate of the quantities produced by the various industries, and its price, PC_i, is given by the component industry prices:

$$\ln PC_i = \sum_j \frac{M_{ji}}{VC_i} \ln PI_j. \tag{B.20}$$

With this commodity price, the quantity, QC_i, is given by (B.13).

B.2.4 Household and General Government Sectors

Finally, we turn to accounts for the two nonbusiness sectors—Households and General Government in table B.1. In the convention of the 1992 benchmark IO table, these sectors do not produce goods and services used as intermediate inputs by other industries. They also do not use intermediate goods, but consume capital and labor services, so that their value added is part of GDP.

The output and input of the Household industry consists of capital service flows from owner-occupied housing and consumers' durable goods. The NIPAs make imputations for the rental-equivalent value of owner-occupied housing, but no imputations are made for the capital services other household durable assets like automobiles and computers. By contrast we treat the flow of services from the stock of consumers' durables symmetrically with the services from housing. We regard all assets that do not depreciate within a year as providing an annual flow of services to be estimated and incorporated into output. We include purchases of new durables in investment rather than personal consumption expenditures. More details are provided in section B.4 below.

The value of capital services for the Household industry is denoted $PKD_{36}KD_{36}$ to be symmetric with the flow of capital services for the business industries. The output of the Household industry consists solely of capital services, so output is not defined as in (B.1) for a business industry, but is equal to input:

$$PI_{36}QI_{36} = PKD_{36}KD_{36}. \tag{B.21}$$

The General Government sector hires a substantial quantity of labor and owns a considerable stock of capital. It is comparable to the larger business industries in size. Table B.1 gives the outputs of the various industries for 2005. The output and input values are

$$PI_jQI_j = PLD_jLD_j + PKD_jKD_j j = 38. \tag{B.22}$$

There is no market for government output, so that the NIPA records industry value-added as the sum of the compensation of labor and the depreciation of capital.[5] The value of the capital service flow using only depreciation is much smaller than the corresponding service flow using the price of capital services described in section B.4. We implement the complete service flow for the government sector and impute the value of capital services and output.

Since there are no markets for the output of the Government sector, there are no output prices and quantities. Following the convention in the NIPAs, we define the quantity of output as an index of capital and labor quantities, so that there is no growth in productivity. The value added from these nonbusiness industries is given in the value-added row in the final demand columns of the USE matrix in table B.2a; Government capital input is \$330.6 billion and Government labor input is \$889.9 billion.

B.2.5 *Data Sources and Adjustments*

Our starting point for constructing a time series of input-output tables is the official benchmark U.S. Inter-Industry Transactions tables produced by the Bureau of Economic Analysis (BEA). These are available on an SIC classification for the years 1977, 1982, 1987, and 1992.[6] The Office of Occupational Statistics and Employment Projections of the Bureau of Labor Statistics (BLS-EMP) uses these benchmark tables to generate a time series of inter-industry transactions tables for 1983–2000 that covers 192 sectors. These data include both Use and Make tables and are structured like the BEA tables. We also use earlier versions of the BLS-EMP data that cover the period 1960–1995.[7] For the post-2000 period all official data are in NAICS and we turn to the BEA gross output data covering 489 NAICS industries. We have bridged these NAICS data to the SIC to extend our series to 2005.

B.2.5.1 *Adjusting the Input-Output Tables to GDP Definitions*

The first step in constructing the BLS-EMP time series of input-output tables is to revise the BEA benchmark tables to conform to a common definition of GDP, including the treatment of software as investment rather than as intermediate input. There are other differences among the benchmark tables, such as the industry classifications, and we have revised the tables to conform to the 1992 conventions.

To interpolate the input-output tables between benchmark years, data on industry output are collected by BLS-EMP. The final demand components are taken from the NIPAs. These include the various categories of personal consumption expenditures and investment, as well as trade data by commodities. The BLS-EMP then adjusts the matrices so that the following identities hold: First, the sum of value-added is equal to GDP. Second the sum over commodities of each of the final demand columns is equal to the C, I, G, X, and M aggregates in the NIPAs. Third, the sum of all inputs in each column j of the Use table equals the value of gross output of industry j. Fourth, the sum of all commodities in row j of the Make table is equal to the output of the domestic industry. Fifth, the sum of all purchases in row i of the Use table is equal to the sum of column i in the Make table and both are equal to the total value of commodity i. This yields a set of consistent input-output tables for all years.

We use the BLS-EMP Use and Make tables that cover 192 sectors from 1983 to 2000 and have reorganized them to produce the IGEM industry classification in Table B.1. The assignments to this industry classification are given in table B.3. The links between the 192 industries and the 35 IGEM industries are direct, except for the Electric Utilities and Gas Utilities. In the first step, the nominal value tables are consolidated and reorganized. The aggregation process involves reallocating nonbusiness sectors such as scrap and rest-of-the-world. These are reallocated to the 35 IGEM industries and final demand. The owner-occupied housing sector is moved to the consumption column and government electric utilities are merged with private utilities to form the IGEM Electric Utilities industry. The BLS-EMP industry, Combined Utilities is divided between Electric Utilities (10%) and Gas Utilities (90%).

We revise the tables for 1998–2000 to match the GDP given in the *Survey of Current Business* for August 2007. Since the BLS-EMP series are based on a previous revision of the NIPAs, we employ the method of iterative proportional fitting, often called the "RAS method." This approach maintains the original values for industry output of each industry and adjusts all elements of the matrix until the value-added rows and final demand columns match the revised GDP.[8]

B.2.5.2 Linking Data Sets

We have linked earlier versions of the BLS-EMP data set, covering 1960–1985 and 1977–1995, to the data set for 1983–2000, extending the series back to 1960. The 1977–1995 data set was used in JHS (2005, chapter 4) and covered 185 industries. The 1960–1985 set was used in Jorgenson (1998). These data are based on earlier benchmarks and differ from the current series in the industrial classification and the definition of investment.

We have consolidated the 185-sector nominal input-output tables to the 35 IGEM sectors the same way as described above for the 1983–2000 data. We take the 1983 Use and Make tables as initial guesses for the 1982 matrices and use the method of iterative proportional fitting to adjust the initial tables to the new column and row totals given by the BLS-EMP industry output series and the final demands from the *Survey of Current Business*, August 2007. The earlier years, 1977 to 1981, are then adjusted in a similar manner, where the initial matrix is a weighted sum of the original and the new 1982 table. We repeat the exercise for the 1960–1977 series by using a 1977 table on the new definitions to revise backwards to 1960. This yields an annual time series of nominal input-output tables covering 1960–2000 that conforms to the latest

Table B.3
Assignment of BLS-EMP IO categories to IGEM 35 Industries

IGEM Industries		BLS 192 Sectors	
1	Agriculture	1	Agricultural production
		2	Veterinary services
		3	Landscape and horticultural services
		4	Agriculture, forestry, and fisheries services, n.e.c.
		5	Forestry, fishing, hunting, and trapping
2	Metal Mining	6	Metal mining
3	Coal Mining	7	Coal mining
4	Oil and Gas Mining	8	Crude petroleum, natural gas, and gas liquids
		9	Oil and gas field services
5	Nonmetal Mining	10	Nonmetallic minerals, except fuels
6	Construction	11	Construction
7	Food Manufacturing	70	Meat products
		71	Dairy products
		72	Preserved fruits and vegetables
		73	Grain mill products and fats and oils
		74	Bakery products
		75	Sugar and confectionery products
		76	Beverages
		77	Miscellaneous food and kindred products
8	Tobacco	78	Tobacco products
9	Textile	79	Weaving, finishing, yarn, and thread mills
		81	Carpets and rugs
		82	Miscellaneous textile goods
10	Apparel	80	Knitting mills
		83	Apparel
		84	Miscellaneous fabricated textile products
11	Lumber and Wood	12	Logging
		13	Sawmills and planing mills
		14	Millwork, plywood, and structural members
12	Furniture	15	Wood containers and miscellaneous wood products
		16	Wood buildings and mobile homes
		17	Household furniture
		18	Partitions and fixtures
		19	Office and miscellaneous furniture and fixtures
13	Paper	85	Pulp, paper, and paperboard mills
		86	Paperboard containers and boxes
		87	Converted paper products except containers

(continued)

Table B.3 (continued)

IGEM Industries		BLS 192 Sectors	
14	Printing and Publishing	88	Newspapers
		89	Periodicals
		90	Books
		91	Miscellaneous publishing
		92	Commercial printing and business forms
		93	Greeting cards
		94	Blank books and bookbinding
		95	Service industries for the printing trade
15	Chemicals	96	Industrial chemicals
		97	Plastics materials and synthetics
		98	Drugs
		99	Soap, cleaners, and toilet goods
		100	Paints and allied products
		101	Agricultural chemicals
		102	Miscellaneous chemical products
16	Petroleum Refining and Coal	103	Petroleum refining
		104	Miscellaneous petroleum and coal products
17	Rubber and Plastics	105	Tires and inner tubes
		106	Rubber products and plastic hose and footwear
		107	Miscellaneous plastics products, n.e.c.
18	Footwear and Leather	108	Footwear, except rubber and plastic
		109	Luggage, handbags, and leather products, n.e.c.
19	Stone, Clay, and Glass	20	Glass and glass products
		21	Hydraulic cement
		22	Stone, clay, and miscellaneous mineral products
		23	Concrete, gypsum, and plaster products
20	Primary Metals	24	Blast furnaces and basic steel products
		25	Iron and steel foundries
		26	Primary nonferrous smelting and refining
		27	All other primary metals
		28	Nonferrous rolling and drawing
		29	Nonferrous foundries
21	Fabricated Metals	30	Metal cans and shipping containers
		31	Cutlery, hand tools, and hardware
		32	Plumbing and nonelectric heating equipment
		33	Fabricated structural metal products
		34	Screw machine products, bolts, rivets, etc.
		35	Metal forgings and stampings
		36	Metal coating, engraving, and allied services

Table B.3 (continued)

IGEM Industries		BLS 192 Sectors	
		37	Ordnance and ammunition
		38	Miscellaneous fabricated metal products
22	Machinery and Computers	39	Engines and turbines
		40	Farm and garden machinery and equipment
		41	Construction and related machinery
		42	Metalworking machinery and equipment
		43	Special industry machinery
		44	General industrial machinery and equipment
		45	Computer and office equipment
		46	Refrigeration and service industry machinery
		47	Industrial machinery, n.e.c.
23	Electrical Machinery	48	Electric distribution equipment
		49	Electrical industrial apparatus
		50	Household appliances
		51	Electric lighting and wiring equipment
		52	Household audio and video equipment
		53	Communications equipment
		54	Electronic components and accessories
		55	Miscellaneous electrical equipment
24	Motor Vehicles	56	Motor vehicles and equipment
25	Other Transportation Equipment	57	Aerospace
		58	Ship and boat building and repairing
		59	Railroad equipment
		60	Miscellaneous transportation equipment
26	Instruments	61	Search and navigation equipment
		62	Measuring and controlling devices
		63	Medical equipment, instruments, and supplies
		64	Ophthalmic goods
		65	Photographic equipment and supplies
		66	Watches, clocks, and parts
27	Miscellaneous manufacturing	67	Jewelry, silverware, and plated ware
		68	Toys and sporting goods
		69	Manufactured products, n.e.c.
28	Transportation	110	Railroad transportation
		111	Local and interurban passenger transit
		112	Trucking and courier services except air
		113	Warehousing and storage

(continued)

Table B.3 (continued)

IGEM Industries		BLS 192 Sectors	
		114	Water transportation
		115	Air transportation
		116	Pipelines, except natural gas
		117	Passenger transportation arrangement
		118	Miscellaneous transportation services
29	Communications	119	Telephone and telegraph communications and communications services, n.e.c.
		120	Cable and pay television services
		121	Radio and TV broadcasting
30	Electric Utilities	122	Electric utilities
		124	Combined utilities (part of)
		178	Federal electric utilities
		183	State and local electric utilities
31	Gas Utilities	123	Gas utilities
		124	Combined utilities (part of)
32	Trade	126	Wholesale trade
		127	Retail trade except eating and drinking places
		128	Eating and drinking places
33	Finance, insurance, real estate	129	Depository institutions
		130	Nondepository; holding and investment offices
		131	Security and commodity brokers
		132	Insurance carriers
		133	Insurance agents, brokers, and service
		134	Real estate
		135	Royalties
34	Services	125	Water and sanitation
		137	Hotels
		138	Other lodging places
		139	Laundry, cleaning, and shoe repair
		140	Personal services, n.e.c.
		141	Beauty and barber shops
		142	Funeral service and crematories
		143	Advertising
		144	Services to buildings
		145	Miscellaneous equipment rental and leasing
		146	Personnel supply services
		147	Computer and data processing services
		148	Miscellaneous business services
		149	Automotive rentals, without drivers

Table B.3 (continued)

IGEM Industries		BLS 192 Sectors	
		150	Automobile parking, repair, and services
		151	Electrical repair shops
		152	Watch, jewelry, and furniture repair
		153	Miscellaneous repair services
		154	Motion pictures
		155	Videotape rental
		156	Producers, orchestras, and entertainers
		157	Bowling centers
		158	Commercial sports
		159	Amusement and recreation services, n.e.c.
		160	Offices of health practitioners
		161	Nursing and personal care facilities
		162	Hospitals
		163	Health services, n.e.c.
		164	Legal services
		165	Educational services
		166	Individual and miscellaneous social services
		167	Job training and related services
		168	Child day care services
		169	Residential care
		170	Museums, botanical, zoological gardens
		171	Membership organizations
		172	Engineering and architectural services
		173	Research and testing services
		174	Management and public relations
		175	Accounting, auditing, and other services
		176	Private households
35	Government Enterprises	177	U.S. Postal Service
		179	Federal government enterprises, n.e.c.
		182	Local government passenger transit
		184	State and local government enterprises, n.e.c.
36	Households	136	Owner-occupied dwellings
38	General Government		

Note: BLS IO categories are those in the input-output data set from the Office of Employment Projections, U.S. Bureau of Labor Statistics; version released December 2001. Notation "n.e.c." is "not elsewhere classified."

SIC-based estimates of industry output from BLS and the annual update of the NIPAs published by the BEA in 2007.

The BLS-EMP followed the conversion from SIC to NAICS by issuing a series of IO tables for 1998–2004 based on 200 NAICS industries. Separately the BEA provided industry output for 489 industries for 1998–2005 based on the NAICS-1997.[9] We first converted the industry output of these 489 NAICS industries to the 35 IGEM industries. In converting the labor data described in appendix C, we used a NAICS-SIC bridge for 1997 provided by the Census Bureau; however, for output we simply assigned each of the 489 industries to one of the 35 IGEM industries. We calculated growth rates from these BEA output data and applied it to the 2000 values.

We use the Make matrix from 2000 to derive SIC commodity values from the industry outputs and use the SIC-based industry output and commodity output series as control totals to extrapolate the 2000 Use and Make tables to 2005. One more input is required to do this extrapolation, namely, an initial guess of the final demand columns. This is taken from the BLS-EMP tables at the 200 NAICS commodity level for 1998–2005. We scale the sum of value added over industries and the sum of the components of final demand to the GDP given in the NIPAs from the *Survey of Current Business* for August 2007. At this point we have the value of industry output at purchasers' prices VQI_{jt} and the values of the intermediate inputs, including noncomparable imports, $PS_{it}QP_{it}^j$ and $PS_{NCI,t}QP_{NCI,t}^j$, for each of the private industries in the period 1960–2005.

B.2.5.3 Generating Value-Added Components

Unfortunately, value added in the BLS-EMP data is not divided among capital and labor compensation and indirect business taxes, as in the BEA benchmark tables. We estimate the value-added components from the *GDP by Industry* data produced by the BEA.[10] Our estimates of the value of labor input are described in appendix B.2 and reflect the sum of the compensation of employees from the NIPAs and the estimated value of self-employed labor compensation. The estimation of the value of capital input is described in section B.4 and includes property compensation, less the imputed value of self-employed labor compensation, plus certain property taxes. After the value of capital and labor compensation are subtracted, the remainder of GDP equals sales taxes net of subsidies.

One important caveat is that the level of the BEA's industry value added is different from the 1992 benchmark input-output data, as explained in BEA (1997). We adjust the *GDP by Industry* data to conform to the rest of the input-output table in the following manner: First, we denote the values of capital input, labor input, and sales taxes that we have derived from the BEA data by VK_{jt}^{BEA}, VL_{jt}^{BEA}, and T_{jt}^{BEA}. Value added for industry j in the BLS-EMP tables is denoted VA_{jt}^{BLS}. Our estimates of the value-added components are derived by scaling the BEA estimates so that they sum to match the total value in the input-output tables. For example, the value of capital services is set as

$$VK_{jt} = VK_{jt}^{BEA} \frac{VA_{jt}^{BLS}}{VK_{jt}^{BEA} + VL_{jt}^{BEA} + T_{jt}^{BEA}}. \tag{B.23}$$

B.2.5.4 Industry Output Prices and Quantities

We begin with the value and price data for industry output at the 192-industry level from the BLS-EMP, covering the period 1972–2000, and aggregate them to the 35 business industries from IGEM, using Tornqvist indexes.[11] The exceptions to this are Communications Equipment and Computer and Data Processing Services, where we replace the BLS prices with BEA prices that are adjusted for quality change.[12] This yields the price deflators, denoted above as PI_{j}. From the value data (VQI) described in section B.2.5.2 and equation (B.8), we obtain the corresponding industry output quantities QI_j.

The behavior of the 35 business industry prices is summarized in figure B.4 where we give the change in industry output prices relative to the overall GDP deflator over the period 1960 to 2005, ranked in order from largest increases to largest declines. The data for this chart are given in the last column of table B.8, which we discuss below. The largest declines in price are in Electrical Machinery, which includes the Electronic Components industry that makes semiconductors, and Industrial Machinery, which includes Computers. After Tobacco, the three largest increases in prices are in the energy-related industries—Petroleum and Gas Mining, Petroleum Refining, and Gas Utilities. With the complete set of industry output prices and the Make table, we then calculate domestic commodity prices PC_i, using (B.20). We do not use the commodity prices that are implicit in the BLS-EMP data. From the industry output prices, we also subtract the sales tax to give the producers' prices in (B.8).

B.2.5.5 Import Prices and Total Supply Prices

The BLS-EMP data set also includes a parallel set of constant dollar Use and Make tables. We use only the data for comparable and noncomparable imports (NCI) that are given in the import column and the NCI row of the Use table. We employ the competitive import data by 192 commodities, many of which are zero, and generate import prices. The value and price data are then aggregated, using the Tornqvist index to give quantities and prices for 35 competitive imports, denoted M_i and PM_i. Noncomparable imports are in the NCI row of the Use table, used by 35 industries and final demand, and we use the BLS-EMP data from the nominal and constant dollar tables, aggregate them and generate 35 + 3 sets of prices for $P_{NCI,j}$.

Given the prices of domestic goods and imported goods, we calculate the total supply quantities and prices using (B.17) and (B.19). These are the prices for intermediate goods. We divide them into the values from our 35-sector Use tables to obtain the quantities of intermediates QP_i^j. The commodity prices and quantities are used to calculate the quantity of energy and non-energy input aggregates using (B.3) and (B.7).

B.2.5.6 Data Issues

There are a number of data issues that arise in constructing quantity indexes of output and inputs and these are discussed in JHS (2005, section 4.4). JHS also includes a comparison of our growth and TFP estimates to other studies that use different data sources. For most industries the growth of output is similar among our estimates, the BLS Office of Productivity accounts, and the BEA *GDP by Industry* accounts. The few substantial differences are discussed in JHS (2005, table 4.4).

We summarize the data issues here. First, the annual value-added data must be reconciled with the benchmark input-output tables.[13] Second, the 1977 and 1982 benchmark tables are based on the 1972 SIC codes, while 1987 and 1992 tables are based on the 1987 SIC codes. Data for *GDP by Industry* are provided for both classifications in the overlap year of 1987 and we have adjusted the old classifications to the new ones, using the shares of each of the old industries in the new industries for 1987. We have made similar adjustments for the older input-output tables. Third, data for 2001 onwards were converted from NAICS to SIC using a fixed bridge. Fourth, we assume that all buyers pay the same price for each commodity, since there is no information about price differences.

B.2.6 *Input, Output, and Prices of Energy Sectors*

In the list of industries in the BLS data set given in table B.3, ten of the 192 BLS industries are assigned to the five energy-related IGEM industries:

(3) Coal Mining
(4) Petroleum and Gas Mining
(16) Petroleum Refining and Coal Products
(30) Electric Utilities (private and government)
(31) Gas Utilities

To represent the input structure for these industries, we present the columns of the 2000 Use table for the industries in table B.4. In the column for Electric Utilities we see that gross output is $319.0 billion, which is split between $112.0 billion for intermediate inputs (35%) and $207.0 billion for value added (65%). The largest intermediate inputs for Electric Utilities are Coal Mining ($15.2 billion), Services ($16.5b), and Petroleum and Gas Mining ($10.9b). Output from Gas Utilities is $50.5 billion and the major inputs are value added ($11.5b), Petroleum and Gas Mining ($26.1b), intra-industry purchases ($6.8b), and Services ($2.1b). Output from Petroleum Refining was $243.7 billion; this is an industry with a volatile share of value added, in 2005 it was 68% and in 2000 it was only 14%. Its major inputs are the feedstock from Petroleum and Gas Mining of $121.5 billion and intra-industry transactions of $33.6 billion.

The use of the energy commodities by the 35 industries and final demand in 2000 are given in table B.5. The five energy-related industries purchase essentially all the commodity output of Coal Mining and Petroleum and Gas Mining, with Chemicals accounting for most of the remainder (rows 3, 4, 16, 30, and 31 of the two mining columns). By contrast, refined oil, electricity, and gas are used in substantial quantities by all industries and Final Demand.

Turning to the detailed MAKE table (table B.6), the total Electric Utilities commodity supplied by U.S. sources is worth $245.8 billion in 2000. Of this total, Private Electric and Gas Utilities industry supplied

Table B.4
Input structure of energy sectors and consumption from the USE table, 2000 (mil. $)

		Coal Mining	Petroleum Mining	Petroleum Refining	Electric Utilities	Gas Utilities	Consumption
1	Agriculture	17	32	57	144	33	56043
2	Metal Mining	0	0	38	0	0	0
3	Coal Mining	1472	0	8	15180	12	109
4	Petroleum and Gas	0	18027	121489	10865	26119	0
5	Nonmetallic Mining	7	6	572	25	8	1
6	Construction	1	406	415	7290	37	22821
7	Food Products	0	0	195	0	0	322566
8	Tobacco Products	0	0	0	0	0	44275
9	Textile Mill Products	54	0	2	32	5	9095
10	Apparel and Textiles	2	1	1	10	2	131930
11	Lumber and Wood	34	17	92	1255	312	636
12	Furniture and Fixtures	0	0	0	3	1	0
13	Paper Products	8	6	346	206	34	22534
14	Printing and Publishing	1	4	13	130	10	30933
15	Chemical Products	164	2023	3966	1444	52	137485
16	Petroleum Refining	674	2069	33587	9200	205	80270
17	Rubber and Plastic	169	29	773	720	91	7894
18	Leather Products	0	1	2	3	1	26278
19	Stone, Clay, and Glass	99	855	989	588	160	1170
20	Primary Metals	62	1382	56	529	96	55
21	Fabricated Metals	285	988	470	1592	415	3570

Table B.4 (continued)

		Coal Mining	Petroleum Mining	Petroleum Refining	Electric Utilities	Gas Utilities	Consumption
22	Industrial Machinery	2243	2998	202	2499	201	305
23	Electronic and Electric Equipment	72	128	88	1836	254	5505
24	Motor Vehicles	39	78	122	2942	19	0
25	Other Transportation Equipment	0	0	1	14	4	0
26	Instruments	2	74	51	1353	24	14041
27	Miscellaneous Manufacturing	2	3	14	100	18	26512
28	Transport and Warehouse	747	1022	5705	7663	313	136024
29	Communications	33	359	361	1386	68	158987
30	Electric Utilities	353	1368	3050	3856	105	129075
31	Gas Utilities	15	1590	12119	8971	6830	37668
32	Trade	668	1795	10302	4649	521	1070687
33	FIRE	732	21818	5443	10284	863	860662
34	Services	923	4612	7168	16465	2095	1870940
35	Government Enterprises	4	8	144	726	73	44724
	Noncompeting Imports	24	2284	879	70	65	51210
	Capital	6402	52184	22084	136527	6656	1394410
	Labor	4624	15352	12112	59742	3719	
	Tax	1292	290	815	10737	1086	
	Gross output	21225	131808	243733	319034	50505	6698412

Table B.5
The use of energy commodities from the USE table, 2000 (mil. $)

		Coal Mining	Petroleum Mining	Petroleum Refining	Electric Utilities	Gas Utilities
1	Agriculture	0	0	7772	3670	227
2	Metal Mining	12	0	489	754	53
3	Coal Mining	1472	0	674	353	15
4	Petroleum and Gas	0	18027	2069	1368	1590
5	Nonmetallic Mining	48	0	1005	709	204
6	Construction	0	0	16087	2535	0
7	Food Products	166	0	2427	3997	1206
8	Tobacco Products	22	0	87	95	11
9	Textile Mill Products	41	1	525	1556	266
10	Apparel and Textiles	6	0	211	553	123
11	Lumber and Wood	3	0	1271	1506	139
12	Furniture and Fixtures	16	0	659	681	119
13	Paper Products	318	19	1955	3913	925
14	Printing and Publishing	0	0	760	1463	236
15	Chemical Products	272	4884	6282	7531	2594
16	Petroleum Refining	8	121489	33587	3050	12119
17	Rubber and Plastic	16	0	760	3110	379
18	Leather Products	2	0	93	134	23
19	Stone, Clay, and Glass	466	3	1735	2796	1233
20	Primary Metals	1169	141	1446	6686	1233
21	Fabricated Metals	10	4	1354	3981	750
22	Industrial Machinery	15	0	1343	3341	514
23	Electronic and Electric Equipment	4	2	1154	3687	408
24	Motor Vehicles	41	1	907	2253	303
25	Other Transportation Equipment	20	0	624	1310	134
26	Instruments	43	0	378	1118	108
27	Miscellaneous Manufacturing	2	0	375	373	77
28	Transport and Warehouse	8	70	48315	6666	133
29	Communications	0	0	810	1995	77
30	Electric Utilities	15180	10865	9200	3856	8971
31	Gas Utilities	12	26119	205	105	6830
32	Trade	21	13	18289	36109	2795
33	FIRE	6	0	3642	19747	1401
34	Services	20	15	18948	29555	2930
35	Government Enterprises	0	0	7919	7731	1851

Table B.5 (continued)

	Coal Mining	Petroleum Mining	Petroleum Refining	Electric Utilities	Gas Utilities
Consumption	109	0	80270	129075	37668
Investment	912	34621	6579	480	42
Government	99	−273	24444	31665	5401
Exports	1592	2055	16164	3826	1278
Imports	−1021	−93679	−77523	−3031	0
Total Domestic Commodity	21111	124376	243289	330303	94366

Table B.6
The supply of energy commodities from the detailed MAKE table, 2000 (mil. $)

Industry \ Commodity	Coal Mining	Petroleum Mining	Petroleum Refining	Electric Utilities	Gas Utilities
Coal Mining	21099				
Petroleum and Gas mining		87321	6917		
Petroleum Refining			207869		
Private Electric Utilities				191961	17485
Gas Utilities				190	49917
Combined Utilities				14810	22511
Government Utilities				38807	5443
All other industries	12	2153	2641	0	54
Total commodity	21111	89475	217426	245769	95410

$207.9, Federal Government Utilities supplied $12.4, and State and Local Government Utilities supplied $26.4 billion. The total gas commodity supplied by Gas Utilities is worth $95.4 billion in 2000. Of this total $72.4 billion comes from Gas and Combined utilities, $17.5 comes from Electric Utilities, and $5.4 from State and Local government enterprises. It is important not to identify gas supplied with the output of Gas Utilities, since this industry does not provide all of gas supplies.

The prices of the various forms of energy have shown substantial movements in the 1960–2005 period, relative to the prices of other commodities. Figure B.1 shows how the prices of the two industries producing primary fuels—coal, oil, and gas—changed relative to the GDP deflator. These graphs are normalized with prices for 1996

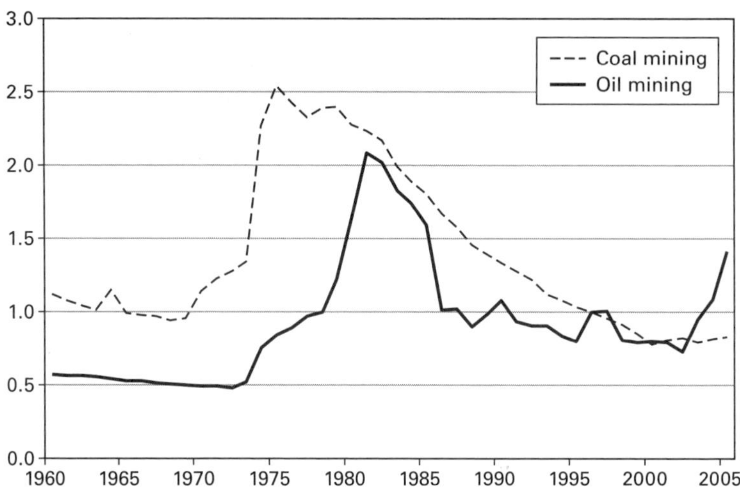

Figure B.1
Prices of primary fuels relative to GDP deflator.

equal to unity. The prices of oil and gas rose from half the 1996 level during the 1960s to twice the 1996 level during the oil shocks of the 1970s. The relatively stable prices of the 1990s gave way to a sharp rise in the mid-2000s. The price of coal also rose substantially in the 1970s, but the decline since then has persisted without a rise in prices in the 2000s.

The secondary energy industries are classified to allow us to distinguish between oil and gas and the prices are given in figure B.2. The prices of Refined Petroleum and Gas Utilities have largely followed the crude oil and gas prices; the rise in refined prices in the 2000s, relative to the GDP deflator, is somewhat larger than the rise in crude prices. The price of delivered electricity showed a very different behavior from the price of coal or oil given that Electric Utilities are highly regulated. After a rise in the 1970s, the behavior of electricity prices is essentially the same as the GDP deflator since 1981.

B.2.7 Output and Intermediate Input by Industry

We next consider gross output levels and growth rates for all 35 industries. The data described above are used in the review of the U.S. economy in tables 3.1–3.3 of chapter 3. That review includes the industry structure in 2005, as well as the growth rates of output and input

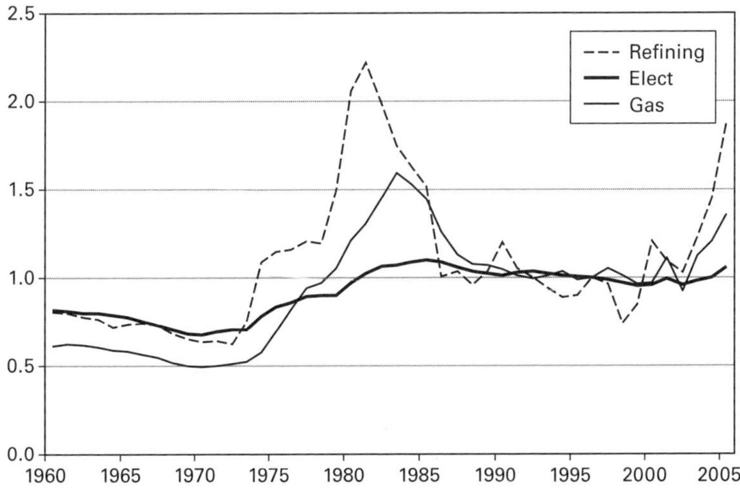

Figure B.2
Prices of refined oil, gas, and electricity relative to GDP deflator.

for the entire 1960–2005 period. Here we provide additional details on the industry characteristics and growth.

B.2.7.1 Output and Inputs in 2005

Table B.1 gives the value of output, energy, and non-energy intermediate inputs, and value added for each industry in year 2005. The largest industry in terms of output is Services ($4354 billion), followed by finance, insurance, and real estate (FIRE, $2752 billion). The five energy sectors together produce a gross output of $1154 billion. This includes substantial intra-industry transactions. In the case of Petroleum and Gas Mining, the output excluding the intra-industry sales is only 86% of industry gross output.

The sum of value added over all sectors is the GDP, $13.6 trillion by our definitions. This is higher than the official $12.5 trillion, due to our imputation of services from consumer durables. In terms of value added, Services is the largest business industry with $2797 billion in 2005, followed by FIRE. The five energy industries have $600 billion worth of value added, or 4.4% of GDP, in 2005.

There is a wide range of variation in the split of gross output between value added and intermediate inputs, as shown in figure B.3. The bars for the five energy industries are light colored while the non-energy industries are in dark bars. Of the three industries with the highest

Figure B.3
Value-added share of output, 2005.

value added to output ratio in 2005, two are energy-related with a large capital input—Petroleum and Gas Mining has a ratio of 71% and Electric Utilities has 65%. At the other end of the scale, the Petroleum Refining and Gas Utilities are heavy intermediate input-using industries with value added to output ratios of about 30%.

International trade plays very different roles in the different sectors. In table B.7 we give exports and (comparable) imports for each of the 26 commodities, as well as the shares of domestic output. The overall ratio of imports to GDP in 2005 is 16%; however, for the individual

Table B.7
Exports and imports, share of commodity output in 2005

	Industry	Export Share	Import Share	Export (bil. $)	Import (bil.$)
1	Agriculture	7.2	7.9	29.2	32.1
2	Metal Mining	8.4	–13.2	2.1	–3.3
3	Coal Mining	7.0	10.8	1.9	2.9
4	Petroleum and Gas	1.4	88.2	3.4	216.6
5	Nonmetallic Mining	4.3	14.1	0.9	3.0
6	Construction	0.1	0.0	1.3	0.0
7	Food Products	6.5	9.2	40.9	57.5
8	Tobacco Products	6.1	5.5	3.2	2.8
9	Textile Mill Products	16.2	29.1	10.5	18.9
10	Apparel and Textiles	15.3	278.9	6.4	116.2
11	Lumber and Wood	4.1	23.7	5.4	30.8
12	Furniture and Fixtures	5.0	41.8	5.0	41.8
13	Paper Products	9.1	15.3	15.3	25.6
14	Printing and Publishing	4.3	4.0	5.6	5.2
15	Chemical Products	17.0	21.6	89.5	113.4
16	Petroleum Refining	6.4	42.1	27.0	176.7
17	Rubber and Plastic	9.2	23.1	17.4	43.4
18	Leather Products	62.6	795.1	4.1	52.2
19	Stone, Clay, and Glass	5.1	18.6	6.5	23.8
20	Primary Metals	8.3	25.6	20.5	63.0
21	Fabricated Metals	7.3	14.8	21.7	44.2
22	Industrial Machinery	29.7	48.4	124.7	203.3
23	Electronic and Electric Equipment	30.2	66.0	100.2	219.4
24	Motor Vehicles	16.5	57.8	72.5	253.2
25	Other Transportation Equipment	29.0	17.5	65.4	39.5
26	Instruments	24.5	34.9	50.9	72.4
27	Miscellaneous Manufacturing	21.4	126.8	12.7	75.1
28	Transport and Warehouse	13.1	–0.5	87.3	–3.3
29	Communications	2.5	0.0	11.5	0.0
30	Electric Utilities	1.5	0.4	6.1	1.6
31	Gas Utilities	1.2	0.0	1.5	0.0
32	Trade	4.3		116.6	
33	FIRE	4.9	0.2	132.7	4.9
34	Services	1.6	0.3	75.9	15.5
35	Government Enterprises	0.3	0.0	0.4	0.0

commodities the share ranges from 253% in Motor Vehicles to zero for services such as Construction and Government Enterprises. For the energy sectors, the import share for Coal was 2.9%, Petroleum and Gas Mining was 217%, and Petroleum Refining was 177%. The United States also exports some coal and the net exports are close to zero over the recent years. There are very small trade flows for Electricity and Gas Utilities. We note that in 2005 the United States was running a substantial trade deficit and a balanced trade configuration would look quite different.

B.2.7.2 The Growth of Industry Output and Prices, 1960–2005

We have described the industry output growth and the contributions to growth of capital, labor, intermediates, and productivity in chapter 3. Table B.8 gives the growth rates of output, energy and non-energy intermediates, as well as the change in prices relative to the GDP deflator over the period 1960–2005. The growth rate of official GDP over this period was 3.3% per year. Industries with output growth exceeding this rate include Rubber and Plastics, Industrial Machinery, Electrical Equipment, Instruments, Communications, Trade, FIRE, and Services. The industries in relative decline are the primary industries (agriculture and mining), Construction, manufacturing industries facing intense import competition, and Utilities. JHS (2005) point out that this pattern is due to rapid productivity growth in IT, leading to rapid fall in prices, increased import competition in low-skill manufacturing, and the shift in demand towards income-elastic commodities as incomes rise.

Turning to intermediate inputs, all but 6 of the 35 industries in table B.8 show a slower growth of energy input than output. This is the result of substantial energy conservation in the U.S. economy, especially in the period of the two oil shocks. The six exceptions are Metal Mining, Construction, Tobacco, Leather, FIRE, and Government Enterprises. Energy input includes purchases of energy for feedstock and should not be interpreted as combustion alone. Fifteen industries had slower growth of non-energy intermediate than output; the other 20 saw intermediate input deepening as a result of increased specialization and outsourcing and biased technical change.

Changes in the output structure comes from four major sources: (1) shifts in supply due to productivity growth, (2) shifts in final demand due to changes in income, (3) shifts in intermediate demands due to biases in technical change, and (4) shifts in demand due to import

Table B.8
Growth in output, inputs, and prices, 1960–2005 (% per year)

		Output	Energy Intermediate	Nonenergy Intermediate	Relative Price
1	Agriculture	2.00	1.39	1.31	–0.85
2	Metal Mining	0.67	1.61	2.34	1.16
3	Coal Mining	2.22	1.36	3.25	–0.67
4	Petroleum and Gas Mining	0.40	–2.78	3.82	2.02
5	Nonmetallic Mining	1.56	0.98	2.05	–0.25
6	Construction	1.60	1.71	2.87	0.84
7	Food Products	2.01	1.31	1.58	–0.63
8	Tobacco Products	–0.83	0.36	0.69	2.41
9	Textile Mill Products	1.17	–0.49	–0.09	–1.67
10	Apparel and Textiles	–0.28	–1.76	–0.96	–1.44
11	Lumber and Wood	2.03	1.62	2.26	0.10
12	Furniture and Fixtures	3.27	2.72	3.13	–0.37
13	Paper Products	2.04	0.96	1.80	–0.29
14	Printing and Publishing	1.83	1.82	1.78	0.59
15	Chemical Products	2.81	1.55	2.67	0.03
16	Petroleum Refining	1.63	1.40	2.51	1.90
17	Rubber and Plastic	4.21	2.49	3.48	–0.87
18	Leather Products	–2.36	–2.01	–2.29	–0.31
19	Stone, Clay, and Glass	1.90	0.89	1.90	–0.12
20	Primary Metals	0.84	0.06	1.04	0.03
21	Fabricated Metals	1.94	1.47	2.00	–0.09
22	Industrial Machinery	5.92	1.90	4.38	–3.44
23	Electronic and Electric Equipment	6.50	1.83	3.66	–4.20
24	Motor Vehicles	3.22	1.66	3.38	–0.84
25	Other Transportation Equipment	1.91	1.82	2.28	–0.05
26	Instruments	4.32	2.27	4.16	–1.06
27	Miscellaneous Manufacturing	2.18	1.32	1.85	–0.57
28	Transport and Warehouse	3.01	2.80	2.91	–0.40
29	Communications	5.65	3.07	5.40	–1.53
30	Electric Utilities	2.94	1.60	3.65	0.58
31	Gas Utilities	–0.45	–0.45	3.78	1.78
32	Trade	3.72	2.62	3.45	–0.54
33	FIRE	4.19	4.32	4.42	0.33
34	Services	3.93	3.37	4.49	1.04
35	Government Enterprises	2.43	3.26	2.86	1.06

Note: Price growth is relative to the GDP deflator.

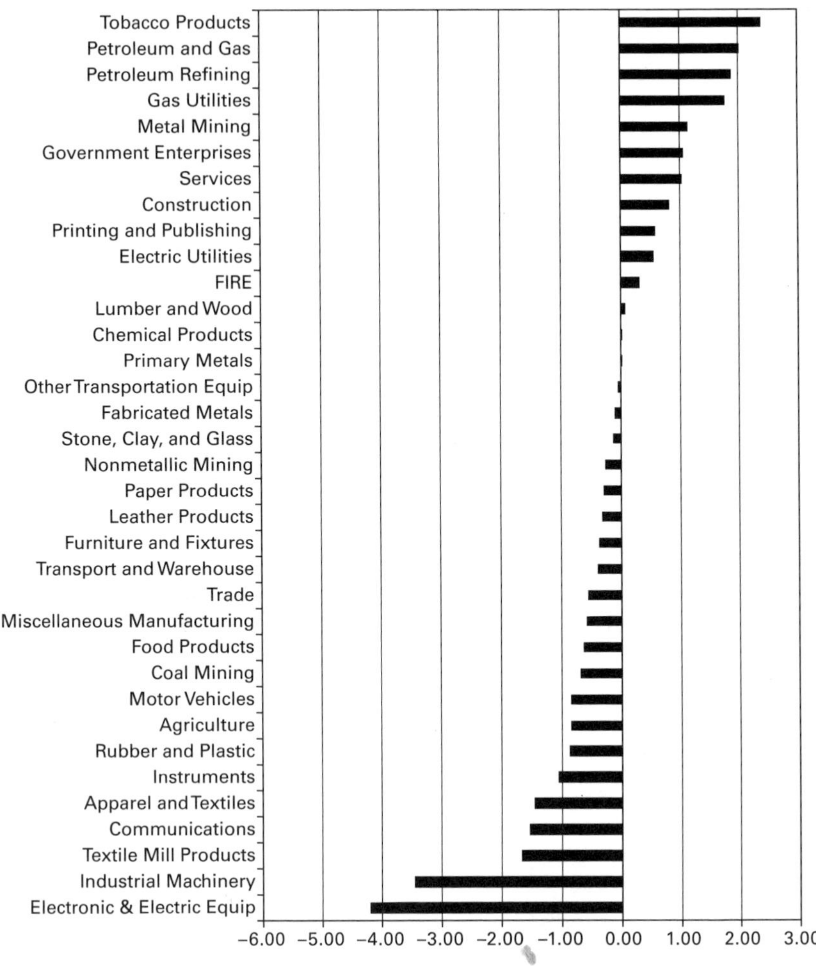

Figure B.4
Growth rate of industry price relative to GDP deflator 1960–2005.

competition. Productivity growth in a competitive economy and in IGEM manifests itself in lower prices. In the last column of table B.8 we give the change in prices of each commodity, relative to the GDP deflator, over the 1960–2005 period. In figure B.4 the price growth is ranked from the biggest rise relative to the GDP deflator to the biggest fall.

Of the four largest increases in relative prices, three are energy-related. Petroleum and Gas Mining prices rose by 2.0% per year followed by Petroleum Refining at 1.9%, and Gas Utilities at 1.8%. The large service industries also had low productivity growth as described in chapter 4 and had a large rise in relative prices; this includes Services, Construction, Government Enterprises, and Printing and Publishing. The relative price of Electricity rose at a 0.58% annual rate. The largest declines in prices were in the Information Technology–related industries—Electrical Machinery (–4.2% per year) and Industrial Machinery (–3.4% per year). The other industries with falling relative prices include Textiles (–1.7%), Communications (–1.5%), and Apparel (–1.4%). The price of coal fell at 0.67% per year (i.e., price at the mine mouth).

The sectors with rapid TFP growth and declines in prices saw the largest growth in demand and this resulted in high growth rates of output. The services saw little productivity growth and higher relative prices, but income effects have increased demand and these industries also had above-average growth rates. Industries that faced sharp international competition such as Textiles and Apparel showed slow or negative growth despite good productivity growth.

The industry performance described above, however, is not uniform over the period 1960–2005 and there is substantial variation in the relative growth rates. In table B.9 we give the growth rates for the subperiods 1960–1973, 1973–1995, and 1995–2005. Overall official GDP growth decelerated from 4.24% per year during 1960–1973 to 2.80% during 1973–1995, and then recovered to 3.15% in the Information Technology boom period (1995–2005). However, at the industry level, some industries kept decelerating while others followed the overall economy.

Many non-IT manufacturing industries, Coal Mining and Electric Utilities showed slowing growth for all three subperiods. In the manufacturing group, Stone-Clay-Glass, Primary Metals, Fabricated Metals, Motor Vehicles, and Miscellaneous Manufacturing followed the "sharp deceleration and then small acceleration" pattern of aggregate GDP. The large non-manufacturing sectors—Construction, Trade, and Services—also followed the aggregate pattern. The IT sectors of Machinery and Electrical Machinery, and Other Transportation equipment had a big acceleration during the 1995–2005 recovery period.

In the energy group, Coal Mining output was decelerating throughout with a sharp drop during 1995–2005. The Electric Utilities also decelerated throughout this period, in this case from an unusually high growth rate during the electrification period of the 1960s. Petroleum and Gas Mining had negative output growth during 1973–1995 but recovered to a small positive growth during 1995–2005. Petroleum

Table B.9
Growth of industry output by subperiod (% per year)

		1960–2005	1960–1973	1973–1995	1995–2005
1	Agriculture	2.00	1.65	1.99	2.11
2	Metal Mining	0.67	1.19	1.32	–0.48
3	Coal Mining	2.21	2.72	2.37	0.82
4	Petroleum and Gas Mining	0.40	2.29	–0.71	0.21
5	Nonmetallic Mining	1.56	3.43	0.64	1.97
6	Construction	1.60	2.52	0.44	2.72
7	Food Products	2.01	2.44	1.83	1.58
8	Tobacco Products	–0.83	0.57	–0.33	–2.63
9	Textile Mill Products	1.17	4.19	1.24	–2.78
10	Apparel and Textiles	–0.28	3.04	1.11	–6.65
11	Lumber and Wood	2.03	4.48	1.32	0.24
12	Furniture and Fixtures	3.27	4.80	2.01	4.27
13	Paper Products	2.04	4.57	2.05	–0.58
14	Printing and Publishing	1.83	3.15	2.06	–0.12
15	Chemical Products	2.81	6.24	1.82	0.93
16	Petroleum Refining	1.63	3.01	1.10	0.64
17	Rubber and Plastic	4.21	7.91	3.64	1.62
18	Leather Products	–2.36	–0.02	–2.78	–4.89
19	Stone, Clay, and Glass	1.90	3.62	0.62	3.07
20	Primary Metals	0.84	3.74	–0.45	1.39
21	Fabricated Metals	1.94	4.14	1.14	1.84
22	Industrial Machinery	5.92	6.51	5.76	7.33
23	Electronic and Electric Equipment	6.50	6.82	6.39	8.40
24	Motor Vehicles	3.22	5.38	2.43	3.33
25	Other Transportation Equipment	1.91	2.51	1.26	3.08
26	Instruments	4.32	4.98	4.65	3.42
27	Miscellaneous Manufacturing	2.18	4.54	0.88	1.91
28	Transport and Warehouse	3.01	4.41	2.80	2.19
29	Communications	5.65	7.09	4.90	5.95
30	Electric Utilities	2.94	5.68	2.37	1.01
31	Gas Utilities	–0.45	4.46	–2.97	–1.69
32	Trade	3.72	4.72	3.27	3.64
33	FIRE	4.19	4.22	4.18	3.99
34	Services	3.93	4.51	3.66	4.02
35	Government Enterprises	2.43	3.02	2.92	1.47
	GDP	3.29	4.24	2.80	3.15

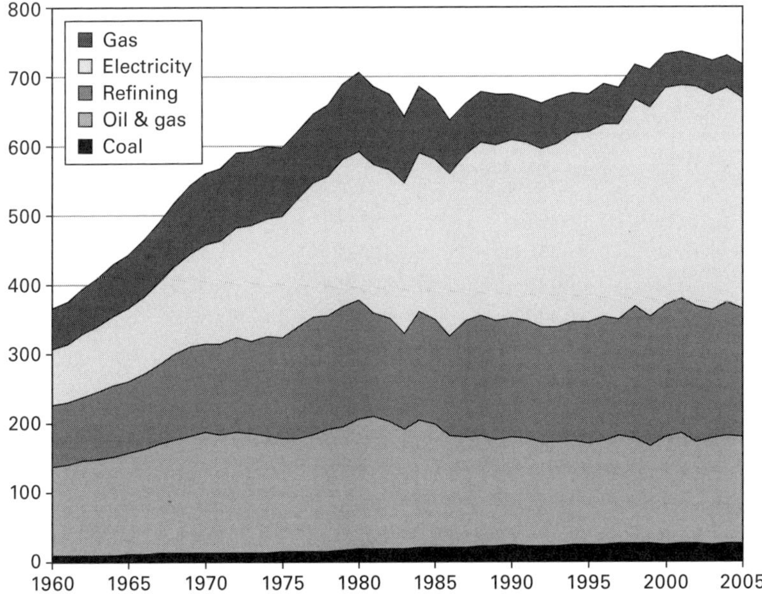

Figure B.5
Output of energy industries (billion $1996).

Refining output also decelerated throughout this period of energy conservation and rising imports.

The complete time series of output for the five energy industries are given in table B.10 and plotted in figure B.5. These are in constant 1996 prices and the nominal values may be derived from the corresponding price data in table B.11. The biggest sector by dollar value is Electric Utilities, which also have the fastest rate of growth over the 1960–2005 period. The next largest sector is Petroleum Refining, which is only growing by 0.64% per year during 1995–2005. As noted, coal output is rising but at a decelerating rate and is the smallest sector by value.

B.3 Measuring Industry Labor Input

In this section we describe the construction of labor input indexes that enter the state-space models of producer behavior presented in chapter 4. The methodology and data sources are discussed in detail in chapter 6 of Jorgenson, Ho, and Stiroh (2005). This methodology is used in many studies, such as Jorgenson, Kuroda, and Motohashi (2007) and Timmer, Inklaar, O'Mahony, and van Ark (2010). We provide a brief

Table B.10
Output of energy industries (producer's prices, billion $1996)

	Coal Mining	Petroleum Mining	Petroleum Refining	Electric Utilities	Gas Utilities
1960	10.01	127.71	88.82	80.94	59.03
1961	9.70	130.90	89.03	84.78	61.20
1962	10.19	135.44	92.30	90.62	65.35
1963	11.04	137.11	97.19	95.35	68.69
1964	10.29	141.50	103.46	100.33	73.89
1965	12.33	145.20	103.73	105.55	76.18
1966	12.88	150.83	107.16	112.78	81.53
1967	13.36	157.06	114.06	119.06	85.58
1968	13.16	162.94	122.52	127.66	91.63
1969	13.51	169.05	127.84	135.57	97.51
1970	14.52	172.71	127.89	143.49	102.13
1971	13.29	169.90	131.40	148.36	106.19
1972	14.33	172.54	136.33	158.58	108.80
1973	14.26	171.89	131.34	169.33	105.45
1974	14.53	168.17	143.05	170.59	102.76
1975	15.61	163.09	144.33	175.40	98.96
1976	16.36	162.33	159.18	184.92	97.93
1977	16.65	166.56	169.97	194.97	98.36
1978	16.02	174.42	164.20	202.42	102.09
1979	18.70	176.31	174.28	211.27	109.80
1980	19.86	186.32	172.13	215.01	112.09
1981	19.71	190.03	148.90	215.03	112.49
1982	20.10	183.12	148.75	214.05	108.45
1983	18.75	172.22	137.86	219.31	95.51
1984	21.49	182.51	156.85	229.05	95.34
1985	21.18	177.03	152.50	230.08	88.16
1986	21.35	160.45	144.74	234.46	77.11
1987	22.05	158.55	166.96	241.80	71.70
1988	22.82	160.08	172.39	250.32	73.24
1989	23.54	153.13	171.18	254.79	71.60
1990	24.72	154.96	171.18	258.12	65.95
1991	23.92	154.86	168.72	257.15	63.93
1992	23.96	149.16	166.51	255.88	66.08
1993	22.68	150.25	165.89	265.13	66.78
1994	24.79	149.69	172.21	271.35	58.10
1995	24.71	146.44	175.77	273.42	54.95
1996	25.35	149.59	179.21	278.04	57.85
1997	26.26	155.46	167.98	281.63	53.36

Table B.10 (continued)

	Coal Mining	Petroleum Mining	Petroleum Refining	Electric Utilities	Gas Utilities
1998	26.96	151.27	191.20	297.44	49.86
1999	26.38	141.25	186.12	302.58	53.84
2000	25.73	154.75	189.50	313.43	48.79
2001	26.82	159.64	193.35	307.63	48.51
2002	26.22	145.99	197.21	315.98	45.44
2003	25.60	152.74	184.86	311.10	47.91
2004	26.50	155.42	192.09	309.55	46.89
2005	27.13	153.19	184.82	303.26	48.23

Table B.11
Industry output price of energy industries

	Coal Mining	Petroleum Mining	Petroleum Refining	Electric Utilities	Gas Utilities
1960	0.250	0.127	0.181	0.183	0.137
1961	0.245	0.128	0.181	0.184	0.141
1962	0.239	0.129	0.178	0.184	0.142
1963	0.235	0.129	0.177	0.185	0.141
1964	0.271	0.127	0.169	0.185	0.139
1965	0.237	0.127	0.176	0.186	0.140
1966	0.242	0.129	0.182	0.185	0.139
1967	0.246	0.132	0.186	0.185	0.139
1968	0.249	0.134	0.181	0.187	0.138
1969	0.266	0.139	0.183	0.190	0.140
1970	0.334	0.144	0.186	0.198	0.145
1971	0.378	0.152	0.197	0.214	0.154
1972	0.410	0.154	0.200	0.226	0.165
1973	0.456	0.176	0.256	0.240	0.177
1974	0.841	0.279	0.402	0.290	0.214
1975	1.028	0.341	0.463	0.338	0.281
1976	1.038	0.381	0.496	0.368	0.349
1977	1.059	0.441	0.550	0.407	0.428
1978	1.164	0.487	0.582	0.439	0.472
1979	1.264	0.645	0.787	0.476	0.554
1980	1.310	0.946	1.184	0.559	0.697
1981	1.405	1.312	1.397	0.644	0.822
1982	1.449	1.350	1.324	0.713	0.970
1983	1.381	1.269	1.213	0.741	1.106

Table B.11 (continued)

	Coal Mining	Petroleum Mining	Petroleum Refining	Electric Utilities	Gas Utilities
1984	1.363	1.253	1.172	0.786	1.102
1985	1.341	1.184	1.127	0.817	1.072
1986	1.267	0.768	0.763	0.827	0.955
1987	1.229	0.794	0.807	0.825	0.883
1988	1.175	0.727	0.775	0.835	0.866
1989	1.163	0.821	0.865	0.858	0.894
1990	1.160	0.936	1.045	0.881	0.911
1991	1.146	0.841	0.949	0.927	0.909
1992	1.121	0.837	0.919	0.950	0.914
1993	1.057	0.853	0.887	0.965	0.953
1994	1.034	0.802	0.855	0.971	0.993
1995	1.015	0.781	0.883	0.989	0.967
1996	1.000	1.000	1.000	1.000	1.000
1997	0.970	1.025	0.979	1.004	1.067
1998	0.939	0.826	0.761	0.994	1.042
1999	0.885	0.825	0.880	0.994	1.007
2000	0.825	0.852	1.286	1.018	1.035
2001	0.877	0.862	1.190	1.084	1.215
2002	0.907	0.804	1.140	1.064	1.027
2003	0.901	1.078	1.390	1.114	1.273
2004	0.950	1.264	1.696	1.165	1.405
2005	0.993	1.699	2.276	1.272	1.637

summary in section B.3.1. We then outline how the data have been updated from JHS (2005) in section B.3.2 and present the results in section B.3.3.

B.3.1 Methodology

The productivity of workers, as measured by their hourly wage rates, varies widely. The highest average wages are observed for the most highly educated male workers in the prime age group. A simple sum of hours worked that ignores differences in productivity fails to capture the impact of substitution among different types of workers. This is highly problematical in a period with large changes in the composition of the workforce like those that took place during 1960–2005.

Table B.12
Classification of civilian labor force for each industry

	No.	Categories
Gender	2	Male; female
Class	2	Employees; self-employed and unpaid
Age	7	16–17, 18–24, 25–34, 35–44, 45–54, 55–64, 65+
Education		
1960–1992	6	0–8 years grade school
		1–3 years high school
		4 years high school
		1–3 years college
		4 years college
		5+ years college
1992+	6	0–8 years grade school
		grade 9–12 no diploma
		High school graduate
		Some college no bachelor's degree
		Bachelor's degree
		More than bachelor's degree

Our objective is to construct a measure of labor input that accounts for the enormous heterogeneity among workers and yet is tractable to implement. For each of the 35 industries in IGEM we classify workers by gender, age (seven groups), educational attainment (six groups), and employment class (two types). In addition, Households and General Government sectors are large employers. The precise definitions of our demographic groups are given in table B.12 for the civilian workers. A slightly different data set is used for military workers in estimating the labor input of General Government.

There is a total of $2 \times 7 \times 6 \times 2 = 168$ types of workers for each industry. Table B.13 gives summary data for the labor input in the 35 industries. There are $168 \times 35 = 5880$ cells for the labor data for these 35 industries, plus 336 additional cells for Households and General Government, for a total of more than 6000 cells altogether.[14]

In describing our methodology, we use the following notation:

$saecj$ subscripts for sex, age, education, class, industry

E_{saecj} employment matrix, number of workers in cell s,a,e,c,j

h_{saecj} average hours per week in cell s,a,e,c,j

w_{saecj} average weeks per year in cell s,a,e,c,j

Table B.13
Employment and labor compensation in 2005

		Employment (000s)	Labor Value (bil. $)	Hourly Cost ($/hr)
1	Agriculture	3,427	150.5	19.2
2	Metal Mining	32	2.8	42.3
3	Coal Mining	80	6.5	36.2
4	Petroleum and Gas	369	38.1	44.2
5	Nonmetallic Mining	108	6.9	29.2
6	Construction	9,107	472.2	26.2
7	Food Products	1,635	83.2	26.8
8	Tobacco Products	31	3.4	57.3
9	Textile Mill Products	348	14.5	22.3
10	Apparel and Textiles	364	15.9	25.0
11	Lumber and Wood	840	35.9	22.8
12	Furniture and Fixtures	479	24.3	27.1
13	Paper Products	526	37.0	35.5
14	Printing and Publishing	1,342	77.7	32.4
15	Chemical Products	940	99.6	53.4
16	Petroleum Refining	115	13.7	58.3
17	Rubber and Plastic	858	43.4	26.2
18	Leather Products	42	2.1	29.5
19	Stone, Clay, and Glass	543	30.7	29.0
20	Primary Metals	527	35.9	34.3
21	Fabricated Metals	1,353	73.3	28.1
22	Industrial Machinery	1,561	124.7	40.3
23	Electronic and Electric Equipment	1,227	98.4	41.3
24	Motor Vehicles	856	71.3	41.7
25	Other Transportation Equipment	759	61.0	40.9
26	Instruments	776	64.5	42.9
27	Miscellaneous Manufacturing	402	20.9	28.5
28	Transport and Warehouse	4,870	247.6	26.7
29	Communications	1,412	112.6	44.1
30	Electric Utilities	822	73.1	49.0
31	Gas Utilities	111	10.4	50.2
32	Trade	32,634	1128.7	22.3
33	FIRE	8,873	726.9	47.7
34	Services	48,331	2293.0	28.8
35	Government Enterprises	1,789	117.7	42.3
	Households	1,313	15.5	9.5
	Government	22,585	1227.7	37.8
	Total Economy	151,388	7661.4	30.3

c_{saej} average hourly compensation of employees in cell s,a,e,j

H_{saecj} hours worked by all workers in cell s,a,e,c,j

H_{lj} abbreviation for H_{saecj}: $l = 1$ is $s = 1, a = 1, e = 1, c = 1, l = 2$ is $s = 1, a = 1, e = 1, c = 2 \ldots, \ l = 168$ is $s = 2, a = 7, e = 6, c = 2$

$L_{l,j}$ labor input of cell l in industry j

$P_{L,l,j}$ price of labor input of cell l

The industry *volume of labor input* is expressed as a Tornqvist index of the effective labor input of the individual components:

$$\Delta \ln L_j = \sum_l \bar{v}_{l,j} \Delta \ln L_{l,j}, \tag{B.24}$$

where $\bar{v}_{l,j} = \frac{1}{2}(v_{l,j,t} + v_{l,j,t-1})$ is the two-period average of the share of the lth type of labor in the value of total labor input in the jth industry:

$$v_{l,j,t} = \frac{P_{L,l,j} L_{l,j}}{\sum_m P_{L,m,j} L_{m,j}}, l = 1, 2, \ldots, 168. \tag{B.24b}$$

To implement this index, we assume that labor input for each category $\{L_l\}$ is proportional to hours worked:

$$L_{l,j} = Q_l H_{l,j}, \tag{B.25}$$

where the proportionality constant, Q_l, differs among workers but is constant over time for each type of worker. For example, an hour worked by a self-employed, male worker, aged 34, with four years of college education, represents the same labor input in 1960 as in 2005.

With assumption (B.25), the labor quantity index in (B.24) can be expressed simply in terms of hours worked:

$$\Delta \ln L_j = \sum_l \bar{v}_{l,j} \Delta \ln H_{l,j}. \tag{B.26}$$

The corresponding *price of labor input* is the ratio of the value of labor compensation to the volume index ($P_{L,j} = VL_j \ / \ L_j$). The total value is

$$P_{L,j} L_j = VL_j = \sum_l P_{L,l,j} L_{l,j}. \tag{B.27}$$

Finally, the *labor quality* index measures the contribution of substitution among the components of labor input to the volume obtained from a given number of hours:

$$Q_{L,j} = \frac{L_j}{H_j}; \ H_j = \sum_l H_{l,j}. \tag{B.28}$$

Labor quality rises and labor input grows faster than hours worked when hours worked by employees with higher marginal products grow faster than hours worked by workers with lower marginal products.[15]

To construct the price and quantity indexes of labor input, we require matrices of average weekly hours worked, average weeks per year, and average hourly labor compensation for 168 types of labor for each year for each industry, h_{saecj}, w_{saecj}, and c_{saej}. We derive total hours worked in cell *saecj* from the number of workers in that cell E_{saecj}, multiplied by the average hours per week and average weeks per year:

$$H_{saecj} = h_{saecj} w_{saecj} E_{saecj}. \tag{B.29}$$

The total compensation for that cell is $c_{saecj} H_{saecj}$. The next section describes how the matrices of employment, hours/week, weeks/year, and compensation/hour are constructed.

B.3.2 Sources of Labor Data

A detailed description of the labor data and its sources can be found in JHS (2005, section 6.3). This covered the 1977–2000 period and we describe two major extensions here. We incorporate the 2000 Census Public Use microdata and link the SIC-based data to the more recent NAICS-based surveys to extend the series to 2005. The employment, hours, weeks, and wage matrices are constructed from household survey data in the decennial Census and annual Current Population Surveys (CPS).

The microdata provide information on gender, age, educational attainment, work status, industry, hours and weeks worked, and wage income for each person in the sample. Issues such as top-coding of income, multiple-job holders, and small sample sizes are addressed in JHS (2005, chapter 6). The challenge for industry analysis has been the change in industry classification from SIC to NAICS. We first discuss extensions for 1960–1990 based on the SIC. We then describe how we incorporated the 2000 Census, which is based on NAICS.

B.3.2.1 Industry Classification

As noted earlier, table B.13 lists the 35 IGEM industries in the business sector, as well as the Household and General Government sectors for which we compute labor input indexes. General Government includes public schools and public hospitals, which are not included in private services. In JHS (2005) 41 business industries are separately identified with considerable detail for the information technology sectors. In IGEM we use a different classification where all two-digit manufacturing industries are distinguished in order to estimate their energy use. The Services industry here is a large composite sector, unlike the more detailed classification of service industries employed in JHS (2005).

Our first step is to estimate employment, hours, weeks, and compensation matrices from the decennial Census. We divide the labor force into 88 sectors that are analyzed in detail in Jorgenson, Ho, Samuels, and Stiroh (2007). The three-digit industry data in the Census and CPS covers about 200 to 300 sectors, depending on the year. These data are first aggregated to the 88-industry classification and then to the 35 IGEM industries.

We estimate initial benchmark matrices for the 88 industries, based on the 1% sample Census Public Use sample covering about one million workers. We then estimate the corresponding matrices for the intervening years, using household data from the CPS *Annual Demographic Survey*, given in the March Supplements.[16] The CPS covers 50 to 100,000 workers during this period and this sample is too small to enable us to estimate such a large matrix directly. Instead, we estimate matrices of lower dimensions used as control totals to adjust the benchmarks. This interpolation for the years between the benchmarks uses the iterative proportional fitting method described in JHS (2005, chapter 6).

Finally, we bring the time series of matrices derived from household data in consistency with data from the U.S. National Income and Product Accounts (NIPAs) derived from establishment surveys. We scale total employment, annual hours worked, and compensation for each industry to the data in the NIPAs, covering 65 industries.[17] We estimate a consistent set of control totals for employment, hours, and labor compensation by applying industry ratios from the household-based matrices described above. The result is a time series of labor data matrices consistent with NIPAs and suitable for applying equations (B.27) and (B.29) to the 35 business industries, Households, and General Government.

An important difference from the NIPAs is our treatment of utilities. The NIPAs have detailed data for private utilities, federal government enterprises, and state and local government enterprises. Private utilities must be disaggregated to obtain electric utilities, gas utilities, and water. Government enterprises must be subdivided into government electric utilities and others. The allocation of sectors not explicitly identified in the NIPAs is done using labor data from the BLS Office of Employment Projections (BLS-EMP) covering 200 sectors that parallels the BLS Input-Output data described above in section B.2.[18]

B.3.2.2 Census 2000 and NAICS

Our second major extension of JHS (2005) is the incorporation of data from the 2000 Census. The estimates in JHS (2005) extrapolate the 1990 Census, using the CPS with a sample size less than one-tenth of the Census. Here we revise the estimates for 1991–2000 by incorporating detailed microdata from the 2000 Census. This represents a major step forward in capturing the trends of the late 1990s, the period of the American growth resurgence discussed by JHS. We are able to capture more accurately the rapidly changing distribution of workers by gender, age, and educational attainment.

The major difference between the 2000 Census and earlier Census data is the change in the industrial classification system from SIC to NAICS. The NAICS classification provides a richer characterization of the now-dominant service industries. We first created matrices of employment, weekly hours, annual weeks, and labor compensation based on the 275 NAICS industries at the three-digit level from the 2000 Census. Next we constructed a link that assigns each of those 275 NAICS industries to the 88 industries based on the SIC.

While some of the 275 industries can be mapped directly into one of the 88 industries, for example, Crop Production is mapped directly to Farms in the SIC system. For other industries, the totals must be split across several three-digit industries. For example, Travel Arrangements and Reservation Services must be mapped into Arrangement of Passenger Transportation, Other Business Services, and Membership Organizations.

We have split industries across three-digit SIC industries, employing ratios from the Current Employment Statistics program of the Bureau of Labor Statistics (BLS).[19] This allocation gives the shares of each NAICS industry going to the corresponding SIC industries. Using this map we convert the Census 2000 benchmark matrices of employment, hours worked, and labor compensation 88 industries based on the SIC data. We thus have a consistent time series for the period 1960–2000.

B.3.2.3 Estimating Self-employment

Our employment class divides the workforce between employees and self-employed and unpaid workers. The wages for employees are reported in the household surveys and total compensation is estimated in the NIPAs. The business income of the self-employed noncorporate business includes the return to the capital as well as labor compensation of self-employed workers. Procedures have to be devised to allocate part of this total to labor compensation. Our method is described in JHS (2005, p. 277) and assumes that self-employed workers cost the same as employees with the same gender-age-education characteristics in each industry.

For the economy as a whole the self-employed are only about 6.9% of the work force in 2000 and our assumption of equal wage rates between employees and self-employed is not numerically significant. However, the proportion of the self-employed varies widely from essentially zero in some manufacturing industries to 70% in health practitioners. The other industries with high self-employment are agriculture, construction, and trade. For these industries the assumption of equal wage rates is important.

B.3.2.4 Extending the Estimates to 2005

The CPS data are classified on a NAICS basis after 2003 and these are treated in a similar manner to the 2000 Census. We first compile the matrices for employment, hours, and compensation on the NAICS classification and then map them to the 88 industries using the 1997 bridge noted in footnote 19. This gives us a set of control matrices with the same definitions for 1960–2005.

B.3.3 Results

B.3.3.1 Employment and Hours Worked

First, in terms of size, there are only 1.50 million workers in the five energy-related industries in 2005, or 0.99% of total domestic employment. This includes both employees and the self-employed. Table B.13 shows that within the energy group, the largest industry is Electric Utilities, private and government, with 822,000 workers, followed by Petroleum and Gas Mining with 369,000.

Table B.14 gives the employment in the five energy industries for all years. Overall, the proportion of workers in the energy group has decreased since 1970, when it employed 1.93% of all workers. Since then services have grown much faster than the primary and manufacturing sectors. Of the energy group, the biggest reductions are in Gas Utilities from 277,000 workers in 1970 to 111,000 in 2005, followed by

Table B.14
Employment in the energy group (1000s)

	Coal	Oil and Gas	Refining	Electric	Gas Utilities
1970	148	281	189	500	277
1971	150	273	187	517	276
1972	163	274	184	471	338
1973	163	283	185	492	335
1974	182	313	190	547	289
1975	215	339	189	556	270
1976	230	355	194	542	288
1977	241	388	200	556	295
1978	236	443	202	568	321
1979	256	485	203	624	303
1980	253	576	198	668	288
1981	238	713	205	682	304
1982	244	721	192	708	287
1983	195	613	187	814	184
1984	200	625	179	848	164
1985	191	596	172	871	152
1986	177	462	164	883	143
1987	162	415	161	907	127
1988	151	419	158	884	163
1989	146	396	155	874	169
1990	147	410	156	900	162
1991	136	410	158	905	165
1992	127	369	155	879	181
1993	113	359	150	873	181
1994	113	352	147	901	145
1995	106	335	143	869	150
1996	99	335	139	853	136
1997	97	354	137	861	118
1998	93	354	135	851	127
1999	87	310	131	822	159
2000	79	321	126	856	118
2001	82	361	124	869	119
2002	81	354	121	866	118
2003	74	348	118	843	114
2004	76	353	115	836	113
2005	80	369	115	822	111

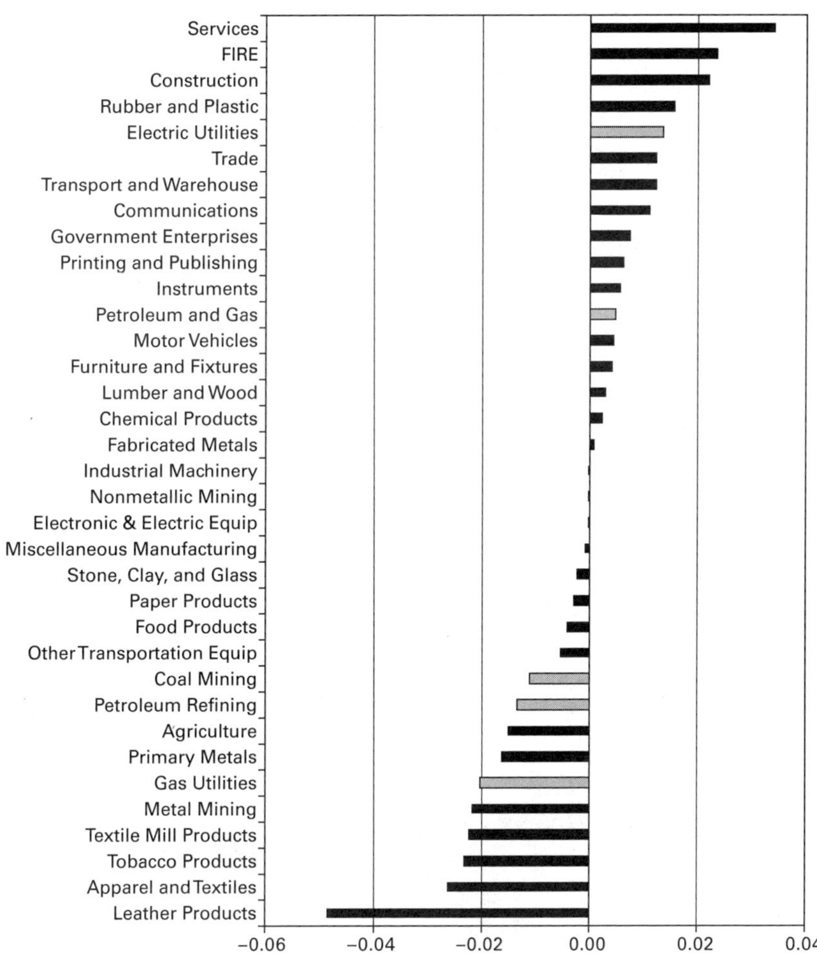

Figure B.6
Growth in industry hours worked, 1960–2005 (% per year).

Coal Mining, which fell from 148,000 to 80,000. The number of workers in Electric Utilities rose from 500,000 to 822,000 over this period.

We measure labor input in terms of total hours worked, not just the number of workers. Figure B.6 gives the growth rate of hours worked over the period 1960–2005, ranking from the fastest to the slowest. The energy industries are again indicated by light-colored bars. The most rapidly growing industry was Services (3.4% per year), followed by Finance, Insurance, and Real Estate (2.4%), and Construction (2.2%).

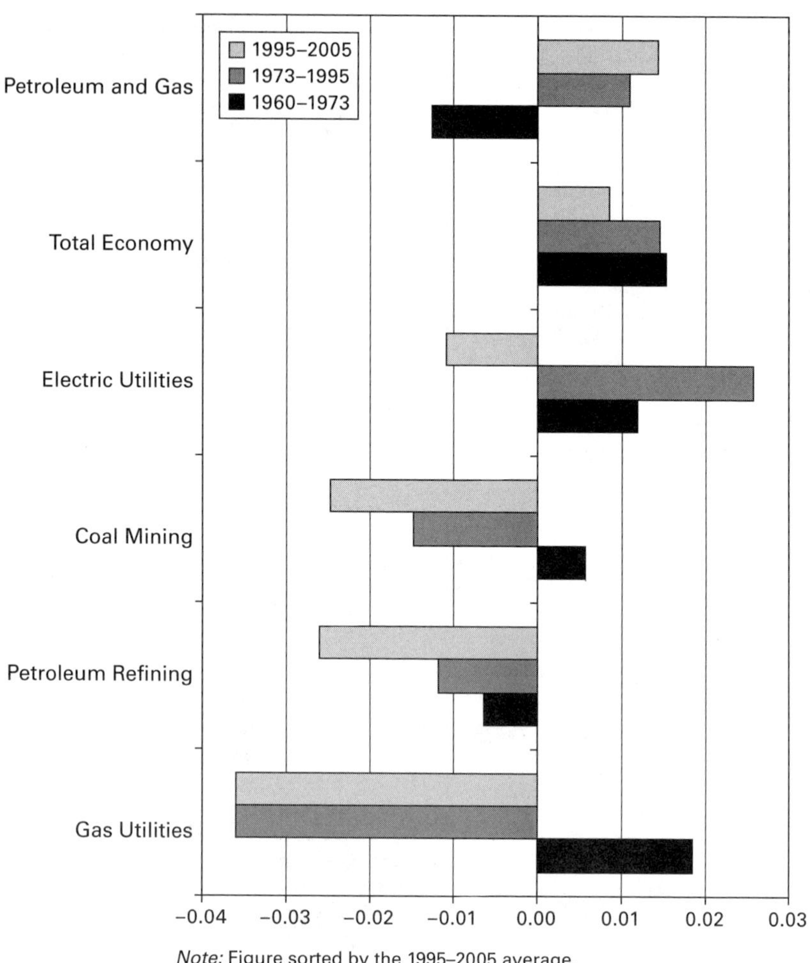

Note: Figure sorted by the 1995–2005 average.

Figure B.7
Growth in hours worked in energy group, by subperiod.

The period 1960–2005 saw considerable electrification. Electric Utilities has the fifth highest growth rate of hours at 1.4% per year. Petroleum and Gas Mining grew at a 0.5% rate. Three of the five energy industries shrank over this period; hours worked in Gas Utilities fell at 2.0% per year, Petroleum Refining at 1.3%, and Coal Mining at 0.6%. These rates should be compared to the national average growth rate of 1.3% per year.

Providing a more detailed picture of the energy group, figure B.7 charts the growth rate of the five industries and the economy average by subperiods 1960–1973, 1973–1995, and 1995–2005. The industries are ranked by the growth rate of the most recent subperiod. We see that during 1995–2005, when the hours-worked growth for the whole economy was 0.84% per year, only Petroleum and Gas Mining exceeded that at 1.4%; the others shrank at rates exceeding 1% per year.

During the 1973–1995 period, which included the oil shocks of the 1970s, Electric Utilities hours grew at 2.6% per year, far exceeding the economy average of 1.4%. Petroleum and Gas Mining grew at 1.1% but Coal Mining, Refining, and Gas Utilities shed hours at a rate exceeding 1.2% per year. In the earliest period, 1960–1973, Gas Utilities expanded hours at 1.8% per year, followed by Electric Utilities at 1.2%, and Coal Mining at 0.2%. Both Petroleum Mining and Refining shrank.

B.3.3.2 Labor Cost

In section B.3.2 above we have observed that there are no direct observations on labor compensation for the self-employed. The last column in table B.13 gives the hourly compensation of workers in year 2005. Household workers are paid the lowest rates, less than $10/hour. Among the business industries Agriculture has the lowest compensation ($19/hour) and Petroleum Refining has the highest at $58/hour. Of course this does not cover the full range of variation in labor compensation. If we had disaggregated the FIRE and Services industries we would find costs exceeding $60/hour. All five of the energy-related industries have labor costs exceeding the economy average of $30.3/hour.

In table B.15 we show how the labor compensation rates have changed over time by reporting the hourly costs for 1970, 1995, and 2005. The relative ranking of the labor costs have not changed a lot during this 35-year span. Petroleum Refining has labor costs among the top three industries in each of these years. Electric Utilities and Gas Utilities also have high labor costs, ranked about five or six during these years. Coal Mining had relatively high hourly compensation in the earlier years but is now closer to the national average. On the other hand, Petroleum Refining had labor compensation rates close to the average in 1970 but the seventh highest rate in 2005.

B.3.3.3 Labor Input and Labor Quality

The growth of industry labor input over 1960–2005 is charted in figure B.8, with industries ranked from the fastest to slowest. Labor input for the whole economy grew at 2.04% per year during this period. The

Table B.15
Compensation per hour ($/hr)

	Industry	1970	1995	2005
1	Agriculture	2.05	10.49	19.21
2	Metal Mining	5.28	28.80	42.31
3	Coal Mining	5.92	25.50	36.16
4	Petroleum and Gas	5.08	26.17	44.23
5	Nonmetallic Mining	4.86	19.78	29.18
6	Construction	5.35	18.68	26.15
7	Food Products	4.21	18.31	26.83
8	Tobacco Products	4.36	36.26	57.27
9	Textile Mill Products	3.32	14.70	22.27
10	Apparel and Textiles	3.53	12.93	24.96
11	Lumber and Wood	4.14	16.20	22.82
12	Furniture and Fixtures	4.01	16.30	27.11
13	Paper Products	4.54	22.58	35.50
14	Printing and Publishing	5.55	20.90	32.43
15	Chemical Products	5.46	30.58	53.37
16	Petroleum Refining	6.57	32.31	58.31
17	Rubber and Plastic	4.34	18.09	26.15
18	Leather Products	3.62	14.99	29.46
19	Stone, Clay, and Glass	4.85	20.56	28.98
20	Primary Metals	5.65	24.76	34.28
21	Fabricated Metals	5.05	20.61	28.11
22	Industrial Machinery	5.28	23.82	40.32
23	Electronic and Electric Equipment	4.76	24.00	41.27
24	Motor Vehicles	6.61	34.62	41.68
25	Other Transportation Equipment	6.13	27.06	40.88
26	Instruments	5.52	26.67	42.89
27	Miscellaneous Manufacturing	4.45	18.73	28.54
28	Transport and Warehouse	5.19	19.49	26.65
29	Communications	5.51	29.57	44.15
30	Electric Utilities	5.60	29.74	49.00
31	Gas Utilities	5.69	29.69	50.22
32	Trade	3.59	14.87	22.33
33	FIRE	4.69	27.45	47.66
34	Services	4.23	19.09	28.77
35	Government Enterprises	4.37	29.39	42.34
36	Households	1.98	7.56	9.45
38	Government	4.71	24.37	37.81
	Total economy	4.25	19.15	29.15

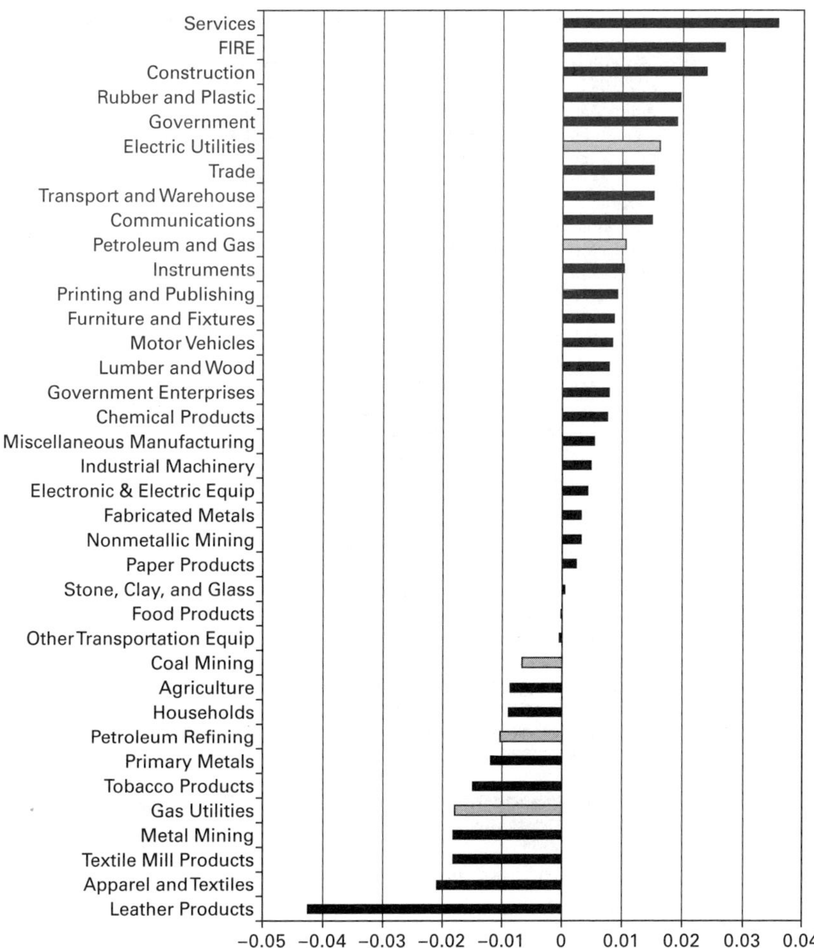

Figure B.8
Growth in industry labor input, 1960–2005 (% per year).

rankings are not identical to those in figure B.6 for the growth of hours worked. The two industries in the energy group with the fastest growth in labor input are also Electric Utilities (1.6% per year) and Petroleum and Gas Mining (1.1% per year). The other three energy-related industries have negative labor input growth, Coal Mining (–0.7%), Petroleum Refining (–1.0%), and Gas Utilities (–1.8%).

The key feature of our methodology is that it allows us to distinguish between total hours worked and labor input adjusted for changes in the composition of the workforce. The quality of labor input in each

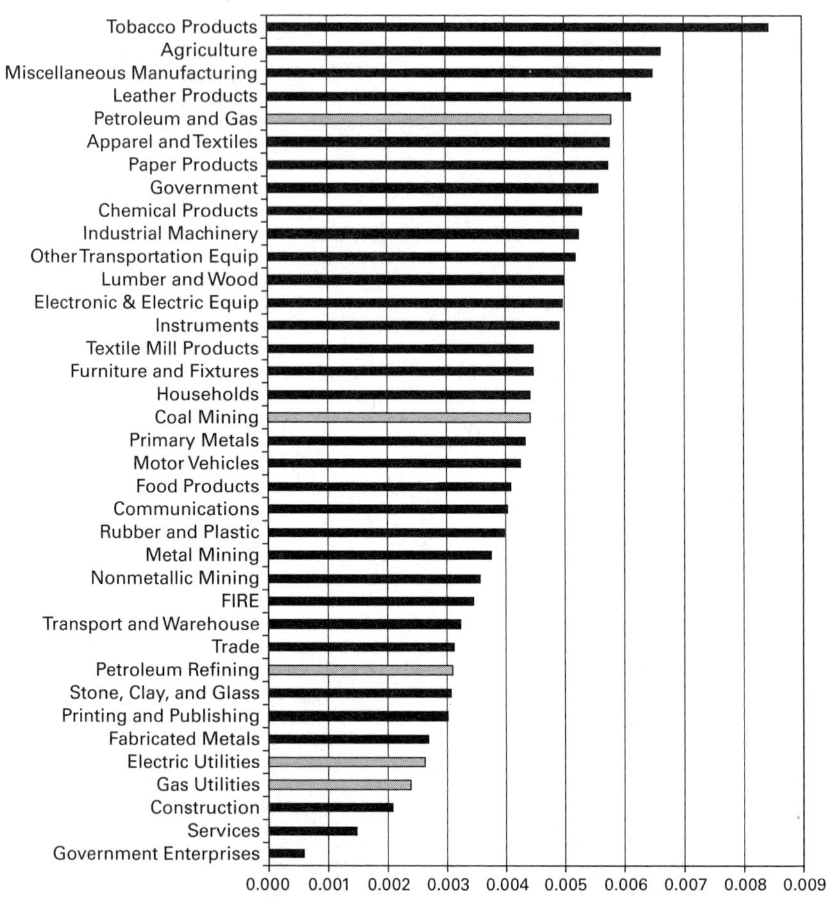

Figure B.9
Growth in industry labor quality, 1960–2005 (% per year).

industry is defined in (B.29) as the ratio of labor input to hours worked. A rise in labor quality reflects a shift in hours worked toward more highly paid workers with higher marginal products, for example, a shift from workers with bachelor's degrees to those with master's or higher degrees.

For the whole economy the labor quality index grew at 0.48% per year during 1960–2005. The gap in growth rates between hours and labor input in Petroleum and Gas Mining means that labor quality was rising at a rapid 0.58% per year during this period. The growth in labor quality for all industries is plotted in figure B.9 with the energy group indicated by light-colored bars.

Tobacco Products has the highest growth in labor quality at 0.85% per year, as the sector shrank with the biggest reduction occurring in groups of workers with the lowest wages. Next is Agriculture, another industry with falling employment and with labor quality rising at 0.66% per year. The three industries with the next most rapid growth of labor quality are Miscellaneous Manufacturing, Leather Products, and Petroleum and Gas Mining. The industries with the slowest growth of labor quality are Government Enterprises (0.06%), Services (0.15%), and Construction (0.21%).

The energy industries that had gains in labor quality below the economy average, are Coal Mining (0.44% per year), followed by Petroleum Refining (0.31%), Electric Utilities (0.26%), and Gas Utilities (0.24%). Over the period 1960–2005 all industries had a positive growth in labor quality. However, as noted in JHS (2005) the changes show a more varied pattern in the more recent period.

To better understand the changes in labor quality growth, we estimate growth by subperiods, as shown in figure B.10. These are ranked by the growth rates in the 1995–2005 period. We see that labor quality in the energy group as a whole grew slower than the total economy rate of 0.45% per year during 1995–2005. In the energy group Petroleum Refining had the fastest growth of labor quality in the most recent decade, while Petroleum and Gas Mining had the slowest at 0.09% per year.

The rankings of industries by growth of labor quality during the 1973–1995 period were quite different. The two energy mining industries had quality growth exceeding 0.7% per year compared to the national average rate of 0.47%. The other industries in the energy group also had substantial quality growth in this period of oil shocks. In the earliest subperiod, 1960–1973, when the national average was growing at 0.53% per year, Electric Utilities, Coal Mining, and Petroleum Refining had labor quality growth less than 0.15% per year. Overall, we conclude that more highly educated workers have been moving towards the high-technology industries identified in JHS (2005) and fewer to the declining energy industries. It must be emphasized that while they are slower than the economy average, all the energy industries showed positive growth in quality in all subperiods.

B.3.3.4 Changes in the Workforce Composition

Changes in labor quality reflect the changing composition of hours worked by gender, class, age, and education. As described in JHS (2005,

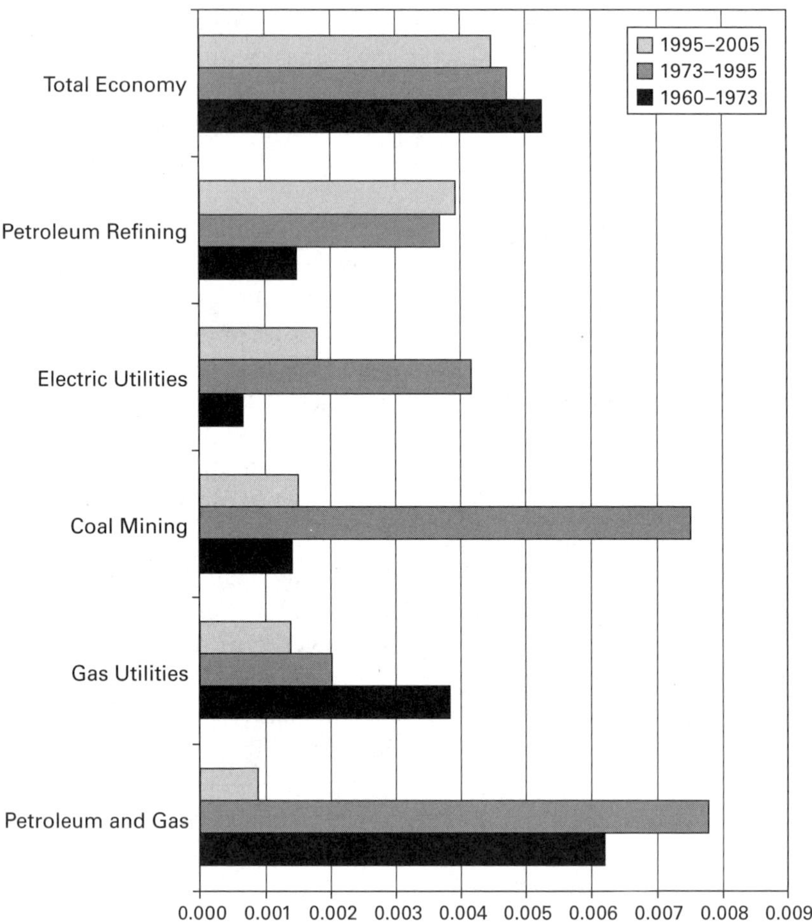

Figure B.10
Growth of labor quality by subperiod (% per year).

chapter 6), the rise in educational attainment for the economy as a whole contributes most to the growth in labor quality, followed by the aging of the labor force. Wages are highest in the prime age group of 45 to 54 years old and this group expanded relative to the younger groups with the maturing of the baby boomers during this period. The rapid entry of women into the labor force in the 1970s led to a fall in the quality index, since they had lower average wages.

To analyze the change in labor quality for the energy group, we tabulate the share of workers with educational attainment of a bachelor's or higher degree in each of the energy industries for 1960, 1970,

Table B.16
Percentage of workers with a college degree or above

	Industry	1960	1970	1980	1990	2005
3	Coal Mining	1.1	2.9	5.4	8.5	9.7
4	Petroleum and Gas Mining	13.3	13.6	19.2	26.4	28.6
16	Petroleum Refining	11.8	15.4	21.7	26.3	31.0
30	Electric Utilities	10.5	6.4	15.0	22.6	25.4
31	Gas Utilities	8.6	8.4	16.5	22.2	26.6
	Total Economy	9.6	12.6	18.7	23.8	30.0

1980, 1990, and 2005 in table B.16. The highest quality growth during 1960–2005 was in Petroleum Gas Mining, one of the two energy industries that expanded its workforce. Educational attainment in Petroleum and Gas Mining rose with the rest of the economy, from only 13.4% with a bachelor's or higher degree in 1960 to 28.6% in 2005.

Coal mining is one of the declining industries in the U.S. economy and has the second largest increase in labor quality among the energy group. Its share of workers with a bachelor's or higher degree rose from 1.1% to 9.7%. Most of the industries in the energy group have lower average educational attainment than the overall economy in 2005. Only Petroleum Refining has a share of workers with more than a bachelor's degree that is higher than the national average of 30.0%. Although the industries in the energy group have lower shares of highly educated workers, their wages are higher than the national average, as shown in table B.15. The relative wages in the energy-mining industries are likely due in part to the higher degree of health and injury risks.

The second important contributor to the change in labor quality is the change in the age structure. In any given period labor compensation rises from the youngest workers up to the age group 45–54 and then declines with age. Thus a workforce that is increasingly young will see falling labor quality, while falling birth rates will generate rising quality. In table B.17 we give the share of the workforce that is in the prime age group, for each of the energy-related industries.

For the entire labor force the share of workers in the prime age group fell from 20.9% in 1960 to 15.9% in 1980 and then rose rapidly to 22.9% in 2005. The age structure for the energy group follows this national trend; however, all five industries have a share of prime-aged workers that is much higher than the national average. In year 2005, the industries with the largest share of prime-aged workers were Coal Mining

Table B.17
Percentage of workers aged 45–54

	Industry	1960	1970	1980	1990	2005
3	Coal Mining	30.5	23.2	15.0	20.2	41.6
4	Petroleum and Gas Mining	22.6	25.2	15.3	15.1	30.1
16	Petroleum Refining	25.7	29.5	17.7	19.5	36.9
30	Electric Utilities	19.9	18.9	18.4	19.5	33.8
31	Gas Utilities	18.9	26.3	24.7	18.7	35.5
	Total Economy	20.9	19.9	15.9	16.1	22.9

Table B.18
Percentage of female workers

	Industry	1960	1970	1980	1990	2005
3	Coal Mining	1.0	2.4	6.0	5.2	6.4
4	Petroleum and Gas Mining	7.9	15.1	16.1	19.5	16.7
16	Petroleum Refining	13.4	13.5	16.2	19.3	18.4
30	Electric Utilities	17.6	15.3	20.7	24.2	25.7
31	Gas Utilities	13.7	11.0	21.5	24.3	25.3
	Total Economy	30.3	35.9	41.3	45.0	46.3

(42%) and Petroleum Refining (37%). Even the lowest share in Petroleum and Gas Mining (30.1%) is much higher than the national average of 22.9%.

Finally, table B.18 presents data on the share of female workers in the energy group over this period. For the workforce as a whole the share rose dramatically in the earlier part of the period, from 30% in 1960 to 41% in 1980, and then rose more slowly to 46.3% in 2005. The energy industries have a far lower share of female workers than the national average: 6% in Coal Mining in 2005, 17% in Petroleum and Gas Mining, and 18% in Petroleum Refining. The change in the female share over time, however, exceeds the national average in some cases; Petroleum and Gas Mining doubled the female share from 8% in 1960 to 17% in 2005.

To summarize: The workers in the energy group are older, mostly male, and less educated than the national average but enjoy wages that are higher than the average. The change in labor quality spans the range seen in the rest of the economy with the slowest change in Electric and Gas Utilities. Differences in growth rates of labor input reflect the large changes in the composition of the energy sector over the period 1960–2005 with the spread of electrification and the rise in domestic mining of petroleum and natural gas.

B.4 Measuring Industry Capital Input

In this section we describe the construction of industry capital input indexes that enter the state-space models of producer behavior presented in chapter 4. The methodology and data sources are described in detail in chapter 5 of Jorgenson, Ho, and Stiroh (2005). We give a short summary of the methodology in section B.4.1, outline how the data are extended 2000 to 2005 in section B.4.2, and provide the results in section B.4.3.

Our calculation of capital input starts with the explicit recognition of the enormous heterogeneity of capital assets. A computer, for instance, has a short service life and a high marginal product per dollar invested, while a commercial building has a long service life and a low marginal product. Recognizing these differences is critical for the measurement of capital input and modeling the future trajectory of the U.S. economy, since investment patterns have changed radically with the rapid substitution toward information technology equipment and software. Information-processing equipment and software accounted for just 11.4% of private fixed investment in 1977 but 25.1% in 2002. Changes at the industry level show even larger swings.

We emphasize the distinction between the installed stock of capital at a point in time and the annual service flow from that stock. The stock of each asset type is associated with an acquisition price, while each service flow is associated with a rental price, the cost of using the asset for a year. When the different asset types are aggregated to obtain total capital services, the weights are the rental prices which are measures of marginal productivity. This methodology is widely used, including by the Bureau of Labor Statistics (BLS) multifactor productivity program and in the new aggregate production account for the U.S. economy constructed by the Bureau of Economic Analysis (BEA) and the BLS.[20] It is also used in the *OECD Manual: Measuring Capital* (Schreyer 2009).

As a result of the distinction between capital stock and capital services, the growth of capital input can be decomposed into two sources—changes in the quantity of capital of each type and substitution among assets. This second effect, which we have denoted as the growth of capital quality, is critical for capturing the dramatic substitution toward information technology (IT) assets like computer hardware, software, and telecomm equipment with relatively short service lives and high marginal products. For the economy as a whole, the annual contribution of capital quality growth to aggregate U.S. output growth increased from 0.90 percentage points for 1973–1989 to 2.27 percentage points for 1995–2002 (JHS 2005, chapter 2).

B.4.1 Methodology

This section presents the methodology used to estimate the flow of capital services in each industry, as expressed in the production function (2.2). We begin with investment by industry and asset class, use the perpetual inventory method to generate capital stocks, and then combine these with national income data on capital income to estimate the rental price of each type of capital. The BEA provides data for 61 types of nonresidential assets in its *Fixed Assets and Consumer Durables* report, and we consolidate these to the 52 assets listed in table B.19. The investment and income data are given for 62 industries, which we reorganize into the IGEM 35 industries. We further add estimates for residential assets, inventories, and land.

B.4.1.1 Notation

We begin by defining measures of investment, capital stocks, and capital input for individual assets. In all cases, we have a price, a quantity, and a value that is the product of the two. The subscript k refers to the specific asset type, j refers to the industry, and t refers to the year. Where possible, we suppress the time subscripts.

For individual assets,

$I_{k,j}$ = quantity of investment

$P_{I,k,,j}$ = price of investment

δ_k = geometric depreciation rate

$A_{k,j}$ = quantity of capital stock at end of period t

$Z_{k,j}$ = quantity of two-period average capital stock

$P_{I,k,j}$ = price of capital stock

$K_{k,j}$ = quantity of capital services

$P_{K,k,j}$ = price of capital services

$Q_{K,k,j}$ = quality index of capital

Table B.19
Depreciation, inflation, and investment by asset type and class

	Asset	Geometric Depreciation	Price Change % per Year 1960–2005	Current Investment 2005 (bil. $)
	Total domestic tangible assets	na	2.67	3,504.8
	Fixed reproducible assets	na	—	3,467.9
	Private:		2.51	3,064.2
	Equipment and software		1.36	946.5
1	Household furniture	0.1375	3.33	1.9
2	Other furniture	0.1179	3.56	36.5
3	Other fabricated metal products	0.0917	3.73	14.2
4	Steam engines	0.0516	3.73	4.3
5	Internal combustion engines	0.2063	4.05	1.2
6	Farm tractors	0.1452	4.22	10.8
7	Construction tractors	0.1633	4.56	3.9
8	Agricultural machinery, except tractors	0.1179	4.12	10.5
9	Construction machinery, except tractors	0.1550	4.29	25.3
10	Mining and oilfield machinery	0.1500	4.50	7.5
11	Metalworking machinery	0.1225	4.00	26.0
12	Special industry machinery, n.e.c.	0.1031	4.27	30.6
13	General industrial, including materials handling	0.1072	3.90	58.7
14	Computers and peripheral equipment	0.3150	–18.37	89.0
15	Service industry machinery	0.1650	3.09	19.0
16	Communication equipment	0.1100	0.98	86.2
17	Electrical transmission, distribution. and industrial apparatus	0.0500	2.68	21.4
18	Household appliances	0.1650	1.97	0.2
19	Other electrical equipment, n.e.c.	0.1834	2.79	6.8
20	Trucks, buses, and truck trailers	0.1917	2.63	96.7
21	Autos	0.2719	2.09	31.9
22	Aircraft	0.0825	4.41	15.0
23	Ships and boats	0.0611	4.17	4.8
24	Railroad equipment	0.0589	3.89	4.6

(continued)

Table B.19 (continued)

	Asset	Geometric Depreciation	Price Change % per Year 1960–2005	Current Investment 2005 (bil. $)
25	Instruments (scientific and engineering)	0.1350	2.89	79.9
26	Photocopy and related equipment	0.1800	0.23	3.6
27	Other nonresidential equipment	0.1473	2.45	56.0
28	Other office equipment	0.3119	0.83	6.2
29	Software	0.3150	–0.88	193.8
	Nonresidential structures		4.74	334.6
30	Industrial buildings	0.0314	4.65	23.0
31	Mobile structures (offices)	0.0556	2.51	0.9
32	Office buildings	0.0247	4.98	46.3
33	Commercial warehouses	0.0222	0.00	0.0
34	Other commercial buildings, n.e.c.	0.0262	4.81	59.3
35	Religious buildings	0.0188	4.72	7.5
36	Educational buildings	0.0188	4.69	14.1
37	Hospital and institutional buildings	0.0188	4.72	24.9
38	Hotels and motels	0.0281	4.71	16.3
39	Amusement and recreational buildings	0.0300	4.71	6.7
40	Other nonfarm buildings, n.e.c.	0.0249	4.70	2.2
41	Railroad structures	0.0166	4.07	5.7
42	Telecommunications	0.0237	3.28	15.6
43	Electric light and power (structures)	0.0211	4.40	21.7
44	Gas (structures)	0.0237	4.46	6.4
45	Local transit buildings	0.0237	0.00	0.0
46	Petroleum pipelines	0.0237	4.49	0.7
47	Farm-related buildings and structures	0.0239	4.73	5.9
48	Petroleum and natural gas	0.0751	5.62	70.2
49	Other mining exploration	0.0450	4.75	3.1
50	Other nonfarm structures	0.0450	4.53	4.2
51	Railroad track replacement	0.0275	0.00	0.0
52	Nuclear fuel rods	0.0225	0.00	0.0

Table B.19 (continued)

	Asset	Geometric Depreciation	Price Change % per Year 1960–2005	Current Investment 2005 (bil. $)
	Residential structures		4.59	759.2
53	1- to 4-unit homes	0.0114	4.67	543.6
54	5-or-more-unit homes	0.0140	4.58	44.3
55	Mobile homes	0.0455	2.49	9.1
56	Improvements	0.0255	4.62	160.7
57	Other residential	0.0227	4.75	1.5
	Consumers durables		1.65	1023.9
61	Autos	0.2550	2.93	227.1
62	Trucks	0.2316	2.51	190.8
63	Other (RVs)	0.2316	2.29	27.0
64	Furniture	0.1179	2.25	79.9
65	Kitchen appliance	0.1500	0.81	36.8
66	China, glassware	0.1650	2.66	36.6
67	Other durable	0.1650	−1.96	85.8
68	Computers and software	0.3150	−14.23	56.5
69	Video, audio	0.1833	1.59	82.7
70	Jewelry	0.1500	3.69	24.3
71	Ophthalmic	0.2750	1.78	76.2
72	Books and maps	0.1650	1.75	58.4
73	Wheel goods	0.1650	4.09	41.8
	Land	—	10.13	—
	Inventories	—	2.84	36.9
	Government:	—	3.58	403.7
	Federal, nonmilitary	—	3.20	37.1
	Structures	—	4.52	9.4
	Office buildings	0.0182	4.62	2.0
	Commercial building	0.0182	4.57	1.1
	Health care	0.0182	4.58	0.6
	Education	0.0182	4.57	0.3
	Public safety	0.0182	4.58	0.3
	Amusement	0.0182	4.58	0.2
	Transportation	0.0285	4.60	0.2
	Power	0.0285	4.39	0.7
	Highways	0.0152	4.53	0.4
	Conservation	0.0152	4.37	2.3
	Other structures	0.0182	4.44	1.4

(continued)

Table B.19 (continued)

Asset	Geometric Depreciation	Price Change % per Year 1960–2005	Current Investment 2005 (bil. $)
Equipment and software	0.1650	2.31	27.7
Software	0.3300	2.52	12.8
Federal, military	—	2.75	78.8
Structures	—	5.22	5.9
Residential	0.0140	5.09	1.6
Industrial	0.0285	4.67	0.6
Military facilities	0.0182	5.23	3.7
Equipment	—	2.41	72.9
Aircraft	0.1375	1.90	13.5
Missiles	0.1100	1.35	3.9
Ships	0.0550	4.27	9.8
Vehicles	0.0825	4.06	3.9
Electronics and software	0.1650	2.23	12.8
Software	0.3300	2.52	5.9
Other equipment	0.1650	2.05	23.0
State and local	—	4.12	287.8
Structures	—	4.61	236.7
Residential buildings	0.0182	4.65	6.4
Office buildings	0.0182	4.64	21.6
Commercial buildings	0.0182	4.61	0.4
Healthcare buildings	0.0182	4.67	4.9
Education	0.0182	4.64	66.2
Public safety	0.0182	4.62	4.4
Amusement	0.0182	4.62	6.7
Transportation	0.0152	4.64	19.4
Power	0.0285	4.43	6.4
Highways	0.0152	4.62	68.1
Sewer	0.0152	4.62	14.5
Water	0.0152	4.21	14.2
Conservation	0.0152	4.40	3.1
Other	0.0182	4.60	0.3
Equipment and software	0.1110	1.91	51.1
Software	0.3300	2.26	10.9

For industry aggregates,

I_j = quantity index of industry investment

$P_{I,j}$ = price index of industry investment

Z_j = quantity index of industry capital stock

$P_{Z,j}$ = price index of industry capital stock

K_j = quantity index of industry capital services

$P_{K,j}$ = price of industry capital services

$Q_{K,j}$ = quality index of industry capital

B.4.1.2 Investment and Capital Stock

The BEA data set provides the nominal investment value and price index for each of the 62 assets. We define the quantity of investment $I_{kj,}$ as the nominal value divided by the price, $P_{I,k,j}$. The adjustment of asset prices to keep quality constant is integral to the construction of tractable measures of capital input, since this greatly facilitates aggregation over different vintages. The best-known example is the price deflators for computers in the U.S. national accounts, which are constructed using hedonic methods. These constant-quality price indexes reflect changes in the productive characteristics and quality of the computers over time.

The BEA data on investment provides industry-specific prices for each asset; for example, each industry pays a different price for automobiles, depending on the commodity bundle of automobiles it purchases. Some of the price estimates are volatile and show wide variations across industries. To avoid this sampling variability, we use the economy-wide price of each asset for all industries. This implies that we are assuming that there are no differences in composition within these 62 asset types across industries. This parallels the use of equal intermediate input prices for each industry in appendix B.1.

Capital stocks are estimated by means of the perpetual inventory method. We assume that the investment of different ages is measured in constant efficiency units and the age-efficiency profile is defined by a constant geometric rate.[21] This allows the capital stock to be expressed as

$$A_{k,j,t} = A_{k,j,t-1}(1-\delta_k) + I_{k,j,t} = \sum_{\tau=0}^{\infty}(1-\delta_k)^{\tau} I_{k,j,t-\tau}, \tag{B.30}$$

where $A_{k,j,t}$ is the stock at the end of period t, and the efficiency of an asset declines geometrically with age at the rate δ_k.

B.4.1.3 Capital Services

We let $A_{k,j}$ represent the installed stock of capital but require the flow of capital services or capital input from that stock over a given period, $K_{k,j}$. The distinction between the stock of capital and the flow of capital services is essential when we aggregate heterogeneous assets with widely different marginal products. We assume that it takes some time for new investment to provide productive services, so that the *capital service flow* is proportional to the average of the current and lagged capital stock:

$$K_{k,j,t} = Q_{K,k,j}\frac{1}{2}(A_{k,j,t} + A_{k,j,t-1})$$
$$K_{k,j,t} = Q_{K,k,j} \cdot Z_{k,j,t} \tag{B.31}$$

where $Z_{k,j,t}$ is the two-period average of the installed capital stock, and $Q_{K,k,j}$ is a factor of proportionality that differs among assets but is constant over time for a given asset. This constant is the quality of capital of type k, so that capital must be measured in units of constant quality. It should be emphasized, however, that IGEM expresses capital input for each industry as a proportion of capital stock that varies over time, reflecting changes in the composition of the stock.

The rental price of capital services or the user cost of capital may be interpreted as an arbitrage equation between two alternatives: earning a nominal rate of return on a bond or buying a unit of capital, collecting a rental, and then selling the depreciated asset. This implies the following equation:

$$(1 + i_{t+1})P_{I,t} = c_{k,t} + (1 - \delta_k)P_{I,t+1}, \tag{B.32}$$

where i_t is the nominal interest, $P_{I,t}$ is acquisition price of capital, $c_{i,t}$ is the rental fee, and δ_k is the rate of economic depreciation. This expression can be rearranged to yield the *rental price of capital services*, which we now write using the notation defined above:

$$P_{K,k,j,t} = (i_{j,t} - \pi_{k,j,t})P_{I,k,j,t-1} + \delta_k P_{I,k,j,t}$$
$$P_{K,k,j,t} = r_{k,j,t}P_{I,k,j,t-1} + \delta_k P_{I,k,j,t} \tag{B.33}$$

where $i_{j,t}$ is the nominal rate of return in industry j, the asset-specific capital gains term is $\pi_{k.j,t} = (P_{I,k,j,t} - P_{I,k,j,t-1})/P_{I,k,j,t-1}$, and $r_{k,j,t}$ is the real rate of return for asset k in j.

Tax considerations play an important role in the capital service price framework, as discussed by Jorgenson and Yun (2001). We use the same information here and account for tax credits, depreciation allowances, corporate taxes, property taxes, debt/equity financing, and personal taxes. This yields the following tax-adjusted cost of capital equation:

$$P_{K,k,j,t} = \frac{1 - ITC_{k,t} - \tau_t Z_{k,t}}{1 - \tau_t} [r_{k,j,t} P_{I,k,j,t-1} + \delta_k P_{I,k,j,t}] + \tau_p P_{I,k,j,t-1} \quad \text{(B.34)}$$

where $ITC_{k,t}$ is the investment tax credit, τ_t is the statutory tax rate, $z_{k,t}$ is the present value of capital consumption allowances for tax purposes, τ_p is a property tax rate, all for asset k at time t.

The real rate of return $r_{k,j,t}$ for asset k in industry j is constructed by assuming that the total value of capital services for each industry equals property compensation, which consists of net interest, capital consumption allowances, inventory valuation adjustments, business transfer payments, corporate profits, and certain indirect business taxes. This property compensation is allocated across all asset classes and our procedure yields an internal rate of return that exhausts capital income. This ensures that all receipts of the producers are paid out to the factors of production and is consistent with constant returns to scale.

The tax treatment of income differs among the corporate, noncorporate, and household sectors. We first assume that the after-tax nominal rate of return $\rho_{j,}$ is the same for all assets in the corporate sector of each industry and estimate this as the rate of return that exhausts corporate property compensation. We then calculate the cost of capital in the noncorporate and household sectors for each industry by assuming that these ownership types enjoy the same tax-adjusted nominal rate of return to equity. This procedure is described in JHS (2005, section 5.2.4) and yields service prices that vary across assets, ownership classes, industry, and time.

B.4.1.4 Industry Aggregation

Equations (B.30) through (B.34) summarize our estimation procedure for the capital service flow and capital service price, $K_{k,j,t}$ and $P_{K,k,j,t}$, respectively, for each asset, industry, and time period. To generate estimates for total capital service flows within an industry, we aggregate over assets. The weights reflect marginal products and rental prices provide the appropriate weights. In aggregating capital stocks and investment, on the other hand, we use acquisition prices as weights.

We use a Tornqvist quantity formula to aggregate the service flows from different capital assets:

$$\Delta \ln K_j = \sum_k \overline{v}_{k,j} \Delta \ln K_{k,j} \tag{B.35}$$

where $\Delta x = x_t - x_{t-1}$ denotes the change between period $t - 1$ and t, and the value share of each type of capital services is

$$v_{k,j} = \frac{P_{K,k,j} K_{k,j}}{\sum_k P_{K,k,j} K_{k,j}}. \tag{B.36}$$

We have used the same subscript k in both the numerator and denominator to avoid excessive proliferation of notation, but the different uses should be clear. The two-period average value share weight is

$$\overline{v}_{k,j,t} = \frac{1}{2}(v_{k,j,t} + v_{k,j,t-1}). \tag{B.37}$$

Substituting (B.31) into (B.35), we obtain the growth of capital input:

$$\Delta \ln K_{jt} = \sum_k \overline{v}_{k,j,t} \Delta \ln Z_{k,j,t}. \tag{B.38}$$

The proportionality constant reflecting the quality of capital input is independent of time and drops out, so that capital input for each industry is derived from stocks and capital service weights for each asset type. The *price index of industry capital services*, $P_{K,j}$, is defined implicitly to make the value identity hold:

$$P_{K,j} K_j = \sum_k P_{K,k,j} K_{k,j}. \tag{B.39}$$

The *quantity of capital stock* in industry j is defined as a similar aggregate over stocks of each asset type:

$$\Delta \ln Z_j = \sum_k \overline{w}_{k,j} \Delta \ln Z_{k,j} \tag{B.40}$$

where the value share weights are the two-period average of

$$w_{k,j} = \frac{P_{I,k,j} Z_{k,j}}{\sum_k P_{I,k,j} Z_{k,j}}. \tag{B.41}$$

The corresponding *price index for capital stock*, $P_{Z,j,t}$, is defined implicitly from the value identity

$$P_{Z,j,t} Z_{j,t} = \sum_k P_{I,k,j,t} Z_{k,j,t}. \tag{B.42}$$

The *quantity of investment* is an aggregate over the investment in each asset class:

$$\Delta \ln I_j = \sum_k \bar{u}_{k,j} \Delta \ln I_{k,j} \tag{B.43}$$

where the value share weights are the two-period average of

$$u_{k,j} = \frac{P_{I,k,j} I_{k,j}}{\sum_k P_{I,k,j} I_{k,j}}. \tag{B.44}$$

Given the quantity, the corresponding *price index for investment*, $P_{I,j,t}$, is defined implicitly from the value identity:

$$P_{I,j,t} I_{j,t} = \sum_k P_{I,k,j,t} I_{k,j,t}. \tag{B.45}$$

Finally, we define *capital quality* $Q_{K,j,}$ for industry j as the ratio of capital input to capital stock:

$$Q_{K,j} = \frac{K_j}{Z_j}. \tag{B.46}$$

Large depreciation rates and rapid downward revaluations for computers implies that these assets have high marginal products, so their weight in the index of capital services greatly exceeds their weight in the index of capital stock. Substitution toward computers as their prices fall implies that capital input grows faster than capital stock, resulting in a higher index of capital quality. It must be emphasized that our definition of capital quality does not refer to improvements across vintages. Asset-specific quality changes are incorporated into the quantity component of each type of capital through the use of constant-quality price deflators. Our measure of capital quality reflects changes in the composition of the industry capital aggregate.

Jorgenson, Ho, and Stiroh (2005) have documented the role of information technology in the remarkable U.S. economic resurgence after 1995. Accordingly, it is critically important to capture changes in the composition of capital resulting from the substitution of IT capital for non-IT capital. To make this distinction empirically, we define IT capital to include computer hardware, software, and telecommunications equipment, and non-IT includes all other assets. The index of industry IT capital services and non-IT capital services are defined, respectively, as

$$\Delta \ln K_{IT,j} = \sum_{k \in IT} \overline{v}_{IT,k,j} \Delta \ln K_{IT,j}$$
$$\Delta \ln K_{NON,j} = \sum_{k \notin IT} \overline{v}_{NON,k,j} \Delta \ln K_{NON,j} \quad \text{(B.47)}$$

where the shares for each type of IT capital or non-IT capital, $v_{IT,k,j}$ and $v_{NON,k,j}$, respectively, are out of total IT capital or non-IT capital for each industry, respectively.

A useful result that follows from Tornqvist aggregation is that the growth in the industry capital service flow defined in equation (B.35) above can also be expressed as a Tornqvist index of these two sub-aggregates:

$$\Delta \ln K_j = \overline{v}_{IT,j} \Delta \ln K_{IT,j} + (1 - \overline{v}_{IT,j}) \Delta \ln K_{NON,j} \quad \text{(B.48)}$$

where $v_{IT,j}$ is the share of IT capital services in total capital services of the industry. Sub-indices of IT and non-IT capital stock and investment are defined in an analogous manner, where the aggregate of each is again a weighted average of the IT and non-IT components.

B.4.1.5 Aggregating Over Industries

In the IGEM we model aggregate investment as a result of intertemporal optimization by the owner of the private national stock of capital. This is described in chapter 2, section 2.3.1. We thus need to construct national series for investment, stocks, and service flows, not just the industry-level series just discussed. In the model we regard the period t's capital services as coming simply from the stock at the end of period $t-1$, not as a more complicated average of the stocks from $t-1$ and t as in (B.31).

Aggregate investment is the Tornqvist index over the total private investment of the 62 asset types:

$$\Delta \ln I_t^a = \sum_{k=1}^{62} \overline{w}_{kt}^I \Delta \ln I_{kt}, \quad \text{(B.49)}$$

where $\overline{w}_{kt}^I$ is the share of type k investment in total private investment. The price of aggregate investment (PII_t) is derived from the (B.49) and the value identity:

$$PII_t I_t^a = \sum_{k=1}^{62} P_{I,k,t} I_{kt}. \quad \text{(B.50)}$$

The aggregate capital stock of type k follows the same accumulation equation (B.30) for each industry:

$$K_{k,t} = K_{k,t-1}(1-\delta_k) + I_{k,t}, \tag{B.51}$$

and the economy-wide private stock of reproducible capital is the Tornqvist aggregate of the $A_{k,t}$'s:

$$\Delta \ln K_t = \sum_{k=1}^{62} \overline{w}_{kt}^K \Delta \ln K_{kt}. \tag{B.52}$$

The total stock of capital includes land and inventories but we ignore that here for simplicity. The price of the aggregate stock (PK_t) is similarly derived from the value equation

$$PK_t K_t = \sum_{k=1}^{62} P_{kt}^K K_{kt};\ P_{kt}^K = P_{I,k,t}. \tag{B.53}$$

Given that (B.49) and (B.52) have different weights, it should be clear that there is no simple aggregate accumulation equation like

$$K_t = K_{t-1}(1-\delta^a) + I_t^a. \tag{B.54}$$

Instead one needs to start from (B.53), substitute in (B.51) and (B.50), and obtain

$$K_t = K_{t-1}(1-\delta_t^a) + \psi_t^I I_t^a \tag{B.55}$$

$$PK_t = \psi_t^{PK} PII_t \tag{B.56}$$

where ψ_t^I, ψ_t^{PK}, and δ_t^a are "aggregation coefficients" that depend on the individual asset prices in the sample period. Since we do not identify 62 different asset types in the model, we simply regard these aggregation coefficients as exogenous in the simulations.

B.4.2 Data

B.4.2.1 Data Sources

The data sources used to estimate capital input by industry are presented by JHS (2005, section 5.3). The starting point is the estimation of capital input by the 60 private economy industries shown in table B.20. This is based on the BEA report, *Fixed Assets and Consumer Durables*.[22] The period covered by this SIC-based data set is 1901–2000. For the 60 industries, we estimate capital input for 57 fixed reproducible assets listed in table B.19, inventories, and land. For the General Government sector, we estimate capital input for 22 assets, divided among Federal (Non-Military), Federal (Military), and State and Local. Our second data source is the *Fixed Asset Tables* on the NAICS basis

Table B.20
Investment by industry, primary BEA data (fixed nonresidential, 2000, bil. $)

	BEA Classifications (SIC)	IGEM Industry	Investment 2000
	Private sector total		1263.3
1	Farms	1	24.5
2	Agricultural services, forestry, fishing	1	14.2
3	Metal mining	2	1.0
4	Coal mining	3	3.3
5	Oil and gas extraction	4	41.5
6	Nonmetallic minerals, except fuels	5	3.4
7	Construction	6	26.3
8	Lumber and wood products	11	4.1
9	Furniture and fixtures	12	2.0
10	Stone, clay, and glass	19	7.9
11	Primary metal industries	20	7.9
12	Fabricated metal products	21	9.0
13	Industrial machinery and equipment	22	21.4
14	Electronic and other electric equipment	23	25.1
15	Motor vehicles and equipment	24	12.7
16	Other transportation equipment	25	6.8
17	Instruments and related prod	26	10.0
18	Miscellaneous manufacturing	27	1.7
19	Food and kindred products	7	19.2
20	Tobacco products	8	0.6
21	Textile mill products	9	3.6
22	Apparel and other textile	10	1.3
23	Paper and allied products	13	10.3
24	Printing and publishing	14	14.2
25	Chemicals and allied products	15	28.9
26	Petroleum and coal products	16	5.0
27	Rubber, miscellaneous plastics	17	11.3
28	Leather and leather products	18	0.2
29	Railroad transportation	28	9.7
30	Local, interurban passenger transit	28	3.1
31	Trucking and warehousing	28	19.7
32	Water transportation	28	3.2
33	Transportation by air	28	33.3
34	Pipelines, except natural gas	28	1.9
35	Transportation services	28	10.4
36	Telephone and telegraph	29	89.4
37	Radio and television	29	23.8

Table B.20 (continued)

	BEA Classifications (SIC)	IGEM Industry	Investment 2000
38	Electric services (utilities)	30	41.4
39	Gas services (utilities)	31	15.1
40	(Water and) sanitary services	34	10.8
41	Wholesale trade	32	100.8
42	Retail trade	32	76.2
43	Depository inst. (banking)	33	39.8
44	Nondepository institutions (nonbanks)	33	73.5
45	Security, commodity brokers	33	19.8
46	Insurance carriers	33	29.8
47	Insurance agents, brokers, and services	33	4.3
48	Real estate	33	111.4
49	Holding and other investment offices	33	16.9
50	Hotels and other lodging places	34	15.0
51	Personal services	34	3.7
52	Business services	34	91.4
53	Auto repair, services, parking	34	23.3
54	Miscellaneous repair services	34	2.6
55	Motion pictures	34	6.6
56	Amusement and recreation services	34	9.6
57	Health services	34	25.8
58	Legal services	34	5.2
59	Educational services	34	2.1
60	Other services, n.e.c.	34	26.0
61	Households		
62	Government		

also provided by the BEA National Accounts.[23] This covers 63 industries, consumer durables, and government fixed assets, and includes investment estimates back to 1947.

We first scale the investment industry data so that it matches nominal investment for the total economy given in the NIPAs. The investment for each industry is allocated to corporate and noncorporate sectors using historical shares. The price deflator for each asset is taken from the national average in the NIPAs. The depreciation rates are based on Fraumeni (1997) except for special adjustments for computers and automobiles, as described in JHS (2005, section 5.3.1). There are two other assets to include, inventories and land. Total inventory change from the NIPA is allocated to the industries using information from the benchmark input-output tables. Land by industry is based on the historical data described in Jorgenson (1990).

The value of capital input is taken from industry-level value added in the Gross Product Originating database maintained by the BEA and described in Lum and Moyer (2000, 2001).[24] This is supplemented by the 192-industry data from the BLS, as described in appendix B. In the earlier SIC-based version, the BEA data include the value of output, value added, and intermediate inputs for the 60 industries in table B.20. The current version based on NAICS covers the same 64 industries mentioned above for the investment data.

We have aggregated the 60 SIC industries from the BEA to match the IGEM 35 industries. Industries such as the Utilities have to be disaggregated for IGEM. For the estimation of capital service prices, we begin with value added in the corporate sector and subtract corporate labor income to estimate the amount of income available to corporate capital. Similarly, we subtract noncorporate labor income from value added, as described in the following section, to obtain the value of noncorporate capital income.

B.4.2.2 Implementation

Our methodology conforms to the international standards recommended by OECD (Schreyer 2001, 2009). The practical implementation of this methodology is discussed in JHS (2005, section 5.3.2). To link the two industry classifications, SIC and the NAICS, we have computed capital input for the 64 NAICS industries for the 2000–2005 period, using the entire time series of NAICS-based investment data and GDP-by-Industry data. We employ the same simple bridge between the SIC and NAICS that we used for output, as described in section B.2.5.2. Each of the NAICS industries is assigned to one IGEM sector and the growth rates for 2000–2005 are applied to the original series for 1960–2000.

The final issue is the allocation of noncorporate income between capital and the labor of the self-employed. We have assumed that the wage of the self-employed for each demographic group is equal to that of the employees, and the residual is then allocated to capital. While this leads to fluctuations in the rate of return for some sectors, the relatively small size of the noncorporate sector in most industries mitigates this effect. As we have noted in section B.3.2.3 when discussing the labor compensation, this is a difficult problem in sectors with high self-employment—agriculture, retail trade, health practitioners, and some services.

B.4.3 Results

B.4.3.1 Investment, Capital Stock, and Services

Table B.19 gives the investment by asset type in year 2005, a few years into the low investment period following the 2001 dot-com crash. Of the $3468 billion investment in fixed reproducible assets, the private sector, including Households, bought $3064 billion and the government bought $404 billion. Within private sector investment, $1783 billion is in residential structures and consumer durables, while $1281 billion is in business equipment and structures. Of the $3064 of private fixed investment, $425 billion is in information and communications technology—computers and peripheral equipment, communications equipment, and software.

Energy-sector investments in structures include electric light and power structures, gas structures, petroleum pipelines, petroleum and natural gas structures, and nuclear fuel rods; these came to $99 billion in 2005, or 30%, of private nonresidential structure investment. This investment pattern is quite different from that in 2000 at the height of the Information Technology boom. In 2000 investment in information technology assets was $457 billion out of a total of $2522 private-sector investment, that is, even higher in nominal terms than the 2005 level. Investment in energy-related structures in 2000 came to only 18% of private structure investment.

During the 1995–2000 period the prices of information technology equipment and software declined dramatically and investment in these assets rose sharply. In figure B.11 we plot the changes in investment goods prices over the period 1960–2005 for the 57 assets. We can see that most goods prices rose at about 3–5% per year with general inflation, but prices of computers fell by 18% per year and communications equipment rose by only 1.0%. The price of electric light and power structures rose at 4.4% per year while petroleum and gas structures rose at 5.6%.

Table B.20 gives investment by industry in year 2000 at the most detailed level in the BEA investment data set.[25] Of the nonresidential business investment of $1263 billion, the energy group share is $106 billion, compared to $101 billion in Wholesale, and $91 billion in Business Services. This energy group investment is 8.4% of business

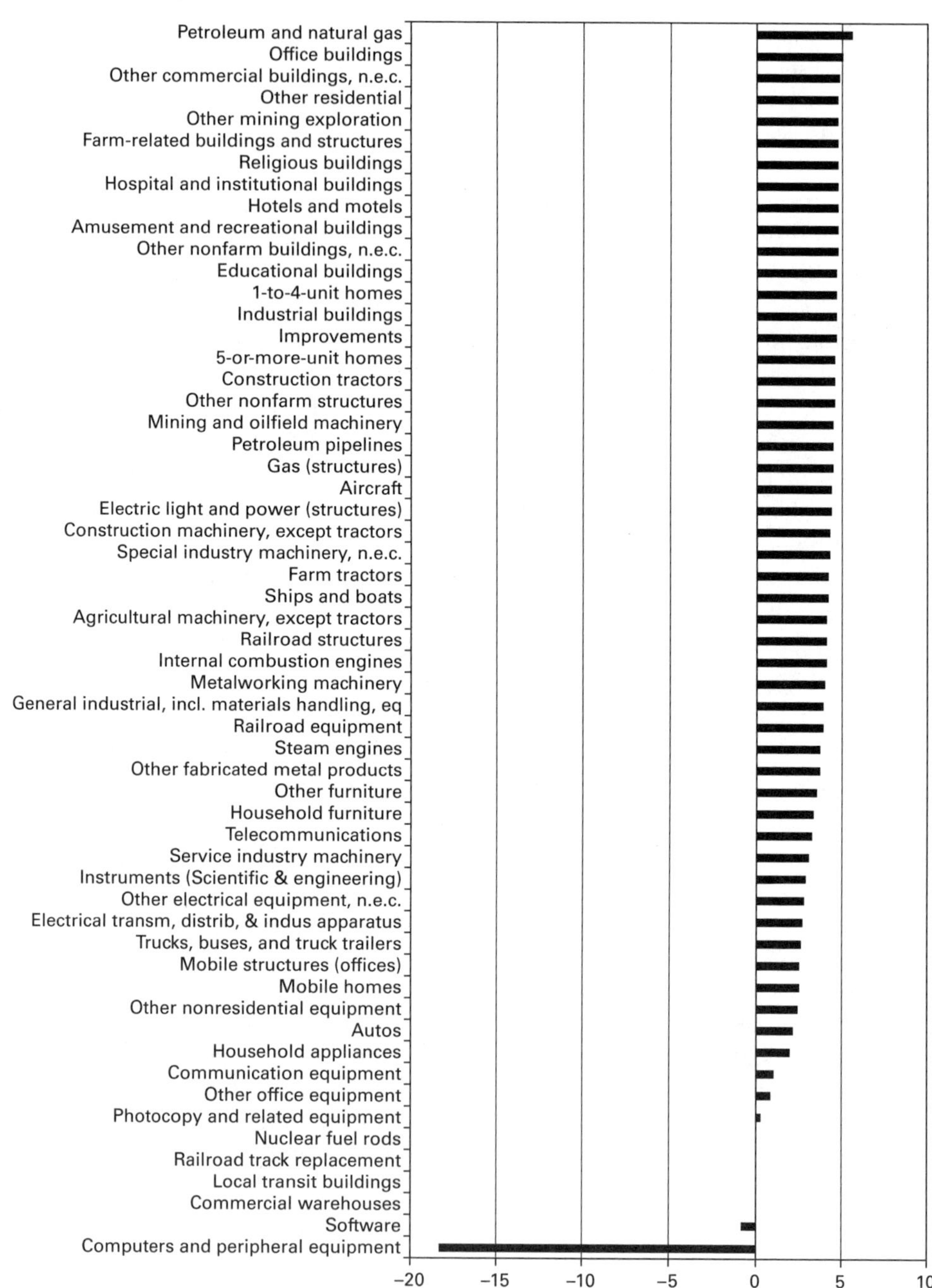

Figure B.11
Average price change by asset, 1960–2005.

investment, quite a bit more than the 4.4% energy group share of total value added. The largest investors are Electric Utilities ($41 billion) and Petroleum and Gas Mining ($41 billion).

Investment is cumulated into capital stocks according to (B.30), using the depreciation rates given in table B.19, for the 60 BEA industries given in table B.20. These stocks are then aggregated to the 35 IGEM industries. Investment by government electric utilities are broken out of total government investment. The stocks at the end of 2000 are given in table B.21. Of the total stock of $37.2 trillion, the General Government owns $5.2 trillion. The rest is owned by the private sector, including households, or government enterprises.

The largest private stocks are in the industries with large land values—FIRE ($5.8 trillion) and Agriculture ($2.9 trillion). The manufacturing group stock of capital in 2000 was $2.9 trillion. The Petroleum Refining industry is only $132 billion. Of the five energy industries, Electric Utilities has the largest stock at $1057 billion, followed by Petroleum and Gas Mining with $462 billion.

The capital stocks generate a flow of annual services given in the second column in table B.21. Given the wide differences in the composition of industry stocks with a larger share of long-lived structures in Real Estate, relative to manufacturing, the service flow is not a fixed proportion of the stocks. Real Estate and Agriculture have a low ratio of service flow to capital stock, while Services and Construction have high ratios. In the last column we show the share of capital input due to IT capital. The Communications, Instruments, and Printing and Publishing industries have the highest shares of IT, exceeding 29%, while Agriculture and Petroleum Refining have the lowest. Four of the five industries in the energy group have low IT shares, less than 6%, the exception being Gas Utilities with a 22% IT share.

B.4.3.2 *Capital Input Changes over Time*

We next consider the change in investment patterns over time. Figure B.12 shows the share of GDP going to private investment, including consumers' durables, over this period. This has been fluctuating between 20% and 25% with a large increase during the economic boom of the late 1990s and a sharp fall after the recession of 2001. Figure B.12 also shows the rapid rise of the IT share of total investment, from 4% in 1960 to a peak of 19% in 2000, before falling back to 16% in the mid-2000s.

Table B.21
Values of capital stock and capital service flows, 2000 (bil. $)

		Capital Stock	Capital Input	IT Share of Capital Input
1	Agriculture	2,878	86.2	1.2%
2	Metal Mining	43	3.8	3.5%
3	Coal Mining	49	8.2	2.9%
4	Petroleum and Gas	462	51.2	2.5%
5	Nonmetallic Mining	33	5.8	3.6%
6	Construction	206	73.5	7.4%
7	Food Products	275	70.8	5.1%
8	Tobacco Products	29	5.6	4.9%
9	Textile Mill Products	72	6.1	8.8%
10	Apparel and Textiles	43	7.1	8.9%
11	Lumber and Wood	70	11.6	4.8%
12	Furniture and Fixtures	35	8.5	7.5%
13	Paper Products	162	30.0	4.7%
14	Printing and Publishing	117	34.6	29.5%
15	Chemical Products	382	102.1	6.5%
16	Petroleum Refining	132	17.1	1.8%
17	Rubber and Plastic	118	22.6	7.3%
18	Leather Products	8	1.4	6.3%
19	Stone, Clay, and Glass	86	18.3	6.6%
20	Primary Metals	187	24.8	4.1%
21	Fabricated Metals	150	43.7	7.7%
22	Industrial Machinery	269	41.6	25.0%
23	Electronic and Electric Equipment	281	71.4	16.5%
24	Motor Vehicles	156	34.2	4.3%
25	Other Transportation Equipment	169	13.9	22.6%
26	Instruments	134	15.8	43.0%
27	Miscellaneous Manufacturing	34	8.3	7.8%
28	Transport and Warehouse	903	75.9	16.6%
29	Communications	859	129.4	53.0%
30	Electric Utilities	1,057	114.3	5.4%
31	Gas Utilities	287	18.4	22.2%
32	Trade	1,979	306.8	24.4%
33	FIRE	5,850	675.6	17.1%
34	Services	1,437	437.1	22.4%
35	Government Enterprises	1,138	78.5	15.9%
	Households	11,897	1,394.4	6.1%
	Government	5,195	290.1	15.9%
	35-industry median	162	30.0	

Note: Household investment includes consumer durables and residential structures.

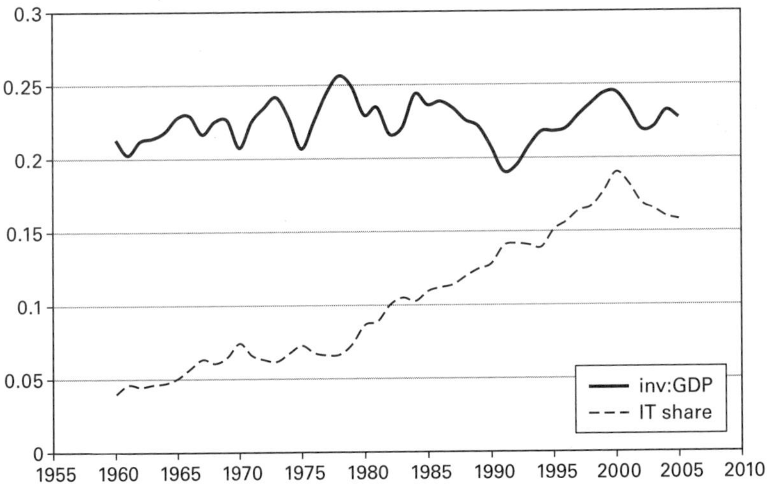

Figure B.12
Investment share of GDP; IT share of total investment.

The fluctuations in investment give rise to corresponding fluctuations in the growth of capital stock. Table B.22 gives the time series of investment and capital stock. It also gives the flow of capital services and the quality index. Recall that (B.46) defines the quality of capital as the ratio of capital services to capital stock. Between 1960 and 2005, the capital stock almost tripled but the flow of annual services quintupled with the quality index rising from 0.64 to 1.19; the capital quality index rose at 1.5% per year during this period.

The growth of private capital stock at the aggregate level conceals a great deal of variation among industries. In table B.23 we give the growth rates of capital stock and capital input over the period 1960–2000. The capital stocks for Electrical Equipment, Industrial Machinery, Instruments, Trade, and Services grow more than 4% per year. At the opposite extreme, capital stocks for Agriculture, Leather, Primary Metals, and Transportation have barely increased.

The capital stock of the energy group grew at a below-average rate in the 1960–2000 period with Coal Mining the most rapid at 3.1% per year and Petroleum Refining the slowest at 1.3%. As we have emphasized, the stock consists of many asset types and these generate very different flows of capital services. The growth rates of capital services are thus quite different from the growth rates of the stock. In this period they are more rapid, reflecting a shift from long-lived to short-lived assets.

Table B.22
Aggregate investment, capital stock, and capital services

	Investment		Capital Stock		Capital Services		
	Price	Quantity	Price	Quantity	Price	Quantity	Quality
1964	0.311	633.0	0.227	11732.7	0.310	1037.4	0.645
1965	0.314	703.1	0.230	12146.3	0.328	1091.9	0.656
1966	0.320	766.6	0.237	12668.4	0.331	1157.2	0.666
1967	0.328	754.5	0.242	13208.8	0.329	1220.7	0.674
1968	0.341	799.1	0.256	13715.3	0.312	1281.6	0.682
1969	0.356	820.6	0.273	14214.6	0.309	1344.7	0.690
1970	0.372	771.6	0.284	14685.3	0.318	1397.2	0.694
1971	0.390	824.8	0.299	15114.7	0.321	1444.8	0.697
1972	0.404	907.1	0.322	15554.5	0.364	1503.5	0.705
1973	0.423	995.4	0.353	16075.3	0.394	1578.5	0.716
1974	0.462	939.4	0.384	16654.7	0.411	1641.5	0.719
1975	0.514	843.8	0.426	17122.6	0.468	1687.8	0.719
1976	0.539	972.6	0.453	17507.0	0.500	1731.9	0.722
1977	0.573	1082.0	0.494	17941.0	0.535	1796.8	0.730
1978	0.614	1186.2	0.529	18493.2	0.570	1879.3	0.741
1979	0.667	1212.9	0.575	19112.8	0.624	1973.3	0.753
1980	0.725	1114.4	0.620	19672.5	0.609	2051.8	0.761
1981	0.793	1171.6	0.675	20164.4	0.658	2126.8	0.769
1982	0.834	1069.1	0.702	20570.1	0.681	2203.1	0.781
1983	0.839	1186.6	0.710	20866.8	0.733	2278.9	0.797
1984	0.852	1444.2	0.741	21290.0	0.795	2376.3	0.814
1985	0.860	1498.9	0.784	21841.8	0.792	2499.7	0.835
1986	0.873	1554.6	0.807	22381.0	0.734	2627.0	0.856
1987	0.891	1602.3	0.843	22872.6	0.787	2750.0	0.877
1988	0.908	1648.1	0.888	23342.1	0.879	2860.5	0.894
1989	0.929	1698.6	0.934	23845.2	0.879	2966.9	0.907
1990	0.944	1676.8	0.943	24310.9	0.881	3066.4	0.920
1991	0.958	1575.0	0.946	24689.0	0.868	3144.6	0.929
1992	0.960	1667.8	0.945	25039.7	0.882	3220.1	0.938
1993	0.973	1775.6	0.947	25448.0	0.876	3314.1	0.950
1994	0.990	1945.9	0.951	25943.4	0.942	3427.6	0.964
1995	1.003	2006.1	0.984	26513.4	0.968	3561.7	0.980
1996	1.000	2161.3	1.000	27120.2	1.000	3718.6	1.000
1997	0.991	2380.0	1.034	27791.2	1.018	3900.5	1.024
1998	0.977	2605.5	1.065	28566.7	0.992	4133.6	1.055
1999	0.972	2834.9	1.108	29389.1	0.971	4365.5	1.083
2000	0.977	2997.1	1.181	30236.5	0.978	4631.4	1.117
2001	0.979	2907.4	1.212	31187.0	0.949	4835.4	1.131
2002	0.976	2947.9	1.230	31827.9	1.014	4998.8	1.145
2003	0.974	3070.1	1.258	32297.4	1.010	5145.2	1.162
2004	0.993	3301.7	1.313	32797.3	1.036	5293.4	1.177
2005	1.016	3466.0	1.389	33383.4	1.160	5450.3	1.191

Note: All prices are normalized to 1.0 in 1996 and all quantities are measured in 1996 dollars, measured in billions.

Table B.23
Growth rates of capital services, stock, and quality, 1960–2000

		Capital Input	Capital Stock	Capital Quality
1	Agriculture	0.79	0.40	0.40
2	Metal Mining	2.28	1.84	0.45
3	Coal Mining	2.38	3.09	−0.71
4	Petroleum and Gas	2.35	2.13	0.22
5	Nonmetallic Mining	3.06	2.87	0.19
6	Construction	3.01	2.75	0.25
7	Food Products	2.51	2.10	0.40
8	Tobacco Products	2.50	1.84	0.66
9	Textile Mill Products	1.99	1.00	0.98
10	Apparel and Textiles	3.22	3.05	0.18
11	Lumber and Wood	2.88	2.14	0.74
12	Furniture and Fixtures	3.61	3.23	0.38
13	Paper Products	3.47	2.92	0.55
14	Printing and Publishing	4.73	3.69	1.04
15	Chemical Products	3.93	3.50	0.43
16	Petroleum Refining	1.77	1.30	0.47
17	Rubber and Plastic	5.09	4.44	0.65
18	Leather Products	0.46	0.09	0.37
19	Stone, Clay, and Glass	2.49	1.77	0.73
20	Primary Metals	1.38	0.75	0.63
21	Fabricated Metals	3.11	2.66	0.45
22	Industrial Machinery	5.65	4.21	1.44
23	Electronic and Electric Equipment	6.20	5.23	0.97
24	Motor Vehicles	2.92	2.58	0.34
25	Other Transportation Equipment	4.54	2.50	2.04
26	Instruments	6.98	5.08	1.90
27	Miscellaneous Manufacturing	3.19	2.66	0.53
28	Transport and Warehouse	1.84	0.40	1.44
29	Communications	6.56	5.56	1.00
30	Electric Utilities	3.28	2.50	0.78
31	Gas Utilities	2.90	2.16	0.74
32	Trade	6.21	4.17	2.04
33	FIRE	4.22	2.84	1.38
34	Services	6.36	4.78	1.58
35	Government Enterprises	4.18	3.92	0.25
	Households	3.92	2.56	1.36
	Government	2.72	2.28	0.44
	35-industry median	3.11	2.66	0.63

Note: All variables are average annual growth rates, in percentages.

The last column of table B.23 gives the growth of capital quality over 1960–2000. With one exception of Coal Mining, the growth in industry capital quality is positive, reflecting a shift towards short-lived assets with higher flows of services per dollar of stock. The biggest increases in capital quality are in Other Transportation Equipment and Wholesale Trade with growth rates exceeding 2% per year. Capital quality in Petroleum Refining rose at a 0.47% rate, while capital quality in Electric Utilities rose at 0.78%.

Another way of viewing the change in the composition of investment is to examine the growth rates of IT capital and non-IT capital given in table B.24. While there are many slowly growing industries with slow growth of output and capital input, all industries had rapid growth of IT capital services. The median growth rate of IT input over 1960–2005 was 20% per year! For Gas Utilities the growth of IT capital input was 24% per year; for Petroleum and Gas Mining, 23%; and for Electric Utilities, 15%. It is clear that the energy group has made much greater use of the new technologies than other industries have.

The United States, like much of the world, saw a sharp deceleration of growth in the 1970s, a period that included the oil shocks. The United States, however, led the world in the acceleration in economic growth after 1995; the 1995–2000 period was the peak of the Information Age as described in JHS (2005). In table B.25 we show the rate of growth of capital during the subperiods 1960–1973, 1973–1995, and 1995–2000.

Most industries had much higher growth during the boom period except for the mining industries—Metal Mining, Coal, and Petroleum and Gas—and the low-skill, labor-intensive industries—Textile, Apparel, Leather, and Tobacco. Petroleum Refining, Electric Utilities, Other Transportation Equipment, and Government Enterprises saw even lower rates of growth. The slow growth of capital input in the energy group relative to the rest of the economy follows the slow growth of output.

The growth of IT investment was even faster than the rapid rate for total investment during the boom of the 1990s. This resulted in a continual rise of the share of total capital input due to IT. As noted above, figure B.12 shows how this share rose from 5% in 1965 to 16% in 1995 and peaked at 19% in 2000 before falling back to 16% in 2005. In table B.26 we show how the IT shares for each industry have been rising during this period. In Gas Utilities the IT share rose from 0.5% in 1973 to 19% in 1995 to 24% in 2005; however, in Electric Utilities the share fell from 7.0% in 1990 to 5.7% in 1995 to 4.9% in 2005. In Coal Mining,

Table B.24
Growth of total, IT, and non-IT capital services, 1960–2005 (% per year)

		Total	IT Capital	Non-IT
1	Agriculture	0.99	20.40	0.93
2	Metal Mining	2.09	17.23	1.83
3	Coal Mining	2.20	17.05	2.02
4	Petroleum and Gas	2.40	22.64	2.22
5	Nonmetallic Mining	2.85	18.08	2.64
6	Construction	3.17	22.97	2.70
7	Food Products	2.15	21.95	1.72
8	Tobacco Products	2.16	17.77	1.77
9	Textile Mill Products	1.27	20.86	0.67
10	Apparel and Textiles	2.71	19.50	2.16
11	Lumber and Wood	2.58	19.28	2.22
12	Furniture and Fixtures	2.80	20.23	2.19
13	Paper Products	2.88	19.83	2.49
14	Printing and Publishing	4.48	25.65	2.49
15	Chemical Products	3.56	23.26	3.08
16	Petroleum Refining	1.73	18.08	1.48
17	Rubber and Plastic	4.57	23.17	3.90
18	Leather Products	0.55	15.21	0.10
19	Stone, Clay, and Glass	2.28	22.02	1.48
20	Primary Metals	0.84	19.35	0.48
21	Fabricated Metals	2.76	21.54	2.17
22	Industrial Machinery	5.15	22.32	3.00
23	Electronic and Electric Equipment	5.44	13.19	4.17
24	Motor Vehicles	2.67	22.51	2.26
25	Other Transportation Equipment	3.32	24.59	1.69
26	Instruments	6.20	23.61	3.75
27	Miscellaneous Manufacturing	2.75	20.20	2.12
28	Transport and Warehouse	2.28	14.70	1.53
29	Communications	6.17	7.62	4.73
30	Electric Utilities	3.18	14.98	2.86
31	Gas Utilities	2.80	24.16	1.88
32	Trade	6.34	26.91	4.46
33	FIRE	3.29	17.11	2.54
34	Services	6.83	21.03	4.64
35	Government Enterprises	4.01	17.74	3.26
	35-industry median	2.80	20.23	2.22

Note: IT capital includes computer hardware, computer software, and telecommunications equipment. Non-IT capital includes all other assets, including inventories and land.

Table B.25
Growth of capital stock, acceleration post-1995 (% per year)

		1960–2000	1960–1973	1973–1995	1995–2000
1	Agriculture	0.40	0.65	0.28	0.32
2	Metal Mining	1.84	3.41	1.42	–0.66
3	Coal Mining	3.09	3.60	3.29	1.25
4	Petroleum and Gas	2.13	1.88	2.46	0.95
5	Nonmetallic Mining	2.87	4.84	1.58	3.39
6	Construction	2.75	4.17	1.28	6.16
7	Food Products	2.10	2.35	1.81	2.61
8	Tobacco Products	1.84	2.59	2.08	–0.86
9	Textile Mill Products	1.00	2.55	0.26	0.10
10	Apparel and Textiles	3.05	5.74	2.30	–0.75
11	Lumber and Wood	2.14	3.84	1.21	1.90
12	Furniture and Fixtures	3.23	4.89	2.55	2.52
13	Paper Products	2.92	3.56	2.87	1.08
14	Printing and Publishing	3.69	4.72	3.27	2.93
15	Chemical Products	3.50	4.57	2.89	2.91
16	Petroleum Refining	1.30	1.83	1.49	–1.30
17	Rubber and Plastic	4.44	6.65	3.18	4.57
18	Leather Products	0.09	1.74	–0.48	–1.81
19	Stone, Clay, and Glass	1.77	2.68	0.85	3.90
20	Primary Metals	0.75	2.42	–0.22	0.27
21	Fabricated Metals	2.66	4.06	1.94	2.50
22	Industrial Machinery	4.21	5.10	3.77	4.51
23	Electronic and Electric Equipment	5.23	5.50	4.98	6.55
24	Motor Vehicles	2.58	3.82	1.77	3.03
25	Other Transportation Equipment	2.50	3.30	2.24	1.06
26	Instruments	5.08	6.25	4.60	3.86
27	Miscellaneous Manufacturing	2.66	4.59	1.71	2.02
28	Transport and Warehouse	0.40	–0.06	0.19	2.67
29	Communications	5.56	6.56	4.82	6.26
30	Electric Utilities	2.50	3.39	2.24	0.83
31	Gas Utilities	2.16	3.25	1.47	2.38
32	Trade	4.17	4.41	3.93	4.67
33	FIRE	2.84	3.67	2.48	2.47
34	Services	4.78	5.53	4.12	6.04
35	Government Enterprises	3.92	5.59	3.47	2.30
	Households	2.56	2.90	2.39	2.51
	Government	2.28	3.02	1.95	1.61
	35-industry median	2.66	3.82	2.24	2.47

Table B.26
IT capital share of total capital input

		1973	1990	1995	2000	2005
1	Agriculture	0.03	0.36	0.92	1.01	0.83
2	Metal Mining	0.92	1.69	5.66	3.54	3.65
3	Coal Mining	0.00	0.63	3.52	2.88	2.97
4	Petroleum and Gas	0.94	1.89	2.92	2.53	1.83
5	Nonmetallic Mining	0.00	1.22	3.05	3.55	3.67
6	Construction	0.83	1.67	6.79	7.53	7.86
7	Food Products	2.72	3.85	4.43	5.12	5.37
8	Tobacco Products	4.79	4.84	4.75	4.90	5.13
9	Textile Mill Products	4.58	4.76	9.61	8.82	5.95
10	Apparel and Textiles	3.85	4.95	8.55	8.94	9.64
11	Lumber and Wood	1.22	2.53	3.69	4.80	4.08
12	Furniture and Fixtures	1.34	7.47	8.19	7.45	7.32
13	Paper Products	1.60	3.83	4.32	4.68	5.04
14	Printing and Publishing	4.22	17.09	26.74	29.17	30.20
15	Chemical Products	0.96	5.03	6.08	6.45	5.65
16	Petroleum Refining	1.80	2.07	3.00	1.79	1.54
17	Rubber and Plastic	3.97	5.79	7.51	7.31	7.84
18	Leather Products	7.49	3.10	3.65	6.18	6.67
19	Stone, Clay, and Glass	1.94	7.34	5.38	6.71	6.67
20	Primary Metals	1.94	4.01	4.29	4.10	2.52
21	Fabricated Metals	2.17	5.16	7.04	7.69	7.67
22	Industrial Machinery	12.67	16.38	19.80	25.00	23.60
23	Electronic and Electric Equipment	10.12	15.47	15.51	16.52	16.46
24	Motor Vehicles	1.36	3.89	4.49	4.30	5.32
25	Other Transportation Equipment	3.46	33.14	17.47	22.00	20.94
26	Instruments	3.72	30.67	45.34	39.12	40.15
27	Miscellaneous Manufacturing	4.43	5.44	6.92	7.74	7.82
28	Transport and Warehouse	2.17	8.37	13.17	14.35	13.15
29	Communications	62.51	54.23	57.11	53.67	46.79
30	Electric Utilities	0.76	6.59	5.68	4.52	4.91
31	Gas Utilities	0.51	11.78	19.10	22.15	24.04
32	Trade	3.34	18.10	22.05	23.05	22.04
33	FIRE	2.84	5.71	8.45	9.93	9.99
34	Services	6.40	25.18	21.45	25.15	29.99
35	Government Enterprises	2.75	9.56	10.53	15.09	16.38
	35-industry median	2.17	5.16	6.92	7.45	7.32

Oil Mining, and Refining the IT shares were much lower, peaking at less than 4%.

In conclusion, the U.S. economy as a whole saw a growth of capital input that exceeded GDP growth, but the energy group grew much more slowly than the average industry. All industries responded to the precipitous decline in IT capital prices with a massive investment in IT capital. While IT capital is relatively less important for the energy group, these industries also saw a rapid growth of IT capital.

B.5 Population and Time Endowment

Section 2.3.7 in chapter 2 describes how the time endowment and leisure demand is defined. Section 6.1.1 describes how the time endowment is projected. Here we describe how the system is implemented for the sample period. The value of aggregate time endowment (eq. 2.59) was given as

$$P_t^h LH_t = VLH_t = \sum_k (1 - tl_t^m) P_{kt}^L \cdot 14 \cdot 365 \cdot POP_{kt} \tag{B.57}$$

where POP_{kt} is the number of people in group k at time t, and $(1 - tl_t^m)P_{kt}^L$ is the after-tax hourly wage of that group. Equation 2.60 gives the Tornqvist index of time endowment. Each person is assumed to have 14 hours per day to spend on work and leisure. The tax rate is the marginal tax on labor income. The demographic groups are the 2 sex, and 6 educational attainment groups given in table B.12; there are 8 age groups in calculating the labor input, but for the time endowment calculation we included a ninth group for those aged 75+.

The population data is the latest revision based on the 2000 Census, that is, the number of people by sex, age, and race for 2001–2007 is revised by the Census Bureau to reflect the 2000 Census.[26] The earlier estimates for 1990–2000 are also re-interpolated with the 2000 Census.[27] The version used here was released by the Census Bureau in 2009. The total for the civilian non-institutional population and resident population plus armed forces overseas are given in table B27. The civilian non-institutional total corresponds to the data in the Current Population Survey and Current Expenditure Survey. The total population corresponds to the graph in figure 6.1 of the sample period population and projected population.

The age structure of the population affects the supply of labor per capita on one hand and the consumption of goods and leisure on the

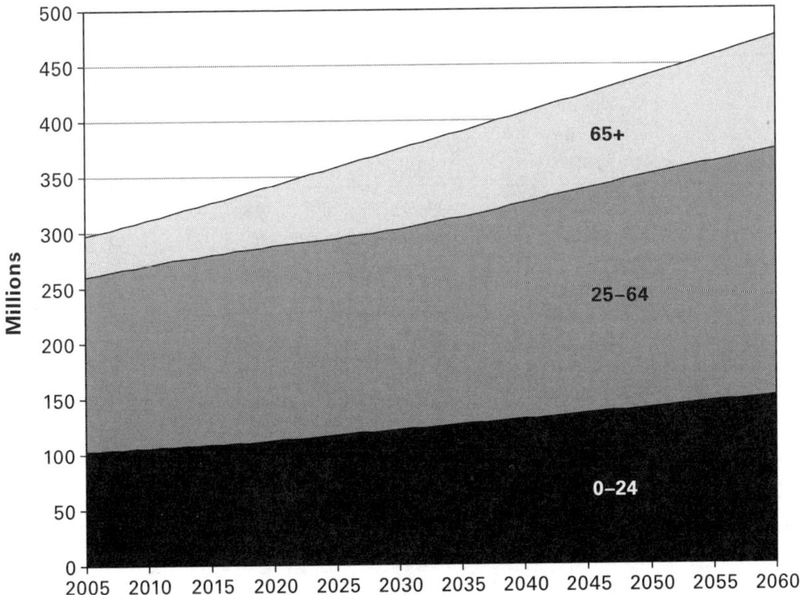

Figure B.13
Projection of U.S. population by age groups.

other hand. The projection of the population by age groups is given in figure B.13 and we can see the rapid aging; the proportion of those aged 65 and older rises from 13.0% in 2010 to 19.3% in 2030 and to 21.4% by 2060. Given the wage-age profile, this aging has a big contribution to the change in the time endowment.

The time endowment, computed using equations B.57 and 2.60, is graphed in figure 6.1 and given in the last column of table B.27. During the sample period, time endowment per capita rose from $37,300 in 1990 to $40,700 in 2007 (measured in 1996 dollars), due to the rising educational attainment and aging. From figure 6.1 we can see that the time endowment per capita continues to rise but not in a smooth manner. In section B.3.3 above we describe how the labor quality index depends on the sex, age, and educational attainment of the workforce. Similarly, the quality index of time endowment (the ratio of time endowment to total hours) may be broken into the sex, age, and educational attainment indices. In figure B.14, the quality index of time endowment is given in the bold line and it rises during the 2010s and then falls to a trough around 2050 before rising again. This pattern is

Table B.27
Population of the United States incorporating the 2000 Census

	Civilian Non-institutional Population (million)	Resident Plus Armed Forces Overseas (million)	Time Endowment (bil. $1996)	Time Endowment per Capita
1990	244.4	250.1	9321	37264
1991	247.7	253.5	9443	37253
1992	251.2	256.9	9560	37215
1993	254.7	260.3	9756	37487
1994	257.9	263.4	9863	37438
1995	261.1	266.6	10059	37737
1996	264.2	269.7	10202	37830
1997	267.5	272.9	10388	38063
1998	270.7	276.1	10578	38312
1999	273.8	279.3	10784	38612
2000	276.9	282.4	10984	38893
2001	279.8	285.3	11168	39140
2002	282.6	288.2	11403	39568
2003	285.1	290.9	11594	39849
2004	287.8	293.6	11776	40108
2005	290.6	296.3	11903	40167
2006	293.4	299.2	12149	40610
2007	296.3	302.0	12290	40691

driven by the age structure. There is an echo of the baby boom, where a rising proportion of young workers, the children of the baby boomers, earn the lowest wage of the various age groups. This change in age distribution also drives the changes in the average level of educational attainment. The index for sex is essentially flat and not plotted. We thus see that our time endowment index differs substantially from a simple measure of labor supply that depends only on total population or only on the working-age population.

B.6 Government Accounts and Taxes

Chapter 5 describes the government accounts in IGEM—how they are constructed from the National Income and Product Accounts (NIPA) for the sample period and how they are projected using forecasts from the Congressional Budget Office (CBO). Table 5.1 gives the tax rates and values of expenditures and revenues for 2005. In this section we

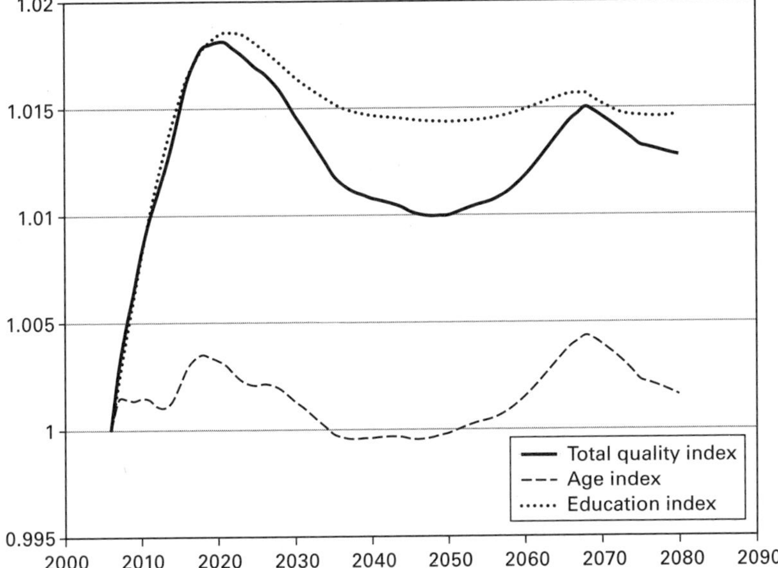

Figure B.14
Time endowment projection: effect of age and educational attainment.

provide some additional detail about the sources of these expenditures and taxes.

The revenue and expenditure accounts of the Federal and the State and Local governments are given in the NIPA at a very detailed level. In this version of IGEM we consider only the consolidated government, adding the Federal and the State and Local, and only the main categories of taxes. The relation between model variables and the National Accounts is given in table B.28. The NIPA tables and line numbers referenced are based on the version in the *Survey of Current Business*, August 2011.

Property taxes are the sum of the State and Local government property tax, the motor vehicle licenses paid by persons and businesses, special assessments, and other taxes on persons and on production. The taxes on capital and labor in IGEM are the sum of the personal income tax and the corporate profits tax, and for simplicity, we include the rents and royalties received by the government. Similarly, the sales tax includes the excise taxes and transfers from businesses, less the subsidies paid.

The expenditure on goods and services, *VGG*, includes the purchases from the private business sector, compensation of government

Table B.28
IGEM Government accounts in relation to the National Accounts

	IGEM Variables	NIPA Table and Line Number	NIPA Names	2005 (bil. $)
Property taxes	*R_P*	Table 3.3. State and local government current receipts and expenditures		
		L8	Property taxes	346.9
		Table 3.4. Personal current tax receipts		
		L10	Motor vehicle licenses	14.0
		L11	Property taxes	6.2
		L12	Other taxes	4.9
		Table 3.5. Taxes on production and imports		
		L36	Motor vehicle licenses	7.9
		L37	Severance taxes	9.1
		L38	Special assessments	6.8
		L39	Other taxes	58.4
		Total		454.2
Capital income plus labor income tax	*R_K* + *R_L*	Table 3.2. Federal government current receipts and expenditures		
		L3	Personal current taxes	931.9
		L8	Taxes on corporate income: Federal Reserve banks	21.5
		L9	Taxes on corporate income: other	319.5
		L15	Rents and royalties	7
		Table 3.3. State and local government current receipts and expenditures		
		L4	Income taxes	251.7
		L10	Taxes on corporate income	54.9
		L15	Rents and royalties	9.8
		Total		1596.3
Sales tax	*R_SALES*	Table 3.2. Federal government current receipts and expenditures		
		L5	Excise taxes	73.5
		L17	Transfers from business	18.7
		L32	Less: subsidies	–60.5

Table B.28 (continued)

	IGEM Variables	NIPA Table and Line Number	NIPA Names	2005 (bil. $)
		Table 3.3. State and local government current receipts and expenditures		
		L7	Sales taxes	402.2
		L18	From business (net)	36.5
		L25	Less: subsidies	–0.4
		Total		470
Import tariffs	*R_ TARIFF*	Table 3.2. Federal government current receipts and expenditures		
		L6	Customs duties	25.3
Wealth tax	*R_ WEALTH*	Table 5.10. Capital transfers paid and received, by sector and by type		
		L37	Estate and gift taxes paid by persons	25.0
		L40	Estate and gift taxes paid by persons	5.3
		Total		30.3
Nontax revenue	R^N	Table 3.2. Federal government current receipts and expenditures		
		L18	From persons	14.9
		Table 3.3. State and local government current receipts and expenditures		
		L19	From persons	56.5
		Total		71.4
Expenditures on goods and services	*VGG*	Table 3.2. Federal government current receipts and expenditures		
		L21	Federal; consumption expenditures	765.8
		L42	Federal; gross government investment	110.5
		Table 3.3. State and local government current receipts and expenditures		
		L22	S&L; consumption expenditures	1212.0
		L35	S&L; gross government investment	281.6
		Total		2369.9

(continued)

Table B.28 (continued)

	IGEM Variables	NIPA Table and Line Number	NIPA Names	2005 (bil. $)
Transfers to domestic residents	G^{tran}	Table 3.12. Government social benefits		
		L3	Social benefits; federal	1,078.0
		L4	Less: benefits from social insurance funds	–894.4
		L27	Social benefits; state and local	404.8
		L28	Less: benefits from social insurance funds	–17.0
		Table 3.14. Government social insurance funds current receipts and expenditures		
		L28	Less: to the rest of the world	–10.6
		Total		560.8
Transfers to rest-of-world	GR	Table 3.2. Federal government current receipts and expenditures		
		L25	Social benefits; to rest of the world	11.2
		L28	To the rest of the world (net)	40.9
		L10	Less: taxes from the rest of the world	–12.1
		Table 3.6. Contributions for government social insurance		
		L32	Less: rest-of-the-world contributions	–4.7
		Total		35.3
Net interest to domestic residents	$GINT$	Table 3.2. Federal government current receipts and expenditures		
		L30	To persons and business	151.5
		L13	Interest receipts	–16.4
		Table 7.11. Interest paid and received by sector and legal form		
		L24	From rest-of-world to federal government	2.4
		Table 3.3. State and local government current receipts and expenditures		
		L24	Interest payments	87.3
		L13	Less: interest receipts	–76.4
		Total		148.4

Table B.28 (continued)

	IGEM Variables	NIPA Table and Line Number	NIPA Names	2005 (bil. $)
Net interest to rest-of-world	*GINTR*	Table 3.2. Federal government current receipts and expenditures		
		L31	To the rest of the world	103.9
		Table 7.11. Interest paid and received by sector and legal form		
		L24	Less: from ROW to federal government	−2.4
		Total		101.5
Interest to social insurance funds	$GINT^{SS}$	Table 3.14. Government social insurance funds current receipts and expenditures		
		L8	Federal; interest received	115.8
		L21	State and local; interest received	4.4
		Total		120.2

Note: The NIPA table and line numbers are those in the *Survey of Current Business*, August 2011.

employees, and capital consumption. This is the sum of both "current expenditures" and "investment" in the NIPA. For transfers and interest paid, recall that we consider the Social Insurance Trust Funds to be part of the household assets, and so social benefits are not counted as government transfers, G^{tran}. There is a separate item for the interest paid to the Trust Funds, $GINT^{SS}$.

Notes

1. See Diewert (1976).
2. The same subscript i is used in the numerator and denominator of equation (B.4) to avoid a proliferation of symbols.
3. In the official U.S. inter-industry transactions tables and in our table B.2, the sum of all noncomparable imports ($196.8 billion) is entered in the noncomparable row of the Import column, with a negative sign. This implies that the column sum of Imports is total (negative) imports and the row sum of noncomparable imports is zero.
4. For example, in the GDP accounts for Personal Consumption Expenditures, the item "footwear" consists of the IO commodities rubber products, leather products, scrap, transportation, and trade. A bridge table linking the two concepts is given for each benchmark year, for 1992 this is table D in the *Survey of Current Business*, November 1997.

5. Note that the treatment of the government industry in the most recent 2002 Input-Output Benchmark in NAICS is different from that in the SIC versions from 1992 and earlier that is used in IGEM.
6. The latest SIC-based tables are described in *Survey of Current Business*, November 1997, p. 36. The benchmark tables for 1997 and 2002 use another classification system, NAICS, that is not comparable to the older systems.
7. The data are available on the Office of Occupational Statistics and Employment Projections website at www.bls.gov/emp/.
8. The method of iterative proportional fitting is described in detail in Jorgenson, Gollop, and Fraumeni (1987), chapter 3.
9. The BEA Gross Output by Industry data may be found at www.bea.gov/industry/gdpbyind_data.htm.
10. These data are described in Lum, Moyer, and Yuskavage (2000) and are available at www.bea.gov/industry/gdpbyind_data.htm.
11. These data are known as the Industry Output and Employment data and are available at www.bls.gov/emp/empind2.htm.
12. The BEA prices are given in the *Gross Output by Detailed Industry* (Lum, Moyer, and Yuskavage 2000). Also, see figure 4.2 in JHS (2005).
13. See BEA (1997). These differences have been eliminated in the most recent version of BEA's industry data.
14. The number of nonzero cells is smaller since the self-employed class is zero for many sectors.
15. Assuming competitive factor markets, workers are paid their marginal products, thus compensation per hour equals the marginal product of labor.
16. The Census data are taken from www.census.gov/census2000/PUMS.html, and the CPS Annual Social and Demographic Supplement is from www.census.gov/cps/.
17. The NIPA data by industry may be seen in *Survey of Current Business*, August 2001, tables 6.2C, 6.3C, 6.4C, 6.7C, 6.8C, and 6.9C. The complete time series is taken from www.bea.gov.
18. See the Employment Projection Program web page, www.bls.gov/emp/empind2.htm.
19. The ratios were downloaded February 2005 from www.bls.gov/ces/cesratiosemp.htm.
20. See BLS (1983) and Harper, Moulton, Rosenthal, and Wasshausen (2009).
21. These assumptions are discussed in JHS (2005), section 5.2.3, which notes that other age-efficiency profiles could also be incorporated into our framework.
22. See Herman (2000).
23. The Fixed Asset Tables are given at the BEA website www.bea.gov/National/FAweb/AllFATables.asp. Table 3.7E gives the equipment investment by industry; table 3.7S provides investment in structures.
24. The GDP-by-Industry data is given at the BEA website www.bea.gov/industry/gdpbyind_data.htm. The updates through 2005 are described in the *Survey of Current Business*, December 2006.
25. Data for investment by each industry is given only for the NAICS classification in 2005. These estimates for 2000 are for the SIC classification in IGEM.
26. The population revisions based on the 2000 Census are in files such as NC-est2006-alldata-P-file**.dat containing the data for "resident plus armed forces overseas population" on the Census Bureau website: www.census.gov/popest/data/national/asrh/2007/2007-nat-af.html.
27. The re-interpolated data are given in the files such as US-EST90INT-07.csv on the web page www.census.gov/popest/data/intercensal/national/index.html.

C Econometric Results

Table C.1
Estimated parameters of industry cost function; top tier $Q(K,L,E,M)$

	1 Agriculture		2 Metal Mining		3 Coal Mining	
α_K	0.171	(0.377)*	0.192	(0.008)	–0.001	(0.667)
α_L	0.166	(1.106)	0.754	(0.040)	0.018	(1.572)
α_E	0.050	(0.232)	0.054	(0.008)	–0.259	(0.777)
α_0	0.266	(1.740)	–0.620	(0.529)	0.098	(1.033)
β_{KK}	0.113	(0.425)	0.057	(0.006)	0.087	(2.974)
β_{KL}	–0.039	(0.408)	0.020	(0.053)	–0.058	(1.226)
β_{KE}	–0.002	(0.277)	–0.036	(0.025)	–0.027	(4.320)
β_{LL}	0.036	(3.377)	–0.290	(0.032)	–0.299	(5.560)
β_{LE}	–0.026	(0.444)	0.012	(0.056)	0.130	(3.858)
β_{EE}	–0.004	(0.024)	0.037	(0.072)	0.019	(1.235)
χ_K	0.025	(0.083)	0.081	(0.084)	0.067	(0.082)
χ_L	0.015	(0.447)	–0.242	(0.084)	0.100	(0.074)
χ_E	0.008	(0.514)	0.018	(0.005)	0.079	(0.022)
χ_P	–0.027	(1.275)	–0.073	(0.010)	–0.114	(0.029)
δ_{KK}	0.247	(1.006)	0.447	(0.161)	0.922	(0.003)
δ_{KL}	0.097	(0.947)	0.116	(0.156)	–0.048	(0.003)
δ_{KE}	0.262	(2.182)	0.002	(0.001)	–0.067	(0.007)
δ_{Kp}	0.069	(3.252)	–0.057	(0.057)	–0.038	(0.046)
δ_{LK}	–0.158	(5.267)	0.779	(0.338)	–0.060	(0.076)
δ_{LL}	0.835	(1.127)	0.558	(0.170)	0.850	(0.010)
δ_{LE}	0.273	(9.924)	–0.325	(3.385)	–0.082	(0.020)
δ_{Lp}	0.000	(3.120)	0.048	(0.078)	0.005	(0.007)
δ_{EK}	–0.137	(14.152)	–0.059	(0.013)	–0.083	(0.050)
δ_{EL}	–0.005	(3.871)	0.010	(0.042)	–0.018	(0.044)
δ_{EE}	1.064	(7.100)	0.658	(0.233)	0.874	(0.020)
δ_{Ep}	0.057	(4.314)	0.007	(0.037)	0.143	(0.052)
δ_{pK}	0.134	(40.125)	0.432	(0.608)	0.134	(0.033)
δ_{pL}	0.057	(6.102)	–0.129	(0.152)	0.332	(0.132)
δ_{pE}	–0.457	(12.978)	–0.119	(1.439)	–0.109	(0.062)
δ_{pp}	0.191	(2.910)	0.085	(0.186)	0.672	(0.059)

*Standard errors in parentheses.

Table C.1 (continued)

4 Petroleum and Gas		5 Nonmetallic Mining		6 Construction		7 Food Products	
−0.077	(0.023)	−0.161	(12.289)	0.060	(0.850)	−0.057	(0.028)
0.058	(0.007)	0.064	(8.921)	0.127	(2.843)	0.276	(0.016)
−0.016	(0.036)	0.045	(14.865)	0.041	(1.432)	0.005	(0.001)
−0.177	(0.118)	−0.046	(28.214)	−0.093	(0.822)	0.101	(0.101)
0.005	(0.080)	0.008	(19.347)	0.037	(0.076)	0.036	(0.060)
−0.017	(0.026)	0.008	(12.750)	−0.004	(0.185)	−0.002	(0.027)
0.021	(0.018)	0.015	(10.008)	0.000	(0.013)	−0.001	(0.008)
−0.042	(0.241)	−0.021	(50.094)	−0.137	(1.028)	−0.045	(0.017)
−0.014	(0.049)	−0.053	(4.590)	−0.016	(0.051)	0.004	(0.022)
0.012	(0.173)	0.052	(36.944)	0.007	(0.025)	0.010	(0.000)
0.056	(0.152)	0.058	(45.136)	−0.025	(0.198)	0.070	(0.034)
−0.029	(0.002)	0.109	(189.898)	0.114	(1.088)	−0.092	(0.022)
0.136	(0.045)	0.025	(27.769)	−0.004	(0.426)	0.012	(0.017)
−0.100	(0.077)	−0.058	(425.450)	−0.034	(0.621)	−0.020	(0.036)
0.875	(0.278)	0.833	(73.238)	0.690	(0.195)	0.724	(0.229)
0.261	(0.139)	0.089	(93.385)	0.085	(3.580)	0.166	(0.111)
−0.045	(0.109)	−0.071	(89.185)	−0.104	(4.318)	−0.607	(0.096)
−0.063	(0.169)	0.067	(132.420)	0.218	(4.097)	0.151	(2.205)
0.136	(0.006)	−0.120	(416.552)	0.075	(0.392)	0.314	(0.147)
0.491	(0.007)	0.718	(46.211)	0.557	(0.192)	0.682	(0.057)
0.019	(0.003)	0.200	(192.076)	−0.130	(0.284)	0.990	(0.619)
−0.013	(0.092)	−0.306	(119.556)	−0.198	(0.994)	0.022	(0.180)
−0.722	(0.011)	−0.038	(77.646)	0.194	(0.385)	−0.040	(0.050)
3.202	(0.022)	0.002	(32.789)	−0.019	(0.361)	0.034	(0.074)
0.803	(0.008)	0.863	(71.712)	0.588	(1.336)	0.816	(0.070)
0.042	(0.038)	0.237	(331.649)	0.072	(1.087)	−0.015	(0.105)
0.197	(0.022)	0.113	(941.232)	−0.099	(0.563)	0.083	(0.198)
0.873	(0.080)	0.045	(27.414)	0.133	(0.281)	0.004	(0.097)
−0.249	(0.017)	−0.002	(334.707)	−0.170	(0.969)	0.023	(0.359)
0.709	(0.187)	−0.028	(687.852)	0.311	(0.624)	−0.276	(0.838)

Table C.1 (continued)

	8 Tobacco Products		9 Textile Mill Products		10 Apparel and Textiles	
α_K	0.063	(0.030)	0.064	(0.005)	−0.020	(0.006)
α_L	0.029	(0.110)	0.141	(0.009)	0.000	(0.000)
α_E	0.021	(0.001)	0.065	(0.043)	−0.001	(0.003)
α_0	−0.318	(0.520)	0.364	(0.040)	−0.324	(1.636)
β_{KK}	0.086	(0.003)	0.011	(0.249)	0.014	(0.012)
β_{KL}	−0.030	(0.062)	0.078	(0.081)	−0.017	(0.023)
β_{KE}	0.000	(0.004)	0.001	(0.069)	0.001	(0.007)
β_{LL}	−0.049	(0.029)	−0.010	(0.016)	0.062	(0.010)
β_{LE}	0.001	(0.005)	−0.017	(0.045)	0.003	(0.028)
β_{EE}	0.002	(0.001)	0.014	(0.169)	0.007	(0.009)
χ_K	0.032	(0.127)	0.022	(0.037)	0.027	(0.010)
χ_L	0.027	(0.126)	0.023	(0.170)	0.047	(0.225)
χ_E	−0.007	(0.006)	−0.011	(0.082)	−0.005	(0.026)
χ_P	−0.012	(0.251)	−0.026	(0.140)	−0.042	(0.288)
δ_{KK}	0.331	(2.937)	0.533	(1.478)	0.844	(0.041)
δ_{KL}	0.851	(4.070)	−0.135	(0.483)	−0.035	(0.007)
δ_{KE}	0.958	(9.272)	−0.029	(2.889)	−0.056	(0.557)
δ_{Kp}	−0.028	(0.564)	−0.016	(1.104)	−0.011	(0.018)
δ_{LK}	−0.204	(0.444)	−0.174	(0.376)	−0.093	(1.127)
δ_{LL}	1.189	(0.564)	0.804	(0.596)	0.864	(0.642)
δ_{LE}	0.815	(9.907)	0.022	(3.116)	0.248	(5.491)
δ_{Lp}	0.006	(0.364)	−0.122	(0.178)	−0.008	(0.061)
δ_{EK}	−0.062	(0.066)	0.092	(0.641)	0.024	(0.123)
δ_{EL}	0.075	(0.096)	0.071	(0.699)	0.011	(0.051)
δ_{EE}	0.342	(0.406)	0.902	(0.086)	0.919	(0.126)
δ_{Ep}	0.002	(0.034)	0.048	(0.354)	0.001	(0.004)
δ_{pK}	−0.015	(3.874)	0.083	(0.546)	0.151	(1.417)
δ_{pL}	0.233	(4.527)	0.054	(1.203)	0.078	(0.529)
δ_{pE}	0.030	(25.983)	−0.154	(1.219)	−0.447	(0.262)
δ_{pp}	0.169	(6.058)	0.104	(1.653)	0.011	(0.053)

Table C.1 (continued)

11 Lumber and Wood		12 Furniture and Fixtures		13 Paper Products		14 Printing and Publishing	
−0.015	(0.012)	0.071	(0.007)	−0.052	(0.054)	0.021	(0.057)
0.053	(0.242)	0.367	(0.018)	−0.003	(0.005)	0.394	(0.019)
−0.036	(0.035)	0.049	(0.000)	0.005	(0.072)	0.046	(0.000)
0.138	(0.197)	0.046	(1.103)	0.110	(0.321)	−0.041	(0.027)
0.016	(0.042)	0.047	(0.007)	0.025	(0.100)	−0.056	(0.089)
0.012	(0.132)	−0.027	(0.002)	−0.006	(0.018)	0.020	(0.044)
−0.002	(0.004)	−0.002	(0.001)	0.008	(0.019)	0.000	(0.001)
−0.001	(0.474)	0.056	(0.028)	0.013	(0.024)	0.087	(0.006)
−0.020	(0.087)	−0.003	(0.009)	0.000	(0.064)	−0.004	(0.011)
0.008	(0.005)	0.011	(0.003)	0.032	(0.004)	0.007	(0.005)
0.015	(0.325)	0.008	(0.187)	0.065	(1.208)	0.054	(0.002)
0.047	(0.040)	0.032	(0.262)	0.022	(1.193)	−0.136	(0.042)
0.028	(0.069)	−0.009	(0.015)	0.053	(0.355)	−0.027	(0.048)
−0.080	(0.172)	0.011	(0.065)	−0.100	(7.518)	0.023	(0.164)
0.798	(0.519)	0.614	(2.996)	0.691	(6.048)	0.471	(0.218)
−0.004	(0.744)	0.048	(1.783)	−0.003	(1.041)	0.003	(0.183)
0.202	(2.006)	−0.030	(4.278)	−0.138	(8.392)	−0.334	(0.058)
−0.075	(0.707)	0.027	(0.686)	0.009	(0.385)	−0.778	(0.829)
0.046	(0.218)	−0.036	(4.586)	0.111	(3.092)	0.474	(0.126)
0.785	(0.273)	0.738	(2.623)	0.878	(1.111)	0.914	(0.022)
−0.195	(0.880)	1.028	(5.812)	−0.246	(8.125)	−2.173	(0.019)
−0.066	(0.320)	−0.003	(0.284)	0.092	(0.827)	1.203	(0.189)
0.059	(0.026)	0.025	(0.214)	−0.230	(1.342)	0.097	(0.160)
−0.086	(0.048)	−0.011	(0.144)	0.051	(0.118)	0.006	(0.044)
0.704	(0.799)	0.752	(0.335)	0.423	(2.694)	0.585	(0.684)
−0.043	(0.116)	0.007	(0.009)	0.035	(0.092)	0.158	(0.215)
−0.094	(0.430)	−0.116	(2.642)	0.540	(27.190)	−0.008	(0.447)
0.323	(1.385)	−0.063	(0.854)	−0.078	(2.381)	−0.069	(0.082)
0.460	(0.154)	0.518	(0.138)	0.371	(43.427)	0.562	(3.184)
0.437	(0.991)	−0.135	(0.967)	−0.073	(1.257)	0.850	(0.763)

Table C.1 (continued)

	15 Chemical Products		16 Petroleum Refining		17 Rubber and Plastic	
α_K	0.151	(0.003)	0.015	(0.014)	–0.046	(0.009)
α_L	0.061	(0.005)	0.016	(0.009)	0.042	(0.010)
α_E	–0.010	(0.002)	0.018	(0.033)	0.037	(0.013)
α_0	–0.045	(0.051)	0.170	(0.109)	–0.113	(0.058)
β_{KK}	0.064	(0.009)	0.033	(0.031)	0.027	(0.005)
β_{KL}	–0.012	(0.032)	0.011	(0.003)	–0.032	(0.012)
β_{KE}	–0.033	(0.054)	–0.049	(0.018)	0.000	(0.009)
β_{LL}	–0.202	(0.078)	–0.009	(0.001)	–0.001	(0.069)
β_{LE}	0.008	(0.004)	–0.035	(0.003)	–0.019	(0.001)
β_{EE}	0.034	(0.014)	0.116	(0.007)	0.018	(0.026)
χ_K	–0.037	(0.017)	0.149	(0.087)	–0.018	(0.002)
χ_L	–0.004	(0.328)	0.003	(0.001)	0.090	(0.002)
χ_E	0.043	(0.061)	0.225	(0.043)	0.015	(0.029)
χ_P	–0.046	(0.480)	–0.026	(0.394)	–0.008	(0.209)
δ_{KK}	0.761	(0.357)	–0.256	(0.047)	0.868	(0.898)
δ_{KL}	0.339	(0.289)	–1.937	(0.306)	0.131	(0.403)
δ_{KE}	–0.038	(0.181)	0.068	(0.174)	–0.034	(2.132)
δ_{Kp}	0.095	(0.040)	0.453	(0.070)	0.014	(0.053)
δ_{LK}	0.024	(0.700)	0.160	(0.005)	0.008	(0.269)
δ_{LL}	0.945	(0.387)	0.962	(0.039)	0.692	(0.128)
δ_{LE}	0.214	(3.349)	–0.022	(0.006)	0.216	(0.644)
δ_{Lp}	0.073	(0.093)	–0.126	(0.077)	–0.016	(0.034)
δ_{EK}	–0.022	(0.383)	0.199	(0.109)	0.002	(0.110)
δ_{EL}	–0.106	(0.442)	–0.478	(0.129)	–0.056	(0.169)
δ_{EE}	0.635	(0.123)	0.663	(0.092)	0.929	(0.165)
δ_{Ep}	0.002	(0.132)	–0.310	(0.061)	0.000	(0.019)
δ_{pK}	0.359	(1.177)	0.125	(0.642)	–0.045	(0.277)
δ_{pL}	–0.059	(0.440)	0.236	(0.773)	0.019	(0.889)
δ_{pE}	0.467	(5.084)	0.013	(0.628)	–0.153	(0.988)
δ_{pp}	0.137	(0.108)	0.130	(0.285)	–0.079	(0.231)

Table C.1 (continued)

18 Leather Products		19 Stone, Clay, and Glass		20 Primary Metals		21 Fabricated Metals	
0.029	(0.028)	0.091	(0.484)	0.076	(0.017)	0.049	(0.061)
0.319	(0.002)	0.516	(0.363)	0.089	(0.016)	0.021	(0.041)
0.024	(0.002)	0.130	(0.209)	0.103	(0.004)	−0.017	(0.004)
0.083	(0.057)	0.062	(0.268)	0.050	(0.140)	0.116	(0.089)
0.006	(0.162)	0.054	(0.169)	0.057	(0.058)	0.047	(0.048)
−0.040	(0.199)	−0.046	(0.253)	−0.021	(0.064)	−0.019	(0.073)
−0.002	(0.010)	−0.004	(0.003)	−0.008	(0.003)	−0.001	(0.004)
−0.077	(0.190)	0.104	(0.709)	0.056	(0.073)	0.042	(0.041)
−0.006	(0.026)	−0.039	(0.356)	−0.051	(0.026)	−0.008	(0.057)
0.011	(0.049)	0.041	(0.084)	0.003	(0.142)	0.011	(0.017)
0.018	(0.052)	0.014	(0.156)	0.138	(0.209)	0.005	(0.011)
−0.004	(0.201)	−0.023	(0.674)	0.026	(0.222)	0.097	(0.010)
−0.002	(0.007)	−0.006	(0.209)	0.048	(0.123)	−0.018	(0.005)
−0.002	(0.076)	0.015	(1.113)	−0.103	(0.066)	−0.026	(0.031)
0.761	(1.055)	0.964	(2.959)	−0.828	(1.475)	0.875	(0.008)
−0.098	(0.923)	0.033	(1.798)	−0.527	(1.155)	−0.033	(0.017)
0.509	(4.193)	0.099	(0.515)	0.947	(0.925)	0.406	(0.053)
0.191	(3.727)	−0.047	(0.304)	0.028	(0.059)	0.009	(0.004)
−0.041	(3.284)	−0.045	(2.645)	0.578	(1.866)	−0.043	(0.002)
0.853	(1.605)	0.883	(3.191)	0.460	(1.133)	0.850	(0.001)
−1.110	(9.322)	−0.060	(3.403)	−0.604	(1.137)	−1.297	(0.008)
−0.148	(4.781)	−0.052	(0.307)	−0.083	(0.079)	0.133	(0.006)
0.047	(0.059)	−0.064	(1.153)	−0.358	(1.093)	0.060	(0.001)
0.031	(0.004)	−0.002	(1.143)	−0.334	(0.642)	0.046	(0.007)
0.790	(0.978)	0.866	(1.026)	1.034	(0.573)	0.998	(0.018)
0.058	(0.230)	0.067	(0.521)	−0.009	(0.011)	0.035	(0.001)
−0.023	(1.114)	−0.225	(5.676)	0.559	(1.194)	0.059	(0.036)
−0.028	(0.342)	0.013	(7.232)	0.571	(0.819)	0.044	(0.037)
0.472	(7.042)	0.152	(4.820)	−0.553	(0.008)	0.105	(0.057)
−0.308	(2.146)	−0.158	(4.131)	0.197	(0.164)	0.125	(0.001)

Table C.1 (continued)

	22 Industrial Machinery and Equipment		23 Electronic and Electrical Equipment		24 Motor Vehicles	
α_K	0.009	(0.011)	0.046	(0.096)	–0.026	(0.002)
α_L	0.018	(0.015)	0.113	(0.045)	0.170	(0.009)
α_E	0.005	(0.001)	–0.003	(0.001)	0.033	(0.001)
α_0	0.099	(0.109)	0.632	(0.427)	0.034	(0.003)
β_{KK}	0.022	(0.003)	0.006	(0.003)	0.010	(0.013)
β_{KL}	–0.009	(0.002)	–0.023	(0.015)	–0.026	(0.022)
β_{KE}	0.000	(0.000)	–0.009	(0.003)	–0.001	(0.001)
β_{LL}	–0.007	(0.023)	0.034	(0.064)	–0.042	(0.031)
β_{LE}	–0.006	(0.000)	–0.008	(0.005)	–0.005	(0.010)
β_{EE}	0.007	(0.001)	0.008	(0.008)	0.004	(0.007)
χ_K	0.023	(0.009)	0.219	(0.013)	–0.013	(0.114)
χ_L	0.036	(0.043)	0.093	(0.020)	0.033	(0.173)
χ_E	0.004	(0.003)	0.304	(0.046)	–0.003	(0.001)
χ_P	–0.258	(0.011)	–0.179	(0.688)	–0.011	(0.256)
δ_{KK}	0.921	(0.051)	0.271	(0.016)	1.174	(0.891)
δ_{KL}	–0.043	(0.009)	–0.679	(0.377)	0.402	(0.470)
δ_{KE}	–0.075	(0.098)	–0.074	(0.077)	–0.102	(1.394)
δ_{Kp}	0.021	(0.005)	–0.006	(0.019)	0.277	(0.523)
δ_{LK}	0.089	(0.439)	–0.300	(0.100)	–0.321	(0.903)
δ_{LL}	0.875	(0.031)	0.678	(0.087)	0.399	(0.407)
δ_{LE}	–0.532	(0.530)	0.157	(0.207)	0.479	(3.881)
δ_{Lp}	0.005	(0.005)	–0.011	(0.049)	–0.271	(0.043)
δ_{EK}	–0.158	(0.032)	–0.870	(0.112)	–0.032	(0.035)
δ_{EL}	0.045	(0.000)	–0.873	(0.057)	–0.062	(0.063)
δ_{EE}	0.717	(0.040)	–0.872	(0.408)	0.763	(0.156)
δ_{Ep}	0.001	(0.001)	0.023	(0.075)	0.038	(0.051)
δ_{pK}	2.497	(1.326)	0.108	(2.698)	0.044	(1.397)
δ_{pL}	–0.087	(0.434)	0.550	(2.189)	–0.053	(0.485)
δ_{pE}	0.704	(0.609)	–0.227	(2.691)	–0.160	(5.697)
δ_{pp}	0.140	(0.137)	–0.479	(0.500)	0.392	(0.088)

Table C.1 (continued)

25 Other Transportation Equipment		26 Instruments		27 Miscellaneous Manufacturing		28 Transport and Warehouse	
−0.038	(0.073)	0.076	(0.014)	0.052	(0.360)	−0.018	(0.006)
−0.013	(0.004)	−0.096	(0.106)	0.383	(0.598)	0.182	(0.053)
−0.028	(0.007)	−0.004	(0.001)	0.000	(0.056)	0.048	(0.045)
0.057	(0.383)	0.230	(0.024)	0.200	(2.659)	0.257	(0.043)
0.020	(0.255)	0.021	(0.011)	0.038	(0.937)	0.045	(0.013)
0.032	(0.125)	−0.006	(0.038)	0.026	(0.627)	−0.039	(0.152)
0.000	(0.002)	−0.002	(0.002)	−0.005	(0.534)	−0.022	(0.088)
0.006	(0.135)	0.102	(0.171)	0.000	(1.448)	−0.091	(0.002)
−0.001	(0.002)	−0.009	(0.005)	0.001	(0.299)	0.004	(0.127)
0.006	(0.021)	0.007	(0.006)	0.010	(0.408)	0.044	(0.032)
−0.005	(0.149)	0.057	(0.077)	−0.005	(0.051)	0.143	(0.120)
0.088	(0.288)	−0.048	(0.111)	0.011	(0.342)	−0.018	(0.024)
−0.003	(0.092)	0.002	(0.001)	0.005	(0.344)	−0.006	(0.058)
−0.173	(1.260)	−0.120	(0.073)	−0.037	(3.953)	0.156	(0.021)
0.925	(0.199)	0.576	(0.286)	0.956	(4.825)	0.364	(0.381)
0.037	(0.501)	−0.070	(0.117)	−0.021	(3.213)	−0.217	(0.262)
−0.075	(2.495)	−0.563	(0.422)	0.556	(12.261)	0.299	(0.115)
0.135	(0.495)	0.004	(0.242)	−0.019	(2.804)	−0.127	(0.291)
−0.463	(0.006)	0.290	(0.375)	−0.689	(13.311)	0.061	(0.009)
0.890	(1.344)	1.021	(0.162)	0.649	(5.449)	0.970	(0.040)
0.242	(7.347)	1.797	(0.656)	0.833	(24.106)	0.326	(0.002)
−0.121	(2.424)	−0.074	(0.423)	−0.166	(0.674)	−0.106	(0.019)
0.043	(0.382)	0.007	(0.006)	0.007	(4.289)	0.054	(0.136)
0.018	(0.181)	−0.002	(0.000)	0.011	(2.376)	0.028	(0.127)
0.765	(0.681)	0.964	(0.073)	0.703	(10.947)	0.592	(0.001)
−0.004	(0.181)	0.004	(0.008)	0.012	(1.176)	−0.537	(0.069)
0.014	(4.953)	0.432	(0.373)	0.262	(67.819)	−0.872	(0.028)
0.413	(2.843)	0.173	(0.164)	0.186	(33.557)	−0.178	(0.043)
−0.190	(13.363)	0.333	(2.107)	1.325	(76.643)	0.489	(0.066)
−0.363	(11.726)	0.334	(0.533)	−0.053	(18.288)	−0.609	(0.108)

Table C.1 (continued)

	29 Communications		30 Electric Utilities		31 Gas Utilities	
α_K	0.085	(0.114)	0.241	(0.015)	–0.255	(0.058)
α_L	0.355	(0.083)	0.064	(0.000)	0.112	(0.044)
α_E	0.079	(0.003)	0.013	(0.030)	0.111	(0.134)
α_0	0.218	(0.086)	0.088	(0.035)	0.041	(0.200)
β_{KK}	–0.021	(0.457)	0.051	(0.051)	0.001	(0.075)
β_{KL}	0.050	(0.247)	0.013	(0.097)	–0.028	(0.060)
β_{KE}	–0.003	(0.033)	–0.024	(0.001)	0.054	(0.159)
β_{LL}	–0.097	(0.209)	0.000	(0.001)	–0.025	(0.003)
β_{LE}	–0.005	(0.004)	–0.019	(0.010)	0.011	(0.068)
β_{EE}	0.002	(0.003)	0.062	(0.024)	–0.108	(0.294)
χ_K	0.070	(0.263)	–0.019	(0.248)	0.168	(0.073)
χ_L	0.040	(0.396)	0.006	(0.156)	0.093	(0.083)
χ_E	–0.025	(0.020)	0.025	(0.058)	0.040	(0.115)
χ_P	–0.036	(0.858)	0.011	(0.163)	–0.405	(0.338)
δ_{KK}	0.907	(2.451)	0.910	(0.666)	0.777	(0.033)
δ_{KL}	0.005	(4.350)	0.390	(0.393)	–0.238	(0.118)
δ_{KE}	0.673	(1.991)	–0.073	(0.477)	–0.147	(0.113)
δ_{Kp}	0.193	(0.346)	–0.057	(0.417)	0.016	(0.343)
δ_{LK}	–0.125	(1.004)	0.035	(0.323)	–0.061	(0.127)
δ_{LL}	0.721	(2.246)	0.865	(0.412)	0.755	(0.270)
δ_{LE}	0.514	(5.529)	0.030	(0.259)	–0.132	(0.073)
δ_{Lp}	0.001	(0.119)	0.147	(0.028)	0.058	(0.132)
δ_{EK}	0.001	(0.004)	0.006	(0.006)	–0.132	(0.242)
δ_{EL}	0.018	(0.040)	–0.279	(0.425)	0.371	(0.425)
δ_{EE}	0.627	(0.271)	1.033	(0.012)	1.044	(0.035)
δ_{Ep}	–0.015	(0.042)	–0.248	(0.288)	–0.152	(0.660)
δ_{pK}	0.085	(1.064)	–0.042	(0.069)	0.348	(0.152)
δ_{pL}	0.059	(1.459)	–0.101	(0.957)	0.596	(1.025)
δ_{pE}	–0.230	(11.335)	0.036	(0.245)	0.506	(0.235)
δ_{pp}	0.405	(0.104)	0.708	(0.851)	0.022	(0.969)

Table C.1 (continued)

32 Trade		33 Finance, Insurance, and Real Estate		34 Services		35 Government Enterprises	
0.112	(0.047)	0.428	(0.017)	0.025	(0.006)	0.157	(0.025)
0.668	(0.011)	0.121	(0.011)	0.075	(0.029)	0.591	(0.004)
−0.015	(0.017)	−0.005	(0.001)	−0.017	(0.003)	−0.003	(0.002)
0.169	(0.001)	0.161	(0.054)	−0.031	(0.010)	0.013	(0.016)
−0.037	(0.037)	−0.128	(0.136)	−0.069	(0.014)	0.108	(0.031)
0.012	(0.095)	0.076	(0.027)	−0.123	(0.022)	−0.046	(0.040)
−0.007	(0.041)	−0.011	(0.007)	0.017	(0.003)	−0.018	(0.004)
−0.095	(0.591)	−0.059	(0.072)	−0.041	(0.017)	−0.042	(0.008)
0.009	(0.059)	0.003	(0.005)	0.008	(0.001)	−0.022	(0.004)
0.020	(0.174)	0.006	(0.011)	0.009	(0.001)	0.021	(0.001)
0.011	(0.000)	−0.025	(0.071)	0.249	(0.149)	0.063	(0.033)
−0.023	(0.012)	0.029	(0.002)	0.167	(0.063)	0.135	(0.005)
0.006	(0.009)	0.001	(0.005)	−0.085	(0.070)	0.039	(0.012)
0.008	(0.027)	−0.002	(0.065)	−0.133	(0.050)	−0.020	(0.050)
0.898	(0.019)	0.726	(0.105)	0.578	(0.163)	1.071	(0.025)
0.040	(0.013)	0.357	(0.524)	−0.585	(0.420)	0.172	(0.125)
−0.007	(0.009)	−0.702	(0.872)	0.840	(0.322)	−0.596	(0.187)
−0.063	(0.003)	0.076	(0.196)	−0.194	(0.007)	−0.140	(0.045)
0.143	(0.000)	0.035	(0.197)	−0.035	(0.036)	0.775	(0.108)
0.885	(0.000)	0.758	(0.102)	0.541	(0.163)	1.025	(0.070)
−0.096	(0.009)	−0.295	(0.639)	0.710	(0.063)	−3.574	(0.198)
0.058	(0.004)	−0.225	(0.136)	0.054	(0.044)	0.165	(0.155)
0.267	(0.006)	−0.039	(0.003)	−0.024	(0.004)	0.152	(0.005)
0.013	(0.021)	0.050	(0.034)	0.298	(0.150)	0.062	(0.029)
0.734	(0.002)	0.620	(0.113)	−0.013	(0.204)	0.285	(0.112)
−0.027	(0.010)	−0.019	(0.001)	0.033	(0.014)	−0.020	(0.005)
−0.320	(0.057)	−0.019	(0.434)	0.136	(0.297)	0.168	(0.078)
0.036	(0.069)	−0.039	(0.675)	0.300	(0.287)	−0.153	(0.114)
−0.064	(0.002)	0.000	(0.148)	−0.017	(1.198)	−0.457	(0.564)
−0.568	(0.049)	0.070	(0.813)	0.190	(0.033)	0.552	(0.144)

Table C.2
Estimated parameters of cost functions of lower tiers: Example for Agriculture (industry 1)

Node		Input	Alpha	Beta1	Beta2	Beta3	Beta4	Beta5
1	Gross output							
2	Energy	Coal Mining	0.000	0.000	0.000	0.000	0.000	0.000
		Petroleum and Gas Mining	0.000	0.000	0.000	0.000	0.000	0.000
		Refining	–0.127	0.000	0.000	0.093	–0.093	0.000
		Electric Utilities	1.127	0.000	0.000	–0.093	0.093	0.000
		Gas Utilities	0.000	0.000	0.000	0.000	0.000	0.000
3	Materials	Construction	0.000	0.000	0.000	0.000	0.000	0.000
		Agriculture Materials	–0.002	0.000	0.154	0.000	–0.033	–0.121
		Metallic Materials	0.000	0.000	0.000	0.000	0.000	0.000
		Nonmetallic Materials	–0.130	0.000	–0.033	0.000	0.018	0.015
		Services Materials	1.132	0.000	–0.121	0.000	0.015	0.106
4	Agriculture Materials	Agriculture	1.386	–0.344	0.344	0.000	0.000	0.000
		Food Manufacturing	–0.386	0.344	–0.344	0.000	0.000	0.000
		Tobacco	0.000	0.000	0.000	0.000	0.000	0.000
		Textile–Apparel	0.000	0.000	0.000	0.000	0.000	0.000
		Wood–Paper	0.000	0.000	0.000	0.000	0.000	0.000
5	Metallic Materials	Fabricated—Other	–0.049	–0.017	–0.025	0.042		
		Machinery Materials	–0.187	–0.025	0.103	–0.077		
		Equipment	1.235	0.042	–0.077	0.035		
6	Nonmetallic Materials	Nonmetal Mining	0.000	0.000	0.000	0.000	0.000	0.000
		Chemicals	1.000	0.000	0.000	0.000	0.000	0.000
		Rubber	0.000	0.000	0.000	0.000	0.000	0.000
		Stone, Clay, Glass	0.000	0.000	0.000	0.000	0.000	0.000
		Misc. Manufacturing	0.000	0.000	0.000	0.000	0.000	0.000

Table C.2 (continued)

Node		Input	Alpha	Beta1	Beta2	Beta3	Beta4	Beta5
7	Services Materials	Transportation	–0.057	–0.002	0.070	0.057	–0.125	0.000
		Trade	–0.027	0.070	–0.009	–0.114	0.052	0.000
		FIRE	–0.015	0.057	–0.114	–0.080	0.137	0.000
		Services	1.099	–0.125	0.052	0.137	–0.065	0.000
		Other Services	0.000	0.000	0.000	0.000	0.000	0.000
8	Textile—Apparel	Textiles	0.123	–0.011	0.011	0.000		
		Apparel	0.877	0.011	–0.011	0.000		
		Leather	0.000	0.000	0.000	0.000		
9	Wood—Paper	Lumber	–0.045	0.158	0.000	–0.158	0.000	
		Furniture	0.000	0.000	0.000	0.000	0.000	
		Paper	1.045	–0.158	0.000	0.158	0.000	
		Printing	0.000	0.000	0.000	0.000	0.000	
10	Other Services	Communications	1.632	–0.051	0.051	0.000		
		Govt. Enterprises	–0.632	0.051	–0.051	0.000		
		Noncomparable Imports	0.000	0.000	0.000	0.000		
11	Fabricated—Other	Metal Mining	0.000	0.000	0.000	0.000		
		Primary Metals	0.017	0.000	0.064	–0.064		
		Fabricated Metals	0.983	0.000	–0.064	0.064		
12	Machinery Materials	Industrial Machinery	0.795	–0.105	0.105			
		Electric Machinery	0.205	0.105	–0.105			
13	Equipment	Motor Vehicles	0.401	–0.131	–0.169	0.300		
		Other Transportation Equipment	–0.137	–0.169	–0.219	0.388		
		Instruments	0.736	0.300	0.388	–0.687		

Table C.3
Change in input bias terms for subtiers (1960–2005)

Node		Components of Node	1 Agriculture	2 Metal Mining	3 Coal Mining	4 Petroleum	5 Nonmetal Mining	6 Construction	7 Food Manufacturing
2	E	Energy							
		Coal	0.000	0.000	–0.253	0.000	0.000	0.000	0.000
		Oil Mining	0.000	0.000	0.000	0.000	0.000	0.000	0.000
		Refining	0.039	0.247	0.237	0.000	0.232	–0.008	0.154
		Electric Utilities	–0.039	–0.151	0.015	0.000	–0.086	0.008	0.079
		Gas Utilities	0.000	–0.096	0.000	0.000	–0.146	0.000	–0.233
3	M	Materials							
		Construction	0.000	0.000	0.000	0.000	0.000	0.000	0.000
		Agriculture Materials	–0.056	0.000	0.000	0.000	0.000	0.016	–0.023
		Metallic Materials	0.000	0.048	–0.015	–0.085	–0.019	–0.046	0.000
		Nonmetallic Materials	0.016	–0.018	–0.014	–0.003	0.007	–0.006	0.000
		Services Materials	0.041	–0.030	0.029	0.088	0.011	0.036	0.023
4	MA	Agriculture Materials							
		Agriculture	–0.050	0.145	0.065	0.139	0.000	0.000	0.037
		Food	0.050	0.000	0.000	0.000	0.000	0.000	–0.033
		Tobacco	0.000	0.000	0.000	0.000	0.000	0.000	0.000
		Textile–Apparel	0.000	0.000	0.301	0.000	0.000	0.000	0.000
		Wood–Paper	0.000	–0.145	–0.366	–0.139	0.000	0.000	–0.004

Table C.3 (continued)

Node		Components of Node	1 Agriculture	2 Metal Mining	3 Coal Mining	4 Petroleum	5 Nonmetal Mining	6 Construction	7 Food Manufacturing
5	MM	Metallic Materials							
		Fabricated–Other Metals	–0.016	0.080	–0.118	0.009	–0.156	–0.044	0.000
		Machinery	–0.032	–0.080	0.118	–0.009	0.156	0.044	0.000
		Equipment	0.048	0.000	0.000	0.000	0.000	0.000	0.000
6	MN	Nonmetallic Materials							
		Nonmetal Mining	0.000	0.000	0.000	0.000	–0.050	0.007	0.000
		Chemicals	0.000	–0.011	–0.075	0.089	–0.015	0.012	–0.024
		Rubber–Plastics	0.000	0.005	–0.166	0.000	0.065	0.022	0.028
		Stone, Clay, Glass	0.000	0.006	0.241	–0.089	0.000	–0.040	–0.004
		Misc. Manufacturing	0.000	0.000	0.000	0.000	0.000	0.000	0.000
7	MS	Services Materials							
		Transportation	–0.018	–0.096	–0.126	0.000	–0.058	–0.016	–0.082
		Trade	–0.021	0.046	–0.051	–0.003	–0.020	–0.201	–0.025
		FIRE	–0.036	–0.150	–0.009	–0.038	0.043	–0.012	0.004
		Services	0.076		0.186	0.028	0.035	0.228	0.185
		Other Services	0.000	0.020	0.000	0.013	0.000	0.000	–0.081
8	TA	Textile–Apparel							
		Textiles	0.089	–0.167	0.000	–0.401	–0.101	–0.096	0.113
		Apparel	–0.089	0.167	0.000	–0.175	0.101	0.096	–0.113
		Leather	0.000	0.000	0.000	0.576	0.000	0.000	0.000

Table C.3 (continued)

Node		Components of Node	1 Agriculture	2 Metal Mining	3 Coal Mining	4 Petroleum	5 Nonmetal Mining	6 Construction	7 Food Manufacturing
9	WP	Wood—Paper							
		Lumber Wood	–0.044	–0.036	–0.056	0.033	–0.572	0.000	0.000
		Furniture	0.000	0.000	0.000	0.000	0.000	0.000	0.000
		Paper	0.044	0.036	0.056	–0.051	0.047	0.000	0.028
		Printing	0.000	0.000	0.000	0.019	0.524	0.000	–0.028
10	OS	Other Services							
		Communications	–0.070	–0.110	–0.170	–0.073	–0.125	–0.038	0.147
		Govt. Enterprises	0.070	–0.182	–0.091	0.000	–0.053	0.038	0.191
		Noncomparable Imports	0.000	0.291	0.261	0.073	0.178	0.000	–0.338
11	FM	Fabricated–Other Metals							
		Metal Mining	0.000	0.123	0.000	0.000	0.000	0.000	0.000
		Primary Metals	–0.026	–0.098	–0.093	–0.088	0.206	–0.110	0.000
		Fabricated Metals	0.026	–0.025	0.093	0.088	–0.206	0.110	0.000
12	MC	Machinery Materials							
		Industrial Machinery	–0.242	0.000	0.000	0.000	0.000	0.022	–0.137
		Electrical Machinery	0.242	0.000	0.000	0.000	0.000	–0.022	0.137
13	EQ	Equipment							
		Motor Vehicles	–0.034	0.213	0.459	0.436	0.000	0.165	0.446
		Other Transportation Equip.	–0.073	0.009	0.000	0.000	0.000	0.046	0.000
		Instruments	0.107	–0.222	–0.459	–0.436	0.000	–0.211	–0.446

Table C.3 (continued)

Node		Components of Node	8 Tobacco	9 Textile	10 Apparel	11 Lumber	12 Furniture	13 Paper	14 Printing
2	E	Energy							
		Coal	–0.017	0.000	0.000	0.000	0.000	0.000	0.000
		Oil Mining	0.000	0.000	0.000	0.000	0.000	0.000	0.000
		Refining	0.169	0.169	0.152	0.135	0.105	0.163	0.132
		Electric Utilities	–0.041	–0.010	–0.031	–0.004	0.016	0.045	–0.025
		Gas Utilities	–0.111	–0.159	–0.121	–0.131	–0.121	–0.207	–0.107
3	M	Materials							
		Construction	0.000	0.000	0.000	0.000	0.000	0.000	0.000
		Agriculture Materials	–0.105	–0.080	–0.080	–0.045	–0.003	–0.148	–0.216
		Metallic Materials	0.000	0.000	0.000	0.000	–0.038	0.000	0.000
		Nonmetallic Materials	0.000	0.082	0.000	0.000	0.006	0.056	0.000
		Services Materials	0.105	–0.002	0.080	0.045	0.034	0.092	0.216
4	MA	Agriculture Materials							
		Agriculture	–0.099	–0.024	0.000	–0.003	0.000	0.000	0.000
		Food	0.000	0.000	0.000	0.000	0.000	0.000	0.000
		Tobacco	0.105	0.000	0.000	0.000	0.000	0.000	0.000
		Textile–Apparel	0.000	0.024	0.000	0.000	–0.043	0.000	0.000
		Wood–Paper	–0.006	0.000	0.000	0.003	0.043	0.000	0.000
5	MM	Metallic Materials							
		Fabricated–Other Metals	–0.084	0.000	–0.087	–0.035	0.000	–0.096	–0.021
		Machinery	0.084	0.000	0.441	–0.005	0.000	0.026	0.068
		Equipment	0.000	0.000	–0.354	0.039	0.000	0.069	–0.047

Table C.3 (continued)

Node		Components of Node	8 Tobacco	9 Textile	10 Apparel	11 Lumber	12 Furniture	13 Paper	14 Printing
6	MN	Nonmetallic Materials							
		Nonmetal Mining	0.000	0.000	0.000	0.000	0.000	0.000	0.000
		Chemicals	0.094	0.000	0.111	–0.012	–0.027	–0.008	–0.057
		Rubber–Plastics	–0.094	0.000	–0.060	0.009	0.034	0.008	0.057
		Stone, Clay, Glass	0.000	0.000	0.000	0.003	–0.007	0.000	0.000
		Misc. Manufacturing	0.000	0.000	–0.051	0.000	0.000	0.000	0.000
7	MS	Services Materials							
		Transportation	0.000	–0.011	–0.037	–0.050	–0.004	–0.041	–0.074
		Trade	–0.005	–0.030	–0.067	0.027	0.018	–0.065	–0.026
		FIRE	0.000	–0.033	0.024	–0.014	–0.016	–0.002	0.050
		Services	0.005		0.122	0.037	0.002	0.107	0.096
		Other Services	0.000	0.000	–0.042	0.000	0.000	0.000	–0.046
8	TA	Textile—Apparel							
		Textiles	0.070	0.000	0.128	0.000	0.000	0.000	0.000
		Apparel	–0.070	0.000	–0.128	0.000	0.000	0.000	0.000
		Leather	0.000	0.000	0.000	0.000	0.000	0.000	0.000
9	WP	Wood—Paper							
		Lumber Wood	0.000	0.000	0.386	0.000	–0.256	–0.008	0.000
		Furniture	0.000	0.000	0.000	0.000	0.294	0.000	0.000
		Paper	0.057	0.000	–0.393	0.000	–0.038	0.008	0.017
		Printing	–0.057	0.000	0.007	0.000	0.000	0.000	–0.017

Table C.3 (continued)

Node		Components of Node	8 Tobacco	9 Textile	10 Apparel	11 Lumber	12 Furniture	13 Paper	14 Printing
10	OS	Other Services							
		Communications	0.029	0.012	–0.007	–0.061	–0.063	–0.069	–0.066
		Govt. Enterprises	–0.073	0.018	0.148	0.061	0.040	–0.006	0.030
		Noncomparable Imports	0.044	–0.030	–0.141	0.000	0.024	0.074	0.036
11	FM	Fabricated–Other Metals							
		Metal Mining	0.000	0.000	0.000	0.000	0.000	0.000	0.000
		Primary Metals	0.000	–0.158	–0.030	0.000	0.000	0.058	–0.187
		Fabricated Metals	0.000	0.158	0.030	0.000	0.000	–0.058	0.187
12	MC	Machinery Materials							
		Industrial Machinery	–0.320	0.000	0.000	–0.059	0.100	–0.041	0.033
		Electrical Machinery	0.320	0.000	0.000	0.059	–0.100	0.041	–0.033
13	EQ	Equipment							
		Motor Vehicles	0.224	0.494	0.654	0.000	0.443	0.035	0.162
		Other Transportation Equip.	0.000	0.000	0.000	0.000	0.000	0.000	0.000
		Instruments	–0.224	–0.494	–0.654	0.000	–0.443	–0.036	–0.162

Table C.3 (continued)

Node		Components of Node	15 Chemical	16 Refining	17 Rubber	18 Leather	19 Stone, Clay	20 Primary	21 Fabricated
2	E	Energy							
		Coal	0.000	0.000	0.000	0.000	–0.024	–0.354	0.000
		Oil Mining	–0.057	–0.234	0.000	0.000	0.000	0.000	0.000
		Refining	0.167	0.230	0.006	0.267	0.219	0.115	0.070
		Electric Utilities	0.113	0.000	0.177	–0.159	0.079	0.242	0.134
		Gas Utilities	–0.223	0.004	–0.183	–0.109	–0.274	–0.004	–0.204
3	M	Materials							
		Construction	0.000	0.000	0.000	0.000	0.000	0.000	0.000
		Agriculture Materials	0.000	0.000	–0.015	–0.036	–0.023	0.000	0.000
		Metallic Materials	0.000	0.000	0.000	0.000	0.000	–0.058	–0.121
		Nonmetallic Materials	–0.094	–0.030	0.019	0.022	–0.022	0.000	0.000
		Services Materials	0.094	0.030	–0.004	0.014	0.046	0.058	0.121
4	MA	Agriculture Materials							
		Agriculture	0.030	0.000	0.152	0.000	0.000	0.000	0.000
		Food	–0.093	0.035	0.000	–0.027	0.000	0.000	0.000
		Tobacco	0.000	0.000	0.000	0.000	0.000	0.000	0.000
		Textile–Apparel	0.000	0.000	–0.125	0.027	0.000	0.000	0.000
		Wood–Paper	0.063	–0.035	–0.027	0.000	0.000	0.000	0.000

Table C.3 (continued)

Node		Components of Node	15 Chemical	16 Refining	17 Rubber	18 Leather	19 Stone, Clay	20 Primary	21 Fabricated
5	MM	Metallic Materials							
		Fabricated–Other Metals	0.030	–0.084	–0.024	0.009	–0.012	–0.262	0.000
		Machinery	–0.030	–0.042	0.024	–0.009	–0.005	0.262	0.000
		Equipment	0.000	0.126	0.000	0.000	0.018	0.000	0.000
6	MN	Nonmetallic Materials							
		Nonmetal Mining	0.000	–0.001	0.000	0.000	–0.019	0.000	0.000
		Chemicals	0.000	–0.084	0.040	0.171	–0.001	–0.099	–0.011
		Rubber–Plastics	0.000	0.046	–0.040	–0.173	0.000	0.006	–0.033
		Stone, Clay, Glass	0.000	0.040	0.000	0.000	0.020	0.093	0.044
		Misc. Manufacturing	0.000	0.000	0.000	0.001	0.000	0.000	0.000
7	MS	Services Materials							
		Transportation	–0.104	–0.317	–0.054	0.014	–0.116	–0.028	–0.008
		Trade	–0.031	0.153	–0.013	–0.065	–0.024	–0.119	–0.049
		FIRE	–0.011	0.059	–0.011	0.059	0.077	–0.020	–0.030
		Services	0.145		0.149	–0.015	0.069	0.167	0.086
		Other Services	0.000	0.000	–0.071	0.008	–0.006	0.000	0.000
8	TA	Textile–Apparel							
		Textiles	0.027	–0.455	0.000	0.018	0.000	–0.151	–0.021
		Apparel	–0.027	0.000	0.000	0.000	0.000	0.067	–0.484
		Leather	0.000	0.455	0.000	–0.018	0.000	0.084	0.505

Table C.3 (continued)

Node		Components of Node	15 Chemical	16 Refining	17 Rubber	18 Leather	19 Stone, Clay	20 Primary	21 Fabricated
9	WP	Wood—Paper							
		Lumber Wood	0.000	0.127	0.000	–0.140	0.060	–0.035	–0.102
		Furniture	0.000	0.000	0.000	0.000	0.000	0.088	0.000
		Paper	0.008	–0.127	0.000	0.140	–0.060	–0.088	0.243
		Printing	–0.008	0.000	0.000	0.000	0.000	0.035	–0.141
10	OS	Other Services							
		Communications	–0.063	–0.009	0.254	–0.070	–0.047	0.114	–0.161
		Govt. Enterprises	0.007	–0.004	0.071	0.070	0.046	0.081	–0.008
		Noncomparable Imports	0.056	0.013	–0.325	0.000	0.001	–0.196	0.169
11	FM	Fabricated–Other Metals							
		Metal Mining	0.078	0.000	0.000	0.000	0.000	–0.019	0.000
		Primary Metals	–0.089	–0.014	0.010	0.000	0.020	0.019	–0.077
		Fabricated Metals	0.012	0.014	–0.010	0.000	–0.020	0.000	0.077
12	MC	Machinery Materials							
		Industrial Machinery	–0.049	–0.095	–0.007	–0.003	0.001	0.008	–0.008
		Electrical Machinery	0.049	0.095	0.007	0.003	–0.001	–0.008	0.008
13	EQ	Equipment							
		Motor Vehicles	0.207	0.216	0.176	0.517	0.332	0.214	0.150
		Other Transportation Equip.	0.000	0.000	0.000	0.000	0.000	0.011	0.000
		Instruments	–0.207	–0.216	–0.176	–0.517	–0.332	–0.225	–0.150

Table C.3 (continued)

Node	Components of Node	22 Industrial Machinery	23 Electric Machinery	24 Motor Vehicles	25 Transportation Equipment	26 Instruments	27 Miscellaneous Manufacturing	28 Transport
2 E	Energy							
	Coal	0.000	0.000	0.000	0.000	0.000	0.000	0.000
	Oil Mining	0.000	0.000	0.000	0.000	0.000	0.000	0.000
	Refining	0.096	0.062	0.134	0.128	0.107	0.210	0.012
	Electric Utilities	0.004	–0.022	0.064	–0.017	–0.052	–0.129	–0.012
	Gas Utilities	–0.101	–0.039	–0.198	–0.110	–0.055	–0.080	0.000
3 M	Materials							
	Construction	0.000	0.000	0.000	0.000	0.000	0.000	0.000
	Agriculture Materials	0.000	0.000	0.000	0.000	0.002	–0.034	0.000
	Metallic Materials	–0.048	–0.040	–0.039	–0.104	–0.028	–0.074	0.000
	Nonmetallic Materials	0.000	0.022	0.018	0.000	–0.001	0.074	0.000
	Services Materials	0.048	0.017	0.021	0.104	0.026	0.034	0.000
4 MA	Agriculture Materials							
	Agriculture	0.000	0.000	0.000	0.008	0.000	0.000	0.000
	Food	0.000	0.000	0.000	0.000	0.000	0.000	–0.079
	Tobacco	0.000	0.000	0.000	0.000	0.000	0.000	0.000
	Textile–Apparel	–0.031	0.000	–0.405	–0.277	–0.035	–0.052	–0.157
	Wood–Paper	0.031	0.000	0.405	0.270	0.035	0.052	0.236

Table C.3 (continued)

Node	Components of Node	22 Industrial Machinery	23 Electric Machinery	24 Motor Vehicles	25 Transportation Equipment	26 Instruments	27 Miscellaneous Manufacturing	28 Transport
5 MM	Metallic Materials							
	Fabricated–Other Metals	0.076	0.137	–0.070	0.083	0.042	–0.087	–0.005
	Machinery	–0.076	–0.137	–0.042	0.023	0.029	0.087	–0.030
	Equipment	0.000	0.000	0.111	–0.107	–0.071	0.000	0.035
6 MN	Nonmetallic Materials							
	Nonmetal Mining	0.000	0.000	0.000	0.000	0.000	0.000	0.000
	Chemicals	–0.032	0.011	–0.004	–0.011	–0.121	–0.020	–0.150
	Rubber–Plastics	0.069	0.009	0.111	–0.029	0.173	–0.003	0.150
	Stone, Clay, Glass	–0.037	–0.020	–0.107	0.040	–0.052	0.000	0.000
	Misc. Manufacturing	0.000	0.000	0.000	0.000	0.000	0.022	0.000
7 MS	Services Materials							
	Transportation	–0.070	0.003	–0.024	0.002	–0.006	–0.001	–0.102
	Trade	0.045	–0.060	0.031	–0.004	–0.047	0.046	–0.048
	FIRE	–0.060	–0.007	0.033	–0.006	0.009	–0.016	–0.017
	Services	0.065		–0.039	0.008	0.054	0.048	0.141
	Other Services	0.021	–0.022	0.000	0.000	–0.010	–0.077	0.025
8 TA	Textile–Apparel							
	Textiles	0.000	0.028	0.061	–0.064	0.000	0.075	0.044
	Apparel	0.000	–0.028	–0.061	0.064	0.000	0.010	–0.044
	Leather	0.000	0.000	0.000	0.000	0.000	–0.085	0.000

Table C.3 (continued)

Node		Components of Node	22 Industrial Machinery	23 Electric Machinery	24 Motor Vehicles	25 Transportation Equipment	26 Instruments	27 Miscellaneous Manufacturing	28 Transport
9	WP	Wood-Paper							
		Lumber Wood	0.012	0.000	0.000	–0.304	0.000	–0.052	0.108
		Furniture	0.000	0.274	0.000	0.352	0.274	0.110	0.000
		Paper	–0.012	–0.274	0.000	–0.048	–0.274	–0.058	–0.019
		Printing	0.000	0.000	0.000	0.000	0.000	0.000	–0.089
10	OS	Other Services							
		Communications	0.000	–0.150	–0.061	–0.065	–0.049	0.187	–0.044
		Govt. Enterprises	0.000	–0.071	–0.081	–0.011	–0.015	0.313	0.000
		Noncomparable Imports	0.000	0.221	0.142	0.076	0.064	–0.500	0.044
11	FM	Fabricated–Other Metals							
		Metal Mining	0.000	0.000	0.000	0.000	0.000	0.000	0.000
		Primary Metals	–0.107	–0.095	–0.029	–0.110	–0.167	–0.058	–0.176
		Fabricated Metals	0.107	0.095	0.029	0.110	0.167	0.058	0.176
12	MC	Machinery Materials							
		Industrial Machinery	–0.168	0.000	–0.043	–0.130	–0.043	–0.067	–0.061
		Electrical Machinery	0.168	0.000	0.043	0.130	0.043	0.067	0.061
13	EQ	Equipment							
		Motor Vehicles	0.282	0.000	0.000	0.000	0.000	0.425	0.168
		Other Transportation Equip.	0.000	0.000	0.000	0.025	0.000	0.045	–0.168
		Instruments	–0.282	0.000	0.000	–0.025	0.000	–0.470	0.000

Table C.3 (continued)

Node		Components of Node	29 Communications	30 Electric Utilities	31 Gas Utilities	32 Trade	33 FIRE	34 Services	35 Government Enterprises
2	E	Energy							
		Coal	0.000	–0.106	0.000	0.000	0.000	0.000	0.000
		Oil Mining	0.000	–0.052	0.076	0.000	0.000	0.000	0.000
		Refining	0.106	0.180	0.000	0.095	0.008	0.132	0.236
		Electric Utilities	–0.106	–0.024	0.000	0.023	0.074	0.028	–0.005
		Gas Utilities	0.000	0.002	–0.076	–0.118	–0.082	–0.160	–0.231
3	M	Materials							
		Construction	0.000	–0.095	0.000	0.000	0.000	0.000	–0.040
		Agriculture Materials	0.000	0.000	–0.003	–0.068	0.000	0.000	0.000
		Metallic Materials	–0.016	0.015	–0.028	0.000	0.000	–0.024	0.020
		Nonmetallic Materials	0.000	0.000	0.000	0.000	0.000	0.000	0.000
		Services Materials	0.016	0.079	0.031	0.068	0.000	0.024	0.020
4	MA	Agriculture Materials							
		Agriculture	0.000	0.000	0.000	0.030	0.137	0.014	–0.049
		Food	0.000	0.000	0.000	–0.002	0.000	0.017	–0.158
		Tobacco	0.000	0.000	0.000	0.000	0.000	0.000	0.000
		Textile–Apparel	0.000	0.000	0.000	0.000	0.000	–0.066	–0.065
		Wood–Paper	0.000	0.000	0.000	–0.028	–0.137	0.035	0.272

Table C.3 (continued)

Node		Components of Node	29 Communications	30 Electric Utilities	31 Gas Utilities	32 Trade	33 FIRE	34 Services	35 Government Enterprises
5	MM	Metallic Materials							
		Fabricated–Other Metals	0.000	–0.032	0.165	–0.090	0.039	–0.016	0.000
		Machinery	0.000	–0.003	–0.165	–0.028	–0.006	0.070	–0.010
		Equipment	0.000	0.035	0.000	0.118	–0.033	–0.054	0.010
6	MN	Nonmetallic Materials							
		Nonmetal Mining	0.000	0.000	0.000	0.000	–0.091	0.000	0.000
		Chemicals	–0.041	–0.029	–0.005	–0.011	–0.034	–0.025	–0.086
		Rubber–Plastics	0.048	0.045	0.007	0.019	0.136	0.028	0.000
		Stone, Clay, Glass	–0.009	–0.016	0.014	–0.007	0.112	0.010	0.086
		Misc. Manufacturing	0.002	0.000	–0.015	–0.001	–0.122	–0.013	0.000
7	MS	Services Materials							
		Transportation	0.000	–0.274	0.077	0.000	0.000	0.000	–0.059
		Trade	0.000	–0.009	0.017	–0.005	0.000	–0.005	–0.046
		FIRE	–0.005	0.052	0.219	–0.036	–0.052	–0.003	0.130
		Services	0.001		–0.330	0.038	0.074	0.014	–0.003
		Other Services	0.004	–0.013	0.016	0.003	–0.022	–0.006	–0.022
8	TA	Textile–Apparel							
		Textiles	–0.121	0.137	–0.011	0.134	–0.121	0.041	–0.124
		Apparel	0.121	–0.137	0.011	–0.134	0.071	–0.060	0.005
		Leather	0.000	0.000	0.000	0.000	0.050	0.019	0.119

Table C.3 (continued)

Node		Components of Node	29 Communications	30 Electric Utilities	31 Gas Utilities	32 Trade	33 FIRE	34 Services	35 Government Enterprises
9	WP	Wood—Paper							
		Lumber Wood	0.083	0.240	0.068	0.013	0.067	0.000	–0.108
		Furniture	0.000	0.000	0.000	0.000	0.000	0.000	0.306
		Paper	–0.024	–0.065	–0.068	–0.086	0.017	0.062	0.015
		Printing	–0.059	–0.175	0.000	0.073	–0.084	–0.062	–0.213
10	OS	Other Services							
		Communications	–0.062	–0.074	–0.181	–0.043	–0.047	–0.002	0.021
		Govt. Enterprises	0.000	0.074	–0.093	–0.024	–0.067	–0.013	0.131
		Noncomparable Imports	0.062	0.000	0.275	0.067	0.115	0.015	–0.152
11	FM	Fabricated–Other Metals							
		Metal Mining	0.000	0.000	0.000	0.000	0.000	0.000	0.000
		Primary Metals	–0.126	–0.048	–0.058	0.016	–0.138	0.000	–0.170
		Fabricated Metals	0.126	0.048	0.058	–0.016	0.138	0.000	0.170
12	MC	Machinery Materials							
		Industrial Machinery	–0.055	–0.004	0.075	–0.134	0.071	–0.042	0.124
		Electrical Machinery	0.055	0.004	–0.075	0.134	–0.071	0.042	–0.124
13	EQ	Equipment							
		Motor Vehicles	0.164	0.194	0.398	0.000	0.151	–0.092	0.167
		Other Transportation Equip.	–0.065	0.000	0.047	0.000	0.000	0.000	–0.167
		Instruments	–0.099	–0.194	–0.445	0.000	–0.151	0.092	0.000

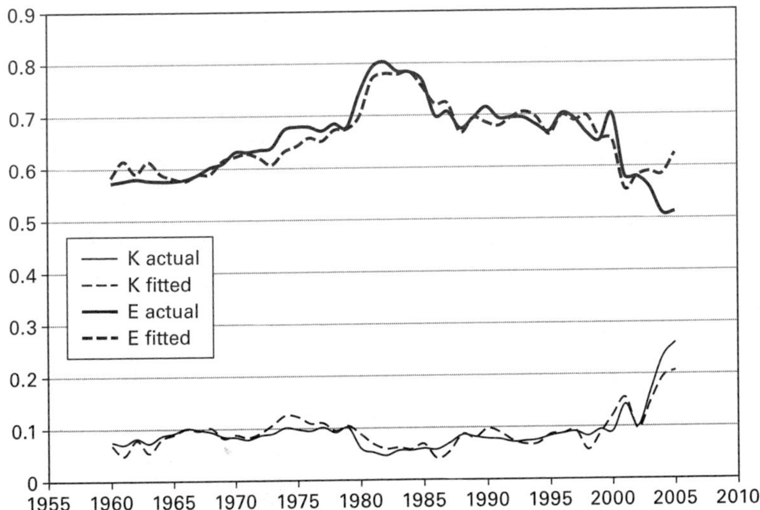

Figure C.1
Fitted vs. actual input shares, Petroleum Refining (industry 16).

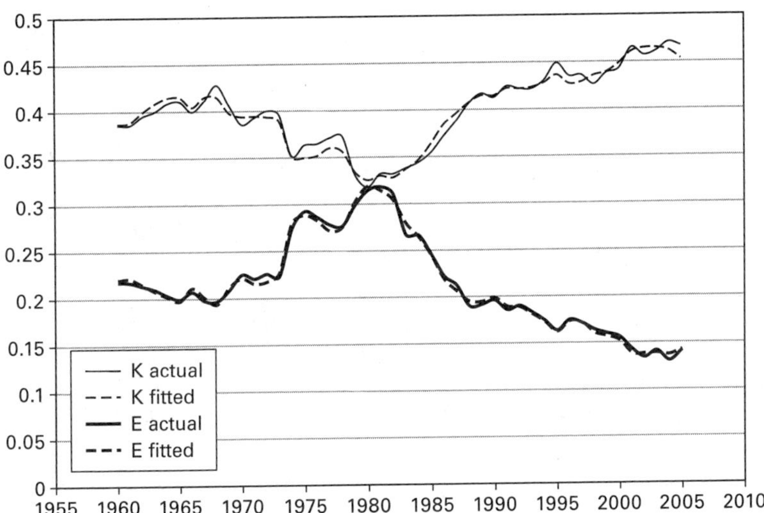

Figure C.2
Fitted vs. actual input shares, Electric Utilities (industry 30).

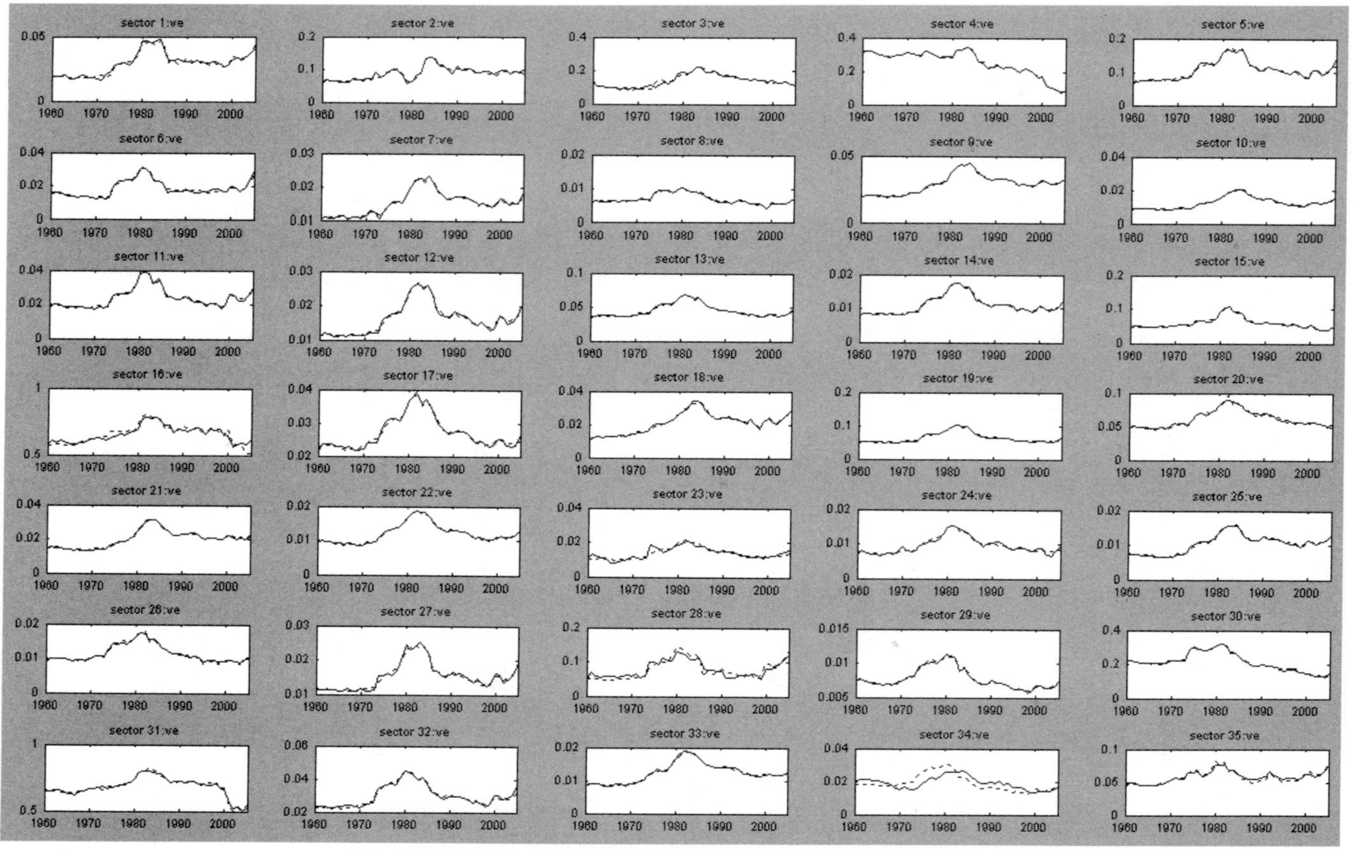

Figure C.3
Fitted vs. actual shares for energy input, all industries.

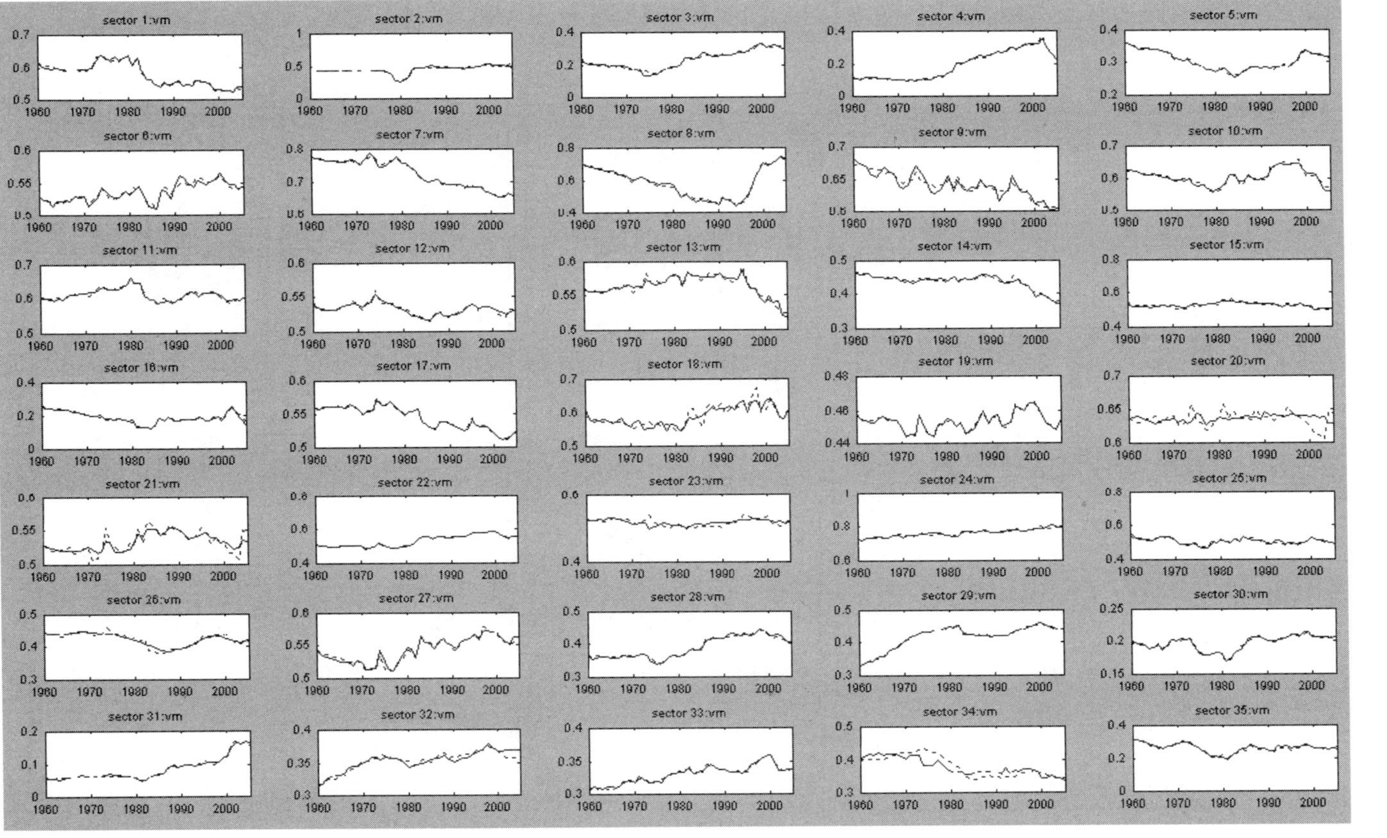

Figure C.4
Fitted vs. actual shares for material input, all industries.

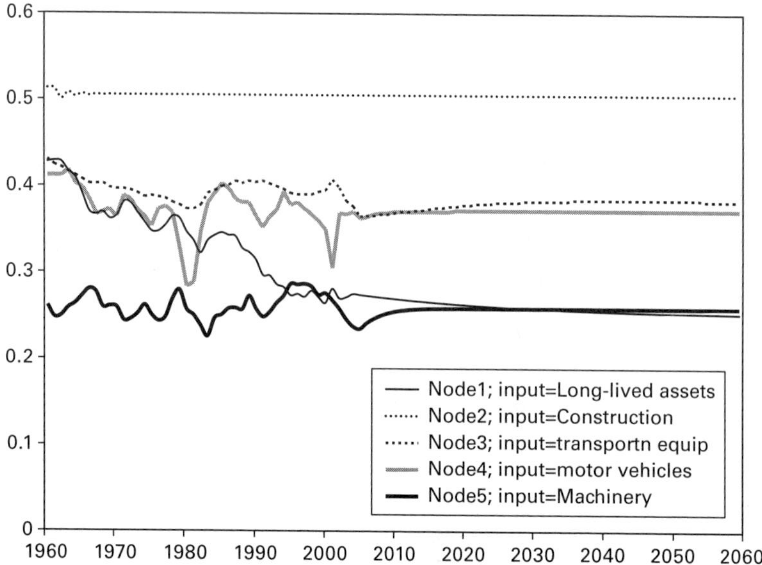

Figure C.5.1
Projection of latent terms in investment nodes (the first input in each node).

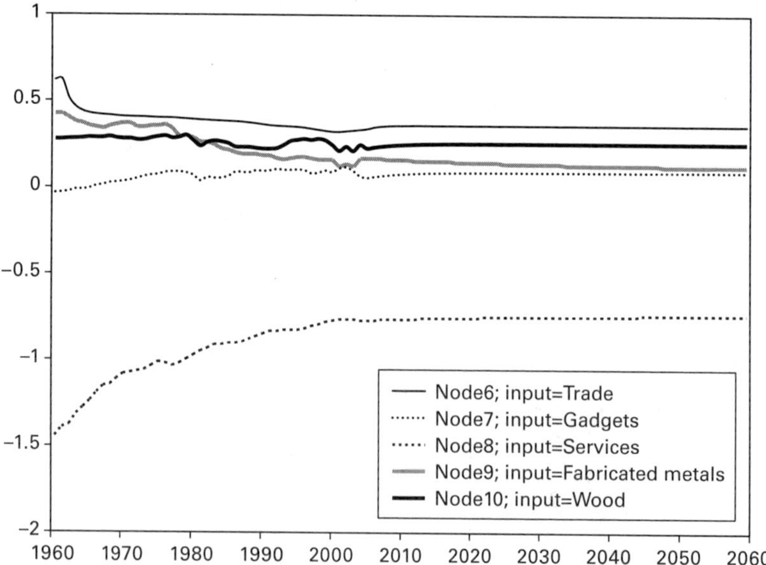

Figure C.5.2
Projection of latent terms in investment nodes (the first input in each node).

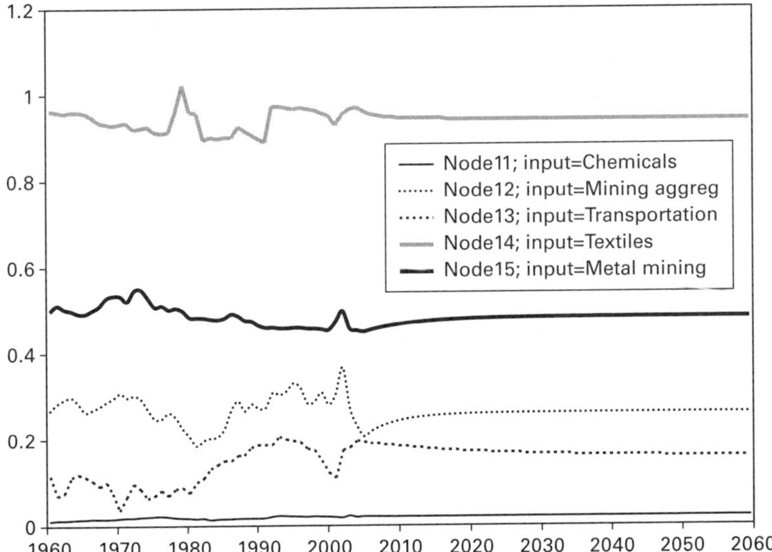

Figure C.5.3
Projection of latent terms in investment nodes (the first input in each node).

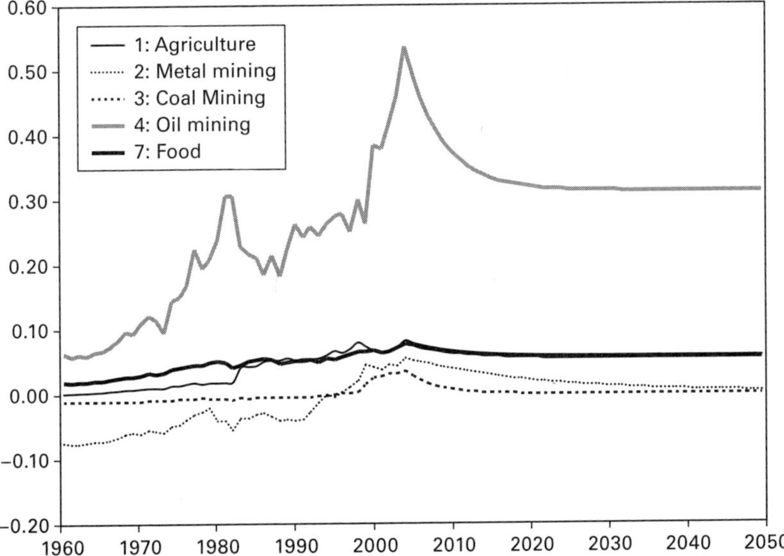

Figure C.6.1
Projection of latent terms in imports.

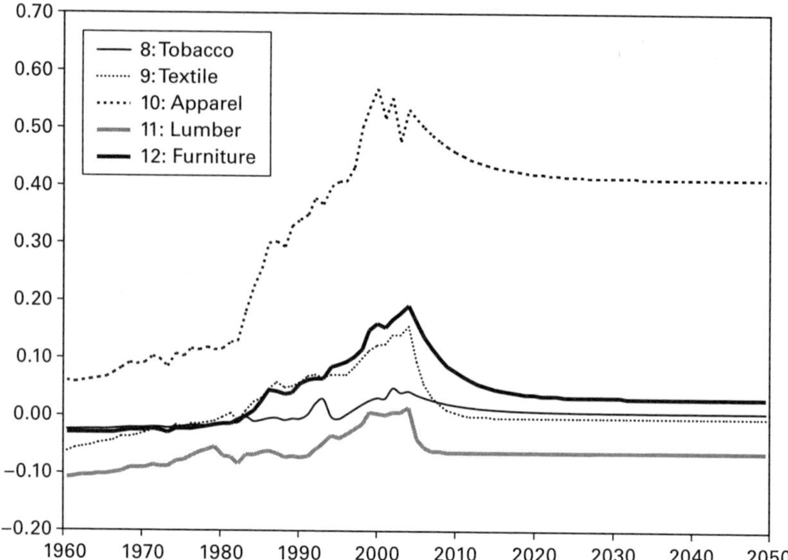

Figure C.6.2
Projection of latent terms in imports.

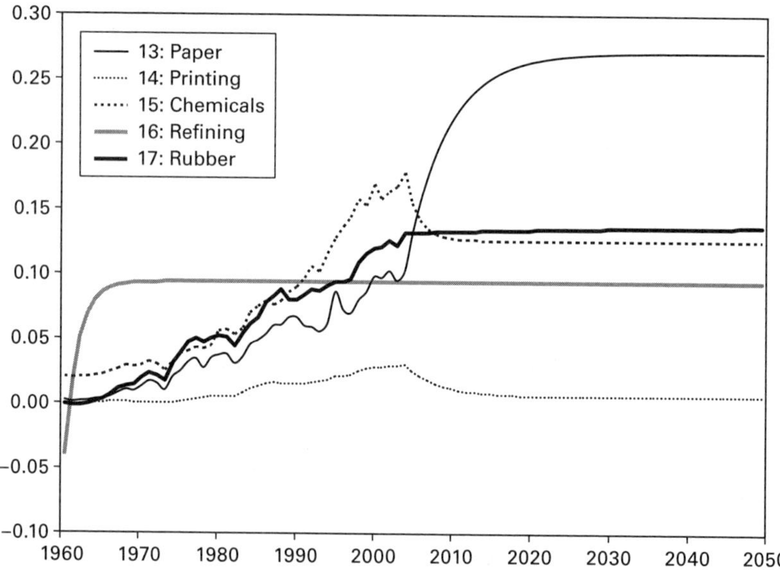

Figure C.6.3
Projection of latent terms in imports.

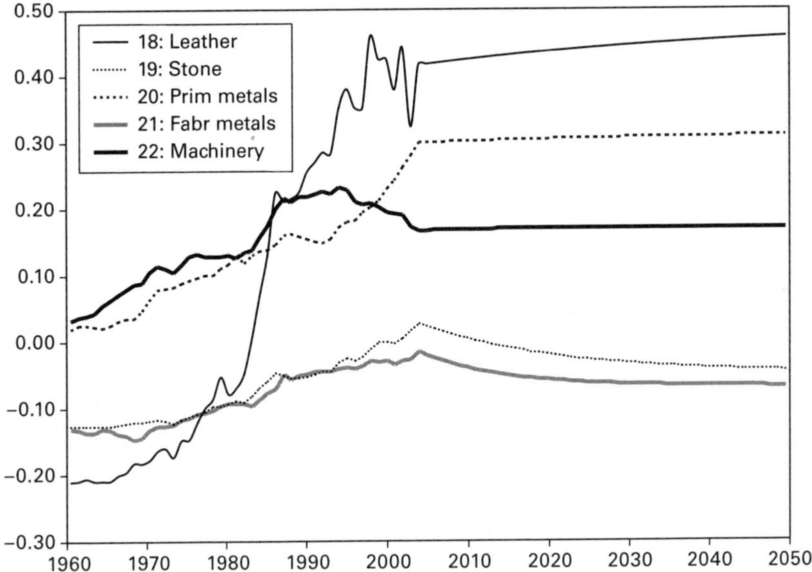

Figure C.6.4
Projection of latent terms in imports.

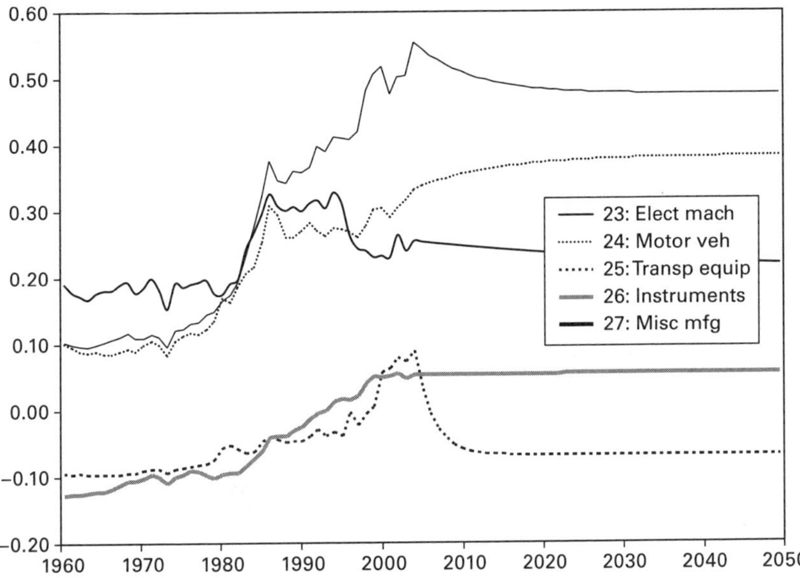

Figure C.6.5
Projection of latent terms in imports.

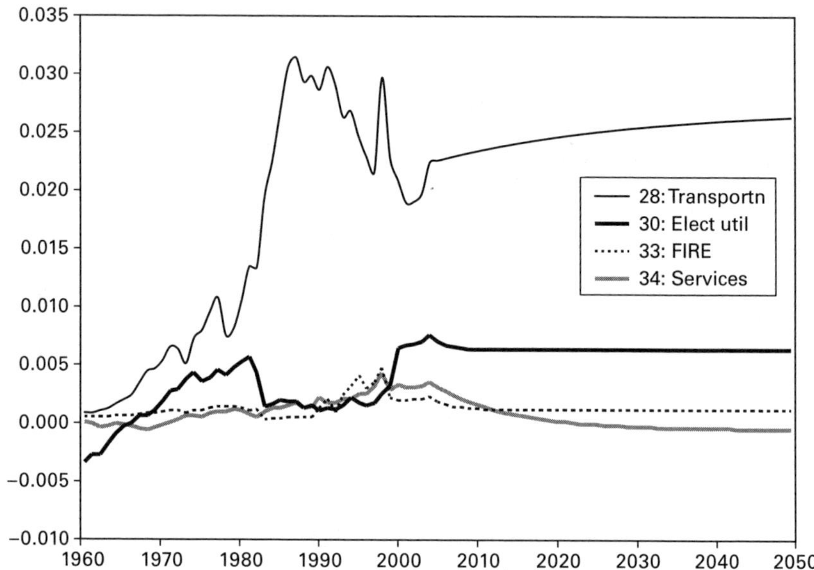

Figure C.6.6
Projection of latent terms in imports.

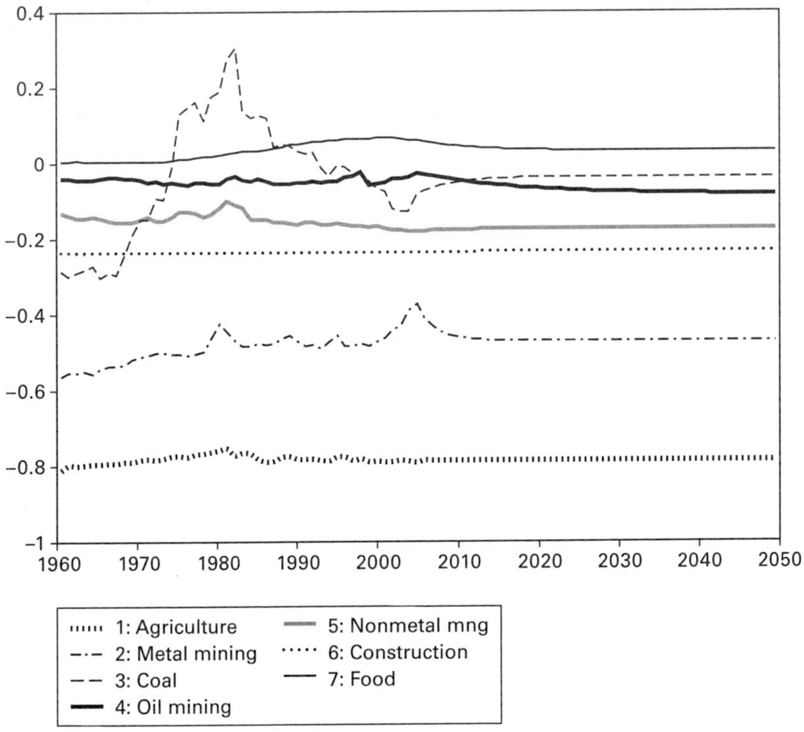

Figure C.7.1
Latent terms for exports.

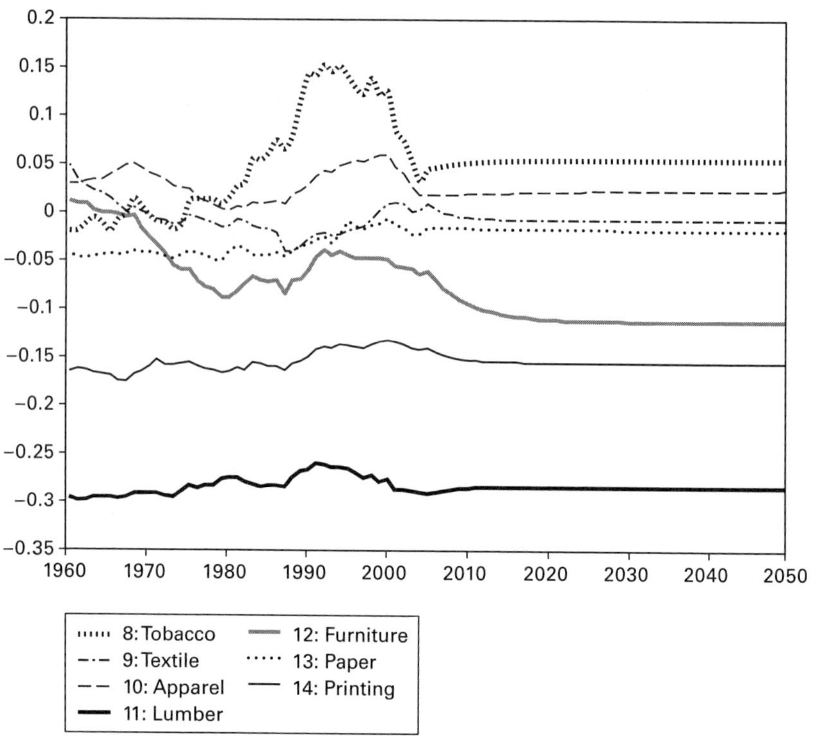

Figure C.7.2
Latent terms for exports.

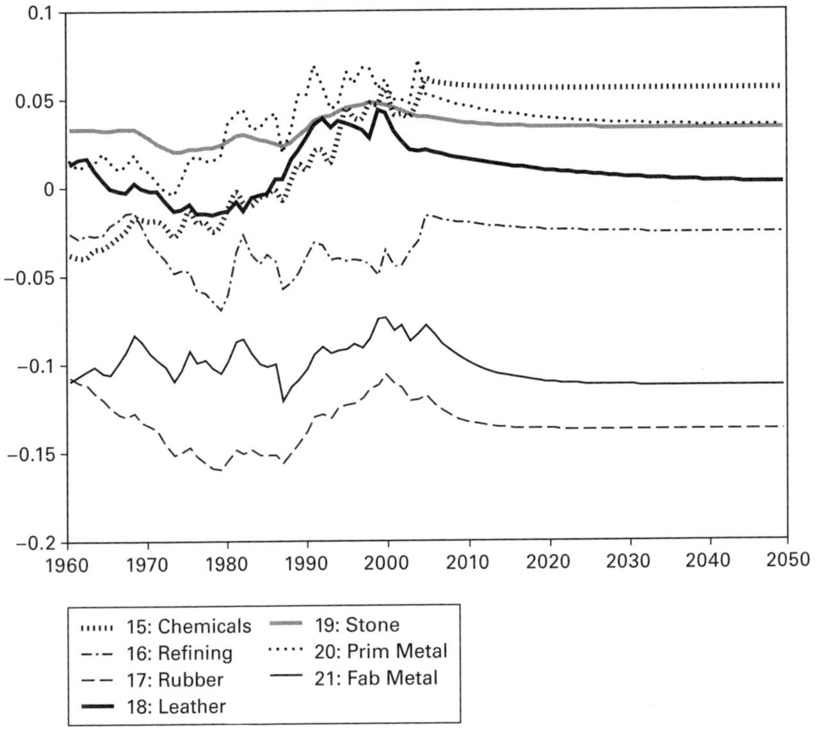

Figure C.7.3
Latent terms for exports.

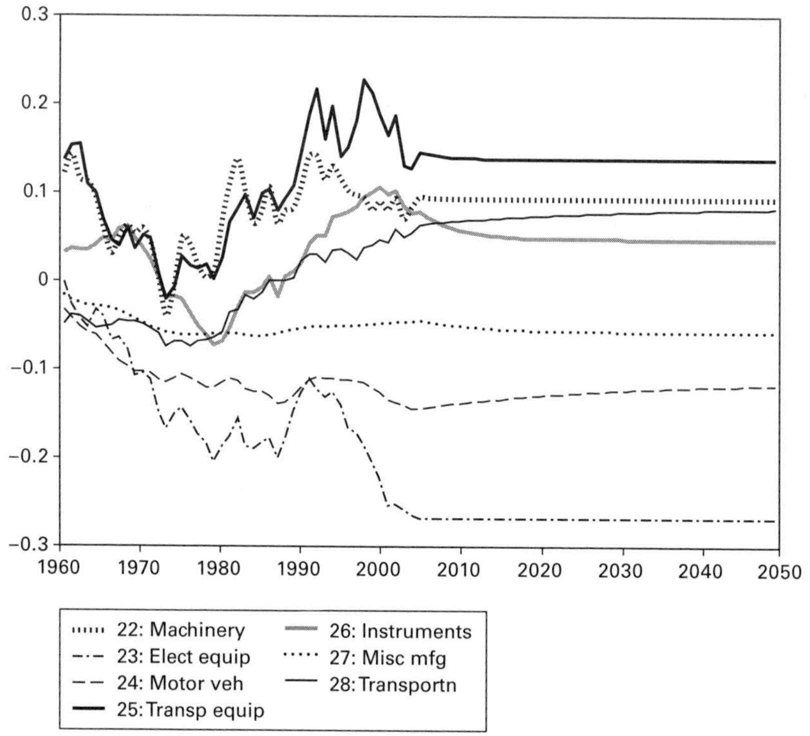

Figure C.7.4
Latent terms for exports.

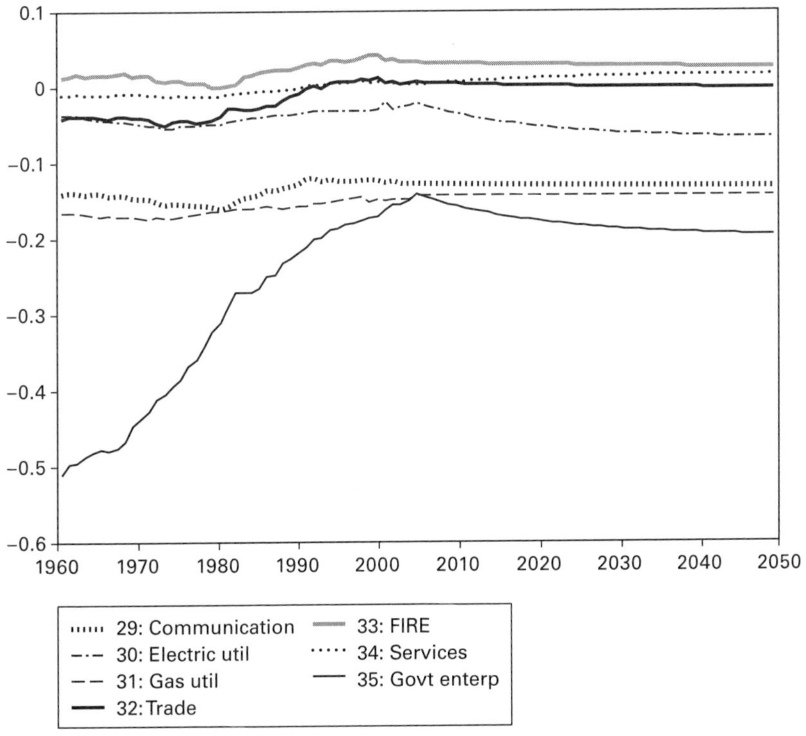

Figure C.7.5
Latent terms for exports.

D Model Solution Algorithm

In chapter 2, section 2.5 we sketched the solution algorithm for IGEM, noting that it is solved using a suite of nested solution algorithms. In this appendix we discuss some of the key details of the implementation. IGEM is implemented in Fortran and C, unlike the more typical approach of using a high-level programming system such as GAMS. The low-level language is more tedious to use but gives us far more flexibility.

D.1 Structure of the Algorithm

The three main modules of IGEM are summarized in table 2.5: (1) an intratemporal module, (2) a steady state module, and (3) an intertemporal module. The intratemporal module computes a complete equilibrium for any given year t conditional on that year's exogenous variables and the two intertemporal variables: K_{t-1} and PFF_t (the capital stock and the value of full consumption). The steady-state module iterates over K_{t-1} and PFF_t, calling the intratemporal module at each iteration, until they satisfy the model's steady state conditions. The intertemporal module iterates over complete trajectories of $\{K_t\}_{t=1}^{T}$ and $\{PFF_t\}_{t=1}^{T}$ until it finds a set that satisfies the model's accumulation and Euler conditions.

In terms of practical implementation, the algorithm begins by using the enhanced version of Newton's method described in section D.2 to compute the model's steady state capital stock and value of full consumption. The algorithm itself is implemented in subroutine *Newton_SS* and the Newton miss distances are computed by *ss_miss*. At each iteration of the steady state module (that is, for each trial pair of $\{K_{ss}, PFF_{ss}\}$), the algorithm invokes the intratemporal module to compute all other steady state variables conditional on the guess of $\{K_{ss}, PFF_{ss}\}$.

After the steady state has been obtained, the intertemporal algorithm begins iterating over the trajectories of $\{K_t\}_{t=1}^T$ and $\{PFF_t\}_{t=1}^T$ using the hybrid intertemporal algorithm described in section D.3. The algorithm is implemented in subroutine *Fair_Taylor* and subroutine *Path* is called at each iteration to evaluate each trajectory. When the intertemporal algorithm converges, the simulation program saves the final transition path for $\{PFF_t\}_{t=1}^T$ (which is formally the model's costate variable), and then writes out a complete set of results for all endogenous variables.

During both the steady state calculation and intertemporal calculations, the intratemporal module is invoked repeatedly. For computational efficiency, it consists of a three-tiered suite of Newton's method algorithms (again, enhanced as described in D.2). The outer tier is implemented in subroutine *Newton_FP* and iterates over the following vector of factor prices and other variables: $\{PKD_t, PKD_{oil,t}, e_t, VII, VGG_t\}$. The corresponding miss distances are computed by subroutine *Intra_miss*. For each iteration of *Newton_FP*, an inner algorithm is called to determine industry output prices conditional on the guessed vector of factor prices. The inner algorithm is implemented in *Newton_PO* and the miss distances are calculated by *PO_miss*. Using a nested structure allows the algorithm to find a solution far more quickly than it would if the complete set of intratemporal equations were solved in a single tier.

D.2 Broyden's Modification to Newton's Method

Broyden (1965, 1973) has developed a procedure that can reduce the number of function evaluations required to solve a system of equations using Newton's method. This section describes how the method works.

Newton's method is an iterative procedure used to find a vector x that satisfies an equation $f(x) = 0$ where f is a vector-valued function. Roughly speaking, a guess of x is refined repeatedly until each element of f is approximately zero. The fundamental relationship used to improve the guess of x can be derived from a first-order Taylor series expansion of f about a trial solution vector x. Suppose that the value of x at iteration k is x_k, and that evaluating f at x_k gives f_k. If the Jacobian of f at x_k is J_k, the Newton adjustment s_k and the new trial solution x_{k+1} are given by the equations

$$s_k = -J_k^{-1} f_k. \tag{D.1}$$

$$x_{k+1} = x_k + s_k. \tag{D.2}$$

In practice, Newton's method is usually implemented as follows. Given a trial solution x_k, the value of f_k is computed. If f_k is not sufficiently close to zero (usually determined by computing $f_k' f_k$), J_k is formed by perturbing each of the n elements of x_k in succession. J_k is then used to determine s_k using equation (D.1), and the new trial solution, x_{k+1}, is found from equation (D.2). For each iteration f must be evaluated $n + 1$ times—once to obtain f_k and n times to produce J_k.

Broyden's modification is a particular way of using f_{k+1} to form J_{k+1} from J_k without additional function evaluations. At each iteration the Jacobian will be less accurate than under the conventional algorithm so more iterations are usually required for convergence. Even so, the computational gain may be substantial since the number of function evaluations per iteration is reduced from $n + 1$ to 1.

The Jacobian updating procedure works as follows. Let $y_k = f_k + 1 - f_k$. Since $y_k / |s_k|$ is the directional derivative of f in the direction given by s_k, y_k can be used to revise the Jacobian. It does not, however, determine a unique adjustment to J_k, so Broyden imposes the additional conditions that the directional derivatives implied by J_k in directions orthogonal to s_k be preserved in J_{k+1}. This produces the updating rule

$$J_{k+1} = J_k + (y_k - J_k s_k)\frac{s_k'}{s_k' s_k}. \tag{D.3}$$

What is really needed for Newton's method, however, is J_k^{-1}. Broyden has also derived an updating formula which operates directly on the inverse, eliminating numerical difficulties which would arise from constantly inverting J. This update is

$$J_{k+1}^{-1} = J_k^{-1} + (s_k - J_k^{-1} y_k)\frac{s_k' J_k^{-1}}{s_k' J_k^{-1} y_k}. \tag{D.4}$$

For the updating method to work, an initial value of J is required. In most cases, this must be constructed by the usual method of perturbing x n times.[1] When a number of similar problems are to be solved, however, the final Jacobian from the previous problem is often a good approximation to the true Jacobian for the next problem. In this case, using the old Jacobian as an initial guess eliminates the n function evaluations at the beginning of the new problem. This results in a substantial increase in the speed of the algorithm and is implemented in the model.

D.3 A Hybrid Intertemporal Algorithm

This algorithm is a generalization of the method due to Fair and Taylor (1983) and exploits the fact that most economic models contain an accumulation equation relating state variables in adjacent periods. It is substantially faster than the ordinary Fair-Taylor algorithm while providing equally accurate results. The method is termed "hybrid" because it employs certain features of multiple shooting (see Lipton et al., 1982) to obtain these improvements in performance. In a sense, multiple shooting and the Fair-Taylor approach are at different ends of a single spectrum. Shooting uses relatively few intermediate points but employs a great deal of information about the problem's dynamic features. Fair-Taylor, on the other hand, uses a large number of points and almost no dynamic information. The method described here lies in between because it uses many points but also a certain amount of dynamic data.

Given a vector valued function A that generates a set of actual values from a vector of expectations E, the problem is to find a vector E which solves the equation

$$E = A(E). \tag{D.5}$$

The Fair-Taylor algorithm proceeds by computing $A(E_k)$ for a trial solution E_k. If A_k is not sufficiently close to E_k, a new trial vector is determined as shown:

$$E_{k+1} = \gamma A_k + (1-\gamma)E_k, \tag{D.6}$$

where $A_k = A(E_k)$, and γ is a parameter used to ensure stability. An important feature of this approach is that the revision of a particular element of E depends only on the corresponding elements of A_k and E_k: no information about adjacent elements is used. In many economic problems, however, E^i and E^{i+1} are related by an accumulation equation. Furthermore, steady state values of E are usually known. Together, these features mean that extending the algorithm to employ information about adjacent periods could lead to a substantial improvement in convergence speed.

An alternative technique can be developed by replacing A with a first-order Taylor series expansion as shown:

$$A(E_{k+1}) \approx A(E_k) + J_k(E_{k+1} - E_k). \tag{D.7}$$

Taking E_{k+1} to be a solution, the left-hand side can be replaced to give

$$E_{k+1} = A_k + J_k(E_{k+1} - E_k). \tag{D.8}$$

Collecting unknown terms on the left yields the equation

$$(I - J_k)E_{k+1} = A_k - J_k E_k. \tag{D.9}$$

For convenience define vector Φ_k and rewrite the equation as

$$\Phi_k = A_k - J_k E_k. \tag{D.10}$$

$$(I - J_k)E_{k+1} = \Phi_k. \tag{D.11}$$

Writing out a small problem in scalar form (where the subscript k on J has been eliminated for clarity):

$$\begin{bmatrix} 1-J_{11} & -J_{12} & -J_{13} \\ -J_{21} & 1-J_{22} & -J_{23} \\ -J_{31} & -J_{32} & 1-J_{33} \end{bmatrix} \begin{bmatrix} E_{k+1}^1 \\ E_{k+1}^2 \\ E_{k+1}^3 \end{bmatrix} = \begin{bmatrix} \Phi_k^1 \\ \Phi_k^2 \\ \Phi_k^3 \end{bmatrix}. \tag{D.12}$$

In practice the true array $I - J_k$ will not be available, and a numerical approximation will have to be used. Often the problem can be set up so that the actuals in period i depend on expectations no farther in the future than period $i + 1$. In the example above, this means that J_{13} will be zero. Further simplification can be achieved by setting the derivatives of the actuals with respect to past expectations to zero. (Note that unlike the previous tactic this is an approximation, since these terms will usually be small but nonzero.) One final approximation is to assume that the remaining partials are the same across periods. This produces the following system:

$$\begin{bmatrix} 1-J_{11} & -J_{12} & 0 \\ 0 & 1-J_{11} & -J_{12} \\ 0 & 0 & 1-J_{11} \end{bmatrix} \begin{bmatrix} E_{k+1}^1 \\ E_{k+1}^2 \\ E_{k+1}^3 \end{bmatrix} = \begin{bmatrix} \Phi_k^1 \\ \Phi_k^2 \\ \Phi_k^3 \end{bmatrix}. \tag{D.13}$$

Finally, expanding the right-hand side gives

$$\begin{bmatrix} 1-J_{11} & -J_{12} & 0 \\ 0 & 1-J_{11} & -J_{12} \\ 0 & 0 & 1-J_{11} \end{bmatrix} \begin{bmatrix} E_{k+1}^1 \\ E_{k+1}^2 \\ E_{k+1}^3 \end{bmatrix} = \begin{bmatrix} A_1 \\ A_2 \\ A_3 \end{bmatrix} - \begin{bmatrix} J_{11} & J_{12} & 0 \\ 0 & J_{11} & J_{12} \\ 0 & 0 & J_{11} \end{bmatrix} \begin{bmatrix} E_k^1 \\ E_k^2 \\ E_k^3 \end{bmatrix}. \tag{D.14}$$

The Fair-Taylor method is equivalent to setting J_{11} and J_{12} to zero. The algorithm can be improved if values of these partials are available, even if they must be found numerically. If the steady state value of E is known, the equation for the last actual can be dropped and the final element of E set directly to the steady state. This helps determine earlier values of E, since the periods are linked by the J_{12} terms in the $I - J$ matrix.

For a model which has one foresight variable, the above system of equations can be solved easily by backward substitution; it is not necessary to use Gaussian elimination or matrix inversion. The new expectation for the last period of the problem above can be found as shown:

$$E_{k+1}^{3} = \frac{1}{1 - J_{11}}\left(A_3 - J_{11}E_k^3\right). \tag{D.15}$$

Earlier periods are found by repeated application of the equation

$$E_{k+1}^{i} = \frac{1}{1 - J_{11}}\left(A_i - J_{11}E_k^i - J_{12}E_k^{i+1} + J_{12}E_{k+1}^{i+1}\right). \tag{D.16}$$

For two or more variables, the method is slightly more complicated because it requires the inverse of matrix $(I - J_{11})$. A typical revised expectation is calculated as

$$E_{k+1}^{i} = (I - J_{11})^{-1}\left(A_i - J_{11}E_k^i - J_{12}E_k^{i+1} + J_{12}E_{k+1}^{i+1}\right). \tag{D.17}$$

Since J_{11} is assumed to be constant over periods, it is only necessary to compute $(I - J_{11})^{-1}$ once for each iteration of the algorithm.

Note

1. In principle, any matrix could be used as an initial Jacobian. However, convergence will usually be slower if it isn't reasonably close to the truth.

References

Acemoglu, Daron. 2002a. Directed Technical Change. *Review of Economic Studies* 69, no. 4 (October): 781–810.

——. 2002b. Technical Change, Inequality, and the Labor Market. *Journal of Economic Literature* 40, no. 1 (March): 7–72.

——. 2007. Equilibrium Bias of Technology. *Econometrica* 75, no. 5 (September): 1371–1409.

Acemoglu, Daron, Philippe Aghion, Leonard Bursztyn, and David Hemous. 2012. The Environment and Directed Technical Change. *American Economic Review* 102, no. 1 (February): 131–166.

Armington, Paul S. 1969. A Theory of Demand for Products Distinguished by Place of Production. *IMF Staff Papers* 16, no. 2 (July): 159–178.

Arrow, Kenneth J., Hollis B. Chenery, Bagicha S. Minhas, and Robert M. Solow. 1961. Capital-Labor Substitution and Economic Efficiency. *Review of Economics and Statistics* 43, no. 3 (August): 225–250.

Attanasio, O., and G. Weber. 1995. Is Consumption Growth Consistent with Intertemporal Optimization? Evidence from the Consumer Expenditure Survey. *Journal of Political Economy* 103, no. 6: 1121–1157.

Barnett, William A., and Apostolos Serletis. 2008. Consumer Preferences and Demand Systems. *Journal of Econometrics* 147, no. 2 (December): 210–224.

Barro, Robert J., and Xavier Sala-i-Martin. 2004. *Economic Growth*, 2nd ed. Cambridge, MA: The MIT Press (first ed. 1995).

Bergman, Lars. 2005. CGE Modeling of Environmental Policy and Resource Management. Ch. 24 in Mäler and Vincent 2005, 1274–1306.

Berndt, Ernst R., and Dale W. Jorgenson. 1973. Production Structure. Ch. 3 in *U.S. Energy Resources and Economic Growth*, ed. Dale W. Jorgenson and Hendrik S. Houthakker. Washington, DC: Energy Policy Project.

Binswanger, Hans P. 1974a. The Measurement of Technical Change Biases with Many Factors of Production. *American Economic Review* 64, no. 6 (December): 964–976.

——. 1974b. A Microeconomic Approach to Induced Innovation. *Economic Journal* 84, no. 336 (December): 940–958.

Binswanger, Hans P., and Vernon W. Ruttan. 1978. *Induced Innovation*. Baltimore, MD: Johns Hopkins University Press.

Blundell, Richard, Martin Browning, and Costas Meghir. 1994. Consumer Demand and the Life-Cycle Allocation of Household Expenditures. *Review of Economic Studies* 61: 57–80.

Blundell, Richard, and Thomas M. Stoker. 2005. Heterogeneity and Aggregation. *Journal of Economic Literature* 43, no. 2 (June): 347–391.

Bond, Charlotte, Teran Martin, Susan McIntosh, and Charles Mead. 2007. Integrated Macroeconomic Accounts of the United States. *Survey of Current Business* 87, no. 2 (February): 14–31.

Bovenberg, A. Lans. 1999. Green Tax Reforms and the Double Dividend: An Updated Reader's Guide. *International Tax and Public Finance* 6, no. 3 (August): 421–443.

Bowles, Erskine, and Alan Simpson. 2013. A Bipartisan Path Forward to Securing America's Future. Moment of Truth Project, Washington, DC, February. www.momentoftruthproject.org/news/bowles-and-simpson-release-new-deficit-reduction-framework.

British Petroleum. 2012. *BP Energy Outlook 2030*. London: British Petroleum Global.

Brock, William A., and Scott M. Taylor. 2005. Economic Growth and the Environment: A Review of Theory and Empirics. Ch. 28 in *Handbook of Economic Growth* 1, ed. Philippe Aghion and Stephen M. Durlauf, 1749–1821. Amsterdam: Elsevier.

Browning, Martin, Angus Deaton, and Margaret Irish. 1985. A Profitable Approach to Labor Supply and Consumer Demands Over the Life Cycle. *Econometrica* 53, no. 3 (May): 503–543.

Browning, Martin, Lars Hansen, and James J. Heckman. 1999. Micro Data and General Equilibrium Modeling. Ch. 9 in *Handbook of Macroeconomics* 1A, ed. John Taylor and Michael Woodford, 543–636. Amsterdam: Elsevier.

Broyden, C. G. 1965. A Class of Methods for Solving Nonlinear Simultaneous Equations. *Mathematics of Computation* 19, no. 92: 531–551.

——. 1973. Some Condition Number Bounds for the (Gaussian) Elimination Process. *Journal of the Institute of Mathematics and Its Applications* 12: 273–286.

Bureau of Economic Analysis. 1997. Note on Alternative Measures of Gross Product by Industry. *Survey of Current Business* (November): 84–85.

——. 2006. Fixed Assets and Consumer Durable Goods for 1995–2005. *Survey of Current Business* 9 (September): 22–33.

Bureau of Labor Statistics. 1983. Trends in Multifactor Productivity, 1948–1981, Bulletin no. 2178. Washington, DC: U.S. Government Printing Office.

Burtraw, Dallas. 2012. *The Institutional Blind Spot in Environmental Economics*. Washington, DC: Resources for the Future, August.

Cass, David. 1965. Optimum Growth in an Aggregative Model of Capital Accumulation. *Review of Economic Studies* 32, no. 3 (July): 233–240.

Chan, Gabriel, Robert N. Stavins, Robert Stowe, and Richard Sweeney. 2012. *The SO_2 Allowance Trading System and the Clean Air Act Amendments of 1990: Reflections on Twenty*

Years of Policy Innovation. Cambridge, MA: National Bureau of Economic Research, January.

Christensen, Laurits R., and Dale W. Jorgenson. 1973. Measuring Economics Performance in the Private Sector. Ch. 5 in Jorgenson, 1995a, 175–272.

Christensen, Laurits R., Dale W. Jorgenson, and Lawrence J. Lau. 1973. Transcendental Logarithmic Production Frontiers. Ch. 4 in Jorgenson 2000, 28–45.

——. 1975. Transcendental Logarithmic Utility Functions. Ch. 1 in Jorgenson 1997a, 125–158.

Clarke, Leon, Christoph Böhringer, and Thomas F. Rutherford. 2009. International, U.S. and E.U. Climate Change Control Scenarios: Results from EMF 22. *Energy Economics* no. 31, S2 (December): S63–S306.

Congressional Budget Office. 2010a. The Budget and Economic Outlook. Washington, DC, January.

——. 2010b. The Long-Term Budget Outlook. Washington, DC, June.

——. 2012. *Choices for Deficit Reduction*. Washington, DC, November. www.cbo.gov/publication/43692.

Dasgupta, Partha S., and Geoffrey M. Heal. 1980. *Economic Theory and Exhaustible Resources*. Cambridge, UK: Cambridge University Press.

Dawkins, Christina, T. N. Srinivasan, and John Whalley. 2001. *Calibration*. Ch. 58 in *Handbook of Econometrics*, ed. James J. Heckman and Edward E. Leamer, 5, 3653–3704. Amsterdam: Elsevier.

Deaton, Angus, and John Muellbauer. 1980. An Almost Ideal Demand System. *American Economic Review* 70, no. 3 (June): 312–326.

DeVuyst, Eric A., and Paul Preckel. 1997. Sensitivity Analysis Revisited. *Journal of Policy Modeling* 19: 175–185.

Diewert, W. E. 1976. Exact and Superlative Index Numbers. *Journal of Econometrics* 4: 115–145.

Diewert, W. E., and Catherine Morrison. 1986. Adjusting Output and Productivity Indexes for Changes in the Terms of Trade. *The Economic Journal* 96, no. 383 (September): 659–679.

Dinan, Terry. 2012. Offsetting a Carbon Tax's Costs on Low Income Households, Congressional Budget Office Working Paper, 2012–2016.

Dixon, Peter B., and Dale W. Jorgenson, eds. 2012. *Handbook of Computable General Equilibrium Modeling* SET, Vols. 1A and 1B. Amsterdam: Elsevier.

Dixon, Peter B., Robert B. Koopman, and Maureen T. Rimmer. 2012. The MONASH Style of CGE Modeling: A Framework for Historical, Decomposition, Forecast and Policy Simulations. Ch. 2 in Dixon and Jorgenson 2012, 23–104.

Dixon, Peter B., and Brian R. Parmenter. 1996. Computable General Equilibrium Modeling for Policy Analysis and Forecasting. Ch. 1 in *Handbook of Computational Economics*, ed. Hans M. Amman, David A. Kendrick, and John Rust, 1, 3–86. Amsterdam: Elsevier.

Dixon, Peter B., and Maureen T. Rimmer. 2013. Johansen's Legacy to CGE Modeling: Originator and Guiding Light for 50 Years. *Journal of Policy Modeling*, forthcoming.

Energy Information Administration. 2012. *Annual Energy Outlook 2012*. Washington, DC: Department of Energy, March.

Environmental Protection Agency. 2000. *Guidelines for Preparing Economic Analyses*. Washington, DC: Environmental Protection Administration, September.

——. 2009. *Waxman-Markey Discussion Draft of the American Clean Energy and Security Act of 2009*. www.epa.gov/climatechange/EPAactivities/economics/legislativeanalyses.html.

——. 2010a. *Guidelines for Preparing Economic Analyses*. Washington, DC: Environmental Protection Administration, December.

——. 2010b. *Inventory of U.S. Greenhouse Gas Emissions and Sinks*. www.epa.gov/climatechange/ghgemissions/usinventoryreport.html.

——. 2011. *Benefits and Costs of the Clean Air Act of 1970: Second Retrospective Study—1990 to 2020*. Washington, DC: Environmental Protection Agency, March.

——. 2012a. *Climate Economics*. www.epa.gov/climatechange/economics/economicanalyses.html.

——. 2012b. *Climate Economic Modeling*. www.epa.gov/climatechange/EPAactivities/economics/modeling.html.

——. 2013. *Inventory of U.S. Greenhouse Gas Emissions and Sinks*. www.epa.gov/climatechange/ghgemissions/usinventoryreport.html.

European Union. 2008. EU KLEMS. www.euklems.net/.

Fair, Ray C., and John B. Taylor. 1983. Solution and Maximum Likelihood Estimation of Dynamic Nonlinear Rational Expectations Models. *Econometrica* 51, no. 4: 1169–1185.

Feng, Guohua, and Apostolos Serletis. 2008. Productivity Trends in U.S. Manufacturing: Evidence from the NQ and AIM Cost Functions. *Journal of Econometrics* 142, no. 2 (January): 281–311.

Fixler, Dennis, and Ted Jaditz. 2002. An Examination of the Difference Between the CPI and the PCE Deflator, Bureau of Labor Statistics Working Paper 361.

Flavin, Marjorie. 1981. The Adjustment of Consumption to Changing Expectations about Future Income. *Journal of Political Economy* 89, no. 5 (October): 974–1009.

Fleck, Susan, Steven Rosenthal, Matthew Russell, Erich Strassner, and Lisa Usher. 2012. A Prototype BEA/BLS Industry-Level Production Account for the United States. *Survey of Current Business* 92, no. 11 (November): 44–50.

Fraumeni, Barbara M. 1997. The Measurement of Depreciation in the U.S. National Income and Product Accounts. *Survey of Current Business* 77, no. 7 (July): 7–23.

——. 2000. The Jorgenson System of National Accounting. Ch. 6 in Lau 2000, 111–142.

Frisch, R. 1959. A Complete Scheme for Computing All Direct and Cross Demand Elasticities in a Model with Many Sectors. *Econometrica* 27, no. 2 (April): 177–196.

Fullerton, Don. 2010. *Six Distributional Effects of Environmental Policy*. Cambridge, MA: National Bureau of Economic Research, January.

Fullerton, Don, and Catherine Wolfram (eds.) 2012. *The Design and Implementation of Climate Policy*. NBER Conference Report, University of Chicago Press.

Gallant, A. Ronald, and Gene H. Golub. 1984. Imposing Curvature Restrictions on Flexible Functional Forms. *Journal of Econometrics* 26, no. 3 (December): 295–321.

Gillingham, Kenneth, Richard G. Newell, and William A. Pizer. 2008. Modeling Endogenous Technological Change for Climate Change Analysis. *Energy Economics* 30, no. 6 (November): 2734–2753.

Goettle, Richard J., and Allen A. Fawcett. 2009. The Structural Effects of Cap and Trade Climate Policy. *Energy Economics* 31, S244–S253.

Gorman, W. M. 1953. Community Preference Fields. *Econometrica* 21, no. 1 (January): 63–80.

——. 1981. Some Engel Curves. In *Essays in the Theory and Measurement of Consumer Behavior*, ed. A. Deaton. Cambridge, UK: Cambridge University Press.

Goulder, Lawrence H. 1995. Environmental Taxation and the Double Dividend. *International Tax and Public Finance* 2, no. 3 (August): 157–183.

——. 2002. *Environmental Policy Making in Economics with Prior Tax Distortions*. Amherst, MA: Edward Elgar.

——. 2004. *Induced Technological Change and Climate Policy*. Arlington, VA: Center for Climate and Energy Solutions.

——. 2013. Markets for Pollution Allowances: What Are the (New) Lessons? *Journal of Economic Perspectives* 27, no. 1: 87–102.

Hall, R. 1978. Stochastic Implications of the Life Cycle–Permanent Income Hypothesis: Theory and Evidence. *Journal of Political Economy* 86, no. 6 (December): 971–988.

Hamilton, James D. 1994. *Time Series Analysis*. Princeton, NJ: Princeton University Press.

Harper, Michael J., Brent R. Moulton, Steven Rosenthal, and David B. Wasshausen. 2009. *Integrated GDP-Productivity Accounts* 99, no. 2 (May): 74–79.

Hayashi, Fumio. 2000. The Cost of Capital, Q, and the Theory of Investment Demand. Ch. 4 in Lau 2000, 55–84.

Herman, Shelby W. 2000. Fixed Assets and Consumer Durable Goods. *Survey of Current Business* 81, no. 9 (September): 27–38.

Hertel, Thomas. 2012. *Applied General Equilibrium Analysis Using the GTAP Framework*. Ch. 12 in Dixon and Jorgenson, 815–876.

Hertel, Thomas, David Hummels, Maros Ivanic, and Roman Keeney. 2007. How Confident Can We Be of CGE-Based Assessments of Free Trade Agreements? *Economic Modelling* 24, no. 4 (July): 611–635.

Hillberry, Russell, and David Hummels. 2012. Trade Elasticity Parameters for a CGE Model. Ch. 18 in Dixon and Jorgenson 2012, 1213–1270.

Ho, Mun S. 2000. Modeling Trade Policies and U.S. Growth: Some Methodological Issues. Ch. 12 in Lau 2000, 327–378.

Holmøy, Erling. 2013. The Development and Use of CGE models in Norway. *Journal of Policy Modeling*, forthcoming.

Holmøy, Erling, and Birger Strom. 2012. CGE Assessments of Fiscal Sustainability in Norway. Ch. 3 in Dixon and Jorgenson 2012, 105–158.

Horridge, Mark, and Kenneth Pearson. 2011. *Systematic Sensitivity Analysis with Respect to Correlated Parameters and Shocks*. West Lafayette, IN: Center for Global Trade Analysis, Purdue University.

Horridge, Mark, Alex Meeraus, Kenneth Pearson, and Thomas F. Rutherford. 2012. Solution Software for CGE Modeling. Ch. 20 in Dixon and Jorgenson 2012, 1331–1382.

Hudson, Edward A., and Dale W. Jorgenson. 1974. U.S. Energy Policy and Economic Growth, 1975–2000. *Bell Journal of Economics and Management Science* 5, no. 2: 461–514.

Hyman, R. C., J. M. Reilly, M. H. Babiker, A. DeMasin, and H. D. Jacoby. 2003. Modeling Non-CO_2 Greenhouse Gas Abatement. *Environmental Modeling and Assessment* 8, no. 3: 175–186.

Jaffe, Adam B., Richard G. Newell, and Robert N. Stavins. 2003. Technological Change and the Environment. Ch. 11 in Maler and Vincent 2003, 461–516.

Jin, Hui, and Dale W. Jorgenson. 2010. Econometric Modeling of Technical Change. *Journal of Econometrics* 152, no. 2 (August): 205–219.

Johansen, Leif. 1960. *A Multi-Sectoral Model of Economic Growth. Contributions to Economic Analysis* 21. Amsterdam: North-Holland.

——. 1974. *A Multisectoral Study of Economic Growth*, 2nd enlarged ed. Amsterdam: North-Holland (first ed. 1960).

Joint Committee on Taxation. 2012. *Present Law and Analysis of Energy-Related Tax Expenditures* (JCX-28–12), Washington, DC: U.S. Congress, March 23.

Jorgenson, Dale W. 1963. Capitol Theory and Investment Behavior. Ch. 1 in Jorgenson 1996a, 1–16.

——. 1966. The Embodiment Hypothesis. Ch. 2 in Jorgenson 1995a, 25–50.

——. 1971. Econometric Studies of Investment Behavior. Ch. 13 in Jorgenson 1996a, 423–478.

——. 1986. Econometric Methods for Modeling Producer Behavior. Ch. 1 in Jorgenson 2000, 1–72.

——. 1990. Productivity and Economic Growth. Ch. 1 in Jorgenson 1995b, 1–98.

——. 1995a. *Productivity, Volume 1: Postwar U.S. Economic Growth*. Cambridge, MA: The MIT Press.

——. 1995b. *Productivity, Volume 2: International Comparisons of Economic Growth*. Cambridge, MA: The MIT Press.

——. 1996a. *Capital Theory of Investment Behavior*. Cambridge, MA: The MIT Press.

——. 1996b. *Tax Policy and the Cost of Capital*. Cambridge, MA: The MIT Press.

——. 1997a. *Aggregate Consumer Behavior*. Cambridge, MA: The MIT Press.

——. 1997b. *Measuring Social Welfare*. Cambridge, MA: The MIT Press.

——. 1998a. *Econometric General Equilibrium Modeling*. Cambridge, MA: The MIT Press.

——. 1998b. *Energy, the Environment, and Growth*. Cambridge, MA: The MIT Press.

——. 2000. *Econometric Modeling of Producer Behavior*. Cambridge, MA: The MIT Press.

——. 2002. *Economic Growth in the Information Age*. Cambridge, MA: The MIT Press.

——. 2005. Accounting for Growth in the Information Age. In *Handbook of Growth Economics*, ed. Phillipe Aghion and Steven Durlauf, 1A, 743–815. Amsterdam: North-Holland.

——, ed. 2009a. *The Economics of Productivity*. Northampton, MA: Edward Elgar.

——. 2009b. A New Architecture for the U.S. National Accounts. *Review of Income and Wealth* 55, no. 1 (March): 1–42.

——. 2012. Comprehensive Tax Reform and U.S. Energy Policy, Hearing on Tax Reform: The Impact on U.S. Energy Policy, Committee on Finance, United States Senate, June 12.

Jorgenson, Dale W., and Barbara M. Fraumeni. 1983. Relative Prices and Technical Change. Ch. 12 in Jorgenson 2000, 341–372.

Jorgenson, Dale W., Richard J. Goettle, Mun S. Ho, and Peter J. Wilcoxen. 2012. Energy, the Environment, and U.S. Economic Growth. Ch. 8 in. Dixon and Jorgenson 2012, 477–552.

Jorgenson, Dale W., Richard J. Goettle, Mun S. Ho, Daniel T. Slesnick, and Peter J. Wilcoxen. 2010. The Distributional Impact of Climate Policy. *B.E. Journal of Economic Analysis and Policy* 10, no. 2: 1–26.

Jorgenson, Dale W., Frank M. Gollop, and Barbara M. Fraumeni. 1987. *Productivity and U.S. Economic Growth*. Cambridge, MA: Harvard University Press.

Jorgenson, Dale W., Hui Jin, Daniel T. Slesnick, and Peter J. Wilcoxen. 2012. Ch. 17 in Dixon and Jorgenson 2012, 1133–1212.

Jorgenson, Dale W., Mun S. Ho, Jon D. Samuels, and Kevin J. Stiroh. 2007. The Industry Origins of the American Productivity Resurgence. *Economic System Research* 19, no. 3 (September): 229–252.

Jorgenson, Dale W., Mun S. Ho, and Kevin J. Stiroh. 2005. *Information Technology and the American Growth Resurgence*. Cambridge, MA: The MIT Press.

Jorgenson, Dale W., Masahiro Kuroda, and Kazuyuki Motohashi. 2007. *Productivity in Asia*. Northampton, MA: Edward Elgar.

Jorgenson, Dale W., and J. Steven Landefeld. 2006. Blueprint for an Expanded and Integrated U.S. National Accounts: Review, Assessment, and Next Steps. In Dale W. Jorgenson, J. Steven Landefeld, and William D. Nordhaus, ed., 2006. Cambridge, MA: NBER Books, National Bureau of Economic Research, Inc. (September): 13–112.

Jorgenson, Dale W., J. Steven Landefeld, and William D. Nordhaus. 2006. *A New Architecture for the U.S. National Accounts*. Cambridge, MA: NBER Books, National Bureau of Economic Research, Inc., September.

Jorgenson, Dale W., Lawrence J. Lau, and Thomas M. Stoker. 1982. Ch. 8 in Jorgenson 1997a, 203–356.

——. 1997. Transcendental Logarithmic Model of Aggregate Consumer Behavior. Ch. 8 in Jorgenson 1997a, 203–356.

Jorgenson, Dale W., and Paul Schreyer. 2013. Industry-Level Productivity Measurement and the 2008 System of National Accounts. *Review of Income and Wealth*, forthcoming.

Jorgenson, Dale W., and Daniel T. Slesnick. 1985. General Equilibrium Analysis of Economic Policy. Ch. 4 in Jorgenson 1997b, 165–218.

——. 1987. Aggregate Consumer Behavior and Household Equivalence Scales. Ch. 5 in Jorgenson 1997b, 219–252.

——. 1997. Aggregate Consumer Behavior and Household Equivalence Scales. Ch. 5 in Jorgenson 1997b, 219–252.

——. 2008. Consumption and Labor Supply. *Journal of Econometrics* 147, no. 2 (December): 326–335.

——. 2013. Measuring Social Welfare in the U.S. National Accounts. Ch. 3 in *Measuring Economic Sustainability and Progress*, ed. Dale W. Jorgenson, J. Steven Landefeld, and Paul Schreyer. Chicago: University of Chicago Press, forthcoming.

Jorgenson, Dale W., Daniel T. Slesnick, and Peter J. Wilcoxen. 1992. Carbon Taxes and Economic Welfare. Ch. 9 in Jorgenson 1997b, 361–399.

Jorgenson, Dale W., and Khuong M. Vu. 2011. The Rise of Developing Asia and the New Economic Order. *Journal of Policy Modeling* 33, no. 5 (September–October): 698–751.

Jorgenson, Dale W., and Peter J. Wilcoxen. 1990. Intertemporal General Equilibrium Modeling of U.S. Environmental Regulation. Ch. 3 in Jorgenson 1998b, 157–194.

——. 1993a. Energy, the Environment, and Economic Growth. Ch. 1 in Jorgenson 1998b, 1–88.

——. 1993b. U.S. Carbon Dioxide Emissions: An Econometric General Equilibrium Assessment. Ch. 6 in Jorgenson 1998b, 253–274.

Jorgenson, Dale W., and Kun-Young Yun. 1990. Tax Reform and U.S. Economic Growth. Ch. 12 in Jorgenson 1996b, 365–410.

——. 2001. *Lifting the Burden: Tax Reform, the Cost of Capital and U.S. Economic Growth.* Cambridge, MA: The MIT Press.

——. 2012. Taxation, Efficiency, and Economic Growth. Ch. 10 in Dixon and Jorgenson 2012, 659–742.

Kalman, Rudolf E. 1960. A New Approach to Linear Filtering and Prediction Problems. *Journal of Basic Engineering*, Transactions ASME, Series D, 82, 35–45.

——. 1963. New Methods in Wiener Filtering Theory. In *Proceedings of the First Symposium of Engineering Applications of Random Function Theory and Probability*, ed. John L. Bogdanoff and Frank Kozen, 270–388. New York: Wiley.

Kim, Chang-Jin. 2006. Time-Varying Parameter Models with Endogenous Regressors. *Economics Letters* 91, no. 1 (April): 21–26.

Kim, Chang-Jin, and Charles R. Nelson. 2006. Estimation of a Forward-Looking Monetary Policy Rule: A Time-Varying Parameter Model Using Ex Post Data. *Journal of Monetary Economics* 53, no. 8 (November): 1949–1966.

Klein, Lawrence R., and Herman Rubin. 1947. A Constant-Utility Index of the Cost of Living. *Review of Economic Studies* 15, no. 2: 84–87.

Kokoski, Mary, Patrick Cardiff, and Brent Moulton. 1994. *Interarea Price Indices for Consumer Goods and Services: An Hedonic Approach*. Washington, DC: Bureau of Labor Statistics.

Koopmans, Tjalling C. 1967. Objectives, Constraints, and Outcomes in Optimal Growth. *Econometrica* 35, no. 1 (January): 1–15.

Lau, Lawrence J. 1977. Existence Conditions for Aggregate Demand Functions: The Case of Multiple Indexes. Technical Report 248. Stanford, CA: Institute for Mathematical Studies in the Social Sciences.

——, ed. 2000. *Research on the Cost of Capital: Past, Present and Future*. Cambridge, MA: The MIT Press.

Leontief, Wassily W. 1951. *The Structure of the American Economy*, 2nd ed. New York: Oxford University Press (first ed. 1941).

——, ed. 1953. *Studies in the Structure of the American Economy*. New York: Oxford University Press.

Lewbel, A. 2001. *The Rank Extended Translog*. Boston, MA: Boston College Department of Economics.

Lipton, David, James M. Poterba, Jeffrey Sachs, and Lawrence H. Summers. 1982. Multiple Shooting in Rational Expectations Models. *Econometrica* 50, no. 5 (September): 1329–1333.

Lucas, Robert E., Jr. 1976. Econometric Policy Evaluation: A Critique. In *The Phillips Curve and Labor Markets*, ed. Karl Brunner and Alan H. Meltzer, 19–46. Amsterdam: North-Holland.

——. 1980. Methods and Problems in Business Cycle Theory. *Journal of Money, Credit, and Banking* 12, no. 4, part 2 (November): 696–715.

Lum, Sherlene K.S., and Brian C. Moyer. 2000. Gross Domestic Product by Industry for 1997–99. *Survey of Current Business* 80, no. 12 (December): 24–35.

——. 2001. Gross Domestic Product by Industry for 1998–2000. *Survey of Current Business* 80, no. 11 (November): 17–33.

Maler, Karl-Goran. 1974. *Environmental Economics: A Theoretical Inquiry*. Baltimore: Johns Hopkins University Press.

——. 1975. Macroeconomic Aspects of Environmental Policy. Ch. 2 in Mills 1975, 27–64.

Mäler, Karl-Goran, and Jeffrey R. Vincent, eds. 2003. *Handbook of Environmental Economics*, 3 vols. Amsterdam: Elsevier.

Marron, Donald, and Eric Toder. 2013. Carbon Taxes and Corporate Tax Reform. Tax Policy Center, Urban Institute and Brookings Institution, February. www.taxpolicycenter.org/UploadedPDF/412744-Carbon-Taxes-and-Corporate-Tax-Reform.pdf.

Mas, Matilde, and Robert Stehrer, eds. 2012. *Industrial Productivity in Europe: Growth and Crisis*. Northampton, MA: Edward Elgar.

McFadden, Daniel. 1963. Constant Elasticity of Substitution Production Functions. *Review of Economic Studies* 30, no. 2: 73–83.

McKibbin, Warwick J., Adele C. Morris Peter J. Wilcoxen, and Yiyong Cai. 2012. *The Potential Role of a Carbon Tax in U.S. Fiscal Reform*. Washington, DC: The Brookings Institution.

McKibbin, Warwick J., and Peter J. Wilcoxen. 1999. The Theoretical and Empirical Structure of the G-Cubed Model. *Economic Modeling* 16, no. 1 (January): 123–148.

——. 2012. A Global Approach to Energy and the Environment: The G-Cubed Model. Ch. 15 in Dixon and Jorgenson 2012, 995–1068.

Mills, Edwin S., ed. 1975. *Economic Analysis of Environmental Problems*. New York: Columbia University Press.

Muellbauer, John. 1975. Aggregation, Income Distribution and Consumer Demand. *Review of Economic Studies* 42, no. 4 (October): 525–543.

Muller, Nicholas Z., and Robert Mendelsohn. 2009. Efficient Pollution Regulation: Getting the Prices Right. *American Economic Review* 99, no. 5 (December): 1714–1739.

Muller, Nicholas Z., Robert Mendelsohn, and William D. Nordhaus. 2011. Environmental Accounting for Pollution in the United States Economy. *American Economic Review* 100, no. 3 (August): 1649–1675.

National Commission on Fiscal Responsibility and Reform. 2010. *The Moment of Truth*. Washington, DC: National Commission on Fiscal Responsibility and Reform, December. www.fiscalcommission.gov/news/moment-truth-report-national-commission-fiscal-responsibility-and-reform.

National Research Council. 2010. *Hidden Costs of Energy: Unpriced Consequences of Energy Production and Use*. Washington, DC: National Academies Press.

NERA Economic Consulting. 2013. *Economic Outcomes of a U.S. Carbon Tax*. Prepared for the National Association of Manufacturers, Washington, DC, NERA Consulting, February.

Newell, Richard G., William A. Pizer, and Daniel Railmi. 2012. Carbon Markets: Past, Present, and Future. RFF Discussion Paper (December): 12–51.

Nordhaus, William D. 2002. Modeling Induced Technical Change in Climate Change Policy. Ch. 9 in *Technological Change and the Environment*, ed. Arnulf Grubler, Neboysa Nakicenovic, and William D. Nordhaus, 259–290. Washington, DC: Resources for the Future Press.

——. 2008. *A Question of Balance: Weighing the Options on Global Warming Policies*. New Haven, CT: Yale University Press.

——. 2010. Economic Aspects of Global Warming in a Post-Copenhagen Environment. *Proceedings of the National Academy of Sciences* 107: 11721–11726.

——. 2012. Integrated Economic and Climate Modeling. Ch. 16 in Dixon and Jorgenson 2012, 1069–1132.

Oehlert, Gary W. 1992. A Note on the Delta Method. *American Statistician* 1, no. 46: 27–29.

Parry, Ian W. H., and Alan Krupnick. 2011. *Is a Clean Energy Standard a Good Way to Move U.S. Climate Policy Forward?* Washington, DC: Resources for the Future Press.

Parry, Ian W. H., and Roberton C. Williams. 2012. Moving U.S. Climate Policy Forward: Are Carbon Tax Shifts the Only Good Alternative? Ch. 10 in *Climate Change and Common Sense: Essays in Honor of Tom Schelling*, ed. Robert Hahn and Alistair Ulph, 173–202. Oxford, UK: Oxford University Press.

Pigou, Arthur C. 1920. *The Economics of Welfare*. London: Macmillan.

Rausch, Sebastian, and John Reilly. 2012. *Carbon Tax Revenue and the Budget Deficit: A Win-Win-Win Solution*. Cambridge, MA: MIT Joint Program on the Science and Policy of Global Change, Report 228, August.

Rausch, Sebastian, Gilbert Metcalf, John Reilly, and Sergey Paltsev. 2010. Distributional Impacts of a U.S. Greenhouse Gas Policy: A General Equilibrium Analysis of Carbon Pricing. In *U.S. Energy Tax Policy*, ed. Gilbert Metcalf, 52–107. New York: Cambridge University Press.

Ross, M. T. 2007. Documentation of the Applied Dynamic Analysis of the Global Economy (ADAGE) Model. Working Paper 07_02. Research Triangle Park, NC: RTI International, Inc., April.

Ruttan, Vernon W. 2001. *Technology, Growth, and Development*. New York: Oxford University Press.

Sandmo, Agnar. 2000. The Double Dividend and the Marginal Cost of Funds. Ch. 6 in *The Public Economics of the Environment*, 109–129. Oxford, U.K.: Oxford University Press.

Schipper, Lee, and Stephen Meyers. 1992. *Energy Efficiency and Human Activity: Past Trends, Future Prospects*. Cambridge, UK: Cambridge University Press.

Schmidt, Sebastian, and Volker Wieland. 2012. The New Keynesian Approach to Dynamic General Equilibrium Modeling: Models, Methods, and Macroeconomic Policy Evaluation. Ch. 22 in Dixon and Jorgenson 2012, 1439–1512.

Schreyer, Paul. 2001. *Productivity Manual: A Guide to the Measurement of Industry-Level and Aggregate Productivity Growth*. Paris: Organisation for Economic Cooperation and Development.

——. 2009. *OECD Manual: Measuring Capital*, 2nd ed. Paris: Organisation for Economic Development and Cooperation (first ed. 2001).

Slesnick, Daniel T. 1992. Aggregate Consumption and Saving in the Postwar United States. *Review of Economics and Statistics* 74, no. 4 (November): 585–597.

——. 1998. Empirical Approaches to the Measurement of Welfare. *Journal of Economic Literature* 36, no. 4 (December): 2108–2165.

——. 2001. *Consumption and Social Welfare*. New York: Cambridge University Press.

——. 2002. Prices and Regional Variation in Welfare. *Journal of Urban Economics* 51, no. 3 (May): 446–468.

Social Security Administration. 2010. *The 2010 OASDI Trustees Report*, www.ssa.gov/oact/tr/2010/.

Solow, Robert M. 1974a. The Economics of Resources or the Resources of Economics. *American Economic Review* 64, no. 2 (May): 1–14.

——. 1974b. Intergenerational Equity and Exhaustible Resources. *Review of Economic Studies* 41: 29–45.

Stone, Richard. 1954. *The Measurement of Consumers' Expenditure and Behavior in the United Kingdom, 1920–38*. Cambridge, UK: Cambridge University Press.

Stoker, Thomas M. 1993. Empirical Approaches to the Problem of Aggregation Over Individuals. *Journal of Economic Literature* 31, no. 4 (December): 1827–1874.

——. 2000. The Cost of Capital and Consumer Behavior. Ch. 8 in Lau 2000, 165–218.

Teplin, Albert M., Rochelle Antoniewicz, Susan Hume McIntosh, Michael G. Palumbo, Genevieve Solomon, Charles Ian Mead, Karin Moses, and Brent Moulton. 2006. Integrated Macroeconomic Accounts for the United States: Draft SNA-USA. Ch. 11 in Jorgenson, Landefeld, and Nordhaus, eds., 2006. Cambridge, MA: NBER Books, National Bureau of Economic Research, Inc. (September): 471–540.

Timmer, Marcel P., Robert Inklaar, Mary O'Mahony, and Bart van Ark. 2010. *Economic Growth in Europe*. Cambridge, UK: Cambridge University Press.

Tietenberg, Thomas, and Lynne Lewis. 2012. *Environmental and Natural Resource Economics*, 9th ed. Englewood Cliffs, NJ: Prentice-Hall.

Tuladhar, Sugandha D. 2003. *Confidence Intervals for Computable General Equilibrium Models*. Doctoral Dissertation. Austin, TX: University of Texas.

Tuladhar, Sugandha D., and Peter J. Wilcoxen. 1999. An Econometric Look at the Double Dividend Hypothesis. *National Tax Association Proceedings*, 57–62. United Nations, Commission of the European Communities, International Monetary Fund, Organisation for Economic Co-operation and Development, and World Bank. 2009. *2008 System of National Accounts*. New York: United Nations.

Uzawa, Hirofumi. 1962. Production Functions with Constant Elasticities of Substitution. *Review of Economic Studies* 29, no. 81 (October): 291–299.

——. 1975. Optimal Investment in Social Overhead Capital. Ch. 1 in Mills 1975, 9–22.

——. 1988. *Optimality, Equilibrium, and Growth*. Tokyo: Tokyo University Press.

Wilcoxen, Peter J. 1988. The Effects of Environmental Regulation and Energy Prices on U.S. Economic Performance. Ph.D. Dissertation, Harvard University.

——. 2000. The Cost of Capital and the Economics of the Environment. Ch. 13 in Lau 2000, 379–406.

Wooldridge, Jeffrey M. 2010. *Econometric Analysis of Cross Section and Panel Data*. Cambridge, MA: MIT Press Books, The MIT Press, edition 2, volume 1.

World Input-Output Database. 2012. Groningen, NL: University of Groningen. www.wiod.org/.

World KLEMS. 2010. www.worldklems.net/.

Yun, Kun-Young. 2000. The Cost of Capital and Intertemporal General Equilibrium Modeling of Tax Policy Effects. Ch. 10 in Lau 2000, 227–272.

Zeldes, Stephen. 1989. Consumption and Liquidity Constraints: An Empirical Investigation. *Journal of Political Economy* 97, no. 2 (April): 305–46.

Index